Data Types
and Structures

Data Types and Structures

C. C. Gotlieb and L. R. Gotlieb

University of Toronto

Prentice-Hall, Inc., Englewood Cliffs, New Jersey   07632

Library of Congress Cataloging in Publication Data

GOTLIEB, C. C.
    Data types and structure.

    Includes bibliographies and index.
        1. Data structures (Computer science)
    2. Programming languages (Electronic computers)
    I. Gotlieb, L. R., (date) joint author. II. Title.
    QA76.9.D35G67   001.6'42   77–25017
    ISBN 0-13-197095-X

Printed in the United States of America

10   9   8   7   6   5   4   3   2   1

PRENTICE-HALL INTERNATIONAL, INC., *London*
PRENTICE-HALL OF AUSTRALIA PTY. LIMITED, *Sydney*
PRENTICE-HALL OF CANADA, LTD., *Toronto*
PRENTICE-HALL OF INDIA PRIVATE LIMITED, *New Delhi*
PRENTICE-HALL OF JAPAN, INC., *Tokyo*
PRENTICE-HALL OF SOUTHEAST ASIA PTE. LTD., *Singapore*
WHITEHALL BOOKS LIMITED, *Wellington, New Zealand*

Contents

v

Preface

Data structures was identified as a distinct subject in ACM's Curriculum 68, which is generally recognized as the first comprehensive formulation of topics to be included in a university program in computing and information sciences. But the scope of the subject was not clearly defined there. As evidenced by the flow of papers, survey articles and books since Curriculum 68, all having some variant of the term "data structures" in their title, there has been a steady evolution in the concept. At first data structures was almost synonymous with graph theory—particularly the theory of lists and trees which lends itself naturally to the description of hierarchical data. Then the concept was extended to include networks, the algebraic theory of sets, relations, lattices, and so on, becoming what is now regarded as *discrete structures*. Following the publications of the Codasyl Task Force it was realized that the mathematical concepts had to be further enlarged by a treatment of *storage structures*, for the fact that data must be represented in computer storage introduces major considerations not present at the mathematical level. The ACM Conference on "Data: Abstraction, Definition and Structure" served to further delineate the subject. In that conference there were several contributions on data types, a concept which appeared in the first versions of Algol, but which until then had not received major attention.

To some the subject of data structures is still the theory of discrete algebraic structures—studied by considering sets of data and the operations on them, by setting up classifications of data types based on the operations, and by devising methods of defining types in computer languages and using the types in applications. We have chosen to regard the storage structure as being an integral part of the data structure, and in Chap. 2, which provides a framework for the rest of the book, the storage structure is explicitly included in the formal definition. Also, throughout the later chapters repeated emphasis is given to methods and problems arising out of the storage representation; for example, the representation of arrays in Chap. 5, and the problems of allocating and deallocating storage in Chap. 8. Because computer storage is so important to data structures, a course on the hardware aspects of computers would be a useful prerequisite to the data structures course for which this book is intended as the text, but such a course is not essential. Because discrete structures *are* essential, Chap. 1 consists of a brief survey of the ideas necessary for an understanding of the book. In many computer science programs a course on discrete structures will be taken as a prerequisite, or simultaneously, with a course on data structures.

There is a natural place for the data structure course in a computing and information sciences program. This place is just *after* the introductory courses in computing, generally devoted to explaining the concept of an algorithm, developing programming style, and introducing the student to one or more programming languages, but just *before* the detailed courses on compiler theory, operating systems, and file systems, which mark a specialist program. Thus a data structures course, and hence this book, is directed at all who propose to specialize in computer science, information science, or system science, and to those in related fields such as applied mathematics or industrial engineering who wish to go at least a little way beyond the elementary courses on computer programming. It is true that only the specialist is likely to have to produce working programs on some of the now highly developed techniques such as sorting and garbage collection discussed in the book. But these processes are so common and so important that an understanding of their principles is part of the basic knowledge which anyone seriously engaged in programming should carry with him. The detail has been suppressed to a basic level.

The concepts of data type and data structures are introduced in Chap. 2, where the framework for later chapters is set up; the common types, strings, lists, arrays, trees, sets and graphs are studied in detail in Chaps. 3 through 7. Beyond these fundamentals the book is intended to bring out certain ideas which we regard as particularly important. These can be summarized as follows:

- There is an intimate association between data type definition and programming language design. Many programming languages have their main justification in their efficient, even brilliant exploitation of some particular data types, and it is pedagogically sound and interesting to use such languages in the presentation of data structures, and to build examples and problems around them. For this reason no single language has been adopted for algorithms. A simple Algol-like language, with sufficient notation to select fields and work with pointer variables, has been adopted. There has been no exposition of programming style, although an effort has been made to express the algorithms in a form acceptable today. It is expected that in many cases the student will rework the algorithms in actual languages such as APL, SNOBOL, PASCAL or PL/I to show how the data structures in the languages lend themselves to implementations of the procedures. To help in this, occasionally an algorithm is expressed in one of these languages.
- Most of the recently developed programming languages allow the user to intro-

duce new data types appropriate to the application being considered. This naturally leads to problems in choosing and designing data structures. Although this process is part of problem solving, and no handbook approach is available, systematic methods of building up and choosing data types and structures are emerging. An illustration of these methods is given in Chap. 7, in order to bring together, in one situation, many of the criteria which have to be applied when comparing and choosing data structures—criteria which appear throughout Chaps. 2 to 7. In addition, a detailed example of data structure design is given in the Appendix.

- The most challenging aspects of describing and representing data are met in attempting to deal with large files and with the file collections of data base systems. File structures and data base management systems are subjects in their own right, and there are whole books on them. But the principles and concepts required to understand them are precisely those required to understand simpler structures. They are more complex because the data volumes are larger, the storage mappings involve multilevel stores, and the basic types are combined into composite ones. But the underlying *structural* aspects are the logical extensions of those encountered in studying the more elementary types, and it is important to bring this out in any serious treatment. Thus Chaps. 9 and 10 are intended to provide the connection between data structures and the more system-oriented subjects of file structures and data base management (generally studied later in the computer science curriculum) and to lay the foundation for the later courses on those subjects.

- Although many aspects of data structures are firmly based in mathematics (especially algebra, graph theory and combinatorics), there are other aspects (centered on programming languages), which are less formal. Thus the subject is still in a state of intensive development. Some of these current developments are introduced in Chap. 2; others are treated in the last chapters. Also, to suggest how future developments might influence data structures, we have included accounts of such topics as associative memories, and data manipulation languages. Although the content of these latter chapters is, inevitably, more subject to change than that of the earlier ones, in our opinion there has been sufficient acceptance of the approaches to justify their inclusion in an undergraduate text.

At the University of Toronto, the data structures course of which this book is the outgrowth, is taken by computer science majors in their third year. At this point they will have had an introductory course on algorithms and structured programming, a course on programming languages (where three or four languages including PL/C, Algol W and SNOBOL are taught), and a course on computer architecture. They will have had experience in working with several types of structures, but no systematic overview of them. The data structures course is necessary prerequisite for most of the advanced courses offered in the senior year. Because the course is taken mostly by students who have not yet had a discrete structure course, and because it is a one-semester subject, it has been customary to teach mainly the material to the middle of

Chap. 7, deferring the later chapters to courses on File Structures and Data Base Systems. The whole book can be covered in a two-semester course. The bibliographic material and reference citations in the footnotes provide the basis to explore any topic for which greater depth is considered desirable.

It is hardly necessary to state that solving problems and doing exercises are essential parts of any course; examples and exercises are given at the end of each chapter. Mathematical formulation and solution of problems are important. But even more important is a thorough understanding of the concepts, so that the student will appreciate for each data type, those features which make it especially suitable for particular applications and problems. It is especially desirable that students should know how to use quantitative methods in system design and evaluation. Many of the end-of-chapter exercises are intended to test understanding, and to encourage familiarity with quantitative comparisons with regard to data structure choices.

Acknowledgments

We are grateful to colleagues, students and others, at Toronto and elsewhere, who have read various sections of the manuscript, making corrections and suggesting changes. Among them we would particularly like to mention M. Bloore, M. Brodie, I. Duff, G. Gonnet, T. E. Hull, J. D. Lipson, F. Lochovsky, E. Schonberg, J. Schwartz, R. Sharma, F. Tompa, and D. Tsichritzis. R. Moenck and R. Perrault (at the Scarborough Campus of the University of Toronto), J. Mylopoulos (at the University of Toronto) and R. Peebles (at the University of Waterloo) have all used preliminary versions of the book in their data structure courses, thereby providing additional experience to our own classroom use of the text.

The careful, detailed comments by the referees on the original manuscript not only helped us avoid mistakes, but have undoubtedly led to a book which is clearer and better organized than it would otherwise have been. We would especially like to acknowledge the contribution of Jeffrey Ullman in this respect.

Finally we would like to express our thanks to Mrs. M. I. Chepely and Mrs. V. Shum, who piloted the manuscript through its many, many versions, doggedly overcoming all the difficulties imposed by text-editors, terminals, computers and authors.

C. C. GOTLIEB
L. R. GOTLIEB

Data Types
and Structures

chapter 1

Mathematical Preliminaries

While a more precise definition of data structures will be given in Chapter 2, it is sufficient for now to regard them as sets of data that can be stored in electronic computers, and on which operations can be carried out. The distinction between data structures and mathematical structures is not sharp, but basically mathematics is concerned with the abstract properties of structures and relations on them rather than how such structures are represented in some device. In this chapter mathematical concepts and notation relevant to the study of data structures are presented.

1.1 Sets and Mathematical Logic

The notion of *set* as a collection of members or elements will be taken as primitive. The following notation is used to denote sets and express simple facts about them. We write

$$x \in X \qquad \text{for } x \text{ is an element, or member, of the set } X$$

$$x \notin X \qquad \text{for } x \text{ is } not \text{ an element of the set } X.$$

When the order in which elements are listed is important, this is indicated explicitly. $\{x_1, x_2, \ldots, x_n\}$ denotes the *unordered set* of elements $x_1, \ldots, x_n$ and $\langle x_1, \ldots, x_n \rangle$ denotes the *ordered set*.

The *index* of an element in an ordered set is the integer that specifies the element's position. The first element may be given either the index 0 or 1. Both the notations x_p and x[p] will be used to specify the pth element of an ordered set.

The *cardinality* of a set, $|S|$, is the number of elements in it. Two important sets are the null set containing no elements, denoted by $\varnothing$, and the power set of a given set A,

1

denoted by $P(A)$. $P(A)$ is the set of all subsets of A. If $|A| = n$, $|P(A)| = 2^n$, since $P(A)$ is constructed by either choosing or deleting each of the elements in A.

Given two sets A and B, we write $A \supseteq B$ or $B \subseteq A$ if every member of B is in A, and say that A includes B or that B is a *subset* of A. B is a *proper subset* of A ($A \supset B$) if there are members in A that are not members of the subset B.

$A = B$ if A and B have the same elements

$A \cup B$ is the set consisting of elements either in A or B

$A \cap B$ is the set whose elements are both in A and B

$A - B$ is the set of elements of A that are not in B

$\bar{A}$ is the set of those elements not in A but which are in some universal set, $X \supset A$, implied to exist.

These definitions may also be considered as definitions of the operators $\cup$ (union), $\cap$ (intersection), $-$ (difference), and $^{-}$ (complement) for which the operands are sets.

For arbitrary sets A, B, and C, the operators $\cup$ and $\cap$ obey certain laws that can be proved directly from the definitions. They are:

Commutative: $A \cup B = B \cup A$ and $A \cap B = B \cap A$

Associative: $A \cup (B \cup C) = (A \cup B) \cup C$ and $A \cap (B \cap C) = (A \cap B) \cap C$

Distributive:
$A \cap (B \cup C) = (A \cap B) \cup (A \cap C)$ and $A \cup (B \cap C) = (A \cup B) \cap (A \cup C)$.

Each of the two operators $\cup$ and $\cap$ distributes over the other.

Example 1.1

Operations on sets can be illustrated by plane figures, called *Venn diagrams*, in which points are regarded as set elements. Figure 1.1(a) illustrates the distributive law

$$A \cup (B \cap C) = (A \cup B) \cap (A \cup C)$$

for the case where $A \cap B \cap C \neq \varnothing$. Similarly, Figure 1.1(b) illustrates the theorem

$$\overline{\bar{A} \cup \bar{B}} = A \cap B,$$

which can be proved from the definitions for the operators. In this book, all the sets will be *countably* (or denumerably) *infinite*; that is, their elements can be placed in correspondence with the integers. Since the number of points in the plane is nondenumerable, the Venn diagrams illustrate that set and set operations are meaningful for sets with an infinite number of elements, even when the number is nondenumerable.

The *Cartesian product* of two sets $A \times B$ is the set of ordered pairs of elements in which the first is a member of A and the second a member of B:

$$\{(a, b) \,|\, a \in A, b \in B\}.$$

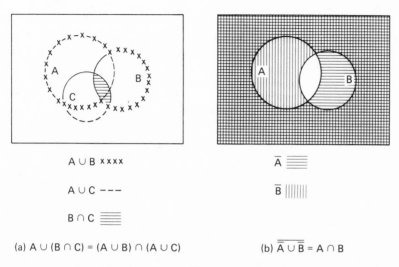

A ∪ B ××××

A ∪ C ---

B ∩ C ≡

A̅ ≡

B̅ ‖‖‖‖‖

(a) A ∪ (B ∩ C) = (A ∪ B) ∩ (A ∪ C)   (b) A̅̅∪̅̅B̅ = A̅ ∩ B̅

Fig. 1.1   Venn-diagram illustrations of set theorems

In addition to sets, other primitive concepts are taken from mathematical logic. $X = \{x \,|\, p(x)\}$ is the set of elements x such that predicate (or statement) p is true. *Boolean variables* take on the values *true* or *false* (also denoted by 1 and 0), and Boolean operations over variables, $\wedge$ (and), $\vee$ (or), and $\neg$ (negation) are defined by truth tables as shown in Table 1.1.

TABLE 1.1   Truth tables for Boolean operators

B A	*true*	*false*	B A	*true*	*false*	A	$\bar{A}$
true	*true*	*false*	*true*	*true*	*true*	*true*	*false*
false	*false*	*false*	*false*	*true*	*false*	*false*	*true*
	$A \wedge B$			$A \vee B$			$\bar{A}$

There is a complete correspondence between sets and Boolean variables, and between set operations and Boolean operations. For example, corresponding to the distributive law for sets, there is the distributive law for Boolean variables:

$$A \wedge (B \vee C) = (A \wedge B) \vee (A \wedge C)$$

and

$$A \vee (B \wedge C) = (A \vee B) \wedge (A \vee C).$$

1.2 Relations

A *binary relation* ρ on the pair of sets X and Y is a subset of the Cartesian product $X \times Y$. If $(x \in X, y \in Y)$ is a member of the subset, we write $x \,\rho\, y$. In particular, a binary relation on the set X is a subset of $X \times X$ (also written as X^2), and is designated (X, ρ).

If M is the set of months, {January, February, . . . , December}, and S the set of seasons, {Spring, Summer, Fall, Winter}, Table 1.2 illustrates the relation "M is a month in S." Members of $M \times S$ belonging to the relations are shown as *true*; others are *false*.

TABLE 1.2   Relation of months and seasons

M	Spring	Summer	Fall	Winter
January	*false*	*false*	*false*	*true*
February	*false*	*false*	*false*	*true*
March	*true*	*false*	*false*	*true*
April	*true*	*false*	*false*	*false*
May	*true*	*false*	*false*	*false*
June	*true*	*true*	*false*	*false*
July	*false*	*true*	*false*	*false*
August	*false*	*true*	*false*	*false*
September	*false*	*true*	*true*	*false*
October	*false*	*false*	*true*	*false*
November	*false*	*false*	*true*	*false*
December	*false*	*false*	*true*	*true*

For finite sets X and Y with n and m elements, respectively, the relation (X, Y, ρ) can be represented by an $n \times m$ matrix of rows and columns corresponding to the elements of X and Y, and in which an entry is 1 iff two elements are related and 0 otherwise. This is the *matrix associated with the relation*. It is a *Boolean matrix* whose elements correspond to the values *true* or *false*. For (X, ρ), the matrix is square. Table 1.3 illustrates the matrix associated with the relation $(\{1, 2, 3, 4,\} <)$.

Note that a binary relation (X, ρ) which determines a subset $R \subseteq X^2$ also defines a complement $\bar{R} = X^2 - R$ and a corresponding complementary relation $(X, \bar{\rho})$. The complementary relation for $(\{1, 2, 3, 4, 5\}, <)$ is $(\{1, 2, 3, 4\} \nless)$, and its members are given by the zero entries in Table 1.3.

TABLE 1.3   Matrix associated with a relation

	1	2	3	4
1	0	1	1	1
2	0	0	1	1
3	0	0	0	1
4	0	0	0	0

The binary relation is not the most general type of relation that might be considered between set elements. We might, for example, consider a ternary relation on three sets as a subset of the Cartesian product $X \times Y \times Z$. However, binary relations have enough complexity to be applicable to a wide variety of problems, and further, it is often useful to regard a ternary relation as a set of binary relations. We can look on the three-dimensional matrix associated with the relation on $X \times Y \times Z$ as a set of X, Y

planes for each $z \in Z$; in effect, there is a binary relation on $X \times Y$ for every z. (Similarly, of course, we can view the ternary relation as a set of binary relations on $Y \times Z$ for each $x \in X$, or on $X \times Z$ for $y \in Y$.)

The relation (X, ρ) is said to be:

Reflexive:	if $x \rho x$ for all $x \in X$
Irreflexive:	if $x \rho x$ for no $x \in X$
Symmetric:	if $x \rho y \Rightarrow y \rho x$ for all $x, y \in X$
Antisymmetric:	if $x \rho y \wedge y \rho x \Rightarrow x = y$ for all $x, y \in X$
Transitive:	if $x \rho y \wedge y \rho z \Rightarrow x \rho z$ for all $x, y, z \in X$.

Relations with different combinations of reflexive/irreflexive, symmetric/antisymmetric, and transitive/nontransitive are interesting both in life and mathemtics. For example, the sibling relationship is irreflexive and symmetric; the relation "x is a substructure of y" is irreflexive, antisymmetric, and transitive. The equivalence relation, and the partial order, considered next, are especially important because they are often encountered.

A relation that is reflexive, symmetric, and transitive is said to be an *equivalence relation*, denoted by E. A *partition*, Π, of a set X, is a family of subsets $X_1, \ldots, X_k \subseteq X$ such that

1. $X_i \neq \varnothing$, all i (the subsets are not empty).
2. $i \neq j \Rightarrow X_i \cap X_j = \varnothing$ (the subsets are disjoint).
3. $\bigcup_i X_i = X$ (the subsets, collectively, make up X).

Given a partition, Π, of X, a binary relation, $E(\Pi)$ is defined on X by making $x_i E(\Pi) x_j$ mean that x_i and x_j are related iff they are in the same subset. It is evident that $E(\Pi)$ is symmetric, transitive, and reflexive, and hence an equivalence relation. It is not difficult to show the converse also: that is, that the existence of an equivalence relation on a set implies a partition. A subset, $C(a)$, of the partition consists of all members such that $xE(\Pi)a$:

$$C(a) = \{x \in X \mid xE(\Pi)a\} \subset X.$$

A commonly cited example of an equivalence relation defined on the integers N is the set of residue classes for a given (integer) modulus k. This is the set of integers remaining after dividing N by k, and it is written $N \bmod k$. Each integer n can be written in the form $i \times k + m$, where i is an integer and $0 \leq m < k$. The effect is a partition of the integers into the residue classes $\{C(0), C(1), \ldots, C(k-1)\}$. For example, if 7 is the modulus, the possible remainders after dividing any integer by 7 are 0, 1, 2, 3, 4, 5, 6, and these represent the residue classes $C(0), \ldots, C(6)$. Integers belonging to $C(1)$ are of the form $7 \times i + 1$.

A *partial order relation* $(X, \leq)$ has the following properties:

1. $x \leq x$ (reflexive).
2. $x \leq y \wedge y \leq x \Rightarrow x = y$ (antisymmetric).
3. $x \leq y \wedge y \leq z \Rightarrow x \leq z$ (transitive).

Sets for which there is a partial order relation between members are called *posets*. From the relation $\leq$ we can define other relations,[1] which may be represented by $\geq$, $<$, and $>$. For example,

$$x \leq y \Rightarrow y \geq x$$
$$x < y \Rightarrow x \leq y \wedge x \neq y.$$

The relation $\geq$ is also a partial order, but $>$ (and also $<$) is irreflexive and hence not a partial order.

Note that $x \not\geq y$ does *not* imply that $x < y$ since the $<$ relation is not defined as the complement of $\geq$. Suppose, for example, that $\geq$ is the inclusion relation on a set; this is a partial ordering, and $X > Y$ is interpreted to mean that Y is a proper subset of X. Given two arbitrary sets, we cannot say that one is necessarily a subset of the other.

If for any two elements $x \geq y \vee x < y$, we have a *linear* or *simple order*. In such a case the members of the poset can be displayed as points on a line, and the set is called a *chain*.

Any finite poset can be represented by a *Hasse diagram* in which:

1. Each distinct element is represented by a point.
2. The relation $x < y$ is represented by a line that rises steadily from x to y.

If x is below y in a Hasse diagram, it does not follow that $x < y$ unless there is a line between them.

Example 1.2

Figure 1.2 shows the Hasse diagram for the poset whose elements are the areas representing subsets in the accompanying Venn diagram. The relation is set inclusion.

Let $(X, \leq)$ be a relation and $X \supseteq Y \supset \varnothing$. Then an element $x \in X$ is an upper bound of Y iff for all $y \in Y$, $y \leq x$. The least element of all the upper bounds of Y

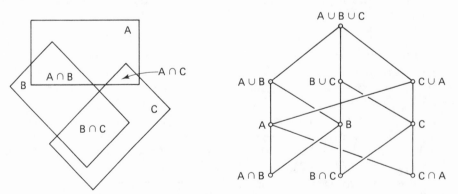

Fig. 1.2 Hasse diagram

[1]There are several common ways of expressing these relations verbally: for example, x has rank less than or equal to y for $x \leq y$, x precedes y for $x < y$, and x is a successor of y for $x > y$.

is the *least upper bound* (LUB) of Y. Similarly, a *greatest lower bound* (GLB) can be defined.

A *lattice* is a poset such that any two elements possess a *least upper bound* and a *greatest lower bound*. The Hasse diagram for a finite lattice always has a single point at the top and at the bottom. (See Fig. 1.3, which illustrates the lattice formed by the power set of $\{a, b, c, d\}$ when inclusion is the relation.) Another example of a lattice can be obtained by taking a set of positive integers $\{1, 2, \ldots, k\}$ and the relation as division without remainder, so that $a \geq b$ means that a is a multiple of b. In this case the least upper bound is the least common multiple and the greatest lower bound is the highest common factor. Other examples of lattices will be found in Section 2.4.

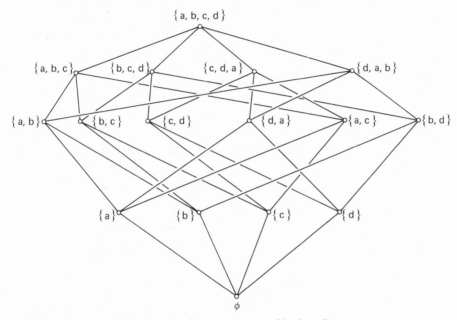

Fig. 1.3   Lattice on power set of $\{a, b, c, d\}$

1.3 Functions, Mappings, and Operators

A slightly different terminology is often used to express many of the same concepts which have just been presented. If X and Y are sets, a *function* $f : X \longrightarrow Y$ is a relation such that if $x f y_1$, and $x f y_2$ where $x \in X$, and $y_1, y_2 \in Y$, then $y_1 = y_2$. For $(x, y) \in f$ we write $f(x) = y$ and say that x is the *argument* and y the *value* of the function. The important restriction on a function, as compared to a relation, is the single value for the given argument. A function $f : X \Longrightarrow Y$ is *onto* or *surjective* iff for every point $y \in Y$ there is at least one point $x \in X$ such that $f(x) = y$.

The set X is called the *domain* of the function f, and the set Y is the *range* of f; y is the *image* of x under f, and $\{x \in X \mid f(x) = y\}$ is the *inverse image* of y, denoted by $x = f^{-1}(y)$.

A function $f: X \Rightarrow Y$ is said to be *one-to-one* or *injective* iff, for every point $y \in Y$, the inverse image $f^{-1}(y)$, when it exists, consists of a single value x. Thus f is injective if the images of distinct points are distinct. A function $f: X \Rightarrow Y$, which is both surjective and injective, is *bijective*. For a bijective function both f and f^{-1} are functions.

The *composition* of two functions, f and g, exists iff the range of f is equal to the domain of g. In that case it is given by

$$h(x) = g(f(x)).$$

It is sometimes desirable to use a functional terminology to describe the relation between two sets X and Y even when there may be several values $y_1, \ldots, y_n$ corresponding to a value $x \in X$. This can be done with the *characteristic function*, F, which is defined with respect to a given subset $X' \subseteq X$. The characteristic function takes on the value 1 or 0 (or alternatively *true* or *false*) according as its argument is a member of X' or not; that is, $F(x) = 1$ if $x \in X'$ and $F(x) = 0$ if $x \notin X'$. Using the characteristic function, the relation (X, Y, ρ) can then be replaced by the *set* of characteristic functions $F_1(X, y_1) \ldots F_k(X, y_k)$, where $y_1 \ldots y_k$ are the set of possible values for Y. The domain of F_1 is the set X and the Boolean relation $y = y_1$; its range is the pair of values 1 or 0.

Example 1.3

Suppose that there is a relation between part number and supplier as shown in Table 1.4, where an entry of 1 means that the part number specified by the row is available from the supplier specified by the column. This relation is not a function,

TABLE 1.4 Part number–supplier relation

Part Number	Supplier		
	A	B	C
105–3	1	0	1
211–1	0	1	0
225–2	1	0	1
436–2	1	1	0

since a given part number may have more than one supplier. However, each column of the relation is a characteristic function for the part number and corresponding supplier.

A *binary operation* on a set X is a function from the set $X \times X$ to a set Y, and may be written $x_1 \cdot x_2 = y$, where $x_1, x_2 \in X$ and $y \in Y$. The operation is *closed* if it is a function from $X \times X$ to X. The binary operation is *commutative* iff $x \cdot y = y \cdot x$ and *associative* iff $(x \cdot y) \cdot z = x \cdot (y \cdot z) = x \cdot y \cdot z$ for all $x \in X$, $y \in Y$, and $z \in Z$.

An *identity element* in a binary operation is an element e such that

$$x \cdot e = e \cdot x = x \qquad \text{for all } x \in X.$$

A *semigroup* is a set X together with an associative binary operation on X. A semigroup with an identity element is called a *monoid*. A *group* is a monoid where for every element $x \in X$ there is an inverse element $x^{-1} \in X$ such that $x \cdot x^{-1} = x^{-1} \cdot x = e$, the identity.

The systems described by sets and relations can be described instead by sets and operators. Thus instead of defining a lattice (X, ρ) as a poset for which any two elements possess a least upper bound and greatest lower bound, we can define binary operators, JOIN and MEET, such that x JOIN y and x MEET y are, respectively, the least upper bound and greatest lower bound for the pair x, y. Then the lattice may be represented by $(X, \text{JOIN}, \text{MEET})$. In the power-set lattice (with inclusion as the relation) the JOIN and MEET operations are set union and set intersection.

This approach leads to algebraic systems and abstract algebras. An (*abstract*) *algebra* $\langle X, f_1, f_2, \ldots, f_k \rangle$ is a system consisting of a set X and a number of operators $f_1 \ldots f_k$, where $f_i: X^{n_i} \longrightarrow X$ is an operator that takes n_i arguments. Important cases are binary, unary, and nil-ary or 0-argument operators (i.e., constants).

As more properties are assumed for the algebra (more operators, associative laws, distributive laws, etc.), more and more structure is imparted to the algebraic system. The abstract algebras then become familiar algebraic systems. Examples are a Boolean algebra with its binary operations $\wedge$ and $\vee$ and unary operation $\neg$ (complementation), and an integral field with its operations over integers. In our study of data structures we shall encounter sets and operators. In general, the variety of operators and number of properties will not be as great as is found in the mathematical structures that are studied in algebra. However, some of the properties will be present, and the concept that operators and their properties determine an algebra is useful in the study of data structures as found in programming languages and computing systems. As an illustration, consider the algebra of strings in the next section.

1.4 Strings and Grammars

Let $V = \{a, b, \ldots, z\}$ be a set of symbols over an alphabet and V^* be the set of strings over the alphabet. Members of V^* are ordered sets of elements of V.

The null string, consisting of zero characters, is denoted by ''. The *concatenation operator*, Θ, is defined such that

$$\langle x_1 x_2 \ldots x_k \rangle \Theta \langle y_1 y_2 \ldots y_l \rangle = \langle x_1 \ldots x_k y_1 \ldots y_l \rangle.$$

Clearly Θ is associative, and '' plays the role of an identity element. ('' is to be distinguished from the string consisting of a single blank character, which will be denoted be $\flat$.) Since

$$\langle x_1 \ldots x_k \rangle \Theta \, '' = \, '' \, \Theta \langle x_1 \ldots x_k \rangle = \langle x_1 \ldots x_k \rangle,$$

the system $(V^*, \Theta, '')$ forms a monoid.

This same system may be described in terms of relations instead of operators. Instead of the concatenation operator, call $x = \langle x_1 \ldots x_k \rangle$ a prefix of $y = \langle y_1 \ldots y_k \ldots y_l \rangle$ iff $x_1 = y_1$, $x_2 = y_2, \ldots, x_k = y_k$ and $k \leq l$. This relation is reflexive, antisymmetric, and transitive, and hence is a partial order. It is often desirable to define a simple order on strings. To do this, assume that there is a simple order

ρ_L on the symbols in the set from which the strings are constructed. When $x\ \rho_L\ y$ we say that x precedes y. This is called the *collating order* or *collating sequence* for the character set. To extend ρ_L to strings, let $\langle x_1 \ldots x_k \rangle$ and $\langle y_1 \ldots y_l \rangle$ be strings where $k \leq l$. Then $\langle x_1 \ldots x_k \rangle\ \rho_L\ \langle y_1 \ldots y_l \rangle$ if one of the following holds:

  (a) $x_1 \rho y_1$, *or*
  (b) $l = k$ and $\langle x_1 \ldots x_k \rangle = \langle y_1 \ldots y_l \rangle$, *or*
  (c) $x_i = y_i$ for $i = 1$ to $j < k$, $x_{j+1} \neq y_{j+1}$ and $x_{j+1}\ \rho_L\ y_{j+1}$.

Otherwise, $\langle y_1 \ldots y_l \rangle\ \rho_L\ \langle x_1 \ldots x_k \rangle$. The ordering so defined is known as the *lexicographic order*. Again, instead of this relation, which holds on strings, it is possible to define a precedence function, Π, so that for strings X, Y,

$$X \Pi Y = \textit{true} \quad \text{iff} \quad X \rho_L Y.$$

In practice it is useful to distinguish the case when the strings are equal (i.e., they match). The precedence function Π will therefore be further specified, so that

$$X \Pi Y = \begin{cases} \textit{less or } -1 & \text{if} \quad X \rho_L Y \wedge X \neq Y \\ \textit{equal or } 0 & \text{if} \quad X = Y \\ \textit{greater or } 1 & \text{if} \quad Y \rho_L X \wedge X \neq Y. \end{cases}$$

Since strings can be regarded as a set V^*, along with the binary concatenation operator Θ and precedence function Π, they represent an instance of an abstract algebra.

The algebra of strings can be extended to model programming languages, and to a lesser extent, to natural ones. First, the prefix relation is generalized to that of a *substring*. Then operators known as *productions* are introduced, to permit the substitution of one substring for another. The production

$$\alpha \beta \gamma \Rightarrow \alpha \delta \gamma$$

means that the substring β in string $\alpha \beta \gamma$ is replaced by the string δ.

A *phrase structure grammar*, G, is a quadruple $\langle V_T, V_N, S, P \rangle$, where

  $V_T =$ set of given symbols called terminals

  $V_N =$ set of nonterminal symbols

  $S =$ designated nonterminal, called the *initial* or *start* symbol

  $P =$ set of productions.

A *sentential form* is a string that is derivable from S by a sequence of productions; a *sentence* is a sentential form consisting of terminal symbols; the *language* of G is the set of sentences. Grammars and languages can be studied formally as production systems or, alternatively, as types of algebras.

An important class of languages is generated by *context-free grammars*, that is, grammars in which every production is of the form

$$U \Rightarrow \delta$$

where U is a single, nonterminal symbol and δ is a string.

Example 1.4

A simple context-free grammar is the generator of strings to be used as identifiers (e.g., the names of variables in ALGOL 60). The components are

$$V_T = \{a, b, c, \ldots, z, A, B, \ldots, Z, 0, 1, \ldots, 9\}$$
$$V_N = \{\text{IDEN, LETTER, DIGIT}\}$$
$$S = \text{IDEN}$$

The set *P* consists of the productions

$$\text{LETTER} \Rightarrow a \,|\, b \,|\, c \,|\, \ldots A \,|\, B \,|\, \ldots \,|\, Z$$
$$\text{DIGIT} \Rightarrow 0 \,|\, 1 \,|\, \ldots \,|\, 9$$
$$\text{IDEN} \Rightarrow \text{LETTER} \,|\, \text{IDEN} \odot \text{LETTER} \,|\, \text{IDEN} \odot \text{DIGIT}$$

In the productions the vertical symbol "|" stands for an alternation operator meaning that the alternatives on either side of it may be selected.

Example 1.5

Another example of a context-free grammar is that which generates arithmetic expressions consisting of sums and products of variables, along with parentheses that indicate the sequence in which the expression is to be evaluated.

$$V_T = \{a, b, \ldots, z, +, -, *, \div, (,)\}$$
$$V_N = \{\text{EXP, TRM, FCT, AOP, MOP, VAR}\}$$
$$S = \text{EXP}$$

The production set, *P*, is

$$\text{EXP} \Rightarrow \text{TRM} \,|\, \text{EXP AOP TRM}$$
$$\text{TRM} \Rightarrow \text{FCT} \,|\, \text{TRM MOP FCT}$$
$$\text{FCT} \Rightarrow \text{VAR} \,|\, (\text{EXP})$$
$$\text{AOP} \Rightarrow + \,|\, -$$
$$\text{MOP} \Rightarrow * \,|\, \div$$
$$\text{VAR} \Rightarrow a \,|\, b \,|\, \ldots z$$

To *derive* a sentence is to exhibit a sequence of productions which yields the sentence from *S*. The following is a derivation for the expression (a+b)*(c+d), which is a sentence of the context-free grammar defined above.

$$\text{EXP} \Rightarrow \text{TRM} \Rightarrow \text{TRM MOP FCT}$$
$$\text{TRM} \Rightarrow \text{FCT} \Rightarrow (\text{EXP}) \Rightarrow (\text{EXP AOP TRM}) \Rightarrow (\text{TRM+FCT})$$
$$\Rightarrow (\text{FCT+VAR}) \Rightarrow (\text{VAR+b}) \Rightarrow (a+b)$$
$$\text{MOP} \Rightarrow *$$
$$\text{FCT} \Rightarrow (\text{EXP}) \Rightarrow (\text{EXP AOP TRM}) \Rightarrow (\text{TRM+FCT})$$
$$\Rightarrow (\text{FCT+VAR}) \Rightarrow (\text{VAR+d}) \Rightarrow (c+d)$$

1.5 Graphs

An alternative way to consider relations is as graphs. A *graph* consists of a (finite) nonempty set of *vertices* or *nodes*, and a set of *edges*, where each edge is an unordered pair of distinct vertices. (Figure 1.4 illustrates a graph.) The *order* of a graph, G, is the

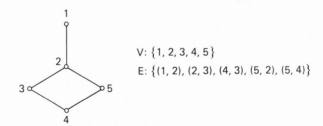

V: {1, 2, 3, 4, 5}

E: {(1, 2), (2, 3), (4, 3), (5, 2), (5, 4)}

Fig. 1.4   Graph

number of vertices in it, and is written $|G|$. The edges define an *incidence relation* between pairs of vertices. Two vertices joined by an edge are *adjacent*; otherwise, they are *independent*. If e is an edge defined by nodes x and y ($e \sim (x, y)$), then e is *incident* with x, y. The only property of the relation assumed so far is symmetry; that is, $(x, y) \in E \Rightarrow (y, x) \in E$, where E is the set of edges.

A graph may be defined so as to have an edge $e \sim (x, x)$. Such an edge is called a *loop*. If the relation is reflexive, there is a loop at every vertex. Also, there may be more than one edge joining a given pair of vertices. (See Fig. 1.5; in such cases the interpretation of the edges as a set has to be relaxed since the pairings are no longer distinct.) If multiple edges are not permitted, the graph is said to be *simple*. The num-

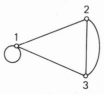

Fig. 1.5   Graph with a loop and multiple edge

ber of edges incident with a vertex is the *degree* of the vertex. In a *regular graph* the degree of every vertex is the same. In K_n, the *complete graph* of order n, every pair of nodes is adjacent (see Fig. 1.6 for the complete graphs up to K_6).

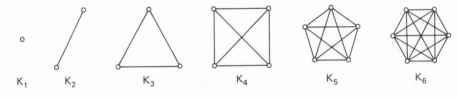

K_1 K_2 K_3 K_4 K_5 K_6

Fig. 1.6   Complete graphs to K_6

A *planar graph* is one that can be drawn in a plane such that any two edges intersect only at vertices. A deep theorem of Kuratowski states than any nonplanar graph contains either of two basic graphs:

1. K_5, the complete *5-graph*,[2] *or*
2. The *utilities graph*, in which there are two sets of three vertices, each vertex being joined to all the vertices in the opposite set (Fig. 1.7).

Fig. 1.7   Utilities graph

In a *transitive graph*, edges $(i,j)(j,k) \Rightarrow (i,k)$. The symmetry property requires that a transitive graph have a loop at each vertex, but these are often assumed to be present and not shown explicitly (Fig. 1.8).

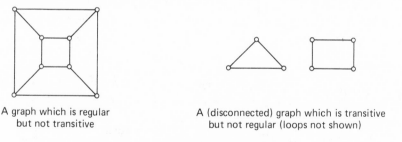

A graph which is regular
but not transitive   A (disconnected) graph which is transitive
                                         but not regular (loops not shown)

Fig. 1.8   Transitive and regular graphs

A graph is *bipartite* if its vertices can be partitioned into two distinct sets, V_1 and V_2, such that every edge has one vertex in V_1 and the other in V_2 (e.g., the utilities graph).

A *subgraph, S*, of G is a graph whose edges are a subset of the edges of G.

A *walk* of a graph G is an alternating sequence of vertices and edges $v_0, x_1, v_1, \ldots,$ v_{n-1}, x_n, v_n, beginning and ending with vertices, in which each edge is incident with the two vertices immediately preceding and following it (Harary, 1969). This walk joins v_0 and v_n, and may also be denoted $v_0, v_1, \ldots, v_n$. It is *closed* if $v_0 = v_n$ and *open* otherwise. It is a *trail* if all the edges are distinct and a *path* if all the vertices are distinct. If the walk is closed and the vertices are distinct, it is a *cycle*. C_n is the cycle with n vertices, and P_n is the straight-line path with n vertices. The length of a walk

---

[2]The complete 5-graph itself need not be present, but rather a graph that is essentially equivalent to it because nodes can be deleted by replacing a pair of edges by a single edge. For example, o———o———o is replaced by o———o.

(path) can be defined by either the number of edges in it, or the number of vertices. We shall find the latter more convenient.

A graph is *connected* if every pair of vertices is connected by a path. A maximal connected subgraph (i.e., a connected subgraph that is not a subgraph of any other connected graph) is a *component* of G. The distance $d(u, v)$ between any two vertices u and v in G is the length of a shortest path between them. In a connected graph, $d(u, v)$ is a *metric*; that is, the following conditions are satisfied:

1. $d(u, v) \geq 0$ with $d(u, v) = 0$ iff $u = v$.
2. $d(u, v) = d(v, u)$.
3. $d(u, v) + d(v, w) \geq d(u, w)$.

An *Eulerian cycle* of a graph includes every edge once, and it is easy to see that one exists if and only if the graph is connected and the degree of every vertex is even. A *Hamiltonian path* includes every vertex once, and although it seems as if Eulerian and Hamiltonian paths should be related, there is, in fact, no simple way of determining whether there is a Hamiltonian path for an arbitrary graph, or finding it if there is one.

Corresponding to the matrix of a relation, it is possible to define the *adjacency matrix*, $A(G)$, of the graph G, where a_{ij} is equal to the number of edges between vertex i and vertex j. If the graph is simple, the adjacency matrix is Boolean. Another matrix that can be associated with a graph is the *incidence matrix* $E(G)$. For a graph with n vertices and m edges, $E(G)$ is a $n \times m$ matrix with $e_{ij} = 1$ if vertex i is incident with edge j, and 0 otherwise.

Example 1.6

The adjacency matrix and incidence matrix for the graph of Fig. 1.9 are given by $A(G)$ and $E(G)$ in Table 1.5. There is an immediate interpretation to the matrix $A^2(G)$.

TABLE 1.5   Adjacency and incidence matrices
for the graph of Fig. 1.9

$$
A(G) = \begin{matrix} 0 & 1 & 0 & 0 & 1 & 1 \\ 1 & 0 & 1 & 0 & 0 & 0 \\ 0 & 1 & 0 & 1 & 1 & 0 \\ 0 & 0 & 1 & 0 & 1 & 0 \\ 1 & 0 & 1 & 1 & 0 & 1 \\ 1 & 0 & 0 & 0 & 1 & 0 \end{matrix}
\qquad
E(G) = \begin{matrix} 1 & 1 & 0 & 1 & 0 & 0 & 0 & 0 \\ 0 & 0 & 0 & 1 & 1 & 0 & 0 & 0 \\ 0 & 0 & 0 & 0 & 1 & 1 & 0 & 1 \\ 0 & 0 & 0 & 0 & 0 & 0 & 1 & 1 \\ 0 & 1 & 1 & 0 & 0 & 1 & 1 & 0 \\ 1 & 0 & 1 & 0 & 0 & 0 & 0 & 0 \end{matrix}
$$

$$
A^2(G) = \begin{matrix} 3 & 0 & 2 & 1 & 1 & 1 \\ 0 & 2 & 0 & 1 & 2 & 1 \\ 2 & 0 & 3 & 1 & 1 & 1 \\ 1 & 1 & 1 & 2 & 1 & 1 \\ 1 & 2 & 1 & 1 & 4 & 1 \\ 1 & 1 & 1 & 1 & 1 & 2 \end{matrix}
$$

An element, a_{ij}^2, in this matrix represents the number of paths of length 2 between vertex i and vertex j in G. Further, if $A''(G)$ is the Boolean matrix such that $a_{ij}'' = 1$ if $a_{ij}^2 \neq 0$, and $a_{ij}'' = 0$ when $a_{ij}^2 = 0$, then $A \vee A''$ is a Boolean matrix that has a 1

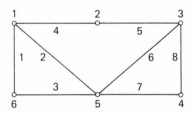

Fig. 1.9   Graph with labeled nodes and edges

present in element (i, j) if there is a path of length 1 or 2 between i and j, and a 0 otherwise. This is easily extended to obtain the *transitive closure* of the path matrix, which has a 1 present in element (i, j) if there is a path between these vertices, and a 0 otherwise.

1.6 Trees

A *tree* is a connected graph with at least two vertices and no cycles (Fig. 1.10).

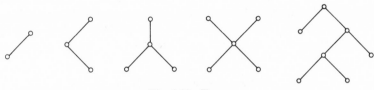

Fig. 1.10   Trees

Let T be a graph with $|T| = n > 1$. Then any of the following are equivalent definitions of a tree:

1. T is connected and possesses no cycles.
2. T is connected and has $n - 1$ edges.
3. T has no cycles and $n - 1$ edges.
4. T contains no cycles, and if a edge is added joining any two nonadjacent vertices, a single cycle is formed.
5. T is connected but loses this property if any edge is deleted.
6. Every pair of vertices is connected by one and only one path.

A *rooted tree* has a designated vertex. A *leaf* is a vertex belonging to only one edge. If T is a subgraph of G, edges of G that appear in T are *branches*; the other edges are *chords* relative to T. A tree *spans* a graph if it is a subtree containing every vertex in G. A graph free of cycles and containing k unconnected components will be called a *forest* of k trees, or a *multiply rooted tree*.

Example 1.7

Figure 1.11 illustrates a tree for the game of $\times$'s and $\bigcirc$'s. The vertices are labeled with the moves and the edges with the square in which the move is made.

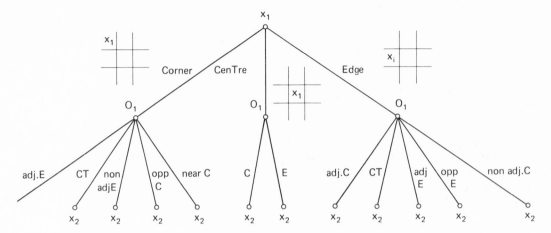

Fig. 1.11   Tree for the game of ×'s and ○'s

The importance of rooted trees derives from the fact that they provide a description of a *hierarchy*, a very common relation. Suppose that $A > B$ is the filial relation, meaning that A is the father of B (and that B is the son of A). From the filial relationship, by transitivity, we derive the "ancestoral" relationship, $A \cdot >$, and also the "descendant" relationship. In a hierarchy the root member is an ancestor of all others; for any two members A and B, either:

1. A is an ancestor of B, or B is an ancestor of A, $A \cdot > B \vee B < \cdot A$, or
2. There is a member ancestral to both A and B, and no descendants of both A
   B, $\exists C | C \cdot > A \wedge C \cdot > B \wedge \not\exists D | A \cdot > D \wedge B \cdot > D$.

Hierarchies occur in so many contexts that many representations are found for them. Figure 1.12 shows alternative representations in the form of:

1. A rooted tree.
2. Sets, in which being an ancestor corresponds to inclusion.
3. Nested parentheses, in which ancestory corresponds to enclosure.
4. Indented lines, in which being a descendant corresponds to indentation to the right.

The representation of trees as sets of nested parentheses is particularly important in notations for algebraic expressions and lists. By induction it can be shown that a parentheses system corresponds to a tree iff it is "well formed." To determine if it is well formed, the parentheses symbols are assigned indexes as follows:

- Left parentheses are numbered consecutively from left to right with the integers 1 to N.
- On the same scan the right parentheses are matched with left by assigning them negative indexes. A right symbol is given a negative number equal to the largest unmatched positive index on its left.

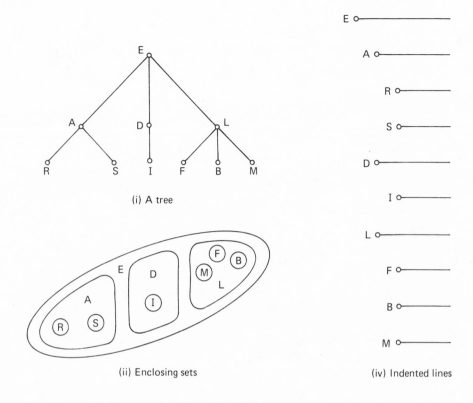

(i) A tree

(ii) Enclosing sets

(iv) Indented lines

(iii) Nested parentheses

Fig. 1.12   Representations of a hierarchy

The system is well formed if and only if there are no unmatched (left or right) parentheses. The indexed parentheses system for the tree of Fig. 1.12 is

$$(\; (\; (\qquad) \; (\qquad) \qquad) \; (\; (\qquad) \qquad) \; (\; (\qquad) \; (\qquad) \; (\qquad) \qquad) \qquad)$$
$$1 \; 2 \; 3 \; -3 \; 4 \; -4 \; -2 \; 5 \; 6 \; -6 \; -5 \; 7 \; 8 \; -8 \; 9 \; -9 \; 10 \; -10 \; -7 \; -1$$

Example 1.8

In an algebraic expression the sequence of operations is indicated by priorities associated with the operators, by parentheses surrounding the operands, or by a mixture of the two. The hierarchy of operations can also be specified by writing the expression as a tree, a form that is completely parentheses-free. Each leaf of the tree is labeled with an operand; each nonleaf node, with an operator. The tree for the expression

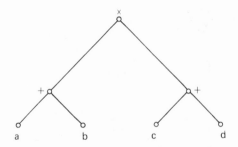

Fig. 1.13   Tree form for the expression $(a + b)*(c + d)$

$(a+b)*(c+d)$ is shown in Fig. 1.13. A program for writing an expression in parenthesis-free notation is given in Algorithm 4.1.

1.7 Directed Graphs

In a *directed graph* or *digraph* a direction is associated with each edge by ordering the vertices. The incidence relation is no longer symmetric. The *dual* of a digraph has the same vertices but all the edges reversed. Note that undirected graphs have complements (defined by the complementary relation) but no duals.

Definitions of connectedness and components require some care, since there are several of each type. Walk, path, and cycle are defined as before, but it is convenient to define *semiwalk*, *semipath*, and *semicycle* in each case allowing either an edge (x, y), or (y, x). Then a digraph is:

(a) *Strongly connected* if there is a path between any two vertices.
(b) *Unilaterally connected* if for any two vertices (x, y) there is a path from x to y *or* from y to x.
(c) *Weakly connected* if there is a semipath between every two vertices.
(d) *Disconnected* otherwise (Fig. 1.14).

Computer flow diagrams are directed graphs. The labels attached to nodes with one outgoing edge specify nonbranching instructions (assignments, arithmetic operations, etc.) or procedures with one exit. Nodes with more than one outgoing edge correspond to branching instructions, or instruction sequences with several possible outcomes (e.g., Boolean predicate conditions). Edges define the instruction sequence path; branches carry labels that indicate the condition met when the path is taken and possibly numbers that give the probability of the branch being taken. Code checking routines, among other things, establish the connection properties of the graph. Figure 1.15 shows the directed graph corresponding to Algorithm 3.1.

A digraph without cycles is *acyclic*. A digraph without semicycles is a *directed tree*. Two types of vertices in acyclic digraphs are of special interest. A *source* is a vertex for which there is a path to any other vertex; a *sink* is the dual. The length of the path from a vertex to the source is the *level* of the vertex. An *in-tree* is a directed tree with a source; an *out-tree* is the dual. Rooted trees can always be regarded as directed, since directions can be assigned to all edges, starting with those at the root.

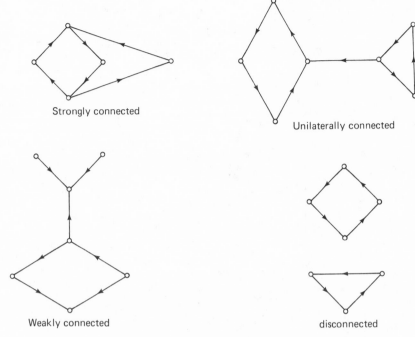

Strongly connected

Unilaterally connected

Weakly connected

disconnected

Fig. 1.14   Connectedness in digraphs

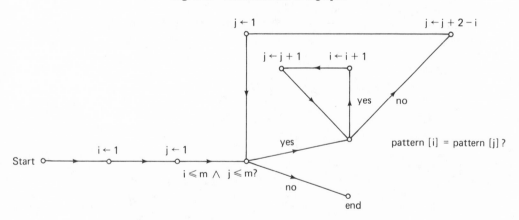

Fig. 1.15   Directed graph representation of Algorithm 3.1

The derivations of a context-free grammar can be represented as a directed out-tree with the start symbol at the root. Since every production has only one symbol on the left-hand side, each production is a rooted subtree. Figure 1.16 shows the generation tree for Example 1.5.

In a *binary out-tree* the out-degree of every vertex is 0, 1, or 2; similarly for a *binary-in-tree*. A *binary tree* is a binary out-tree or a binary in-tree. In an *extended*

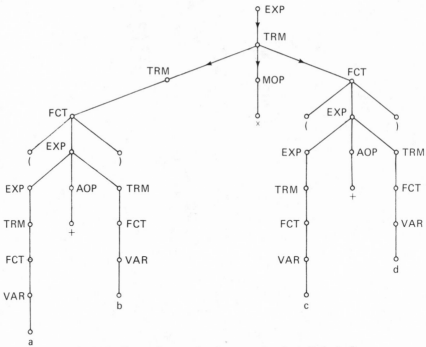

Fig. 1.16 Generation tree for the expression $(a + b)*(c + d)$

binary tree the in (or out)-degree of every vertex is 0 or 2. A *complete* binary tree has leaves only at the last or next-to-last level.

Figure 1.17 shows a binary out-tree. The two edges with dotted lines extend the tree.

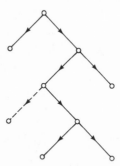

Fig. 1.17 Binary out-tree

Example 1.9

Figure 1.18 shows an in-tree that represents the merging of 12 reels of magnetic tape, each initially sorted, to produce a combined, 12-reel, sequenced file. The numbers at the nodes represent the lengths of the subfiles during stages of the merge. It is assumed that a three-way merge is possible, so that the maximum in-degree of any

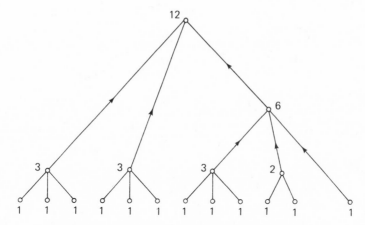

Fig. 1.18   In-tree representing the merging of tape files

vertex is three. The time for a merge is limited by the tape-reading speed, and the total sorting time is proportional to the sum of the numbers below the root. This particular tree, with a sum of 29, represents the most efficient merge for a 12-reel file. It is constructed by the same method used to construct a Huffman coding tree (see Section 3.5).

1.8 Timing Behavior of Algorithms

The term *isomorphic* (also applicable to relations and algebras) describes graphs that are essentially the same. Two graphs are isomorphic if there is bijective mapping from the nodes of one to the nodes of the other which preserves the incidence relation. In Fig. 1.19 the graphs (a) and (b) are isomorphic under the mapping

$$1 \Longrightarrow 5'$$
$$2 \Longrightarrow 2'$$
$$3 \Longrightarrow 3'$$
$$4 \Longrightarrow 4'$$
$$5 \Longrightarrow 1'$$

Any edge for a pair of nodes on the left-hand side is mapped into an edge for the corresponding right-hand side nodes. Similarly, the (nonrooted) trees (c) and (d) are isomorphic. Two graphs can be established as being isomorphic if a permutation of rows and columns of the adjacency matrix of one (corresponding to a renumbering of the vertices) makes the matrix identical to that of the other. Since there are $n!$ permutations of the rows for a matrix of order n, this suggests, as is the case, that testing arbitrary graphs for isomorphism can be a time-consuming procedure for any but very small values of n.

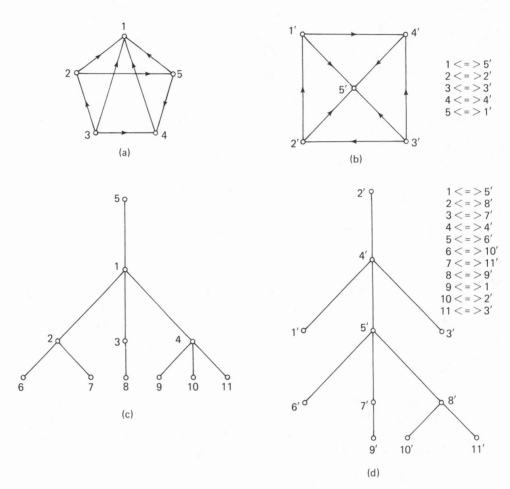

Fig. 1.19 Isomorphic graphs

The time for carrying out all the mathematical algorithms described or suggested in this chapter can be analyzed and expressed in terms of parameters of the problems. It is necessary to distinguish between the time for the worst case and the expected time. To determine the latter measure, a population is implied; usually it is based on a sample that is random in some sense, but it is not obvious that such samplings correspond to situations which arise in practice. For graphs the important parameters are n, the number of vertices, and m, the number of edges, and the timing results are expressed using the mathematical notation $O(f(n, m))$ where $f(n, m)$ is a function of n and m.

For example, to find the transitive closure of a graph, there is a well-known algorithm whose execution time can be shown to be $O(n^3)$. By this it is meant that if T is the expression for the computed execution time for the algorithm, the highest power of n in T is n^3, and $\lim_{n \to \infty} T = Kn^3$. An algorithm whose execution time is $O(f(n, m))$ is said to be of *complexity* $f(n, m)$. The constant K, known as the *iteration constant*, is characteristic of the computer on which the algorithm is run and on the way in which the algorithm is coded. On detailed analysis it can often be expressed as a linear combination of a few basic operations (additions, multiplications, comparisons, etc.). If two different algorithms for the same procedure, A_1 and A_2, have terms $K_1 n^{p_1}$ and $K_2 n^{p_2}$, and $p_1 < p_2$, it is usual to regard A_1 as being more *efficient* than A_2, but the iteration constants K_1 and K_2 are also important. If $K_2 \ll K_1$, the advantage of A_1 may not appear until n is very large.

Transitive closure provides a case in point. There is an algorithm for transitive closure with complexity $n^{2.8}$, but the iteration constant is so large that the n^3 algorithm is usually preferred, especially since it can have an expected performance that is $O(n^2)$.[3] For most algorithms the execution time takes such forms as $O(n \log n)$ or $O(n^3)$, and in particular, the complexity is bounded by n^p, where p is a constant independent of n. There are problems, of which graph isomorphism and finding Hamiltonian paths are examples, for which it is not known whether there exist algorithms that run in time $O(n^p)$.

Exercises

1. Let (Y, m) be a poset where m means "multiple of." Draw the Hasse diagrams for

    $$Y = \{30, 15, 10, 6, 5, 3, 1\}$$
    $$Y = \{30, 15, 10, 6, 5, 3, 2, 1\}$$
    $$Y = \{30, 15, 12, 10, 6, 5, 4, 3, 2, 1\}$$
    $$Y = \{30, 10, 6, 5, 3, 1\}.$$

    Which of these are lattices?
2. Show that $(P(X), \subset)$, where $X = \{1, 2, 3\}$, and (Y, m), where $Y = \{30, 6, 10, 15, 2, 3, 5, 1\}$ and m means "multiple of," are lattices having the same Hasse diagram.
3. Write a computer program that will determine from the matrix associated with a relation whether the relation is:
    (1) A chain.
    (2) A lattice (construct the LUB and GLB tables).
    (3) A poset.
    (4) None of these.
    Test your program by displaying the result on appropriate examples.
4. Indicate the properties (symmetric/antisymmetric, reflexive/irreflexive, transitive/nontransitive) of the following relations:
    (a) Course x is a prerequisite for course y.
    (b) Course x is a prerequisite or corequisite for course y.
    (c) x is a teammate of y.
    (d) x is a classmate of y.

---

[3]P. E. O'Neil and E. J. O'Neil, "A Fast Expected Time Algorithm for Boolean Matrix Multiplication and Transitive Closure," in *Combinatorial Algorithms*, R. Rustin, ed. (New York: Academic Press, 1973), pp. 59–68.

(e) x is a blood relative of y.

(f) x is connected to y by marriage.

(g) x is a customer of y.

(h) Countries x and y maintain diplomatic relations.

What are the partitions in the equivalence relations? Of the eight possible property combinations, which are missing? Name relations that correspond to these.

5. Let E and F be equivalence relations. Show that $E \cdot F$ is an equivalence relation iff $E \cdot F = F \cdot E$.

6. Suppose that we have a set of six blocks, $B_1, \ldots, B_6$, where:

(1) B_1 is a red cylinder.

(2) B_2 is a red sphere.

(3) B_3 is a green cube.

(4) B_4 is a green cylinder.

(5) B_5 is a blue sphere.

(6) B_6 is a blue cube.

(a) Which of the following relations are functions?

      (block number, color), (block number, shape), (shape, color), (color, shape)

(b) How can a function be defined on color versus shape?

7. Let $f: A \longrightarrow B$ be a function, and if $S \subset A$, define $f(S) = \{f(s) \,|\, s \in S\}$. Show that $f(S \cap T) = f(S) \cap f(T) \ \forall S, T \subseteq A \Leftrightarrow f$ is $1:1$.

8. Find all ways of completing the following table of the binary operation $*$ to achieve a monoid.

$*$	a	b	c
a	c	b	a
b			b
c		a	

9. A context-free grammar is *ambiguous* if there is a sentence having two distinct derivations. The grammar G has the form $G = \langle \{S, A, B\}, \{a, b\}, S, P \rangle$, where P is the set of productions $S \longrightarrow bA \ \ S \longrightarrow aB \ \ A \longrightarrow a \ \ B \longrightarrow b \ \ A \longrightarrow aS \ \ b \longrightarrow bs \ \ A \longrightarrow bAA \ \ B \longrightarrow aBB$.

(a) Show that G is ambiguous.

(b) Show that the language of G consists of strings having an equal number of a's and b's.

10. A bijective map, $p: X \longrightarrow X$ is called a *permutation*. Let $p^k(X) = p(p^{k-1}(X)), k \geq 2$. Show that for every finite set X there is an integer n such that $p^n(X) = I$, the identity mapping. Find the smallest n for the mapping

$$(1, 2, 3, 4, 5) \longrightarrow (4, 1, 5, 3, 2).$$

11. The Boolean matrix $A''(G)$ can be defined directly from the adjacency matrix, $A(G)$, for a graph G. This is done by the Boolean product

$$a_{ij}'' = \bigvee_k (a_{ik} \wedge a_{kj}),$$

where a_{ij}'' is the row i, column j, terms of A'', and $\bigvee_k$ is the "or" operation extended over all terms in row i and column k. Show that the same result is obtained as for the definition based on $A^2(G)$ given in Example 1.6. Using the Boolean product, calculate the transitive colsure of the adjacency matrix for the graph of Fig. 1.9.

12. Write a computer program that takes the set of vertices and set of edges of an undirected graph as input, and lists the connected components as output. [*Hint:* One method is to construct the adjacency matrix and transitive closure of the path matrix (see Example 5.1). Another method is based on constructing a spanning tree (or forest) for the graph (see Algorithm 7.2).]

13. Write a program that accepts the set of vertices and edges of a graph as input and which then:
   (1) Displays the adjacency and incidence matrices.
   (2) Determines if the graph is bipartite.

14. Prove that a set of nested parentheses corresponds to a tree if and only if it is well formed.

15. A *clique* of a given graph is a maximal complete subgraph (i.e., a complete subgraph that is not itself a subgraph of any other subgraph). Devise algorithms for finding the smallest and largest cliques of a given graph represented by its adjacency matrix. What is the complexity of the algorithms?

16. (a) Draw the dual graphs for (1) K_n, (2) C_n, (3) an n-star graph (n vertices all connected to one at the center), and (4) the bipartite graph in which the constituent sets have n_1 and n_2 vertices.
   (b) What construct in the dual corresponds to a component of a given graph? A clique?
   (c) What is the complexity of the algorithm for finding the dual of a given graph represented by (1) its adjacency matrix, and (2) its incidence matrix?

17. The edge density of a graph is the number of edges/number of possible edges [it is therefore $m/n(n-1)$ for a directed graph and $2m/n(n-1)$ for an undirected graph]. In a random graph of density p, there is a probability p that an edge is present joining two randomly chosen vertices. Write a computer program for generating random graphs. Estimate the number of components in a random graph with n vertices and density p, and test your estimate on the generated examples.

Bibliography

More complete information on algebraic structures, including the definitions of groups, Boolean algebras, fields, and so on, can be obtained in any book on modern algebra (see, for example, MacLane and Birkhoff, 1967). The terminology used for graphs mainly follows that given in Harary (1969), where proofs of the Kuratowski and other theorems can be found. Other books are Deo (1974) on graph theory, and those of Korfhage (1947), Preparata and Yeh (1973), and Tremblay and Manohar (1975) on discrete structures. Further definition and theorems on graphs are introduced in Chapters 6 and 7 as they are needed. Formal languages are described in Hopcroft and Ullman (1969). For a discussion of the analysis of graph theoretical algorithms, see Corneil (1975).

CORNEIL, D. G., "The Analysis of Graph Theoretical Algorithms," in *Proceedings of the Fifth South-Eastern Conference on Combinatorics*, F. Hoffman et al., eds. Winnipeg, Manitoba: Utilitas Mathematica Publishers, Inc., 1975, pp. 3–38.

DEO, N., *Graph Theory with Applications to Engineering and Computer Science*. Englewood Cliffs, N.J.: Prentice-Hall, Inc., 1974.

HARARY, F., *Graph Theory*. Reading, Mass.: Addison-Wesley Publishing Company, Inc., 1969.

HOPCROFT, J. E., AND J. D. ULLMAN, *Formal Languages and Their Relation to Automata.* Reading, Mass.: Addison-Wesley Publishing Company, Inc., 1969.

KORFHAGE, R. R., *Discrete Computational Structures.* New York: Academic Press, Inc., 1974.

MACLANE, S., AND G. BIRKHOFF, *Algebra.* New York: Macmillan Publishing Co., Inc., 1967.

PREPARATA, F. P., AND R. T. YEH, *Introduction to Discrete Structures.* Reading, Mass.: Addison-Wesley Publishing Company, Inc., 1973.

TREMBLAY, J. P., AND R. MANOHAR, *Discrete Mathematical Structures with Applications to Computer Science.* New York: McGraw-Hill Book Company, 1975.

chapter 2

Basic Concepts and Definitions

Data structures is the study of how data are organized for use by computers. In this chapter a framework is set up for the approach taken in later chapters. The place of data structures in the overall study of computers, programming languages, and mathematics is examined. Basic concepts and terms are introduced and formal definitions for data types and data stuctures are developed.

2.1 Structures and Processes

The distinction between "things" and "processes" originates in our sense of reality and logic, and the two concepts find many expressions—substances and reactions in chemistry, nouns and verbs in grammar, arguments and functions (or operands and operators) in mathematics. Yet at a deeper level this distinction is not always tenable. We recognize things by the way they behave when subjected to processes. Certainly, the *representation* of a process is a thing. Every time a program (i.e., the representation of a process) is submitted to an operating system, it is clearly the data (i.e., a thing) for some other process. In the context of the subject matter of this book, any definition of data must be accompanied, explicitly or implicitly, by the operations over the data. This need to look at the operations on data at the same time one looks at data has been recognized in most studies of data organization.

There are general theories (e.g., the theory of automata) which deal with computations globally, encompassing in their purview data, programs, and computational devices. In this book a more restricted point of view is taken. In spite of the difficulty of distinguishing between things and processes, attention is focused on things that are called data, and on operations on such data. No attempt is made to set up a descriptive system which can at the same time represent data and the computer, regarded here as a device that effects operations on data, either directly by means of its built-in hardware and microprograms or through the intermediary of macro-instructions and sub-routines. However, the data must be represented in the store or memory of the computer in order that it can be operated on, and this affects the approach fundamentally.

One consequence of this representation requirement is that the subject matter of data structures overlaps with those aspects of computer system design that are concerned with the storage of data, in particular, coding theory, storage devices, and addressing mechanisms. But it is not only the hardware aspects of storage which have to be considered. Within the general area of software there are techniques that focus particularly on storage systems and management (i.e., on processes that control and make use of the data representation). Both compilers and operating systems play roles in the allocation and deallocation of storage arising out of the creation and deletion of data elements. Also, the general application area of information retrieval is concerned with the organization of data to facilitate search and access. The operations of search, access, creation, and deletion of data may be regarded as basic, arising out of the fact that the data are stored in computers; they are present regardless of other uses made of the data. The study of data structures will therefore overlap with those topics in programming systems and programming languages, and with those application areas, where these operations are encountered.

In attempting to set up a precise description of how data are organized in computers, it is natural to turn to mathematics, particularly to abstract algebra. In an algebra $\langle X, F \rangle$, the set X and operators f[1], ..., f[n] of F permit an immediate correspondence with data and with computer instructions on the data, the two aspects that have to be considered together. The notion of a type algebra, as seen in Chapter 1 for a lattice, group, and so on, is carried over to data type for which the operations are those which are performed on computer data. It then becomes possible to give rigorous descriptions of the simple and complex data types which are discussed in later chapters (strings, arrays, lists, and so on), to define formal operations on these types, and to use mathematical techniques to show that programs using the types will operate correctly. This approach, which has been developed by a number of authors[1-3] is consistent with that taken here, but generally throughout this book the rigorous definitions and proofs are omitted in favor of a less formal presentation. (However, an example of the formal definition is presented in Section 4.2.1.) The reason for the informal approach in part is that the formal techniques have so far been applied to only a limited set of data types. But even more important, as already noted, to an understanding of how data are manipulated in computers, the mathematical definition must be supplemented by a description of the way in which the data are represented within the computer store.

---

[1] C. A. R. Hoare, "An Axiomatic Basis for Computer Programming," *Communications of the ACM*, **13**, no. 10 (Oct. 1969), 576–853.

[2] D. Scott, "Outline of a Mathematical Theory of Computation," in *Proceedings of the Fourth Annual Princeton Conference on Information Sciences and Systems* (Princeton, N.J.: Department of Electrical Engineering, Princeton University, 1970), pp. 169–76.

[3] T. A. Standish, "Data Structures—An Axiomatic Approach" (Cambridge, Mass.: Bolt, Beranek and Newman, Inc., Aug. 1973), *Report 2639.*

The terms *logical structure* and *storage structure* have generally been adopted for the mathematical aspect of data, and the representation within storage respectively. The storage structure is the feature that distinguishes the subject of data structures from pure mathematics. Special attention is given here to storage structures, and this aspect of the subject is less amenable to mathematical formalism, connected as it is with the computer as a physical device governed by software modules that manage the storage representations.

Thus the subject of data structures can be viewed as lying in the intersection domains of three broader subjects—mathematics, computer hardware, and computer software (Fig. 2.1). Although the subject is not sharply delineated, the study of how to organize collections of data in a computer, starting with very primitive data elements corresponding to a bit or character, and proceeding up to the very large units found in files and data base systems, is important and it has resulted in a large body of practical and theoretical knowledge.

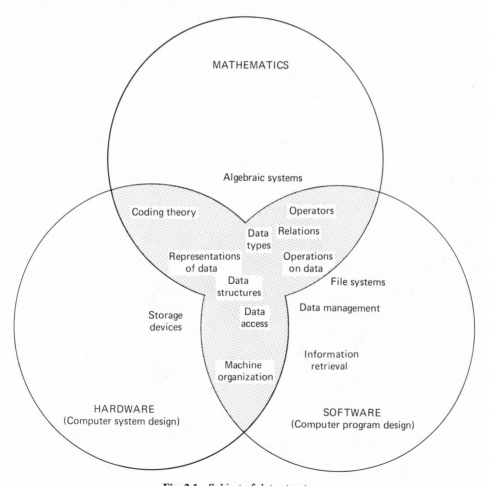

Fig. 2.1 Subject of data structures

The notion of type was not explicitly formulated in the early programming languages, although some primitive types were actually present. Even when types were first recognized and made explicit by the type declaration in ALGOL 60,[4] only a few were identified. One reason for designating types was to make possible checks on the consistency of statements by ensuring that correct values were being used for functions and variables. More important, the type declaration plays a role in facilitating storage allocation. Later still in the development of programming languages, features were incorporated to permit construction of user-defined data types. These allow a programmer to work with concepts that are natural to the application being programmed, and to defer until later considerations of how the types are to be represented. The ability to work this way is a principal feature of the *stepwise refinement of problems*, which is the basis of structured programming. It is for this reason that languages such as SNOBOL and ALGOL 68[5] provide the user with the ability to construct data types, and that the study of data types and data structures is of continuing importance.

In the remainder of this chapter abstract definitions of data type and data structure will be developed. These definitions are intended to be applicable to programming languages and systems where there are either implicit or explicit types, by providing a setting in which the data definition facilities can be viewed.

2.2 Integer Data Type

The term *integer*, abbreviated **int**, commonly denotes the set of values $\{0, \pm 1, \pm 2, \ldots\}$, together with the operations $+, -, *, \div$ (division with remainder), which work on pairs of integers. This view changes when integers are represented on a computer. Since they must be stored in cells of finite size, the computer really deals with a ring of integers modulo some large value, I. There are further considerations regarding the radix of the number system and the way negative numbers are represented.

The fact that in computers, integers are stored in memory locations or cells, means that it is possible to represent integer *variables*. Logically, these are named items that assume integer values. They are operated on as integers and can be assigned (and used to impart) values. Physically, integer variables are realized by associating *identifiers* (terminal strings of a grammar for generating names) with memory locations, via a storage mapping. A specific name generated by the grammar is written $id^{\mathbf{int}}$, or simply *id* if the grammar is not a special one for integers. If *id* is an identifier for a variable of type **int**, the mapping can be written (using a notation of ALGOL 68)

$$id \Rightarrow \widehat{id},$$

where $\widehat{id}$ is a member of the set of memory addresses capable of storing integers.[6]

In practice, the mapping is effected by some kind of table in which *id* is associated

---

[4]P. Naur, J. W. Backus, *et al.*, eds., "Report on the Algorithmic Language ALGOL 60," *Communications of the ACM*, **3**, no. 5 (May 1960), 299–314.

[5]A. van Wijngaarden, B. J. Mailloux, J. E. L. Peck, and C. H. A. Koster, eds., *Revised Report on the Algorithmic Language ALGOL 68* (Berlin: Springer-Verlag, 1976).

[6]$\widehat{id}$ will usually be represented as an integer, expressed in a base that is determined by the accessing mechanism of the storage device. It is read as "the address for the identifier $\widehat{id}$."

with $\widehat{id}$. This table is usually called the *symbol table*, and an entry is made into it when the variable is first named. Here we shall call the table the *storage map*, $S^{int}(id)$, to serve as a reminder that it can be regarded as a function, which takes as its argument identifiers of integer variables.

The *value* of a variable is defined to be the contents of the memory cell associated with the identifier. If $VAL(x)$ denotes the value of the variable x, and id is the identifier for a variable of type **int**, then

$$VAL(id) = i,$$

where

$$i \in V = \{0, \pm 1, \pm 2, \ldots, \pm I\}$$
$$I = \text{largest integer capable of being represented in a register.}$$

Writing $CON(x)$ for the contents of the location whose address is x, we have

$$VAL(id) = CON(\widehat{id}).$$

The semantic interpretation[7] of an assignment statement such as

$$num \Leftarrow 3$$

is obtained by noting that the effect is to make

$$CON(\widehat{num}) = 3.$$

When a variable is named on the right-hand side of an assignment statement such as

$$id \Leftarrow id + 1,$$

its value must be determined (it must be *dereferenced*, in ALGOL 68 terminology) before the addition is carried out, so the effect of the statement is to make

$$CON(\widehat{id}) = VAL(id) + 1$$

or, alternatively,

$$CON(\widehat{id}) = CON(\widehat{id}) + 1.$$

We have seen that the concept of a variable has both logical and physical aspects. These can be expressed formally. The data structure for *variables of type* **int** is defined by the quintuple

$$\langle V^{int}, O^{int}, G^{int}, M^{int}, S^{int} \rangle,$$

where

$V^{int} = $ set of values from the domain of integers
$O^{int} = $ set of operations and relations on members of V^{int}
$G^{int} = $ grammar for generating names of integer variables, $L(G^{int})$
$M^{int} = $ set of cells, each capable of storing an integer value
$S^{int} = $ storage mapping from $L(G^{int})$ to M^{int}

---

[7]These notions of variable, value, and calculation can be formalized, as for example in J. McCarthy, "A Formal Description of a Subset of ALGOL," in *Formal Language Description Languages for Computer Programming*, T. B. Steel, Jr., ed. (Amsterdam: North-Holland Publishing Company, 1966), pp. 1–12; or P. Wegner, "The Vienna Definition Language," *Computing Surveys*, **4**, no. 1 (Mar. 1972), 5–63.

With this notation, the *logical structure* of integer variables—a set of named items taking on integer values, together with operations on the items—is modeled by the triple $\langle V^{int}, O^{int}, G^{int}\rangle$, and it can be regarded as designating the *type*. The *storage structure*, which may be regarded as an association of variables with storage, or as an access mechanism for going from names to addresses, is expressed by the triple $\langle G^{int}, M^{int}, S^{int}\rangle$. The data structure is thus a union of the data type and storage structure.[8]

2.3 Model for Primitive Data Types

It is clear how to extend the model discussed above to certain types other than **int**. For example, if a variable *var1* can take on real values expressed as floating-point numbers, the variable name will be mapped onto a member of M^{real}, a set of locations capable of storing numbers of type **real**. M^{real} may be a distinctly different set than M^{int}. Note also that the operators for which *var1* can be an operand are quite different from the operators associated with integers. The extension to Boolean variables (data type **boolean**), and to variables that can take on the value of a single character belonging to the character set capable of being represented in memory (data type **char**) is also obvious. We have in these respective cases storage locations capable of storing a truth value (true or false), and characters.

The four data types described so far—**int**, **real**, **boolean**, and **char**—are considered primitive because computers are designed to handle them directly. In particular, computers have memory locations built to store values for these types, and instruction sets capable of operating on them.[9] In addition to these types, there is another which is usually recognized as primitive. This is the type **pointer**, abbreviated **ptr**. Making an assignment to a pointer variable corresponds to setting an address, an operation that is always included in the basic set of machine instructions. Another operation tests whether two pointers have the same value.

If pointer assignments such as

$$link \Leftarrow \hat{y}$$

are possible, it will be necessary to include in the programming language a method of semantically interpreting $\hat{y}$ (i.e., finding the address of an identifier).

There are varying opinions on the desirability of having pointers in high-level languages. Objections to the use of pointers were first raised by Hoare,[10] and others

---

[8]There is no accepted definition of the term "data structure" and some authors do *not* include in it the storage mapping as we have done. The definitions given here have been adopted because they maintain distinct meanings for data type and data structure, and they are consistent with the meaning of many writers. $\langle V^{int}, O^{int}\rangle$ is commonly referred to as the *abstract data type* **integer**. We have included G in the concept of type because we wish to deal with integer variables, not just integer values.

[9]Most computers handle Boolean variables, not as a single bit, but as an ordered set of k bits, where k is characteristic of the word length of the machine (i.e., as Boolean vectors). Similarly, the logical instructions operating on Boolean variables operate on all the bits in the word.

[10]C. A. R. Hoare, "Hints on Programming Language Design," *ACM SIGACT/SIGPLAN Symposium on Principles of Programming Languages* (Boston, Oct. 1–3, 1973).

have argued against them as well.[11,12] Generally, the problems created by using pointers for data descriptions are similar to those in using *goto* statements in programs. More specifically, the objections are:

1. Pointers are easily misused. In PL/I, for example, the ADDR function yields the absolute address of a variable, and therefore allows one to define a pointer as referencing a variable of one type, and yet set it to point to a variable of another type. This can result in invalid operations and other errors.
2. Pointers allow one to refer to a common data object by multiple names, a phenomenon called the "alias variable" problem. Alias variables make it more difficult to construct modular programs, and to verify program correctness, since it is necessary to allow for the consequences of variables having multiple identities throughout the program.
3. A pointer may be left dangling. This happens when it is set to point at storage which is subsequently deallocated, either explicitly or because the program has left the block in which the declaration is valid.
4. The indiscriminate use of pointers may prevent the use of built-in techniques that take advantage of hardware devices provided to speed up processing. An example of such a device is a pipeline control unit in which a sequence of instructions, held in the pipeline, is simultaneously decoded. The instructions can then be executed in rapid succession, provided the referenced data items can be accessed quickly enough. But pointers make it easy to separate data items into different parts of an auxiliary store, and if this happens, the effectiveness of the pipeline is lost.

Although early languages such as FORTRAN and ALGOL were designed without pointers, and even later languages, such as APL and SETL, have done without them, the facilities provided by pointers are too valuable to be given up. As will be seen in later chapters, pointers make it easy to link lists, and allow simple realizations of trees and other kinds of data structures which can grow or diminish with program execution. Moreover, it is often highly *desirable* to share a common data item among several processes without making a separate copy for each process, and pointers provide an effective mechanism of doing this.

It has been suggested that programming languages should have one or more recursive data types as primitives to replace **ptr**.[13] The idea is to define data types such as **list** and **tree**, in which pointers arise naturally, recursively, along with operations that permit their creation, growth, and diminution, In this way dynamic data types are available, but their pointers are hidden, so the programmer is prevented from introducing constructs which are likely to cause trouble.

Somewhat less restrictive is the device of using *typed pointers* or *reference* types,

[11]R. Kieburtz, "Programming Without Pointer Variables," *ACM SIGPLAN Notices*, **8**, no. 2 (1976), 95–107.

[12]D. M. Berry, Z. Erlich, and C. J. Lucena, "Correctness of Data Representations: Pointers in High Level Languages," *ACM SIGPLAN Notices*, **8**, no. 2 (1976), 115–120.

[13]Kieburtz; see footnote 11.

that is, pointers whose data types are dependent on the type of variable they reference. For example, **real-ptr** *loc* declares that *loc* is a pointer variable whose values are addresses of real numbers. This is the solution adopted in such languages as SIMULA,[14] ALGOL 68, PASCAL,[15] and EUCLID.[16] With typed pointers, some, but not all, of the undesirable effects of using pointers (e.g., illegal references) are avoided, or are less likely to occur. It is for this reason, and also because of the view that graphs and lists are general data types whose realization is naturally effected with pointers, that typed pointers will be adopted in this book.

Summing up, the data structure for a variable of type **prim**, where **prim** is one of **int**, **real**, **boolean**, **char**, or **ptr**, can be described by the quintuple

$$\langle V^{prim}, O^{prim}, G^{prim}, M^{prim}, S^{prim} \rangle,$$

where

V^{prim} = set of values from a given domain characteristic of the primitive type; a value, $v \in V^{prim}$, will be called a *datum*

O^{prim} = Set of operations (and relations) on members of V and L(G)

G^{prim} = grammar for generating names, $L(G^{prim})$, for variables of type **prim**

M^{prim} = set of cells, each capable of storing *prim* values

S^{prim} = storage mapping from $L(G^{prim})$ to M^{prim}.

As was the case for integer variables, the logical structure is described by the triple $\langle V^{prim}, O^{prim}, G^{prim} \rangle$, while the storage structure is represented by $\langle G^{prim}, M^{prim}, S^{prim} \rangle$. Before this model is extended to handle more complex data structures, some points should be noted.

First, we do not mean to suggest that each data type necessarily has its own distinct naming scheme G, address space M, or storage mapping function S. In a given programming language, any of G, M, or S could be common to several types. The type superscripts are used to reflect type-dependent differences when they do occur. In particular:

- While identifiers in a program may initially be mapped through a common symbol table, there will generally be differences in storage allocation, depending on type. Therefore, S is more accurately pictured as a composition of several functions, some of which may be type-dependent.
- Normally, the same set of cells holds values of all types, However there may be differences in the way this set is addressed, depending on the type of the values being stored. For example, the address space for S/370 integers is a restricted subset of that for S/370 characters. Hence, while M^{int} and M^{char} physically comprise the same cells, the differing superscripts reflect a real distinction.

[14]O. Dahl, B. Myhrkaug, and K. Nygaard, "The SIMULA 67 Common Base Language," Norwegian Computing Center, Forksningsveiven 1B (Oslo 3, Norway, 1968).

[15]K. Jensen and N. Wirth, *Pascal User Manual and Report* (Berlin: Springer-Verlag, 1974).

[16]B. W. Lampson *et al.*, "Report on the Programming Language Euclid," *ACM SIGPLAN Notes*, **9**, no. 2 (1977).

Second, O, the operator set, is not the set of all conceivable operations on its associated items. It will be a subset, determined by considerations such as efficiency and the purpose of the system that underlies the model. For example, O^{real} might or might not include exponentiation, depending on the environment in which variables are being modeled.

A third point concerns *constants*, or *literals* as they are commonly known in assembler language. Logically, these can be thought of as unnamed items that have been initialized to values. Since they cannot be referred to by name, the values cannot be changed. Physically, the value must be stored somewhere, and accessed somehow; this is normally done by treating its denotation (i.e., a character string, sometimes enclosed by quotes representing the value) as a name. Thus there is a physical, but not logical naming mechanism for constants, and this can be expressed using the notation above by dropping the grammar component from the logical structure. Hence a model for real constants is given by $\langle V^{real}, O^{real} \rangle$, together with $\langle G^{real}, M^{real}, S^{real} \rangle$.

2.4 Composite Data Types

Primitive types can be concatenated or composed to form composite types. To illustrate, suppose that a variable named *pair* may take as its value an ordered pair of integers. The grammar G is the rule for naming such a variable (e.g., the ALGOL 60 rule of any string starting with an alphabetic character) along with the rule for identifying the two integer items. The two items might be designated by

$$pair[1], pair[2]$$
$$pair_1, pair_2$$
$$\text{first } (pair), \text{ second } (pair)$$

or by any other naming mechanism considered appropriate.

Given a storage mapping for **int**, a mapping function for *pair* naturally suggests itself, that is, to map the first item into the memory cell that would be allocated to *pair* had it been designated of type **int**, and the second item into the next consecutive cell. In other words, set

$$\widehat{pair}[1] = \widehat{pair} \text{ and } \widehat{pair}[2] = \widehat{pair} + 1$$

Although G, M, and S have been designated for *pair*, not enough has been specified to say that a data structure is known or even that there is a data type for which *pair* is a variable. The operations allowable on *pair* have not been given, and several quite different sets of arithmetic operations are conceivable. For example, *pair* might be a double-length integer, in which case the addition, subtraction, multiplication, and division rules for double-length integers would apply; alternatively, it might be a complex number with *pair*[1] being interpreted as the real part and *pair*[2] as the imaginary part, in which case the rules for complex arithmetic apply; or still again *pair* might be a rational fraction with *pair*[1] as the numerator, *pair*[2] as the denominator, and yet another set of arithmetic operations. Thus we have three different types of variables (say, **double-length, complex,** and **rational**) with the same storage structure $\langle G, M, S \rangle$ but different operation sets.

As suggested by the example, the specification for a variable of composite type **c** is essentially the same as that for a primitive type, that is, a quintuple

$$\langle V^c,\ O^c,\ G^c,\ M^c,\ S^c \rangle.$$

The various components will now be described.

1. A value in the set V is built up from primitive values in a way that is characteristic of the type.

Systematic ways of building up composite types will be presented shortly, and in the chapters that follow the commonly encountered composite types—strings, lists, stacks, arrays, and trees—will be examined in detail. We start by considering composite types which have values built up from ordered sequences of primitive values or of previously defined composite values. Before showing how to do this, we note that designating a type as an ordered sequence of possible literals is a simple extension of primitive types. Just as the type **boolean** can be specified by the equation

$$\textbf{boolean} = \langle \text{false, true} \rangle,$$

so we can define a type season by

$$\textbf{season} = \langle \text{winter, spring, summer, fall} \rangle.$$

Operations for such types follow immediately from the fact that an ordering has been assigned to the values. For example, the relational operators are valid, so winter $\langle$ spring, and true$\rangle$ false; also a unary predecessor operator is meaningful, so pred (fall) = summer.[17]

The notation above suggests how to specify a composite type from an ordered sequence of previously defined types. This can be done by writing a *specification statement* of the form

$$\textbf{comp type}c = \langle \textbf{type1}\ var1,\ \textbf{type2}\ var2,\ \ldots,\ \textbf{type}m\ varm \rangle \qquad (2.1)$$

where *vari* is an identifier for a variable of **type***i*, previously defined. Each of the positions occupied by *var1*, ..., *varm*, is called a *field*.

As an example, if a programming language did not already have **array** as a built-in data type, it might be desirable to specify a three-demensional vector by

$$\textbf{comp 3-vector} = \langle \textbf{real}\ xcoord,\ \textbf{real}\ ycoord,\ \textbf{real}\ zcoord \rangle.$$

A declaration of the form

$$\textbf{3-vector}\ origin,\ destination$$

would have the effect of creating two instances of **3-vector**, one named *origin*, the other *destination*, both of them consisting of triplets of reals, with the names *xcoord*, *ycoord*, and *zcoord*.

As another example, in Chapter 4 it will be seen that lists are built up from items which are instances of a data type that might be called **entry**. A possible specification for entry is

$$\textbf{comp entry} = \langle \textbf{datum}\ info,\ \textbf{entry-ptr}\ link \rangle \qquad (2.2)$$

---

[17]In PASCAL the generic name *scalar types* is given to types defined in this way; in EUCLID they are termed *enumeration types*.

where *info* is an identifier of type **datum** and *link* is an identifier of the type **entry-ptr**. The significance of *link* is that it contains a pointer to another instance of **entry**. **Datum** itself may be a composite type with two fields, its definition given by

$$\textbf{comp datum} = \langle \textbf{string } key, \textbf{ boolean } flag \rangle. \qquad (2.3)$$

In an actual programming language, specifications such as (2.1), (2.2), and (2.3) would contain information about the size of the fields and the format of values occupying them, where these are not automatically known. The notation adopted here is similar to that found in several programming systems, but it is not taken from any particular one, and for simplicity, size and format data have been omitted.

Note that in Eq. (2.1), **type***i* may be a primitive type, or it may itself be composite. But there is a restriction: it must not introduce recursion—the situation where a type is defined in terms of itself—into the definition. In other works, the specification of **type***i* must not contain **type***i* or any type which, directly or indirectly, has **type***i* in its specification.[18]

The other members of the quintuple are discussed in greater length in later sections of this chapter. For now we note the following:

2. O^c is the set of operators for which variables of type **c** serve as operands: it is described in detail in the next section.
3. $L(G^c)$ consists of the set of names for variables of the given data types, as well as of the names of fields within the type specifications.
4. M^c is the set of locations in which variables can be stored.
5. S^c is a mapping from $L(G) \Rightarrow M$; it is discussed in Section 2.7.

As before, $\langle V^c, O^c, G^c \rangle$ is the logical structure for variables of type **c**, $\langle G^c, M^c, S^c \rangle$ is the storage structure, and the whole complex, $\langle V^c, \dots, S^c \rangle$, is the data structure for the type.

2.4.1 Composition, Recursion, and Type Lattices

Types defined by a **comp** specification can be viewed as the Cartesian product of the constituent types. From Eq. (2.1), we may write

$$\textbf{type c} = \textbf{type1} \times \textbf{type2} \times \dots \times \textbf{type}m,$$

meaning that a variable of **type c** is constructed by choosing a variable of **type1**, a variable of **type2**, and so on. For this reason the term *Cartesian product* can be used to describe generic types defined by a **comp** specification.

Another way of expressing this is to recall that an ordered list is a vector or tuple. A vector, with components $c[1], \dots, c[k]$, is a mapping from the integers $1, \dots, k$ into the components. Thus we construct Cartesian product types by mappings from one list of types (the integers) on which order is defined, into another list.

There are other ways to combine types. When the domain of one function is equal to the range of another, the two can be combined by composition. Composite types

---

[18]The possibilities for composite declarations are more limited here than they are, say, in ALGOL 68. In that language a precise set of prohibitions, called *shielding rules*, guard against the possibility of recursion.

can be defined similarly, and by this technique it is possible to declare, for example, a stack of complex numbers, or a pointer to a vector of integers. Because the storage structures for composite types are inevitably more complicated than those for simple types, questions arise as to whether there should be any restrictions on how the compositions can be effected.

Restricting the depth of compositions to an arbitrary number of levels is possible, but unsatisfying. For example, in some languages it is useful to regard an array of dimension n as a vector whose components are arrays of $n - 1$ dimensions, and a depth restriction would have the effect of limiting the dimension of arrays. A consequence of not restricting depth of composition is that an unbounded number of types can occur. Still, some other restrictions on composition may be desirable. Most language designers have not felt it necessary to provide for a pointer that points to another pointer, although the feature is found occasionally (e.g., in ALGOL 68). More important, as already noted, when a new composite type is defined in terms of those previously declared, it is essential that the chain of definitions terminate. In other words, there must be no circularity in the type definition. (There may be, nevertheless, types such as **list** or **tree** which themselves are inherently recursive.) The notion that composite types are defined in terms of simpler ones, and that there are no cycles in the definitional chain, implies structure to the system of possible types, and this we proceed to investigate.

Union: If **t1** and **t2** are given types, the union of **t1** and **t2**, **t1** $\cup$ **t2**, defines a data type for which variables may be either of type **t1** or type **t2**. The union may be regarded as a "broadening" of its argument types; there are fewer restrictions on a variable of type **t1** $\cup$ **t2** than on a variable of type **t1** or type **t2**. The union type is necessary in a programming language where statements such as

$$\text{if c then } x = p \text{ else } x = q \tag{2.4}$$

are allowed, and p and q have been declared as variables of different types. As an example, suppose that we introduce the Pascal notion of *subrange type*, defined as the restriction of a previously defined scalar type to a subset of the domain, specified by upper and lower bounds. Thus if **t1** is **int**(f1:ℓ1), where $f1 \leq \ell1$, and **t2** is **int**(f2:ℓ2), $f2 \leq \ell2$, then **t1** $\cup$ **t2** is **int**(min(f1,f2):max($\ell1,\ell2$)). In Eq.(2.4), if p is of type **int**(0:20), and q of type **int**(10:30), then $0 \leq p \leq 20$, and $10 \leq q \leq 30$, so x is of type **int**(0:30). As another example, p might be of type **int** and q of type **real**, and x would be either **int** or **real**, constituting a new type which might be called **number**. **Number** variables are either integers, or reals expressed in floating-point notation, but not both; the precise nature of an addition operation on two **number** variables will depend on which data types the variables happen to be. Still another example arises when one wishes to have pointers that can reference either of two different data types. In an application, for example, there might be data objects of type **head-of-family** and type **dependent**. A **person** pointer that can reference either of these data objects could be defined by

$$\textbf{person-ptr} = \textbf{head-of-family-ptr} \cup \textbf{dependent-ptr.}$$

If a pointer *arrow* has been declared to be of type **person-ptr** certain selected fields such as *name* at *arrow* could be valid for both of the constituent types **head-of-family** and

dependent: others such as *earnings* at *arrow* or *school* at *arrow* might apply to only one type.

Intersection: If **t1** and **t2** are types, the intersection of **t1** and **t2**, written **t1/t2**, is the data type for variables that are of *both* types **t1** and **t2**. The effect of intersection is to "narrow" the arguments. There are more restrictions on a variable of type **t1/t2** than on one of type **t1** or **t2**, since such a variable must be a valid operand for any operator associated with **t1**, and also for any operator associated with **t2**. As an example, if **t1** is **int**(0:20) and **t2** is **int**(10:30), then **t1/t2** is type **int**(10:20). As another example, encountered in hashing, it is desirable to regard keys, represented as strings, as both integers, **int**, and character strings, **string**. As an integer, arithmetic operations such as additions and divisions can be carried out on a key; as a character string, selection operations that remove characters can be performed. Keys therefore of data type **int/string**.

Defining union and intersection over types makes it possible to construct a formal theory of types in the same way that we were able to define a lattice over sets, where set union corresponded to the JOIN operation in the lattice, and set intersection to MEET (Section 1.3).

Example 2.1

It is particularly easy to envisage the lattice if the data types are nested intervals, **int**(fi:ℓi) for different *i*. JOIN and MEET correspond to union and intersection as defined above. When defining the MEET of two subrange types for which the intervals have no values in common, it is necessary to introduce a **null** type, just as the null set is needed in the lattice of sets. **Null** is the minimum element of the lattice. The maximum type, **max**, is defined **int**(min fi:max ℓi). **Null** and **max** have the properties that

$$\left.\begin{array}{l} \textbf{max JOIN int}(\text{fi}:\ell i) = \textbf{max} \\ \textbf{null MEET int}(\text{fi}:\ell i) = \textbf{null} \end{array}\right\} \text{for all interval types } \textbf{int}(\text{fi}:\ell i).$$

Figure 2.2 shows the lattice obtained by applying union and intersection to the three subrange types **int**(0:20), **int**(10:40), and **int**(30:50).

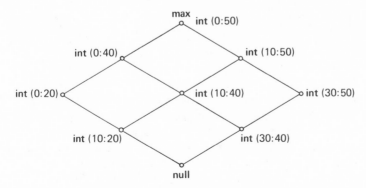

Fig. 2.2   Lattice of subrange types

When there is an interpretation to both union and intersection of data types, as in the example just considered, then both the MEET and JOIN are meaningful, and the full lattice can be shown. As another simple example of a full lattice, consider the data type **key**, which, as pointed out, can be regarded as the intersection type of integer **int** and character string **string**. Since both integers and character strings are represented as bit strings, **bit-string** can be regarded as the type formed by union of **int** and **string**. A variable of type **bit-string** may be an integer or character string. The lattice is shown in Fig. 2.3. In general, the JOIN operation (i.e., union) is always applicable. **Max** can be

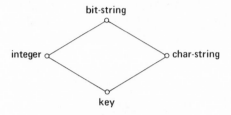

Fig. 2.3   Lattice of string types

regarded as a universal or undefined type; if one is given information that a variable is of type **max**, then no information is available for distinguishing among the possible lower types (lower since the lattice reflects a partial ordering on all the types).

There are times when the union operation is easily interpreted but there is no obvious meaning to intersection. Suppose, in the example previously cited under union, that besides data types for **person**, **dependent**, and **head-of-family**, a dependent type may be either a **spouse** or a **child**, and that we want typed pointers which can reference variables of type **spouse**, **child**, **head-of-family**, and **person**. The structure shown in Fig. 2.4 is applicable to this situation. This is an example of a *semilattice*, where only

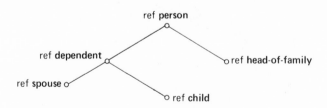

Fig. 2.4   Semilattice of typed pointers

one of the operators (JOIN, in this case) is meaningful. It is technically possible to make a complete lattice by introducing a pointer to a data type, called **nobody**, say, and make the MEET of any pair of types equal to **nobody.** But to do so is somewhat artificial, and it is probably better to leave the structure as a semilattice.

The lattice representation of types is interesting, if for no other reason than that it reveals the structure, in the form of a partial ordering, which is present, and it is therefore a unifying concept, particularly for *extensible languages* which feature user-defined data types. Nevertheless, the formal theory of types will not be pursued here, except to note that there are important processes for whose implementation knowledge of the type is helpful. These include storage assignment, code checking, garbage collection, and choice of representation. Even in extensible languages (e.g., ALGOL 68 and SETL) it is possible to determine the type of many (although not all) defined variables at compile time.[19] Since it is useful to know a variable's type, and a type code is very often explicitly present in the symbol table as part of the information carried with the variable's identifier, it is natural to think of having an instruction that yields the type on inquiry. This could easily be done for primitive variables, even though it might be more difficult for every composite type. It is only recently that programming languages have been provided with this capability. The reason may be, in part, that the processes which use knowledge of type are not under direct programmer control but rather, are embedded in the language processor and operating system. Thus explicit inquiries about type, and use of type codes, were regarded as low-level language capabilities, which were better not placed at the disposal of application programmers in a high-level language.

2.5 Operators for Types

The operator set for a data type will, as already noted, be a large, perhaps open-ended, set of operators, functions, and relations. For a primitive data type, such as **boolean**, many of the operators (e.g., $\neg$, $\wedge$, $\vee$) will be part of the instruction set of the computer. Certain others (e.g., NAND) may be realized as macro-instructions or subroutines. More complicated data types will have complex operations associated with them. Methods of specifying the operation set to be associated with a defined type will be outlined in the next section. Here we focus attention on operations that are common to all, or nearly all, types. Thus, if data elements are stored, the necessity of retrieving them can be taken for granted, so that selection and searching operations are needed. Similarly, it will be necessary to have an assignment operation which allows a value to be assigned to a component. Assignment is a universal operator, applicable to every data type; a related operation is that which enables one to determine whether two assigned values are identical. Selection is applicable to every nonprimitive type.

Among the operators of the logical structure which take a variable, v, or items, $v[i]$, as their operands, there are some that imply changes in the storage when they take effect. For example, before a set of values can be assigned to a composite variable, storage must be allocated for the constituent items. The user may have available operations which allocate storage independently of setting a value; if not, the first assignment to a composite variable will require storage to be provided. Storage alloca-

---

[19]See A. M. Tenenbaum, "Type Determination for Very High Level Languages," *Report NSO-3*, Courant Institute of Mathematical Sciences (New York University, New York, Oct. 1974); also, P. Cousot and R. Cousot, "Static Determination of Dynamic Properties of Generalized Type Unions," in Proceedings of ACM Conference on Language Design for Reliable Software, D. B. Wortman (ed.), *Sigplan Notices,* **12**, no. 3 (March 1977), 77–94.

tion is discussed in the next section and again in Chapter 8. Here the emphasis is on the operations as part of the logical structure or algebra for the data type, and a general classification of operators is outlined. Specific instances that relate to the data type under consideration are presented in succeeding chapters. Usually, a class of operators will be denoted by a Greek letter in uppercase, and a particular member of the class by a Greek letter in lowercase. The names stand for the class as a whole, and within a class there may be several members or subclasses.

Operators are limited in their applicability to the data types associated with them, but they may also be valid only for variables with certain identifiers, of for specified durations of a program. For example, a "file write" might be permitted only for files with certain names or to certain users. We shall use the term *scope* to describe the set of statements and class of variables for which an operator is valid.

Select (Σ):   This operator selects a particular item or field within a variable. The notation $\sigma(item\text{-}id, field\text{-}id)$ can be used to specify selection of a field named *field-id* from a variable named *item-id*. When the item selected is to be designated by its position, this can be written $\sigma(item\text{-}id, i)$ where i is an integer, or an expression which yields an integer value. Thus in the example of the previous section, if *list1* is declared as the identifier for a Cartesian product data type whose components are all of type **entry**,

$$\sigma(list1, 3)$$

selects the third member of this list,

$$\sigma(\sigma(list1, 3), info)$$

selects the subitem named *info* of this member, and

$$\sigma(\sigma(\sigma(list1, 3)info)), key)$$

selects the *key* field of this subitem.

This notation, although precise, is awkward when many levels of selection are present. Selection is the device by which identifiers are qualified so that a general identifier named in a **comp** declaration becomes specific. It is therefore an important and necessary operation, and with varying notations it is found in all programming languages. In PL/I, for example, the *id2* field of item *id1* would be designated by *id1. id2*. In SNOBOL or ALGOL 68, it would be *id2(id1)*. When selection takes place according to position, the usual subscript notation is convenient, especially for arrays. Arrays provide an example where the selection operation for the data type is built into the programming language, and conventional ways of implementing this are described in Chapter 5. In particular situations we shall feel free to adopt a compact notation for selection.

Note that the selection operation implies that the **comp** declaration for the item variable has been given, in which case the operation can be implemented as a sequence of indexing, masking, and logical operations. Thus in the example just given, knowing that *list1* items are a sequence of entries, described by

$$\textbf{comp entry} = \langle \textbf{datum } \textit{info}, \textbf{entry-ptr } \textit{link} \rangle$$

and knowing further the **comp** for **datum**, it is possible to construct the selector $\sigma(\sigma(\textit{list1}, 3), \textit{info})$. Many operators are really a composition of primitive operators, one of which is selection.

Restructure (Π) (e.g., Order, Permute):   The effect of (Π, *id*) is to leave the number of items unchanged, but to alter the sequence in some way. An example might be a permutation operator, which, given the set of indexes $1 \ldots n$, for the items $d[1] \ldots d[n]$, permutes the items in some systematic way to produce a rearrangement (e.g., to produce $d[2], d[3], \ldots, d[n], d[1]$).

Extend (Θ₊) and Contract (Θ₋) (e.g., Insert, Delete, Merge):   These are operators which insert (or delete) an item in a variable. Such operators would have to be accompanied by, or imply, a selection operator that indicates precisely where the extension (deletion) is to take place. Examples are:

1. Addition of an item to the end of a list.
2. Dropping the first component of a vector.

Variations of these operators could take pairs of variables as the operands (e.g., concatenation of strings), or could operate on fields of a named item.

Retrieve (R):   This is a generic name for a class of operations of which the following might be an example:

LOCATE(**type-name**, *field-id*, v)—returns the addresses for all variables of type **type-name** which have value, v, in the field *field-id*.

Retrieve operations involve searching and selection, a subject that is considered in Section 4.6.

Assignment Operations (⟸ or α):   These also could have either items or fields as operands. Assuming that a field of a given variable is specified, there will be suboperations which:

- Allocate storage and create an entry in S if the variable is named for the first time.
- Select the field whose value is to be assigned (i.e., *dereference* the right-hand side of the statement).
- Calculate an address for the left-hand side.
- Store the selected item in the calculated address.

Figure 2.5 (suggested by ALGOL 68) illustrates the process of assigning, to the variable identified by *varx*, the value of *vary*. The left-pointing arrow, ⟸, commonly used to denote assignment, is suitable when values are copied into all fields. For the more general case, when an assignment can be made to a particular field, we can write

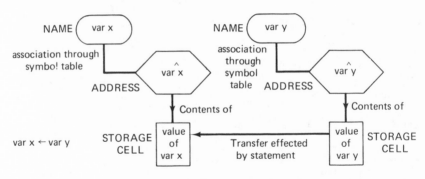

Fig. 2.5 Assignment statement

α(*item-id, field-id*, y) to indicate that a value y has been given to the named field of the variable identified by *item-id*.[20]

Equate (≡) (Equivalence declaration):   This is a statement about the identity of the addresses associated with variables, and really belongs to storage management, but it is mentioned here to contrast it with assignment. If *varx* and *vary* are the identifiers for two variables, the result of *varx* ≡ *vary* is to make $\widehat{varx} = \widehat{vary}$. This is illustrated in Fig. 2.6.

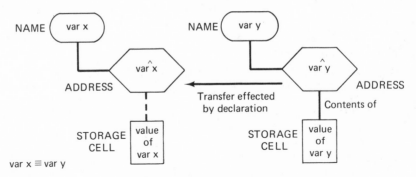

Fig. 2.6 Equivalence declaration

Many specific instances of the operators described here will be encountered in later chapters, as well as different kinds of operators altogether. Those described here should be sufficient to illustrate the principal classes and give some indication of the variety to be found in common data types.

2.6 Type Specification and Checking

Even when types were included in earlier languages, their definition was regarded as part of the semantics of the language, and they were not formally described. In more

---

[20]Adopting a notation of Standish (see footnote 3).

recent languages it has been realized that careful specification of types could be of considerable aid in helping verify the correctness of programs. Three different aspects of types are involved in the process of verifying that programs have been written correctly.

- There must be no inconsistencies or unresolvable ambiguities in the specification of a composite type.
- The implementation of the type (including its storage representation) must be verifiably consistent with the functional definitions.
- It should be possible to ensure that the way in which a variable is used, and the values it takes on, are either consistent with the type specification, or are made consistent by well-defined rules.

These aspects are considered in this section.

2.6.1 Specification

The specification of a type must include some kind of declaration similar to the **comp** which is used throughout this book, and a way of associating the type with its valid set of operations. For composite types, the operations can be described by means of macros or subroutines: for primitives, operations are likely to be built into the hardware, but they may also be defined as subroutines. In any case, for an extensible language with extendible types, it is necessary to be able to bind the applicable operation set to the data type. In essence, the specification is a definition of the syntax and semantics for the type operators. Such definitions are needed because it is often convenient to use the same symbol for different purposes. For example, $+$ is used for addition of both integers and reals, even though addition is very different for numbers represented in floating-point notation than it is for integers. Moreover, $+$ is frequently used to represent union of sets, and concatenation of tuples and strings. Making a single operator applicable to variables of different types is called *overloading* the operator, and with overloading it is especially important to be able to describe the effects of operators precisely. The process of collecting in one place, separate from the application program, all information relevant to a type abstraction and its implementation is known as *encapsulation*. The more explicit the encapsulation, the more automatic can be the process of checking that a type has been correctly specified.

    SIMULA was the first language that allowed a programmer to specify subroutines for the operators associated with a *class*, the concept in SIMULA which corresponds to type. Later languages have gone even further than SIMULA toward encapsulation of types. As an example, we give the following definition for a type *vector*, having three dimensions, as expressed in the Madcap 3 programming language.[21]

[21]M. B. Wells and F. L. Cornwell, "A Data Type Encapsulation Scheme Utilizing Data Base Language Operators," *ACM SIGPLAN Notices*, **8**, no. 2 (1976), 170–178.

$$
\text{VECTOR} \Leftarrow \$ <
$$

$$
\langle \text{real}:3 \text{ items} \rangle
$$

$$
\downarrow \text{pls}: \ll (u,v):@ \text{ VECTOR};
$$

$$
\langle u_i' + v_i' : 0 \leq i < 3 \rangle @ \text{ VECTOR} \gg;
$$

$$
\downarrow \text{mns} \ll (u,v):@ \text{ VECTOR};
$$

$$
\langle u_i' - v_i' : 0 \leq i < 3 \rangle @ \text{ VECTOR} \gg;
$$

$$
\downarrow \text{bye}: \ll u:@ \text{ VECTOR}; \; c:\text{real};
$$

$$
\langle u_i' \cdot c : 0 \leq i < 3 \rangle @ \text{ VECTOR} \gg;
$$

$$
\downarrow \text{eql}: \ll (u,v):@ \text{ VECTOR};
$$

$$
(\forall_{0 \leq i < 3} \; u_i' = v_i') \gg
$$

$$
> \$
$$

The assignment is delimited by the special brackets \$⟨...⟩\$, and the first declaration indicates that **vector** consists of three reals. Each of the operations, pls (for $+$), mns, bye (for multiplication by a constant), and eql (a Boolean predicate), has its definition. Within a definition the prefix operator @ indicates that the formal parameters named are instances of the type being defined. The ′ (accent) suffix operator indicates that the operand is of the type declared; for example, in pls, u_i' and v_i' are to be treated as type **real**. This particular vector has exactly three components; to specify vectors with arbitrary numbers of components, it is necessary to include parameters in the type specification.

Specifying a type by describing the operators and subroutines that may use variables of the given type for operands explains how programmers should use the type. But it does not help in establishing that the type definition is correct, that the implementation of the type as carried out by the storage mapping is consistent with the specification, or that the variable assignments are valid. To validate the first two of these, it is necessary to carry out a special verification procedure based on the actual implementation. An example of such a verification will be given when stacks are discussed in Section 4.2.1 There the implementation is straightforward, and the verification procedure correspondingly simple. The verification procedure may be lengthy if the implementation and type operations are more complicated. In general, an inductive process consisting of two steps is useful[22]:

1. Verify that all created instances of the data type satisfy the axioms.
2. Verify that all operations on a type instance which satisfy the axioms leave the instance so that it still satisfies the axioms.

The proof procedures, even if tedious, are comparatively straightforward, and lend

---

[22]For a more detailed discussion, see B. Wegbreit and J. M. Spitzen, "Proving Properties of Complex Data Structures," *Journal of the ACM*, **23**, no. 2 (Apr. 1976), 389–396.

themselves to automatic methods. In this way one important part of programs, that relating to the specification and implementation of composite data types, becomes subject to formal verification.[23]

2.6.2 Value Checking

Assertions about the types of variables are assertions about possible values that the variables may assume. Since an assignment is an assertion about the equality of values, every assignment implies a consistency condition on the types of the variables that occur on the left- and right-hand sides. In physics this condition leads to a relation on the dimensionality of variables in an equation. For example, in mechanics, when the equation

$$F = 6\pi\eta av$$

is developed for the viscous force on a sphere of radius a moving with velocity v through a fluid of viscosity η, a dimensional check is carried out to verify that the units of the quantities are consistent. In this case force has the dimensions of mass $\times$ acceleration (i.e., $[MLT^{-2}]$, where M is mass, L length, and T time), velocity has dimension $[LT^{-1}]$, a has dimension L, and η has dimension $[ML^{-1}T^{-1}]$. The dimension of the right-hand side of the equation is

$$[ML^{-1}T^{-1}][L][LT^{-1}],$$

which is the same as that of the left-hand side, so the equation is consistent. This is not a complete verification of the correctness of the equation—in particular, nothing is proved about the correctness of the dimensionless constant 6π, but consistency is a *necessary* condition for correctness.

In computer programs the same consistency condition must hold between the left- and right-hand sides of an assignment (although there may be a type conversion, as explained in the next section). Therefore, a test which ensures that the values being assigned to a variable are consistent with those permitted by the type is a useful program-checking technique. With compilers, an important decision must be made as to whether the value checking should be done dynamically, during program execution, or statically: for example, when the program is being read in, compiled, or when a new block is entered. Since the value of a variable can be changed anywhere within a block, dynamic checks are necessary to be completely sure that permitted values are always used. But because it can be prohibitively expensive to increase the execution time of a key inner loop in a program by adding validity checks, it is usual to carry out such checks statically. The situation is illustrated by checks on the index values of array variables. If, during matrix multiplication, every time an array element is selected a test is done to ensure that the indexes lie within specified bounds, multiplication will be dominated by the time required for these tests. There are, in fact, computers that

---

[23]An example of a more complicated verification procedure, one for the type **symbol table**, is given by J. Guttag,"Abstract Data Types and the Development of Data Structures,"*Communications of the ACM*, 20, no. 6 (June 1977), 396–404.

have built-in hardware to do the tests, but even then the processing time is increased significantly, and compromise solutions on validity testing are usually preferred. One possibility is to have array-bound checking as an option, which is switched on when a program is being debugged, and off during normal execution. Another possibility is to check the initial value of assignments (this can be done statically on block entry, for example), but not the later values during execution. It may be possible to establish by induction that once an initial value is correct, subsequent computed values will also be correct. This is one of the accepted techniques for proving programs to be correct, but such techniques are far from standard, even with structured programs. The usual situation is that language processors have some restricted form of validity checking, which is useful for detecting errors but is not guaranteed to find all instances of invalid values.[24]

2.6.3 Type Conversions

The problem of checking the validity of values is further complicated because there may be "errors" of type in a program which one wants to override, or let pass, possibly with a warning message. Such a case occurs in FORTRAN, where an assignment such as

$$X = 20 + 4.51 \times 10^2$$

is permitted, even though the two operands have different types. There is an arbitrariness in deciding whether the result should be a **real** (in which case 20 is converted to type **real**) or an integer (in which case 4.5×10^2 should be converted to **integer**). The decision can be represented as a property of the $+$ operator. Whenever an operator is overloaded, so that it can have operands from different value sets, a type-conversion table has to be associated with it, showing the result for all valid combinations of operand types. The ALGOL 68 coercion table for the binary operator $+$ is shown in Table 2.1.

TABLE 2.1   ALGOL 68 type conversion for operator $+$

Type of:		Type of Result					
First Operand	Second Operand	**int**	**real**	**compl***	**char**	**string**	Other
int		int	real	compl	Undefined	Undefined	Undefined
real		real	real	compl	Undefined	Undefined	Undefined
compl*		compl	compl	compl	Undefined	Undefined	Undefined
char		Undefined	Undefined	Undefined	string	string	Undefined
string		Undefined	Undefined	Undefined	string	string	Undefined
Other		Undefined	Undefined	Undefined	Undefined	Undefined	Undefined

***compl** is a complex number type, consisting of a pair of reals.

[24]For further discussion, see P. Henderson "An Approach to Compile-Time Type Checking," in *Information Processing*, (Amsterdam: North-Holland Publishing Company, 1977), pp. 523–527.

In the description of ALGOL 68, where there is a very extensive treatment of type conversion, the process of changing one type to another during the execution of an instruction is known as *coercion*. It is pointed out that even the simplest processes involve coercion.[25] For example, the declaration **real** x is a short form for

$$\textbf{ref real } x = \hat{x}$$

which means that the address of x is to be associated with the reference (identifier) for a real variable x. **Ref real** x, as the name of a real, is a different type from x, and so the declaration implies something about a type derived from the type actually named. Similarly, the assignment

$$z \Leftarrow y+2$$

requires a dereferencing of the variable y (i.e., a conversion from the name y to an integer) in order to obtain the value, so here also a form of coercion is involved. Altogether eight kinds of coercion are identified, including (besides the two above), widening, proceduring (creating parameterless routines) and deproceduring (calling routines). The contexts in which each of the eight kinds of coercion may be applied are carefully spelled out, and the standard prelude for ALGOL 68 (a section that explains the built-in features for the standard version of the language) contains tables like Table 2.1, for unary and binary operators, and for logical relations.

In order to say more about methods of specifying types, type checking, and type conversion, it would be necessary to go much deeper into the details of particular programming languages than would be justified here. Questions relating to data type lie at the interface between the subjects of data structures and programming languages, and both subjects are continuing to evolve.

2.7 Storage Mapping

When a composite data type is mapped into storage, a decision has to be made about how the fields of an item are to be mapped onto the cells available for primitive data elements. Typical cell sizes are the number of bits required for a Boolean value (bit), a character (byte), an address, and an integer (word); the varieties present vary from machine to machine. Thus, whereas variables may be defined in terms of items and fields at the logical structure level and so be independent of the computing system, the storage structure will be machine- and implementation-dependent.

For a composite variable at certain levels of use (e.g., the application programmer), it may be enough to know that the identifier for an instance of the type is mapped into M, as was the case for a primitive variable. At other levels (e.g., the system programmer) it may be necessary to know precisely how *all* the fields of V are mapped into M. This mapping may be characteristic of the data type (as it is for an **array**) or it may be partially under programmer control (as is usually the case for a **list**).

[25]For a discussion, see C. H. Lindsey and S. G. van der Meulen, *Informal Introduction to ALGOL 68*, (Amsterdam: North-Holland Publishing Company, 1971), especially Chap. 5.

2.7.1 Storage Allocation

The process of assigning storage and a value to a variable is known as *binding the variable*.[26] There is a considerable advantage in deferring the storage allocation, if possible, to immediately before execution of the statement in which the variable occurs. The reason is that in programs, the size (i.e., the storage requirements) of variables can vary considerably, and by deferring the binding it will be possible to allocate the exact amount of storage needed.

Among the stages of a program at which storage allocation can be carried out, the following may be identified:

- Statement read-in time.
- Program read-in time.
- Block entry time.
- Compile time (during the translation phase).
- Program load time (when the program is transferred from secondary storage and various subprograms are assembled).
- Execution time.

Not all these times are present in every system: in an interpretive, time-shared system such as APL, for example, allocation must occur at execution. Since there are so many possibilities in time when allocation can take place, the storage mapping function, as already noted, is not an isolated program but rather a sequence of processes that take place during the various stages between program read-in and execution. Because the transformation from the written program to the one finally executed takes place in many small steps, it is useful to view the translation as being carried out on a sequence of distinct, "virtual" computers. The first member of this sequence is a device programmed in the language in which the problem is conceived; the last is the real computer using machine language; in between there are virtual machines using perhaps the procedural language defined by a compiler, an assembly language, and so on. This concept of virtual machines has proved useful in structured programming and in designing programming languages intended to be transferable from one computing system to another. Each invocation of a program segment furthering storage allocation and value binding may be regarded as a change from one, more abstract, virtual machine to a more concrete one. On the first virtual machine the logical structure defines the mapping of data into the variables arising in the formulation of the problem. On the last, the actual computer, the data are stored in the memory locations.

For a Cartesian product data type, the **comp** declaration indicates the number and kinds of storage cells that have to be allocated for an instance of the data type. The allocation of storage cells and the assignment of values to a data item may be valid for only part of a program. The set of statements over which a storage allocation (or value assignment) holds is called the *scope* of the allocation (assignment). The main

---

[26]This is only one example of binding, which in general defines a function (or sometimes a relation) on a variable, taking the identifier as the argument. Other examples are the association of an attribute with an identifier, and of a type with an identifier (i.e., a declaration).

purpose of a scope indication is to allow the storage for variables that are not to be used again to be made available for further use (i.e., to be *deallocated*). Deallocation is as important as allocation, and the two are discussed in Section 8.3.

Block structure, as introduced in ALGOL 60, provides an elegant method of specifying scope. In programming languages where parallel processing or cooperating programs are possible, additional techniques are necessary, but for the relatively simple programs presented in this book, the ALGOL-like declaration of a primitive variable will be taken to indicate that the requested storage is to be reserved for it. Usually the variable will be named in an explicit type declaration, but even if this has not been done, it is to be assumed that preceding the first assignment, storage has been allocated to hold the values. In Section 4.3, where linked lists are discussed, a CREATE instruction which has the effect of allocating storage for an item on the list will be explicitly written when needed.

2.7.2 Classification of Mappings

From the processing requirements for the data, a programmer may know that the use of one item is always followed by the use of another, or that access to one field of a variable is usually accompanied by access to another. Since it is not always possible to arrange that items needed together are stored together, the basic technique of attaching pointers to fields is used to facilitate access of related items and fields. The use of a pointer may be regarded as imposing a successor condition on the data which is implemented in the storage mapping. Storage assignment through the use of pointer variables is one of a number of techniques in storage mapping. Frequently, the techniques are hidden in the automatic storage allocation procedure, and hence only subject to programmer control in part, if at all. Nevertheless, it is often important to understand storage mappings to utilize the logical data structure efficiently.

The basic property of computer storage is that addresses are specified by consecutive integers. A consequence is that for any address, $\hat{a}$, there is a successor address, $SUC(\hat{a})$, uniquely defined.[27] Let $\hat{d}[i,j,k]$ represent the address of the kth cell in the mapping for the jth field of item $d[i]$. Since the cells of a field are simply numbered as they occur, it follows that $\hat{d}[i,j,1] < \hat{d}[i,j,2] \ldots < \hat{d}[i,j,n[i,j]]$, where $n[i,j]$ is the number of cells required for the jth field of $d[i]$. That is, the cells within a field have a sequential order, determined by the addressing scheme of the storage devices. Almost always, a stronger condition is imposed on a mapping of a field, namely that the cells be *contiguous* (i.e., that no vacant cells are permitted between the storage cells required for a field). The contiguity condition may be expressed by writing

$$\hat{d}[i,j,k+1] = SUC(\hat{d}[i,j,k]).$$

Unless otherwise stated, contiguity will be assumed to hold for the cells into which a field is mapped. A set of contiguous storage cells will be called a *block*, and the assump-

---

[27]For the usual case where there are different cells, it will be necessary to introduce $SUC(\hat{a})^{prim}$ to obtain a unique successor, but, as indicated, it will be assumed from the context that the type of cell is known.

tion just made can be expressed by saying that a field is mapped into a storage block. The storage for a set of fields may also be contiguous, as may be that for a set of items, but contiguity for these will *not* be assumed unless explicitly stated. Since contiguity is present for the cells of a field, when the total number of cells required for the field is known, it is meaningful to use the notation $\hat{d}[i,j]$ for the address of field j in $d[i]$. This can be interpreted as an address characterizing the set of cells whose addresses are $\langle \hat{d}[i,j,1], \ldots, \hat{d}[i,j,n[i,j]] \rangle$, or more simply as $\hat{d}[i,j,1]$, the address of the first cell of the block.

One mapping which is frequently encountered is that which adds a constant to every address in a given set of addresses. Such a mapping is a *storage relocation*, and the ability to do this is basic to a modern operating system. The fields within a variable can be made relocatable by locating them relative to the address of the first field, called the *base address*. In such a case we have

$$\hat{d}[i,j] = \hat{d}[i,1] + \mathrm{f}(j),$$

where $\hat{d}[i,1]$ is the base address and $\mathrm{f}(j)$ is a function of the field position.

It will henceforth be assumed that fields are relocatable in this way. When this is the case, and $\mathrm{f}(j)$, the storage mapping function for fields, is known, it is meaningful to use the notation $\hat{d}[i]$ for the address of an item, even in a composite data structure where an item is mapped into a set of addresses; $\hat{d}[i]$ can be regarded as the base address for the field of the item, Given $\mathrm{f}(j)$, the field selection operator, $\sigma(d[i],j)$ can be constructed.

Although contiguity is not assumed for fields or items, somewhat weaker conditions may be imposed. The mapping may be such, for example, that the addresses of successive fields are always either monotonically increasing or monotonically decreasing, in which case the mapping on fields will be said to be *sequential*. Mathematically,

$$\hat{d}[i,\bar{j}] > \hat{d}[i,j] \text{ whenever } \bar{j} > j$$

or

$$\hat{d}[i,\bar{j}] < \hat{d}[i,j] \text{ whenever } \bar{j} > j.$$

The mapping for items may also be sequential, but this will generally not be assumed to be the case. Figure 2.7 illustrates a mapping that is contiguous for cells within a field and sequential for fields within an item, but neither contiguous nor sequential on items.

Another way of characterizing mappings is whether the address depends solely on the position (i.e., on the indexes i, j), in which case it will be called an *indexed* mapping, or whether it also depends in some way on the value of the item, in which case it will be called a *content-addressed mapping*.

Two kinds of indexed mappings are commonly encountered:

1. $\hat{d}[i]$ is given as the ith entry in a table of addresses (i.e., the ith member of an ordered set).
2. $\hat{d}[i]$ is a linear function of i (i.e., $\hat{d}[i] = \mathrm{p}i + \mathrm{q}$, where p and q are constants). The is a *linear addressing scheme* or linear mapping.

The general case of content-addressed mappings is expressed by

$$\hat{d}[i] = \mathrm{f}(d[1], \ldots, d[i-1], d[i]).$$

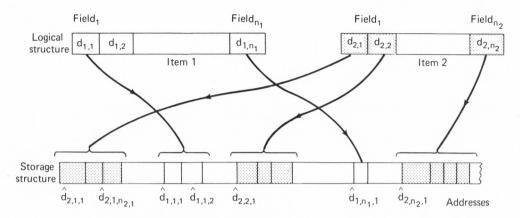

Fig. 2.7 Storage mapping of items and fields into cells

An important special case is the *linked list* mapping. In a linked list the composition of an item is specified by a declaration of the form

$$\textbf{comp item} = \langle \textbf{type-c } \textit{info}, \textbf{ item-ptr } \textit{link} \rangle,$$

where **type-c** is a data type for the composite subitem *info*. The mapping property of a *linked list* is that the *link* field defines the address of the successor to an item. We have, using the selector notation,

$$\hat{d}[i] = \text{SUC } \hat{d}[i-1] = \sigma(d[i-1], \textit{link}).$$

The general content-addressed mapping is illustrated by *hash coding*. In such a mapping the first step in calculating $\hat{d}$ is to use d as the argument of a function that yields a number, random in some sense, from which d is determined by a simple rule. The name hashing comes from the fact that there are advantages if the function, for the domain of d, yields values distributed uniformly over the range of permitted addresses. For most items the address depends only on the value of the item [i.e., $\hat{d} = \text{f}(d)$], but if the location calculated happens to be occupied, a rule must be given for finding a substitute. Hash coding has been the subject of a great deal of investigation and it is discussed further in Section 4.6.3.

In summary, there are four basic storage mappings.

1. Contiguous: storage is densely filled.
2. Indexed: addresses are determined by position number.
3. Linked: a field points to the address of the successor.
4. Hash-based: addresses are randomized within a range.

Mapping functions can combine several of the basic addressing techniques. As a common example, a list may be stored in a contiguous region as long as the number of items does not exceed a fixed limit, l. When this limit is passed, a pointer variable contains a link or *chaining address* to an *overflow area*—another contiguous region for additional items (see Fig. 2.8). All the mappings in this book will be one of these four basic types, or a combination.

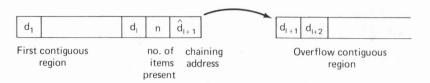

Fig. 2.8 Contiguous mapping with chain-linked overflow region

2.7.3 Example

A simple example will serve to show how the constructs described in this chapter allow one to specify data types appropriate to an application, and how these types lead to storage mappings and data structures. The data for the example is a bridge deal, which, in conventional form, is displayed in Fig. 2.9(a).

The specifications for the data types are written in the language in which the application is being programmed. By slightly varying the specification, the language processor can be made to produce two different storage mappings, one based on an array and the other on a linked list. (Linked lists and arrays are discussed in Chapters 4 and 5 of this book, respectively, but the concepts are undoubtedly familiar from elementary programming, and here we are only interested in the fact that they make use of indexed and linked mappings, the second and third of the four kinds just discussed.)

We start by specifying a data type **card,** derived from specifications for types **rank** and **suit.** (Note first that the digit 0 is used to denote the value 10, and that single letters are used for clubs, diamonds, hearts, and spades, as well as for jack, queen, king, and ace, so that all ranks and suits can be represented by a single character.) The specifications are:

$$\textbf{rank} = \langle 2, 3, 4, 5, 6, 7, 8, 9, 0, J, Q, K, A \rangle \tag{2.5}$$

$$\textbf{suit} = \langle C, D, H, S \rangle \tag{2.6}$$

$$\textbf{comp card} = \langle \textbf{rank } r, \textbf{suit } s \rangle. \tag{2.7}$$

Next it assumed that the data type **sequence** is one which the processor is capable of implementing. A **sequence** is a set item of identical types (**cards,** in this case), and part of the implementation is that the name of the sequence, followed by an integer in parentheses, results in the selection of the named element. A **sequence** corresponds to an array (actually a vector here), and it will be seen in Chapter 5 that one of the standard ways of implementing an array is to set up an indexed mapping of the components. Also, in the specification the minimum and maximum indexes are given. Thus

$$\textbf{card-sequence } (1:13) \; \textit{north}$$

denotes a sequence variable named *north,* whose values consist of 13 cards, identified by the integers 1 to 13. The data type **deal** is specified as four such sequences

$$\textbf{comp deal} = \langle \textbf{card-sequence}(1:13)\textit{north}, \textbf{card-sequence}(1:13)\textit{south},$$

$$\textbf{card-sequence}(1:13)\textit{east}, \textbf{card-sequence}(1:13)\textit{west} \rangle. \tag{2.8}$$

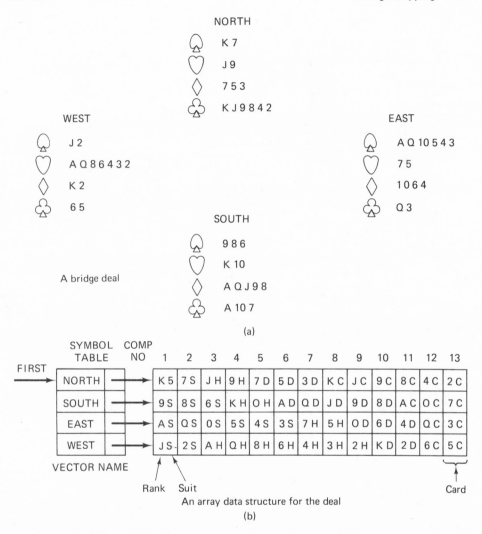

Fig. 2.9(a)   Bridge deal

The effect of the specification (2.8) is that a language processor constructs a mechanism for setting up four **card-sequences**, with names as given, every time a variable of type deal is declared. For example, if *first* is of type **deal**, space for four such card-sequences, with names *north*, *south*, *east*, and *west*, is reserved. The actual values for the cards may not be assigned until later (e.g., when the data are read in, or when the program enters the block in which *first* is declared). Figure 2.9(b) shows the data structure after the values have been assigned. The value for the expression *north* (*first*)[4] is the fourth card of *north*'s hand in deal *first*, namely 9H.

The structure of Fig. 2.9(b) faithfully captures all the facts about the data. The operations for the data types have not been discussed, but it is easy to envisage selec-

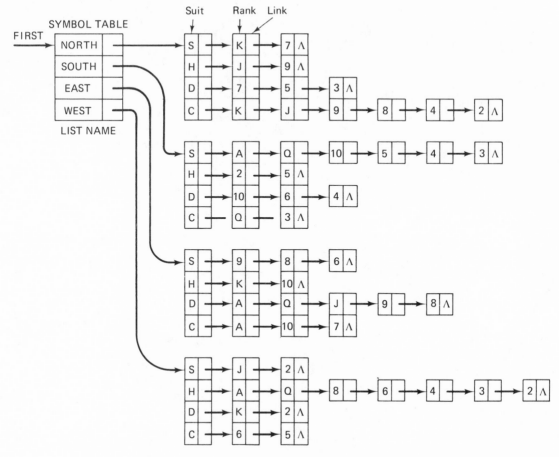

A linked data structure for the deal

Fig. 2.9(b)

tion operators that yield a particular card or rank, for example, as well as other operators important for the application, such as one to compare the rank of cards in a given suit. Nevertheless, the structure of Fig. 2.9(b) does not quite correspond to the display of Fig. 2.9(a). In the latter, a player's hand is shown with suits of varying length rather than as fixed-length vectors of 13 cards, and to represent such a suit, a data type with a varying number of items is needed. To have the language processor recognize this possibility, we can write

rank-sequence(0 *up to* 13)

to specify a data type consisting of a sequence (of values for **rank** variables) containing between 0 and 13 entries. After specifying **rank** as in Eq. (2.5), a data type **hand** is specified as consisting of four **rank-sequences**, named *clubs*, *diamonds*, *hearts*, and *spades*:

$$\textbf{comp hand} = \langle\textbf{rank-sequence}(0 \; up \; to \; 13)clubs,$$

$$\textbf{rank-sequence}(0 \; up \; to \; 13)diamonds,$$

$$\textbf{rank-sequence}(0 \; up \; to \; 13)hearts,$$

$$\textbf{rank-sequence}(0 \; up \; to \; 13)spades\rangle. \qquad (2.9)$$

Finally, **deal** is composed of four **hands**:

$$\textbf{comp deal} = \langle\textbf{hand} \; north, \textbf{hand} \; south, \textbf{hand} \; east, \textbf{hand} \; west\rangle. \qquad (2.10)$$

It is possible to make the language processor, on recognizing the words *up to*, implement the sequence data type as a linked list. Another possibility is that sequence is implemented *either* as an array *or* as a linked list, the choice being determined by features of the program. Assuming that the representation *is* a linked list, Fig. 2.9(c) shows the data structure after the card values have been assigned.

The example illustrates the independence of data type and storage structure. In both instances, the **comp** specification is implemented as a contiguous mapping of the named constituents. The sequence implementation can be either an indexed-mapping or a linked list, so that different data structures result from essentially the same type specifications. This question of alternative choices for data structures is considered again in Section 7.1, where a more elaborate example is given.

2.8 Evaluating Data Structures

One criterion for evaluating a data structure, or for comparing two different structures that might be used for solving a problem, is to calculate the storage requirements as a function of the parameters of the problem. But equally important criteria derive from the efficiency of the algorithms which use the data structure, and we saw in Chapter 1 that timing efficiency is a complex factor. The situation is made more complicated because it is difficult to attach relative importance to the various algorithms of interest. The usual approach is to determine the timing for certain "basic" operations (e.g., creating an instance of the data type, searching, insertion, and deletion). If somehow the relative frequencies of these basic operations can be estimated, then an overall timing cost can be established. Knowing these relative frequencies is equivalent to knowing something about the frequency distributions for the parameters of the problems to which the algorithms are applied. In the absence of such knowledge, it is common to make certain assumptions regarding randomness. When manipulating (undirected) graphs, for example, it is common to assume that the graph population has a given edge density, ρ, and that the edges are uniformly distributed. By this is meant that for a graph with n vertices, the probability of any given edge being present is the same, and is equal to $\rho \cdot n \cdot (n - 1)/2$, since the number of edges for a complete graph is $n \cdot (n - 1)/2]$. Although such assumptions are useful in that they make possible a more detailed comparison of different algorithms, they are not often applicable to the data processed by computers. To give an obvious example, it is not valid to assume that frequency distribution of the letters in strings corresponding to words in a natural language, or names in a list of surnames, is uniform.

The relative importance of storage and timing efficiency is even more difficult to establish than the relative importance of operation types. One of the characteristic features of computer algorithms is that there is very often a trade-off between storage and time. An algorithm can be made to run faster by using a data structure that requires more storage, or conversely, storage can be saved at the expense of execution efficiency. Time and again throughout this book we shall point out instances of such trade-offs. Examples are the efficiency of finding a substring within a string versus the cost of maintaining redundant information in the storage mapping (Section 3.2.2), efficiency of deleting entries in a linked list versus the cost for storing back pointers (Section 4.3.1), and the efficiency of accessing components in a sparse matrix versus the cost of storing zero components (Section 5.4). If one knows the relative cost of storage and central processor time, this may be used in determining an overall criterion for a storage structure, but the multiplicity of trade-offs often makes such determination conditional on unknown factors.

Besides the factors already mentioned, there are others which are even less precisely measurable but which can nevertheless be decisive. Among these are the cost of setting up a problem (writing programs, debugging, embedding them in an existing system) versus the cost of execution (running a number of cases). Also, it is very difficult to attach a cost or value to environmental factors such as security (protection against either inadvertant or deliberate unauthorized access to the program) and integrity (establishing the correctness and consistency of the data). A detailed treatment of these latter factors, forming part of what is generally known as "data management," is beyond the scope of this book.

Exercises

1. Look up the Peano axioms as a method of specifying the operations on the integers (consult an algebra text).
   (a) Is this the minimal set of operations, O^{int}, for producing the integers?
   (b) How is O^{int} realized in the computer and what mechanisms are there for enlarging the set when necessary?
2. Identifiers have certain operations defined for them; for example, string values can be assigned, and they can be compared lexicographically.
   (a) Does this allow one to define a data type **identifier**?
   (b) Can a data type **label** be defined? (Assume that labels are strings which locate instructions.)
   Justify your answers.
3. Show that the union and intersection operations defined for types are commutative and associative.
4. Suppose that there are, in an application, data types corresponding to **dependent, head-of-family, spouse,** and **child,** and further that a **dependent** can be a **spouse** or **child,** and a **family** is a set consisting of the **head-of-family** and all **dependents.** Complete the lattice over these types.
5. Define a specific operation, corresponding to each of the general operations in Section 2.5, for the data types **string** and **array**. Compare your operations with equivalent ones in SNOBOL and APL.

6. Show that a variable of Cartesian product type, all of whose components are either primitive or variables of Cartesian product types, can be regarded as a tree in which the leaves are variables of primitive type. What is the graph structure if only types (and not variables) are associated with the nodes, and if the type for each node must be distinct?

7. Look up how variables of Cartesian product type are specified in some standard programming languages (e.g., COBOL, PL/I, ALGOL 68). How are the size and format of the fields specified in each case?

8. Using a vector as an example, show why it can be desirable to introduce a parameter into a type specification. What other examples of type specification are there in which a parameter would be convenient?

9. Typeless languages have been designed in which the only data type is **bit string**. Discuss the advantages and disadvantages of such a language. How might checking be accomplished? [See M. Richards, "BCPL: A Tool for Compiler Writing and System Programming," *AFIPS Conference Proceedings*, Vol. 34. Montvale, N.J.: AFIPS Press, 1969, pp. 557–1566. Also, C. J. Higley, "Type Checking in a Typeless Language," *The Computer Journal*, **19**, no. 2, (May 1976), 166–169.] Is APL a typeless language?

10. Suppose **t1** and **t2** are types. Is the type **t1-ptr** $\cup$ **t2-ptr** the same as (**t1** $\cup$ **t2**)**-ptr**? Justify your answer.

11. The following declarations are given:
    > **int** a;   **char string** b;
    > **bit string** = **int** $\cup$ **char string**
    > **bit string** c;

    Which of the following assignments are valid, and which invalid?

    $$a \Leftarrow 1977; \quad a \Leftarrow \text{``}1977\text{''};$$

    $$b \Leftarrow 1977; \quad b \Leftarrow \text{``}1977\text{''};$$

    $$c \Leftarrow 1977; \quad c \Leftarrow \text{``}1977\text{''}.$$

    Justify your answers, and indicate what takes place in computer storage for the valid cases.

12. (a) Indicate some conditions which the value set for a variable of type **deal** must satisfy if the data is to be valid.
    (b) How can these conditions be applied to the storage structure?
    (c) At what point in the program should they be applied?

13. (a) Regarding **procedure** as a data type, describe the features of V, 0, and G which characterize **procedure**.
    (b) Do the same for **decision-table**. Would a **decision-table** be a **procedure**?

14. Indicate the type of storage mapping (contiguous, linked, indexed, or hash-based) that might be used for the following data representations (more than one may be applicable).
    (a) Entries in a compiler symbol table.
    (b) Items on a stack.
    (c) Items in a queue.
    (d) Components of a FORTRAN array.
    (e) Fixed-length records on a magnetic tape.
    (f) Blocked records on a magnetic tape.
    (g) Entries in a file directory.
    (h) Variable-length records on a magnetic disk.

15. (a) In the example of Section 2.7.3 suggest O, an operator set, for each of the types **rank, suit, card, card-sequence, deal, rank-sequence,** and **hand.**

(b) What specifications are needed to establish a data type **trick** consisting of one card drawn from each hand?

(c) What other data types are needed to represent the play of bridge? The bidding?

16. What reasons are there to favor one of the two storage mappings in the example of Section 2.7.3? (*Hint:* Consider the operations needed for developing play of the hand.)

17. (a) Specify data types that could be used to represent the board position in (1) checkers; (2) chess.

(b) What operations should be associated with the types?

Bibliography

Although primitive data types were introduced in ALGOL in the late 1950s, subsequent advances were slow in coming, with the exception perhaps of the realization that strings were a recognizable type with distinctive operations. For a time much of the writing on data structures focused on addressing schemes and access to data, corresponding to what we have termed the selection process (see, for example, D'Imperio, 1969, and Rosenberg, 1971). The Report of the Codasyl Data Base Task Group (1971) played an important role in distinguishing between the logical structure and storage structure. A paper by Earley (1971) developed the notions of data in terms of graph concepts, and Hoare (1972) suggested the axiomatization of data types and the use of this approach in developing techniques for proving correct implementations of types. Extensible languages appeared in sufficient number that a conference was held on them in 1969 (see Christensen and Shaw, 1969), and they have continued to increase in variety and number (Solntseff and Yerzerski, 1974). As already noted, many of the well-known current languages (SNOBOL, PL/I, PASCAL, ALGOL 68) contain specific features for user-defined types, and more recent languages go further toward formal type definition and abstraction (see, for example, Wulf, 1974). Additional ideas on the use of abstract data types in programming are to be found in Liskov and Zilles (1974), Flon (1975), and the Proceedings of Conference on Data: Abstraction, Definition and Structure (1976). An important outgrowth of the interest in data structures has been the work on data bases, particularly developments on the relational model of data, which are described and referenced in Chapter 10.

When data structures have been considered to any depth in books, the treatment has usually been combined with related topics, for example, discrete structures (Berztiss, 1971), programming languages (Harrison, 1973), or programming style (Wirth, 1976). Other books have emphasized applications (Lewis and Smith, 1976) and algorithms (Tremblay and Sorensen, 1976, and Horowitz and Sahni, 1976), but the distinction between data type and data structure is usually not sharply drawn. Knuth (1974, 1973) continues to be the definitive reference for source material and detailed mathematical properties of many of the data types described in this book.

BERZTISS, A. T., *Data Structures: Theory and Practice*, 2nd ed., New York: Academic Press, Inc., 1975.

CHRISTENSEN, C., AND C. J. SHAW, eds., "Proceedings of the Extensible Language Symposium." *ACM SIGPLAN Notices*, **4** (Aug. 1969).

Codasyl Data Base Task Group Report. New York: Association for Computing Machinery, Inc., 1971.

D'IMPERIO, M. E., "Data Structures and Their Representation in Storage," in *Annual Review in Automatic Programming*, Vol. 5. New York: Pergamon Press, Inc., 1969, pp. 1–75.

EARLEY, J., "Toward an Understanding of Data Structures." *Communications of the ACM*, **14**, no. 10 (Oct. 1971), 617–627.

FLON, L., "Program Design with Abstract Data Types." Report of the Department of Computer Science, Carnegie-Mellon University, Pittsburgh, Pa., 1975.

HARRISON, M. C., *Data Structures and Programming*. Glenview, Ill.: Scott, Foresman & Company, 1973.

HOARE, C. A. R., "Notes on Data Structuring," in O. J. Dahl, E. W. Dijkstra, and C. A. R Hoare, *Structured Programming*. New York: Academic Press, Inc., 1972.

HOROWITZ, E., AND S. SAHNI, *Fundamentals of Data Structures*. Woodland Hills, Calif.: Computer Science Press, Inc., 1976.

KNUTH, D. E., *The Art of Computer Programming:* Vol. 1, *Fundamental Algorithms*, 2nd ed., 1974; Vol. 3, *Sorting and Searching*, 1973. Reading, Mass.: Addison-Wesley Publishing Company, Inc.

LEWIS, T. G., AND M. Z. SMITH, *Applying Data Structures*. Boston: Houghton Mifflin Company, 1976.

LISKOV, B., AND ZILLES, "Programming with Abstract Data Types." *ACM SIGPLAN Notices*, **9**, no. 4 (Apr. 1974). 50–59.

"Proceedings of Conference on Data: Abstraction, Definition and Structure." *ACM SIGPLAN Notes*, **8**, no. 2 (1976).

ROSENBERG, A., "Data Graphs and Addressing Schemes." *Journal of Computer and System Sciences*, **5** (June 1971), 193–238.

SOLNTSEFF, N., AND A. YERZERSKI, "A Survey of Extensible Programming Languages," in *Annual Review in Automatic Programming*, Vol. 7. New York: Pergamon Press, Inc., 1974, Part 5, pp. 267–307.

TREMBLAY, J. P., AND P. C. SORENSEN, *An Introduction to Data Structures with Applications*. New York: McGraw-Hill Book Company, 1976.

WIRTH, N. K., *Algorithms + Data Structures = Programs*. Englewood Cliffs, N.J.: Prentice-Hall, Inc., 1976.

WULF, W. A., "'ALPHARD': Toward a Language to Support Structured Programs." Report of the Department of Computer Science, Carnegie-Mellon University, Pittsburgh, Pa., 1974.

chapter 3

Strings

A string is a composite data object, built up from the primitive type **char**. If we adopt the logical view of a string as a sequence of zero or more characters, the method for generating objects of type **string** can be regarded as a grammar with two productions, $D \Rightarrow$ " (where " represents the empty, or *null*, string), and

$$D \Rightarrow ch \ D$$

where *ch* represents any value of type **char**.

In early programming languages, strings appeared only as constants used for input and output. The absence of operations on them permitted a straightforward storage mapping—consecutive characters stored consecutively in memory. As the theory of language processors developed, it was recognized that every processor needs a lexical scanner to assemble, from the input stream of symbols, sequences to be interpreted as data, as scanner instructions, program instructions, and so on. Accordingly, string-handling primitives were invented, and eventually languages with the concept of a string variable were introduced.

In this chapter we examine ways of representing and manipulating strings. After a discussion of basic string representation at the machine level, and string variables and operations, more sophisticated string processing is considered.

3.1 Basic String Representation

Certain aspects of the hardware design bear fundamentally on string representation. The two most obvious such features are the character set and its encodings, and the choice of cell sizes that make up the primary store.

3.1.1 Character Set

The history of the evolution of character sets is long and complicated. Among the factors that must be considered are:

- The range of characters to be accommodated. These include numerals, alphabetic characters in upper- and lowercases, punctuation marks and other special symbols (non-Roman letters, delimiters, and separators), and control characters appropriate to the hardware.
- Conservation of storage.
- Compatibility with earlier systems of encodings.
- Ease of distinguishibility of character subsets (e.g., numerals from other characters).
- Incorporation of error-detection and error-correction features (e.g., parity bits).

The PL/I 48-character set, its EBCDIC (Extended Binary Coded Decimal Interchange Code) encoding, and the corresssponding keypunch code are shown in Table 3.1.[1] EBCDIC is an 8-bit code used by the S/360–370 computers. It can represent up to 256 symbols, although a substantial number of code values remain unassigned. Observe from Table 3.1 that the EBCDIC values for the alphabet preserve the lexicographic order normally associated with the letters.

There has been slow progress toward standardization of codes, and Table 3.2 shows the American Standard Code for Information Interchange (ASCII).[2]

The 7-bit ASCII code is shown in Table 3.2 The 16 rows correspond to the 4 leftmost bits of the character code; the 8 columns are determined by the 3 low-order bits. Thus ampersand (&)—the row 6 (0110) column 2 (010) entry—is 0110010 in ASCII. Columns 0 and 1 of the chart contain symbols used in data transmission; for example, ETX (0011-000) means "end of text." An eighth bit can be adjoined at the left of each code group to provide parity checking, that is, to indicate whether the number of 1's in the other 7 bits is even or odd. This provides (at the cost of some redundancy) error detection at the character level. If the parity bit is set so that the total number of 1's in a 4-bit group is even, then an odd-parity condition means that one or three bits are in error. This may be enough resolution if errors are infrequent and single bit errors the most common kind. At greater cost (more check bits), codes can be designed to detect and enable correction of errors in specific positions.[3]

3.1.2 Cell Size

We shall use the term *cell* to denote an addressable unit on a machine. In the past, the choice of cell size depended on the purpose of the computer. Business data-processing machines were generally character- or *byte*-oriented: their cell size was the

---

[1] *IBM OS/360 PL/I(F) Language Reference Manual*, Form GC28-8201-3 (IBM Corporation, June 1968), p. 244.

[2] *U.S.A. Standard Code for Information Interchange* (Washington, D.C.: ANSI Publication X3.4, 1968).

[3] R. K. Richards, *Digital Design* (New York: Wiley–Interscience, 1971), Chap. 5.

TABLE 3.1   PL/I 48-character-set encodings

Character	360 EBCDIC (Decimal)	Hollerith Punch Positions
A	193	12–1
B	194	12–2
C	195	12–3
D	196	12–4
E	197	12–5
F	198	12–6
G	199	12–7
H	200	12–8
I	201	12–9
J	209	11–1
K	210	11–2
L	211	11–3
M	212	11–4
N	213	11–5
O	214	11–6
P	215	11–7
Q	216	11–8
R	217	11–9
S	226	0–2
T	227	0–3
U	228	0–4
V	229	0–5
W	230	0–6
X	231	0–7
Y	232	0–8
Z	233	0–9
0	240	0
1	241	1
2	242	2
3	243	3
4	244	4
5	245	5
6	246	6
7	247	7
8	248	8
9	249	9
Blank	64	Space
.	75	12–8–3
(	77	12–8–5
+	78	12–8–6
$	91	11–8–3
*	92	11–8–4
)	93	11–8–5
−	96	11
/	97	0–1
,	107	0–8–3
'	125	8–5
=	126	8–6

TABLE 3.2 ASCII code chart

b_3					0	0	0	0	1	1	1	1
b_2					0	0	0	1	0	0	1	1
b_1					0	1	0	1	0	1	0	1
b_7	b_6	b_5	b_4	Row	Column: 0	1	2	3	4	5	6	7
0	0	0	0	0	NUL	DLE	SP	0	@	P	`	p
0	0	0	1	1	SOH	DC1	!	1	A	Q	a	q
0	0	1	0	2	STX	DC2	"	2	B	R	b	r
0	0	1	1	3	ETX	DC3	#	3	C	S	c	s
0	1	0	0	4	EOT	DC4	$	4	D	T	d	t
0	1	0	1	5	ENQ	NAK	%	5	E	U	e	u
0	1	1	0	6	ACK	SYN	&	6	F	V	f	v
0	1	1	1	7	BEL	ETB	´	7	G	W	g	w
1	0	0	0	8	BS	CAN	(	8	H	X	h	x
1	0	0	1	9	HT	EM	)	9	I	Y	i	y
1	0	1	0	10	LF	SUB	*	:	J	Z	j	z
1	0	1	1	11	VT	ESC	+	;	K	[	k	{
1	1	0	0	12	FF	FS	,	<	L	\	l	|
1	1	0	1	13	CR	GS	–	=	M	]	m	}
1	1	1	0	14	SO	RS	.	>	N	∧	n	~
1	1	1	1	15	SI	US	/	?	O	—	o	DEL

number of bits required to encode the character set, and they could reference characters in blocks up to a fixed size. Typical cell sizes ranged from 6 to 10 bits. The popularity of the IBM S/360–370 series, together with the growing adoption of the ASCII set, has resulted in a standard character size of 8 bits.

In computers designed especially for numeric computation, the cell, or word size, is determined by the precision (number of digits) considered sufficient for integers and floating-point numbers. Typical cell sizes on today's word machines range from 16 to 60 bits.

For elementary string handling, word machines are not as efficient as byte-addressable ones. On the latter, a string can be represented in a straightforward way—succeeding characters placed in consecutive memory locations. Individual characters are easy to extract, and such machines can usually search large blocks of them with a single instruction.

On a word machine, characters can be quickly accessed if they are stored one per cell. However, this wastes most of the space in a word; to use all of it, several characters can be *packed* (combined) into one location. Character extraction then becomes more complicated, as the undesired portion of a word where a given character is located must be masked out with logical operations. Thus there is a space/time trade-off between the packed and unpacked representations. Regardless of how strings are represented, scanning them is more costly on a word machine, because only one or two words can be referenced in one instruction.

Modern general-purpose computers (the S/370, for example) permit both byte and word addressing, so string handling need not mean compromises in efficiency. Moreover, for some operations, consecutively storing characters is not the best storage mapping, with the consequence that cell size is not always so important.

3.1.3 Literals

If only very simple operations are to be carried out on a string (e.g., it is only to be read and printed), and the string is not too long, it can be referred to merely by quoting its value. A string referenced this way is called a *literal string*, or simply a *literal*; as for literals of primitive type, it is modeled by dropping the naming mechanism, G, from the logical structure for strings. Literals can be designated in several ways, for example, by surrounding them with special characters, or by having the lexical analyzer recognize them as terminal productions of a special grammar (such a grammar is *not* a naming mechanism, as the literals cannot be assigned to). It is even possible not to distinguish them at all; where data are understood to be of string type (as might be the case with parameters of macros), it may be enough to specify string length.

Literal strings resemble another type, *numeric*, which is always present, even in programming languages where types are not explicitly recognized. Numeric constants (usually integers or reals) are referred to by quoting their value. They are recognized by the lexical scanner and are used when the fixed or "one-time" nature of values make variables unnecessary. Similarly, numerals are found as operands in data transfer

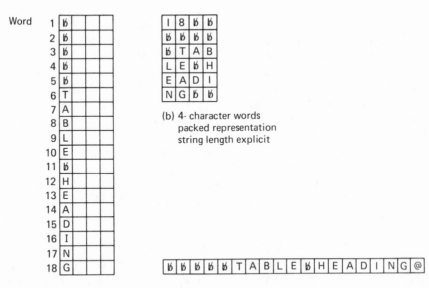

(a) 4-character words
    unpacked representation
    string length implicit

(b) 4- character words
    packed representation
    string length explicit

(c) Single byte characters
    End-of-string delimiter

Fig. 3.1 Possible storage representations for a literal string

statements (e.g., input/output operations, or as parameters of macro-instructions which process strings).

Because literals (and numerals) are not referenced by name, it is unnecessary to have an entry in the symbol table for them. On byte machines they can be stored on a character-per-location basis. On word machines there is the question of whether or not to pack characters. Since the only operations on literals are transfers which move them from one part storage to another, the packed representation will have little effect on processing time, while saving space; on the other hand, it may not be worth packing only a few small strings.

There must be some method of designating the length a of string, either explicitly (e.g., by including an integer which is interpreted as the number of characters), or implicitly (e.g., by specifying the length in the parameter list where the literal appears). Figure 3.1 illustrates some simple storage representations that might be used in conjunction with an output instruction DISPLAY 'ƀƀƀƀƀTABLEƀHEADING'.

3.2 String Variables

Once strings can be identified by names that are distinct from the string value, the language possesses the ability to handle string variables. The storage mapping for such variables will depend on the nature of the string operations chosen to be implemented. These can range from simple character extraction to complex pattern matching, and, not surprisingly, the more elaborate operations require more flexible string representations. In this section we shall look first at a few "basic" string operations and then at some storage mappings that might support them. The operations are basic in the sense that they are typical of string-handling facilities found in many programming languages. In the next section, more sophisticated string handling is presented by way of SNOBOL, a language designed specifically for string manipulation.

3.2.1 Basic Operations

In Section 2.5, operations for composite data types were classified according to general function (e.g., assignment, selection, retrieval, etc.). From these categories, we now present some specific operations that one might want for string processing. Characters will be denoted by small (and possibly subscripted letters) a, b, and c. Let *string1* have the value $a[1]a[2] \ldots a[m]$, and *string2* have the value $b[1]b[2] \ldots b[n]$, where $1 \leq n \leq m$.

1. *Assignment* ($\Leftarrow$)
   The target (left side) must be a variable of type *string*. The source can be a literal, string variable, or the *null* (empty) string. For example,

   $string \Leftarrow$ 'abc'; *string* now has the value 'abc'

   $string \Leftarrow string1$; *string* is now $a[1]a[2] \ldots a[n]$

   $string \Leftarrow$ ''; *string*'s value is null.

2. *Substring Selection* (σ)
   σ (*string1*, i, j), where $1 \leq i \leq i + j - 1 \leq m$, extracts from *string1* the sub-string of length j, starting at the ith character; thus σ (*string1*, i, j) = a[i]a[$i+1$] $\ldots$ a[$i+j-1$]. Setting $j = 0$ yields the null string.

3. *Substring Retrieval* (R)
   A simple retrieve operation returns the number of characters in a string:

   $$\rho \ (\textit{string1}) = m, \text{ the current length of } \textit{string1}$$

   $$\rho \ ('') = 0; \text{ the null string has length } 0.$$

   More complicated is that operation which finds, in a string, the first occurrence of a given string:

   $$\imath \ (\textit{string1}, \textit{string2}) = \text{smallest } k, \ 1 \leq k \leq m,$$

   such that σ (*string1*, k, ρ (*string2*)) = *string2*, and 0 if *string2* occurs nowhere in *string1*.

4. *Concatenate* (θ)
   string1 θ *string2* = a[1]a[2] $\ldots$ a[m]b[1]b[2] $\ldots$ b[n].

The following two operations are presented for their own sake, although they are expressed in terms of the operations above. We do not suggest that this is how they would be implemented.

5. *Insert* (θ_+)
   θ_+ (*string1*, i, *string2*) inserts *string2* into *string1* following the ith character. The result is to set *string1* to

   $$\sigma \ (\textit{string1}, 1, i) \ \theta \ \textit{string2} \ \theta \ \sigma \ (\textit{string1}, i+1, \rho \ (\textit{string1}) - i);$$

   for example, θ_+ (*string1*, 3, 'abc') sets *string1* to a[1]a[2]a[3]abca[4]a[5] . . a[m].

6. *Delete* (θ_-)
   θ_- (*string1*, i, j) deletes, from *string1*, the substring σ (*string1*, i, j). Thus *string1* is set to

   $$\sigma \ (\textit{string1}, 1, i-1) \ \theta \ \sigma \ (\textit{string1}, i+j, \rho \ (\textit{string1}) - (i+j-1));$$

   for example, θ_- (*string1*, 3, $m-2$) = a[1]a[2].

7. *Replace* (α)
   This last operation is presented as an instance of partial assignment mentioned in Section 2.5. For precision it is expressed in terms of operations already introduced.

   $$\alpha \ (\textit{string1}, i, j, \textit{string2})$$

   replaces σ (*string1*, i, j) with *string2*. Thus *string1* is set to

   $$\sigma \ (\textit{string1}, 1, i-1) \ \theta \ \textit{string2} \ \theta \ \sigma \ (\textit{string1}, i+j, \rho \ (\textit{string1}) - (i+j-1));$$

   for example, α (*string1*, 2, 1, 'abc') replaces a[2] in *string1* by 'abc', thus changing *string1* to a[1]abca[3]a[4] $\ldots$ a[m].

These operations represent basic capabilities found, in one form or another, in programming languages that permit string processing. For example, in PL/I, σ and ι appear, respectively, as the functions SUBSTR and INDEX. Partial assignment (α) is possible using SUBSTR (as a target, or *pseudo-variable*) or VERIFY, with the restriction that the replacement string have the same length as the original. To perform insertion (up to maximum string length) or deletion, on the other hand, SUBSTR and concatenate ($\|$) must be used in combination as was done above. In APL, substring selection, retrieval, and length-preserving replacement are available through the powerful indexing and subscripting facilities. The expansion and contraction operators, used in conjunction with the aforementioned ones, enable one to perform insertion and deletion. String processing in APL is further illustrated in Chapter 5. In SNOBOL, substring selection, retrieval, and modification do not require explicit references to character positions and string length: rather they are part of the more general pattern matching/replacement capability.[4]

The preceding string operations are low-level in the sense that they involve lengths and positions. To show how a more string-oriented operation would be expressed with these functions, we present a small program for the command "Replace, in *text*, each instance of *old* by *new*."

Example 3.1

Program to "Replace in *text* each instance of *old* by *new*"

```
string text, old, new;
integer search-start, old-start;
boolean replacing;
search-start ⟸ 1 ;
replacing ⟸ true ;
do while (replacing) ;
        /* look for first occurrence of old in text, starting at search-start */
        old-start ⟸ search-start−1 + ι (σ (text, search-start,
          ρ (text)+1−search-start), old) ;
        if old-start > 0 then
        do ;                          /* if found */
              α (text, old-start, ρ (old), new) ; /* replace */
              /* and resume search following substitution */
              search-start ⟸ old-start + ρ (new) + 1;
              if search-start > 1 + ρ (text) − ρ (old) then
                    replacing ⟸ false; /* end of text */
        end
        else replacing ⟸ false; /* stop if no old */
end
```

[4] We have not attempted, in the prototype operations, to specify what happens if actual parameters are assigned incorrect values, so that the operation becomes meaningless. For example, in *Delete*, j must be ≥ 0; if it is not, some error action must be taken. Reference should be made to the actual operators of the specific languages to see what form these actions take.

3.2.2 Storage Mappings for String Variables

The values of string variables can be stored in the same way in which literals were stored (Fig. 3.1). However, as a variable's contents are accessed through an identifier, the storage map must include a symbol table entry. This entry may contain a pointer to the location of the string, or it may be possible to store the value itself in the symbol table. There are also several ways of designating string length—directly specifying the length, including an end-of-string delimiter, carrying pointers to the first and last characters, and so on. Figure 3.2 illustrates possible storage mappings for the assignment operations

string1 ⇐ 'abcdefg'

string2 ⇐ 'bcd'.

Symbol Table Area

String identifier	Reference Type	Pointer (0) or Direct (1)
string1	0	a[1]
string2	1	bcd

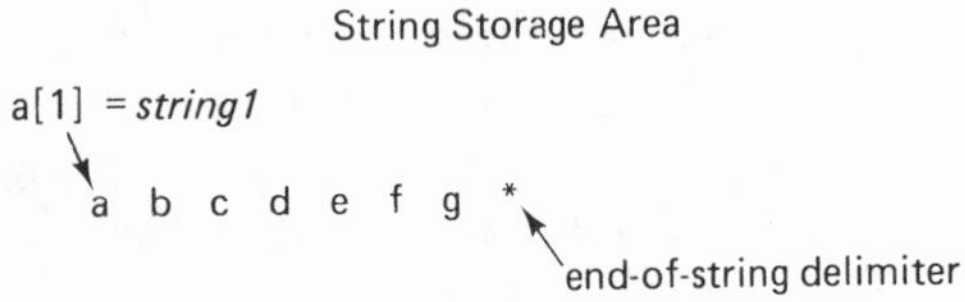

Symbol Table Area

String identifier	Pointer	String length
string1	a[1]	7
string2	a[2]	3

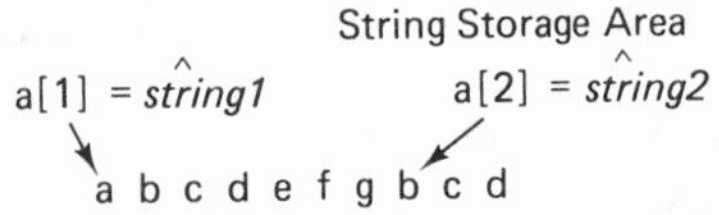

Symbol Table Area

String identifier	Initial pointer	Final pointer
string1	a[1i]	a[1f]
string2	a[2i]	a[2f]

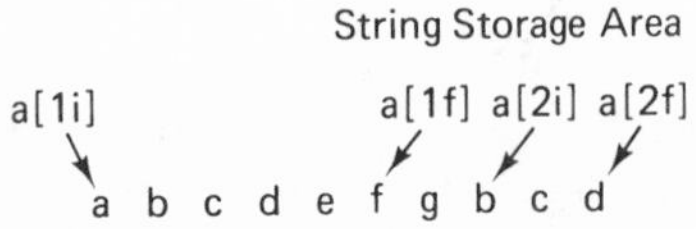

Fig. 3.2 Simple mappings for string variables

When string operations other than assignment are of particular interest, it may be worthwhile to modify the storage mapping for strings in order to make these operations efficient. Suppose, for example, that there are many assignments where one string is a substring of another, and that it is highly desirable to take advantage of savings in storage arising out of such circumstances. One way of doing this is to replace the initial and final reference pointers, which normally denote the beginning and end of a string (Fig. 3.2), by a *pair* of numbers. The first of the pair points to the address in string storage where a number of strings are to be found; the second names a forward *offset* (or backward offset, in the case of the final pointer) which specifies how many characters are to be skipped before the particular named string begins (Fig. 3.3). Note that in this case, *string2* can be recognized as a substring of *string1* simply by exam-

Symbol Table Area   String Storage Area

	Initial Pointer	Offset	Final Pointer	Offset
string1	a[1i]	0	a[1f]	0
string2	a[1i]	1	a[1f]	−3

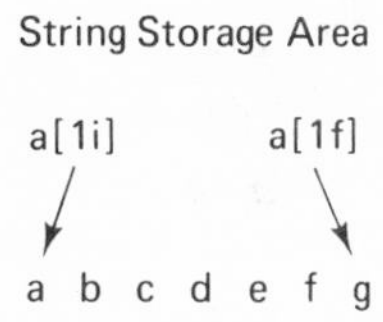

a[1i]   a[1f]

a b c d e f g

Fig. 3.3   String storage with pointer offsets

ining the pointers. However, if the assignments to the two strings had been made in reverse order, it would not have been possible, with the storage map just described, either to save the storage or to recognize the substring relationship. Whether the savings in storage and in execution time are worth the cost of enlarging the symbol table so as to include the offsets is something that cannot be further determined without information about the application in mind. The answer depends on how frequently string assignments arise of the type that allow the savings to be effected.

So far, nothing has been said about how operations that change string length might affect the storage mapping. In an interpretive system, this presents no problem; since a variable must be looked up each time it is referenced during execution, it can be reallocated when necessary and the symbol table updated to reflect the new address and length information. For compiled programs, the address of a variable is resolved during the translation phase by consulting the symbol table each time an identifier occurs and inserting the address into the code generated. Since this address remains fixed for the scope duration, the length of a string cannot vary beyond an initially specified amount. If the length is stored with the string, it can be changed during execution, just as the string's contents can, so the string can effectively vary in length up to a maximum. In PL/I, strings of this type are declared by specifying a maximum length and the attribute VARYING.

If string length is stored in the symbol table, it too will be compiled into all code referencing the string. For example, any interrogation of length will always give the value initially placed in the symbol table. In PL/I, strings are of this type, unless declared VARYING. Some of the effect of varying length can be achieved in a fixed-length string by *padding*, that is, filling in the trailing character positions with some insignificant character (usually a blank), called a *filler*. For example, if *string3* is of fixed length 4, the assignment *string3* ⟸ 'CAT' would place 'CATƀ' in the storage area for the string.

To implement true variable-length strings, a compiler would have to generate calls to execution-time allocation routines whenever an operation could change string length, and keep an execution-time symbol table of sorts so the variable could be located. This is expensive and detracts from the efficiency of a compiled system. Another possibility is to represent strings as linked lists of characters. A typical list element would consist of a group of characters followed by a pointer. The address of the string could then be resolved (as that of a fixed list head) at compile time, while operations that change the string (e.g., insertion, deletion) would translate as list-processing routines (see Section 4.3).

Figure 3.4 illustrates a linked allocation for the string assignment $string4 \Leftarrow$ 'abcdefgh' together with the result of the the insertion $\Theta_+ \, (string4, \, 4, \, 'wxyz')$. Each

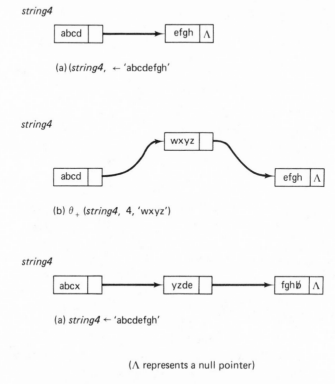

(∧ represents a null pointer)

Fig. 3.4 Linked allocation to support variable-length strings

element consists of a four-character string followed by a (4-byte) pointer. This makes space utilization 50 percent of what it would be were the string stored on a character-per-location basis. Moreover, on a byte machine, a linked representation makes searching through a string less efficient, because the character-scanning instructions cannot be used to best effect if pointer chains have to be followed. Note, also, that although insertion and deletion are simplified, they still might require movement between list elements. For example, if the insert in Fig. 3.4 were $\Theta \, (string4, \, 4, \, 'xyz')$, some rearrangement would be needed to get the desired result of Fig. 3.4(c). This could be avoided by using list elements consisting of a single character and a pointer. Space allocation then drops to 20 percent and scanning becomes even less efficient, but insertion and deletion are extremely simple.

A linked representation for strings thus permits the implementation of variable-length strings at the cost of storage space. Moreover, given this king of mapping, some operations can be made more efficient than others at the cost of additional space. These trade-offs are typical of those which occur in data structure selection.

The question of an appropriate storage mapping for strings may be complicated by the garbage collection problem. In particular, suppose that advantage has been taken of substring relationships to reduce storage, as was done in Fig. 3.3. If the scope of the assignment *string2* ⇐ 'bcd' changes so that the assignment is no longer valid, it is not possible to release the storage for *string2* as long as the first assignment still holds. Because of the storage mapping, garbage collection cannot be initiated as soon as the scope changes. This is a classic problem and methods of dealing with it are discussed in Section 8.3.

3.3 String Processing in SNOBOL

Since it is useful to regard the processing of either computer languages or natural language text as string processing, programming languages have been developed in which the string is the basic data type. The best known of these is SNOBOL (along with its variant SPITBOL), which is, in turn, an outgrowth of an earlier language, COMIT. SNOBOL finds a permanent place in the repertory of programming languages because the range of operations it provides for strings is not easily duplicated in other languages, even those which have powerful notations and processing abilities. In particular, it generalizes the string to a data type called **pattern**, which really defines classes of strings, and it provides the ability to search for instances of a pattern. SNOBOL has evolved to a general-purpose language, SNOBOL4, complete with arithmetic and data structuring facilities. Here, however, the focus is on the representation of strings and patterns. Some language features are discussed, but the reader is referred to Griswold, Poage, and Pololnsky (1971) for a detailed description of SNOBOL4 at the user level.[5]

3.3.1 Pattern Matching

SNOBOL is a string-oriented language and, as such, adopts concise notations for describing common string operations. For example, the concatenation operator is not represented at all; the assignment

$$\text{STRING1} = \text{'ABC' 'DEF'}$$

assigns string 'ABCDEF' to the variable STRING1. Aside from simple assignments, processing in SNOBOL centers around the pattern-matching facility. A typical statement has the form

label subject pattern = object :S(*stmt1*)F(*stmt2*).

This says "In string *subject* look for a string specified by *pattern*, and replace it by the string *object*. On success (an instance of *pattern* was found), go to the statement labeled *stmt1*; otherwise (failure), go to the one labeled *stmt2*." *Subject* and *object* are of type **string**; *label, stmt1,* and *stmt2* are identifiers used as labels; and *pattern* is of type **pattern**, a datatype that enables the user to specify classes of strings for matching purposes. The replacement part of the statement above is optional, as are the label and goto portions.

[5]For SNOBOL4 implementation, see Griswold (1972). Griswold (1975) presents numerous SNOBOL examples and applications.

Any string can be used as a pattern. In addition, patterns are built up from strings by two operations, alternation (|) and concatenation (indicated as remarked above, by simple juxtaposition). If PAT1 and PAT2 are patterns, PAT1 | PAT2 is a pattern that matches any string specified by either PAT1 or PAT2. The concatenation PAT1 PAT2 matches any string consisting of a string specified by PAT1 followed by one matched by PAT2. For example, following the assignments

$$SUIT = 'S' | 'H' | 'D' | 'C'$$

$$FACE = 'K' | 'Q' | 'J'$$

$$FACECARD = SUIT\ FACE,$$

the pattern FACECARD will match any of the 12 strings from 'SK', 'SQ', and 'SJ', on through to 'CK', 'CQ', and 'CJ'. If the assignment

$$DEAL = 'SAS2HJD10C2'$$

is made, the statement

$$DEAL\ FACECARD =$$

locates the 'HJ' in DEAL and replaces it by the null string (represented by the empty right side); that is, 'HJ' is deleted from DEAL.

When concatenation and alternation appear together (e.g., PAT1 PAT2|PAT3 PAT4), concatenation has precedence. The order can be changed by bracketing [e.g., PAT1 (PAT2|PAT3) PAT4], or by using intermediate variables, as was done above to construct FACECARD.

For use in building patterns, SNOBOL provides various primitives. For example:

1. LEN (*n*): matches any string of length *n*.
2. SPAN (*string1*): matches the longest string consisting only of characters appearing in *string1*.
3. BREAK (*string1*): matches anything up to (but not including) the first occurrence of a character in *string1*.
4. ARBNO (*pat*): matches zero or more consecutive appearances of strings matched by the pattern *pat*.

These primitives are used in constructing patterns just as strings were above. With the definitions

$$NUMBER = SPAN\ ('0123456789')$$

$$SIGNED = + | -,$$

the pattern SIGNED NUMBER can be used to recognize strings denoting signed integers of arbitrary length (e.g., -3, $+16$, -20022).

In SNOBOL a variable can be associated with a pattern component and set to the substring matched by that component during the match. The assignment can be made conditional upon the entire pattern match succeeding (using the operator .), or it can be made regardless of the outcome (using the operator $). If the pattern

$$NUMBER\ .\ WHOLE\ '\ .\ '\ NUMBER\ .\ FRACTION$$

is matched against '3.14', the match will succeed, setting WHOLE to '3' and FRACTION to '14'.

SNOBOL permits a degree of user control over the pattern-matching logic, or scanner. For example, the scanner will look for alternatives in the (left to right) order that they are specified. Thus matching of individual patterns can be made more efficient if the relative frequencies of individual components are known. Normally, matching is performed in the *unanchored* mode; that is, a pattern will be sought anywhere in the subject string. To restrict matches to those which start at the beginning of a string, the keyword &ANCHOR is set to 1.

In its most general form, SNOBOL pattern matching works by backtracking; at any point, if one alternative fails, the scanner backs up to try the second. If all possibilities fail, the scanner moves on, looking again for the first alternative. Often, backtracking can be avoided by use of heuristics; for example, an alternative can be disregarded if there are not enough characters left in the subject for a successful match. Normally, the scanner operates using shortcuts to make matching more efficient (*quickscan* mode); when full backtracking is desired, it can be forced by setting &FULLSCAN to 1.

One of most powerful features of SNOBOL pattern matching is the ability to defer evaluation of a pattern until it is used in a matching statement. Suppose that we want to recognize strings of the form $\{WW \mid W \in \{A \cup B\}*\}$, that is, any string of A's and B's whose first half matches its second. The pattern

$$POS(0) \; ARBNO \; ('A' | 'B') \; \$ \; W \; *W \; RPOS \; (0)$$

will do this.[6] The * before the W postpones construction of a pattern for W until an instance of ARBNO ('A'|'B') has been matched. When it has, the matched substring will be assigned to W, which can then be searched for. When the pattern above is matched against a string of A's and B's, the scanner will operate as follows:

Starting at the beginning of the string (POS (0)), ARBNO ('A'|'B') matches the null string and assigns it to W. W will then be matched immediately (since attempts to match the null string always succeed), but unless the entire string is null [RPOS (0) is the same string position as POS (0)], the whole match will fail. The scanner will then back up to the beginning, where ARBNO ('A'|'B') will match one character and assign it to W. The next text character will then be compared with W. If it matches and is the last string character (RPOS(0)), an instance of WW has been found; otherwise, the scanner backs up to the beginning, matches *two* characters, and assigns them to W. The process repeats until either the entire string is determined to be an instance of WW, or ARBNO ('A'|'B') matches more than half the string, in which case the whole pattern cannot succeed.

The pattern just presented recognizes a *context-sensitive language*. This is a class of languages generated by phrase structure grammars with rules of the form $\alpha \Rightarrow \beta$, where $\alpha, \beta \in \{V_N \cup V_T\}*$ and $|\alpha| \leq |\beta|$. While the SNOBOL recognizer was easy to construct, it is harder to find a grammar which produces the language (Exercise 4).

---

[6]This pattern illustrates some of the scanner features we have discussed, but for efficiency, backtracking (and therefore ARBNO) should be avoided. The pattern

$$POS(0) \; LEN \; (SIZE \; (*TARGET) \; / \; 2) \; \$ \; W \quad *W \; RPOS(0),$$

when matched against a string TARGET, has the same effect and, moreover, avoids dependence on the alphabet. The pattern can be further modified to avoid explicit reference to the subject string.

3.3.2 SNOBOL Data Representation[7]

The basic SNOBOL cell, called a *descriptor*, consists of three fields—type (T), flag (F), and value (V) (see Fig. 3.5). The V field either stores an actual data value (if it is of type **real** or **integer**), or points to a data object (string, pattern, array, etc.). The type field contains an integer that identifies the type (although it is convenient to display instead a mnemonic letter, e.g., S for string, P for pattern, I for integer). The F field contains bits or flags which describe certain properties of the descriptor; in particular, an A flag indicates that V is a pointer.

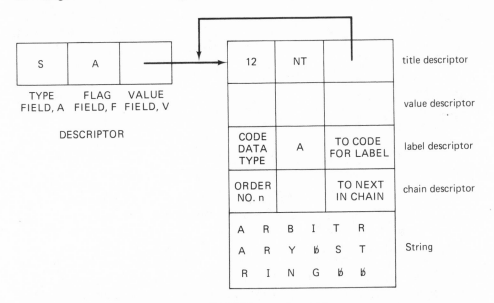

Fig. 3.5   SNOBOL natural variable

In SNOBOL, every string is represented as a *natural variable*. This is a block made up of descriptors followed by sufficient space to store the string value. Figure 3.5 shows a descriptor pointing to a natural variable for 'ARBITRARYⱡSTRING'. The four descriptors function as follows:

1. The title descriptor contains the string length in the T field and the value NT in the flag field. N identifies the structure as a natural variable and T indicates that this is a title descriptor. The V field contains a self-pointer, which may point elsewhere during garbage collection.

2. The value descriptor enables the string to act as a variable that may take on different values. For example, if the value descriptor in Fig. 3.5 were $\boxed{\text{I} \mid 0 \mid 3}$, the natural variable 'ARBITRARYⱡSTRING' would be interpreted as having the value 3. By changing the descriptor to $\boxed{\text{S} \mid \text{A} \mid \quad}$→{VALUEⱡ1},

[7]The representations shown here are those described by Griswold, *Macro Implementation*.

where {VALUEβ1} stands for a natural variable similar to that of Fig. 3.5 but with 'VALUEβ1' in the string field, 'ARBITRARYβSTRING' assumes a **string** value, namely 'VALUEβ1'.

3. The label descriptor is used when string is the label of a statement. The V field then points to the corresponding block of code.

4. All natural variables (i.e., all strings) are organized in a symbol table. The location of string is determined by computing, from that string, two numbers, c and n. The first, c, identifies the head of a chain of natural variables in which the string is to be found (or inserted, if it has just been created). The V field of the chain descriptor is the link to the next natural variable in this chain. The chain is ordered by n value, which is stored in the T field of the chain descriptor.

Item 2 points out one of the interesting aspects of SNOBOL, that any string may serve as a name for a variable: all it requires is a meaningful value descriptor field. On the other hand, only identifiers, a restricted subset of strings, can be directly *assigned* values. To treat an arbitrary string as a variable, the indirect reference ($) is used. The statement

$$\$'ARBITRARYβSTRING' = 'VALUEβ1'$$

will set the value descriptor of the natural variable for 'ARBITRARYβSTRING' (Fig. 3.5) to $\boxed{\text{S} \mid \text{A} \mid \ }\rightarrow${VALUEβ1}. Consequently, the statement

$$X = \$'ARBITRARYβSTRING'$$

sets the value descriptor of the natural variable for 'X' to

$$\boxed{\text{S} \mid \text{A} \mid \ }\rightarrow\{VALUEβ1\}.$$

Some assignments using indirect reference are illustrated in Fig. 3.6. The statement $W = 4$ places $\boxed{\text{I} \mid \text{0} \mid \text{4}}$ in the value descriptor for (natural variable) W(①).

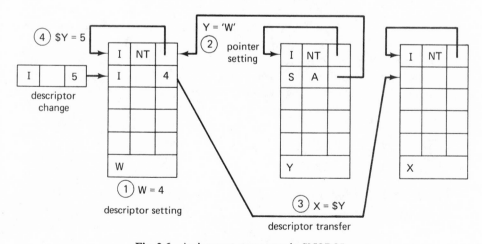

Fig. 3.6 Assignment statements in SNOBOL

Y = 'W' places $\boxed{\text{S} \mid \text{A} \mid \ \ }$ →{W} in the value descriptor for Y(②). Now consider the assignment X = \$Y. Y has the value 'W', so X is set to \$'W', i.e., the value descriptor of W is copied into that for X(③), giving X the value of 4. Finally, \$Y = 5 sets \$'W' to 5; that is, the value descriptor for W is replaced by $\boxed{\text{I} \mid 0 \mid 5}$ (④).

SNOBOL patterns are represented in very much the same way as strings are. Each pattern component is described by four descriptors. Figure 3.7 illustrates how a simple

descriptor type

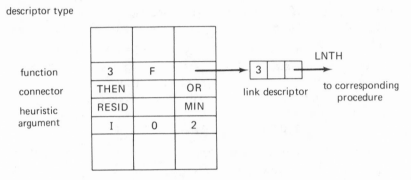

Fig. 3.7   Pattern component of LEN(2)

pattern, LEN(2), would be represented. The descriptors function as follows:

1. Pattern components are realized as procedures that construct the patterns, and the *function* descriptor contains a pointer to the procedure for the component. (To be consistent with other procedures, the call is performed indirectly, through a link descriptor.) The T field contains a "3" or a "2", according to whether an argument is or is not needed for the component.
2. The *connector* descriptor contains an offset, THEN, to the next (concatenated) component in the T field, and to the alternate (OR) component in the V field. The offsets are given as the number of descriptor words from the beginning of the pattern (e.g., as 4d for four descriptors).
3. The *heuristic* descriptor contains information useful in the heuristic procedures employed to match pattern components. RESID gives the minimum number of characters which must be present if the subject string is to match the constituents that follow, and the sum RESID + MIN is the number of characters in untried instances of the current pattern element.
4. The *argument* descriptor gives the number of arguments in conventional integer form.

The pattern of Fig. 3.7, LEN(2), matches any string consisting of two characters. Figure 3.8 shows the storage representation for the pattern 'B' LEN(3)|'BRE' LEN(2). Note the title descriptor, which serves as a heading for the whole block; also that multiple calls to each pattern procedure are effected through a single link descriptor.

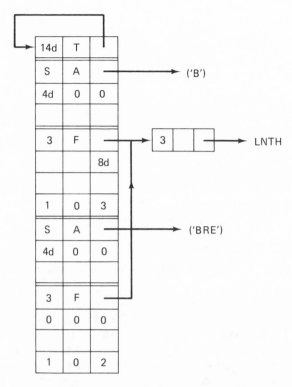

Fig. 3.8   Pattern for 'B' LEN(3)|'BRE' LEN(2)

3.4 String Matching

By allowing patterns to vary dynamically, and by supplying numerous pattern functions, SNOBOL enables a user to perform very elaborate pattern matching. The cost of this elegance and flexibility is efficiency—as patterns are changed and functions invoked during a match, the number of alternatives to be tried can grow quickly. Frequently, however, matching only involves comparing one character string against another. It then becomes possible to match very efficiently (i.e., without ever backing up the pattern string). We now present such a linear pattern-matching algorithm. The discussion (and Algorithm 3.3, in particular) is based on a work by Knuth, Morris, and Pratt.[8]

Suppose that we want to find the first instance of a pattern string *pattern*[1] . . . *pattern*[m] in a target *text*[1] . . . *text*[n], $m \leq n$. (Here *pattern*[i] denotes $\sigma(pattern, i, 1)$, the ith character of *pattern*.) An obvious approach is the following. Align *pattern* with the leftmost m characters at *text* and start matching. When a mismatch occurs, shift *pattern* right one character and restart matching from its first position. Continue

[8]D. E. Knuth, J. H. Morris, Jr., and V. R. Pratt, "*Fast Pattern Matching in Strings*," SIAM J. Computing, **6**, 2 (June 1977), 323–350.

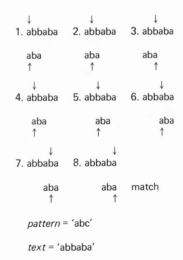

Fig. 3.9   Locating 'aba' within 'abbaba' using "naive" algorithm

until either *pattern* matches or there are no more characters to match in *text*. Figure 3.9 illustrates the method when searching for 'aba' in 'abbaba'. Algorithm 3.1 is a formal version of what has just been described. On termination, $i > m$ indicates that *pattern* has been found starting at $j-1$, otherwise, it occurs nowhere in *text*.

Algorithm 3.1 works by backtracking; when it finds a mismatch, it backs up to *pattern*[1], shifts *pattern* one right, and restarts matching. In the worst case (no pattern found), each of m pattern characters will be compared to at most n in *text*, making the run time $O(m \cdot n)$. However, an analysis of the operation as illustrated in Fig. 3.9 suggests that some comparisons are unnecessary.

Algorithm 3.1   String matching with backtracking

```
integer i, j, m, n;
string pattern[1:m], text[1:n];
i ⇐ j ⇐ 1;
do while i ≤ m ∧ j ≤ n;
   if pattern[i] = text[j] then
   do /* keep matching */
      i ⇐ i+1; /* bump pattern position */
      j ⇐ j+1; /* and text position */
   end
   else
   do /* backtrack */
      j ⇐ j+2−i;
      i ⇐ 1;
   end
end
```

After step 3 of that example, the algorithm unsuccessfully compares *pattern*[1] with *text*[2] and then *text*[3]. Yet information from the pattern can eliminate these compares. First, by definition of the matching process, the last k characters matched are the first k of *pattern;* following step 3, it has been determined that *pattern*[1] = *text*[1] and *pattern*[2] = *text*[2]. Since *pattern*[1] $\neq$ *pattern*[2], there is no point in shifting *pattern* right one place and comparing it to *text*[2]. Also, *pattern*[1] = *pattern*[3], which did not match *text*[3]; thus step 5 of Fig. 3.9 is unnecessary. Given a mismatch at *pattern*[3], *pattern* should be shifted three characters right before matching restarts (at step 6). With the elimination of steps 4 and 5, each character in the target is examined only once. Backtracking has been avoided by suitable pre-analysis of the pattern.

In general, suppose that σ(*pattern*, 1, $i-1$) has been matched with σ(*text*, $j-i+1$, $i-1$), and that *pattern*[i] $\neq$ *text*[j] (Fig. 3.10, top two rows). If the matching algorithm

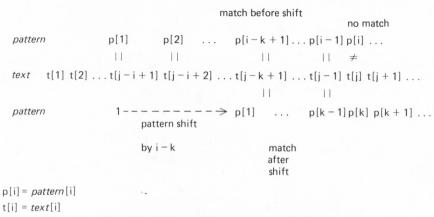

p[i] = *pattern* [i]

t[i] = *text*[i]

Fig. 3.10 Matching linear patterns by shifting

is not to backtrack, the next operation must do one of two things:

1. Shift *pattern* right some number of places to compare *text*[j] with *pattern*[k], $k < i$; *or*
2. compare the next target character *text*[$j+1$] with some character in *pattern*.

At this point it has only been determined that *text*[j] *does not* match *pattern*[i]. Therefore, *text*[$j+1$] cannot be examined until either *text*[j] is determined to be part of a potential substring match, or ruled out of one; in other words, choice (i) must be investigated.

If the pattern is to be shifted, it must be moved right until a prefix σ(*pattern*, 1, $k-1$) ($1 \leq k < i$) of the portion of *pattern* already matched matches the last $k-1$ characters of σ(*text*, 1, $j-1$) (Fig. 3.10, bottom two rows). At this point, *pattern*[k] can be compared with *text*[j]; if it matches, we proceed with choice 2, comparing *text*[$j+1$] with *pattern*[$k+1$]; otherwise, the shift process just described is repeated. Note that it can be repeated at most i times without checking *text*[$j+1$]; after that *pattern* will be left of *text*[j].

In the discussion of Fig. 3.9, it was suggested that the required amount of shift could be computed from the pattern alone. To see this, consider the description of the shift process above (refer also to Fig. 3.10). When $pattern[i] \neq text[j]$, the pattern is shifted right so that $text[j]$ is compared to $pattern[k]$, where k is the largest prefix of the pattern matched so far, which matches the last $k-1$ text characters. But the last $i-1$ text characters comprise $\sigma(pattern, 1, i-1)$, so this prefix must match a substring of *pattern*, namely $\sigma(pattern, i-k+1, k-1)$. However, there is more information available. Since $pattern[i] \neq text[j]$, the compare after the shift is guaranteed to fail unless $pattern[k] \neq pattern[i]$. Therefore, on a mismatch at $pattern[i]$, we know the next pattern character to compare with the current target one (i.e., how much to shift *pattern*). It is simply $pattern[k]$ for the largest $k < i$ such that

1. $\sigma(pattern, 1, k-1) = \sigma(pattern, i-k+1, k-1)$.
2. $pattern[k] \neq pattern[i]$.

Call this k $next[i]$, and note that $i-next[i]$ specifies the actual amount of shift. If no such k exists, $text[j]$ has been eliminated from any match, so matching restarts by comparing $pattern[1]$ with $text[j+1]$. As this represents a shift of i positions, $next[i]$ can be taken as zero.

If a *next* table can be precomputed efficiently, backtracking will be eliminated from Algorithm 3.1. Algorithm 3.2 is essentially Algorithm 3.1 modified to use a *next* table on a mismatch rather than backtrack. Again, *pattern* has been found starting at $text[j-1]$ if, on termination, $i > m$. Operation of the algorithm is illustrated in Fig. 3.11.

Algorithm 3.2   Pattern matching without backtracking (Algorithm 3.1 modified to use a *next* table)

```
integer i, j, m, n;
string pattern[1:m], text[1:n];
i ⇐ j ⇐ 1;
do while i ≤ m ∧ j ≤ n;
   if pattern[i] = text[j] then
   do /* keep matching */
      i ⇐ i+1;
      j ⇐ j+1;
   end
   else
   if next[i] > 0 then
      i ⇐ next[i]; /* shift pattern right by i-next[i] */
   else
   do              /* restart matching from pattern[1] */
      i ⇐ 1;
      j ⇐ j+1;
   end
end
```

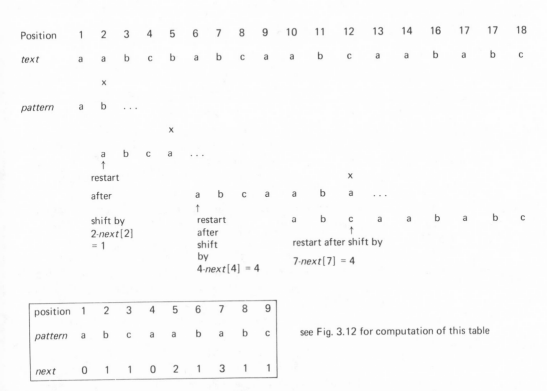

Fig. 3.11   Pattern matching using Algorithm 3.2

In Algorithm 3.2, i and j can be incremented at most n times. The shift "$i \Leftarrow next[i]$" never reduces i below zero, so it too can be executed at most n times. Thus, the total running time is $O(n)$. This is an improvement over $O(m \cdot n)$, assuming that the *next* table can be computed with comparable efficiency. Before this is done, however, we shall argue that Algorithm 3.2 is correct (i.e., that it finds a match if and only if one is there). The backtracking version (Algorithm 3.1) satisfies this requirement because it works by exhaustive search. Since Algorithm 3.2 differs only in the action taken on a mismatch, it must be shown that such action never causes a match to be overlooked. But, by definition, $i=next[i]$ represents the least amount of shift to the next potential match. The algorithm is therefore correct if the *next* table is computed properly, a problem now considered.

One approach to computing $next[1:m]$ for *pattern*, a string of length m, is to first look for $next[m]$. We start by comparing *pattern* against itself shifted by one, and keep shifting right until some prefix matches a suffix of $\sigma(pattern, 1, m-1)$. Then, if the character following the prefix is not *pattern*[m], *next*[m] is set to the length of that prefix; otherwise shifting and matching continue.

Suppose that after some number of right shifts, a prefix $\sigma(pattern, 1, i-1)$ matches $i-1$ positions in *pattern* ending at $pattern[j-1]$, and that $pattern[i] \neq pattern[j]$; that is,

$$
\begin{array}{ccc}
\text{p}[1] & \cdots & \text{p}[i-1]\ \text{p}[i] \\
\| & & \| \quad \not\Vert \\
\text{p}[1] \cdots \text{p}[j-i+1] \cdots \text{p}[j-1]\ \text{p}[j] &
\end{array}
$$

Because *pattern* is being matched against itself, information not present it in general case is available here. First, $next[j]$ can be set to i, since by repeated shifting, $\sigma(pattern, 1, i-1)$ has been determined to be the *longest* prefix that matches $\sigma(pattern, j-i+1, i-1)$ and satisfies $pattern[i] \neq pattern[j]$. Second, for $k = 1$ to $i-1$ (i.e., the last $i-1$ characters matched), $next[j-i+k]$ can be set to $next[k]$, as it has been established that $pattern[j-i+k] = pattern[k]$ for the same range. Thus new *next* entries can be computed if previous ones are available.

Now unless $i = m$, *pattern* must be shifted right again in an attempt to compute $next[m]$. However, the situation resembles the case above, when $pattern[i]$ failed to match the jth target character—unless *pattern* is shifted past $pattern[j]$, the only shifts worth pursuing are those for which a prefix of the $i-1$ pattern characters just matched agree with some suffix of the last $i-1$ target characters matched. In other words, the amount of shift desired is exactly that specified by $i-next[i]$. After a shift by this amount, matching resumes at $pattern[j+1]$ if $next[i]$ was zero and $pattern[j]$ otherwise. On a mismatch, *next* is computed for the positions just scanned, and the pattern is shifted again.

The discussion above suggests that computing the *next* table can be treated as a special case of the general matching algorithm if we can ensure that, on a mismatch, at the ith pattern position, $next[1]$ through $next[i]$ are available for computing new entries and specifying shifts. This is the basis for Algorithm 3.3, and a straightforward induction argument shows that the required values are ready when needed. Except for steps assigning to *next*, the algorithm is just a rearranged version of Algorithm 3.2, with *pattern* serving as both pattern and target. Variables i and j indicate, respectively, pattern and target positions. As long as a prefix of *pattern* is matching some portion of *pattern*, i and j are incremented, and *next* entries are computed from previous values. On a mismatch, $next[j]$ is set to i, and the pattern is shifted right until some prefix agrees with $\sigma(pattern, 1, j)$ (lines 4 and 5). Matching then resumes at positions $i+1$ and $j+1$. Figure 3.12 illustrates how the algorithm would work on the string 'abcaababc'.

The timing analysis for Algorithm 3.3 is similar to that for Algorithm 3.2. Informally, each iteration either shifts the pattern or examines a new target character, making the run time proportional to the length of *pattern*. More precisely, the outer **do while** is executed exactly $m-1$ times since j is incremented by one each time through. The inner loop (lines 4 and 5) reduces i, possibly down to zero on each execution. Since i starts at 0, is incremented $m-1$ times, and is never less than zero, this loop can be executed at most m times. The *next* table can therefore be computed in time proportional to pattern length. Thus a pattern of length m can be located in a target of length n in time $O(m+n)$. Note that this is independent of alphabet size.

Algorithm 3.3 can be extended, to find, for example, all occurrences of *pattern* in *text*. Also, a slight gain in efficiency can be made by eliminating some redundant comparisons. These and similar results are left for the exercises. The basic idea of linear-time pattern matching, using a table of shifts efficiently computed by matching the pattern against itself, remains unchanged.

Algorithm 3.3   Computing the *next* table

```
      integer i, j, m, next[1:m];
      string pattern[1:m];
 1.     i, next[1] ⟸ 0;
 2.     j ⟸ 1;
 3.     do while j < m;
 4.       do while i > 0 ∧ pattern[i] ≠ pattern[j];
 5.         i ⟸ next[i];
        end
 5.     i ⟸ i+1;
 7.     j ⟸ j+1;
 8.     if pattern[i] = pattern[j] then next[j] ⟸ next[i];
 9.                          else next[j] ⟸ i;
      end
```

Target Position	1 2 3 4 5 6 7 8 9
next Table	0 1 1 0 2 1 3 1 1

	Target		Action during iteration
		a b c a a b a b c	
	1	ⓐ b ...	*next*[2] ← 1
Iteration # x indicates position of mismatch with target. Matching starts at circled letter.	2	ⓐ b ...	*next*[3] ← 1
	3	ⓐ b c ...	*next*[4] ← *next*[1] = 0 *next*[5] ← 2
	4	a ⓑ c ...	*next*[6] ← *next*[2] = 1 *next*[7] ← 3
	5	a ⓑ c	*next*[8] ← *next*[2] = 1 *next*[9] ← *next*[3] = 1

Fig. 3.12   Computing *next* table for 'abcaababc' using Algorithm 3.3

3.5 Data Compression

Among the transformations which can be carried out on a string, one of obvious interest is that which reduces its length without losing any of the information content. This reduces the storage requirement for it and increases the effective capacity of a communication channel on which it is transmitted. Communication theory, based on the theory of information conceived by Claude Shannon, is concerned with the storage and transmission of messages (i.e., strings of characters). Information theory starts by introducing a quantitative measure for the information content of a message, and goes on to develop methods for representing the message by encoding the characters or character sequences comprising it, in efficient ways.

3.5.1 Encodings

The definition of the information in a message is based on the notion of the "surprise" imparted by the knowledge that the message, regarded as the occurrence of a particular event, has transpired. Thus if we are told that a certain message having a high probability of occurrence is received, there is little surprise in knowing this fact. Specifically the surprise associated with a message having a probability p of occurring is defined as $-\log p$, and the information H associated with a set X of N messages is defined to be the average surprise.[9] If p_i is the probability of finding the ith message,

$$H(X) = -\sum_{i=1}^{N} p_i \log p_i \qquad \text{where } \sum_{i=1}^{N} p_i = 1.$$

This measure (which is analogous to entropy in thermodynamics) has certain properties which are desirable as a measure of information:

- It is always positive ($0 \leq H < \infty$).
- It has its maximum value when $p = 1/N$. This corresponds to the intuitive notion that we are given most information when told that a particular one of a number of equally likely events has occurred.
- Consider the message set C, found by taking the cross product, $A \times B$, of two independent sets A and B. It is easy to show that

$$H(C) = H(A) + H(B). \tag{3.1}$$

This additive property is what one would expect for the information imparted by unconnected events.

A basic theorem of information theory relates the information content of a message set, X, to the average length of an encoding for the messages, formed by representing them in terms of characters chosen from a d-character alphabet in such a way that each message can be unambiguously associated with its encoding. If message i is represented

---

[9]The base of the logarithms here, and everywhere else in this book, unless explicitly stated otherwise, is 2.

by a sequence of l_i characters, this theorem states that the average length

$$\bar{L} = \sum_{i=1}^{N} p_i l_i \geq \frac{H(X)}{\log d}.$$

The *efficiency* of an encoding system is defined to be $H(X)/\bar{L} \log d$, and the *redundancy* is given as $1 - efficiency$. Information theory shows that encoding which are arbitrarily close to unit efficiency exist, and provides constructive measures for finding them.

Example 3.2

As an illustration of these ideas, suppose that we have eight messages, identified by the letters a, . . . , h, with equal probabilities as shown in column 2 of Table 3.3. The information content,

$$H(X) = \sum_{i=1}^{8} - p_i \log p_i = 8 \times \tfrac{1}{8} \times 3 = 3.$$

If we choose to represent these in an alphabet consisting of the binary digits 0 and 1, then $d = 2$, so

$$\bar{L} \geq \frac{3}{1} = 3 \text{ bits.}$$

The notation in which the messages are represented by the 3 bit numbers $000, \ldots 111$ is an efficient (nonredundant) encoding. Note that $H(X)$, which is a pure number, can be thought of as the length in bits for a nonredundant encoding, or as the number of binary choices required to identify a message on the average.

TABLE 3.3

Message	p	Binary Encoding for p	p'	Efficient Encoding for p'
a	0.125	000	1/2	0
b	0.125	001	1/4	10
c	0.125	010	1/8	110
d	0.125	011	1/16	1110
e	0.125	100	1/32	11110
f	0.125	101	1/64	111110
g	0.125	110	1/128	1111110
h	0.125	111	1/128	1111111

If the messages have the probabilities shown in column 4, $H(X) = 1/2 \times 1 + 1/4 \times 2 + 1/8 \times 3 + 1/16 \times 4 + 1/32 \times 5 + 1/64 \times 6 + 1/128 \times 7 + 1/128 \times 7 = 127/64$, so we can look for an encoding where the average message length is less than 2 bits. This requires short codes for the most frequently occurring messages. In column 5, an encoding that has this property is shown and it is clearly efficient, for

$$\bar{L} = 1/2 \times 1 + 1/4 \times 2 + \ldots + 1/128 \times 7 + 1/128 \times 7 = 127/64.$$

It is obviously necessary to be able to decipher messages unambiguously. A desirable property is that messages can be deciphered one character at a time, without having to read the whole message before the translation starts. In this example the sequence 111100111111110 is immediately deciphered as "eahb." This property of instant decipherability will be present if no message has a code that is the beginning of another message's code. Such encodings are said to have the *prefix* property.

Codes can have many other useful properties, such as the ability to detect an error in a message, or to both detect and correct an error and coding theory is a fully developed theory in its own right, for which it is necessary to go to special books for further details. We conclude this section by giving an algorithm, due to Huffman, for constructing an optimal encoding (i.e., one with minimum redundancy) having the prefix property (Algorithm 3.4). The algorithm, which is described as the construction of a tree, is given for the case of an alphabet with two characters. On completion, the leaf nodes will carry the optimal encodings.

Algorithm 3.4   Huffman encoding of messages

    1. Let the message set be the leaf nodes of a tree whose nodes carry a weight factor equal to the probability of the message occurrence.
    2. Join the two nodes of least weight to a parent node to which is attached a weight equal to the sum of the weights of its descendents.
    3. Continue this process (using nodes of least weight) until the tree has a single root (with weight $= 1$ since $\sum\limits_{i=1}^{N} p_i = 1$).
    4. Assign the codes 0 and 1 to the nodes immediately descending from the root.
    5. Descending from the root, assign codes to all nodes, each pair of descendents receiving the code $L0$ and $L1$, where L is the code label of the parent.

In the general case where there are N messages and d digits in the alphabet, d nodes are combined in step 2. There may be a nonleaf node in the tree with fewer than d branches, and it is necessary to ensure that this, if it happens, takes place at the very first step. This is accomplished by combining d nodes the first time, if $(N-1) \bmod (d-1) = 0$, and $(N-1) \bmod (d-1) + 1$ nodes otherwise. In step 4 the codes $0, 1, \ldots, (d-1)$ are assigned to the branches, and similarly the codes $L0, L1, \ldots, L(d-1)$ in step 5.

As an illustration of the use of the algorithm, consider a very simple set of three messages, a, b, c, with probabilities of 0.6, 0.3, and 0.1, respectively. Figure 3.13 shows the Huffman tree for a two-digit alphabet, resulting in the encoding $a = 0$, $b = 10$, $c = 11$. For this encoding,

$$H(X) = -0.6 \log 0.6 - 0.3 \log 0.3 - 0.1 \log 0.1 = 1.295,$$

$$\bar{L} = 0.6 \times 1 + 0.3 \times 2 + 0.1 \times 2 = 1.4$$

and the efficiency is $1.295/1.4 = 92.5$ per cent. To obtain a more efficient system, we can encode pairs of messages, $aa, ab, ac, \ldots, cc$. These have probabilities 0.36, 0.18,

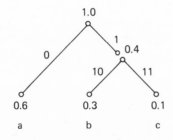

Fig. 3.13 Huffman tree

0.06, . . . , 0.01, assuming independence of successive messages. The Huffman tree for message pairs, along with the binary encoding that results, is shown in Fig. 3.14. For this system,

$$\bar{L} = 0.36 \times 1 + 0.18 \times 3 + 0.18 \times 3 + 0.09 \times 4 + 0.06 \times 4 + 0.06 \times 4$$
$$+ 0.03 \times 5 + 0.03 \times 6 + 0.01 \times 6 = 2.67.$$

Recalling that $H(x)$ for a single message is 1.295 and that messages are considered independent, the entropy for a message pair [using Eq. (3.1)] is 2×1.295. The efficiency is $2(1.295)/2.67 = 95.8$ percent.

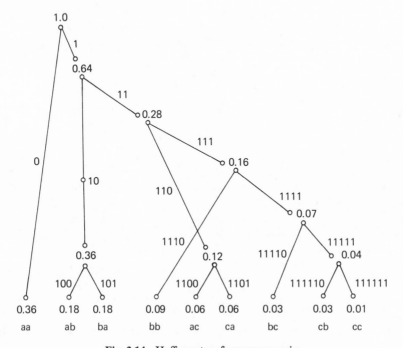

Fig. 3.14 Huffman tree for message pairs

If the encoding of Fig. 3.13 is used for a pair of messages, the efficiency remains 92.5 per cent, since the messages are independent. Thus by being ready to consider two message sequences, a more efficient encoding has been achieved. By taking longer message sequences, the efficiency can be increased still more, but the improvement comes slowly.

3.5.2 Substitutions

Huffman encoding is most effective when there is a small number of message types, a few of which account for a relatively high proportion of text. The savings become less dramatic as the number of message types increase and the frequencies become more uniform. In information processing, one often finds that the number of different messages is either effectively undetermined in advance (e.g., when the units are words of English text), or too large to justify a variable-length encoding (e.g., the ASCII character set). In such cases it is more practical to compress by replacing only selected portions of the text with shorter codes. This selection can be performed in two ways:

1. Dynamically—scaning the text and replacing "obviously" redundant sequences by shorter ones.
2. In advance—analyzing the text to determine groups to be replaced and the codes to replace them with.

Perhaps the most common form of dynamic compression is *run-length encoding*, often used to eliminate strings of blanks or zeros. This is done by substituting for each run of k zeros (or blanks) ($2 < k \leq 9$) an unused character (e.g., @), followed by the integer k. Thus AB200003940000052600D000 becomes AB2@4394@552600D@3. If there are no unused characters in the alphabet set, some rarely used one may be chosen as the blank indicator, and when the character actually appears in the string it is recorded twice; the repetition serves to distinguish it from the blank indicator. Even with this complication, the translation of actual strings into compressed strings (and vice versa) is easy.

Often it is easier to delete a whole field rather than use run-length encoding. For example, a record may have fields that are not applicable to all records in the file. Other fields may be required to accommodate a maximum-size value, while the average size is considerably less. The record might thus contain a large number of zeros and blanks which do not occur in sequences long enough to be worth encoding. In such a case, compression can be done by *bit mapping*. A bit map at the front of a record indicates the presence or absence of field values. For example, a map of '100110' for a six-field record says that only the first, fourth, and fifth field values need to be stored. The appropriate number of zeros or blanks can be inserted for the other fields on decompression. In Fig. 3.15, names may occupy up to 32 characters. Since most are shorter, a bit map is used to indicate the number of 8-character blocks actually needed.

Although blank compression and bit mapping can be effective, there are many situations where they are not applicable, and if compression is to be done, the substi-

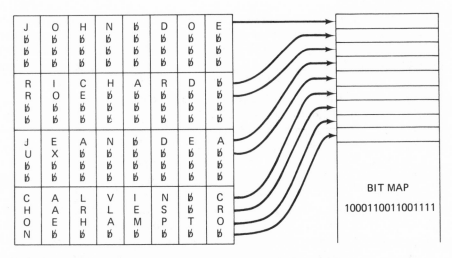

Fig. 3.15   Blank word compression by bit mapping

tutions must be identified in advance. At the expense of some possible compression, encoding is often simplified by confining replacement to predetermined pattern types. In processing language text, the word is a natural compression unit, as often a few word types account for a relatively large fraction of the textual material. In several studies, the number of distinct vocabulary entries in English textual material varied from 10 to 15 percent of the total text. For specialized sources (e.g., military documents) the fraction was even less.[10]

The compression achievable by word encoding is limited by two factors. First, in any natural language such as English, the most common words (the, of, a, to, and, in) are short. Second, words in natural language seem to obey *Zipf's law:* The frequency of the nth most common word is proportional to $1/n$. This means that the space savings become less and less as progressively more words are encoded. In such cases it is often possible to increase the number of usefully replaceable message types by encoding digrams (letter pairs) instead of words. If every digram in the text can be replaced by a single character, 50 percent compression will be obtained, and savings of close to this have been reported. For a discussion of the merits of word and digram encoding, see Lesk.[11]

A variation on compressing selected words is to encode all words in the texts as unique fixed-point numbers.[12] Basically, the idea is to regard a word (i.e., a sequence of nonblank characters) as a number in a system whose radix is the alphabet size. The

[10]E. S. Schwartz, "A Dictionary for Minimum Redundancy Encoding," *Journal of the ACM*, **10**, no. 4 (1963), 414–439.

[11]M. E. Lesk, "*Compressed Text Storage.*" Computer Science Technical Report 3, (Murray Hill, N.J.: Bell Telephone Laboratories, Nov. 1970).

[12]W. D. Hagamen and others, "Encoding Verbal Information as Unique Numbers," *IBM Systems Journal*, **11**, no. 4 (1972), 278–315.

degree of compression achievable through this technique compares with that obtained by encoding either most frequent words or digrams.[13]

The most general compression methods find commonly occurring substrings, called *patterns*, and replace them with strings of shorter length. This approach has had some success,[14,15] but there are drawbacks. First, the preprocessing (determining the most frequent patterns) is expensive, owing to the large number of candidates, and complicated by such considerations as the fact that the choice of one pattern may affect the usefulness of previous ones. For example, suppose 'ere' is marked for replacement, and subsequently, 'here', 'there', and 'where' are all chosen for substitution; then assuming that longer patterns are replaced before shorter ones, the code for 'ere' will probably have been wasted, along with the effort in determining the substitution.

Second, encoding arbitrary strings can hamper text searching, because it can cause a piece of text to be encoded in different ways. For example, if 'ingɒl' is replaced by '#' and 'ingɒt' by '@', then 'string' will appear as 'str#' in the context 'string lists', and as 'str@' in the context 'string trees'. Thus a search for all instances of 'string' will have to contend with alternate patterns. In general, it may be undesirable to encode patterns which cross field boundaries, because updating that is confined to change of a single datum becomes more expensive when neighboring fields are also affected.

Finally, the algorithm for replacing patterns with their encodings requires some strategy; the "obvious" method of moving through the text, substituting for the longest initial substring of the input that is a pattern, is not always best. For a discussion of this and other aspects of general substitution, see Rubin.[16]

Once the strings to replace have been determined, they must be encoded; one method is to replace them by codes from the machine's character set which do not appear in text. EBCDIC has 256 values, fewer than half of which are used for upper- and lowercase characters, numbers, and punctuation marks. This leaves codes for about 180 words, each of which can be compacted into a single byte. More generally, tables are set up to compress the strings into their encoded representations, and likewise for decompression when the encodings are to be printed. The storage requirements for these tables can be very large, offsetting to some extent the savings in the text, but for large files the general experience is that compression using tables is worthwhile.[17]

[13]Bruce Hahn, "A New Technique for Compression and Storage of Data," *Communications of the ACM*, **17**, no. 8 (Aug. 1974), 434–436.

[14]J. P. McCarthy, "Automatic File Compression," in *Proceedings of the International Computing Symposium 1973*, A. Gunther and others, eds. (Amsterdam: North-Holland Publishing Company, 1974), 511–516.

[15]A. Mayne and E. B. James, "Information Compression by Factorising Common Strings," *The Computer Journal*, **18**, no. 2 (May 1975), 151–160.

[16]F. Rubin, "Experiments in Text File Compression," *Communications of the ACM*, **19**, no. 11 (Nov. 1976), 617–623.

[17]P. A. Alsberg, "Space and Time Savings Through Large Data Base Compression and Dynamic Restructuring," *Proceedings of the IEEE*, **63**, no. 8 (Aug. 1975), 1114–1422.

Exercises

1. Use Algorithm 3.3 to compute a *next* table for the following patterns:
    ABRACADABRA, ISSISSIPPI, BABBABAB.
2. Modify Algorithm 3.2 to:
    (a) Find all occurrences of *pattern* in *text*.
    (b) Find the longest repeated occurrence of *pattern* in *text*.
3. Modify Algorithm 3.2 to match more than one pattern in parallel, stopping when one
    of the alternatives is found. Is there a better alternative to using multiple *next* tables and
    pattern pointers? (*Hint:* See if the process can be made to depend on alphabet size rather
    than the number of patterns.)
4. Give a context-sensitive grammar for $\{WW \mid W \in \{a \cup b\}*\}$.
5. Show the effect of the following SNOBOL operations, using diagrams similar to Fig. 3.6:
    (a) $X = \$Y + 2$.
    (b) $\$3 = \text{'TEST'}$.
    (c) $\$*X = 2$.
6. Write a SNOBOL program that will read a text (consisting of words, punctuation marks,
    and blanks), and will identify all palindromes (phrases which start and end with a word,
    and which read the same forward and backward, neglecting spaces and punctuation,
    e.g., "Madam, I'm Adam").
7. Construct a sequence of SNOBOL patterns that recognize the grammar of Example 1.5.
    (*Hint:* Use unevaluated expressions.)
8. Write a program that examines a given text for every occurrence of each member of a
    set of strings, and prints out the location of all places in the text where each string is
    found.
9. A concordance is a list in which the place of occurrence of every word in a given text is
    cited, along with the surrounding context of the word. Write a program which:
    (a) Prepares a concordance for a given text—the context should be the line in which the
        entry is found.
    (b) Skips words that belong to a given "omission list" of common words such as "the,"
        "of," "his," and "and."
10. Encode the message set of Example 3.2 as triplets of messages, aaa, aab, . . . , ccc. Con-
    struct the Huffman tree and calculate the efficiency for triplet encoding. Compare it
    with the efficiency for encoding single messages and message pairs.
11. The following data (see reference cited in footnote 10) shows the frequency of occur-
    rence for the 15 most common words in a sample of English text for which the total
    count was 19,710 words. Assuming that an alphabetic character is equivalent to $\log 26$
    $= 4.7010$ bits, what is the average length in bits for these words? Suppose that a text
    were to consist *only* of these words with frequencies as shown, and they were encoded
    optimally, using four characters. What would the average length be? Construct an
    optimal encoding for the set.

Word	the	of	a	to	and	in	that	he
Frequency	1192	677	541	518	462	450	242	195
Word	is	at	on	for	his	are	be	
Frequency	190	181	174	157	138	124	123	

12. (a) Let $p_1, \ldots, p_R$ be the set of input groups for which substitutions are to be made in a compression algorithm. Suggest algorithms for scanning the text to carry out the substitutions. (Allow for the possibility that one group is a prefix to another.)

(b) Assuming that the encoded lengths are given, how can the shortest encoding be achieved?

(c) Suggest methods for determining the input groups. (See the references in footnotes 14 and 16.)

13. When surnames are part of a long record, it is often useful to have an abbreviation for them. Two such abbreviations are the Russell Soundex Code and Name Compression. These are constructed as follows.

Russell Soundex Code

1. The code consists of an alphabetic prefix which is the first letter in the surname followed by three digits.
2. Ignore W and H.
3. A, E, I, O, U, and Y are defined as separators, but they are not coded.
4. Other letters are coded according to the table shown, until three digits are reached.

Letter	Code Digit
B, P, F, V	1
D, T	3
L	4
M, N	5
R	6
C, G, J, K, Q, S, Z, X	2

5. When a letter is coded with the same digit as its predecessor, it is ignored unless there is a separator between the two.
6. Zeros are added as necessary.

Name Compression

1. Delete the second of any pair of identical consonants.
2. Delete A, E, I, O, U, and Y except when the first letter in the name.

Construct the coded and compressed forms for a number of similar name pairs (e.g., Fischer, Fisher; MacLain, McLaine). What advantages are there to having these the same? What are the relative advantages and disadvantages of the two methods of abbreviation? [From *Social Issues on Computing*, C. C. Gotlieb and A. Borodin (New York: Academic Press, Inc., 1974), reprinted with permission.]

14. The ASCII standard recommends the use of both vertical and horizontal parity checks for messages. The horizontal check is the eighth bit of the encoded character; the vertical check is an extra row which sets the parity for the sum of all digits in a given column. For example, the message 23456 with horizontal parity odd, and vertical parity even, is encoded as follows:

Message Character		Bit Position							Horizontal Parity (Odd)
		7	6	5	4	3	2	1	
2	First	0	1	1	0	0	1	0	0
3	Second	0	1	1	0	0	1	1	1
4	Third	0	1	1	0	1	0	0	0
5	Fourth	0	1	1	0	1	0	1	1
6	Fifth	0	1	1	0	1	1	0	1
Vertical parity (even)		0	1	1	0	1	1	0	1

In the example, what condition must hold for the bit at the lower right to be correct for both horizontal and vertical parity? What is the redundancy (ratio of bits transmitted to bits in the message, exclusive of checks) in this system? Show that an undetected error must have an even number of incorrect bits, greater than two, in compensating positions, and give an example.

15. In a language with "low-level" string operations, of the type described in Section 3.2.1 (e.g., PL/I, PASCAL), write programs to convert integers to and from Roman numerals. (A description of the Roman numeral system can be found under the entry "number" in most general college dictionaries.)

16. String-processing facilities are being implemented on a machine that is character- and word-addressable. Each word can store four characters or a pointer, and most strings will be longer than four characters. Compare the following representations with respect to (1) storage efficiency, (2) ease of scan for a given substring, (3) ease insertion and deletion, and (4) speed of insertion and deletion.

    (a) Linear mapping, one character per byte [as in Fig. 3.1(c)].
    (b) Linear mapping, one character per word [Fig. 3.1(a)].
    (c) Linked mapping, each item consisting of a word (with up to four characters) and a pointer (Fig. 3.4).
    (d) Linked mapping, each item is a word containing one character, and a pointer.

    Can you think of other representations that would be competitive with those above?

Bibliography

Some aspects of character sets are discussed in Chapter 6 of Martin (1972), and in Fletcher (1974). Chapter 5 of Richards (1971) deals with codes for error detection and correction.

String operations and their realization in some current programming languages is the subject of Housden (1975). Madnick (1967) discusses string representations to support basic string operations.

The standard reference for SNOBOL is Griswold, Poage, and Polonsky (1971). For information about implementation, and a deeper understanding of SNOBOL operations, see Griswold (1972). Griswold (1975) shows how SNOBOL4 can be applied to a wide variety of data-manipulation problems.

Linear pattern matching is also presented by Aho, Hopcroft, and Ullman (1974).

Huffman encoding is discussed in any book on information theory. A good reference is Ash (1965). A brief but readable survey on compression is given by Ruth and Kreutzer (1972). For detail on various techniques, see the references in footnotes 10 through 17, and Moore et al. (1977).

AHO, A. V., J. E. HOPCROFT, AND J. D. ULLMAN, *The Design and Analysis of Algorithms.* Reading, Mass.: Addison-Wesley Publishing Compony, Inc., 1974.

ASH, R. B., *Information Theory.* New York: Wiley–Interscience, 1965.

FLETCHER, J. G., "Characters in a Dialogue." *DATAMATION* (Oct. 1974), 42–47.

GRISWOLD, R. E., *The Macro Implementation of SNOBOL4.* San Francisco: W. H. Freeman & Company, 1972.

GRISWOLD, R. E., *String and List Processing in SNOBOL4 Techniques and Applications.* Englewood Cliffs, N.J.: Prentice-Hall, Inc., 1975.

GRISWOLD, R. E., J. F. POAGE, AND I. P. POLONSKY, *The SNOBOL4 Programming Language*, 2nd ed. Englewood Cliffs, N.J.: Prentice-Hall, Inc., 1971.

HOUSDEN, R. J. W., "On String Concepts and Their Implementation." *The Computer Journal*, **18**, no. 2 (May 1975), 150–156.

MADNICK, S. E., "String Processing Techniques." *Communications of the ACM*, **10**, no. 7 (July 1967), 420–424.

MARTIN, J., *Introduction to Teleprocessing.* Englewood Cliffs, N.J.: Prentice-Hall, Inc., 1972.

MOORE, G. B., J. L. KUHNS, J. L. TREFFTS, AND C. A. MONTGOMERY, "Accessing Individual Records from Personal Data Files Using Non-unique Identifiers." *NBS Special Publication 500-2*, U.S. Department of Commerce, National Bureau of Standards, 1977.

RICHARDS, R. K., *Digital Design.* New York: Wiley–Interscience, 1971.

RUTH, S. S., AND P. J. KREUTZER, "Data Compression for Large Business Files." *DATAMATION*, **18**, no. 9 (Sept. 1972), 62–66.

chapter 4

Simple Lists

The term "list" is used very generally in computing to describe a broad collection of data types. In all of them there is an ability to list or enumerate the members of the set that make up the list, and this can be taken as the characteristic property.

The *list* consists of ordered sets of *entries*. An entry may be an item with fields (as in Chapter 2) or it may be a list itself. The ordering represents a successor relationship between entries and it can arise from the logical structure (e.g., a chronological order based on the time when the entry is first encountered, a lexicographic order based on the value of a field) or from the storage structure.

The ordering of list entries gives information about a successor/predecessor relation between entries. But displaying list entries as a contiguous linear sequence is not adequate for expressing all such relationships. For example in Fig. 4.1 it is not possible to specify the prerequisite relationships as shown, by a single, contiguous, linear list of courses. A similar problem arises because we have defined a list in a way that permits a sublist to be an entry. Some method is needed to specify that a given entry can be followed both by sublists and by other entries of the main list. An additional problem arises if the sublists may have entries in common and it is not wanted to keep multiple copies of the shared entries [Fig. 4.1(b)]. In Fig. 4.1(b), when MILLER is found on a particular list, some way of designating its successor on that list is needed. The way to meet these difficulties is to include pointers as part of the data in order to indicate successor relationships. In a general list, the fields of an entry may include pointers to other entries. Except for the next section, this chapter is mainly concerned with simple lists, a term which is explained in that section, but where, essentially, any entry has only *one* successor.

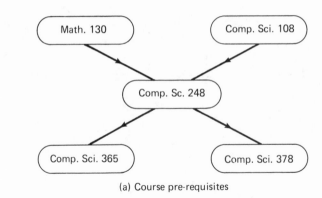

(a) Course pre-requisites

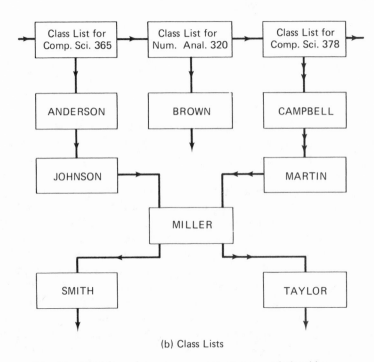

(b) Class Lists

Fig. 4.1   Need for pointers to represent successor relationships

In the terminology of Chapter 2, the logical structure for a **list** consists of

1. V—a set of composite values. A particular instance of a list consists of an ordered set of entries or lists. Any field of an entry whose value uniquely identifies that entry is a *key*, so there is a one-to-one mapping from keys to the entries of a list.

2. O—a set of operators, including Search, Insert, and Delete, and of relations, including a successor/predecessor relation between list entries. From these

it is possible to construct a procedure for traversing the list and enumerating entries.

3. G—a method of naming lists, entries, keys, and other fields so that they can be selected.

Lists are so basic to programming that some type of list-processing facility, however primitive, is found in every programming language. A method of naming list variables is desirable. If lists cannot be named, a common approach is to name the first entry, specify the way in which entries are to be linked, and provide a mechanism for identifying entries in terms of the linking mechanism. The first entry, called the *header*, may be regarded as the name for the list. Since we are assuming that the list is an *ordered* set of entries, the header is unambiguous.

Most basic list operators involve searching the list. The search may be carried out for an entry in a specified position (fixed, or relative to some other entry) or for an entry with a given value or values in one or more fields. Very often efficiency of search is the prime consideration in organizing a list. In the simplest organization all entries are chained in a consecutive sequence. If nothing is known about the sequence of entries, to search for a given key, say *goal*, it will be necessary to scan the entries in turn. The search time will be proportional to the time required to compare *goal* with the key of a typical entry, and the expected number of comparisons is a measure of its cost. The minimum number of comparisons is 1, and the maximum N, where N is the number of entries.

The expected number of comparisons $= \sum_{i=1}^{N} i \cdot p_i$, where p_i is the probability of finding the key in the ith position. If the keys are equally likely to occur at any position, then $p_i = 1/N$, and the expected number of comparisons for finding an entry known to be present, defined as $E_p(N)$, is equal to $(1/N) \sum_{i=1}^{N} 1 \cdot i = (N+1)/2$. Thus the search cost for this case of equally likely entries is $O(N)$.

On the other hand, if an entry's position number or index is known and the entries all occupy the same number of storage cells, it can be selected immediately—for example, by a fetch instruction in which an index register is set with the position value. In this case, which may be regarded as optimal, the search time is *independent* of the size of the list and may be written $O(1)$, meaning a constant. These two situations, where the search cost is linearly dependent on the number of entries, and where it is a small constant independent of the number of entries, represent the extreme cases. Generally, a linear dependence on N will be acceptable only for very short lists; for large N it is necessary to look for an organization where the search time, if not constant, at least increases more slowly than linearly. The classical method of binary search is such an organization. Searching lists is discussed further in Section 4.6.

Another critical factor about lists is their behavior under conditions when the list is highly dynamic (i.e., when there are frequent additions and deletions to it). Deletions require searches; additions may or may not, depending on whether or not the entry must be inserted in a specified position. Beyond this the storage management can be important. Assuming that unlimited storage is *not* available, the storage allocated to a deleted entry must eventually be returned to the set of storage cells available for assignment to new entries.

Lists are such general data structures that it is impossible to set up a comprehensive classification scheme for them. However, particular kinds of lists are characterized by their successor relationships, by their behavior under searching, additions and deletions, by the operations permitted on them, and by their storage representations. These features are examined in detail in the sections that follow. Before doing so, it is useful to make one more distinction in terminology. Data structures such as lists (and trees), which grow or shrink as needed entries are added and deleted, are sometimes called *dynamic*. This is in contrast to *static* structures, such as arrays, where the size or dimension of an item is relatively constant. It is true that in these latter cases, the dimension can be a parameter of the structure, and its value set can be set or changed, but once storage for a static data item is assigned, in most programs, the size is likely to be constant for some appreciable time. In dynamic structures on the other hand, insertions and deletions are very frequent, and there is a continual adjustment in the size of the structure as the program is being executed.

4.1 List Types and Representations

In this section we establish a correspondence between lists and directed graphs, and examine how the storage mappings considered in Chapter 2 give rise to different types of lists.

4.1.1 Lists as Graphs

The successor relationships that are present in the entries of a list, either implicitly through contiguity, or explicitly through pointers, suggest an immediate correspondence between lists and directed graphs. In this correspondence the nodes of the graph are entries, while the edges are represented either by contiguity or by pointers. The advantage of establishing such a correspondence is that in graph theory there is a highly developed body of mathematics that can provide a theoretical basis for the study of lists.

The simplest graphs are P_n, the straight line with n vertices, and C_n, the cycle with n vertices. Lists corresponding to these are *chains* and *rings* (or *circular lists*), and they will be called *simple*. The important property of a simple list is that it can be traversed completely by following successors from an initial entry. A chain has an entry with no predecessor, and another with no successor; a ring does not have such entries, but an initial or header entry will be designated for it.

The next level of complexity is when a list can contain an entry that itself is a list of entry values. For example, $\langle a, \langle b, c \rangle, \langle \langle d, e \rangle, \langle f, g \rangle \rangle \rangle$ is a list of three entries, two of which are lists. Recalling the nested parentheses notation for trees in Section 1.6, it follows that the graph corresponding to this list can be identified with a tree. Actually, there are *two* methods of interpreting even a simple list such as $\langle a, b, c \rangle$ as a rooted directed graph. (Rootedness and direction are desirable in recognition of the fact that the list has an initial entry, and is ordered.) In the first interpretation there is a directed edge between the beginning of the list and each member in it. The ordering of list entries induces an ordering of the edges. In the second interpretation the edges of the graph correspond to contiguity of entries. The list enclosed by parentheses is regarded as a directed chain, with the root pointing to the first entry [Fig. 4.2(a)]. These two interpretations give rise to two different trees for the list $\langle a,\langle b,c,\rangle,\langle\langle d,e\rangle,\langle f,g\rangle\rangle\rangle$ [Fig. 4.2(b)]. These trees may be regarded as equivalent, in the sense that they represent the same list. A tree is a generalization of a simple list in that entries may have *either* more than one predecessor or more than one successor

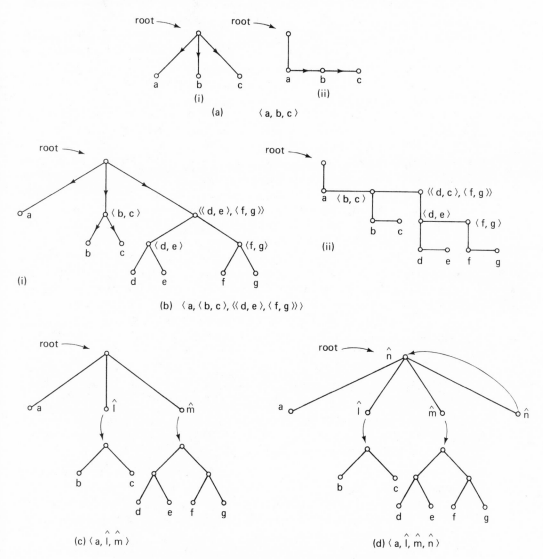

Fig. 4.2 Representations of lists as rooted, directed graphs

but not both. Consider the case of only one predecessor; if any predecessor link is broken, the list becomes disconnected. Recalling the property of a tree that it is a connected graph which loses this property if any edge is deleted, it follows that lists in which the header has no predecessor, and all other entries have exactly one, correspond to trees.

A still higher level of complexity arises when list entries can contain pointers. Some additonal naming or labeling convention is needed for the pointers. The conventional notation for labeling statements in a program is to display them at the beginning followed by a semicolon. But a label is a value in the domain of a pointer variable, just as an address is, and we can use the notation $\hat{l}$ to designate the pointer value corresponding to the label l. The label for a list may be regarded as the value of a pointer variable which names the header entry or the root of the corresponding graph. If the label for $\langle b,c \rangle$ is $\hat{l}$, that for $\langle \langle d,e \rangle, \langle f,g \rangle \rangle$ is $\hat{m}$, and that for the whole list, $\langle a, \langle b,c \rangle, \langle \langle d,e \rangle, \langle f,g \rangle \rangle \rangle$ is $\hat{n}$, then Fig. 4.2(c) shows the corresponding list structure with pointers.

Once pointer or labels are allowed in lists the corresponding graphs need no longer be trees. Thus the list $\langle a, \hat{l}, \hat{m}, \hat{n} \rangle$, labeled as $\hat{n}$, can be interpreted as one that contains itself as an entry, and it is possible to draw a graph [Fig. 4.2(d)] to represent it. The graphs corresponding to lists with arbitrary pointers are still rooted and directed, but they can contain cycles and are, in effect, general graphs. General, arbitrary graphs are very difficult structures to deal with. We saw in Chapter 1 that there are no efficient ways of finding Hamiltonian paths for them, and this can give rise to corresponding difficulties in enumerating the list entries. Also, to determine whether two n-node graphs are essentially the same (i.e., isomorphic) may require a computation of $O(n!)$. It follows that if lists are identified with arbitrary graphs, it can be very expensive to find whether two given lists are the same, or if one contains the other as a sublist. To keep lists manageable for search and enumeration, some restrictions are needed on their pointers, restrictions that have the effect of limiting their corresponding graphs. In this chapter we consider mainly simple lists, and in Chapter 6, lists that are identified with trees. More general lists and graphs are considered in Chapter 7.

LISP: The first computer language built upon lists as a basic data type was LISP, introduced by John McCarthy.[1] In LISP all data are represented by *symbolic expressions* (called S expressions), which can take two forms:

1. Atoms, consisting of strings or numeric constants (e.g., abc, 4.15).
2. A pair of S expressions, represented by the constituents separated by a dot and surrounded by parentheses [e.g., $(S_1 \cdot S_2)$].

Note that this definition of S expression is recursive. S expressions can be identified with binary trees in which the left and right subtrees correspond to the constituents of an S expression, and atoms correspond to labels attached to the leaves. Atoms are strings, and the storage mappings described in Section 3.1 can be used for them, but

---

[1]J. McCarthy, "Recursive Functions of Symbolic Expressions and Their Computations by Machine," Part 1, *Communications of the ACM*, **3**, no. 4 (Apr. 1960), 184–195.

here we simply show them as a box containing the value. The storage mapping for an S expression is a pair of pointers in which the first, called *car*, points to the first (left) constituent, and the second, called *cdr*, points to the second (right) constituent.[2] Figure 4.3 shows some simple S expressions along with their binary tree forms, and storage representations.

Three primitive operators in LISP make it possible to dissect S expressions and build complicated ones from simple constituents. If A and B are S expressions:

> CONS[A; B] constructs the S expression (A·B)
>
> CAR[(A·B)] yields A, the first constituent of its argument
>
> CDR[(A·B)] yields B, the second constituent of its argument.

(CAR and CDR applied to atoms are undefined.) These operators can be applied sequentially, so that we have the following results, using the examples of Fig. 4.3.

> CAR[(((A·B)·C)·D)] = ((A·B)·C)
>
> CDR CAR[(((A·B)·C)·D)] = C   (this is written as CDAR)
>
> CONS[CDR(((A·B)·C)·D); CAR(((A·B)·C)·D)] = (D·((A·B)·C)).

In order to reduce parentheses and simplify notation, a special null atom called NIL is introduced, and the S expression (A·(B·(C·(D·NIL)))) is abbreviated to (A B C D). Such an expression is called a *List*, and it also has the simplified storage representation shown in Fig. 4.3(e). In Fig. 4.3(f) the algebraic expression (*(+(AB))(−(CD))) is shown in List form.

Three other primitive operations in LISP are:

EQ[A; B], which takes on the value *true* if A and B are the same atomic symbols, and *false* otherwise.

ATOM[A], which is *true* if A is an atom and *false* otherwise.

COND[$p_1 \Rightarrow e_1$; $p_2 \Rightarrow e_2$; ... ; $p_n \Rightarrow e_n$], which takes on the value e_k where p_k is the first true predicate. It is undefined if no p_k is true.

From these primitives more complicated expressions and various standard functions are constructed. An unusual feature of LISP which has far-reaching consequences is that programs are themselves written as S expressions, so that we have here a case in point of the equivalence between program and data referred to in Section 2.1. Execution of a program is the evaluation of an S expression.

Although in its pure theoretical form as outlined here, S expressions are trees, in practical implementation of LISP it is necessary to refer to S expressions and modify their contents. This need arises, for example, because it is desirable to represent an S expression that is common to several parts of a program, only once. For these reasons, two additional operators are provided. RPLACA[x; y] replaces CAR[x] with y.

---

[2]These names are carryovers from the terminology for the two halves of a storage register on the IBM 7090, the computer on which LISP was first implemented. *Car* stands for "contents of the address register" and *cdr* (pronounced "cooder") for "contents of the decrement register".

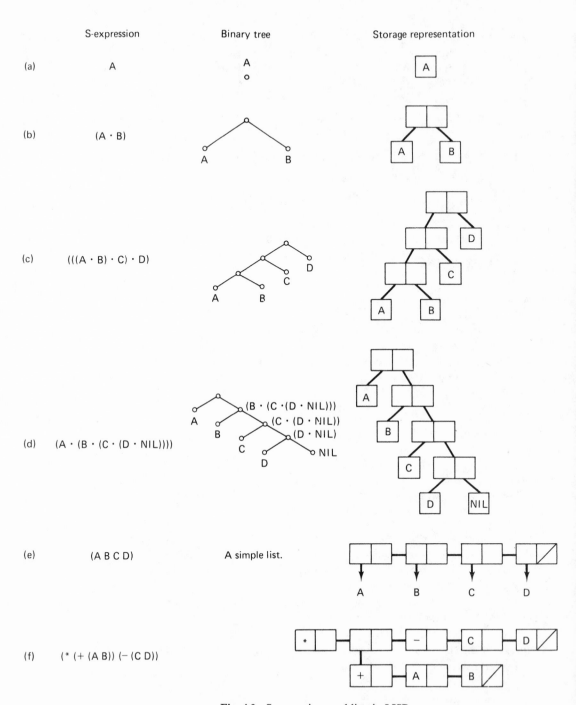

Fig. 4.3 S expressions and lists in LISP

Its effect can be described by

$$RPLACA[x, y] = CONS[y; CDR[x]].$$

Similarly,

$$RPLACD[x; y] = CONS[CAR[x]; y].$$

With these operators it becomes possible to construct LISP structures which are not trees and which may have cycles. For example, the effect of RPLACD[((A·B)·(A·B)); CAR((A·B)·(A·B))] is to create the acyclic graph of Fig. 4.4(a) in which the common subexpression is represented only once. The effect of RPLCD[CDR[RPLCD[(A·B); (C·D)]]; (A·B)] is to create the circular structure of Fig. 4.4(b). Manipulating such lists can give rise to the problems encountered in dealing with arbitrary graphs.

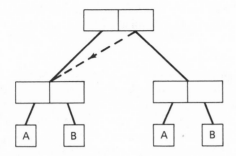

(a) RPLACD [((A · B) · (A · B)); CAR ((A · B) · (A · B))]

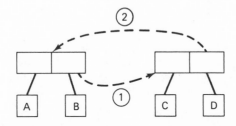

(b) RPLACD [CDR [RPLACD [(A · B); (C · D)]] ; (A · B)]

Fig. 4.4 Creation of nontree structures in LISP

4.1.2 Storage Representation

When lists are represented in the computer, the storage mapping must provide the address of every entry. By means of this mapping, access paths from the header entry to any other entry in the lists are defined. Any of the mappings described in Section 2.6—contiguous, indexed, hash-based, or linked—can be used. Which *is* used depends on a number of considerations, such as the type of searches conducted, the relative importance of searches, additions and deletions, and the need to conserve storage. When the number of entries is very large, there will not be sufficient space in the high-speed store for the full list, and auxiliary storage is needed. Lists for which two (or more) levels of storage are used in the storage mapping are called *files*, and these are discussed in Chapter 9.

The storage mapping, besides representing the mapping for entries, must also reflect the internal structure of the entries. Since entries are ordered sets of fields, a **comp** declaration, as described in Chapter 2, will provide the necessary information. In the examples in this chapter there will be such a specification for each entry type of the list that is being considered. For example, if a typical linked list entry consists of a key in the form of a string, a bit flag that may be 1 or 0, and two pointers, the specification could take the form

$$\textbf{comp entry} = \langle \textbf{string } key, \textbf{ boolean } flag, \textbf{ entry-ptr } link1, \textbf{ entry-ptr } link2 \rangle$$

where, as usual, *key*, *flag*, *link1*, and *link2* are identifiers for the fields. A single list may have several types of entries, in which case each type will be specified by its own **comp** declaration.

A note about the representation of list keys is necessary. Although keys are often alphanumeric, the collating sequence determines a sequential ordering for them. They can be interpreted as integers in the radix system whose base is the size of the character set, and then converted to decimal integers by using standard radix conversion techniques. Therefore, the keys in a list will be regarded either as strings or as decimal integers, whichever is convenient. Even if string keys are not converted to integers, the lexicographic order on the strings still makes it meaningful to compare them, so that a relational expression of the form $key1 > key2$, for example, has a Boolean value **true** or **false**.

4.1.3 Directories

In a general list, entries may have a variable number of fields, each of which may be of variable size. The storage mapping and searching algorithms must take this variability into account. But there is a considerable simplification, particularly in searching, if the entries *are* fixed in size. This can be accomplished, in effect, by dividing the list into two parts. One part, the *directory*, consists of a list of keys and addresses. The other part, called the *attribute* data, is in a separate storage area containing information relating to the keys. At the cost of one extra storage access, the attributes can be retrieved after a desired key is located in the directory.

The essential feature of directories is that they are devices for managing lists. The principal operations on them are searching for an entry, and insertion and deletion of entries. They are particularly advantageous when the list entries vary in size, but even when list entries are already of fixed size, directories are often used to separate keys from the attribute fields. If the list is being modified frequently, it may be easier to change the address field of the directory entries than to move long items which may occupy several computer words. Similarly, an entry may be deleted from a list by marking a flag field in the directory and the deletion deferred for a special pass over the whole list, at which time values no longer needed are erased. Often we shall simply represent a list by its directory, with the understanding that there is an additional storage area where the attribute fields are to be found. Sometimes only the key list will be shown, with the further understanding that the keys are accompanied by addresses pointing to the attribute fields.

Any of the standard storage mappings may be used for a directory. Since the entries are usually fixed in size, the most common mapping is indexed and the directory is of type **array** (see Chapter 5). But directories may also take the form of a table of contiguous entries which is scanned sequentially or by binary search, using techniques described in Section 4.6. Directories play a principal role in files, where the large number of entries makes it critically important to be able to search efficiently. With files especially, a somewhat more general form of directory, called an *index*, is commonly employed. An index consists of a list of *selected* keys (or parts of keys), which determines an address indicating where the search for a desired key is to be initiated. There is also a rule for continuing the search (e.g., examine consecutive entries starting with that located by the index). The term "index" is suggestive of the thumb index of a directory, where the searching procedure is the one just described. An index, like a directory, may also be based on an indexed (i.e., positional) mapping for its entries. Indexes are discussed further in Chapter 9.

Figure 4.5 illustrates some of the list types described in this section. In Fig. 4.5(a) entries consist of a key and a variable number of attribute fields. The entries are mapped contiguously, and the storage mapping would have to contain some method of indicating the entry structure. This might take the form of separators between fields and entries, count fields as part of an entry, or be a separate map showing how the entries are composed. Figure 4.5(c) illustrates a directory. The directory entries are stored contiguously; the attributes mapping is linked. For searching purposes the variable-length entries have been effectively converted to fixed size.

4.2 Lists with Controlled Access Points

One way to keep the retrieval time in a list independent of the number of items, even when additions and deletions are permitted, is to limit the places where changes can be made. This also makes it easy to name entries, since reference can be made only to those at the specified locations. There are several kinds of lists with controlled access points, of which two are particularly important:

1. *Stack* (also called a *pushdown list*)—A chain in which insertions and deletions can be made at one end, called the *top*.
2. *Queue*—Insertions are made at one end of the list (the rear) and deletions at the other (the front).

Stacks and queues arise naturally in a great many processes, not only in computing, but in any situation where traffic flows are generated. Whenever a sequence of data items is to be processed, and some item is encountered for which the processing is to be deferred, stacks and queues are used for holding the item until processing can be carried out. Which is employed depends on the service discipline (i.e., the scheduling rules applicable to deferred items). For a stack, the item most recently entered is pro-

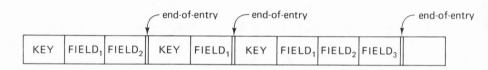

(a) A contiguous chain with variable sized entries

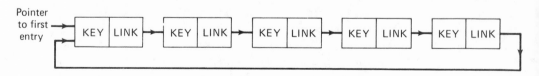

(b) A circular linked list or ring

Simple lists

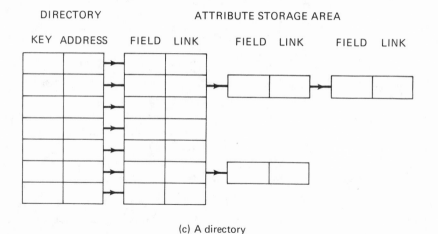

(c) A directory

Fig. 4.5   Storage representation of lists

cessed next (LIFO—last in, first out); for a queue the oldest item is processed next (FIFO—first in, first out).

Figure 4.6(a) and (b) illustrates lists with controlled access, along with the "switching diagrams" sometimes used to describe them.

4.2.1 Stacks

Using the notation of Section 2.5, the operation of inserting the value of a variable, *var*, onto a stack *S* can be expressed as $S\theta$ *var*. The word PUSH is commonly used to describe this operation, and we can write PUSH (*S,var*) for insertion, which may even be elided to PUSH(*var*) if there is only one stack. A deletion operator can be defined

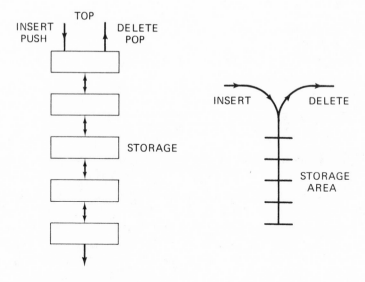

(a) STACK OR PUSHDOWN LIST

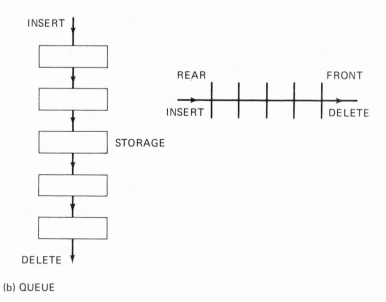

(b) QUEUE

Fig. 4.6 Representations of lists with controlled access

as the inverse of insertion, but it is useful to separate recovery of the entry at the top of the stack and decrementing of the stack. POP(S) results in the deletion of the top entry; TOP(S) yields the value of the top entry.

A stack is easily implemented by using an indicator, p, to keep track of the top position in a vector S. The operation PUSH(S,*var*) is carried out by

$$S[p+1] \Leftarrow var; p \Leftarrow p+1$$

(In practice, p would not be allowed to exceed a maximum size.)

For the POP operation it is necessary to check that the stack is not empty. POP(S) is realized by

if $p=0$ **then return** "STACKERROR" **else** $p \Leftarrow p-1$

Similarly, TOP(S) is realized by

if $p=0$ *then* TOP(S) $\Leftarrow$ "ERROR" *else* TOP(S) $\Leftarrow$ S[p].

"STACKERROR" is an indication that an invalid stack has been encountered, and "ERROR" is an indication that a nonexistent entry has been called from a stack.

Using a position indicator and a vector is not the only way to represent a stack. It is also possible to implement a stack by a chained list as described in the next section. Regardless of how the stack is implemented, in accordance with the definition of Chapter 2, it is a composite data type which is specified by the operations performed on it. It is, in fact, possible to give a quite rigorous definition of the stack data type in terms of the operations set O^{stack}, and this will be done here because it illustrates how the informal definition of type outlined in Chapter 2 can be formalized in a way that is useful for establishing the correctness of an implementation.

Suppose, for the sake of definiteness, that the type of *var* in $S \theta var$ is **int**, so that we wish to define a data type that we may call **int-stack**. In addition to the operators PUSH, POP, and TOP already considered, it is necessary to have some mechanism, denoted by CREATE, say, for creating a stack. The four stack operations are formally described in O^{stack}.

1. CREATE: $\rightarrow$ STACK
2. PUSH   : STACK $\times$ INTEGER $\rightarrow$ STACK
3. POP   : STACK $\rightarrow$ STACK $\cup$ "STACKERROR"
4. TOP   : STACK $\rightarrow$ INTEGER $\cup$ "ERROR"

The second line here indicates that PUSH is an operator (i.e., a function) requiring two arguments of type **int-stack** and **int**, and it maps these into a variable of type **int-stack**. According to the third line, the POP operation can result in either an **int-stack** or "STACKERROR" message. These four specifications are not in themselves sufficient to describe the stack. We must convey additional information about the operators; for example, if an integer is pushed onto the stack and a POP is performed immediately thereafter, the result is to recover the integer and leave the stack as it was originally. The four operators are subject to the following conditions, which may be regarded as axioms for them.

5. TOP(PUSH(S,I)), $= I$
6. TOP(CREATE) $=$ "ERROR"
7. POP(PUSH(S,I)) $= S$
8. POP(CREATE) $=$ "STACKERROR"

It can be shown that O^{stack} with its axioms *are* sufficient to define a stack completely, although it is not trivial to prove that the specification is consistent and nonredundant. Any implementation based on a storage structure that satisfies these axioms will turn out to be correct. For example, using a vector to represent the stack, we can implement the four operations as noted.

Operation	Results	
CREATE	Allocate storage to S and set $p \Leftarrow 0$:	
PUSH (S, I)	$S[p+1] \Leftarrow I; \, p \Leftarrow p+1$	
TOP (S)	**if** $p=0$ **then** "ERROR"	**else** $S[p]$
POP (S)	**if** $p=0$ **then** "STACKERROR"	**else** $p \Leftarrow p-1$

For these definitions, it is possible to verify whether the axioms (5)–(8) hold:

5. PUSH(S,I) sets $S[p+1]=I$ and $p \Leftarrow p+1$.
   An application of TOP returns $S[p]$, which is I.
6. L.H.S. = TOP(CREATE)
   $\quad$ = TOP(S) with $p=0$
   $\quad$ = "ERROR"
   $\quad$ = R.H.S.
7. PUSH(S,I) sets $S[p+1]=I$ and $p \Leftarrow p+1$
   An application of POP decrements p, leaving S at its original state.
8. L.H.S. = POP(CREATE)
   $\quad$ = POP(S) with $p=0$
   $\quad$ = "STACKERROR"
   $\quad$ = R.H.S.

Since the axioms do hold, we can be satisfied that the implementation of a stack in terms of a vector is correct. The important point here is that the definition of a stack in terms of O^{stack} and its axioms has been separated from the storage mapping. Therefore, programs in a high-level language can use the data type **int-stack** with confidence. The question of how **int-stack** is realized is one that can be deferred to the language processors.[3]

In compiling programs it turns out that with a single stack it is possible to translate from a source language, using statements with multiple, nested operations, into a target language with instructions using binary operators, free of parentheses (and hence immediately interpretable as machine code). Even more remarkably, by using one stack and a single scan of statements, it is possible to execute statements in an ALGOL-like language, allowing full use of nested block structure, recursive routines, and dynamic allocation of storage.[4]

---

[3]This example, suggested by Hoare, has become the standard one for illustrating the axiomatic approach to defining the operator set, O, of a data type.

[4]P. Wegner, *Programming Languages, Information Structures, and Machine Recognition* (New York: McGraw-Hill Book Company, 1968).

Because stacks are so useful, they have been built into the design of some machines, in particular the Burroughs B-5000 and its successors. Many computer instructions are binary operations, where only two operands are needed, so that providing a mechanism that allows access to the top two elements of the stack (without erasure) is sufficient for compilation and execution. This makes it easy to construct an inexpensive stack by using high-speed registers for the top two positions, and core memory for the others. The stack implementation is a combination of hardware and micro-programmed software.

The use of a stack to convert simple arithmetic statements into a parentheses-free form suitable for interpretation or compilation is illustrated in Algorithm 4.1.

Algorithm 4.1   Parentheses removal

```
integer stackpri; string target, tokens;
comp entry = ⟨integer pri, string token⟩;
entry source, pair ; entry-stack lifo;
target ⟸ 'b' ; PUSH(lifo,0,'b') ; /*initialize*/
do while end-of-file = false ;
   read (source) ;
   stackpri ⟸ pri(source) ; tokens ⟸ token(source) ;
   if stackpri = 0 then target ⟸ target θ tokens θ b; /*identifier*/
   else if tokens = '(' then PUSH(lifo, source);
   else if tokens = ')' then
   do
      do while token(lifo) ≠ '(' ;
         POP(lifo, pair);
         target ⟸ target θ token(pair) θ b ;
      end
      POP(lifo, pair); /*delete '('*/
   end
   else
   do
      do while stackpri ≤ pri(lifo) ;
         POP(lifo, pair);
         if token(pair) = '(' then call error; /*parentheses unbalanced*/
         target ⟸ target θ token(pair) θ b;
      end
      PUSH(lifo, source);
   end
end
if token(lifo) ≠ ';' then call error; /*incomplete statement*/
```

The statements are strings that have been preprocessed by a lexical scanner which recognizes them as a sequence of *tokens*. The tokens are identifiers, numerals, operators, and delimiters (i.e., separating characters), and the scanner attaches a precedence number to each according to the values shown in Table 4.1, thereby constructing an integer–token pair. For example, the statement

$$num \Leftarrow (a+b)*(c-d);$$

is transformed into

$$\langle 0, num \rangle, \langle 1, \Leftarrow \rangle, \langle 2, (\rangle, \langle 0, a \rangle, \langle 3, + \rangle, \langle 0, b \rangle, \langle 2,) \rangle$$
$$\langle 4, * \rangle, \langle 2, (\rangle, \langle 0, c \rangle, \langle 3, - \rangle, \langle 0, d \rangle, \langle 2,) \rangle, \langle 1, ; \rangle.$$

TABLE 4.1   Operator precedences

Token Type	Precedence
String, numeral	0
$\Leftarrow$, ;	1
(,)	2
+, −	3
* ÷	4
↑ (exp)	5

It is assumed that there is a "read" operation which reads a pair produced by the lexical scanner into a variable called *source*, as long as an end-of-file condition has not been encountered. A working stack, called *lifo*, is capable of storing a pair and a selection operation can be performed to examine its contents without a POP. The output of the program is a string called *target*, which would be the input to the next phase of the program where interpretive or compiled code is generated.

The results of the interpretation or compilation phase would be the statement as a sequence of operations in which the conventional precedence rules of arithmetic apply (exponentiation taking precedence over multiplication, which in turn takes precedence over addition, etc.). Only simple statements are processed by the program as shown, but it can be extended to deal with more complicated statements which have unary (as well as binary) operators, subscripted variables, and operators specified by reserved words (such as **if**, **else**, and **goto**). Likewise, the error checking is primitive, but can be made more elaborate. The program can process a sequence of statements. Figure 4.7 illustrates the contents of the stack and target for the sample statement.

Another example of the use of a stack for deferred processing is given by Algorithm 6.1, which traverses binary trees. Often several stacks are needed in a program. If there are two stacks, they can be paired to share common storage by having one list count up while the other counts down (Fig. 4.8). Overflow will not occur until the total number of entries in both stacks exhausts the storage assigned. Note that each stack has a *fixed base* address (i.e., the origin is set initially and does not have to be changed). If there are more than two stacks, it is not possible to assign storage so that they all have fixed base addresses, and at the same time there is overflow only when the total memory is exhausted.

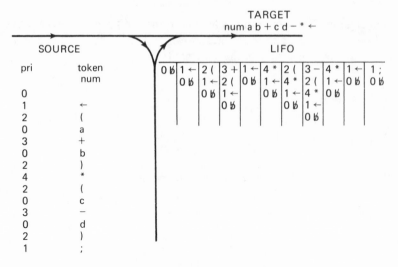

Fig. 4.7   Removal of parentheses with a stack

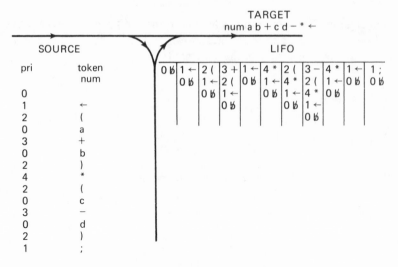

Fig. 4.8   Pair of stacks

4.2.2 Queues

To represent a queue two pointers to the storage region, F (front) and R (rear), can be maintained. Insertions are made at the rear, and deletions taken from the front. One possible implementation is in terms of a vector with Q, with $Q[F+1]$ pointing to the front and $Q[R]$ to the rear. The number of components is $R-(F+1)+1 = R-F$, and with this convention the CREATE operation may be interpreted as producing the queue with $F=R=1$ having zero components.

The operation by which the contents of a variable, *var*, are appended to the queue is accomplished by

$$Q[R+1] \Leftarrow var \;;\; R \Leftarrow R+1.$$

Likewise, deletion (i.e., removing the front element) is effected by $F \Leftarrow F+1$.

There are some difficulties that must be overcome in the implementation. Since F and R are always increasing, the queue is continually being translated in its storage area, and a considerable amount of storage may have to be reserved for it, even though the portion in actual use may be small. If the queue arrives at an empty state, which can be recognized by F and R becoming equal, the two pointers can be reset to 1, but this may not happen often enough to prevent the useful storage from drifting away from the base address. The usual solution is to set aside M locations, $Q[1], \ldots, Q[M]$, arranged implicitly in a circle, with $Q[1]$ following $Q[M]$. We then have

Insertion: **if** $R = M$ **then** $R \Leftarrow 1$ **else** $R \Leftarrow R+1$; $Q[R] \Leftarrow var$

Deletion: **if** $F = M$ **then** $F \Leftarrow 1$ **else** $F \Leftarrow F+1$;

When $R < F$, the queue contents are located in $Q[F+1], \ldots, Q[M], Q[1], \ldots, Q[R]$, and the number of entries is given by $R-F+M$.

In this it is assumed that M storage spaces are sufficient and that no attempts are made to delete entries from an empty queue. To ensure these conditions, tests must be incorporated, for example, preceding insertion:

if *no-of-entries* = M **then goto** *overflow*, where *overflow* is a section of the program that extends the storage for the queue.

Similarly, prior to deletion the test is:

if $R = F$ **then goto** *underflow*, where *underflow* is a part of the program dealing with an empty queue.

When queues are used in application, they are classified according to:

- The process governing the arrival rate of items.
- The process determining the time spent in the queue waiting for service.
- The number of servers and service discipline.
- The storage capacity.

The arrival process and service times are specified by distributions, $A(t)$ and $B(x)$, where

$$A(t) = \text{probability that the time between arrivals} \leq t$$

$$B(x) = \text{probability of service time} \leq x.$$

In the standard notation for queues these parameters are named. Thus $A/B/m$ represents a queue with m servers, whose arrival rate distribution is the given function, A, and whose service time distribution is the given function, B. If the storage capacity is infinite, it may not be mentioned; otherwise, its value is appended.

Given the queue, what is usually wanted in the flow problems where queues arise is the expected behavior for individual items and for the queue as a whole. This includes such quantities as the expected waiting time, the average number of items in the queue, and the idle time for servers. One commonly made assumption about arrivals is that they are generated by a birth process with a constant birth rate, λ. This corresponds to an arrival rate governed by the Poisson distribution, where

$$\text{probability of } n \text{ arrivals between } t \text{ and } t + dt = \frac{e^{-\lambda}}{n!}\lambda^n \, dt,$$

and it is easily shown that the average interarrival time $= 1/\lambda$. The behavior of queues where the arrival and service distributions are simple (e.g., M/M/1, a single server queue with exponential arrival and service times) is readily calculated. For more general distributions and queue disciplines the problems are much more difficult, and simulation techniques are used to obtain results.[5]

---

[5] For a concise treatment of queues, see A. D. Allen, "Elements of Queueing Theory for System Design," *IBM Systems Journal*, **14**, no. 2 (1975), 161–187.

The representation of the **queue** data type in terms of a vector with two pointers, simple as it is, is adequate for describing both queues whose parameters are given mathematically, and those for which the distribution types must be given as observations. The functional dependence of the front pointer, F, on time corresponds to that of the arrival distribution, and the behavior of the rear pointer, R, corresponds to the service time distribution. Also, the parameter M corresponds to the storage capacity $R-F$ of the queue. Thus the representation has the ability to describe complicated queues, even those which are not readily amenable to mathematical analysis.

4.3 Simple Linked Lists

We have already seen (Section 2.6.2) that a *linked list* implies a storage structure in which the address for an entry is obtained by interpreting a field as a pointer that locates the successor entry. List entries are structured as the concatenation of two or more items, some of which carry the information about the data in the entry, and at least one of which is a pointer to a successor entry. If the entry datum is a string, a suitable definition might be

$$\textbf{comp entry} = \langle \textbf{string } \textit{info}, \textbf{ entry-ptr } \textit{link} \rangle,$$

where *info* and *link* are the names of the constituent items.

This declaration describes the entry *type*. In addition, we need some method of referring to the individual entries of a list so that it is possible to designate selector operators which permit assignments and other operations on individual data elements. Now a reference to the header entry will appear in some symbol table, either in the form of a name or a pointer to it. So for a simple list at least, if the *position index* of an entry were known, it would be possible to construct a path to it, and therefore the position *could* serve as the name. But to refer to list entries in this way would, in effect, treat all lists as vectors. The main point of using *linked* lists is to be able to refer to entries *without* having to keep track of their position from the beginning, especially in such operations as insertion and deletion.

The alternative to using position to identify list entries is to reference them by a pointer. Accordingly, when p has been declared as an **entry** pointer, the notation

$$@p$$

will be used to denote "the instance of **entry** referenced by the **entry-pointer** variable p." It is also necessary to be able to specify a selection operation which refers to the *info* field of entry. Using previously defined notation this could be written as $\sigma(@p, \textit{info})$ or $\textit{info}(@p)$; the latter more concise form will be used.

Related to the use of pointers to reference entries, is the possibility of deriving an address (i.e., a pointer from an identifier). Recall that $\hat{x}$ stands for "the address of x." The ability to carry out an assignment operation such as

$$p \Leftarrow \hat{x}$$

will mean that there is some system-supplied or hardware function that is capable of finding the address of an identifier and using it for assignment and possibly other operations. The address of an identifier is of course available from the symbol table, and some programming languages, notably PL/I with its ADDR operation, do provide the capability of working with addresses. Note, however, that it becomes impossible to restrict the domain of the operator or the kinds of arithmetic carried out on addresses. Thus, while such unrestricted use of addresses and pointers is permitted in assembly languages, it is regarded as controversial for high-level languages, because it can lead to complicated data structures whose correctness is difficult to verify. These caveats notwithstanding, for descriptive purposes it is useful to be able to discuss the effect of an address assignment such as

$$p \Leftarrow \widehat{listhead}$$

and we shall occasionally use the notation.

4.3.1 Insertions and Deletions

With entries referenced by pointers, insertions and deletions in linked lists are carried out by changing pointers. For example in Fig. 4.9(a), to delete the entry which follows that referenced by the pointer variable *pvar*, the instruction sequence

$$temp \Leftarrow link\ (@pvar)$$

$$link\ (@pvar) \Leftarrow link\ (@temp)$$

is performed. Here *temp* is a temporary pointer and the effect is to change the link of the entry referenced by *pvar* from *j* to *k*. The deletion can be effected without *temp*, but the sequence is not as clear. To insert an entry referenced by the variable *qvar* into the linked list so as to *follow* the entry referenced by *pvar*, the instructions are [Fig. 4.9(b)]

$$link(@qvar) \Leftarrow link\ (@pvar)$$

$$link(@pvar) \Leftarrow qvar.$$

It is the ease of insertion and deletion which makes linked lists so useful, but when insertions can be made anywhere, the storage mapping is not sequential, even for simple lists. As a consequence, to search a linked list for a particular item (e.g., for a specified key), one has to be prepared to examine every member in it, and the expected number of comparisons for *sequential lists* is $(N + 1)/2$ (see Section 4.6.1).

It is usual to terminate linked lists by assigning a special null pointer, Λ, to the final entry, but another possibility is to end the list with a special key whose value is larger than any key that can arise. Alternatively, it is sometimes desirable to maintain a *count* field in the header, indicating the number of entries in the list. The expected search time for missing entries can be shortened by keeping the list ordered according to key value, but this gain is at the expense of insertion. If the list is not maintained in order, insertions might as well be made at the beginning of the list. Thus ordering according to key value is worthwhile only when the frequency of searches is appreciably greater than the number of insertions or deletions.

It is obvious that the efficiency of searching a linked list will be increased if the list is maintained so that the most frequently used items are near the beginning (i.e.,

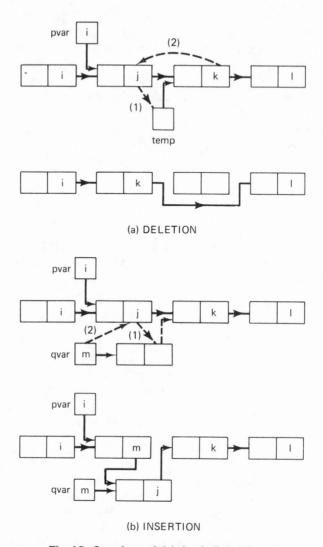

(a) DELETION

(b) INSERTION

Fig. 4.9 Insertion and deletion in linked lists

ordered according to key frequency). Even when it is not known a priori which items are used most frequently, much of the advantage of this ordering can be obtained by maintaining the list in a *self-organizing* fashion. In this organization whenever an entry is referenced, it is moved to the head of the list.[6] For linked lists, moving an entry is particularly easy. Frequently used items will always be near the beginning, and the

[6]The strategy, although obvious, is not the best one for a self-organizing list. It is better to promote the referenced entry only one place by transposing it with its predecessor. See R. Rivest, "On Self-Organizing Sequential Search Heuristics," *Communications of the ACM,* **19**, no. 12 (Feb. 1976), 63–67.

general effect is clearly similar to that in which the entries are sequenced according to frequency of reference.

Besides the link that points to the successor, the storage mapping for a list may contain other links or other information to facilitate important, commonly occurring operations. There are applications where it is necessary to enter the list at an arbitrary item, not just at the header, and then to be able to refer back to the header. This can be done by replacing the null pointer at the end of the list with a pointer back to the header, making the list into a ring. If it is important to find the header quickly, it may be desirable to include a link to the header in *every* entry, rather than having to search a circular list sequentially until the last item, pointing to the header, is encountered.

In lists that can be entered in arbitrary places (as in Fig. 4.9), one cannot delete a referenced item because there is no way of finding the predecessor to change its link. Even if access is restricted to the header, it is useful to know predecessor links. Consider a program in which list entries are being scanned sequentially for possible deletion. When the item to be deleted is encountered, the link of its predecessor must be available. Thus it is necessary to keep in the working space *two* items, the one currently under examination and its predecessor. If deletion is a very frequent occurrence, so that it must be done efficiently, it may be worth storing the link to the predecessor in *every* item. Such a list, with forward and back pointers (successor and predecessor links) is called a *two-way chain list*. A two-way chain can be searched efficiently either forward or backward, and insertions and deletions can be made preceding a named entry.

Different combinations of extra link fields are possible. For example, one might choose a representation with two links per entry; one of these always points to the successor; the other points to the header and to the predecessor for alternate items. In this way only one extra link is needed for fast location of either the header or the predecessor. The cost of such a storage mapping is a somewhat more complicated program for insertion and deletion, since the use being made of the pointer has to be examined. Figure 4.10(a) to (c) illustrates the storage mappings just mentioned. All of these are for simple lists; although there are more than one link fields to an entry, each entry has at most one predecessor and one successor. Instruction sequences for insertion and deletion, similar to those for the one-way chain, are straightforward.

4.3.2 Constructing Linked Lists

Consider now the problem of constructing a linked list, given a set of data values. This is the same as the problem of inserting a sequence of entries into a list, and what is clearly needed is a source of "empty" entries each capable of storing a value. This need is met, in programming languages with list processors, by providing an operation of the form

CREATE (**entry**, *arrow*),

where *arrow* is a variable of type *entry-ptr*. The effect of CREATE is to allocate an entry, which may be referenced as

@arrow,

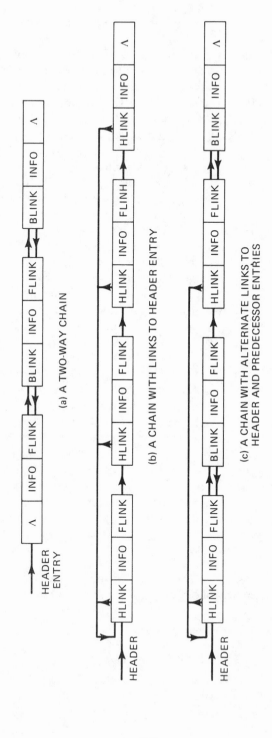

(a) A TWO-WAY CHAIN

(b) A CHAIN WITH LINKS TO HEADER ENTRY

(c) A CHAIN WITH ALTERNATE LINKS TO
HEADER AND PREDECESSOR ENTRIES

Fig. 4.10 Simple lists with extra links

and to assign the address of that entry to *arrow*. As usual, the *link* field may be referenced by *link(@arrow)*.

The use of the CREATE operation is illustrated in Algorithm 4.2 for constructing a linked list. In this example, integer data items are read and assembled into a list; *listhead* is the address of a header entry, the *info* field of which contains the number of data items in the resulting list.

Algorithm 4.2 Constructing a linked list

```
integer i ; entry-ptr listhead , current, next ;
comp entry = ⟨integer info, entry-ptr link⟩ ;
CREATE (entry, listhead) ;
info (@listhead) ⟸ 0 ; /*initialize count*/
current ⟸ listhead ;
do while end-of-file = false ;
    read(i) ;
    CREATE (entry, next) ;
    info (@next) ⟸ i ; /*enter datum*/
    link (@next) ⟸ Λ ;
    info (@listhead) ⟸ info (listhead) + 1 ; /*increase count*/
    link (@current) ⟸ next ; /*link last item to this one*/
    current ⟸ next ;
end
```

4.4 List Processing in Programming Languages[7]

The need for list-processing facilities in programming languages was first recognized in artificial intelligence applications. There, heuristic searching of trees representing problem goals and subgoals required data structures that were easy to modify and could vary greatly in size. Special languages to manipulate linked lists, notably IPL-V[8] and LISP, were developed early. LISP has survived as a working language because of its theoretical importance and powerful generality, but IPL-V was replaced, first by packages added on to more widely used languages (e.g., SLIP[9] onto FORTRAN), and eventually by list-processing features built into languages such as PL/I, SNOBOL, PASCAL, and ALGOL 68.

From the previous sections of this chapter, it is reasonably clear what features a programming language should have to facilitate the construction and manipulation of linked lists. Needed are:

[7]According to the usage of this chapter the term list processing includes manipulation of any type of list—whether the storage mapping is contiguous, hash-based, or linked. In certain contexts it has come to mean the processing of *linked* lists, and it will be used in this way for this section.

[8]A. Newell and others, eds., *Information Processing Language-V Manual*, 2nd ed. (Englewood Cliffs, N.J.: Prentice-Hall, Inc., 1965).

[9]J. Weizenbaum, "Symmetric List Processors," *Communications of the ACM*, 6, no. 9 (Sept. 1963), 524–544.

1. A method of defining a list entry, built up as a composite from primitive data types.
2. A method of declaring pointers (preferably typed), of assigning values to pointers, and of referring to entries through pointers.
3. A method of creating list entries by allocating storage for them, with pointer assignments as needed.
4. A method of deallocating storage for entries and lists.

Feature 4, although perhaps not as obvious as the others, is particularly important. Lists find their best use in applications when new entries are continually being introduced and old ones discarded. Unless there is an efficient method for garbage collection (i.e., releasing the storage for entries not needed any longer to the available pool from which allocations are made), sooner or later the storage will be exhausted in even modest programs. Thus the garbage collector is an important constituent of a list-processing package.

Widely used systems such as LISP and SNOBOL have efficient garbage collectors built into them, but in some languages (e.g., PL/I and PASCAL) the task is left to the programmer. For the "programming language" used in this book, a suitable deallocation primitive might be FREE ($@p$), the interpretation being "release the storage for the item pointed at by p. (This is essentially the PL/I FREE statement.) A problem with this function is that after its execution, there may be pointers referencing storage no longer available to the program. If this is a possibility, the programmer is faced with the prospect of keeping track of references and checking them each time FREE is invoked. This is not a concern with automatic garbage collection because, in general, an item will not be freed if there are other items which point to it (Chapter 8).

We continue this section by looking at some of the list-processing facilities in PL/I. The discussion is motivated by a simple program, UNION (Algorithm 4.3), which takes two linked lists and constructs the union on the field labeled INFO.

Algorithm 4.3

```
1    UNION: PROC(A,B) RETURNS(POINTER);
2        DECLARE
            1 ITEM BASED(ITEM_PTR),
                            /* FORMAT FOR LIST ENTRY */
                2 INFO BIN FIXED,
                2 NEXT POINTER,
            (A,B,                   /* INPUT LISTS */
            ITEM,CURRENT_A,CURRENT_B,
                            /* WORKING VARIABLES */
            TEMP_PTR,RESULT) POINTER,
            FROM_A BIT(1);
3        CURRENT_A = A;   CURRENT_B = B;
5        IF A ¬= NULL|B ¬= NULL THEN
6        DO;
7            ALLOCATE ITEM;
```

```
8              ITEM.NEXT = NULL;
9              RESULT = ITEM_PTR; /* POINTER TO FIRST ITEM OF
                               RESULT */
10      END;
11      ELSE RESULT = NULL;    /* NO RESULT IF INPUTS ARE
                               EMPTY */
12      DO WHILE (CURRENT_A ¬= NULL|CURRENT_B ¬= NULL);
13        IF CURRENT_A = NULL THEN FROM_A = '0'B;
15        ELSE
          DO; /* LIST A NOT EXHAUSTED */
16            FROM A = '1'B;
17            IF CURRENT_B ¬= NULL THEN
18                IF CURRENT_A → ITEM.INFO >=
                               CURRENT_B → INFO THEN
19                    DO; /*TAKE INFO VALUE FORM LIST A ON
                          EQUALITY */
20                        IF CURRENT_A → INFO = CURRENT_B
                                       → INFO THEN
21                        CURRENT_B = CURRENT_B → NEXT;
22                        ELSE FROM_A = '0'B; /* AND FROM B IF B
                                       VALUE LOWER */
23                    END;
24            END;
25        IF FROM_A THEN
26        DO;                    /* A CONTRIBUTES TO UNION */
27            INFO = CURRENT_A → INFO;
28            CURRENT_A = CURRENT_A → NEXT;
29        END;
30        ELSE                   /* B CONTRIBUTES */
          DO;
31            INFO = CURRENT_B → INFO;
32            CURRENT_B = CURRENT_B → NEXT;
33        END;
34        IF CURRENT_A ¬= NULL|CURRENT_B ¬= NULL THEN
35        DO; /* A,B OR BOTH NOT EMPTY − MERGE
                  CONTINUES */
36            TEMP = ITEM_PTR;
37            ALLOCATE ITEM;
38            NEXT = NULL;
39            TEMP → NEXT = ITEM_PTR; /* LINK LAST
                                       ELEMENT TO
                                       THIS ONE */
40        END;
41      END; /* WHILE EITHER LIST NOT EXHAUSTED */
42      RETURN(RESULT);
43  END UNION;
```

As remarked, one component of a list-processing facility is the mechanism for specifying composite types which can be used as list entries. In PL/I this is done with *structure* variables. Line 2 of UNION contains a declaration for a structure, ITEM, composed of an integer field named INFO and a pointer field called NEXT. Field selection is performed by concatenating identifier names (separated by periods) down to the level desired. Thus the NEXT field is referred to as ITEM.NEXT (UNION, line 8). If there is no ambiguity, the prefix can be dropped; in line 38, NEXT is used instead of ITEM.NEXT because there is no other variable or field identifier with that name in the procedure. The abbreviation could also have been used in line 8.

It is often useful to regard fields of a structure as themselves being structures; this is the purpose of the level numbers that precede the field names. As an example, the INFO field of an item could be further specified as a structure of two subfields, KEY and NAME, by the declaration

DECLARE 1 ITEM,

2 INFO,

3 KEY BIN FIXED,

3 NAME CHAR(20),

2 NEXT POINTER;

In the notation of Chapter 2, composite structures are types that can be defined by *comp* declarations. To build lists, it is necessary to create instances of these types and link them together. In PL/I, a structure to be used in this way is declared as BASED. Associated (in the declaration) with the BASED variable is a pointer which will receive the address when an instance of that variable is created. In line 2 of UNION, ITEM is declared BASED on ITEM_PTR. When an instance of ITEM is created by the ALLOCATE statements in lines 7 and 37, ITEM_PTR is set to the location of the newly created ITEM. ITEM_PTR is not explicitly named in those statements because it is the pointer upon which ITEM is declared to be based; to designate a pointer other than the base as recipient of the address, the form ALLOCATE ITEM SET(P) would have been used.

In the notation for expressing algorithms in this book, every pointer is bound to a particular type; thus *info* (@p) unambiguously selects the field named *info* from the instance of the type pointed at by *p*. In PL/I, pointers are untyped; a pointer may be declared as the base for a particular variable, but it can be set with any address. The instance of a structure ITEM referred to by pointer P is indicated by P → ITEM. Thus in line 18, CURRENT_A → ITEM.INFO means "the INFO field of the instance of ITEM at address CURRENT_A." Recalling that in UNION, the qualification ITEM. is unnecessary, the selection can be accomplished simply by CURRENT_A → INFO. If the qualifying pointer is the one on which the variable is based, it can be taken as implicit and be omitted; in lines 8 and 27, ITEM·NEXT and INFO appear instead of, respectively,

ITEM_PTR → ITEM.NEXT and ITEM_PTR → INFO.

To indicate that a pointer does not currently identify any instance of a variable, it can be given the value NULL. In PL/I, it is wise to initialize pointers to NULL, since otherwise their values cannot be regarded as meaningful when the program is entered. In line 38 of UNION, the NEXT field of the newly created ITEM is set to NULL to indicate the end of the linked list. Also, pointers should always be tested for NULL when there is any doubt about their value, or an error may result.

The operation of UNION is fairly straightforward. The inputs point to lists which, for testing, were constructed by a PL/I version of Algorithm 4.2, and the mechanics of building the union list are essentially those of that program. Note, however, that in line 36, it is necessary to save the address of the current instance of ITEM before a new instance is created, because line 37 redefines ITEM_PTR. Then, the old allocation can be linked to the new one (line 39).

We have outlined the features of PL/I list processing as it applies to data in main memory. Linked structures can be stored on external devices, but first the pointers must be converted to OFFSETS relative to the start of a designated AREA in which all the items have been allocated; otherwise, being absolute addresses, they would probably not refer to the right locations when read back in. For details of this and other aspects of based variables, see the *PL/I Language Reference Manual*.[10]

4.5 Inverted Lists

So far, not much structure has been assumed about the *info* field of a list entry; in most of the diagrams it has been shown as a single field, and sometimes the presence of a key has been noted. Usually, however, it will consist of several, perhaps many, attributes. Thus an *info* field, examined in detail, might take on the structure illustrated in Fig. 4.5(a). In general, the mapping that associates a key with an attribute is many-to-one (i.e., many keys may have a given value of an attribute). If the mapping is bijective (i.e., there is a one-to-one correspondence between the values for the key and those for a particular attribute), that attribute can serve equally well as a key for the entry. For example, the key data needed to distinguish an employee uniquely might be his name and address, and an attribute be a unique employee number. Then the employee number, requiring a shorter, simpler (probably numeric) field, serves to identify the employee and can be used instead as a key.

Very frequently, given a list it is desired to know the set of keys that have a given attribute value (i.e., the inverse corresponding to an attribute). Usually, this inverse will *not* be a function, since there will be more than one key having the given value. To avoid having to search a list when keys corresponding to given attribute value are wanted, it is possible to maintain, along with the original list, the inverted relation. Such a list, whose domain consists of attribute values, and whose range contains keys having a specified attribute value, is known as an *inverted list*. A given list gives rise to a set of inverted lists; in fact, there will be one list for each value of every attribute of interest.

[10]IBM System/360 Operating System, *PL/I(F) Language Reference Manual*, IBM Form GC 28-8201-3.

4.5.1 Examples of Inverted Lists

As an example of an inverted list, suppose that the entries on a personnel list contain fields of descriptive information on employees, including employee number, city of employment, department, and job type. Besides the original list (which may or may not be arranged according to the employee number), it would clearly be useful in certain applications to maintain inverted lists according to the attributes *city*, *dept*, and *job*. Table 4.2 illustrates a main list with inverted lists constructed on each attribute. Note that the complete set of inverted lists requires more storage than the original list because the employee number is repeated on each attribute list. Moreover, the

TABLE 4.2   Inverted lists constructed on a list of employees

Main Personnel List

Employee Number	City	Department	Job
105–26	N.Y.	MARKT.	SALES
136–90	CHI	ACCT.	TYP–1
603–28	CHI	MANF.	MACH.
329–51	N.Y.	D.P.	PROG.
174–85	MTL	ACCT.	ACCT.
604–02	L.A.	MANF.	FORMN.
324–83	CHI	D.P.	PROG.
341–90	N.Y.	MARKT.	SALES
600–77	L.A.	ACCT.	TYP–2
603–29	MTL	MARKT.	SALES

Inverted Lists

City List	Employees
N.Y.	105–26, 329–51, 341–90
CHI	136–90, 603–28, 324–83
MTL	174–85, 603–29
L.A.	604–02, 600–77

Department List	Employees
MARKT.	105–26, 341–90, 603–29
ACCT.	136–90, 174–85, 600–77
MANF.	603–28, 604–02
D.P.	329–83, 324–83

Job List	Employees
SALES	105–26, 341–90, 603–29
TYP–1	136–90
TYP–2	600–77
MACH	603–28
PROG.	329–51, 324–83
ACCT.	174–85
FORMN.	604–02

inverted list does *not* replace the original list. If all the attributes of a given employee are required, it is necessary to go to entries in the original list. When both the original and the inverted lists are kept to simplify searching for attributes, addition or deletion of any item in the original list must be accompanied by changes in corresponding entries of the inverted lists.

For another example of the use of inverted lists, suppose that a list contains entries describing documents (either original articles or summaries in an abstract journal), where each entry contains the following data:

1. A sequentially assigned accession number.
2. Author.
3. Title.
4. Source identification.
5. A set of standardized *descriptors* (also called *key words* or *index terms*) which describe the contents of the entry.
6. The text of the article or abstract (this may be optional).

The basic information retrieval problem in such a system is to retrieve documents whose contents are relevant to queries posed by the user. The queries, as well as documents, can be described in terms of the descriptors, and so the problem becomes one of finding documents with given descriptors. An obvious approach is to maintain an inverted list for each descriptor. Queries may be expressed as the logical combination of descriptors, and so the search procedure becomes one of taking unions and intersections of the sets determined by the descriptors.

There are two observations about inverted lists which may provide some insight into why there are so many applications involving them. The first is that an inverted list can be regarded as defining a subset of the original list items, membership in the subset being determined by the presence of some attribute value (i.e., by satisfying some characteristic function). Thus a list and the inverted lists constructed on it are a system of sets and subsets, a commonly occurring system in mathematics. (See Example 7.1.) The second observation is that inverted lists serve the purpose of effecting a *search-by-attribute value*. If we regard access-by-address (also called *direct access*) and access-by-key, as two forms of accessing data, then access-by-value (or *access-by-content*) is a third. Two examples of lists organized to aid access-by-value in everyday life are the index of a book (where the text corresponds to the main list) and the classified pages in a telephone directory, which lists entries according to the type-of-service attribute. In data processing, access-by-value is of considerable importance, and a great deal of effort has been directed toward being able to do it quickly and economically.

4.5.2 Multilists

In the inverted lists just considered, the lists contained the directory keys for each attribute value. In practice, pointers to the entries are more common because they allow faster access to the original data. To illustrate, suppose that employees are

TABLE 4.3   Personnel list with directory and data storage area

Directory		Data Storage Area			City Pointer Values				
Employee Number	Storage Area Address	Address	Employee Number	City	N.Y.	CHI	MTL	L.A.	Pointer
					viii	vii	x	ix	
105–25	i	i	105–26	N.Y.					Λ
136–90	ii	ii	136–90	CHI					Λ
174–85	v	iii	603–28	CHI					ii
324–83	vii	iv	329–51	N.Y.					i
329–51	iv	v	174–85	MTL					Λ
341–90	viii	vi	604–02	L.A.					Λ
600–77	ix	vii	324–83	CHI					iii
603–28	iii	viii	341–90	N.Y.					iv
603–29	x	ix	600–77	L.A.					vi
604–02	vi	x	603–29	MTL					v

hired according to the sequence shown in the main personnel list of Table 4.2 and, as each employee is engaged, the relevant data are set up in a storage area. For reasons that will be clear shortly, suppose also that the address of the storage areas increases monotonically as they are assigned. The first two columns of Table 4.3 show the directory, sorted by employee number. Instead of listing keys in an inverted list, as was done in Table 4.2, pointers to the storage areas are to be listed. Thus the inverted list on the attribute *city* takes the following form (assuming that last entries are listed first):

City	Pointer to Initial Location	Pointers to Subsequent Locations	
N.Y.	viii	iv	i
CHI	vii	iii	ii
MTL	x	v	
L.A.	ix	vi	

To identify the employees with a given attribute (i.e., find their employee numbers), the first field in the address indicated by the pointer is consulted. As for any inverted list, there is a separate list for each attribute value, in this case four of them. Now each of these four lists may be regarded as a chain in which the *info* value is the same. Since *info* is common, it may be taken out of the data field and stored in a header entry at the beginning of the chain, and all that need be stored in the data field is the chaining address to the next item. Moreover, since *city* is a single-valued function of employee, any employee is on at most one chain and contains at most one chaining address. Thus a single pointer location can be reserved for the addresses in all four chains, along with a separate header block which identifies the attribute value and gives the start of each. Table 4.3 shows the data storage area for the *city* attribute, and Table 4.4 shows the linked list for the three attributes *city*, *dept*, and *job*, along with the necessary header blocks. An organization such as that in Table 4.4, where there is a separate chain for each value of each attribute, along with header blocks to start the chains, is called a *multilist*.

TABLE 4.4   Multilist form of inverted list

Directory		Multilist Pointers					Header Blocks		
Employee Number	Address	Address	Employee Number	City	Department	Job	City Value	Length	Pointer
105–26	i	i	105–26	Λ	Λ	Λ	N.Y.	3	viii
136–90	ii	ii	136–90	Λ	Λ	Λ	CHI	3	vii
174–85	v	iii	603–28	ii	Λ	Λ	MTL	2	x
324–83	vii	iv	329–51	i	Λ	Λ	L.A.	2	ix
329–51	iv	v	174–85	Λ	ii	Λ			
341–90	viii	vi	604–02	Λ	iii	Λ	Department Value	Length	Pointer
600–77	ix	vii	324–83	iii	iv	iv			
603–28	iii	viii	341–90	iv	i	i			
603–29	x	ix	600–77	vi	v	Λ	ACCT	3	x
604–02	xi	x	603–29	v	viii	viii	MARKT	3	ix
							MANF	2	vi
							D.P.	2	vii
							Job Value	Length	Pointer
							SALES	3	x
							TYP–1	1	ii
							TYP–2	1	ix
							MACH	1	iii
							PROG.	2	vii
							ACC'T	1	v
							FORMN	1	vi

The multilist, unlike the inverted list, can replace the original personnel list. However, it is necessary to introduce modifications when one wants to find *all* the data for a given employee—his or her city, department, and job. To do so for the employee with personnel number 341–90, for example, the directory can be entered and the reference to data storage viii followed. There, the pointer in the first field can be recognized as a city pointer, but *which* city is not known. If the pointer value is followed to the end of the chain, and the final value contains, instead of Λ a reference to the header, the city *can* be identified. Similarly, the other pointer lists must be made circular, with final values referencing the headers. The disadvantage of this technique is that it is very slow to follow the chains, and to print a list of all the attributes for each employee would be prohibitively expensive. It is possible to use additional linking, for example storing occasional pointers to the headers along the chain, but the structure then becomes more complex, and it may be simpler to store the main personnel list along with the multilist.

Compared with inverted lists using pointer references, the main difference in multilists is that the pointers are stored with the data rather than being collected in separate lists for each attribute value. Multilists were first proposed by Prywes and Gray,[11] and the relative merits of inverted lists and multilists are discussed by Inglis.[12] The general conclusion is that multilists are more efficient for updating operations in which the value of a field is being changed, but less efficient for searching and retrieval. This is what one would expect in the light of the fact that multilists are linked lists, where insertions and deletions are efficient, and searches are expensive. Additional points are that there are difficulties with multilists (but not with inverted lists) if attributes are not single-valued, and that searches for the absence of an attribute are easier to carry out with multilists than with inverted lists.

4.6 Searching a Simple List

In this section the principal methods of searching a simple list are considered. These are sequential scan, binary search, and key-to-address calculation. Locating an entry through indexing, which may be regarded as a method of avoiding search, is discussed in Chapter 5. To make the problem concrete, the list can be regarded as a directory.

4.6.1 Sequential Scan

Although the main point about sequential search of a simple list of N items is that the search time is $O(N)$ for a random distribution of entries, there are some techniques that can help to shorten or simplify the search. For example, it is not necessary to know the number of entries in order to test when the end-of-list has been reached during the search. Instead, the list can be terminated with a key, say Ω, which is greater than any possible search argument, and the end-of-list recognized when Ω is encountered. In this way even if the list is dynamic, it is not necessary to keep a record of its length (although this may be desirable for other reasons).

Ordering the list offers no advantage in a sequential search if the requests for entries are distributed uniformly and a search is being made for an entry known to be present. However, if searches can be made for entries not in the list, there *is* an advantage to maintaining the list in increasing (or decreasing) value of key. Once a key larger than that being sought is encountered, the search can be terminated, and for random keys this will save looking at about half the list, so that the gain is $qN/2$, where q is the probability of the entry being absent.

[11]N. S. Prywes and H. J. Gray, "The Multi-List System for Real-Time Information Storage Retrieval," in *Proceedings of IFIP Congress 1962* (Amsterdam: North-Holland Publishing Company, 1962), pp. 112–116.

[12]J. Inglis, "Inverted Indexes and Multi-List Structures," *The Computer Journal*, 17, no. 1 (Feb. 1974), 59–63.

To see this, suppose that a list has N distinct keys, each with equal probability of occurrence, and that we are searching for an entry that has an a priori probability p of being present, and $q = 1 - p$ of not being present. The expected number of comparisons, $E(N)$, is $p \cdot E_p(N) + q \cdot E_a(N)$, where $E_p(N)$ is the expected number when the entry is known to be present, and $E_a(N)$ is the expected number when the entry is absent. There are two cases:

1. The list is not ordered.

$$E_p(N) = \sum_{i=1}^{N} i \cdot p(i) \qquad \text{where } p(i) \text{ is the probability that a match}$$
$$\text{is found with the } i\text{th key.}$$

From the assumptions $p(i) = 1/N$,

$$E_p(N) = \frac{1}{N} \sum_{i=1}^{N} i = \frac{N+1}{2}.$$

When the entry is absent, the expected number of comparisons $E_a(N) = N + 1$, since the whole list must be searched until the key is encountered. Therefore, the expected number of comparisons for an unordered list

$$E(N) = \frac{p(N+1)}{2} + q(N+1) = (N+1)\left(1 - \frac{p}{2}\right).$$

2. The list is ordered.

When the entry is present, $E_p(N) = (N+1)/2$, as before.

When the entry is absent, $E_a(N) = \sum_{i=1}^{N} (i+1) \cdot p(i)$, since $(i+1)$ comparisons are needed to exceed the key, and $p(i) = 1/N$, as before.

$$E_a(N) = \frac{1}{N} \sum_{i=1}^{N} i + 1 = \frac{N+3}{2}.$$

$E(N)$, the expected number of comparisons for an ordered list $= p(N+1)/2 + q(N+3)/2$, and the expected savings due to ordering the list $= q(N+1) - q(N+3)/2 \approx qN/2$.

As has already been mentioned, if the expected frequencies of encountering entries vary, the entries should be sequenced in decreasing frequency. In this way the search is terminated early for the commonly occurring items. In many applications, a few particular keys are retrieved very frequently. A commonly observed rule of behavior is that 20 percent of the entries generate 80 percent of the requests for retrieval. Bringing these active entries to the beginning of the list can greatly shorten the expected search time for a serial scan.

4.6.2 Binary Search

If the list entries are stored contiguously, are fixed in size, and are in sequence according to value of the key, the classical method of binary search achieves a search time that is $O(\log N)$. The search is initiated by comparing the key being sought with the entry in the middle of the list, or that preceding the middle, if N is even. This divides the original list into two sublists, and the result of the comparison determines whether the key has been found, or in which of the upper or lower sublists the search is to be continued. If the search has not terminated, the selected sublist is taken as a new list to be searched, and recursive continuation of the process will eventually either yield the desired key or reveal that it is missing. Algorithm 4.4 describes the search.[13]

Algorithm 4.4 Binary search

```
procedure binary_search (name, f, l, place);
integer f, l, i, place ; string name, temp;
if f > l then place ⇐ −1; /*missing*/
else
do
    i ⇐ ⌊(f+l)/2⌋; /*bisect current table*/
    temp ⇐ key(table[i]); /*get key at bisection*/
    if temp = name then place ⇐ i; /*found*/
    else if temp > name then call   binary_search (name, f, i−1, place);
    else call binary_search (name, i+1, l, place); /*search lower half*/
end
end binary_search;
```

The list to be searched is a directory for which the keys are strings having some maximum length. The result sought is the index or position in the directory of the entry with the given key value *name*. On procedure call, besides the value *name*, the indices f and l of the first and last directory entries are given. This directory is in the form of an array, called *table*, and prior to using the procedure (i.e., global to it) it is assumed that there have been declarations which define the form of a table entry and the table. These take the form

comp entry $= \langle$**string** *key*, **attribute-ptr** *address*$\rangle$

entry array *table*$[1 : l-f+1]$.

On procedure exit, *place* is set to either the desired index, or the value -1, to show that there is no entry with key value *name*.

For a list whose number of entries is of the form $N = 2^p - 1$, where p is an integer, binary_search will identify a key that is in the table by making at most p comparisons. If $2^p - 1 < N \leq 2^{p+1} - 1$, at most $p + 1$ comparisons are needed. It follows that the number of comparisons is bounded by $\lceil \log (N + 1) \rceil$ and the search time is $O(\log N)$. Because this is significantly better than the $O(N)$ of a sequential

[13]Algorithm 4.4 is written using recursive calls, because this is so natural for the process. For an efficient program this should be rewritten using iteration. For a discussion of the desirability of avoiding *goto*'s in this iteration, see D. Knuth, "Structure Programming with *goto* Statements," *ACM Computing Surveys*, **6**, no. 4 (Dec. 1974), 261–301.

scan, the binary search is a commonly accepted way of searching long lists. However, it is important to note some qualifications about its use:

1. Table entries must be stored contiguously and be of uniform size.
2. For small N (e.g., $N < 10$) the overhead involved in calling and initiating the binary-search routine will probably make sequential search better.
3. Binary search requires that the list be maintained in sorted order. As will be seen in Section 4.7, many sorting programs are $O(N^2)$ or $O(N \log N)$, so sorting is more costly than (a single) search. This may not be important if the list can be sorted once and for all.
4. On insertion, the new entry must be placed in its correctly sequenced position. Since entries are stored contiguously, this will involve moving entries. Similarly, deletion will eventually require removal of entries (although this may be deferred). Thus binary search is good for searching, but relatively expensive for insertion and deletion.
5. Methods described next are significantly faster than binary search for very large N.

4.6.3 Interpolation Search

Binary search makes no use of any information that might be known about the list (or table) being searched. Sometimes, a great deal is known, including the precise nature of the distribution of key values over the keyspace domain, but this is rare. What is *not* unusual, however, is to know the extreme values of the keys, say *Kmin* and *Kmax*, and it is natural to ask how this information might be useful in speeding up the search.

Because of the lexicographic order induced by the collating sequence, all keys have numeric equivalents, even those based on alphanumeric characters. Given a list of keys, ordered monotonically, a simple assumption that might be made about the position of a given key, K, is that the distance of K from the origin is proportional to the fraction of the total key range covered by K. More precisely, if *min* and *max* are the addresses in which *Kmin* and *Kmax* are stored, and $\hat{K}$ is the address of K,

$$\frac{\hat{K}-min}{max-min} = \frac{K-Kmin}{Kmax-Kmin}.$$

To convert $\hat{K}$ to an (integer) address, this is rewritten as[14]

$$\hat{K} = min + \left\lceil \frac{max-min-1}{Kmax-Kmin} \cdot (K-Kmin) \right\rceil. \tag{4.1}$$

In effect, we are performing a linear interpolation, based on the key value to estimate the address of K. If the key which is actually present in the address so determined is not that being sought, the interpolation search continues in exactly the same way as

---

[14]Interpolation search has been known for a long time, but it has had limited use because there can be convergence difficulties for arguments near the boundaries. The -1 is introduced in ($max-min-1$) to overcome these difficulties. See G. H. Gonnet, *Interpolation and Interpolation Hash Searching*, Report CS 77-02, 1977; Department of Computer Science, University of Waterloo, Waterloo, Ontario, Canada.

did the binary search. Let the value produced by the right-hand side of Eq. (4.1) be called $E_1(K)$, the first estimate for the address of the unknown key, K. If the key at this estimated address is too large, then *max* and *Kmax* are replaced by $E_1(K)$ and the key at $E_1(K)$, respectively, and Eq. (4.1) is used again to obtain a new estimate, $E_2(K)$. If the key at the estimated address is too small, then *min* and *Kmin* are replaced by $E_1(K)$ and the key at $E_1(K)$, and these are used in Eq. (4.1) to obtain $E_2(K)$. The search is continued until K is found, or if the entry is missing, until the table has been contracted to the two entries min and max, neither of them containing K.

Interpolation search is illustrated in Table 4.5 using an example which will be useful for the section on hashing that follows. The keys are the first three letters of the months of the year, interpreted as numbers expressed in radix 26, and converted into base 10 integers (col. 2). *Kmin* = Apr = 407, *Kmax* = Sep = 12287. Taking $0 = \text{A}\hat{\text{p}}\text{r}$, and $11 = \hat{\text{S}}\text{ep}$, Eq. (4.1) becomes

$$\hat{K} = \left\lceil \frac{10(K-407)}{11880} \right\rceil.$$

The program for searching is given in Algorithm 4.5. The list of keys is an array *table*, which has been constructed in a procedure global to this one, where *Kmin* and *Kmax*, the minimum and maximum key values, and *min* and *max*, the corresponding storage address bounds, were declared. As shown, these quantities will be altered during the program; to avoid producing global side effects, they should be replaced by working variables, *lowkey hikey*, *low* and *hi*, at the beginning. The appropriate specifications are

comp entry = ⟨**int** *key*, **attribute-ptr** *address*⟩

entry array *table* [*min*: *max*].

TABLE 4.5   Interpolation search

		Address Using Algorithm [Eq. (4.1)]			Search Table, Ordered by Key Value		
Month	Base 10 Value	First Iteration	Second Iteration	Third Iteration	Address	Month	Key
Jan	6097	5			0	Apr	407
Feb	3485	3	4		1	Aug	526
Mar	8129	7			2	Dec	2134
Apr	407	0			3	Feb	3485
May	8136	7	8		4	Jan	6097
Jun	6617	6			5	Jul	6615
Jul	6615	3	6		6	Jun	6617
Aug	526	1			7	Mar	8129
Sep	12287	11			8	May	8136
Oct	9535	8	9	10	9	Nov	9173
Nov	9173	8	9		10	Oct	9535
Dec	2134	2			11	Sep	12287

Algorithm 4.5   Interpolation search

> **procedure** interpolation_search (*table, arg, place*);
> **int** *arg, place, Kmax, Kmin, max, min*;
> **entry array** *table* [*min : max*];
> *place* $\Leftarrow max$; /*initialize search address*/
> **do while** *key*(*table* [*place*])$\neq arg \wedge (max-1) > min$;
>
> $$place \Leftarrow min + \left\lceil \frac{(max-min-1)}{Kmax-Kmin}(arg-Kmin) \right\rceil;$$ /*estimate location
> of search key*/
>
> **if** *key* (*table*[*place*]) $< arg$ **then do**;
>   *min* $\Leftarrow key$ (*table*[*place*]);
>   *Kmin* $\Leftarrow key$(*table*[*min*]); **end** /*replace lower boundary*/
> **else if** *key* (*table*[*place*]) $> arg$ **then do**;
>   *max* $\Leftarrow key$ (*table*[*place*]);
>   *Kmax* $\Leftarrow key$ (*table*[*max*]); **end** /*replace upper boundary*/
> **end**
> **if** *key* (*table*[*place*]) $\neq arg$ **then**
>   *place* $\Leftarrow {}^{-}1$; /*missing entry*/
> **end** interpolation search

The search key, K, is called *arg* in Algorithm 4.5. On exit, an address *place* contains the location of *arg* if *arg* is present in the table, or $^{-}1$ of it if it is not. Initially, *place* is set to *max*, so the algorithm will work correctly in the special case that it is entered with *arg=Kmax*.

It will be noted in Table 4.5 that the address of seven of the twelve months are calculated correctly on the first iteration, four of the months require two iterations to find the address, and one requires three. Thus the average search length is $(7 \times 1 + 4 \times 2 + 1 \times 3)/12 = 1.5$. Because use is being made of the information at the extreme ends of the search table, one would expect that linear interpolation, based on using Eq. (4.1), will be faster than binary search for uniformly distributed keys. It turns out that the expression for the expected number of comparisons in a list with N entries is $\log \log N + O(1)$, so that under the given conditions, interpolation search *is* faster than binary search.[15] If the key distribution is not uniform, but known, interpolation search can still be done by estimating the address from the cumulative distribution function, but the procedure can become appreciably more complicated. Moreover, because the keys must be ordered monotonically for interpolation search (as for binary search), insertion (and hence constructing the list) is a relatively expensive operation. The hashing methods that are described next do not have these disadvantages, and with good choice of the parameters that appear in those methods, they are even faster than interpolation search.

[15]See G. A. Gonnet (footnote 14) and also A. C. Yao and F. F. Yao, "The Complexity of Searching an Ordered Random Table," *Proceedings of the Conference on the Foundation of Computer Science*, Houston (Oct. 1976), pp. 173–176.

4.6.4 Key-to-Address Calculation

Constructing a list can be regarded as repeated searching for absent entries and inserting them into the list. Alternatively, constructing the list can be viewed as a mapping from the keyspace into the address space of the list entries. Interpolation is just one method for accomplishing this mapping by a key-to-address calculation. The mapping must be single-valued (i.e., each key must ultimately be mapped into a unique address), but as happens with interpolation, it cannot be expected that the *first* estimate of an address produced by the mapping function will necessarily be unique. Distinct keys that are (initially) mapped into the same address are known as *synonyms* or *collisions*. It is clearly desirable, both for searching and constructing a list, to have a mapping function that keeps the number of collisions small. But very often programmers choose similar names for a group of logically related identifiers (e.g., $x1, x2, x3$). Unless precautions are taken, addresses calculated for such nearly identical keys are likely to be the same, and hence give rise to a large number of synonyms. We are thus led to look for methods of key-to-address calculation, other than linear interpolation, methods which, if possible, will keep the number of collisions low. The general approach is to apply a transformation to the keys, scrambling them in some way to produce nearly random numbers interpreted as addresses, which results in their being scattered throughout the search table. Such table construction and searching methods are known as *scatter storage* or *hashing* techniques.

Before hashing is considered in detail, one general observation can be made about the key-to-address calculation performed for constructing the search table. To keep the number of collisions low, it is desirable that the N keys be mapped into more than N address locations in the search table. A simple argument shows the reason for this. Suppose that exactly N locations are provided for the N keys, and consider the situation when the last key is being entered. There is precisely one vacancy somewhere in the table for it. Any address calculation function will have to be used iteratively, and in the situation just described, one must expect a large number of collisions until the vacancy is located. In general, more and more collisions are likely to be encountered as the search table becomes progressively fuller. The ratio number-of-keys/table size is known as the *load factor*, α, and this parameter plays an important role in hashing. Recall that for binary and interpolation search, the table size was just equal to the number of entries (no vacancies being allowed), so that one of the ways we seek to improve the search time is by making $\alpha < 1$, thereby reducing the frequency of collisions in the address calculation.

4.6.5 Hashing

The general approach to hashing is to divide the problem of key-to-address mapping into two almost separate subproblems.

1. Find a hashing function, $h(x)$, whose range of values for the actual key domain approximates a uniform distribution over some interval, say 0 to $M-1$.
2. Find a scheme for resolving collisions (i.e., assigning distinct addresses) to keys that hash into the same number.

Because hashing is so heavily used for identifier directories in language processors, as well as in searching of lists and files, it has been the subject of intense investigation. Some of the basic results appeared in Dumey,[16] Peterson,[17] and Buchholz[18]; important surveys are given by Morris, and by Maurer and Lewis,[19] and there is a comprehensive treatment in Knuth.[20] In this section we examine a few principal techniques for subproblems 1 and 2 above, indicating how the performance differs, and how it depends on parameters of the technique such as the load factor.

Finding a Hash Function: Besides mapping the N keys uniformly into the address range 0 to $M-1$, the hash function, $h(K)$, should be easy to compute. Extensive tests have been carried out on functions in which a very short sequence of computer instructions scrambles the digits to produce a number to be interpreted directly as an address. Among the sequences that have been tried are those which:

- Extract digits in selected positions, and combine them using logical or arithmetic operations.
- Square the key and extract digits from selected positions (the midsquare method).
- Convert the key to a number in a new radix and then select digits.
- Multiply or divide the key by suitably chosen factors.

For most of the methods there are circumstances that can generate runs of synonyms. Methods based on multiplications or division, where the factors are carefully chosen, seem to have the most consistently good performance.[21]

The division method is particularly easy to use, for taking

$$h(K) = K \bmod M$$

allows the result to be interpreted directly as a number in the address range 0 to $M-1$. There are certain choices for M which are obviously poor. For example, M even always maps even keys into even-numbered addresses and odd keys into odd-numbered addresses; M equal to a power of r, the radix of the number system, will make h a selection operation in which certain digits of the key are merely dropped. Making M a prime not simply related to r usually produces a good hashing function.[22]

[16]A. I. Dumey, "Indexing for Rapid Random-Access Memory Systems," *Computers and Automation*, **5**, no. 12 (Dec. 1956), 6–9.

[17]W. W. Peterson, "Addressing for Random-Access Storage," *IBM Journal of Research and Development*, **1**, no. 2 (Apr. 1957), 130–146.

[18]W. Buchholz, "File Organization and Addressing," *IBM Systems Journal*, **2** (June 1963), 86–111.

[19]R. Morris, "Scatter Storage Techniques," *Communications of the ACM*, **11**, no. 1 (Jan. 1968), 38–43, and W. D. Maurer and T. G. Lewis, "Hash Table Methods," *ACM Computing Surveys*, **7**, no. 1 (Mar. 1975), 5–19.

[20]D. Knuth, *The Art of Computer Programming, Vol. 3, Sorting and Searching* (Reading, Mass.: Addison-Wesley Publishing Company, Inc., 1973).

[21]V. Y. Lum, P. S. T. Yen, and M. Dodd, "Key-to-Address Transform Techniques, A Fundamental Performance Study on Large Existing Formatted Files," *Communications of the ACM*, **14**, no. 4 (Apr. 1971), 228–239.

[22]What must be avoided is having the radix raised to some small power equal to an integer [i.e., $r^c \neq i$ (modulo M) where c an i are integers].

Multiplicative methods are similar to the midsquare method in that k is multiplied by a constant C, and selected digits of the product are interpreted directly as the address. C can be chosen so that h exhibits desired properties (e.g., it maps arithmetic sequences of keys such as K, $K + d$, $K + 2d, \ldots$ into distinct addresses).

Column 3 in Table 4.6 shows the hashing address calculated for the list of months, using

$$h(K) = K \bmod 19$$

There are three sets of synonyms *Feb* and *Apr*, *Mar* and *Oct*, *Aug* and *Sep*, so that even in this example the hashing function produces fewer collisions than did the linear mapping.

TABLE 4.6   Organizing a list by hashing

Key k					Separate Chained Lists		Combined Chained Lists	
String	Base 10 Value	k Mod 19	Table Row Number	Open Address-ing Key	Key	Chaining Address	Key	Chaining Address
Jan	6097	17	0	ꞵꞵꞵ	ꞵꞵꞵ	Λ	Oct	Λ
Feb	3485	8	1	ꞵꞵꞵ	ꞵꞵꞵ	Λ	ꞵꞵꞵ	Λ
Mar	8129	16	2	ꞵꞵꞵ	ꞵꞵꞵ	Λ	ꞵꞵꞵ	Λ
Apr	407	8	3	Jul	Jul	Λ	Jul	Λ
May	8136	4	4	May	May	Λ	May	Λ
Jun	6617	5	5	Jun	Jun	Λ	Jun	Λ
Jul	6615	3	6	Dec	Dec	Λ	Dec	Λ
Aug	526	13	7	ꞵꞵꞵ	ꞵꞵꞵ	Λ	ꞵꞵꞵ	Λ
Sep	12287	13	8	Feb	Feb	80	Feb	9
Oct	9535	16	9	Apr	ꞵꞵꞵ	Λ	Apr	Λ
Nov	9173	15	10	ꞵꞵꞵ	ꞵꞵꞵ	Λ	ꞵꞵꞵ	Λ
Dec	2134	6	11	ꞵꞵꞵ	ꞵꞵꞵ	Λ	ꞵꞵꞵ	Λ
			12	ꞵꞵꞵ	ꞵꞵꞵ	Λ	ꞵꞵꞵ	Λ
			13	Aug	Aug	130	Aug	14
			14	Sep	ꞵꞵꞵ	Λ	Sep	Λ
			15	Nov	Nov	Λ	Nov	Λ
			16	Mar	Mar	160	Mar	18
			17	Jan	Jan	Λ	Jan	Λ
			18	Oct	ꞵꞵꞵ	Λ	Oct	Λ
			80		Apr	Λ		
			130		Sep	Λ		
			160		Oct	Λ		

Resolving Collisions: Linear probing—going to the next list entry in storage to find the address of a key that hashes into a position already occupied—is representative of a general class of methods, in which the table is searched systematically for an available position in which to place a synonym. Such methods are called *open address-ing*. There are also other techniques. One simple method, called *chaining*, is to keep synonyms in a linked list. If the N keys are mapped with reasonable uniformity into

M entries of a primary list, and each entry points to a secondary sublist, then searching the key list of length N is replaced, on the average, by search of a sublist of length N/M. Even if $M < N$, which is permissible, the sublists are short compared to N, on the average, so the search for synonyms is efficient. In addition, there are techniques for combining the sublists to simplify storage management. If the sublists are kept in a distinct storage area so that access to them is relatively expensive, it is worth setting up a mechanism whereby several synonyms are examined in the primary list before fetching the sublist where the other synonyms are to be found. This is done by dividing the primary list into *buckets*, each of which contains b synonyms. The bucket technique is particularly appropriate for files when the entries must be kept in auxiliary storage. Consideration of hashing with buckets is deferred to Chapter 9.

Before discussing the open addressing and chaining method of resolving collisions, it is helpful to consider the case of *uniform hashing*, based on the assumption that the hashing function distributes the keys randomly into the M locations of the hash table. To have such a hash table, whenever a collision is encountered, a truly random method would be needed to determine where the next probe should be made, which in effect means a different hashing function for each successive probe. (It is permissible, however, to use one of the accepted generators for pseudo-random numbers.) Suppose that N keys have been entered, by uniform hashing, into a table with M locations. Let $E_p(N)$ be the expected number of probes to find an entry present in the table, and $E_a(N)$ be the expected number of probes to determine that an entry is missing. Note that $E_a(N)$ will be the number of probes required to place an $(N+1)$st entry into the table. We have

$$E_a(N) = \sum_{i=1}^{N+1} i \cdot p_i$$

where p_i = probability that *exactly* i probes are required to show that the entry is missing

= probability that probes $1 \ldots (i-1)$ fail to find a vacancy (i.e., reveal collision) and probe i succeeds

$$= \frac{N}{M} \cdot \frac{N-1}{M-1} \cdots \frac{N-i+2}{M-i+2} \cdot \left(1 - \frac{N-i+1}{M-i+1}\right) \qquad 1 < i \leq N+1.$$

Therefore,

$$E_a(N) = 1 \cdot \left(1 - \frac{N}{M}\right) + 2 \cdot \frac{N}{M}\left(1 - \frac{N-1}{M-1}\right) + \cdots$$

$$+ N \cdot \frac{N}{M} \cdot \frac{N-1}{M-1} \cdots \frac{2}{M-N+1}\left(1 - \frac{1}{M-N+1}\right)$$

$$+ (N+1) \cdot \frac{N}{M} \cdot \frac{N-1}{M-1} \cdots \frac{1}{M-N+1} \cdot 1$$

$$= 1 + \frac{N}{M} + \frac{N}{M} \cdot \frac{N-1}{M-1} + \cdots + \frac{N \cdot (N-1) \cdots 1}{M \cdot (M-1)(M-N+1)}.$$

By induction on N, this sums to $1/(1 - N/M + 1)$. [Note that $E_a(N) = 1$ if $N = 0$, and $E_a(N) = M + \frac{1}{2}$ if $N = M - 1$, as should be the case.] But

$$\frac{N}{M + 1} \approx \frac{N}{M} = \alpha \text{ (the load factor)}. \tag{4.2}$$

Therefore,

$$E_a(N) = \frac{1}{1 - \alpha}.$$

To find $E_p(N)$, note that the number of probes required to find a key is just equal to the number that were needed to insert it. The average number for inserting N keys = (number for insertion when table is empty + number for insertion when table has one entry + $\cdots$ + number for insertion when table has $N - 1$ entries). Therefore,

$$E_p(N) = \frac{1}{N} \sum_{i=0}^{N-1} E_a(i) \approx \frac{M}{N} \int_0^\alpha \frac{dx}{1 - x}$$

$$\approx -\frac{1}{\alpha} \log (1 - \alpha). \tag{4.3}$$

Although there should really be different hash functions on every probe for Eqs. (4.2) and (4.3) to hold, the situation is approximated reasonably well if one hash function, $h1(K)$, is used for the initial entry, and a second, $h2(K)$, to calculate an offset for continuing the search on collision. In Fig. 4.11, the plots for $E_p(N)$ and $E_a(N)$ versus α are shown. For $\alpha < 0.8$, $E_p(N) < 2$, but for $\alpha = 0.5$, already $E_a(N) = 2$ and the number of probes for both successful and unsuccessful search becomes large once the table is more than three-fourths full.

For collision resolution, open addressing cannot be expected to behave as well as uniform hashing, since there is bound to be some clustering of keys, and these are likely to map into neighboring addresses with a somewhat higher probability of collision than for the uniform distribution. For open addressing it can be shown that[23]

$$E_a(N) \approx \frac{1}{2}\left[1 + \frac{1}{(1 - \alpha)^2}\right]$$

$$E_p(N) \approx \frac{1}{2}\left(1 + \frac{1}{1 - \alpha}\right). \tag{4.4}$$

These are also shown in Fig. 4.11, and they exhibit an even more rapid rise with increasing load factor than does uniform hashing. Modifying linear probing by attempting to place keys in locations $h(K) + \delta$, $h(K) + 2\delta$, and so on, after collision, where δ is a constant other than 1, does not alter the behavior.

There is some gain to be had in loading the hash table in two passes. During the first pass, addresses are calculated as long as there are no collisions; during the second pass, addresses for collisions are calculated. This has the effect that all items for which there are no synonyms will always go directly into their hash-calculated positions;

---

[23]These results, along with those given in Eqs. (4.5) and (4.6) are developed in Knuth, *The Art of Computer Programming*, Vol. 3, 517–521.

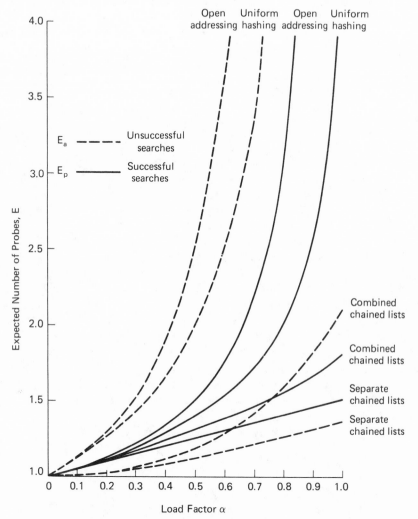

Fig. 4.11 Number of probes in hashing for different methods of synonym resolution

however, if the list is a dynamic one, with insertions and deletions, separation into two passes is not applicable.

When collisions are resolved by maintaining a separate sublist starting from each hashed address, the length of each sublist is $N/M = \alpha$. If $M < N$ (i.e., $\alpha > 1$), the sublists are stored as separate lists in a separate storage area away from the primary table of M entries. An analysis shows that for this case of separate lists,

$$E_a(N) = \alpha + e^{-\alpha}$$

$$E_p(N) = 1 + \frac{\alpha}{2}.$$

(4.5)

Table 4.6 shows the list organization for separate lists of the previous example, using a chaining address to point to the sublists (three in this case).

It is possible to maintain sublists for each set of synonyms by having only a primary table, with $M > N$. The technique is essentially that of open addressing, except that a synonym is located by a chaining address rather than by a search through consecutive entries. When an entry is being inserted, even if it is not a synonym of some earlier entry, its calculated address may be occupied because it was used on some earlier chain. In this case the new entry is simply added onto the earlier chain. In effect, the sublists are combined in the primary table. Thus in Table 4.6 in the columns under "Combined Chained Lists," *Oct* hashes into row 16, which is already occupied by *Mar*, and therefore a chaining address to 18, the first vacancy after 16 is attached to the *Mar* entry. If any other key were also to hash into 16, it would be appended to this sublist. Had there been an entry that hashed into 18, it, too, would have to be appended to the *Mar*, *Oct* sublist. Note that in this method each entry is placed exactly in the same address that it would be according to the linear probing scheme, because the rule for placing synonyms is precisely the same as that for that method. The difference is that the chaining address directs the search more quickly than in open addressing. The price of the shorter search time is the extra storage required for the chaining field.

Analysis of this combined sublist method of chaining shows that

$$E_a(N) \approx 1 + \frac{e^{2\alpha} - 1 - 2\alpha}{4}$$

$$E_p(N) \approx 1 + \frac{1}{8\alpha}(e^{2\alpha} - 1 - 2\alpha) + \frac{\alpha}{4}.$$

(4.6)

The curves for expected number of probes using chaining are also shown in Fig. 4.11. The significant difference from those for uniform hashing and open addressing is that there is no longer a sharp rise as the hash table becomes full. Even for $\alpha = 1$, for example, the number of probes for a successful search is less than 2. *The important feature of all hash-table methods is that the expected search is independent of the number of entries N, and for carefully designed tables its expected value can be reduced to less than 1.5 probes per search.* It is this feature that makes hashing so popular.

Important as this advantage is, there are nevertheless some qualifications about hashing. It is difficult to be certain that the hashing function is satisfactory without an empirical study on the actual keyset being used, and even with such a study if the keyset changes dynamically, the function may not remain satisfactory. The time for computation of the hash function does add to the search time. Also, two neighboring keys, K' and K'', will not hash into neighboring addresses. It might be desirable, for example, to store the entries for two names that are spelled nearly the same (e.g., Smith and Smythe) close together. Finally, hashing presents some problems on additions and deletions. If additions cause the number of entries, N, to increase, it might be desirable to increase the table size, M, particularly if open addressing is used. This means recalculating the hash address for every entry, in other words, total reorganization.

Deletions, especially, need careful attention. One cannot delete a key, either in the open addressing or chaining method of resolving collisions, by simply replacing the key (and chaining address) by a null entry. To do so would interrupt the searching path for certain entries other than that being deleted. Suppose in Table 4.6 with open addressing that the entry for *Jan* were to be deleted by inserting a null string in address 17, and a search for *Oct* subsequently requested. The search would initiate at address 16 and continue to 17, where the blank encountered would give the false indication that there was no entry for *Oct*. Similarly, in combined chained lists, deleting an entry can destroy search paths.

One method of handling the deletion problem is to include a deletion bit in the directory. Initially, all deletion bits are 0, and when an entry is deleted, the appropriate bit is set to 1. During the search process, searching is terminated on encountering a blank key only if the deletion bit is 0. The disadvantage of this technique is that the list is not shortened, as far as search is concerned, by removing entries (although new entries that hash into an address previously occupied by a deletion can be placed in the vacated address). With chaining, the standard techniques of deletion from linked lists can be used to remove entries completely, so that they do not have to be skipped over during a search.

We conclude this section on hashing by giving an algorithm for searching a hash table that has combined, chained sublists (Algorithm 4.6). The entries in the hash table have three fields $\langle key, chain, address \rangle$, where *chain* points to the next list entry to be interrogated, and *address* points to the attribute fields. The declarations for **entry** and *table* are:

comp entry $= \langle$**string** *key*, **int** *chain*, **attribute-ptr** *address*$\rangle$

entry array *table*[1 : M]

Given a key value *name*, convert (*name*) interprets it as an integer, k. If *name* is located, *place* is set with its position; if *name* is *missing*, *place* is set with the negative value of the place where it would appear. It would not be difficult to modify the program so that new entries could be added to the table if they were found to be missing. If this were done, it would be necessary to initialize the table by setting all keys to 'ƀ' and all chaining address to Λ.

Algorithm 4.6   Searching a hash table with chaining

```
procedure, hash_search (name, place) ;
integer k, M, place, chainval ; string name, keyval;
    k ⇐ convert(name) ; place ⇐ k mod M;
    chainval ⇐ chain(table[place]);
    keyval ⇐ key(table[place]);
    do while keyval ≠ name ∧ chainval ≠ Λ;
            place ⇐ chainval; /*continue search*/
            chainval ⇐ chain(table[place]);
            keyval ⇐ key(table[place]);
    end
    if keyval ≠ name then place ⇐ − place; /*missing*/
end hash_search;
```

4.7 Internal Sorting

We conclude the chapter with a discussion of sorting. Even though many of the techniques on lists are intended to make it unnecessary to keep them in sorted order, after the very basic operations of insertion, deletion, and searching, sorting is undoubtedly the most common process to which lists are subjected. The performance characteristics of a sorting method are those of interest in any computing process: the dependence of the expected processing time on N, the number of entries, best and worst cases for the processing times as affected by the key distribution, the working storage required, and so on. A large number of sorting methods have been described (Lorin, 1975), and most are capable of mathematical analysis (Knuth, 1973). In this section we consider five that are very different from one another, and between them illustrate many (but not all!) of the characteristics of the numerous methods described in the literature. The descriptions are informal in that no algorithms are presented. Instead, the methods are illustrated by showing, in each case, how the sort proceeds on a sample set of 16 three-digit numbers that were selected at random. As well, there is a discussion of the expected sorting time. When the number of items is large, which is the usual case in data-processing applications, secondary storage devices are need d for the lists and for the sorting algorithm. Methods in which the entire lists are accommodated in high-speed storage are called *internal sorts*, as opposed to *external sorts*, where auxiliary storage is needed. Consideration of external sorting is deferred to Chapter 9.

4.7.1 Sorting by Linear Insertion

Perhaps the most obvious way of sorting is to take in turn each key of the list to be sorted, and insert it in its correct place in the linear list of previously sorted keys. The process starts with the first entry in its original place, and in general, a key to be inserted is compared with entries already present until a greater one is encountered.

When this happens, all the following entries which have already been sorted are moved down one location to make room for the insert, and the next candidate for insertion is taken. The process is illustrated in Table 4.7 on a sequence of 16 three-digit keys chosen at random. The italicized entry in each column shows the entry being inserted.

TABLE 4.7   Insertion sorting

Initial list											
711	*711*	711	711	*146*	146	*053*	053	053	053	053	...053
802		*802*	802	711	*302*	146	146	146	146	146	146
855			*855*	802	711	302	*150*	150	150	150	150
146				*855*	802	711	302	302	302	302	187
302					*855*	802	711	*516*	516	516	*201*
053						*855*	802	711	*537*	537	215
150							*855*	802	711	*569*	302
516								*855*	802	711	516
537									*855*	802	537
569										*855*	569
591											591
860											717
215											802
988											855
187											860
201											988

The time to insert a key and hence the sorting time will be determined by two kinds of operations:

1. The number of comparisons.
2. The number of entries that have to be moved.

These depend on the initial arrangements of the keys. Their values for the cases when the list is already sorted and when the list is in reverse order are obvious (Table 4.8).

TABLE 4.8   Operations for insertion sorting

	Number of Comparisons	Number of Moves
List initially ordered	$N(N - 1)/2$	0
List in reverse sequence	$(N - 1)$	$N(N - 1)/2$
Expected for random distribution	$N^2/4$ (approx.)	$N(N - 1)/4$

To calculate the expected number of moves for a randomly ordered list, note that when the ith key is being inserted, it can be expected to go into the middle of the list, requiring half of the $i - 1$ keys already there to be moved. Therefore, the expected number is $= N(N - 1)/4$. Thus for all cases the sorting time for insertion is $O(N^2)$.

Insertion is typical of a number of methods in which the sorting time is $O(N^2)$. Other examples of such sorts are selection and exchange methods, where passes are made over the list, and during each pass the least (or greatest key) from those not already sorted is selected. The sort time is determined by the number of passes, $O(N)$, and the number of comparisons and key exchanges made during a pass [also $O(N)$, for randomly arranged keys]. These methods are easy to understand and program, and there are some which are relatively better than others, but the $O(N^2)$ factor, greater than the time for methods to be considered next, makes them useful only for dealing with short lists. If during the sort, a binary search is used to locate where the key is to be inserted, then insertion sorting is improved, but the method remains $O(N^2)$ because of the need to move entries.

4.7.2 Sorting by Merging

In sorting by merging, the basic process is the merging of two input lists, each of which is already sorted, to form a single, sequenced output. Because the inputs are sorted to start with, it is only necessary to scan them sequentially, during which a choice is made as to which contributes an entry to the output.

A list of sequenced entries is called a *run*.[24] We can always start by regarding the initial list of N items as N input runs of length 1. In the first merging pass, two runs of length 1 are merged to form a run of length 2, by exchanging the entries, if necessary, to place them in ascending order (alternatively, the list can be sorted in descending sequence of keys). This exchange is carried out pairwise, over the whole list, at the end of which there are $N/2$ runs of length 2. (If N is odd, we can imagine adding a dummy entry with key Ω, greater than any existing key.) On the next merging pass, the runs of length 2 form the inputs, and the outputs are runs of length 4 ($N/4$ of them if N happens to be a multiple of 4). The process is continued until there is a single sorted run.

In the process as described, on the jth merging pass, the input runs are sequences of length 2^{j-1}. By writing the program so that the input runs in a merge pass are of arbitrary length, two advantages are achieved. It is not necessary to pad the last pair of runs with dummy keys (but there will have to a copy instead of a merge on the last step when the number of input runs is odd), and it is possible to take advantage of any initial ordering that happens to be present, by regarding the initial list as a set of given runs. Table 4.9 shows how the runs are built up on successive merge passes for the 16 numeric keys of the previous example.

Assuming the method is that of fixed run lengths, when there are N keys there are $\lceil N/2 \rceil$ runs after the first pass, $\lceil N/4 \rceil$ after the second, and so on, so that the number of passes is m, such that

$$\frac{N}{2^{m+1}} < 1 \le \frac{2^m}{N};$$

that is,

$$m = \lceil \log N \rceil.$$

---

[24]The term *string* is used in much of the literature on sorting for this. However, *string* has become so accepted as meaning a sequence of characters that we prefer to follow Knuth in adopting *run* for a monotonic sequence of keys.

TABLE 4.9   Merge sorting with variable-length runs

Initial List	After Merging Pass		
	1	2	3
711	146	053	053
802	302	146	146
855	711	150	150
	802	215	187
146	855	302	201
302		516	215
		537	302
053	053	569	516
150	150	591	537
516	215	711	569
537	516	802	591
569	537	855	711
591	569	860	802
860	591	988	855
	860		860
215	988		988
988			
187	187	187	
201	201	201	

During a merge pass there will be N comparisons and copies, and something less than N exchange operations, so that the time of a pass is $O(N)$. Hence the total time for sorting by merging is $O(N \log N)$. Extra work space is needed, equal to that occupied by the list, when inputs are rewritten as outputs. When the merge pass uses variable-length runs, for random keys, as a first approximation, we can expect that there will be $N/2$ runs initially. This is equivalent to saying that there will be one less pass, so that the sorting time will be $O(N \log N/2) = O(N \log N - N)$ which is still $O(N \log N)$. Instead of merging two input runs during a merge, it is possible to merge k runs by doing a k-way comparison to determine which entry is passed to the output, in which case the merge is said to be of *order* k. With a merge of order k, the sorting time will be $O(N \log_k N)$, i.e., the time is decreased by a factor $\log_2 N/\log_k N = \log k$.[25]

The $N \log N$ behavior makes merging a desirable sorting method, particularly for magnetic tape files where the number of entries is large, and the serial scan of runs is well suited to magnetic tape capabilities.

4.7.3 Quicksort

Many other methods of sorting achieve an expected sort time of $O(N \log N)$. The basis of these methods is to partition the list in some way which can be described in terms of constructing a binary tree on the partitions. One such method is Quicksort,

---

[25]Some of this saving may be lost because of the time required for a k-way comparison of keys rather than a two-way comparison.

which was first described by C. A. R. Hoare[26] and which has received considerable attention because with suitable choice of a critical parameter, called the *pivot*, it can be very fast. After a pass the pivot ends up in its correct final place in the list, with all lesser keys being placed before it, and all greater keys, after. The two partitions are placed on a stack, and the smaller one is partitioned again in the same way. The process continues, new partitions being added to the stack until a single key results, after which a partition is taken from the stack for processing. The sort is complete when the end of a partition finds the stack empty.

The method of constructing the partitions is illustrated in Table 4.10 using the sample list. It is assumed that the pivot is selected as close to the middle of the list as possible. The pivot is transferred to a temporary location, and replaced by the first member of the list, creating a vacancy at the beginning. Two pointers, TOP and BOT, mark the beginning and end of the partition. The TOP pointer starts moving down the list. If it finds a key less than the pivot, it moves it up into the vacancy, and continues down until it encounters a key greater than the pivot (in the example this happens immediately with key 802). The BOT pointer then starts moving up the list until it encounters a key less than the pivot (this occurs when key 150 is encountered in Table 4.10). On this event the key pointed at by BOT is moved into the vacancy, and replaced by the key pointed at by TOP. After this exchange, TOP and BOT have moved closer together, all keys above TOP are less than the pivot, while all keys below BOT are greater than the pivot. The scan continues with TOP moving down until a key greater than the pivot is encountered, when BOT starts to move up again. When TOP and BOT meet, the pivot is inserted into the vacancy and a pass is complete, the partition having been achieved.

TABLE 4.10   First partition pass in Quicksort

	711	—	150	150	150	150
	802	802←TOP	—	053	053	053
	855	855	855←TOP	—	146	146
	146	146	146	146←TOP	—	156
	302	302	302	302←BOT	302←TOP	302
	053	053	053←BOT	855	855	855
	150	150	802	802	802	802
PIVOT	156	711	711	711	711	711
	537	537	537	·	·	537
	569	569	569	·	·	569
	591	591	591			591
	860	860	860			861
	215	215	215			215
	988	988	988			988
	187	187	187			187
	201	201←BOT	201	201	201	201
			PIVOT = 156			

Figure 4.12(a) shows the tree with the pivot at the root, the lesser partition attached as a left subtree and the greater partition as a right subtree. The subtree with the fewest number of keys not completely sorted is processed next, in this case the set consisting

[26]C. A. R. Hoare, "Quicksort," *The Computer Journal,* **5**, no. 1 (Apr. 1962), 10–15.

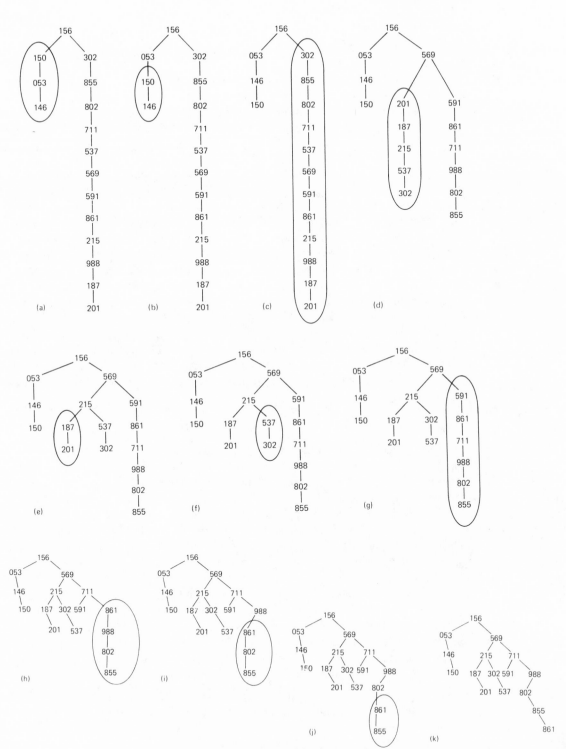

Fig. 4.12 Tree growth in Quicksort

of 150, 053, 146. Figure 4.12(b) to (k) shows how the sort continues. At each pass one new key is correctly positioned and the identified sublist is selected next for partitioning.

The number of comparisons in a pass depends on the pivot selected. If, for a partition with p keys, the smallest key should happen to be selected, then $(p - 1)$ comparisons will be needed to complete the pass. The worst situation will arise if the smallest key is selected on *every* pass, in which case the number of comparisons will be $\sum_{p=1}^{N} (p - 1)$ [i.e., $O(N^2)$], and the sorting method will behave like insertion or other exchange methods. The best situation occurs when the median key is selected as the pivot, in which case the two partitions are as equal as possible. If the keys are random numbers, choosing a pivot in a particular position will yield an expected number of comparisons approximately equal to $1.4N \log N$.[27] Variants on Quicksort adopt different methods of selecting the pivot in order to protect against nearly worst case situations and some, based on sampling the keys, reduce the number of expected comparisons to about $1.1N \log N$, which is close to the optimal case of choosing the median every time. The sorting time depends on the number of exchanges and on pointer manipulations, as well as on the number of comparisons, but the number of comparisons gives a good overall indication of the performance.

Quicksort is one of the best all-purpose sorting routines. Another fast, general-purpose method is that proposed by Shell, based upon a combination of merging and exchanging.[28] It is very difficult to determine the order of Shell's method, but limiting cases behave like $O(N \log N)$, and empirically, $O(N^{1.25+\epsilon})$, where ϵ is small, gives a good estimate.

4.7.4 Digital Sorting

Digital or *radix sorting* is the method used in mechanical sorting of punched cards. In it, a pass consists of examining the digits in a given digital position of the key, starting with the least significant, and dispersing the entries into buckets according to the digit value—10 buckets if the keys are expressed as numbers in base 10. After a *dispersion* pass[29] the entries are collected into a single list, those in bucket 0 first, bucket 1 second, and so on, and then a dispersion pass is performed on the next higher significant digit of the key. The process is continued to the collection pass of the last (most significant digit) of the largest key. Table 4.11 illustrates the process on the sample set of keys.

If the number of buckets is r, the radix of the number system in which the keys are expressed, and the largest key is K, then the number of dispersion passes is equal to the number of digits in $K = \lceil \log_r K \rceil$. The time for a dispersion (or collection) pass will be proportional to N, so that the total sorting time is $O(N \log_r K)$. This behavior is quite different from the $O(N^2)$ of the insertion sort or the $O(N \log N)$ of merging. If $\log_r K \ll \log N$, then radix sorting will be significantly faster than merging. This is

---

[27]This multiplier is determined by the expected depth of a "random" tree (see Section 6.4).

[28]D. L. Shell, "A High-Speed Sorting Procedure," *Communications of the ACM*, **2**, no. 7 (July 1959), 30–33.

[29]Also called a *distribution* pass.

TABLE **4.11**   Digital sorting

After Dispersion Pass

Initial List	1	Bucket	2	Bucket	3	Bucket
711	150	0	201	0	053	0
802	860		802		146	1
855	711	1	302		150	
146	591		711	1	187	
302	201		215		201	2
053	802	2	516		215	
150	302		537	3	302	3
516	053	3	146	4	516	5
537	855	5	150	5	537	
569	215		053		569	
591	146	6	855		591	
860	516		860	6	711	7
215	537	7	569		802	8
988	187		187	8	855	
187	988	8	988		860	
201	569	9	591	9	988	9

likely to occur if the key space is densely filled (i.e., many of the possible keys are actually present), particularly if repeated keys can arise. On the other hand, if the keys contain a large number of digits, and there are few of them, radix sorting will be expensive relative to merging.

During a dispersion it is conceivable that all the entries will be deposited in one bucket, making the working storage for a radix sort potentially of size Nr, an amount that may not be negligible. This can be reduced by monitoring the buckets to see if they become full.

4.7.5 Sorting by Address Calculation

Sorting by address calculation is essentially the same as constructing a table by linear interpolation. Assuming that there are no repeated keys, every entry being looked up will be missing. After estimating the address of an entry, it is inserted into the list in its correct position, moving previous entries as needed to make place for it.

The sorting time is essentially determined by the frequencies of two kinds of operations (besides the time required to calculate an address): the number of comparisons, and the number of entries that have to be moved to make room for one being inserted. The load factor, α, plays the same role as it did in interpolation search and hash coding. If $\alpha \approx 1$, there are likely to be frequent collisions and moves, particularly as the last keys are being inserted. If α is small, collisions are rare, but after all insertions are made, the table has to be scanned to compress the N entries into consecutive table positions.

Table 4.12 illustrates the sort for the 16 numbers of the example using a linear estimator for the address with $\alpha = \frac{2}{3}$. The address for a key, K, is estimated as

$$\hat{K} = \lfloor K \cdot 24/1000 \rfloor$$

During the distribution pass there are 23 comparisons and 3 moves; during the compression pass there are 24 comparisons and 15 moves. If the estimator for the address is good, so that there are few collisions, then the time for the distribution pass is bounded by the searching time, which is $O(N \log \log N)$ even for $\alpha = 1$. The time for the compression pass is $O(M) = O(N/\alpha)$. Thus the dependence of sorting time on the number of entries is a function that is almost linear. This makes address calculation the fastest sorting method, subject to the critical condition that there is a good estimator for the key address. It is not necessary, of course, that the key address be linearly proportional to the key value; what must be known is the cumulative key distribution. Moreover, the variance for the distribution must not be large (i.e., keys must be close to their calculated addresses). In practice, the key distribution and its variance are seldom known, and this has inhibited the use of address calculation as a sorting method.

TABLE 4.12   Distribution pass on sorting by address calculation ($M = 1.5N$)

Key K	Calculated Address $\lfloor K \cdot 24/1000 \rfloor$	Storage Address	Key			
711	17	0	053			
802	19	1				
855	20	2				
146	3	3	146			
302	7	4	150			
053	1	5	215	187		
150	3	6		215		201
516	12	7	302	302		215
537	12	8				302
569	13	9				
591	14	10				
860	20	11				
215	5	12	516			
988	23	13	537			
187	4	14	569			
201	4	15	591			
		16				
		17	711			
		18				
		19	802			
		20	855			
		21	860			
		22				
		23	988			

Exercises

1. Let Δ stand for an undefined value of an attribute of type **real**, and $+\Delta$ for a value that is ≥ 0. Give examples when it might be desirable to assign such values. If O is a binary operator (e.g., $+$, $-$, $\times$, max, or min) are there any instances where the result of an

operation, one of whose operands is undefined, does *not* result in an undefined value? Can a key be undefined?

2. A doubly chained list consists of entries defined by
    comp entry = ⟨**entry-ptr** *flink*, **string** *info*, **entry-ptr** *blink*⟩
    Write instruction sequences to:
    (a) Delete the entry referenced by a pointer variable *pvar*.
    (b) Delete the entry following that referenced by *pvar*.
    (c) Insert an entry, referenced by a pointer *qvar*, so as to follow a list entry referenced by *pvar*.
    (d) Construct a list of entries with given *info* values.

3. Using an appropriate language, write routines for binary search and sequential search. Let

    $$a = \text{time required to execute an assignment instruction}$$
    $$t = \text{time for a transfer of control}$$
    $$c = \text{time for a comparison}$$
    $$o = \text{time for any other instruction.}$$

    Find N, the number of items beyond which binary search is faster, as a function of the above parameters. Look up the parameters for an available computer and determine N in this case.

4. What corresponds to the successor relationship between entries in a hash-based list? Is any use made of this relationship? Is there an occasion to determine the predecessor of an entry?

5. A *dequeue* (double-ended queue) is a list for which insertions and deletions may be made either at the beginning or end of the list. Suggest a suitable set of operators for a dequeue. Write instructional sequences that make a pair of stacks behave like a dequeue.

6. Give an algorithm of determining whether an S expression in LISP is well formed.

7. Give the S expression and storage structure for the algebraic expression $(a*b+c) \div (a*b+d)$. Apply a replace operator to this S expression which has the effect that the storage representation of $(a*b)$ appears only once.

8. Modify UNION (Algorithm 4.3) to carry out list intersection.

9. Give a linked-list representation for polynomials $P(x, y, z)$ whose coefficients are of the form coeff $\cdot x^a \cdot y^b \cdot z^c$ where a, b, and c are integers. Modify Algorithm 4.3 so as to carry out addition of such polynomials. Use the addition algorithm to construct an algorithm for multiplying polynomials.

10. Show that the implementation of a stack by a linked list satisfies O^{stack} and its axioms.

11. Give the operation set, O^{queue} for a queue, and the axioms that must be satisfied. Show that the implementations in terms of (a) a vector; (b) a doubly linked list are valid.

12. Using a language conveniently available to you, write a program that reads in the personnel list of Table 4.2, and sets up the inverted lists on the City, Department, and Job attributes. Write routines that:
    (a) Add entries into the system.
    (b) Delete entries.
    (c) Change an attribute value.

13. Compare multilists and inverted lists with respect to:
    (a) Changing the value of an attribute.
    (b) Adding or deleting an entry.
    (c) Searching for an entry with a given attribute.

Do this by defining parameters for the list, and estimate the times in terms of these parameters. (See the reference in footnote 11.)

14. Write the binary search routine (Algorithm 4.4) as an iteration rather than a recursion.

15. In hashing with linear probing, the number of comparisons required to locate an entry is equal to the number required to insert it when the table was being constructed. Is this also true for interpolation search? What other operations, besides comparisons, are important in constructing a table for iterative interpolation search?

16. Change Algorithm 4.5 to make it into an algorithm for *constructing a table* that can be searched by linear interpolation.

17. Derive the expressions in Eq. (4.4) for the search time when using a hash table with open addressing.

18. Choose as a set of keys the names at the beginning of 50 consecutive pages in the telephone book. Construct a hash table on these keys using:
(a) $\alpha = 0.8$.
(b) Linear probing.
(c) Several hashing functions, including selection of characters, midsquaring, and division by a prime.
Compare the observed expected search times (for both missing and present entries) with the theoretically computed values.

19. The methods described for searching a list with N items have times which are $O(N)$, $O(\log N)$, and $O(1)$. Identify as many methods as you can with each order. Why should a higher-order method ever be used?

20. Write computer programs for each of the sorting methods described in Section 4.7. Test your programs on five sets of 100 random numbers. Draw up a table, comparing the programs with respect to:
(a) Program length.
(b) Working storage requirements.
(c) Execution time.
(d) Time to write and debug the program.

21. Some sorting methods have the property that the sequence of keys which are equal in the original list is retained in the sorted list.
(a) Why might this property be useful?
(b) Which of the sorting methods described in Section 4.7 have this property?

22. In the first round of a tournament sort, keys are compared in pairs, the winner (i.e., lower key) in each pair being promoted to the second round. (If there is an odd number of keys, one is automatically given a by and promoted.) Successive rounds are carried out in the same way, until the overall winner (the lowest key in the list) is found. To find candidates for the next highest key, it is only necessary to promote the loser of rounds involving the overall winner, and follow through contests which start with the promoted key.
(a) Using the data of Section 4.7, draw a binary tree to represent a tournament sort.
(b) Taking the number of comparions as a measure, what is the order of the time required to find the overall winner?
(c) For the whole sort?
(d) What is the order for the time needed to find the first k winners?
(e) How does this compare with the time needed for other methods?
(f) What working storage is needed in a program for a tournament sort?

Bibliography

In many respects lists can be regarded as the universal data type, so that a large fraction of the literature in computing is related to the subject matter of this chapter. Historically, it was through LISP that attention was focused on lists, and that language continues to be important as a tool for innovative applications (see Weissman, 1967). For a reference manual on the LISP programming language, see LISP 1.5 (1969). Although linked lists have been understood for a long time, it is only recently that it has become accepted that they are too useful to be omitted in programming language design (see Baecker, 1975). Graphic applications have been a particularly rich source of linked list data structures (Williams, 1971, and Sexton, 1972). Sorting, as a topic amenable to mathematical analysis, is of special interest, and surveys and books on it continue to appear periodically (Gotlieb, 1963; Martin, 1971, and Lorin, 1975). Searching is perhaps the most important application in data processing and information retrieval. Detailed mathematical treatments of various topics, including binary search and hashing, are to be found in Knuth (1973).

BAECKER, H. D., "Areas and Record-Classes." *The Computer Journal*, **18**, no. 3 (Aug., 1975), 223–226.

GOTLIEB, C. C., "Sorting on Computers." *Communications of the ACM*, **6**, no. 5 (May 1963), 194–201.

KLEINROCK, L., *Queueing Systems*, Vol. 1, *Theory*; Vol. 2, *Computer Applications*. New York: John Wiley & Sons, Inc., 1975.

KNUTH, D., *The Art of Computer Programming*, Vol. 3, *Sorting and Searching*. Reading, Mass.: Addison-Wesley Publishing Company, Inc., 1973.

LISP 1.5 Programmers Manual, 2nd ed. Cambridge, Mass.: MIT Press, 1969.

LORIN, H., *Sorting and Sort Systems*. Reading, Mass.: Addison-Wesley Publishing Company, Inc., 1975.

MARTIN, W. A., "Sorting." *Computing Surveys*, **3**, no. 4 (Dec. 1971), 147–174.

PRICE, C. E., "Table Lookup Techniques." *ACM Computing Surveys*, **3**, no. 2 (June 1971), 49–65.

SEXTON, J. H., "An Introduction to Data Structures with Some Emphasis on Graphics." *The Computer Journal*, **16**, no. 9 (Sept. 1972), 444–447.

WEISSMAN, C., *LISP 1.5 Primer*. Belmont, Calif.: Dickenson Publishing Company, 1967.

WILLIAMS, R., "A Survey of Data Structures for Computer Graphic Systems." *Computing Surveys*, **3**, no. 1 (Mar. 1971), 1–21.

chapter 5

Vectors and Arrays

The term *vector* has a precise meaning in mathematics and physics: an ordered list of numbers, called *components*, which are interpreted as coordinates in a multidimensional space. From this follows the concept of a matrix (a vector whose components are vectors), along with certain transformational properties of the matrix. We shall use the term *vector* in a more general sense, to denote an ordered list of components, all of the same data type. Thus a list of five alphabetic strings will be a vector and the value of, say, the third component, regarded as a variable, will be the third string. Ordering means a correspondence with the positive integers, 0, 1, ..., and so another way of defining a vector is to say that it is a mapping from the integers to a set of components all of the same data type.

The *dimension value* of a vector is an integer, equal to the number of components. The time at which the value becomes known is a matter of some importance. If it is known early enough (compile time, or even block entry time), an indexed storage mapping function, S^{vector}, can be set up to reserve storage for all the components, and so provide efficient access. In this case the components of a vector can be written as $a[i]$, where $1 \leq i \leq n$ is the index of the component and n is the dimension value. (Alternatively, the component index may be allowed to range between p and q, in which case $n = q - p + 1$.) Another implication of knowing the number of components is that any operation defined for a pair of components can be extended to hold for a pair of vectors having the same dimension value. When the dimension value of the vector is not known until execution time, as happens with interpreters, a dynamic storage mapping function, based on linked lists for example, may be more convenient. However, an indexed mapping can be used in this case also, if an upper bound for the dimension value can be given.

The definition of vector is readily extended. Let a vector be one-dimensional array. An s-dimensional array is a set of component values identified by the ordered set of indices $\langle i_1, i_2, \dots, i_s \rangle$, where $1 \le i_j \le n_j, j = \langle 1, \dots, s \rangle$. More generally, the integer indices may range from $p_1 \le i_1 \le q_1, \dots, p_s \le i_s \le q_s$ with $n_j = q_j - p_j + 1$. The array components will be written as $d[i_1, \dots, i_s]$. By distinguishing the first index, the array may be regarded as a vector of dimension value i_1, whose components are arrays of dimension $s-1$. If the second index is distinguished, it is a vector of dimension value i_2, whose components are again arrays of dimension $s-1$, and so on. These different interpretations mean that different storage mappings can be used for the same array, resulting in different access paths to the components. The ordered list $\langle n_1, \dots, n_s \rangle$ is the *dimension list* of the array, and the number of components for the array is $\prod_{i=1}^{s} n_i$.

The number of dimensions, s, is the *rank* of the array.[1] As with vectors, knowing the dimension list in advance can be used to advantage in setting up the storage mapping function, and we consider this next.

5.1 Storage Mappings for Arrays

Assuming that one cell is required for a component, $d[i]$, S^{vector} can be specified by[2]

$$\hat{d}[i] = \hat{d}[p_1] + i - p_1,$$

with the first component being stored in $\hat{d}[p_1]$, and the last in $\hat{d}[p_1] + (q_1 - p_1)$. For a matrix, the storage mapping function can be written as a linear function of the two indices:

$$\hat{d}[i_1, i_2] = a + b \cdot i_1 + c \cdot i_2.$$

One equation for determining the constants a, b, and c results from the conditions that the first component is stored in $\hat{d}[p_1, p_2]$. Thus

$$\hat{d}[p_1, p_2] = a + b \cdot p_1 + c \cdot p_2.$$

Other conditions are obtained by deciding how successive components are to be stored. If, for example, two consecutive components in the same row are to be stored in contiguous cells (with the last component of one row being followed by the first component of the next), we have

$$\hat{d}[i_1, p_2] = \hat{d}[i_1 - 1, q_2] + 1 \qquad p_1 < i_1 \le q_1$$

and
$$\hat{d}[i_1, i_2] = \hat{d}[i_1, i_2 - 1] + 1 \qquad p_2 < i_2 \le q_2.$$

---

[1] In linear algebra, the rank of an array is the number of *linearly independent* rows and columns, so the rank is not equal to the number of dimensions if the determinant vanishes. We shall use the term "rank" in this somewhat looser way.

[2] In this chapter we make frequent use of the notation $\hat{d}$ for the address of d, even though, as indicated in Section 4.3, high-level programming languages do not usually permit calculating addresses explicitly. The address mapping function for rectangular arrays given by Eq. (5.1) is built into the programming language, and the user sees it in the form of the component selector, $d[i]$. The address mapping function for other types of arrays discussed in Section 5.3 may be user-defined, perhaps realized with the aid of pointers.

Solving for a, b, and c leads to the storage mapping function, S^{matrix}, defined by

$$\hat{d}[i_1,i_2] = \hat{d}[p_1,p_2]+(i_2-p_2)+(i_1-p_1)n_2.$$

Relative to $\hat{d}[p_1,p_2]$, the address of the first component, the addresses of the other components displayed in matrix form are

$$0,1,2,\ldots,1\cdot n_2-1$$
$$1\cdot n_2,\ldots,2\cdot n_2-1$$
$$\cdot$$
$$\cdot$$
$$\cdot$$
$$(n_1-1)\cdot n_2,\ldots,n_1\cdot n_2-1.$$

Alternatively, the matrix could be stored so that the components of each *column* occupy consecutive storage locations.

For an s-dimensional array, storing the components as above, so that two components are in consecutive locations when the last index increases by one, the storage mapping function, S^{array}, generalizes to[3]

$$\hat{d}[i_1,\ldots,i_s] = \hat{d}[p_1,\ldots,p_s]+(i_s-p_s)+(i_{s-1}-p_{s-1})n_s$$
$$+(i_{s-2}-p_{s-2})n_{s-1}\cdot n_s+\cdots$$
$$+(i_1-p_1)n_2\cdot n_3\cdots n_s. \tag{5.1}$$

As a particular example, the three-dimensional array defined by $0\leq i_1\leq 2$, $0\leq i_2\leq 1$, $0\leq i_3\leq 3$ has the address mapping function

$$\hat{d}[i_1,i_2,i_3] = \hat{d}[0,0,0]+i_3+4\cdot i_2+8\cdot i_1.$$

The components are stored in 24 consecutive locations, the sequence of components being

$$d[0,0,0],d[0,0,1],d[0,0,2],d[0,0,3]$$
$$d[0,1,0], \qquad\qquad \ldots,d[0,1,3]$$
$$d[1,0,0], \qquad\qquad \ldots,d[1,0,3]$$
$$d[1,1,0], \qquad\qquad \ldots,d[1,1,3]$$
$$d[2,0,0], \qquad\qquad \ldots,d[2,0,3]$$
$$d[2,1,0],d[2,1,1],d[2,1,2],d[2,1,3].$$

To simplify the calculation of addresses, Eq. (5.1) can be written as a recursion

$$\hat{d}[i_1,\ldots,i_s] = \hat{d}[p_1,\ldots,p_s]+\sum_{j=1}^{s}(i_{s-j+1}-p_{s-j+1})\cdot A_{s-j+1},$$

where

$$A_s = 1 \quad \text{and} \quad A_{j-1} = n_j\cdot A_j.$$

---

[3]Alternatively, components with descending sequence numbers can be mapped into consecutive cells. Permutation of the indexes produces different, but equivalent mappings.

In effect, the components are calculated by nested multiplication. To access a component, we need to calculate $\sum_{j=1}^{s} (i_{s-j+1} - p_{s-j+1}) \cdot A_{s-j+1}$. But p_{s-j+1} and A_{s-j+1} are known as soon as the dimension limits are known. These can be calculated and stored in a special array known as a *dope vector*. It is common to store:

1. s, the rank of the array.
2. p_j, q_j; $j = 1, \ldots, s$ for checking that only valid (existing) components are referenced.
3. $\prod_j n_j$, the total number of components.
4. A_{s-j+1}, $j = 1, 2, \ldots, s$.
5. $\hat{d}[p_1, \ldots, p_s] - \sum_{j=1}^{s} p_{s-j+1} A_{s-j+1}$.

Altogether, these require $3s+3$ locations. For a component, the displacement from the base address is

$$\sum_{j=1}^{s} i_{s-j+1} \cdot A_{s-j+1},$$

so that the access time is proportional to the rank, but not directly dependent on the number of components in the array. For a matrix, nine storage locations are required for the dope vector; only one multiplication and two additions are needed to calculate the address of a component.

5.2 Array Processing

Arrays are so important in numerical analysis, applied mathematics, and engineering that even in languages where there are few explicit data types, or none at all, a storage mapping essentially equivalent to that described above is built into the system. In this sense **array** is like primitive types and type **string**, and different from, say, a linked list or user-defined types, in that the programmer does not have to specify how the array components (i.e., items) make up the array. Further, the selector functions are built into the language through the mechanism of subscripting. In APL, the array is the *universal* type. Computers have been built in which array operations are built into the hardware—not only in the form of APL machines, but also as devices with special array-processing arithmetic units. In this section we shall examine APL to indicate the range of array operations available in it, and to show how arrays can serve as the basis for other types, particularly linked lists.

5.2.1 APL

In APL the primitive types are **boolean, integer, real**, and **character**; **array** is the only composite type. In spite of the language's extensive use and the large literature on applications, details on storage representation are rare, and various realizations of the language inevitably differ. For our purposes it is adequate to assume that a representation such as that shown in Fig. 5.1 is used. The essential features are:

1. X ← (1, 2, 3, 4, 5)   Set up entry in value storage area.
                          Set pointer ①

2. Y ← (5, 4, 3, 2, 1)   Set up entry in value storage entry.
                          Set pointer ②

3. Y ← X   Copy entry in value storage entry.
                          Set deletion bit = 1 in old values for Y.
                          Set pointer ③

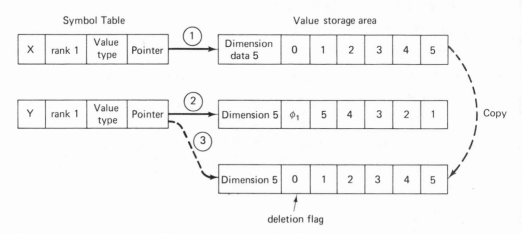

Fig. 5.1   Assignment operators in APL

- There is a symbol table for identifiers, and a value storage area.
- The symbol table entries contain
    the variable identifier
    the rank of the variable
    a type indicator
    a pointer to where the value is stored
  These fields are fixed in size, so standard directory searching techniques can be used.
- The value storage contains
    dimension data for the array
    the value
    a flag to mark entries available for deletion (garbage collection bit)

An important restriction is that an array may be the value of only a single variable. This means that in the assignment

$$Y \Leftarrow X$$

the value of the array X must be recopied, and a pointer from Y set up for it. This feature, along with the deletion bit, simplifies storage allocation and deallocation, at the cost of extra space.

The APL instruction set is very rich; besides the usual arithmetic, logical, and relational operators, many common mathematical operations can be expressed directly. The notation is extremely concise, the same symbol often being used to mean different things depending on the context. As examples, Table 5.1 shows some operators that yield a scalar result.

TABLE 5.1   Examples of scalar functions in APL

Notation	Explanation
$\times Y$	Signum Y; equals 0 if $Y = 0$, -1 if $Y < 0$, $+1$ if $Y > 0$
$* Y$	e^Y
$X * Y$	X^Y
$\lceil Y$	Ceiling of Y; smallest integer $\geq Y$
$X \lceil Y$	Larger of X and Y
$! Y$	Factorial Y
$X ! Y$	Binomial coefficient $\binom{Y}{X}$; number of combinations of Y things taken X at a time
$\circledast * Y$	Natural logarithm of Y
$X * Y$	Logarithm of Y to base X

Most interesting are the operations involving vectors and arrays.[4] An especially important process is *reduction*, designated by an operator, followed by /, followed by an array. The result is to apply the operator successively to all array components; thus $+/V$ means the sum of the components of V, and $\lceil /V$ means the largest component in V. Some of the basic operators are illustrated in Table 5.2, along with the results of their application based on the following assignments:

$$S \Leftarrow 3$$

$$V \Leftarrow \langle 10,11,12,13,14 \rangle \qquad W \Leftarrow \langle 5,4,3 \rangle \qquad A \Leftarrow \langle 1,0,1 \rangle$$

$$M \Leftarrow \begin{matrix} 1 & 2 & 3 \\ 4 & 5 & 6 \\ 7 & 8 & 9 \\ 10 & 11 & 12 \end{matrix} \qquad N \Leftarrow \begin{matrix} 3 & 2 \\ 5 & 6 \\ 4 & 1 \end{matrix}$$

---

[4]Because the array is such a general data type, in which, for example, subscripts may be arrays, and because the language is an interpreter, in which subscripts are evaluated at execution type, efficiency considerations are important. For a discussion, see A. Hassitt and L. E. Lyon, "Efficient Evaluation of Array Subscripts of Arrays," *IBM Journal of Research and Development*, **16**,, no. 2 (Jan. 1972), 45–57.

TABLE 5.2   Some array operations in APL

Notation	Explanation	Result
$3\uparrow V$	Selects first three elements of V	10 11 12
$3\downarrow V$	Drops last three elements of V	10 11
$M[3;1]$	Selects component in row 3, column 1	7
$M[2\ 4;]$	Selects rows 2 and 4	4 5 6 10 11 12
ρM	Dimension list of M	4,3
V,W	Concatenation	10,11,12,13,14,5,4,3
$V\iota 12$	Position of first occurrence of 12 in V	3
$+/V$	Reduction (i.e., repeated summation over components)	60
$+/M$	Reduction over columns of M	22 26 30
A/M	Compression (i.e., column selection of M according to A)	1 3 4 6 7 9 10 12
$A\backslash N$	Expansion of N according to A	3 0 2 5 0 6 4 0 1

It is necessary to go to an APL reference manual to obtain a proper idea of the extensiveness of the notation. APL's acceptance depends as much on its convenient mechanisms for defining procedures and for assigning work spaces and files as it does on notational precision. But perhaps three more examples will serve to illustrate its notational conciseness.

- When the operator ρ is used with two arguments, the argument preceding the operator specifies a reshaping or restructuring of the vector (or array) following the operator. Moreover, components in the second operand are repeated as necessary so that the specified structure can be built. Thus

$$2\ 3\ \rho\ V \text{ results in } 10\ 11\ 12$$

$$13\ 14\ 10.$$

- Certain combinations of operators are defined. For example, $M +.\times N$ yields ordinary matrix multiplication or *inner product* resulting, for the assignments above, in

$$25\ 17$$

$$61\ 44$$

$$97\ 71$$

$$133\ 98.$$

$M\ O_1.O_2\ N$, where O_1 and O_2 are operators, yields a generalized inner product.

- $S \bigcirc V$ specifies a rotation (i.e., left circular shift) of V, S places. It results in 13, 14, 10, 11, 12 for the values of S and V given.

$X \bigcirc M$, where M is a matrix and X is a vector, specifies a rotation of the rows of M. The dimension of X must equal the number of rows, and the rotation for the ith row is given by $X[i]$. Thus

$$0\ 1\ 2\ 3 \ \phi\ M \text{ results in}$$

1	2	3	(no rotation)
5	6	4	(rotation by one)
9	8	7	(rotation by two)
10	11	12	(rotation by three).

The columns of M are rotated by specifying $X \bigcirc [1]M$, where ρX matches the number of columns.

$$1\ 2\ 3 \ \phi[1]\ M \text{ gives}$$

4	8	12
7	11	3
10	2	6
1	5	9.

$\bigotimes M$ specifies a transposition of the matrix M.

To illustrate the use of APL, we now show how strings and lists can be represented and manipulated.

5.2.2 String Operations in APL

APL does not have an explicit string data type; strings are simply arrays of characters. The variety of array operations, and the fact that the language is interpreted, enable most of the basic string operations of Section 3.2 to be realized in a straight-forward manner. Some examples follow.

Substring Selection: Following the assignment $TEXT \leftarrow 'STRINGS'$, $TEXT[3]$ produces $'R'$. $TEXT[3\ 4\ 5\ 6]$ yields $'RING'$, and in general, if V is a vector of numbers representing valid positions in $TEXT$, $TEXT[V]$ will select the corresponding characters. An APL version of $\sigma\ (TEXT,I,J)$ is $TEXT[^-1+I+\iota J]$; the expression in the brackets uses the *index generator* ι to produce the vector $\langle I,I+1,\ldots,I+J-1\rangle$, which specifies the required substring.

Insertion: $TEXT \leftarrow (I \uparrow TEXT), NEW, (I-\rho TEXT) \uparrow TEXT$ effectively inserts NEW into $TEXT$ following the Ith character. This is done by concatenating the first I characters of $TEXT(I \uparrow TEXT)$, NEW, and the last $(\rho TEXT)-I$ characters, and re-assigning the result to $TEXT$; $\rho TEXT$ gives the length of the string. The operators take ($\uparrow$) and catenate (,) are illustrated in Table 5.2. Note that $TEXT[\iota I]$ could have been used instead of $I \uparrow TEXT$; it is often the case that different operator combinations can be used to achieve the same result.

Deletion and Partial Assignment: As for insertions, the interpretive nature of APL leads to straightforward implementations of substring deletion and partial assignment. The statement

$$TEXT \leftarrow ((I-1)\uparrow TEXT), NEW, (I+J-1-TEXT)\uparrow TEXT$$

replaces, in *TEXT*, the substring of length *J* starting at position *I* with the string *NEW*. If *NEW* is omitted, or is null (''), the effect is to delete the specified substring.

Substring Matching: The operator ι, when used as a *dyadic* (two-argument) function, locates the first instance of a character in a given string. If *TEXT*='*STRINGS*', then $TEXT\iota'R'$=3, and $TEXT\iota'A'$=8, one longer than $\rho TEXT$, to indicate that '*A*' is not present. More generally it is useful to be able to locate the first occurrence (or all instances) of one string within another. A simple implementation of the index operation is provided by the function *LOCATE* [Fig. 5.2(a)]. Given a string *PAT* to be located in *TEXT*, *LOCATE* first determines all possible starting positions for a match (line 2). Then it proceeds to check them in turn, stopping as soon as *PAT* is found (line 6). If *PAT* is not present, or is null, a value of zero is returned (lines 1 and 4).

$$\nabla LOCATE[\square]\nabla$$

```
    ∇   PLACE←TEXT LOCATE PAT;FIRST;L
[1]     →(0=ρPAT)/PLACE←0
[2]     FIRST←(PAT[1]=TEXT[ιL])/ιL←0⌈1+(ρTEXT←,TEXT)
        −ρPAT←,PAT
[3]     L←0
[4]  TEST:→((L←L+1)>ρFIRST)/PLACE←0
[5]     PLACE←FIRST[L]
[6]     →(PAT≠TEXT[⁻1+PLACE+ιρPAT])/TEST
    ∇
```

(a)

$$\nabla FIND[\square]\nabla$$

```
    ∇   PLACE←TEXT FIND PAT
[1]     PLACE←(⁻1↓∧≠(⁻1+ιρPAT)⌽((PAT←,PAT)∘.=TEXT),
        (ρPAT)ρ0)ι1
    ∇
```

(b)

Fig. 5.2   APL programs for LOCATE and FIND

Most of the operations used in *LOCATE* are illustrated in Table 5.2. The assignment $PAT \leftarrow, PAT$ uses the *monodic* (unary) operator *ravel* (,) to ensure that *PAT* is a vector; otherwise, if it were a single character, it would be considered a scalar of length zero and indexing problems would result. A branch (indicated by $\rightarrow$) to any expression with the value zero (line 1) causes an exit from the program.

APL operations are so elaborate and compact that it is possible to write a one-line version of *LOCATE*. *FIND* [Fig. 5.2(b)] is such a function; it returns the first location of

PAT in *TEXT* if *PAT* is present, and $1+\rho TEXT$ otherwise.[5] The operation will be illustrated for the inputs *TEXT*='*STRING PROCESSING*' and *PAT*='*ING*'.

After ensuring that *PAT* is a vector, each character in *PAT* is compared to every character in *TEXT* $((PAT\leftarrow, PAT)\circ.=TEXT)$. The result is a 3×17 matrix whose *I,J*th entry is 1 if *PAT*[*I*]=*TEXT*[*J*], and 0 otherwise:

$$00010000000000100$$

$$00001000000000010$$

$$00000100000000001.$$

The occurrence of an instance of *PAT* is indicated by a diagonal string of 1s from top row to bottom. To recognize this, row two can be rotated left one position, row three two positions, and so on $(^-1+\iota\rho PAT)\phi)$, and a logical AND applied to each column $(\wedge\neq)$. However, to prevent certain circular permutations of *PAT* from being found in *TEXT*, a column of 0s is catenated to the matrix $(,(\rho PAT)\rho 0)$ before these two operations are carried out. This catenation results in a spurious zero in the column-reduced matrix. It is dropped $(^-1\downarrow)$, and the resulting vector, here

$$00010000000000100,$$

is searched for the first occurrence of a 1 $(\iota 1)$.

5.2.3 List Representation in APL

Although APL does not have composite types or pointers, the array facilities make it easy to represent and manipulate linked structures. As an example, we show how to do this for LISP-type structures.[6]

Recall from Section 4.1 that the basic LISP item, or S expression, is either an atom (i.e., a character string), or a pair of LISP items, denoted by CAR and CDR. There is also a list-terminator symbol, NIL. Atomic items can be stored in a string, *DATA*, and referenced by an integer pair, the first giving the starting location and the second the string length. A nonatomic item, essentially a pair of pointers to other S expressions, can be stored as a two-row matrix, the top row representing CAR and the bottom CDR. To provide addressability, the matrix is stored as a slice of a three-dimensional array, *ITEM*, the *i*th item being denoted by *ITEM*[*I*;;].

With the means of referring to atoms and composite items specified, the matrix representing a composite item can be described in further detail. The *i*th item, *ITEM*[*I*;;], is a 2×3 matrix defined as follows. The second index identifies the pointer cell within the pair, i.e. 1 for CAR, 2 for CDR. The third index specifies (up to) three attributes about the cell:

[5]This function illustrates the versatility of APL and the conciseness that can be achieved in writing programs. It also illustrates that programs, especially one-liners, can be difficult to interpret, and that their inefficiency is often hidden. This method of pattern search is less efficient than that given in Section 3.4, where the search time was a linear function of the length of the string being examined.

[6]The technique was suggested in H. Katzan, Jr., "Representation and Manipulation of Data Structures in APL," in "Symposium on Data Structures in Programming Languages," J. Tou and P. Wegner eds., *SIGPLAN Notices*, **6**, no. 2 (Feb. 1971), 366–397.

- If *ITEM[I;J;1]*=0, the cell is a pointer, in which case *ITEM[I;J;2]* gives the pointer value and *ITEM[I;J;3]* has a value of zero.
- If *ITEM[I;J;1]*=1, the call refers to an atom, in which case *ITEM[I;J;2]* refers to the starting address in *DATA* and *ITEM[I;J;3]* gives the string length.
- If *ITEM[I;J;1]*=2 the cell has the value *NIL;* the remaining fields have the value 0.

Basically, then, a list item is a pointer pair stored as a slice of a three-dimensional array; a pointer is a three-element vector which refers to an atom, another item, or has the value *NIL.* To create items, two functions, *CREATE* and *CONS*, are provided [Fig. 5.3(a)]. *CREATE* takes a character string, appends it to *DATA*, and returns a pointer to it. *CONS* takes two pointers, *laminates* them to form a 2 × 3 matrix representing a composite it:m (*CAR*,[0.5]*CDR*), and adds it to the item list by joining it with *ITEM* along the latter's first coordinate (*ITEM*,[1]*CAR*,[0.5]*CDR*). The value returned is a pointer to this newest slice of *ITEM*.

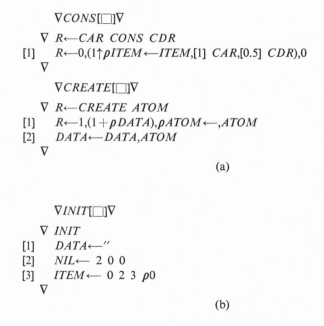

∇*CONS*[□]∇

∇ *R←CAR CONS CDR*
[1]   *R←0,(1↑ρITEM ←ITEM,[1] CAR,[0.5] CDR),0*
∇

∇*CREATE*[□]∇

∇ *R←CREATE ATOM*
[1]   *R←1,(1+ρDATA),ρATOM ←,ATOM*
[2]   *DATA←DATA,ATOM*
∇

(a)

∇*INIT*[□]∇

∇ *INIT*
[1]   *DATA←"*
[2]   *NIL← 2 0 0*
[3]   *ITEM← 0 2 3 ρ0*
∇

(b)

Fig. 5.3   APL programs for CONS, CREATE, and INIT

To illustrate the use of *CONS* and *CREATE*, we will construct a tree for the list (∗(+(AB))(−(CD))) (Fig. 4.3). First, *INIT* [Fig. 5.3(b)] is called to set up needed global variables and define *NIL.* Then the following assignments are made:

EXPR←(CREATE 'B') CONS NIL
EXPR←(CREATE 'A') CONS EXPR
EXPR←(CREATE '+') CONS EXPR
EXPR1←(CREATE 'D') CONS NIL

$$EXPR1 \leftarrow (CREATE \ 'C') \ CONS \ EXPR1$$
$$EXPR1 \leftarrow (CREATE \ '-') \ CONS \ EXPR1$$
$$EXPR1 \leftarrow EXPR \ CONS \ EXPR1$$
$$EXPR \leftarrow (CREATE \ '\times') \ CONS \ EXPR$$

Following these assignments, *DATA* and *ITEM* have the values shown in Fig. 5.4(a). *PRINT* (Fig. 5.5) is a recursive function that assembles (in global variable *OUTPUT*) a preorder listing of the atomic nodes in a tree. Applied to various subtrees of *EXPR*

$$DATA$$
$$BA + DC - \times$$

$$ITEM$$

$$'B' \leftarrow 1 \quad 1 \quad 1$$
$$2 \quad 0 \quad 0 = NIL$$

$$'A' \leftarrow 1 \quad 2 \quad 1$$
$$0 \quad 1 \quad 0$$

$$'+' \leftarrow 1 \quad 3 \quad 1$$
$$0 \quad 2 \quad 0$$

$$'D' \leftarrow 1 \quad 4 \quad 1$$
$$2 \quad 0 \quad 0$$

$$'C' \leftarrow 1 \quad 5 \quad 1$$
$$0 \quad 4 \quad 0$$

$$'-' \leftarrow 1 \quad 6 \quad 1$$
$$0 \quad 5 \quad 0$$

$$0 \quad 3 \quad 0$$
$$0 \quad 6 \quad 0$$

$$'*' \leftarrow 1 \quad 7 \quad 1$$
$$0 \quad 7 \quad 0$$

$$EXPR$$

(a)

$$LPRINT \ EXPR$$
$$\times + AB - CD$$
$$LPRINT \ CAR \ EXPR$$
$$\times$$
$$LPRINT \ CDR \ EXPR$$
$$+ AB - CD$$
$$LPRINT \ CDR \ CDR \ EXPR$$
$$- CD$$
$$LPRINT \ CAR \ CAR \ EXPR$$

(b)

Fig. 5.4 LISP structures in APL

```
        ∇CAR[☐]∇

     ∇ R←CAR X
[1]    →(X[1]>0)/(R←NIL)[2]
[2]    R←ITEM[X[2];1;]
     ∇

        ∇CDR[☐]∇

     ∇ R←CDR X
[1]    →(X[1]>0)/(R←NIL)[2]
[2]    R←ITEM[X[2];2;]
     ∇

        ∇PRINT[☐]∇

     ∇ PRINT X
[1]    →(∧/X=NIL)/0
[2]    →(X[1]=0)/PRINTCAR
[3]    OUTPUT←OUTPUT,DATA[⁻1+X[2]+ιX[3]]
[4]    →0
[5]    PRINTCAR:PRINT CAR X
[6]    PRINT CDR X
     ∇

         ∇LPRINT[☐]∇

      ∇ R→LPRINT X
[1]     OUTPUT←"
[2]     PRINT X
[3]     OUTPUT
      ∇
```

Fig. 5.5 APL programs for CAR, CDR, and PRINT

(via a driver, *LPRINT*), it produces the equivalent prefix code [Fig. 5.4(b)]. *CAR* (*CDR*) takes a pointer and returns a pointer to the left (right) sublist. For convenience, *CAR* (*NIL*) and *CAR* (atom) return *NIL*.

Although only basic functions have been presented, it is clear that more complicated LISP-type primitives can be implemented without difficulty. It should be noted that list construction by a sequence of assignments, as was done above, is tedious and was offered here only as an example. It is easy to write an APL routine that accepts a list expression, for example,

$$(*(+A\ B)\ \ (-(C\ D)))$$

and constructs the appropriate list. For mathematical expressions, Algorithm 4.1 can be used to produce trees from infix input. All that is required is to:

1. Process the input from right to left (to produce prefix instead of postfix code).
2. Call *CREATE* when an atom (i.e., a token) is recognized, and *CONS* when a stack reduction is called for.

5.3 Block and Sparse Arrays

It often happens that special arrays occur with a significant number of components with zero values. Common examples are a diagonal matrix, which can simply be regarded as a vector, and a triangular matrix, where it is sufficient to specify the lower (or upper) triangle [see Fig. 5.6(a) and (b)]. In such cases it is desirable to find a storage mapping function that does not require space for the zero values. This is easily done for the lower triangular matrix by taking

$$\hat{d}[i,j] = \hat{d}[1,1] + \frac{i(i-1)}{2} + (j-1) \qquad 1 \leq i \leq n, 1 \leq j \leq i.$$

Another commonly occurring matrix with many zeros, shown in Fig. 5.6(c), is the tridiagonal matrix, $d[i,j]$, where $1 \leq i \leq n$, $j = 1,2$ for $i = 1$, $j = i-1,i,i+1$ for $i < i < n$, and $j = n-1,n$ for $i = n$. For this the storage mapping function may be taken as

$$\hat{d}[i,j] = \hat{d}[1,1] + 2(i-1) + j - 1.$$

Alternatively, the tridiagonal matrix may be regarded as three n-component vectors with elements given by $d[i+1,i]$, $d[i,i]$, $d[i,i+1]$, and a storage map constructed for each vector.

Each of the matrices in Fig. 5.6(a) to (c) may be regarded as a special case of a more general block matrix. For example, the diagonal matrix is a special case of a block diagonal matrix, which takes the form

$$\begin{matrix} D_1 & 0 & \ldots & 0 \\ 0 & D_2 & \ldots & 0 \\ . & . & \ldots & \\ 0 & 0 & \ldots & D_n, \end{matrix}$$

where $D_1, \ldots, D_n$ are square matrices, and the 0's represent matrices whose components are all zero [Fig. 5.6(d)]. Similarly, a triangular matrix generalizes into a block triangular matrix [Fig. 5.6(e)], and a tridiagonal matrix into a band matrix [Fig. 5.6(f)]. These three block matrices, in turn, are examples of more general block matrices, and Tewarson[7] gives 10 canonical forms for block matrices, two others of which are illustrated in Fig. 5.6(g) and (h).

The diagonal, triangular, and tridiagonal matrices have, respectively, n, $n(n+1)/2$, and $3n-2$ nonzero components. For the diagonal and tridiagonal matrices, the ratio of the number of nonzero components to the number in the full rectangular matrix is $1/n$ and $3/n-2/n^2$. In each case this is $O(1/n)$, and becomes vanishingly small for very large n, so that these matrices are called *sparse*. In general, if N is the number of components for a matrix $D[i_1, \ldots, i_s]$, where $1 \leq i_1 \leq n_1, \ldots, 1 \leq i_s \leq n_s$, the matrix will be sparse if $N \ll \prod_{i=1}^{s} n_i$.

[7]R. P. Tewarson, "Computations with Sparse Matrices," *SIAM Review*, **12** (1970), 527–543.

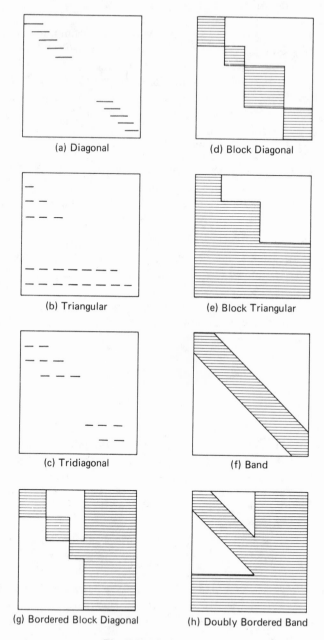

(a) Diagonal

(b) Triangular

(c) Tridiagonal

(d) Block Diagonal

(e) Block Triangular

(f) Band

(g) Bordered Block Diagonal

(h) Doubly Bordered Band

Fig. 5.6 Block matrixes

A matrix may have a considerable number of zeros but not be sparse (e.g., the triangular matrix). Any matrix that has a significant number of zeros can be brought into one of the canonical forms by permutation of its rows and columns. The advantages of representing a block matrix in canonical form may be considerable. Besides the savings in not having to store the zero components, operations using the matrix may be faster and more accurate. However, unless one knows the context of the problem in which the matrix arises, it may be difficult to say *which* of the canonical forms would be most appropriate (i.e., would give rise to the largest blocks of zero components). Reduction to a canonical form is a combinatorial problem (see Tewarson, 1973, for a discussion).

Our interest is in methods of specifying the storage mapping function for the components, but before considering these, it is instructive to see one example of the techniques for converting a matrix to block form. The techniques are easily understood if the matrix is interpreted as the adjacency matrix of a directed graph. Algorithm 5.1 describes a process for reducing a matrix to block triangular form.[8] The reduction is based on finding a permutation of the rows and columns (equivalent to a renumbering of the components) that brings connected components into blocks.

Example 5.1

An example of the application of Algorithm 5.1 is illustrated in Fig. 5.7, for the matrix M, displayed in Table 5.3. The matrices that appear during the reduction are shown in Table 5.4. The reduction can be applied to any matrix, even one that has few nonzero entries, but in such a case the condensation graph would contain only one or two components, the order of the largest being of the same order as the original matrix, so there would be no simplification.

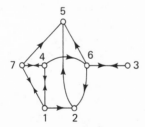

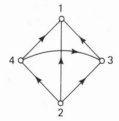

(a) D, the graph corresponding to adjacency matrix for the given matrix

(b) D*, the condensation of D — one node for each strongly-connected component

Fig. 5.7   Graphs arising in the reduction of a matrix to block triangular form

---

[8]The time for the method described here is dominated by the time taken to find the strongly connected components for the digraph in step 2, which in turn is dominated by the time for transitive closure, $O(n^3)$. There is a more efficient method for finding the connected components, based on representing the graph as a list of nodes, each with its outgoing edges and finding a spanning tree. Then the time is $O(n + m)$, where m is the number of edges.

Algorithm 5.1   Reduction of a matrix to block triangular form

Step Number	Operation	Comment
1.	Form the digraph D associated with the given matrix M.	Replace M by a matrix A, in which $$a[i,j] = \begin{cases} 1 & \text{if } m[i,j] \neq 0 \\ 0 & \text{otherwise} \end{cases}$$ A is the adjacency matrix of D.
2.	Determine the strongly connected components of D. In each strongly connected component there is a path between every pair of points.	The method adopted here is to find the transitive closure of the adjacency matrix. Each set of identical rows determines the vertices of a strongly connected component.
3.	Form D*, the condensation of D. D* has one vertex for every strongly connected component in D. A* is the adjacency matrix for D*.	$a*[i,j] = 1$ iff there is a path from component i to component j; D*, being acyclic, has at least one vertex of in-degree zero, since the path length is bounded.
4.	Order the strong components of D* so that A* is lower block triangular.	This is always possible, since only one directed edge can connect two strong components. Start with the component of in-degree 0 and continue.
5.	Reorder the nodes of A to obtain A' such that A' is lower block triangular.	Suppose that row n_i of A* is mapped into the set of rows, S_i, and $s_k^i \in S_i$. Renumber s_k^i $\Rightarrow s_k^{i'} = \sum_{j=1}^{i-1} |S_j| + k$. The result is A', a permutation of the rows of A. Rows in the same set S_i of A* will receive consecutive row numbers in A'. As i increases in A*, the row numbers of A' will increase monotonically. As a result, since A* is block triangular, A' will also be block triangular.
6.	Replace each entry of A' by the entry of M to which it corresponds, to obtain M' = M in block triangular form.	A substitution.

TABLE 5.3 Reduction to block triangular form

```
a  b  0  c  0  0  d          n  0  0  0  0  0  0
0  e  0  0  f  0  0          f  e  0  0  0  0  0
0  g  h  0  0  i  0          0  g  h  i  0  0  0
j  0  0  k  0  1  m          g  0  p  r  0  0  0
0  0  0  0  n  0  0          0  b  0  0  a  c  d
0  0  p  0  q  r  0          0  0  0  1  j  k  m
s  0  0  t  u  0  v          u  0  0  0  s  t  v
M, original form             M', block triangular form
```

TABLE 5.4 Matrices appearing during reduction of M

```
1  1  0  1  0  0  1
0  1  0  0  1  0  0
0  1  1  0  0  1  0
1  0  0  1  0  1  1
0  0  0  0  1  0  0
0  0  1  0  1  1  0
1  0  0  1  1  0  1
```
(a) A, adjacency matrix corresponding to M

```
1  1  1  1  1  1  1
0  1  0  0  1  0  0
0  1  1  0  1  1  0          identical rows indicate
1  1  1  1  1  1  1          common vertices in D*
0  0  0  0  1  0  0
0  1  1  0  1  1  0
1  1  1  1  1  1  1
```
(b) Transitive closure of A

Corresponding rows in A
```
1  0  0  0      5
1  1  0  0      2
1  1  1  0      3,6
1  1  1  1      1,4,7
```
(c) A*, adjacency matrix of condensate

Row of A* i	$\lvert S_i\rvert$	s^i_k, Rows of S_i			$\sum_{j=1}^{i-1}\lvert S_j\rvert$	Renumbered Rows, $s^i_k{}'$		
		$k=1$	$k=2$	$k=3$		$k=1$	$k=2$	$k=3$
1	1	5			0	1		
2	1	2			1	2		
3	2	3	6		2	3	4	
4	3	1	4	7	4	5	6	7

(d) Renumbering the rows of A to obtain A′

```
1  0  0  0  0  0  0
1  1  0  0  0  0  0
0  1  1  1  0  0  0
1  0  1  1  0  0  0
0  1  0  0  1  1  1
0  0  0  1  1  1  1
1  0  0  0  1  1  1
```
(e) A′ = A, reordered into lower block triangular

5.4 Storage Mappings for Block and Sparse Arrays

In looking for storage mappings for sparse arrays, two possibilities suggest themselves immediately. These, as well as methods that derive from them, are easily envisaged for the case of rectangular matrices, as a simple example will show. Let the matrix D have r rows and c columns, and the components be $d[i,j]$ where $1 \le i \le r$, $1 \le j \le c$. We assume that the number of nonzero components $N \ll r \cdot c$.

Example 5.2

Suppose that the matrix D to be stored is

$$1 \ 0 \ 2$$
$$2 \ 3 \ 0$$
$$0 \ 0 \ 0$$
$$0 \ 1 \ 0.$$

In order to provide a comparison basis for methods that take advantage of sparseness, consider the dope vector already developed for general arrays. For a rectangular array of dimension 4×3, Eq. (5.1) becomes, with $d[1,1] = 0$,

$$\hat{d}[i,j] = (j-1)+(i-1)3 = 3i+j-4.$$

The dope vector quantities are

1. 2
2. (1,4), (1,3)
3. 12
4. 1,3 $\Big\}$ These are the coefficients in the equation for $\hat{d}[i,j]$.
5. −4

If the full vector and all the coefficients are stored, 21 locations are needed; for an $r \times c$ matrix, $r \cdot c + 9$ locations are required.

The second obvious technique is to store only the nonzero components, along with a position identifier. If the row and column indices are stored, the array takes the form

$$1(1,1) \ 2(1,3) \ 2(2,1) \ 3(2,2) \ 1(4,2).$$

In this case the storage requirements are $3N$.

The dope vector method is efficient for accessing components, but inefficient with respect to storage for block and sparse matrices. The method based on storing a component and its position indices is efficient for storage but inefficient for component access. To find a given component can take N comparisons; even if some kind of binary search is devised, so that the access time becomes $O(\log N)$, for large N this would still be much greater than the constant time, independent of matrix size, which characterizes the dope vector method. Also, when components are changed, the usual cost of insertion and deletion manifests itself if one attempts to use binary search.

What is desired is a method that has the rapid access feature of indexing, and the low storage cost of recording only nonzero components. It will be recalled that the search time for a hash table entry is essentially independent of the size of the table. By constructing a hash table for nonzero components, using as key a linear combination of the indexes ($3i+j$, in this example), we have a mapping for the array which is $O(N)$ for storage requirements and $O(1)$ for component access. But hash tables have a property which makes them unsuitable for storing sparse arrays. In most applications involving arrays, it is very seldom that one requires access to a single component; calculations (e.g., matrix multiplication or inversion) almost always proceed by accessing in serial fashion all the components of a row or column. The very nature of the hash table organization is that the components are scattered throughout the table. Each component of a row must be retrieved independently, and the access time for a whole row will be the sum of the access times for each entry in the row. Because of this feature, although hash tables have been used for storing sparse matrixes, they are considered unattractive, and we look for other methods. What is presented in this section are variants of the two basic methods, with different trade-offs with respect to storage and component access time.

Techniques based on storing the components and position indicators will be called *row–column* methods, because in some sense these positional indices are specified. They have storage requirements $O(N)$, that is, of the form aN, where a is some integer, 3 in the example above. Techniques derived from use of dope vectors will be called *auxiliary array* methods. The auxiliary will *not* be the dope vector, which provided an access method dependent only on the rank of the array being stored, and independent of the values of the dimension indices. Assuming that the array being stored is a matrix, as in the example, the expression for the storage requirement of an auxiliary array takes the form $O(r \cdot f(c))$, where $f(c)$ is a function that depends on the number of columns in the matrix. The total storage requirement is given by an expression of the form $a'N + r \cdot f(c)$; the advantage depends upon a' being less than a above, and $f(c)$ being less than c. For example, $f(c)$ can be $\bar{c}$, the average number of nonzero columns $= N/r$, and the total storage, including that for the components, $N + r \cdot \bar{c}$. Since there is symmetry with respect to rows and columns, there will be another auxiliary array method with storage requirements $N + c \cdot \bar{r}$, where $\bar{r}$ is the average number of nonzero components in a column.

5.4.1 Row–Column Methods

In examining row–column methods, it may first be noted that a straightforward linear search for a given component makes the access time $O(N)$. To achieve a binary search, it is necessary to order the components in a systematic way.

One possibility is to store with each nonzero component a *pseudo-address* (i.e., the relative address it would have if the full array were to be stored). For the example matrix D, the quantities are

$$1(0),\ 2(2),\ 2(3),\ 3(4),\ 2(7).$$

For a two-dimensional array this technique requires a total storage of $2N$ and, with binary search, access time $O(\log N)$. The cost for this improvement over $3N$ storage and $O(N)$ access is only that for calculating the pseudo-addresses, so for all but the very smallest N, this method is an improvement over direct row–column storage.

Another way of organizing the component systematically is to store all the components of a given row contiguously. Each row takes the form

New row symbol	row no.	col.no. of first comp.	comp. value	col.no. of next comp.	comp. value	...	col.no. of last comp.	comp. value

The storage requirement is $2N+2r$. However, binary search cannot be carried out directly, since the rows take up a variable number of locations, depending on the number of nonzero components there are for the row. The difficulty can be overcome by keeping a row directory which lists the beginning and final addresses in storage where the components for the row are to be found. This requires r locations and a search costing $O(\log r)$. Once the row is accessed, a binary search can be carried out on the column index. The time for row i will be $O(\log c[i])$, where $c[i]$ is the number of nonzero components present. Overall, the search time for this method, based on a directory-plus-contiguous-component list, becomes $O(\log r + \log c(max))$, where $c(max)$ is the maximum number of columns in any row. Alternatively, by setting up a column directory, the storage requirements would be $2N+2c$, and the search time $O(\log c + \log r(max))$. A row–column method with a directory as part of the storage mapping can be regarded as a combination of the two basic methods, since the directory is really an auxiliary array to facilitate component access.

As already noted, in many matrix operations the requirements are similar to those encountered in matrix multiplication, where access is wanted to *all* the components in a given row (along with knowledge of the column indices), or all the components in a given column. This can be accomplished with a *linked list representation* for a sparse array in which all the components in a given row or column are linked together. Assuming that *both* row *and* column access are needed, then for each nonzero component, five quantities will be required. These are

1. The row index.
2. The column index.
3. A pointer to the next component in the same row.
4. A pointer to the next component in the same column.
5. The component value.

In addition, there will be header blocks for each row and column (i.e., row and column directories), so that the total storage is $5N+2(r+c)$. Figure 5.8 illustrates the linked list representation for the sample matrix D, using both row and column pointers.

The time for accessing a single component using a linked list is bounded by $O(\log r + c(max))$, which is greater than that for the directory-plus-contiguous-component method. However, the time to access *all* the components in a given row is also $O(\log r + c(max))$, which is the same as for that method, so that the time to

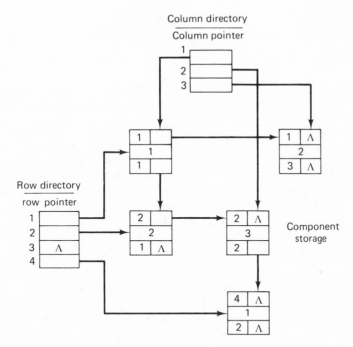

(b) Representation of example matrix, D

Row no.	Row pointer
Component value	
Column no.	Column pointer

(a) Entry Format

Fig. 5.8   Linked list representation of a sparse matrix

process matrices as a whole is not increased by using the linked list. Also, if single components have to be added or deleted, the usual advantages of linked lists manifest themselves.

5.4.2 Auxiliary Array Methods

The first auxiliary array method to be considered is based on the use of a bit map. As was seen in Section 3.5, bit maps are often used in data compression, and setting up a storage mapping that eliminates the need to store nonzero components is really a problem in data compression. For the example matrix D, the bit map is

$$1\ 0\ 1$$
$$1\ 1\ 0$$
$$0\ 0\ 0$$
$$0\ 1\ 0.$$

(It is the adjacency matrix of the graph corresponding to the matrix.) If w is the number of bits in a computer word, then each row requires $\lceil c/w \rceil$ words, so the total storage for components plus bit map is $N + r \cdot \lceil c/w \rceil$. With a bit map it is still necessary to devise an efficient way of accessing components, and this depends on the availability of computer instructions for manipulating words regarded as bit streams. As with row–column methods, it is useful to maintain a row directory which gives the location in the component storage area of the first component for each row. Masking and indexing techniques can then be used to locate a given column entry.

With bit maps, the full array is maintained for specifying positions. It is possible instead to keep a compressed array that contains only summary data, and we consider such methods next. These summary data are the *number* of nonzero components, rather than their position. To illustrate what is needed, assume that the data to be stored have been presented as a complete array and that it is desired to calculate and use the auxiliary array.

It is necessary to introduce some additional notation for parameters of the matrix; this is given in Table 5.5. Suppose now that a contiguous mapping is used to store each row, starting with the component $d[rf, cf[rf]]$. For row i all the components from $cf[i]$ to $cl[i]$ are stored, including zero components. The components of row 1 are stored

TABLE 5.5   Sparse matrix parameters

	Row		Column
r	number of rows	c	number of columns
rf	first row	cf	first column
rl	last row	cl	last column
$\bar{c}$	average number of columns in a row	$\bar{r}$	average number of rows in a column
$cf[i]$	first column of row i	$rf[j]$	first row of column j
$cl[i]$	last column of row i	$rl[j]$	last row of column j
$cw[i] = cl[i] - cf[i] + 1$ = column width of row i		$rw[j] = rl[j] - rf[j] + 1$ = row width of column j	
$\overline{cw} = \dfrac{1}{r}\sum\limits_{i=1}^{r} cw[i]$ = average column width		$\overline{rw} = \dfrac{1}{c}\sum\limits_{j=1}^{c} rw[j]$ = average row width	
$cw = \max\limits_{i} cl[i] - \min\limits_{i} cf[i]$ = column band width		$rw = \max\limits_{j} rl[j] - \min\limits_{j} rf[j]$ = row band width	

$$N = \text{number of components}$$
$$r \cdot \bar{c} = N \leq r \cdot \overline{cw} \leq r \cdot cw \qquad\qquad c \cdot \bar{r} = N \leq c \cdot \overline{rw} \leq c \cdot rw$$

first, followed by those for row 2, and so on. With this scheme, the storage mapping equation becomes

$$\hat{a}[i,j] = \hat{a}[rf, cf[rf]] + j - cf[i] + \sum_{k=rf}^{i-1} cw[k].\qquad(5.2)$$

Note that for $cf[i] = p_2$ and $cl[i] = q_2$, this reduces to the two-dimensional case of Eq. (5.1), as it should. To calculate an address, a generalized dope vector, that is, a *dope array* with components $(-cf[i] + \sum_{k-1}^{i-1} cw[k])$, can be stored for $i = 1, 2, \ldots, r$. As already noted, in this auxiliary array the number of components depends on r, the *value* of the dimension index, rather than on s, the number of dimensions, as was the case for dope vectors. The access time for components is not increased, but the storage for the auxiliary array is now r locations, and for the components $r \cdot \overline{cw}$ locations, to make a total of $r \cdot (\overline{cw} + 1)$. The ratio of the storage requirements using the auxiliary mapping array to the requirements when using the dope vector is $r \cdot (\overline{cw} + 1)/(r \cdot c) + 2$, so the saving is $O(\overline{cw}/c)$, a quantity that reflects the sparseness of the matrix.

Although the technique just described has been presented as a variant of using dope vectors, it can also be viewed as a data compression formed from an *augmented bit map* of the matrix. This can be seen in Table 5.6, where the example matrix D and the augmented bit map are shown, along with $A = cf[i]$, $B = \sum_{k=rf}^{i-1} cw[k]$, and $C = B - A$.

TABLE 5.6   Dope array for D

D			Augmented Bit Map			A	B	C = B−A
1	0	2	1	1	1	1	0	−1
2	3	0	1	1	0	1	3	2
0	0	0	0	0	0	0	5	5
0	1	0	0	1	0	2	5	3

The bit map for D contains a 1 in places where D has a nonzero component, and a 0 elsewhere; the augmented bit map has a continuous string of 1s in each row, starting with the first nonzero column for the row, and ending with the last. The component list stored for D is

$$1, 0, 2, 2, 3, 1$$

and the address mapping function is

$$\hat{a}[i,j] = 1 + C[i] + j \qquad \text{(assuming that } \hat{a}[1,1] = 1).$$

Thus $\hat{a}[4,2] = 1 + 3 + 2 = 6$ (i.e., the sixth entry in the component list). Note that storage has been reserved for one component which is actually zero. This arises because of the indexed nature of the access, and such a vacant storage call is needed wherever there is a 1 in the augmented bit map which corresponds to a 0 in the actual bit map. Another way of deriving an augmented bit map and an auxiliary array is to take the j component first. In this case the alternative modified bit map for D and the auxiliary array components are shown in Table 5.7.

TABLE 5.7   Alternative auxiliary array for D

		1	0	1
		1	1	0
Augmented bit map		0	1	0
		0	1	0
	A'	1	2	1
	B'	0	2	5
	C' = B'−A'	−1	0	4

The component storage is 1, 2, 3, 0, 1, 2, and the address mapping function is $d[i,j] = 1+i+C[j]$. This time the storage requirements are $c(\overline{rw}+1)$. The relative advantage of the two choices depends on the value of $r \cdot \overline{cw}$ versus $c \cdot \overline{rw}$.

The technique just described is suitable for block triangular, diagonal, or band matrices [Fig. 5.6(d), (e), and (f)]. By introducing extra indices it is not difficult to generalize it to bordered types of band matrices. Also it can clearly be generalized to higher-dimensional arrays; an array of dimension s will require an $(s-1)$-dimensional dope array, and there will be $s!$ ways of defining one. The storage savings may be appreciable only for relatively sparse arrays.

In practice it is not necessary to *calculate* the auxiliary array, as has just been done. In applications using sparse matrices, the full matrix is never generated. Instead, sets of nonzero components are generated, for example the set of components in a given row, and along with these there are indices showing where the sets are to be found. These indices correspond to the row and column directories already mentioned. Alternatively, they can be regarded as *pointers*, and the auxiliary array for locating nonzero components can be viewed as a pointer array.

5.4.3 Pointer Arrays

Figure 5.9 illustrates how the components for the matrix D of the example can be accessed by a pointer array P. When D is a matrix, P is a vector P[i]. There is one pointer component for each row of D, r altogether. A null pointer value is entered for a

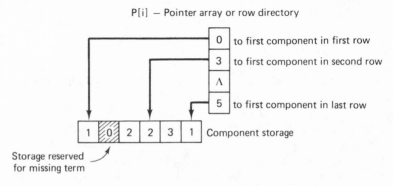

Fig. 5.9   Pointer array for a sparse matrix of rank 2

row that has all nonzero components. Taking addresses relative to that of the first component,

$$\hat{d}[i,j] = P[i]+j,$$

where $P[i]$ is the address of the first nonzero component in row i. Comparing with Eq. (5.2) and assuming $\hat{d}[rf,cf[rf]] = 0$, we have

$$P[i] = -cf[i] + \sum_{k=rf}^{i-1} cw[k].$$

The equivalence between auxiliary arrays and pointer arrays is obvious, the difference being only in the interpretation of the quantity that determines the address.[9]

The method is readily generalized. When D has rank s, a pointer array, $P[i_1, \ldots, i_{s-1}]$, is needed.

$$\hat{d}[i_1, i_2, \ldots, i_s] = P[i_1, i_2, \ldots, i_{s-1}] + i_{s-1}.$$

This pointer may itself be accessed in terms of a lower-dimensional pointer array.

Example 5.3

Figure 5.10 illustrates the pointer array required to access the three-dimensional array $d[i,j,k]$, where $1 \leq i \leq 4$, $1 \leq j \leq 3$, $1 \leq k \leq 2$, and of the 24 possible components, only 8, with indices as shown, are actually present. The location of a com-

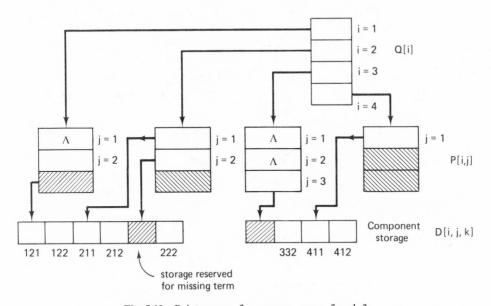

Fig. 5.10 Pointer array for a sparse array of rank 3

[9] The auxiliary array is very similar to the trie organization to be described in Section 6.3. The main difference is that in the trie, the pointers are included with the data rather than being stored in a separate array as is done here.

ponent is given by

$$\hat{d}[i,j,k] = P[i,j] + k,$$

where $P[i,j]$ is a two-dimensional pointer array. Here P is sparse, so the technique can be applied again using a pointer vector Q to access its components.

$$\text{Thus } \hat{P}[i,j] = Q[i] + j,$$

where $Q[i]$ is a four-component pointer vector. For example, to find $d[3,3,2]$, we follow the pointer $Q[3]$, take $j = 3$ to get the address of the pointer $P[3,3]$, and then take $k = 2$ to find the location of the component. In this example 10 locations are needed for the components and 12 for the pointers, so that compared with storing the full array, almost no storage savings result, but depending on the pattern for missing components, pointer arrays can result in less storage being required. Again, certain positions must be reserved in both the component and pointer storage, because of the indexed nature of the access at each level, even though the contents of the positions are irrelevant. The number of empty cells depends on the selection order of the indices. It is not necessary that the first index, i, be the one that corresponds to the one-dimensional pointer vector $A[i]$. Any other index could be used, and as with the dope vector, there are $s!$ possible permutations, each giving rise to a different pointer array. Moreover, each pointer array is specific to the set of components that are present in the matrix, D. If components are added or deleted, a new mapping is needed.

It is possible to modify the pointer array (and likewise the dope array considered in the last subsection) so that no storage is allotted to zero-component elements. The method will be illustrated on the two-dimensional matrix, D, which has served as the example throughout this section. The technique is to store with each component, its column index j, but to use, as before, a pointer vector for access to the rows. Figure 5.11 shows the storage mapping for D using this method. The total storage require-

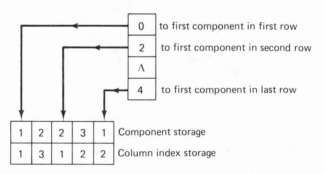

Fig. 5.11   Modified pointer array for a sparse matrix of rank 2

ments become $2N + r = 2r \cdot \bar{c} + r$, as compared with $r(\overline{cw} + 1)$ before. Thus the storage savings depend on the value of $2\bar{c}$ compared with $\overline{cw}$. There is a time cost, however because indexed access is now made only to the first element of a row. After that the, terms in component storage have to be examined until the desired j index is encountered. The search time will be $O(\overline{cw})$ [or $O(\log \overline{cw})$ if binary search is utilized], and this extra time for access has to be traded off against storage savings. For sparse matrices of the kind that arise in very large linear programming problems, for example, the storage savings may justify the approach described here. This is essentially the storage mapping adopted in at least one sparse matrix package.[10] The method is a combination of the two described at the beginning of the section, in that indexing is used for one of the dimensions and column specification for the other. Looking at it another way, it can be regarded as a variant row–column method, in that only partial specification of the row–column is included with the component storage.

Exercises

1. Suggest storage mapping functions for the tetrahedral array with components $d[i, j, k]$, where:
   (a) $0 \leq k \leq j \leq i \leq n$.
   (b) $0 \leq i \leq j \leq k \leq n$.
2. Write APL routines corresponding to Algorithm 5.1 for:
   (a) Deletion of the Nth entry from a list.
   (b) Changing the Nth entry from STRING1 to STRING2.
   (c) Finding the (first) number for an entry with a given string value.
3. Write APL functions, with suitable parameters and operators to realize:
   (a) A STACK.
   (b) A QUEUE.
   (c) A DEQUEUE (see Exercise 5, Chapter 4).
4. Determine the complexity of the expression for the time required to perform substring searches using the APL programs shown in Fig. 5.2.
5. Introducing extra parameters as needed, develop a storage mapping equation suitable for bordered block diagonal matrices. What are the storage requirements for the matrix and dope array? Do the same for doubly bordered band matrices.
6. When a matrix is block diagonal, what form do the associated graph and its corresponding adjacency matrix take? Give an algorithm, similar to Algorithm 5.1, for reducing a matrix to block diagonal form.
7. Construct a hash table for storing and retrieving the components of the matrix of Example 5.4. What is the average access time per component for your table? Per column?
8. Let the density of a square matrix of order n with N nonzero components be $\rho = N/n^2$. For a random matrix the probability of a given component being nonzero is ρ. Derive expressions for the storage required to represent a random matrix of density ρ using:
   (a) A dope vector.
   (b) A row directory-plus-contiguous component scheme.
   (c) A doubly linked list.
   (d) A bit map.
   (e) An auxiliary dope array (or augmented bit map).
   (f) A pointer vector to rows.
   (g) A pointer vector with column indexes for nonzero components.

[10]See J. M. McNamee, "Sparse Matrix Package," *Communications of the ACM* **14**, no. 4 (Apr. 1971), 265–267.

9. Using the results of Exercise 8, draw up a table showing the storage requirements for each representation when $n = 25$, 50, and 100 and $p = 0.01, 0.05, 0.1$, and 0.25.
10. For each of the representations in Exercise 8, give the complexity of the expression for the time to access
    (1) An individual component.
    (2) A row.
11. Write programs for solving the set of linear equations

    $$Ax = b,$$

    where A is an $n \times n$ matrix and x and b are vectors, by Gauss–Jordan elimination:
    (a) When A is represented by a doubly linked list.
    (b) When A is represented with the aid of an auxiliary array.
12. One of the standard methods for inverting a matrix A is to express it as the product

    $$A = LDU,$$

    where

    > L is lower triangular and $l[i, i] = 1$
    >
    > U is upper triangular and $u[i, i] = 1$
    >
    > D is diagonal.

    Give storage mapping functions for L, D, and U, so that only n^2 locations are needed altogether.
13. What parameters are needed to represent a sparse three-dimensional array? Use a display similar to Table 5.5 to identify them. Give the equation for the storage mapping function and show that it reduces to Eq. (5.1) for $s = 3$ when the array bounds are constant along lines and planes.
14. Write programs for multiplying sparse matrices:
    (a) When the matrices are represented by doubly linked lists.
    (b) When the storage mapping is realized by a pointer vector.
15. Suppose that in a certain application it is frequently necessary to border a matrix by adding a new row and column, or reduce it by deleting the last row and column. Which of the representations discussed in this chapter would be efficient for these operations? (Specify your interpretation of efficiency.)

Bibliography

Dope vector techniques for handling relatively static full arrays have long been standard. They are built into programming languages to the point where they are all but transparent to users (although when debugging, it may be necessary to know precisely how components are stored, or what happens when array bounds are exceeded). Designing storage for extendible arrays (arrays whose dimension can vary dynamically) is a more open topic, still under development. (See, for example, Rosenberg, 1975).

Sparse matrices appear continually in numerical analysis and conferences on them are held periodically. (See Reid, 1971, and Rose and Willoughby, 1972.) Although interest centers on applications and matrix manipulations, the data structures also receive attention (Duff, 1976, Pooch and Nieder, 1973).

Gilman and Rose (1974) is a highly readable presentation on learning APL interactively.

BUNCH, J. R., AND D. ROSE, *Sparse Matrix Computation*. New York: Academic Press, Inc., 1976.

DUFF, I. S., *A Survey of Sparse Matrix Research* (HL 76/485). Computer Science and Systems Division. Harwell, England: Atomic Energy Research Establishment, 1976.

GILMAN, L., AND A. J. ROSE, *APL/360 An Interactive Approach*, 2nd ed. New York: John Wiley & Sons, Inc., 1974.

POOCH, V. W., AND A. NIEDER, "A Survey of Indexing Techniques for Sparse Matrices." *ACM Computing Surveys*, **5**, no. 2 (June 1973), 109–133.

REID, J. K., ed., *Large Sparse Sets of Linear Equations*. New York: Academic Press, Inc., 1971.

ROSE, D. J., AND R. A. WILLOUGHBY (ed.,) *Sparse Matrices and their Applications*. New York: Plenum Press, 1972.

ROSENBERG, A. L., "Managing Storage for Extendible Arrays." *SIAM Journal on Computing*, **4**, no. 3 (Sept. 1975), 287–306.

TEWARSON, R. P., *Sparse Matrices*. New York: Academic Press, Inc., 1973.

chapter 6

Tree Directories

In this chapter we examine in greater detail two of the data structures studied earlier—directories and indexes, particularly indexes that are organized as trees. When a directory is stored as a sequential list and keys are located by binary search, there is a tree *process* associated with it, for the initial entry establishes a root, and the upper and lower sections of the directory correspond to the left and right branches of a binary tree. However, when the list is simple sequential, this tree is not part of the *organization* of the directory—in particular, it is not part of the storage mapping. In all the structures of this chapter the tree is built into the storage mapping.

The trees corresponding to directories, in common with other graphs which correspond to lists, are rooted and directed. Also, as noted in Section 4.1, the set of outgoing edges from a vertex is ordered. In trees as described in Chapter 1, no ordering would necessarily have been assumed for the filial set, $f_1, \ldots, f_k$ attached to vertex v in Fig. 6.1(a). Now this ordering *is* significant, and hence there is also an ordering to the edges, $e_1 \sim (v, f_1), \ldots, e_k \sim (v, f_k)$. In particular, this makes the binary tree with

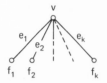

(a) a multi-branched tree

(b) distinct binary trees

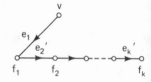

(c) binary tree transform of (a)

Fig. 6.1 Trees with ordered edges

186

edges $\langle l, r \rangle$ attached to vertex v different from the binary tree with edges $\langle r, l \rangle$ [Fig. 6.1(b)].

Ordering the edges permits a definition of a rooted, directed binary tree which is different (but essentially equivalent) to that given in Section 1.7. If a single root node and the null tree consisting of no nodes are accepted as trees, then a (rooted directed) binary tree is one of:

(a) The null tree.
(b) A root node.
(c) A root node having a binary left tree and a binary right tree.

This recursive definition is useful in that it immediately suggests recursive algorithms for tree processing (e.g., for traversing all the nodes). While recursive algorithms are logically simple and easy to program, it is often desirable to look for iterative forms that are not recursive, in order to avoid the extra instructions that are always present when routines are called recursively.

Determining whether two trees are isomorphic is a much more manageable problem than determining whether two (general) graphs are isomorphic. For trees with ordered edges, establishing isomorphism is particularly straightforward because the ordering immediately leads to a canonical traversal for the trees. In fact, there is more than one obvious canonical traversal, and these are considered in Section 6.2.

There are several different ways in which directories can be organized as trees, and these will be presented in the next section. When the description of a tree contains no information about the storage representation (i.e., only the nodes and edges, along with their labels are shown), the tree will be called a *logical tree*. When a storage structure is shown, the representation will be called a *storage tree*. Since edges can be realized as pointers, for each logical tree there is an immediate storage tree in which every node is shown with an ordered set of pointers to its filial set. This storage tree is called the *natural representation* by Knuth, but it is not the only one of interest. In addition to pointers for the filial set attached to a node, there may be an address field pointing to information about the node. For example, if the node corresponds to a key of an item, there will usually be a pointer to the associated attributes; as was the case previously with directories, this pointer will often be implied.

Before we consider the varieties of trees, it is necessary to introduce some additional terminology. To illustrate the terms, and to give examples of the kinds of tree directories as well as the operations on them, it is helpful to be able to work with small sets of sample keys. The set of keys that is generated by GK, the following context-free grammar, will be taken for this purpose.

$$V_T = \{*,w,x,y,z,\ a,e,i,o,u,l,m,n\}$$

$$V_N = \{\text{name, 1charname, 2charname, 3charname,} \\ \text{2ndchar, 3rdchar}\}$$

$$S = \text{key}$$

and the productions are:

$$\text{key} \Rightarrow \text{name} *$$

$$\text{name} \Rightarrow 1\text{charname} \,|\, 2\text{charname} \,|\, 3\text{charname}$$

$$1\text{charname} \Rightarrow w \,|\, x \,|\, y \,|\, z$$

$$2\text{charname} \Rightarrow 1\text{charname} \; 2\text{ndchar}$$

$$2\text{ndchar} \Rightarrow a \,|\, e \,|\, i \,|\, o \,|\, u$$

$$3\text{charname} \Rightarrow 2\text{charname} \; 3\text{rdchar}$$

$$3\text{rdchar} \Rightarrow l \,|\, m \,|\, n.$$

As a particular subset of the keys that can be generated by GK, we take the set K,

$$\langle xal*, \; wan*, \; wil*, \; zol*, \; yo*, \; xul*, \; yum*,$$

$$wen*, \; wim*, \; zi*, \; yon*, \; xem*, \; wul*, \; zom* \rangle.$$

A key in the set K will be called an *actual* key, as distinct from the *possible keys* of GK.

Note that all keys are terminated by * for reasons that will become clear shortly, when character-by-character searching of keys is discussed. The terminator is not needed in searching methods that examine the whole key. It will be assumed that * precedes ϸ (which precedes *a*) in the lexicographic sequence for characters. Note also that K is ordered, but *not* according to lexicographic value. Its members can be thought of as names, and the ordering might represent the sequence in which they are encountered in some application. If the 14 keys are listed in lexicographic sequence, the particular ordered set K, which reflects the order in which the keys have been inserted in the tree, can be associated with the permutation, Π_K, of the integers 1 to 14 given by $\langle 6, 1, 3, 13, 9, 8, 11, 2, 4, 12, 10, 7, 5, 14 \rangle$. Here *xal*∗ is the sixth key in the lexicographic ordering of K, *wan*∗ is the first, and so on. This will be called the *permutation sequence* for K.

6.1 Varieties of Tree Directories

We start by classifying nodes according to the data associated with them. If a node's datum is a character in a specified position of the key, it will be called a *character node;* if the datum is a key, the node will be called a *key node*. The fact that a position is associated with a character node carries with it the implication that the datum for a successor to that node will be in the *next* position of the key. For key nodes no such relationship is implied.

A tree in which every node is a character node is called a *positional* or *digital tree*. If the tree is such that every node has an outgoing edge for every possible character in the alphabet, it will be called a *multidimensional index*.

Example 6.1

Figure 6.2 shows the multidimensional index for GK. Each node of the tree has associated with it a string formed by concatenating the characters encountered in traversing a path from a root to the node in question. A string associated with an

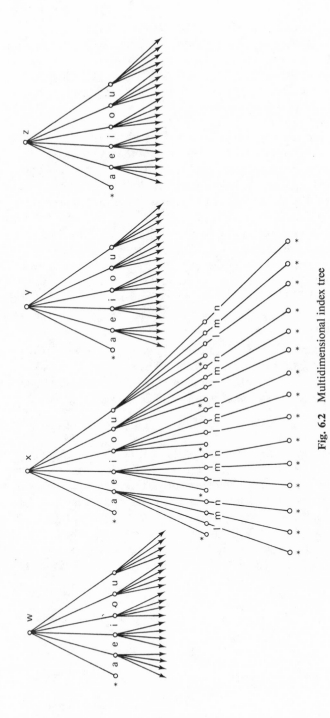

Fig. 6.2 Multidimensional index tree

189

interior node of the tree is a prefix of a possible key; a string associated with a leaf is a possible key. Actual keys are distinguished from possible keys in that the pointers to the attributes (not shown in the tree of Fig. 6.1) contain nonnull addresses, while the pointers for nonoccurring keys have null addresses. The lexicographic ordering on the keys of GK is preserved in the multidimensional index by regarding the edges that emanate from a node as being ordered.

Searching in a positional tree is initiated by comparing the first character in the key being sought with the characters at the root of the multiple-rooted tree. The search proceeds along the tree corresponding to the matching character. At this tree a branch is selected according to the second character in the key. This branching on successive key characters continues, either until all characters of the key have been matched, or until there is no match, in which case the key is missing. Examples of searching algorithms are given in the next section, but here the reason for including a termination character with each key can be noted. This is needed because the name part of one key is allowed to be a prefix of some other (e.g., *yo* is a prefix of *yon* in the keyset K). Such possibilities create a problem when choosing a storage representation for the logical tree. When a search for *yon* is initiated and *yo* is encountered, there must be some way of knowing whether the pointer that is stored in a node points to the attributes of *yo*, or to a continuing search path. Two solutions are:

1. Keep distinct pointers for attributes and continuation paths. This means reserving at least *two* pointers in each node.
2. Append a termination character to every key, and make the matching pointer a continuation address, unless it is associated with a terminator.

We shall choose the second method. Although the key length is increased by one extra character, this method seems to be best overall with respect to storage and extra processing time. Every actual key can be thought of as being terminated by a blank, and it is possible to test for ƀ as the terminator. But it is generally accepted that no significance should be attached to blanks that precede or follow a message, and it is less confusing to introduce an explicit end-of-key symbol, here taken to be *.

A positional tree can be constructed so that only *actual* keys are represented. Such a tree can be formed from Fig. 6.2 by pruning all branches that lead to nonoccurring keys. In the pruned tree the lexicographic order of K is preserved. One might attempt to show the permutation sequence by drawing the different positional tree of Fig. 6.3,

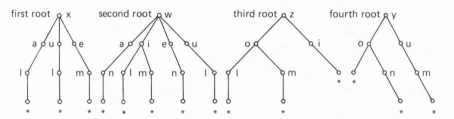

Fig. 6.3 Positional tree for a set of keys

but this tree still does not carry the *full* information about the sequence. If the permua-
tion sequence were important, information about it would have to be attached to the
keys. A positional tree in which there are paths (from a root to a leaf) corresponding
only to actual keys in a keyset will be called a *de la Briandais tree*, after its proposer.[1]
Another type of positional tree, called a *trie*,[2] in which the number of paths is intermediate to the number of actual keys and the number of possible keys, will be described
in Section 6.3, where positional trees are considered further.

Returning to consideration of trees with key nodes, a binary rooted tree can be
derived from partitioning the set of keys according to the key associated with any
node. The given node is the root of the tree; keys lexicographically *less* than the root
key are attached to the left subtree of the node, and those lexicographically *greater* are
attached to a right subtree. The resulting tree will be called a *lexicographic binary tree*.
A tree on a lexicographically ordered set of keys is "grown" by taking the first key
encountered as root, attaching the second key to be encountered onto the left or right
branch according as it precedes or follows the root, attaching the third as a leaf key
following a path from the root, and so on. The logical lexicographic tree for the first
five members of K is shown in Fig. 6.4(a). The natural representation for this logical
tree is shown in Fig. 6.4(b). In both representations the * terminator has been omitted.
Assuming that there is too much data about the key to be stored in the node, the
natural tree directory has *three* pointers (including that which points to key attributes),

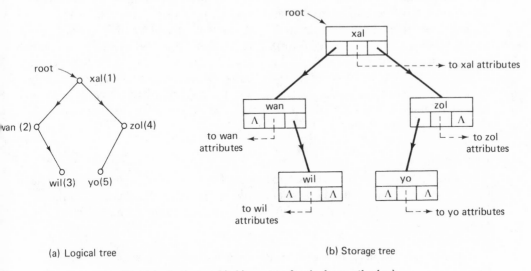

(a) Logical tree   (b) Storage tree

Fig. 6.4 Lexicographic binary tree for ⟨*xal,wan,wil,zol,yo*⟩

[1]R. de la Briandais, "File Searching Using Variable Length Keys," in *Proceedings of the Western Joint Computing Conference, 1959,* pp. 259–298.

[2]A name apparently deriving from re*trie*val, suggested by Fredkin, who first proposed this data structure for information retrieval. See E. Friedkin, "TRIE Memory," *Communications of the ACM,* **3,** no. 9 (Sept. 1960), 409–499.

but the structure is nevertheless called a binary tree because the key string in a node defines a binary partition of possible keys. For a different permutation sequence, a different lexicographic tree results. Figure 6.5 shows the logical tree when the first five keys are $\langle wil,zol,wan,xal,yo \rangle$.

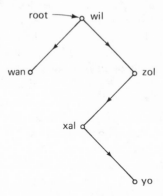

Fig. 6.5   Lexicographic binary tree for $\langle wil,zol,wan,xal,yo \rangle$

It might appear as if positional trees are multiway and lexicographic trees are binary, but there are binary positional trees and multiway lexicographic trees (the latter are considered in Section 6.5.3). There is a simple transformation by which any rooted multiway tree with ordered edges can be converted into a rooted, binary tree.[3] Suppose that the multiway tree contains a subtree consisting of a node n, connected to the filial set $\langle f_1,f_2,\ldots,f_k \rangle$ [Fig. 6.1(a)]. Then the subtree can be replaced by a binary subtree consisting of a chain $\langle f_1,\ldots,f_k \rangle$, and an edge from n to f [Fig. 6.1(c)]. As a particular case, the multirooted tree consisting of the vertices $v_1,\ldots,v_p$ can be replaced by the chain $\langle v_1,\ldots,v_p \rangle$. The transformation is equivalent to changing from one interpretation of a simple list as a rooted tree, to the other interpretation as a directed chain. (See Section 4.1.)

Example 6.2

Figure 6.6 shows the binary tree equivalent for the rooted, multiway positional tree of Fig. 6.3. In the multiway positional tree, the position of a character in the key is equal to the level of the corresponding node in the tree, but this is no longer true for the binary version.

Later in this chapter, trees will be described which are either generalizations of those already presented in that they are unions of several types, or are more specific in that additional conditions are imposed on a type previously described. A *hybrid tree* (Section 6.6) can have either character nodes, or nodes that contain any substring of a key. A *threaded tree* is one in which data giving information about the tree structure is inserted into storage tree node links which would otherwise be null. This infor-

---

[3]For a generalization of the graphs for which the transformation is possible, see John L. Pfaltz, "Representing Graphs as Knuth Trees," *Journal of the ACM*, **22**, no. 3 (July 1975), 361–366.

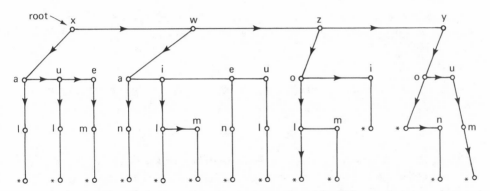

Fig. 6.6   Binary tree equivalent of rooted, multibranched tree of Fig. 6.3

mation is redundant, but it is useful in searching and in tree-processing algorithms. In later sections also, trees will be considered where conditions are imposed on the tree structure, for example on the relative sizes of the left and right subtrees attached to the root of a binary tree, or on the ratio between the maximum and minimum number of branches that may be attached to a nonleaf node in a multiway tree. These conditions enable useful bounds to be set on the time required to carry out important operations. Trees with such conditions will be called *constrained trees*. Trees with nodes in which several strings can be stored are particularly useful in file directories, and they are considered in Chapter 9.

6.2 Operations on Trees

Since tree directories are particular kinds of lists, the operations usually performed on lists—Search, Insert, Delete and Enumerate—are of primary interest. When searching trees, as in searching a simple list, the number of comparisons will be taken as a measure of the searching time. Expressions for the time to carry out the operations above will be derived later, but in this section some preliminary results are developed both for binary and multiway trees.

6.2.1 Searching and Traversal in Binary Lexicographic Trees

We first consider binary lexicographic trees.

Searching: In such trees, the algorithm to locate an entry with a given key follows immediately from the recursive definition of the tree.

- If there is no tree, the entry is not present.
- Compare the given key with that at the root.
- If the keys are equal, the entry has been located.
- If the given key is less than that at the root, search the left subtree.
- If the key is greater, search the right subtree.

In locating an entry, suppose first that the entry is known to be present in the directory. Each key comparison increases the depth by one, so that the number of comparisons required to locate entry i is l_i, its level. (The root is taken to be at level 1.) The expected number of comparisons if all N entries are equally likely to occur is

$$E_p(N) = \frac{1}{N} \sum_{i=1}^{N} l_i. \tag{6.1}$$

If entries do not have equal probability of occurrence, and p_i is the observed frequency (or node weight) for key k_i, then

$$E_p(N) = \frac{1}{W} \sum_{i=1}^{N} l_i p_i \qquad \text{where } \sum_{i=1}^{N} p_i = W. \tag{6.2}$$

To allow for the possibility of unsuccessful searches, first note that an unsuccessful search is performed to insert a new entry, which is accomplished by attaching a new leaf onto the tree. To represent *all* unsuccessful searches, let the lexicographic tree constructed on the given set be extended; that is, a pair of "vacant" leaves is *attached* to every original leaf of the tree, and one "vacant" leaf is *attached* to every internal node not already of out-degree 2.

Example 6.3

Figure 6.7 shows the extended tree for the lexicographic tree on the keyset K. In the extended binary tree, all of the N original nodes of the lexicographic tree have

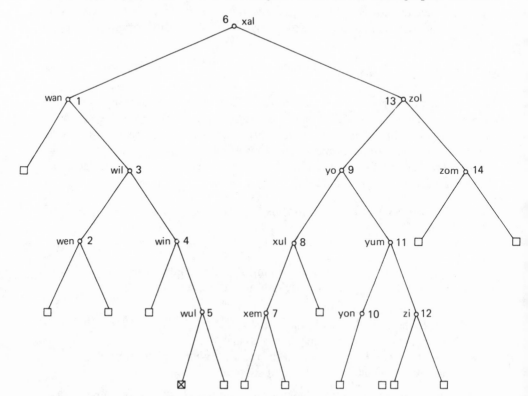

Fig. 6.7   Extended lexicographic tree for a keyset

out-degree 2. The extended tree therefore has $2N$ edges and $2N + 1$ nodes, so that $N + 1$ vacant nodes were added. Each vacant node represents the set of all keys that fall lexicographically between two actual keys of the original tree. In Fig. 6.7, if x is a possible key in the node X, then $wim < x < wul$.

To obtain an expression for the number of comparisons when searches may be either successful or unsuccessful, let $q_0, q_1, \ldots, q_N$, be the frequencies associated with the vacant nodes.[4] Then if l'_j is the depth of the vacant node with frequency q_j, the expected number of comparisons, allowing for unsuccessful searches, is given by

$$E(N) = \frac{1}{W}\left[\sum_{i=1}^{N} p_i l_i + \sum_{j=0}^{N} q_j(l'_j - 1)\right].\tag{6.3}$$

$$W = \sum_{i=1}^{N} p_i + \sum_{j=0}^{N} q_j$$

is called the *weight* of the tree. Equation (6.3) will serve as the basis for finding *optimal* search trees, for which the expected search time is minimized. Useful as such trees are, minimum average search time is not the only criterion one might wish to apply. For example, the search time can obviously range between 1 and N (the latter for a chain) and it might be desirable to minimize the *maximum* search time. Also, the times for insert and delete are important. Insertion is straightforward, but deletion clearly needs attention, since the subtree rooted at the node being deleted must be reattached to the tree. It is conceivable (as turns out to be the case) that minimizing the search time might result in poor average insertion/deletion times, and some trees that are less than optimal for one type of operation would still be preferable when all three are taken into consideration.

Traversal: Frequently, one wishes to traverse all the nodes of a tree, that is, per-form a walk through the tree in some systematic fashion in order to carry out a process at each node. For binary trees, three methods of traversal are possible, depending on the permutations of root, left subtree, and right subtrees.[5] These are called *preorder*, *symmetric*, and *postorder traversal*.

Preorder Traversal

- Visit the root.
- Traverse the left subtree in preorder sequence.
- Traverse the right subtree in preorder sequence.

The listing for the nodes of the binary tree rooted at *zol* in Fig. 6.7, traversed in preoder is

zol, yo, xul, xem, yum, yon, zi, zom.

The name "preorder" comes from the method of writing parenthesized algebraic ex-pressions in parentheses-free form. The *prefix* form of an algebraic expression is just

---

[4] q_i = probability that the key being sought lies between k_i and k_{i+1}
q_0 = probability that the search argument precedes k_1
q_N = probability that the search argument follows k_N.
[5] There are six permutations, but three of them are reflections of the other three.

the preorder listing of the nodes when the expression is presented as a binary tree. Thus in Fig. 1.13 the prefix representation of the expression (a+b)*(c+d) is given by the preorder listing of the nodes in the tree (i.e., *,+,a,b,+,c,d).

Symmetric Traversal

- Traverse the left subtree in symmetric sequence.
- Visit the root.
- Traverse the right subtree in symmetric sequence.

The listing for the nodes of the subtree rooted at *zol* in Fig. 6.7, traversed in symmetric order, is

xem, xul, yo, yon, yum, zi, zol, zom.

This is precisely the lexicographic order, as it must be, from the way in which lexicographic trees are defined.

Postorder Traversal

- Traverse the left subtree in postorder sequence.
- Traverse the right subtree in postorder sequence.
- Visit the root.

Postorder corresponds to the *postfix* form of parentheses-free expressions, in which the operator follows the operands. For the tree of Fig. 1.13, the postorder listing is

a,b,+,c,d,+,.*

For the subtree rooted at *zol* in Fig. 6.7, the postorder listing is

xem, xul, yon, zi, yum, yo, zom, zol.

A binary tree is not unambiguously defined when one of the above listings is given. For example, both trees in Fig. 6.8 have the same preorder listing: *a, b, c, d*. However, if the binary tree has all nodes to a given level, or if both the preorder and postorder listings are given, it is possible to reconstruct the tree unambiguously.[6]

Recursive algorithms for tree traversal are easy to write. Programs without explicit recursion can be written by using a stack. Let *lifo* be a stack capable of storing pointers,

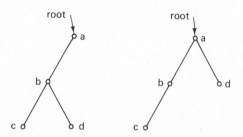

Fig. 6.8   Different binary trees with the same preorder listing

[6]Knuth, *Fundamental Algorithms*, p. 239.

and *root* be a pointer variable which references the root of a tree whose nodes are described by

$$\textbf{comp node} = \langle \textbf{node-ptr } \textit{llink}, \textbf{string } \textit{key}, \textbf{node-ptr } \textit{rlink} \rangle.$$

Assuming that visiting a node consists of printing the key at that node, Algorithm 6.1 describes a procedure for visiting a tree in symmetric sequence. Similar algorithms will carry out preorder or postorder processing.

Algorithm 6.1

```
procedure symmetric_list (root);
node-ptr root, ptr-stack lifo;
    lifo ⟸ Λ; /*initialize*/
    do while root ≠ Λ ∨ TOP(lifo)≠Λ;
        do while root ≠ Λ;
            PUSH(lifo, root);
            root ⟸ llink(@root);
        end /*youngest unlisted descendant found*/
        POP(lifo, root);
        if root ≠ Λ then
        do
            PRINT key(@root);
            root ⟸ rlink(@root);
        end
    end
end symmetric_list
```

6.2.2 Traversal and Search in Multiway Trees

For multiway, ordered trees, two methods of traversal and search suggest themselves: *depth-first* and *breadth-first*. In depth-first traversal, after the root is listed, the subtrees rooted at its filial set are listed in order. This is carried out recursively. For the subtree rooted at *w* in Fig. 6.3, this yields[7]

$$w,a,n,*,i,l,*,m,*,e,n,*,u,l,*.$$

This is just the preorder listing of the nodes in the corresponding binary tree (Fig. 6.6), and from the way in which the corresponding tree was constructed, it will be clear that this must be so.

In breadth-first traversal, the root is listed, then the nodes in the first level are listed in order, then those at the second level, and so on. For the *w*-rooted subtree of Fig. 6.3 this results in

$$w,a,i,e,u,n,l,m,n,l,*,*,*,*,*.$$

[7]In the context of this example, where the multiway tree is a positional tree, depth-first and breadth-first listings are not particularly meaningful, but in other contexts these traversals are important.

The expected search time in a multiway tree with N nodes can be written as

$$T(N) = a \cdot h + b \cdot \sum_{j=1}^{h} f(n_j), \tag{6.4}$$

where
$\quad\quad h =$ number of levels
$\quad\quad n_j =$ number of nodes at level j
$\quad\quad a =$ time to move from one level to the next
$\quad\quad f(n_j) =$ function dependent on the searching method within a level
$\quad\quad b =$ multiplier, characteristic of the time to access a node within a level.

Genealogical Searches and Threaded Links: The algorithms just described for traversal lead to simple algorithms (given later in this chapter) for finding the location of a given key. But certain other kinds of search are not easy to carry out. This is because in the storage tree representations of the logical trees described so far, all the pointers go in one direction: from a father to its filial set, or from one member of a filial set to the next member in sequence (from a child to its next younger sibling, to continue with the family terminology already adopted). Sometimes one wishes to determine the father of a node, or an older brother, and in the representations presented so far, this is difficult to do. The situation is very much like that encountered in trying to determine the predecessor of a given entry in a simple list. If we do not want to traverse the whole list, keeping track of predecessors on the way, it is necessary to have both forward and backward pointers (Fig. 4.10). Extra pointers inserted into a tree to provide (redundant) information about the tree structure, additional to that needed for establishing the filial relationship, are known as *threaded links*, and a tree with such pointers is a *threaded tree*. There turns out to be a very nice way of inserting threaded links in the binary tree equivalent of a multiway tree.[8]

A binary storage tree with N nodes has space for $2N$ links, of which only $N - 1$ are actually used to specify the tree edges. This leaves $N + 1$ possible links for information which is useful for searches of the type indicated. Suppose that a multiway tree is represented by its binary equivalent and that it is frequently necessary to find the father of a given key. In the storage tree corresponding to the binary tree (see Fig. 6.6), the eldest son relationship is established by the pointer in the left link, and the right link is the pointer to a node's next younger sibling. It follows that the right link of the youngest member of a filial set is null, and this is therefore a good candidate for a threaded link. If it is set to point back to the father, then the ability to trace ancestors is provided; also, since the father points to the oldest member of his filial set, the thread makes it possible to find older siblings of a given node.

Example 6.4

Figure 6.9 shows the storage representation of the binary tree rooted at w in Fig. 6.6, when threaded links as described have been added. There is a threaded link at each internal node not of out-degree 2. Once the nodes that have threaded links are identi-

---

[8]This technique was proposed in A. J. Perlis and C. Thornton, "Symbol Manipulation by Threaded Lists." *Communications of the ACM*, **3**, no. 4 (Apr. 1960), 195–204.

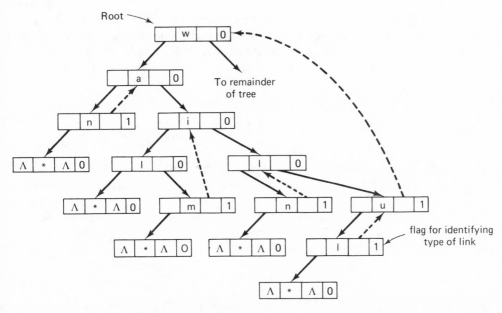

Fig. 6.9   Binary storage tree with right-threaded links

fied, it is not difficult to establish *where* the threads should point. In a symmetric listing the youngest sibling of a filial set is followed immediately by the father. Thus one only has to look at the successors of every youngest sibling in the symmetric listing in order to find the targets of the threaded links. For the tree of Fig. 6.9, the symmetric listing is

$$*,n\ddagger,a,*,l,*,m\ddagger,i,*,n\ddagger,e,*,l\ddagger,u\ddagger,w.$$

As can be seen, the youngest member of each filial set (identified by ‡ in the listing) is followed immediately by his father. Similarly, a path of left links in a binary tree traces the line of descent through the oldest son. When it is terminated because there are no more descendants, the left link becomes available for storing information that might be useful.

Using threaded links has its costs. In the storage mapping it is necessary to reserve a bit in every link to serve as a flag which distinguishes between ordinary links and threaded links. Also, the insertion and deletion algorithms will necessarily be more complex. But if genealogical type traces are important, the presence of the threaded links justifies these complications.

6.3 Positional Trees

We now examine in somewhat greater detail the three kinds of positional trees described earlier.

6.3.1 Multidimensional Indexes

The two features that are of particular importance for any directory are the storage requirements and the time to access or search for an entry. In a multidimensional index, storage is provided for every possible character that can occur at each level of the logical tree. At any level, access to the next level is obtained by applying an indexing operation, in which the character determines the index value. In effect, then, there is no search, only a constant access time at each level, and the number of comparisons to find a key becomes

$$E(N) = a \cdot h$$

where

$$a = \text{constant}$$
$$h = \text{number of characters.}$$

Not only is the access time simply proportional to the number of characters in the key, but the iteration constant can be expected to be small since only a few instructions are needed at each level.

If there are n_i possible characters in the ith position of the key (in addition to the end-of-key delimiter *), and keys can terminate at any level, then for a key of length h, the number of possible keys is given by

$$N = \sum_{j=1}^{h} \prod_{i=1}^{j} n_i \tag{6.5}$$

Assuming that the n_i are not too different in value, N will be $O\left(\prod_{i=1}^{h} n_i\right)$, reflecting the fact that about half the nodes are leaves. Writing $\prod_{i=1}^{h} n_i = \gamma^h$, where γ is the geometric mean of the number of characters, we have

$$N \approx \gamma^h \quad \text{or} \quad h = \log_\gamma N.$$

Thus in the multidimensional index, the access time is (approximately) proportional to the logarithm of the number of keys.

With regard to both storage requirements and access time, the multidimensional index behaves like a multidimensional array. The short access time is very desirable, but when the number of possible keys is much larger than the number of actual keys, as certainly happens when keys are constructed from alphabetic strings, the storage requirements are too great. The situation is very similar to that encountered with sparse matrices. It is necessary to look for some method that uses less storage, without, if possible, increasing the access cost too much.

6.3.2 De la Briandais Trees

A *de la Briandais tree* is a positional tree with character nodes in which keys correspond to a path from root to leaf, and every leaf corresponds to a key. In the original proposal the tree was multiway, but when the binary equivalent of a multiway tree is formed, the natural representation immediately leads to a storage representation with two links, and to simple algorithms for searching, insertion, and deletion.[9] Figure 6.10 shows the binary storage tree for the sample keyset, K. The left links of * nodes point to the storage area where attributes for the corresponding keys are to be found.

---

[9] In the literature these are often referred to as *doubly chained trees*.

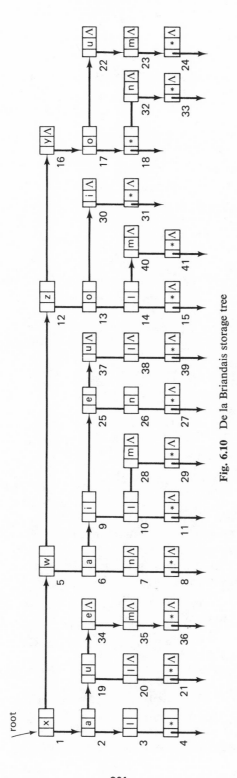

Fig. 6.10 De la Briandais storage tree

201

Algorithm 6.2 describes the searching procedure. A pointer, *root*, references the root of the tree, which has nodes described by

comp node = ⟨**node-ptr** *match*, **string** *info*, **node-ptr** *mismatch*⟩.

Algorithm 6.2   Searching a de la Briandais tree

```
procedure tree_search1 (root, key, index, place);
int index; node-ptr root, place;
string key; boolean searching;
   place ⟸ root;
   index ⟸ 1;
   seaching ⟸ place ≠ Λ ; /*initialize*/
   do while searching;
      if info (@ place) = key[index] then
      do
         if key[index] ≠ * then place ⟸ match (@ place);
         else searching ⟸ false;
         index ⟸ index + 1;
      end /*take next char.*/
      else
      do /*check next member of filial set*/
         if mismatch (@ place) = Λ then searching ⟸ false;
         else place ⟸ mismatch (@ place);
      end
   end
end tree_search1
```

The identifier, *key*, is a string, and *key*[*index*] selects the current character. Whether the key is present or not, a pointer *place* is set to point at the node where the search ended. On exit, the value of *index* indicates the last unmatched character; for a successful search it is one greater than the number of characters in the key.

The technique of representing linked lists by arrays (Section 5.2.3) is equally applicable to trees. Let *tree*[*j,k*] be an *array* where *j* references the row (corresponding to the node) and *k* the field. By interpreting *root* as an integer pointer to a row, and replacing

$$info (@ root) \text{ by } tree [root, 2]$$

$$match (@ root) \text{ by } tree [root, 1]$$

$$mismatch (@ root) \text{ by } tree [root, 3],$$

Algorithm 6.2 is valid. Table 6.1 shows the array for *tree* when the keys are inserted in the order given.

The insertion algorithm is a combination of searching and constructing a linked list. Algorithm 6.3 describes the procedure. It starts with a call to tree_search1 to determine *index*, the position of the first character to be inserted, and *place*, the pointer to the node where the insertion is to start. (If the key was found by tree_search1, tree_

TABLE 6.1 Array representation for de la Briandais tree

j Node Number	k = 1 Match	k = 2 Character Value	k = 3 Mismatch	j Node Number	k = 1 Match	k = 2 Character Value	k = 3 Mismatch
1	2	x	5	22	23	u	Λ
2	3	a	19	23	24	m	Λ
3	4	l	Λ	24	@ yum*	*	Λ
4	@ xal*‡	*	Λ	25	26	e	37
5	6	w	12	26	27	n	Λ
6	7	a	9	27	@ wen*	*	Λ
7	8	n	Λ	28	29	m	Λ
8	@ wan*	*	Λ	29	@ wim*	*	Λ
9	10	i	25	30	31	i	Λ
10	11	l	28	31	@ zi*	*	Λ
11	@ wil*	*	Λ	32	33	n	Λ
12	13	z	16	33	@ yom*	*	Λ
13	14	o	30	34	35	e	Λ
14	15	l	40	35	36	m	Λ
15	@ zol*	*	Λ	36	@ xem*	*	Λ
16	17	y	Λ	37	38	u	Λ
17	18	o	22	38	39	l	Λ
18	@ yo*	*	32	39	@ wul*	*	Λ
19	20	u	34	40	41	n	Λ
20	21	l	Λ	41	@ zom*	*	Λ
21	@ xul*	*	Λ				

‡@ xal* is a pointer to the data associated with the key xal*.

Algorithm 6.3 Insertion into a de la Briandais tree

```
procedure tree_insert(root, key, place);
int index; node-ptr key, place, next; boolean adding; string key;
call tree_search1 (root, key, index, place);
if index = ρ(key) + 1 then return;
CREATE (node, next);
mismatch (@ place) ⇐ next;
adding ⇐ key [index-1] ≠ * ; /*initialize*/
    do while adding;
        mismatch (@ next) ⇐ Λ;
        info (@ next) ⇐ key [index];
        place ⇐ next; /*new node inserted*/
        index ⇐ index+1;
        if key [index−1] ≠ * then
        do
            CREATE (node, next);
            match (@ place) ⇐ next;
        end
        else adding ⇐ false;
    end
end tree_insert
```

203

insert is bypassed.) After the key is inserted into the tree, *place* indicates where the pointer to data associated with the key is to be located. Deletion would be somewhat more complex. A node (including the terminator) can be deleted only if its *mismatch* link is null. The deletion must be started with the last character. Since links pointing back up the tree are not present, a record of the search path must be kept in temporary storage. This is precisely the situation in which threaded links are useful; deletion would be greatly simplified, but at the expense of insertion, which would require updating of the links. Without threaded links, the path down to the node being inserted can be stored in a stack.

At each level of the de la Briandais tree, the search time will be the time required to search the filial set. If n_i is the average number of nodes encountered at level i, and we make the assumption that the nodes are equally likely to occur, the expected number of comparisons for the ith level $= (1 + n_i)/2$. If the average number of levels is $\bar{h}$, the expected number of comparisons

$$E_p(N) \approx \sum_{i=1}^{\bar{h}} \frac{1 + n_i}{2} \approx \bar{h} \cdot \frac{\bar{n} + 1}{2},$$

where $\bar{n} = (1/\bar{h}) \sum_{i=1}^{\bar{h}} n_i$ is the size of the filial set averaged over all levels.

Thus for the de la Briandais tree, the search time is $O(\bar{n} \cdot \bar{h})$. As an approximation, we can take $N \approx \bar{n}^{\bar{h}}$, from which $\bar{h} \approx \log_{\bar{n}} N$. This is only an approximation because, going back to the multiway tree, it is clear that the out-degree of a node depends not only on the level, but also on the value of the nodes. (In English, for example, consonant characters are likely to be followed by a vowel, and the character q has only one possible successor.) Therefore, the expected number of nodes in the de la Briandais tree is a rather complicated function of the keyset. Still, accepting the approximation, the searching time is $O(\bar{n} \log_{\bar{n}} N)$, which is the same kind of dependence on N as in the multidimensional index. However, the iteration constant will be appreciably greater for the de la Briandais tree than that for the multidimensional index, since it is the expected time to search a level by linear search, rather than the time to locate a character by indexing.

Although the storage requirements for the de la Briandais tree are difficult to estimate, depending as they do on the grammar for constructing keys, it is apparent that as the ratio of actual keys to possible keys increases, the extra storage required grows slowly with the number of entries. As more actual keys are added, the situation is approached where only one or two new nodes per key are needed, one for the last character (if it is not already present) and one for the terminator. It is this property that is reflected in the equation $\bar{h} \approx \log_{\bar{n}} N$. In Fig. 6.10, 41 nodes (each capable of storing a character and two pointers) are needed for the key set K. This may be compared with 54 characters (including terminators) needed to store the keys as strings. If additional keys are added, the storage advantage of the de la Briandais tree, as compared to trees in which every key must be stored in full, becomes even more significant.

The de la Briandais representation has been used with considerable success in storing a very large dictionary of English words,[10] but its long search time makes it impractical compared to other methods. However, there are several techniques that can be used to shorten the search. Since the members of a filial set are linked in a chain through their right links, any of the techniques considered earlier for shortening the search in simple list can be applied. For example, the filial list can be maintained in sequence according to the alphabetic value of the node. In this case missing entries will be detected as soon as the node value is exceeded and the search time for them shortened accordingly. If the relative access frequencies for the different characters are known, characters that are used most often can be placed at the beginning of the list. Even if it is necessary to assume that all keys are equally likely to occur, this implies something about frequencies of the characters. As in any linked list, the members within a filial set should be ordered so that those with the largest frequencies (i.e., the largest number of terminal nodes attached to their subtrees) are at the highest level in the tree. They will then be encountered first.

Example 6.5

Figure 6.11 shows the de la Briandais binary tree of Fig. 6.10 with the nodes reordered so as to satisfy the criterion just described and minimize the search time. For the tree of Fig. 6.10,

$$E_p(N) = \frac{4 + 5 + 6 + 5 + 6 + 7 + 7 + 8 + 6 + 7 + 6 + 6 + 8 + 8}{14} = \frac{89}{14}.$$

For the optimal tree of Fig. 6.11,

$$E_p(N) = \frac{4 + 5 + 5 + 6 + 7 + 5 + 6 + 7 + 6 + 7 + 6 + 6 + 8 + 8}{14} = \frac{86}{14}.$$

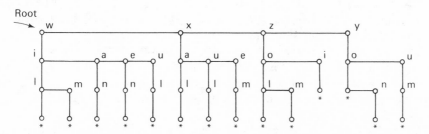

Fig. 6.11   Optimal binary tree for equally likely keys

Still another possibility for shortening the search is to make a *ternary* choice at each node instead of a binary choice. In the trees considered so far, each node determines a two-way branch, according as the key character matches or does not match the character stored in the node. By adding a third link, we can branch according as the key character is less (*llink*), equal to (*clink*), or greater than (*rlink*) the character stored

---

[10]S. M. Lamb and W. H. Jacobson, "A High-Speed Large-Computing Dictionary System," *Mechanical Translation*, **6** (Nov. 1961), 76–107.

in the node. A lexicographic comparison is being made at each node, so that using a ternary node is really equivalent to having a tree that is both positional and lexicographic. A tree with such nodes is a special case of the hybrid tree considered in Section 6.6.

6.3.3 Trie Directories

A *trie* is a positional tree in which the filial set following a character is represented as a pointer vector, with each component pointing to a member of the filial set.

Example 6.6

Figure 6.12 illustrates the logical trie for the keyset K, and Fig. 6.13 shows a corresponding storage tree. When searching for a key (or inserting one into the directory), a pointer is followed for each character in the key; *which* pointer is determined by an indexing operation based on the value of the character. Thus to search for *wul∗*, the tree is entered at the root. An indexing operation on *w* results in the second pointer being followed, since *w* is the second of the possible characters that appear. Another indexing operation on *u*, the second character in the key, results in the sixth pointer being followed from the location determined by the first pointer. Another comparison with *l* results in the choice of the second pointer. Following this leads to an ∗, which is recognized as the terminator, and a pointer leads to the attributes.

Within a level of the trie, the search time is constant and very fast; the number of levels is equal to the number of characters in the key. Altogether the search time is $O(a \cdot h)$, where a is a small constant, so that the trie behaves like the multidimensional index with regard to access. With regard to storage, the requirements for the trie will usually lie between those for the multidimensional index and the de la Briandais tree. The trie, like the de la Briandais tree, is formed by pruning the multidimensional index. But, because of the indexed nature of the access, whenever there is a pointer to *one* member of a filial set, space is reserved for pointers to *all* members of the set. The whole structure is very much like the pointer array for sparse matrices described in Section 5.4. Knuth estimates that for a k-way trie in which branching is terminated when there are s or fewer pointers emanating from a node, altogether $N/(s \cdot \ln k)$ character nodes will be needed.[11]

As already mentioned, in the storage implementation of the trie, it is necessary to reserve, in the filial set, a pointer for each possible character. For keys consisting of alphabetic characters, this means 27 pointers, one for the terminator and one for each letter of the alphabet. For keys in GK, where a given character can occur only in a particular level, it is possible to construct a simple table that gives the unique pointer position for each character (Table 6.2). The storage nodes for the pointer vectors need only contain enough pointers for the largest filial set (six in this case).[12] If one were

---

[11]Knuth, *Sorting and Searching*, Sec. 6.3.

[12]For the sake of uniformity, provision has been made for an ∗ in the first character of the key, but such a key would not be assigned. We can regard ∗ as a key that lexicographically precedes all existing keys, similar to Ω, which lexicographically follows all keys.

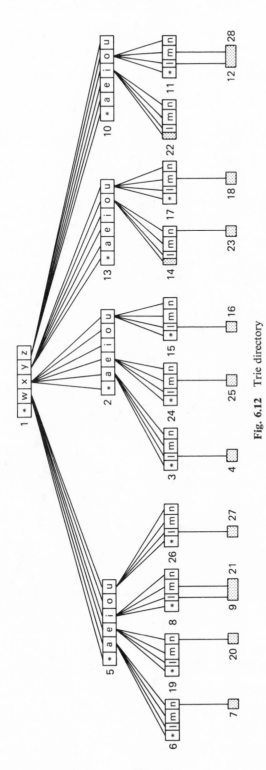

Fig. 6.12 Trie directory

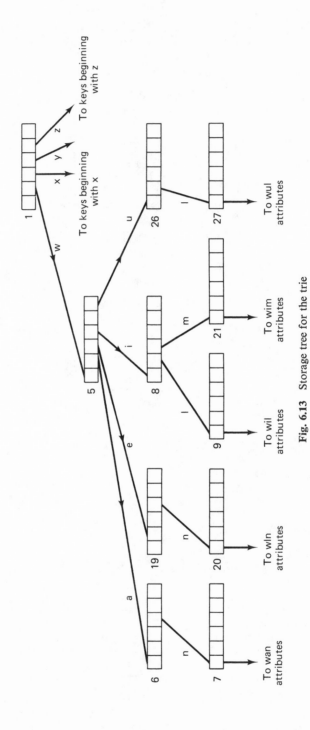

Fig. 6.13 Storage tree for the trie

prepared to use a different kind of node at each level, then level 1 nodes would need only four pointers, and level 3 nodes four. Note that it is not necessary to store the character values for the nodes; these are implied by the pointer that is chosen.

TABLE 6.2   Pointer number for characters

Character	* a b c d e f g h i j k l m n o p q r s t u v w x y z
Pointer Position	1 2 – – – 3 – – – 4 – – 2 3 4 5 – – – – – 6 – 2 3 4 5

Algorithm 6.4 shows how very short the searching program is for the trie directory. Nodes are described by the declaration

$$\textbf{comp node} = \langle \textbf{node-pointer array } p[1:6] \rangle,$$

Algorithm 6.4   Searching a trie

```
procedure trie_search(root, key, place);
int i, j; node-ptr root, place;
int-array num[1:27]; string key;
i ⇐ 1; j ⇐ num[key[1]]; /*initialize*/
    do while key[i] ≠ * ∧ p[j](@ root) ≠ Λ
            root ⇐ p[j](@ root); /*new subtree*/
            i ⇐ i+1;              /*new character*/
            j ⇐ num [key[i]];
    end
    place ⇐ p[1] (@ root); /*locate pointer*/
end trie_search
```

where p[1:6] is a vector of dimension 6, each of whose components is a pointer to a node. The notation p[j](@root) describes the selection of the jth pointer in the node referenced by *root*. Again *key* is a vector, and *key*[i] identifies the character in the ith position. *Num* [*key*[i]] specifies the pointer position in a node for the character *key*[i] according to Table 6.2. On exit, the parameter *place* is a pointer to the data for the key being sought if the key is present. It contains Λ if the key is missing (it is assumed that the trie has been initialized by putting Λ in all pointer positions).

As before, if the trie were to be represented as an array, the program would be very similar. Table 6.3 shows the array that would result if the keys in K were to be inserted in the sequence given by Π_K.

6.4 Lexicographic Trees

We return to consider lexicographic trees. These are constructed by inserting keys into the tree by comparing the key value with nodes starting at the root, and following left or right branches depending on whether the key being inserted is less than or greater than the one with which it is being compared. Our main interest is in minimizing the search time for lexicographic trees, but first two observations can be made.

TABLE 6.3   Array representation for trie

Row Number	Pointer					
	1	2	3	4	5	6
1	Λ	5	2	13	10	Λ
2	Λ	3	24	Λ	Λ	15
3	Λ	4	Λ	Λ	Λ	Λ
4	@ xal*‡	Λ	Λ	Λ	Λ	Λ
5	Λ	6	19	8	Λ	26
6	Λ	Λ	Λ	7	Λ	Λ
7	@ wan*	Λ	Λ	Λ	Λ	Λ
8	Λ	9	21	Λ	Λ	Λ
9	@ wil*	Λ	Λ	Λ	Λ	Λ
10	Λ	Λ	Λ	22	11	Λ
11	Λ	12	28	Λ	Λ	Λ
12	@ zol*	Λ	Λ	Λ	Λ	Λ
13	Λ	Λ	Λ	Λ	14	17
14	@ yo*	Λ	Λ	23	Λ	Λ
15	Λ	16	Λ	Λ	Λ	Λ
16	@ xul*	Λ	Λ	Λ	Λ	Λ
17	Λ	Λ	18	Λ	Λ	Λ
18	@ yum*	Λ	Λ	Λ	Λ	Λ
19	Λ	Λ	Λ	20	Λ	Λ
20	@ wen*	Λ	Λ	Λ	Λ	Λ
21	@ wim*	Λ	Λ	Λ	Λ	Λ
22	@ zi*	Λ	Λ	Λ	Λ	Λ
23	@ yon*	Λ	Λ	Λ	Λ	Λ
24	Λ	Λ	25	Λ	Λ	Λ
25	@ xem*	Λ	Λ	Λ	Λ	Λ
26	Λ	27	Λ	Λ	Λ	Λ
27	@ wul*	Λ	Λ	Λ	Λ	Λ
28	@ zom*	Λ	Λ	Λ	Λ	Λ

‡@ *xal** is a pointer to the data associated with the key *xal**.

1. Constructing the lexicographic tree is equivalent to performing a sort on the keyset. After the tree is completed, traversing it in symmetric fashion will produce the list in lexicographic order. When the tree of Fig. 6.7 is traversed in symmetric order, the sequence ⟨*wan, wen, wil, win, wul, xal, xem, xul, yo, yon, yum, zi, zal, zom*⟩ results. Putting it another way, the permutation

$$\Pi_K = \langle 6, 1, 3, 13, 9, 8, 11, 2, 4, 12, 16, 7, 5, 14 \rangle,$$

corresponding to the original sequence of the keys, has been converted to the natural sequence ⟨1, 2, . . . , 14⟩. Sorting by constructing a lexicographic tree is called, appropriately enough, *Treesort*.

2. Suppose that the keys are sorted, and a tree is constructed by inserting keys in the sequence in which they would be encountered as a binary search is performed on the series members in turn. The resulting tree is shown in Fig. 6.14. The first key to be inserted is *xem*, since it has position $\left\lfloor \left(\frac{1+14}{2} \right) \right\rfloor = 7$ and it is

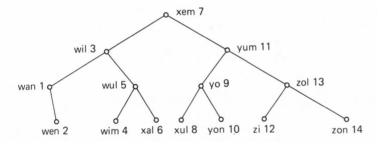

Fig. 6.14 Complete lexicographic tree

the first key that would be encountered in a binary search on *wan*. The second to
be inserted is *wil*, since it would be encountered next. The insertion is continued
in this way until all nodes have been entered. The tree is complete (i.e., there are
leaves only at the last two levels). It also has the property that for any node, the
orders of its left and right subtrees differ by at most one. This follows from
the fact that if *l* and *f* are the rank (i.e., the positions in the ordered list) of the
extremal nodes of a subtree, the root will have rank $\lfloor(l+f)/2\rfloor$. A complete
tree will not be unique unless it is completely filled at every level, since $\lceil(l+f)/2\rceil$
could equally well be chosen as the construction rule.

6.4.1 Optimal Trees with Equally Weighted Keys

For a given *N*, a complete binary tree will have the minimum height (i.e., number
of levels). If all the keys have equal weight (i.e., are equally likely to occur), then the
optimal tree, that with minimum expected search time, must be complete. For if a
noncomplete subtree is present, it can be replaced by a complete tree with a shorter
search time. It follows that the optimal tree must have *every* subtree complete and is
therefore complete itself.

In a complete tree when all keys have equal weight, $E_p(N)$, the number of comparisons required for a successful search is given by Eq. (6.1). From this it is easy to
derive an expression for a binary tree in which all levels, down to and including the
*h*th, are filled. Such a tree will be called *completely filled* and be denoted by B_h. For it,
the number of nodes $N = 1 + 2 + \ldots + 2^{h-1} = 2^h - 1$, and $h = \log(N + 1) \approx
\log N$. If $I(N)$ is the path length, summed over all *N* nodes for this tree, then

$$I(N) = 1 + 2 \cdot 2 + 3 \cdot 2^2 + \ldots + h \cdot 2^{h-1}$$
$$2I(N) = 1 \cdot 2 + 2 \cdot 2^2 + \ldots + h \cdot 2^h$$
$$I(N) = h \cdot 2^h - (1 + 2 + \ldots 2^{h-1})$$
$$= 2^h \cdot (h - 1) + 1.$$

Thus for B_h, the expected number of comparisons on a successful search,

$$E_p(N) = \frac{I(N)}{N} = \frac{2^h(h-1) + 1}{2^h - 1} = (h - 1 + 2^{-h})(1 - 2^{-h})^{-1}$$

$$\approx h - 1 + \frac{h}{2^h} \approx \log(N + 1) - 1 + \frac{\log N}{N} \qquad (6.6)$$

By induction on N it can be shown that this same approximation holds for a complete tree that is not filled [i.e., one for which $2^h < N + 1 < 2^{h+1}$]. The maximum search time is $h \approx \log{(N + 1)}$, so that the difference between the maximum and the average number of comparisons is only 1. This should not be surprising, since in a filled tree half the nodes are at the bottom level.

6.4.2 Random Binary Lexicographic Trees

When a lexicographic tree is grown by inserting keys into the tree randomly, it will usually have long and short branches. The worst situation arises when a tree is constructed by inserting the members of a lexicographically ordered set in turn, in which case the tree will be a chain of N entries, and the expected number of accesses of a random search is $(N + 1)/2$. The question arises whether a randomly constructed tree is highly skewed and behaves like this worst case, or it is more like the complete tree whose search time is $O(\log N)$. To answer this, note that there is a lexicographic tree, T_j, associated with each permutation, Π_j, of the natural numbers $1, \ldots, N$. Taking the trees corresponding to the $N!$ permutations and computing the average search time over all of these gives the search time for a random tree.

Before doing this it is necessary to define some additional terms on paths lengths in binary trees, and derive relationships between them. Let $I_j(N)$ be the sum of the path lengths over all internal nodes in the extended binary T_j constructed on the permutation $\Pi_j(N)$, and $L_j(N)$ be the sum of the path lengths over all leaf or external nodes. Since there are N internal, and $N + 1$ external, nodes,

$$I_j(N) = \sum_{i=1}^{N} l_i(T_j) \qquad \text{where } l_i \text{ is the level of internal node } i$$

$$L_j(N) = \sum_{i=0}^{N} l'_i(T_j) - 1 \qquad \text{where } l'_i \text{ is the level of external node } i.$$

$$(6.7)$$

In each case l_i or l'_i is measured by the number of nodes encountered in traversing a path from the root to the node in question, with the root having level 1.

For the tree T_j constructed on $\Pi_j(N)$,

$$E_p(N) = \frac{I_j(N)}{N} \quad \text{and} \quad E_a(N) = \frac{L_j(N)}{N} + 1.$$

$$(6.8)$$

Averaging over all $N!$ trees,

$$E_p(N) = \frac{1}{N!} \sum_{j=1}^{N!} \frac{I_j(N)}{N} = \frac{I(N)}{(N \cdot N!)}$$

$$(6.9)$$

$$E_a(N) = \frac{1}{N!} \sum_{j=1}^{N!} \frac{L_j(N)}{N} + 1 = \frac{L(N)}{(N + 1)!},$$

$$(6.10)$$

where

$$I(N) = \sum_{j=1}^{N!} I_j(N) \quad \text{and} \quad L(N) = \sum_{j=1}^{N!} L_j(N).$$

Thus to find the average search times for successful and unsuccessful searches in a randomly grown tree we could evaluate $I(N)$ and $L(N)$. In fact, this is unnecessary, since there is an equation relating $E_p(N)$ and $E_a(N)$.

There is an immediate connection between $I_j(N)$ and $L_j(N)$. In computing $I_j(N)$, any internal node, which, by virtue of its level number contributes m to $I_j(N)$, will contribute $m + 1$ to $L_j(N)$. Thus $I_j(N)$ and $L_j(N)$ differ by 1 for each internal node in $I_j(N)$, and altogether

$$I_j(N) = L_j(N) - N$$

$$\sum_{j=1}^{N!} I_j(N) = \sum_{j=1}^{N!} L_j(N) - N \cdot N!,$$

and from Eqs. (6.9) and (6.10),

$$E_p(N) = \frac{N+1}{N} E_a(N) - 1. \tag{6.11}$$

This equation, which relates the expected lengths for successful and unsuccessful searches in a binary tree, was discovered by Hibbard.[13] To illustrate it, the tree T_K, for the permutation $= \langle 6, 1, 3, 13, 9, 8, 11, 2, 4, 12, 10, 7, 5, 14 \rangle$, was shown in Fig. 6.7. For this tree

$$I_K(N) = 1 + 2 \cdot 2 + 3 \cdot 3 + 4 \cdot 4 + 4 \cdot 5 = 50$$

$$L_K(N) = 1 \cdot 2 + 2 \cdot 3 + 4 \cdot 4 + 8 \cdot 5 = 64$$

and

$$L_K(N) - I_K(N) = 14 = N.$$

Another equation between $E_p(N)$ and $E_a'N)$ is obtained by observing that the number of comparisons needed to find a key is exactly one more than is needed to enter the key into the tree. The same is true for the expected numbers.

$$E_p(N) = 1 + \frac{E_a(0) + E_a(1) + \ldots + E_a(N-1)}{N}. \tag{6.12}$$

Combining this with Eq. (6.11) yields

$$(N+1)E_a(N) = 2N + E_a(0) + E_a(1) + \ldots + E_a(N-1).$$

To solve this recurrence equation for $E_a(N)$, we write

$$NE_a(N-1) = 2(N-1) + E_a(0) + \ldots + E_a(N-2).$$

Subtracting this from the previous equation,

$$(N+1)E_a(N) - NE_a(N-1) = 2 + E_a(N-1)$$

or

$$E_a(N) = E_a(N-1) + \frac{2}{N} + 1.$$

Substituting repeatedly, and noting that $E_a(0) = 1$, gives

$$E_a(N) = 2\left(\frac{1}{2} + \frac{1}{3} + \ldots + \frac{1}{N} + 1\right). \tag{6.13}$$

Writing H_N for the harmonic series $1 + 1/2 + \ldots + 1/N$, this becomes

$$E_a(N) = 2H_{N+1} - 2.$$

[13]T. Hibbard, "Some Combinatorial Properties of Certain Trees," *Journal of the ACM*, **9**, no. 1 (Jan. 1962), 11–28.

Now $\lim\limits_{N\to\alpha} H_N = \ln N - \gamma$, where $\gamma =$ Euler's constant $= 0.57722$. The approximation becomes good only for relatively large N, but, accepting it,

$$E_a(N) \approx 2\ln(N+1) - 2\gamma - 2 \approx 1.386 \log N - 3.15. \tag{6.14}$$

Also,

$$E_p(N) = \frac{N+1}{N} E_a(N) - 1 \approx 2\ln(N+1) - 2\gamma - 3$$

$$= 1.386 \log N - 4.15. \tag{6.15}$$

Since $E_p(N) \approx \log N$ for the complete tree, the time to find a key in a randomly constructed tree is only 40 per cent greater. Thus in spite of the possibility that a random tree might have $E_p(N) = (N+1)/2$, most such trees will not be too different from the complete tree. For T_K in Fig. 6.7,

$$E_a(N) = \frac{64}{15} = 4.27 \qquad E_a(N) = 2H_{N+1} - 2 = 2\cdot 3.318 - 2 \approx 4.64$$

$$E_p(N) = \frac{50}{14} = 3.51 \qquad E_p(N) = \frac{15}{14} \cdot E_a(N) - 1 \approx 3.96.$$

For the complete version (Fig. 6.14), $E_p(N) = 45/14 = 3.21$.

The searching algorithm for a lexicographic tree is very similar to those already studied. Algorithm 6.5 gives the procedure. Nodes are described by the declaration

comp node $= \langle$**node-ptr** *llink*, **attribute-ptr** *clink*, **node-ptr** *rlink*, **string** *info*$\rangle$.

On exit, the pointer *place* indicates where a match was found, or to which node the key should be attached if it is not already in the tree.

Algorithm 6.5   Searching a lexicographic tree

```
procedure tree_search2(root, key, place);
node-ptr root, place; string key;
boolean searching;
place ⇐ root;
searching ⇐ place ≠ Λ; /*initialize*/
    do while searching;
        if key = info (@ place) then searching ⇐ false; /*key found*/
        else if key < info (@ place) then
            do
                if llink (@ place) = Λ then searching ⇐ false;
                else place ⇐ llink (@ place); /*continue on left*/
            end
        else do
                if rlink (@ place) = Λ then searching ⇐ false;
                else place ⇐ rlink (@ place); /*continue on right*/
            end
    end
end tree_search2
```

Deletion, as always, is somewhat more complicated than insertion, but a consideration of possible cases soon reveals how to do it.

- Deleting a node that is a leaf, or has either no left subtree or no right subtree
  presents no problem. In the former case, nothing has to be done except to set a
  pointer to Λ (and release the storage for the deleted node). In the latter case, the
  root of the subtree which is present replaces the deleted node. For example, in
  Fig. 6.7 *wul* is deleted by setting the pointer to it (i.e., the *rlink* of *wim*) to Λ.
  Also *wan* is deleted by making the pointer to it point to its right subtree, rooted
  at *wil*; similarly, *xul* is deleted by making the pointer to it point to its left subtree rooted at *xem*.
- If a node that has both left and right subtrees is to be deleted, it can be replaced
  by its lexicographic successor, the first node encountered in a symmetric traversal of the right subtree of the deletion node. This successor will always have its
  llink value $= \Lambda$, and therefore when it is removed, either no new moves are
  needed, or *its* right subtree has to be reattached at the point of deletion. Thus
  in Fig. 6.7, *xal* is deleted by replacing it with *xem*, its successor; since *xem* is a
  leaf, no further moves are needed. In Fig. 6.5 *wil* is deleted by replacing it with
  xal its successor; *xal* is replaced by the root of its right subtree, *yo*.

With these rules a deletion procedure is easily written. For the deletion it is necessary to reconstruct the path from the root to the node being deleted. The obvious way
to do this is by recording the path in a stack, but a technique due to Schorr and Waite,
based on pointer reversal, makes it possible to avoid using a stack (see Section 8.4).

Besides the times for search, insertion, and deletion of entries in a search tree, the
time to *construct* a random tree is of interest. This will be measured by the total number
of comparisons made as keys are added. For a random tree with N keys, the total
number of comparisons to construct the tree

$$= E_a(0) + E_a(1) + \ldots + E_a(N-1)$$

$$\approx \sum_{j=1}^{N-1} [2 \cdot \ln (j+1) - 2\gamma - 2] \approx 2 \cdot \ln N! - 3.15N.$$

Applying Stirling's approximation,

$$\ln N! \approx (N + \tfrac{1}{2}) \ln N - N.$$

The number of comparisons to construct a random tree is therefore about

$$1.386N \log N - 5.15N + 0.69 \log N \qquad \text{which is } O(N \log N).$$

It follows that the order of the expected time for Treesort is the same as that when
sorting the keys by merging or Quicksort.

6.5 Constrained Trees

Although the number of comparisons to find a key in a random tree is $\approx 1.4 \log N$,
in worst cases it can go as high as N. If trees with hundreds of thousands of names are
to be constructed, one would like to guard against extreme cases, and in this section

techniques for doing so are examined. All of them are based on placing some constraints on how the tree grows as new nodes are inserted. The effect of the constraints is to prevent the height of the tree (i.e., the maximum level) from becoming too great.

6.5.1 Height-Balanced Trees

The first type of constrained trees to be proposed was the *height-balanced tree*, in which for any node, the height of the left and right subtrees may differ by at most 1.[14] Figure 6.15 illustrates some height-balanced trees, along with one where the height constraint is violated at one node.

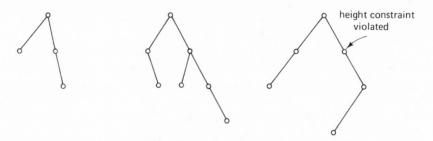

Fig. 6.15   Height-balanced trees

It is not too difficult to obtain bounds on the search path length for height-balanced trees. These are found by looking for trees that have the least and greatest heights within the constraint. The completely filled tree, B_h, has least height of all N-node trees, and it is height-balanced, so that the lower bound is determined from $N = 2^h - 1$ or $h_{min} = \log(N + 1)$. To determine h_{max}, we can ask what is the minimum number of nodes possible in a completely filled tree of height h. If F_h is such a tree with root v, and its left and right subtrees are F_l and F_r, we can write $F_h = \langle F_l, v, F_r \rangle$. Now one of F_l or F_r must be of height $h - 1$, say F_l, and the other, F_r, of height $h - 1$ or $h - 2$. Since F_h has the *minimum* number of nodes, F_l must be of the form F_{h-1}, and F_r of the form F_{h-2}: that is,

$$F_h = \langle F_{h-1}, v, F_{h-2} \rangle.$$

Writing $|F_h| = N$, for the order of the tree,

$$|F_h| = 1 + |F_{h-1}| + |F_{h-2}|. \tag{6.16}$$

If F_1 and F_2 are taken as trees of one and two nodes, respectively, the next few members are shown in Fig. 6.16. They are known as the *Fibonacci trees*. Their orders are determined by the well-known Fibonacci series, 0, 1, 1, 2, 3, 5, 8, 13, . . . , whose terms

---

[14]These are also called *AVL trees*, after the initials of the authors who first described them. See G. M. Adel'son-Vel'skii and E. M. Landis, "An Algorithm for the Organization of Information," *Doklady Akademii Nauk SSSR*, **16**, no. 2 (1962), 263–266 (Russian). English translation in *Soviet Math. Doklady*, **3** (1962), 1259–1262.

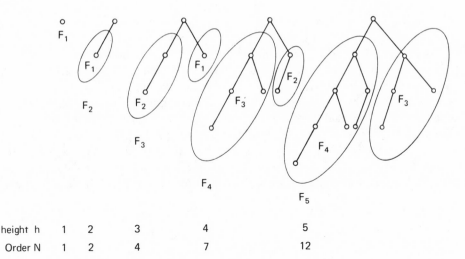

height h	1	2	3	4	5
Order N	1	2	4	7	12

Fig. 6.16　Fibonocci trees

satisfy the difference equation

$$f_{n+2} = f_{n+1} + f_n \qquad \text{where } n = \ge 0 \quad \text{and} \quad f_0 = 0, f_1 = 1. \tag{6.17}$$

From this and Eq. (6.16) it follows that

$$|F_h| = f_{h+2} - 1 = N.$$

Solution of the difference equation for the Fibonacci numbers (available in standard texts) yields

$$f_n = \frac{1}{\sqrt{5}}(\Phi^n - \bar{\Phi}^n) \qquad \text{where } \Phi = \frac{1}{2(1 + \sqrt{5})} \quad \text{and} \quad \bar{\Phi} = \frac{1}{2(1 - \sqrt{5})},$$

from which

$$\frac{\Phi^h}{\sqrt{5}} - 1 < f_h < \frac{\bar{\Phi}^h}{\sqrt{5}} + 1.$$

Hence

$$\frac{\Phi^{h+2}}{\sqrt{5}} - 1 < f_{h+2} = N + 1,$$

and taking logarithms to the base 2,

$$(h + 2) \cdot \log \Phi < \log (N + 2) + \log \sqrt{5}$$

and

$$h_{\max} < 1.44 \log (N + 2) - 0.33. \tag{6.18}$$

Thus for a height-balanced tree with N nodes,

$$\log N < h < 1.44 \log (N + 2).$$

The *expected* path length for height-balanced trees is difficult to calculate, but empirical evidence indicates that it behaves like $\log N + c$, where $c \approx 0.25$.[15]

---

[15]Knuth, *Sorting and Searching*, p. 460.

Both insertion and deletion in height-balanced trees need an analysis of cases. For insertion to be efficient, it is necessary to carry a balance flag in each node. The flag is "equal," "left," or "right" according as the left and right subtrees rooted at the node have the same height, the left is greater, or the right is greater. When a new node is being inserted, it may be necessary to rearrange the tree, and the flag makes it unnecessary to retrieve the complete path in order to determine which parts of the tree are affected. It turns out that there are two basic cases where adjustments are needed (two others are reflections), and these are illustrated in Fig. 6.17 (the flags there are designated by balance signs). In the first case, $B+$, the node being inserted lexicographically, follows B in the range $\langle A, B \rangle$ specified by the node pair where the imbalance occurred, [Fig. 6.17(a)]. The correction is to apply a rotation, R1, in which the root is moved

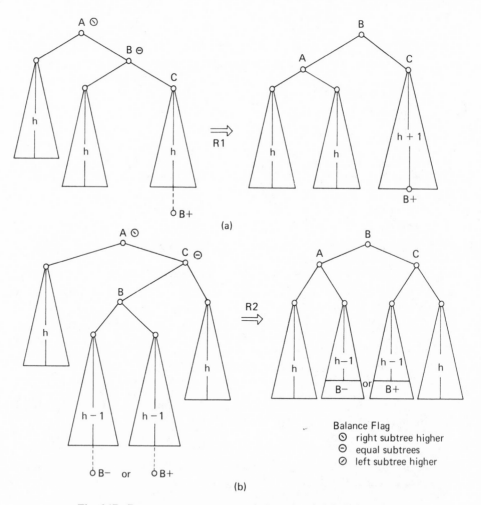

Fig. 6.17 Rearrangements to restore balance in a height-balanced tree

down one, and a subtree pointer is reattached to the old root. In the second case the node being inserted, lies within the lexicographic range $\langle A, B, C \rangle$ of the part of the tree requiring rearrangement. It may precede B [shown as $B-$ in Fig. 6.17(b)], or follow B (shown as $B+$). The correction is to apply a "double rotation," R2, in which the roots of two subtrees are reattached.

Example 6.7

Figure 6.18 illustrates the growth of the height-balanced tree constructed on the permutation Π_K representing the keyset $\langle xem, \ldots, zom \rangle$. During the growth seven rearrangements were required, the last two of type R1 and the others of type R2. Although this is a considerable number of rearrangements, the effect in each is local, and only a few pointer changes are needed to carry one out. When deleting a key, however, it is possible that rearrangements will be propagated. The situation is illustrated in Fig. 6.19, where the key 6 in the height-balanced tree constructed on $\langle 6, 1, 3, 13, 9, 8, 11, 2, 4, 12 \rangle$ is to be deleted. As in deletion from a simple lexicographic tree, the basic rule is to replace the node being deleted by its lexicographic successor. The resulting move can necessitate rotations of the same types as were encountered during insertion. These rotations may, in turn, initiate rotations that can be propagated all the way down the tree. However, in both insertion and deletion, the upper bound on the tree is proportional to the height of the tree and is therefore $O(\log N)$ in each case.

When programming the deletion algorithm in a height-balanced tree, it is convenient to use a stack for recording the path from the root to the place being sought. As in other deletion algorithms, there are advantages in recording threaded links for retracing.

Although the insertion and deletion algorithms are more complicated than for unconstrained lexicographic trees, height-balanced trees have other advantages than just guaranteeing that the search time will not be too long. Using them, it is also possible to develop good algorithms for concatenating and partitioning keysets.

6.5.2 Weight-Balanced Trees

Since a complete tree has the property that the left and right subtrees at any root are nearly of the same order, one might attempt to construct well-balanced trees by restructuring after insertion so as to maintain completeness. This is not satisfactory, because inserting a single node into a complete tree can propagate a series of moves that affects half the tree. Nievergelt and Reingold suggest, instead, that a parameter p be allowed to determine the possible imbalance between left and right subtrees.[16] Rearrangements become necessary only when the imbalance factor is exceeded, so p can be adjusted to achieve a desirable compromise between keeping the search time short and reducing the frequency of tree rearrangements.

[16]J. Nievergelt and E. M. Reingold, "Binary Search Trees of Bounded Balance," *SIAM Journal on Computing*, **2**, no. 1 (Mar. 1973), 33–43.

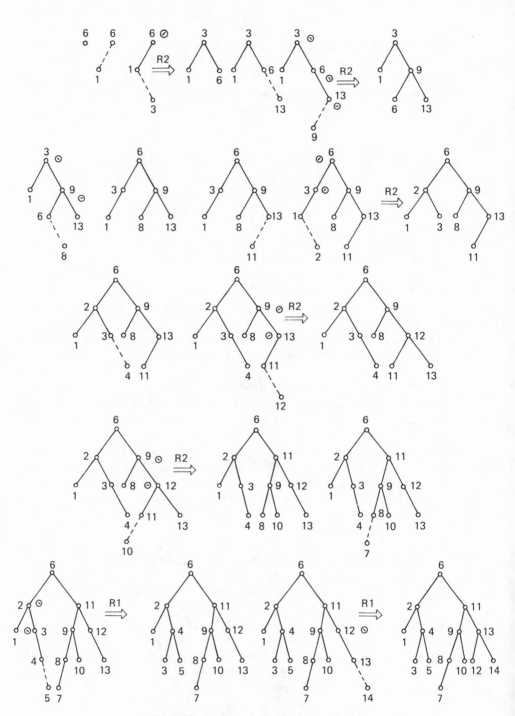

Fig. 6.18 Growth of a height-balanced tree

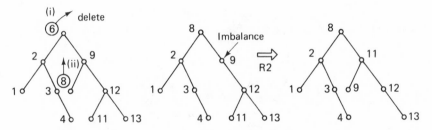

Fig. 6.19 Deletion in a height-balanced tree

Let $T_N = \langle T_l, v, T_r \rangle$ be a binary tree on N vertices, where T_l is the left subtree, T_r the right subtree, and the root v is a single vertex. Then

$$|T_N| = N = |T_l| + |T_r| + 1.$$

The *root balance* of T, $\rho(T)$, is defined as

$$\rho(T_N) = \frac{|T_l| + 1}{N + 1}.\tag{6.19}$$

It follows at once that

$$0 < \frac{1}{N+1} \le \rho(T) \le \frac{N}{N+1} < 1.$$

A binary tree, T_N, is said to be of *bounded balance* α, or of type BB[α], for $0 \le \alpha \le 1/2$, if:

1. $\alpha \le \rho(T) \le 1 - \alpha$.
2. Both T_l and T_r are BB[α].

For completely balanced trees B_h, $N = 2^h - 1$ and $\rho(T) = 1/2$, so they are BB[1/2]. The Fibonacci trees can be shown to be of type BB[1/3]. These two kinds of trees play limiting roles because there are no trees with $1/3 < \alpha < 1/2$.

To see this, suppose that T is not completely balanced, (i.e., is not a member of the set BB[1/2]). Then T must have subtrees that are not BB[1/2]. Let T' be the smallest such tree. Since T' is minimal, both its subtrees, T'_l and T'_r, are completely balanced, with, respectively, $2^l - 1$ and $2^r - 1$ nodes ($l \ne r$ since T' is not BB[1/2]). Therefore,

$$\rho(T') = \frac{2^l}{2^l + 2^r} = \frac{1}{1 + 2^{r-l}}$$

which is $\le 1/3$ or greater than $1/2$ according as r is greater or less than l.

Although height-balanced and weight-balanced trees seem alike superficially, they are quite different in that neither class contains the other. Thus the tree (B_2, v, F_4) shown in Fig. 6.20 is of type BB[1/3], but it is not height-balanced. Also the balance at the root of the height-balanced tree (F_h, v, B_h) is

$$\frac{1}{1 + \sqrt{\frac{5}{4}} \left(\frac{4}{1 + \sqrt{5}} \right)^{h+2}},$$

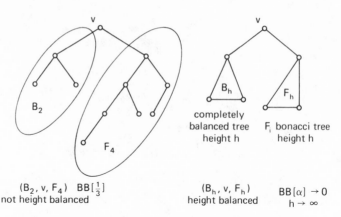

completely
balanced tree F_i bonacci tree
   height h   height h

(B_2, v, F_4) $BB[\frac{1}{3}]$
not height balanced

(B_h, v, F_h) $BB[\alpha] \to 0$
height balanced $h \to \infty$

Fig. 6.20   Height-balanced and weight-balanced trees

which approaches 0 as $h \Rightarrow \infty$, so that keeping a tree height-balanced does not assure that any nonzero weight balance will be maintained.

The main results of interest about weight-balanced trees are their average and maximum search path lengths, h_{av} and h_{max}. By induction on N, it is not difficult to show that if T is BB[α], then

$$h_{max} \leq \frac{\log(N+1) - 1}{\log(1/1 - \alpha)}.$$

Also,[17]

$$h_{av} = E_p(N) \approx \frac{1}{H(\alpha)}\left(1 + \frac{1}{N}\right)\log(N+1) - 2. \tag{6.21}$$

where

$$H(\alpha) = -\alpha \log \alpha - (1 - \alpha)\log(1 - \alpha).$$

Although h_{max} can get large for arbitrarily small α, even for $\alpha = 1/3$, which leads to moderately skewed trees, $1/H(\alpha) \approx 1.09$. For such trees of type BB[1/3], the maximum search length is only 9 per cent greater than for a completely balanced tree, and the average search length is increased by 3 per cent.

There are two costs in maintaining a tree to be of BB[α].

1. It is necessary to store the root balance with each node and update this quantity as insertions and deletions are made.
2. If changes violate the condition $\alpha \leq \rho \leq 1 - \alpha$, the tree has to be rearranged. Provided that $\alpha \leq 1 - \sqrt{2}/2$ (0.2228), it can be shown that one of the same two kinds of rotations R1 and R2 encountered with height-balanced trees will restore the weight balance. It is possible that a single insertion will give rise to a chain of rotations. But if the trees are assumed to be distributed so that the root balance is uniform in the range $(\alpha, 1 - \alpha)$, it can be shown that the number of rotations per insertion is less than $2/(1 - 2\alpha)$. This is independent of N so that the cost of rebalancing is not excessive.

[17]J. Nievergelt and C. K. Wong, "On Binary Search Trees," in *Information Processing 71*, Vol. 1 (Amsterdam: North-Holland Publishing Company, 1972), pp. 91–98.

Example 6.8

The insertion and deletion algorithms for weight-balanced trees are comparable with those for height-balanced trees. Figure 6.21 shows the weight-balanced tree grown on the keyset K. Note that inserting key 10 caused two rearrangements.

The root balance information carried in each node of a weight-balanced tree turns out to be useful for other operations on trees. Such operations as finding the kth item, the qth quartile, or the number of keys that lie lexicographically between two given keys can be carried out in time $O(\log N)$, because of the ρ factor present in each node.

6.5.3 Multiway Lexicographic Trees

Still another way of controlling the growth of trees and preventing them from becoming too highly skewed is to depart from binary trees, allowing more than two branches at a node. The basic technique is to store several keys at a node, along with pointers that indicate a continuation path according to the position of the key being sought in the key list. Figure 6.22 shows the node for a multiway lexicographic tree. There are $m - 1$ keys, $k_1, \ldots, k_{m-1}$ ordered lexicographically, and m pointers $p_1, \ldots, p_m$ in each node. Let $p[j]$ be the pointer taken when the key, k, is being compared with those in the nodes. Then

$$j = \begin{cases} 1 & \text{if } k \leq k_1 \\ i & \text{if } k_{i-1} < k \leq k_i \qquad i = 2, \ldots, m-2. \\ m & \text{if } k_{m-1} < k \end{cases} \qquad (6.22)$$

The determination of which path to take at a node thus depends on a series of comparisons, rather than on *two*, as it does for binary trees.

To obtain trees with desirable properties, certain restrictions are placed on the trees. In one class of multiway trees:

- The number of pointers is allowed to range between m and $m/2$.
- The depth of all leaves is the same.

Trees defined in this way are called *B trees* of order m. They find their most important application in the construction of file directories, and further consideration of them is deferred to Chapter 9.

A restricted type of B trees, called *2–3 trees*, in which $m = 3$, was proposed by Aho, Hopcroft, and Ullman.[18] In such trees:

- Every node has one or two keys and hence (with the possible exception of the root) either two or three branches.
- All leaves are at a constant depth.[19]

---

[18]A. V. Aho, J. E. Hopcroft, and J. D. Ullman, *The Design and Analysis of Computer Algorithms* (Reading, Mass.: Addison-Wesley Publishing Company, Inc., 1974).

[19]The 2–3 trees illustrated in Aho, Hopcroft, and Ullman have every key at a leaf. This means that same keys are repeated in the internal nodes. In the tree illustrated here, each key is stored only once, and not every key is present at a leaf.

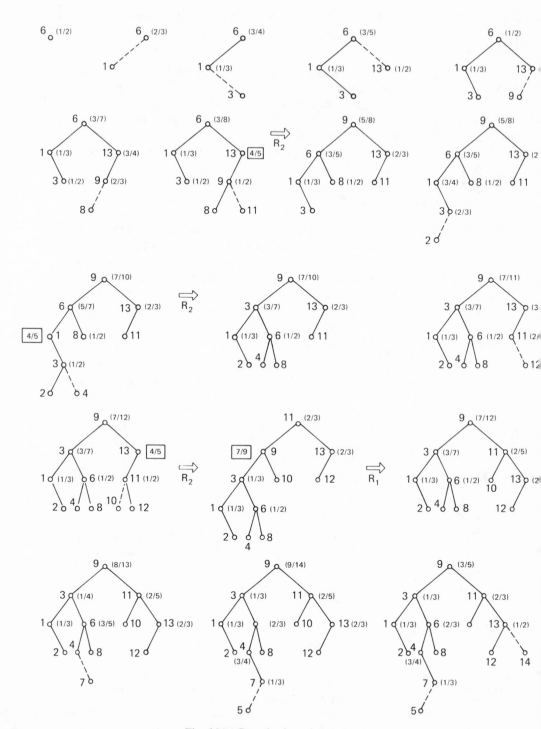

Fig. 6.21 Growth of a weight-balanced tree

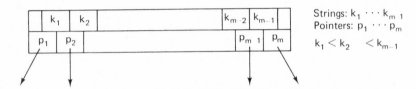

Fig. 6.22   Node for multiway lexicographic tree

If N is the number of keys and h the depth of the tree, $2^h \le N \le 3^h$, and $h \le$ log $N \le 1.59h$, since log 3 = 1.585. Therefore, the search path length for a 2–3 tree is $O(\log N)$.[20]

A new key is inserted into a 2–3 tree by following a path from the root to a leaf first as in a binary lexicographic tree. If the result of inserting the key produces three nodes in the leaf, the leaf splits, and the middle key migrates upward to the father. This, in turn, may cause a splitting, resulting in a further migration, and so on, to, possibly, a new root.

Example 6.9

Figure 6.23 shows stages in the development of the 2–3 tree grown on $\langle xal, wan,$ ..., $wul, zom \rangle$. In Fig. 6.23(i), at the addition of *wil*, the original root is split and a new level is added. Addition of *xem* [shown in Fig. 6.23(ii)] causes splitting at two levels and a new root. The tree on the 14 keys is shown in Fig. 6.23(iii).

Deletion in 2–3 tree is a special case of deletion in B trees, and is discussed in Section 9.3.2.

6.6 Trees with Unequally Weighted Nodes

A complete lexicographic tree on a set of keys, representing as it does a binary search, is the tree with minimum average path length (i.e., search time) when all keys are equally likely to occur. It is natural to ask what the minimum tree will be if the keys have different probabilities of occurrence. If we construct a tree with only internal nodes, so that every search ends in a key being found, from Eq. (6.2) the expected number of comparisons

$$E_p(N) = \frac{1}{W} \sum_{i=1}^{N} p_i l_i,$$

---

[20]A. C. Yao has shown that for random 2–3 trees, if N is the number of keys, $n(N)$, the number of nodes satisfies the inequality

$$0.70N < n(N) < 0.79N.$$

(See *On Random 3–2 Trees*, Technical Report UIUC DCS-R-74-679, Department of Computer Science, University of Illinois at Urbana–Champaign, Oct. 1974.) If we take $n(N) \approx 0.75N$ and assume that the average branching ratio is constant at each level, it follows that the height of a random 2–3 tree, $h \approx 0.83$ log N. In converting search path length to search time, it must be remembered that a node inquiry may require *three* key comparisons rather than two as in a lexicographic tree.

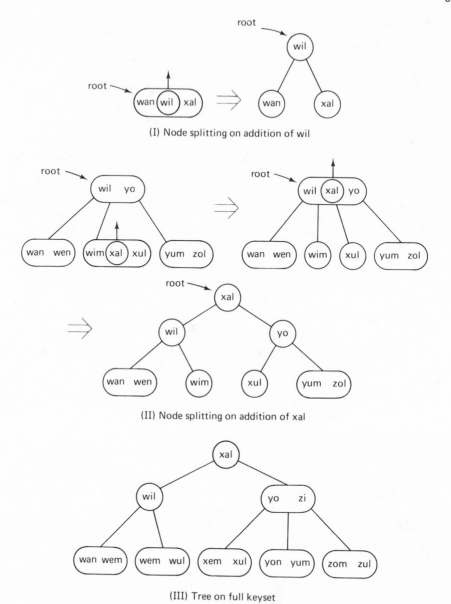

(I) Node splitting on addition of wil

(II) Node splitting on addition of xal

(III) Tree on full keyset

Fig. 6.23   Growth of a 2–3 tree

where p_i is the frequency of k_i. The goal is to construct an optimal lexicographic tree in which this expression is minimized. In comparing the expected number of key comparisons for different trees of the same order, the normalizing factor $1/W$ can be omitted, and the total path length can be used instead of the average path length. In effect, what is being calculated is $I(N)$, the internal path length for the tree. A property of optimal trees that has already been noted is that every subtree must be optimal, for if there were one that was not, the path length of the overall tree could be shortened by optimizing the subtree. This suggests a method of constructing an optimal tree, analogous to the rule that to optimize the search in a simple list, the most frequently occurring items should be entered first. Thus we might try to construct an optimal tree by choosing the node with the largest frequency as the root. This partitions the remaining nodes into two subsets. The same construction rule is to be applied to each subset, and the process continued until all keys have been entered.

Example 6.10

As an example consider keys: B, D, F, H, with frequencies 1, 5, 4, 3, respectively. According to the procedure just outlined, D, the key with the largest frequency, is selected for the root. This partitions the remaining keys into the set B with $p_1 = 1$, and F, H with $p_3 = 4$, $p_4 = 3$. The key B is a tree with a single node, and F, having the larger frequency, is taken as the root of the subtree for (F, H). The tree so constructed is shown in Fig. 6.24(a) (along with all the other lexicographic trees for this

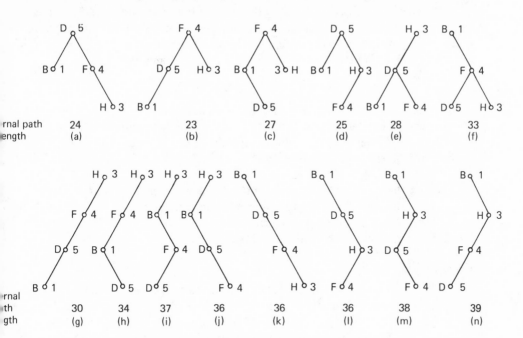

Fig. 6.24 Lexicographic binary trees on ⟨B,D,F,H⟩

keyset). It has an internal search path $I(N) = 5 \cdot 1 + 1 \cdot 2 + 4 \cdot 2 + 3 \cdot 3 = 24$. For the optimal tree, shown in Fig. 6.25(b), $I(N) = 23$. In fact, the procedure described will produce a chain whenever the lexicographic ordering $k_1 < k_2 < \ldots < k_N$ has a monotonic sequence of frequencies $p_1 < p_2 < \ldots < p_N$, so it is clearly inadequate.

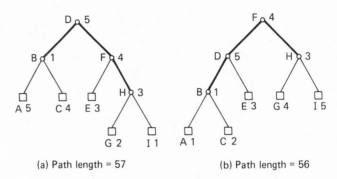

(a) Path length = 57   (b) Path length = 56

Fig. 6.25   Optimal lexicographic binary trees

6.6.1 Optimal Lexicographic Binary Trees

The method of constructing the *optimal* tree was given by Knuth, who generalized a problem that had been solved earlier to the case in which keys may be missing or present. The problem can be stated formally as follows.[21] Given the set of lexicographically ordered keys $\langle k_1, \ldots, k_N \rangle$ with expected frequencies $\langle p_1, \ldots, p_N \rangle$, and the frequencies $\langle q_0, \ldots, q_N \rangle$, where q_i is the frequency that there will be a search for a missing key lying between k_i and k_{i+1}, it is required to construct a binary tree for which the keys listed in symmetric sequence are $\langle k_1, \ldots, k_N \rangle$, and for which

$$\sum_{j=1}^{N} p_j l_j + \sum_{k=0}^{N} q_k (l'_k - 1)$$

is minimized. Here l_j or l'_k is the level of the node in the tree, measured by the number of nodes encountered in traversing a path from the root to the node in question.

The external node weights influence the shape of the optimal tree. Figure 6.25 shows two different optimal trees where the internal node weights are the same as for the trees of Fig. 6.24, but the weighting for the external nodes is different.

The fact that every subtree of an optimal tree is optimal leads to a method of constructing the optimum. The procedure is to construct optimum trees of higher and higher order. For a given set of consecutive nodes, the only tree that need be retained for the next stage is the one with minimal path length.

Example 6.11

The process is illustrated in Fig. 6.26. At the first stage the weights and path lengths of the four subtrees rooted at the internal nodes B, D, F, and H are calculated. At the second stage it is necessary to compute all the optimal two (internal)-node trees that can occur. The first of these is the tree containing the internal nodes (B, D) and it can be rooted at B or D. Calculation reveals that the tree rooted at D is optimal and it is retained for further constructions. Similarly, for the two-node trees constructed on (D, F), the one rooted at D is optimal, and for the trees constructed on (F, H), that rooted at F is optimal. At the next stage trees with three internal nodes are needed;

---

[21]Knuth, *Sorting and Searching*, Sec. 6.2.2.

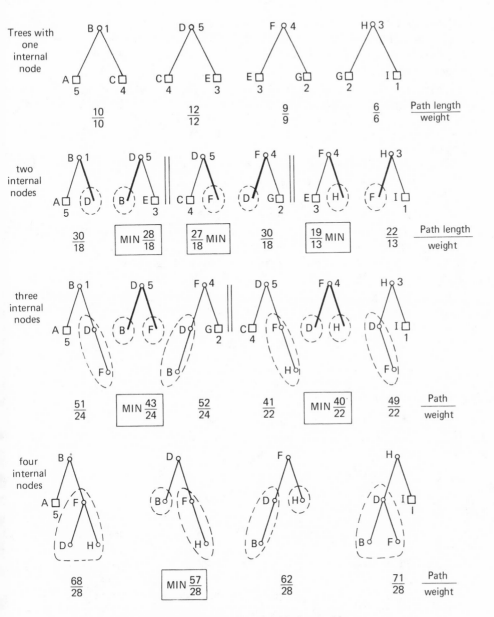

Fig. 6.26 Construction of optimal lexicographic tree

there are two such trees, with nodes (B, D, F) and (D, F, H). The trees containing (B, D, F) can be rooted at B, D, or F. Calculation reveals that the one rooted at D is optimal. Similarly, the (D, F, H) tree rooted at F is optimal. In the final stage, where the tree is constructed on all internal nodes, it may be rooted at B, D, F, or H. Calculation reveals that the one rooted at D is optimal. At any stage any subtrees needed for the calculation are available from earlier stages. (These are encircled in Fig. 6.26.) For example, at the final stage in computing the path length for the tree rooted at F, the optimal tree on (D, B) is needed, and also the tree rooted at H. All the information for these trees (path length and weights) is already available.

To describe the process in mathematical terms, let $c(i, j)$ be the cost (i.e., the path length) of the optimum tree with weights $(q_i, p_{i+1}, q_{i+1}, \ldots, p_j, q_j)$, where $0 \le i \le j \le N$. Further, let $w(i, j) = p_{i+1} + \ldots + p_j + q_i + \ldots + q_j$ be the sum of the weights for these nodes. We have that $c(i, i) = 0$, and $w(0, N)$ is the sum of the weights for the whole tree.

From the principle of subtree optimality,

$$c(i, j) = w(i, j) + \min_{i < k \le j} (c(i, k - 1) + c(k, j)) \qquad i < j. \qquad (6.23)$$

This equation is illustrated in Fig. 6.27. The calculation procedure is to determine $c(0, 1), c(1, 2), \ldots, c(N - 1, N)$, then $c(0, 2), c(1, 3), \ldots, c(N - 2, N)$, and so on to $c(0, N)$. Table 6.4 shows the matrices developed for Example 6.11.

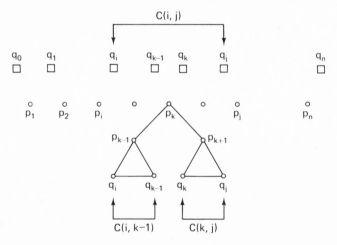

Fig. 6.27 Searching for the optimal tree

In practical applications of this algorithm, the number of nodes can be very large, so that the dependence on N of the time to construct the tree and of the working storage needed is of some importance. To find the minimum over k, it is necessary to evaluate Eq. (6.23) $j - i$ times for $i < j$ and $j = 1 \ldots N$. The total number of operations is

$$\sum_{j=1}^{N} \sum_{i=1}^{j} (j - i) \approx \frac{N^3}{6}$$

or $O(N^3)$. The storage needed for $c(i, j)$ and $w(i, j)$ is $O(N^2)$. The $O(N^3)$ time to compute the optimal tree is expensive but it can be reduced to $O(N^2)$. If $r(i, j)$ denotes the root of the optimal tree defined on nodes with weights $(q_i, p_{i+1}, \ldots, q_j)$, Knuth shows that

$$r(i, j - 1) \leq r(i, j) \leq r(i + 1, j).$$

This means that in Eq. (6.23) the minimum does not have to be sought over the range $i \leq k \leq j$, but rather over the narrower range $r(i + 1, j) - r(i, j - 1) + 1$. The effect is to make the total number of evaluations $O(N^2)$.

TABLE 6.4   Matrices needed for determining the optimal lexicographic tree of Fig. 6.26

	Weight of Subtree, $w(i, j)$						Cost of Subtree, $c(i, j)$				
	j						j				
i	0	1	2	3	4	i	0	1	2	3	4
0	0	10	18	24	28	0	0	10	28	43	57
1		0	12	18	22	1		0	12	27	40
2			0	9	13	2			0	9	19
3				0	6	3				0	6
4					0	4					0

☐ the cost for the minimal tree over all the nodes

6.6.2 Nearly Optimal Trees

Even with a reduction to $O(N^2)$ for the time to construct an optimal tree, the requirements for both time and storage are prohibitive for large N (e.g., $N > 100$). What is needed is a rule like the one based on taking the internal node with the greatest weight as root. The feature of this rule is that it suggests a top–down construction of the tree, in which once the root is estimated, very little else is needed by way of computation or storage. The maximum has to be determined repeatedly for the subtrees, but by sorting the weights, this can be done in time $O(N \log N)$. But taking the largest weighted node as root is inadequate, among other reasons because it takes no account of the missing key frequencies. Another simple rule is to choose as the root that key which minimizes the difference in weights of the left and right subtrees. Such a root will be called a *centroid*. Building a tree by taking centroids works well for the examples of Figs. 6.24 and 6.25—in fact, the optimal tree is obtained in all three cases. For example, for the tree of Fig. 6.25(b) we have

Node	A	B	C	D	E	F	G	H	I
Weight, w_i	1	1	2	5	3	4	4	3	5
$\sum w_i$	1	2	4	9	12	16	20	23	28

centroid

centroids for second level

It is possible to obtain a bound on the difference in cost between an optimal tree and a nearly optimal tree constructed by taking the centroid as root repeatedly. If C_{opt} is the cost for an optimal tree and C_{cen} the cost for the tree based on taking centroids, P. J. Bayer that has shown[22]

$$\frac{H}{\log 3} \le H - P\left(\log \frac{H}{P} + \log e - 1\right) \le C_{opt} \le C_{cen} \le H + 2,$$

where H, the entropy function already encountered in the Huffman encoding problem (Section 3.5), is given by

$$H = -\sum_{j=1}^{N} p_j \log p_j - \sum_{k=0}^{N} q_k \log q_k$$

and

$$P = \sum_{i=1}^{N} p_i.$$

Even though the choice of centroid for root provides a bound on the departure from optimality, it does not always produce a good tree. In failing to take account of the individual p's, a node with a very low weight might be selected as root, even though an adjacent node might be heavily weighted. A slight shift to this adjacent node could significantly reduce the path length. As an illustration, suppose that the p weights are $\langle 2, 28, 1, 28, 2 \rangle$. Choosing the centroid as root produces a tree with path length 125. By taking one of the nodes with weight 28 as root, the path length is reduced to 97 (Fig. 6.28). Combining the rules of estimating the centroid and attempting to choose heavily weighted nodes as high-level roots does produce good nearly optimal trees.

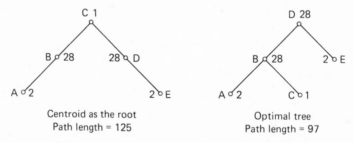

| Centroid as the root | Optimal tree |
| Path length = 125 | Path length = 97 |

Fig. 6.28   Example where choosing the centroid as root leads to a poor tree

This can be done by calculating the position of the centroid, and then examining the nodes in its neighborhood for a little way to see if there is one that is a local maximum. If there is, this local maximum is selected as the root, thus determining a partition on the remaining nodes, and a new nearly optimal tree is constructed for each partition. If an algorithm based on this rule is programmed so as to construct the optimal tree when the partitions become small enough, very good results are obtained. F, the fraction of the nodes over which the search for a local maximum is conducted, and s, the size of the partition for which there is a switch to the optimizing routine, are made parameters of the algorithm. Experimental tests on a wide variety of nearly optimal trees constructed in this way indicate that the path lengths are usually within 1 or 2 per cent of the optimum, and rarely exceed the optimum by more than 3 per cent.[23]

Figure 6.29 shows the result of an experiment in constructing optimal and nearly optimal trees on a sequence of trees, including some with a very large number of nodes. The data for this experiment comprises a file of 144,486 distinct surnames drawn from a list of 1 million names.[24] The frequencies associated with the names are the frequencies in the original list. A point such as $N = 15$ on the curve is obtained by selecting those 15 names for which the frequencies $p_1, \ldots, p_{15}$ are greatest. The q's are then found by counting—thus q_1 is the number of names alphabetically preceding the name alphabetically lowest on the list, q_2 is the frequency of names lying between the two lowest on the list, and so on. The effect of this way of choosing N, the p's, and q's is that $\sum p_i + \sum q_j$ is a constant, equal to 1,002,343. A number of interesting observations can be made from the curve:

1. Where it is possible to construct optimal as well as nearly optimal trees (up to $N = 150$), the search lengths differ by less than 2 per cent.
2. Initially (up to $N \approx 1000$) the search time is $O(\log N)$. This behavior is what would be expected for an optimal tree with uniform weighting of nodes.
3. As N becomes large (>5000) the search time becomes relatively insensitive to increasing the number of nodes. This is because later names extend the tree, but they have low frequencies, so that relatively few search paths terminate in them. At $N = 144,486$ the q's are all zero and the average search path is 12.2. This may be compared with $\log 144,486 - 1 \approx 19.5$, which would be the average for a tree with uniformly weighted nodes.

Example 6.12

The 15 most common names were selected from the Canadian census file, along with the p and q frequencies, computed in the manner just described. Figure 6.30 shows the optimal tree for this list. It has an average path length of 3.734. An algorithm for constructing nearly optimal trees using the technique described above yielded the same tree, because the algorithm was designed such that the cutoff value of s, for which there was a switch over from nearly optimal to optimal construction, was 15. For the tree based on the 25 most common names, the two methods provided different trees, the search length of the nearly optimal tree being greater by about 1 per cent.

---

[23]W. A. Walker and C. C. Gotlieb, "A Top–Down Algorithm for Constructing Nearly Optimal Lexicographic Trees," in *Graph Theory and Computing*, R. Read, ed. (New York: Academic Press, Inc., 1972), pp. 303–323.

[24]These million names themselves were selected by drawing every tenth name from the Canadian census file.

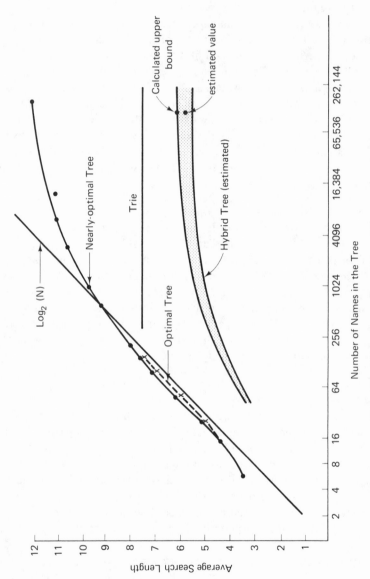

Fig. 6.29 Dependence of search length on number of names

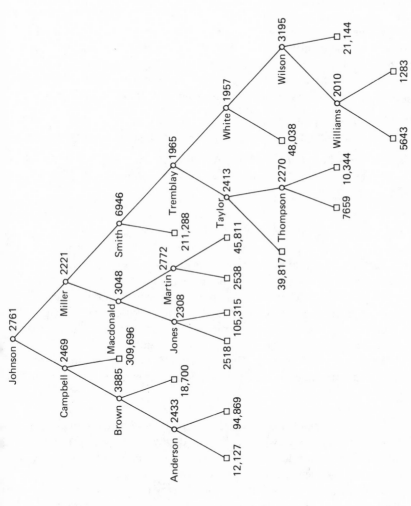

Fig. 6.30 Optimal lexieographic tree on the 15 most common names in the Canadian Census

6.7 Hybrid Trees

The last type of search tree that we shall consider are the *hybrid trees*, in which the nodes are generalized so that they may be either character nodes, as in a trie, or nodes similar to those in a lexicographic tree but containing a string that is not necessarily a complete key.[25] The character nodes contain a pointer for each of the possible characters which can occur in the position being investigated. The string nodes can contain keys or any substring of a key, along with three pointers corresponding to "less," "equal," and "greater." In the storage tree implementation of the hybrid tree, it is convenient to store a type identifier "s" or "c," which identifies the node type, and a length field in the case of string nodes. As usual, a search is conducted by tracing a path from the root of the tree. It may terminate at either a root or an internal node of the tree. At each node there is an associated key constructed obtained by concatenating:

- Characters defined by pointers taken in character nodes.
- Strings found in a string node if the path proceeds along the equal pointer.

When a path terminates in a *, the end-of-key delimiter, the attributes are located either by the * pointer in a character node, or by the equal pointer in a string node.

Example 6.13

A hybrid tree on the keyset K is shown in Fig. 6.31. As an illustration of the search procedure, suppose that the key *wim*∗ is being sought. When the tree is entered, the character identifier indicates that the root is a character node. The pointer corresponding to *w*, the second of the five possible characters in the first position, is followed by a node that is again of type character. The pointer corresponding to *i*, the fourth possible character, is then taken to the third level, where a string node of length 2 is found. Therefore, the next two characters in the key being sought, *m*∗, are compared with *l*∗, the contents of the string node. There is no match and *m*∗ > *l*∗, so the search is continued along the "greater" pointer. There a character node of length 2 is found. The suffix being sought, *m*∗, matches the string stored, so the equal pointer locates the attributes of *wim*∗.

The tree of Fig. 6.31 is one of many hybrid trees that could be constructed on the keyset K. The question arises as to which is best, and why choose a hybrid tree over a "pure" positional tree or pure lexicographic tree. It must first be noted that when searching algorithms are implemented for a hybrid tree, a comparison at a character node turns out to require an execution time which is very close to that needed for a comparison at a string node. This is because a branch instruction, determined by an index register (which is how an inquiry at a character node is implemented), requires about the same number of basic machine instructions as does a three-way comparison

[25]W. A. Walker and C. C. Gotlieb, "Hybrid Trees: A Data Structure for Lists of Keys," in *Proceedings of 1972 ACM-SIGFIDET Workshop on Data Description, Access and Control*, A. L. Dean, ed. (New York: Association for Computing Machinery, 1972), pp. 189–211.

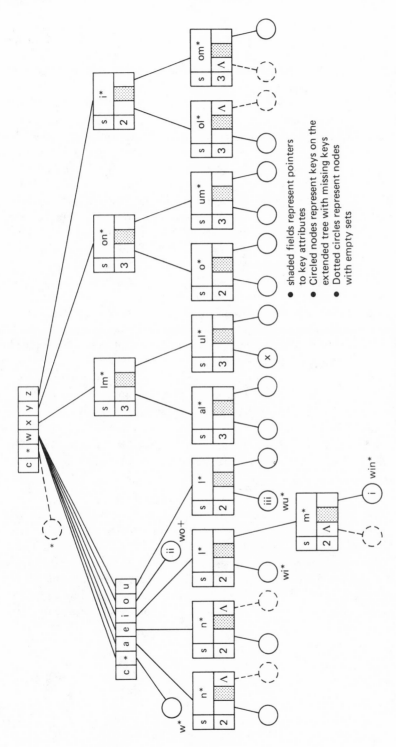

- shaded fields represent pointers to key attributes
- Circled nodes represent keys on the extended tree with missing keys
- Dotted circles represent nodes with empty sets

Fig. 6.31 Hybrid tree

237

of string values.[26] The significance of this is that for the hybrid tree, as for the positional tree or lexicographic tree, the path length is a reasonable measure of the search time to find a key, and the average path length of the tree is an acceptable measure of the searching efficiency for the whole tree.

In the tree of Fig. 6.31 the internal path length for the 14 keys is $3 \times 2 + 10 \times 3 + 1 \times 4 = 38$. This may be compared with 45, the internal path length for the complete tree, which is the optimal lexicographic tree on the keyset K in Fig. 6.14. Further, the storage for the hybrid tree is that needed for 14 string nodes, plus the storage for two character nodes, and this is scarcely greater than that for the lexicographic tree. For the trie in Fig. 6.12 on the keyset K, the internal path length is 56, and the storage is required for 28 character nodes (assuming that the leaves are also character nodes).

This suggests that hybrid trees may offer significant advantages over lexicographic trees or tries if the overall requirements of search time and storage are considered. It also raises the question of how to determine *optimal* hybrid trees when frequencies are assigned to the keys, and when searches for missing keys can occur.

To construct the optimal *lexicographic* tree on the keyset K, it is necessary and sufficient to know the frequencies of the keys, p_i, $i = 1, \ldots, N$, and the frequencies, q_j, for searches between each pair of keys when they are lexicographically ordered. Each q_j, it will be recalled, represents a frequency sum for all keys ranging between p_j and p_{j+1}. To construct the optimal hybrid trees, more information is needed about the frequencies between a pair of actual keys than just the sum of the frequencies of the missing keys. To see why, consider the keys that lie between *wim*∗ and *wul*∗ in the keyset K. When the hybrid tree in Fig. 6.31 is extended, there are three distinct "vacant" nodes between *wim*∗ and *wul*∗. These correspond respectively to

1. The key *win*∗.
2. The set of keys $\langle$*wo*∗, *wol*∗, *won*∗, *wom*∗$\rangle$. Collectively these may be designated as *wo*+, which may be called the *extension* of *wo*.
3. The key *wu*∗.

The key *win*∗, extension key *wo*+, and key *wu*∗ are members of what can be called an *augmented set* on K. If the frequencies for these three augmented keys are known, a path length can be calculated for that part of the hybrid tree in Fig. 6.31 in which there are keys that fall between *wim*∗ and *wul*∗.

To know what frequencies are needed for *any* possible hybrid tree constructed on the keyset K, we can go to the trie of Fig. 6.12 and enumerate all the members of the augmented set for K by completing the trie. The tree is completed by adding a vacant node to every node that is not an actual key. Thus for keys between *xem*∗ and *xul*∗, the following members are present:

1. *xen*∗.
2. $\langle$*xi*∗, *xil*∗, *xim*∗, *xin*∗$\rangle$ or *xi*+.
3. $\langle$*xo*∗, *xol*∗, *xom*∗, *xon*∗$\rangle$ or *xo*+.
4. *xu*∗.

---

[26]For evidence on this, see W. A. Walker, *Hybrid Trees as a Data Structure.* (Ph.D. thesis, Department of Computer Science, University of Toronto, 1975), pp. 2–22.

Knowing the frequencies for the augmented set on K will ensure that sufficient information is available to calculate the path length of a hybrid tree. In the particular tree of Fig. 6.31, all that is necessary to construct the path length for the tree is the frequency associated with the box X, which contains keys in

$$\{x \in X \,|\, xem* < x < xul* \}.$$

This frequency is available as the sum of the four frequencies above.

In this example the keys have a maximum length of three characters. If no maximum is specified, an extension key will have an infinite number of members in it. For example, if keys of any length are constructed on the alphabet $\{a,b,c\}$, then there is an infinite number of keys in ab+, all < ac, including

$$\langle aba*, abaa*, \ldots, abba*, \ldots, abbba* \ldots \rangle.$$

However, given a maximum key length, it is not difficult to construct the augmented set for a given keyset and trie. Then given the frequencies in the augmented set, the search path for any hybrid tree can be constructed. By a generalization of the procedure for constructing an optimal lexicographic tree, an *optimal hybrid* tree can be constructed.

The tree of Fig. 6.31 is optimal for equal frequencies of the 14 keys $\langle wan*, \ldots, zom* \rangle$ and no weights attached to the external nodes. To construct a hybrid tree on a set with missing keys it is necessary to know or estimate frequencies for the keys in the augmented set. Such information has to be gathered from statistics on searches for missing keys, in the same way as must be done for frequencies of vacant nodes in the lexicographic tree. As for the lexicographic tree, the algorithm for an optimal hybrid tree becomes impractical for large N, and it is necessary to investigate procedures to construct nearly optimal trees on large keysets.

In developing a top–down method, besides looking for the root of a new subtree at each stage, a decision has to be made whether the root should be a character node or a string node, and if a string node is chosen, what length the string should be. It is clear that a character node should be chosen whenever, for a character in a given position, there are keys in which most of the possible characters in the alphabet follow the given one. However, even this intuitive rule has to be modified if some of the keys have unusually large frequencies. Methods of constructing good nearly optimal hybrid trees are beyond the scope of this book, but it seems that the entropy, $H = -\sum p_i \log p_i$, already encountered in Huffman trees and weight-balanced trees, provides a useful criterion in determining what kind of node to choose as root.[27]

The search cost for an optimal hybrid tree will be less than the cost for the trie, or for the optimal lexicographic tree, since these are special cases of the hybrid tree. For small N, the optimal lexicographic tree will give the better lower bound, but the cost for the trie is independent of N, since only the number of characters in the key is involved, and hence for large N it will give the better lower bound. It is difficult to estimate the *expected* cost for hybrid trees, but on large keysets, using a character node at the first two or three levels is bound to produce significant reductions. In Fig. 6.30,

---

[27]For a further discussion, see Walker, *Hybrid Trees*, Chap. 5.

besides showing the dependence of the search length for the nearly optimal lexicographic trees on N, there is also displayed the constant search length for the trie, and estimates on the search length for the hybrid trees based on using trie nodes on the first three levels for very large keysets.

6.8 Comparisons

Table 6.5 summarizes the results on the maximum and expected search times for the various types of tree directories considered in this chapter. It would be possible to include columns for insertion and deletion times, but these are rather similar to those for search. The positional trees constitute a distinct class, and the results are not quite comparable with other types, much in the same way as the cost for radix sorting is not quite comparable with the cost for other methods because of the dependence on different key parameters.

TABLE 6.5   Comparison of search cost and storage requirements for different trees

Search Cost: Number of Comparisons

Tree Type	Maximum	Expected	Estimated Storage Requirements
Multidimensional index	$h + 1$	$\bar{h} + 1$	$A \cdot N = A \cdot m^h / m - 1$
De la Briandais trie	$m \cdot (h + 1)$ $h + 1$	$(1 + \bar{n}) \cdot (\bar{h} + 1)$ $\bar{h} + 1$	$(2A + 1) \cdot (\bar{n} + 1)^h / \bar{n}$ $A \cdot m \cdot N / \ln m \Vert$
Complete lexicographic	$\log (N + 1)$	$\log (N + 1) - 1$	$N (\bar{h} + 3A)$
Random	N	$1.386 \log (N + 1)$	$N(h + 3A)$
Height-balanced	$1.44 \log (N + 1)$	$\log N + 0.25$†	$N(\bar{h} + 3A + 1)$
Weight-balanced	$\dfrac{\log (N + 1) - 1}{\log (1/1 - \alpha)}$	$\log (N + 1)/H(\alpha)$	$N(\bar{h} + 3A + 1)$
2–3	$\log N + 1$	$0.82 \log N + 1$‡	$N(1.5\bar{h} + 2.25A)$
Optimal node weighted	$H + 2$§	Not applicable	$N(\bar{h} + 3A)$
Optimal hybrid	$\min (h + 1, H + 2)$	Not applicable	$A \cdot m \cdot N/4 \ln m$ $+ N(\bar{h} + 1 - \log_m N + 3A)$¶

N = number of keys
h = height of tree = maximum number of characters in key for multidimensional index or trie (excluding end-of-key terminator)
$\bar{h}$ = average number of characters in key (excluding delimiter)
n_{max} = number of character types in key alphabet
$n_{max} + 1 = m$
$\bar{n}$ = number of character types averaged over position within key
$\bar{h} \approx \log_{\bar{n}} N$
If $|T|$ = order of left subtree, $\alpha \leq |T_l|/N + 1 \leq 1 - \alpha$.
$H(\alpha) = -\alpha \log \alpha - (1 - \alpha) \log (1 - \alpha)$
$H = -\sum p_j \log p_j - \sum q_k \log q_k$ for a node-weighted tree
A = number of bytes/address field.

†See reference in footnote 15.
‡See reference in footnote 19.
§See reference in footnote 21.
‖See reference in footnote 11.
¶See reference in footnote 25.

Formulas for estimating the storage requirements are also shown in Table 6.5. The following assumptions are made about the storage representations for nodes:

- The number of nodes in the de la Briandais tree is approximated by $(\bar{n} + 1)^h/n$.
- In a trie, with $(n_{max} + 1)$ characters, where multiway branching is terminated when there are s or fewer pointers emanating from a character node, $N/s \cdot \ln(n_{max} + 1)$ storage nodes are needed (see footnote 11). If the trie is continued until there is only one pointer, $N/\ln(n_{max} + 1)$ character nodes are needed, each requiring $(n_{max} + 1)A + 1$ bytes.
- Lexicographic trees have a field for the key (requiring one byte per character) and three address fields (each requiring A bytes).
- Weight-balanced and height-balanced tree each require an extra byte for storing the balance data.
- The 2–3 trees require about $0.75N$ nodes (see footnote 19), where there are up to two keys and three addresses in each.
- Hybrid trees are constructed by using character nodes until there are $s = 4$ pointers emanating. (There are arguments to show that this is reasonable.) After that, string nodes are used. In using character nodes, the length of the keys are reduced from $\bar{h}$ to $(\bar{h} - \log_{n_{max}+1} N)$ characters. (See the reference in footnote 25.)

Although these formulas are useful for comparison and design of tree directories, they are all based on one-level storage devices. When N becomes large (and some of the equations are only valid if this is true,) it is necessary to use secondary storage, in which case these equations have to be modified, often in important ways. Trees on files with secondary storage devices are considered in Chapter 9.

Exercises

1. Rewrite Algorithm 6.1 for tree traversal, so that it uses iteration (instead of recursive calls) and does not use a stack. [See D. Knuth, "Structured Programming with Go To Statements," *ACM Computing Surveys*, **6**, no. 1 (Dec. 1974), 261–301. Also, W. A. Buckhard, "Nonrecursive Traversals of Trees," *The Computer Journal*, **18**, no. 3 (Aug. 1975), 227–230.]
2. Modify Algorithm 6.1 to traverse the tree in (a) preorder; (b) postorder sequence.
3. Write an algorithm for deleting a key in a positional binary tree.
4. Draw the binary tree with right-threaded links for the subtree rooted at x in Fig. 6.3.
5. (a) Modify Algorithm 6.3 so as to include right-threaded links on insertion of keys into a binary positional tree.
   (b) Write the algorithm for key deletions.
   (c) Compare the insertion/deletion algorithms, with and without the threaded links, and estimate the savings for deletion and costs for insertion because of the extra links.
6. Given the preorder and postorder listings of the nodes of a tree, develop an algorithm to specify the tree in parenthesized notation.
7. (a) Suggest a target for left-threaded links in a binary tree (i.e., pointers that are null because the line of descent through the eldest son is terminated).
   (b) In what situations would your target be useful?
   (c) Give an algorithm for locating the target.

8. Write key insertion and deletion algorithms for the trie.
9. (a) Draw the tree that results if the positional tree of Fig. 6.3 is converted to a ternary tree in which each node contains three branches, according as the key character is less than, equal to, or greater than that stored in the node.
   (b) What is the average search time (expressed in number of comparisons) for the full keyset?
10. Each node of a tree may be regarded as having two successors, its first descendant and its next sibling. By representing an ordered list of successors either as a vector or as a linked list, we get four representations of a tree.
    (a) Of the four possible representations for positional trees described in Section 6.3, which is missing?
    (b) Under what circumstances might the missing representation be a good one?
11. Write a procedure for deleting a node in a lexicographic binary tree.
12. (a) Give a complete tree for the keyset K other than that shown in Fig. 6.14.
    (b) How many complete trees are there for N keys?
13. Show that Eq. (6.6) is an approximate expression for the number of comparisons required for a successful search in a complete tree that is *not* filled.
14. (a) Write an algorithm which, given a set of keys, produces a *complete* lexicographic tree for the set.
    (b) State the algorithm for adding a new (arbitrary) key so as to keep the tree complete.
    (c) What is the complexity of the expression for the number of comparisons?
15. Delete the keys in the tree of Fig. 6.18 in reverse sequence to that in which they were entered, introducing rotations as needed to maintain the height balance.
16. Write algorithms for insertion and deletion in a height-balanced tree.
17. Write algorithms for insertion and deletion in a weight-balanced tree.
18. (a) If the same key is inserted and then deleted in a lexicographic binary tree, is the final tree identical with the original one?
    (b) Is this also true for deletion followed by insertion?
    (c) If the final tree is different, what is the result of a sequence of paired operations? Investigate the situation for constrained trees.
19. Delete the keys in the tree of Fig. 6.21, in reverse sequence to those in which they were entered, introducing rotations as needed to maintain the weight balance.
20. Show that for a tree in BB[α],

$$h_{max} \le \frac{\log (N + 1) - 1}{\log (1 - 1/\alpha)}.$$

21. Let $T(N)$ be the number of lexicographic binary trees constructed on N distinct keys.
    (a) Show that $T(N)$ satisfies the recursion relation

$$T(N) = 2 \sum_{j=0}^{N} T(j)T(N - j - 1) - N \bmod 2 \cdot T^2(M),$$

    where

$$M = \left\lfloor \frac{N - 1}{2} \right\rfloor, \qquad T(0) = 1, \qquad T(1) = 1.$$

    (b) Tabulate $T(N)$ for $N = 2$ to 14.
22. Show that a Fibonacci tree is BB[1/3].
23. Develop an algorithm for finding the number of keys that lie between two given keys, k_1 and k_2, in a weight-balanced tree. Show that the number of comparisons is $O(\log N)$.
24. Redraw the 2–3 tree of Fig. 6.23 so that every key is at a leaf.

25. Give the algorithm for deleting a node in a 2–3 tree.
26. Program the algorithm for finding an optimal lexicographic tree with weighted nodes.
27. Construct the full augmented set for the keyset K.
28. Fill out Table 6.5 using parameter values for the keyset K.
29. The following list of "names" is given, each with an equal probability of occurrence:

$$wxw,\ wxz,\ wzw,\ wzy,\ wzz,\ yyw,\ yyx,$$

$$zww,\ zwx,\ zwy,\ zyw,\ zyx,\ zyy,\ zyz.$$

(a) Construct an optimal binary search tree with character nodes for these names. What is the average search time?

(b) What would be the average search time for an optimal lexicographic binary search tree with string nodes?

(c) Note that there are two names with prefix *wx*, three with prefix *wz*, two with prefix *yy*, three with prefix *zw*, and four with prefix *zy*. Construct an optimal lexicographic tree with string nodes for these five prefixes using the given weights. What is the average search time to identify the first two letters in this way? Construct a hybrid tree, taking advantage of this.

Bibliography

Binary search trees and tree directories have been the subject of intense investigation since the early 1960s. Surveys on the results are presented by Severance (1974) and Nievergelt (1974). Even with such interest, there is a large body of mathematical theory relating to trees, especially about enumerations and combinatoric properties, which has not found its way into practical use. For examples, see Knuth (1973) and Moon (1970).

KNUTH, D. E., *The Art of Computer Programming:* Vol. 1, *Fundamental Algorithms*, 2nd ed., 1973; Vol. 3, *Sorting and Searching*, 1973. Reading, Mass.: Addison-Wesley Publishing Company, Inc.

MOON, J. W., "Counting Labelled Trees." *Canadian Mathematical Monographs, no. 1*, 1970.

NIEVERGELT, J., "Binary Search Trees and File Organizations." *ACM Computing Surveys*, **6**, no. 3 (Sept. 1974), 195–207.

SEVERANCE, D. G., "Identifier Search Mechanisms: A Survey and Generalized Model." *ACM Computing Surveys*, **6**, no. 3 (Sept. 1974), 175–194.

chapter 7

Structures for Sets

and Graphs

In Chapter 1 sets and graphs were seen to be basic mathematical data types. The importance of both derives from the fact that a great many problems, both abstract and applied, are naturally formulated in terms of these types and the operations defined over them. In this chapter we are interested in representations for the types (i.e., in storage mappings and structures.) It turns out that neither for sets nor graphs is there one representation that is suitable for all operations and processes. In each case there are alternatives, some best for certain operations, and others better in different contexts. For this reason the dominant theme of the chapter is *not* the particular data structures, but the relation between the data structure—more precisely the storage mapping, S, and the operation set, O, for the type.

7.1 Data Structures for Sets

Sets differ from lists in that the members of a set must be distinct, a condition not necessarily imposed on lists. Concatenating two sets will not in general produce a set, and the applicable *operation* is set union. Sets also differ from ordered lists (even if the lists have distinct elements), which will be called *tuples*. In the systematic development of set theory, tuples are brought into the framework by defining them as sets of sets. Thus, an ordered pair $\langle a, b \rangle$ is defined as

$$\langle a, b \rangle = \{\{a\}, \{a, b\}\}. \tag{7.1}$$

This definition does not depend on a definition for the integers (which are themselves constructed from the notion of sets), and also permits one to say when ordered pairs are equal; for example,

$$\langle a, b \rangle = \langle c, d \rangle \qquad \text{iff } a = c \quad \text{and} \quad b = c.$$

244

The definition of a tuple is built up from that of an ordered pair. There are, nevertheless, difficulties with the definitions. For one, it follows that

$$\langle a, b \rangle \cap \langle x, b \rangle = \varnothing$$

since there are no elements common to the sets associated with these two tuples. Under most interpretations it would be desirable that b be regarded as the intersection. Second, the definition given in Eq. (7.1) would require redundant use of storage in any computer realization of it. Finally, since the tuple is ordered, it is natural to take advantage of the ordering imposed by memory when that tuple is stored. On the other hand, sets are not considered as being ordered, and we may not wish to attach meaning to the order imposed on them by storage, so that there is a mismatch if tuples are identified with sets. The consequence is that it is desirable to regard sets and tuples as distinct data types, even though theoretically tuples can be derived from sets. A definition of a tuple that naturally leads to using its order in the storage representation, and which also yields the desired results for intersection, can be based on the integers. Each member of the tuple is associated with an integer in a mapping (i.e., the tuple is indexed). Thus

$$\langle d_1, d_2, \ldots, d_n \rangle = \{\langle d_1, 1 \rangle, \ldots, \langle d_n, n \rangle\}.$$

This definition requires that an ordered pair be accepted as a primitive concept, but it is nevertheless useful. With it the SELECT operation on a tuple is naturally effected by specifying the number or index of the wanted element, so for all practical purposes tuples are vectors.

Sets, as the most primitive concept in mathematics, have profound problems associated with them. To avoid logical difficulties, such as Russell's paradox, it is necessary to impose restrictions on how they can be constructed, not allowing, for example, sets that can have themselves as members.[1] When considering operations for which set members and sets are operands, it is desirable to introduce the concept of type, and this gives rise to the question of whether sets should be constructed with members of differing types. One can arrive at meaningless conclusions by, to use a common saying, "trying to compare apples and oranges." In building up sets, possible constituents are:

- Atomic types, including integers, reals, characters, strings, and Boolean values.
- Sets constructed on atomic types.
- Tuples (i.e., ordered lists of atomic types).
- References to sets or tuples in the form of literals (labels or addresses) and variables (identifiers and pointers whose domains are atomic elements).

Most implementations of sets allow several of these constituents. Including the last presents problems, but there have been attempts to deal with them.[2] But even if

---

[1] Russell's paradox arises by attempting to define a set, S, as the set of all sets that are not members of themselves. The paradox comes about by asking whether S is a member of itself. Both answers, yes and no, are self-contradictory.

[2] Earley uses the terms *atomic objects* and *identity objects*; the latter describes set members that are variables, as opposed to *atomic objects*. See J. Earley, "High Level Operations in Automatic Programming," *SIGPLAN Notices*, **9**, no. 3 (Apr. 1974).

only atomic types are allowed in the construction of sets, the problem of choosing a best storage mapping, S^{set}, is nontrivial. The best choice depends critically on the operations, O^{set}. The primitive operators, set union, intersection, and difference, are obviously of interest, but beyond these, sets are applicable to so very many problems that it is necessary to have some idea of the applications in mind in order to know which operations are important.

Example 7.1

To illustrate the operations needed for set manipulation applications, we consider a now classic problem, whose statement and solution was given by P. Hall in 1935. Given a family of nonempty subsets S_i of a set S, $i = 1, \ldots, m$, the problem is to determine when it is possible to choose $a_i \in S_i$, $i = 1, \ldots, m$, such that $a_i \neq a_j$ for $i \neq j$. This is known as finding a set of *distinct representatives* for the sets S_i. One interpretation is that it is the problem of electing presidents of a set of clubs with overlapping memberships, such that every club has a president, and nobody is president of more than one club. There are other interpretations and also generalizations of the problem. Hall showed that a necessary and sufficient condition for a set of distinct representatives to exist is that for all $j \leq m$, the union of any j subsets must contain at least j members. As an example, suppose that

$$S = \{g, t, a, f, v\};$$

$S_1 = \{g, t, a, f, v\}$, $S_2 = \{a, t\}$, $S_3 = \{t, g, f\}$, $S_4 = \{v, t\}$, and $S_5 = \{a, g\}$. The Hall condition is satisfied, and one set of discrete representatives is given by the mapping $\{\langle S_1, f\rangle, \langle S_2, v\rangle, \langle S_3, g\rangle, \langle S_4, t\rangle, \langle S_5, a\rangle\}$.

The statement of the Hall condition suggests that it might be necessary to calculate all unions of the sets S_i, to determine whether a set of discrete representations exists. In fact, this can be avoided. By considering flows in networks, Ford and Fulkerson (1962) showed not only how to reduce the computation, but also how to solve a more general problem. In their formulation the network to be considered is one in which the sets S_i are all connected to a single source. The set elements, which we designate as a_j, are connected to a single sink. From each S_i there is a connecting path to all the a_j's that are members of it. The connections are such that only unit flows can take place along a path from the source, or a path to the sink, but arbitrarily large flows can occur along a path from an S_i to an a_j. (See. Fig. 7.1.) The existence of a set of distinct representatives is equivalent to asking whether the maximum flow in the network is equal to the number of sets (i.e., m units). A set of distinct representatives certainly implies a (maximum) flow of m, since unit flow can take place from the source, to every S_i, to the representative, to the sink. The following argument shows that the converse is also true.

If the flow is maximum there is a flow from the source to every S_i; likewise, there is a flow from m of the a_j's to the sink. It follows that each of these m a_j's is connected to *some* S_i. Suppose that any set with the smallest number of connections (i.e., of least cardinality), say S_p, is selected, and all paths from it, except a single one, say

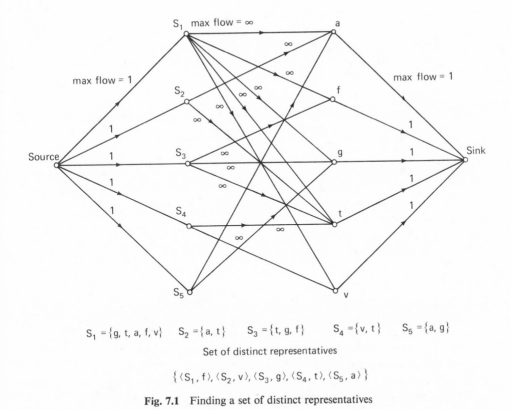

$$S_1 = \{g, t, a, f, v\} \quad S_2 = \{a, t\} \quad S_3 = \{t, g, f\} \quad S_4 = \{v, t\} \quad S_5 = \{a, g\}$$

Set of distinct representatives

$$\{\langle S_1, f \rangle, \langle S_2, v \rangle, \langle S_3, g \rangle, \langle S_4, t \rangle, \langle S_5, a \rangle\}$$

Fig. 7.1 Finding a set of distinct representatives

that to a_q, are deleted. Also delete all other paths *to* a_q. The network now consists of a path from source to sink through S_p and a_q, along with the rest of the network of $m - 1$ sets and $m - 1$ elements, say N_{m-1}. Previously there were $m - 1$ units flowing through N_{m-1}, and since the capacity of any link from an S to an a is unbounded, N_{m-1} can clearly still sustain a flow of $m - 1$ units. Therefore, a_q can be chosen as a representative for S_p; N_{m-1} is a network that has a maximum flow of $m - 1$ units for which the Hall conditions still hold, and the argument can be continued until a complete set of distinct representatives is chosen.

An algorithm for finding a set of distinct representatives follows immediately from the Ford–Fulkerson solution. An informal version, using set theoretic notation, is given by Algorithm 7.1. Our purpose is to see which set primitives are needed in a problem of this type. The operations that appear are those for constructing a set, choosing an element from the set, finding a minimum, and set difference and union. It is assumed that there have been declarations to the effect that S_i, $i = 1, \ldots, m$, are sets whose members are a_j, $j = 1, \ldots, n$, $n \geq m$. *Reps* is a set of integer pairs, $\langle i, j \rangle$, where S_i is represented by a_j, and *unmatched* is the set of integers, initially $\{1, \ldots, m\}$, whose indices specify sets that have not yet been assigned a representative.

Algorithm 7.1   Finding a set of distinct representatives

$reps \Leftarrow \emptyset$;

$unmatched \Leftarrow \{1, 2, \ldots, m\}$; /*initialize representatives and unmatched
$\qquad\qquad\qquad\qquad\qquad\qquad\qquad$ set indices*/

do while $|unmatched| \geq 0 \wedge \forall_{\underset{i \leq m}{}} S_i \neq \emptyset$;

$\quad p \Leftarrow i \,||\, S_i| = \min_{i \in unmatched} |S_i|$; /*select the set of smallest cardinality*/

$\quad$ choose $a_q \in S_p$; /*select a member in this set*/

$\quad reps \Leftarrow reps \cup \langle p, q \rangle$; /*augment $reps$ with new assignment*/

$\quad unmatched \Leftarrow unmatched - \{p\}$;

$\quad$ **for** $i \in unmatched$

$\quad\quad$ **do** $S_i \Leftarrow S_i - \{a_q\}$; /*remove latest rep. from unmatched sets*/

$\quad\quad$ **end**

end

if $unmatched \neq \emptyset$ **then** print 'none';

else print $reps$;

In order to show more generally how O^{set} influences S^{set}, we shall assume that O^{set} consists of the eight operations and functions shown in Table 7.1. These will be called *macros*, because it is easy to imagine them as being realized either as a sequence of built-in microprogrammed instructions, or as short sequences of instructions to be inserted in-line in programs. Five different storage representations, R_j, will be considered, where $1 \leq j \leq 5$. The system we shall assume is one where there are set variables, and hence a symbol table containing set names. Each set can have only

TABLE 7.1 O^{set}—macros for sets

Macro	Effect
1 MEMBER (x, S)	*True* if $x \in S$ and *false* otherwise.
2 CHOOSE (x, S)	Select an element x such that $x \in S$; successive invocations of CHOOSE yield different elements.
3 MAX (S)	The maximum element of S, where the ordering relation on the elements is determined by the collating sequence.
4 PART (x, S)	Creates two sets, $S_1 = \{y \in S \,|\, y \leq x\}$ and $S_2 = \{z \in S \,|\, z > x\}$.
5 UNION (S_1, S_2)	Creates a set that is the union of S_1 and S_2; members common to S_1 and S_2 appear only once in the result.
6 DIFF (S_1, S_2)	Creates a set consisting of elements in S_1 not present in S_2.
7 BOTH (S_1, S_2)	The result is $S_1 \cap S_2$.
8 CONSTRUCT $(S, a_1, \ldots, a_n)$	Given the data structure and storage mapping S^{set}, atomic values $a_1, \ldots, a_n$ are assigned as the members of S.

atomic members which require a fixed number of bytes,[3] but for R_1, the set members are assumed to be the integers. In the symbol table, the number of elements in the set $|S| = n$ is stored along with the pointer to the storage area in which the elements are to be found. The five storage structures are described in Table 7.2 and illustrated in Fig. 7.2.

TABLE 7.2   Set data structures

Representation	Description
R_1	Possible set members are numbered according to their values (using lexicographic equivalents if they are strings). Each set is represented by a characteristic vector, where component $c_i = 1$ if the ith value is a member of the set, and $c_i = 0$ if the value is absent. The rank of the vector $=$ size of the value domain.
R_2	Each set is a contiguous, *unordered* list.
R_3	Each set is a contiguous *ordered* list, the ordering being that of the values of the members.
R_4	Each set is represented as an individual hash table, H_i, corresponding to S_i. For simplicity, we assume linear probing in resolving collisions.
R_5	Each set is represented as a height-balanced, binary tree constructed on values of its members.

The cost for executing the ith macro in Table 7.1 on the jth mapping, R_j, can be expressed as $c_{ij} \cdot F_{ij}$, where F_{ij} is a function and c_{ij} is the iteration constant (see Section 1.8). The F_{ij} are shown in Table 7.3. Most of the entries in this table are immediately available from the results of Chapters 4 and 6, but it should be noted that UNION, DIFF, and BOTH have been defined in a way which assumes that the resultant set is a new creation (not just one of the previous sets with modified entries), and this affects the timing. For example, $c_{12}F_{12}$ is the cost of determining MEMBERship in an unordered list. This was called $E_p(n)$ [or $E_a(n)$] in Chapter 2, and the cost was $O(n)$, so that $F_{12} = n$. To determine the c_{ij} precisely, it is necessary to distinguish between average costs and maximum costs. In most cases the ratio of these is a constant, independent of the size of the set, but to be definite, we shall assume that maximum cost is meant. This assumption may affect the way certain data structures are implemented. For example, it may require that the load factor of the hash table not be greater than a predetermined factor, and it was because of it that a *balanced* lexicographic binary tree was chosen rather than a randomly given tree. But with suitable qualifications, the F's of Table 7.3 can be accepted as showing the functional dependence of the maximum cost on the number of entries.

Entries in Table 7.3 that have not already been found in earlier chapters are readily determined. For R_1 it is assumed that in the instruction set of the computer there are available the logical operations "and," "or," and "not," on bit vectors. These allow

---

[3] If it were desirable to have atomic members of variable length, as would be necessary if strings could be elements, a pointer to the end of the storage area could be included.

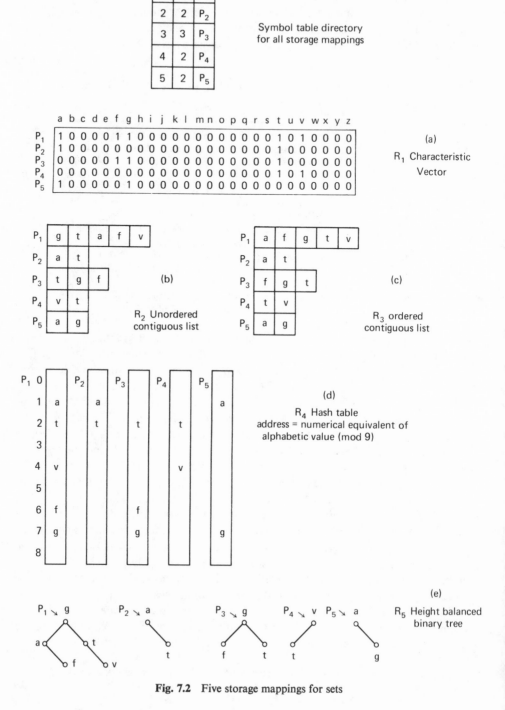

Fig. 7.2 Five storage mappings for sets

250

TABLE 7.3 Cost of executing set macros with different data structures (execution time $= c_{ij} \cdot F_{ij}$)

Data Structure Macro	R_1 Characteristic Vector	R_2 Unordered List	R_3 Ordered List	R_4 Hash Table	R_5 Height-Balanced Binary Tree
1 MEMBER (x,S)	constant	n	$\log n$	constant	$\log n$
2 CHOOSE (x,S)	constant	constant	constant	n	$\log n$
3 MAX (S)	$n_{\max}$	n	constant	n	$\log n$
4 PART (x,S)	$n_{\max}$	n	$\log n$	n	n
5 UNION (S_1,S_2)	$n_{\max}$	$(n_1 + n_2)\log\min(n_1, n_2)$	$n_1 + n_2$	$\max(n_1, n_2)$	$\log[(n_1 + n_2)!/\max(n_1!, n_2!)]$
6 DIFF (S_1,S_2)	$n_{\max}$	$(n_1 + n_2)\log\min(n_1, n_2)$	$n_1 + n_2$	$\max(n_1, n_2)$	$\log[(n_1 + n_2)!/\max(n_1!, n_2!)]$
7 BOTH (S_1,S_2)	$n_{\max}$	$(n_1 + n_2)\log\min(n_1, n_2)$	$n_1 + n_2$	$\max(n_1, n_2)$	$\log[(n_1 + n_2)!/\max(n_1!, n_2!)]$
8 CONSTRUCT $(S,a_1,\ldots,a_n)$	$n_{\max}$	n	$n\log n$	n	$n\log n$

$|S| = n \qquad |S_1| = n_1 \qquad |S_2| = n_2$

set union, intersection, and difference to be carried out. Assuming that there are too many components to be represented in a single word, the time is proportional to n_{max}, the cardinality of the maximum set size. Membership is accomplished by looking for a 1 bit in a specified position. It can be determined in a constant time by setting an index register with the numerical value of the member being sought to find a word that is tested against the set. It is assumed that consecutive invocations of CHOOSE will yield different set elements. If a record is kept of the result of the last invocation, choosing a member can be accomplished in a constant time.

Using the data structure R_2, procedures for realizing UNION, DIFF, and BOTH can take $O(n_1 \cdot n_2)$, but for large sets it will be worth ordering the smaller set and using a binary search to test for the presence of elements of the larger. This makes these times $O(n_1 + n_2) \log \min (n_1, n_2)$.

For R_3, CONSTRUCT requires sorting, so F_{83} is $n \log n$. After sorting, MEMBER can be carried out by binary search, making F_{13} equal to $\log n$. If UNION is carried out by a straightforward merging of S_1 and S_2, F_{53} is $n_1 + n_2$. The times for carrying out the macros with a height-balanced tree representation follow from the searching and inserting algorithms given in Chapter 6. Note that MAX is effected by following right links of the tree, so that F_{35} is $\log n$; and that PART is accomplished by tree traversal, so that F_{45} is n. Choosing a member involves a partial descent into the tree, and hence F_{25} is $\log n$.

In each row of Table 7.3, the entry which is least (i.e., shows lowest-order dependence on n) is in boldface. The fact that there is no column for which all the entries are smallest shows that no one data structure is most efficient for all the macros. From the discussions of efficiency in Sections 1.7 and 2.8, it will be realized that even if we assume that a particular problem can be programmed using only the macros given here, Table 7.3 does not contain *all* the information needed to carry out a proper comparative evaluation of the data structures. For example, the iteration constants, c_{i1}, are small for the characteristic vector structure because they all contain a factor, $1/w$, where w is the word size in bits. This makes the method very efficient for sets with only a few members. But if it is not desired to use integer numbers to represent the members, then a dictionary for converting the names to integers is needed. This could be a hash table or some kind of array, but additional costs are then incurred. Moreover, the F_{ij} as shown are only the limiting forms of functions that contain several terms, each with some multiplier. These extra terms can influence the relative costs, so that the limiting forms, valid for sets of large cardinality, may not present an accurate picture for the problem of interest.

From Table 7.3 it can be inferred that for applications in which the operations UNION, DIFF, and BOTH dominate, a hash table data structure is likely to be most effective. This same organization would be best where insertions and deletions are of principal concern. For applications involving rank determinations and partitioning, the ordered list is likely to be best. Where both insertions and ranking are important, the tree might be best, even though it is never best for a *particular* operation. For sets of small cardinality the characteristic vector may be best. The unordered list has little to recommend it, except that choosing a member takes a time that is independent of cardinality. These conclusions, however, must be qualified by the considerations raised in the previous paragraph, and the overall conclusion is *that there is no one data structure best for all set manipulation problems.* Thus Aho, Hopcroft, and Ullman, in their discussion of data structures for set manipulation problems (Chapter 4 in the *Design and Analysis of Computer Algorithms*), consider all the structures mentioned here in the light of the particular set of operations that are important to the applications in which the sets arise.

Given the application, the following is a suggested strategy for determining the program with least execution costs.

- Code the macros in terms of the instruction set available for the computer, determining the iteration constants c_{ij}. (These will be expressed in terms of the execution times for the operations, and as such will be machine dependent.)
- Program the application in terms of the macros, determining the frequencies of occurrence, f_i. [The f_i will depend on parameters of the problem (e.g., the number of variables, the frequencies of certain searches, and so on).]
- Assuming that the macros dominate the execution, T, the execution time using the jth data structure, is given by

$$T_j = \sum_{i=1}^{8} f_i \cdot c_{ij} \cdot F_{ij}.$$

- Choose the data structure for which T_j is a minimum.

7.1.1 Data Structure Design

Before leaving the question of choosing the best structure for sets, it is interesting to speculate on whether the preceding approach to the design of data structures can be made systematic, or even automated, so as to be applicable in other situations, even when additional considerations such as saving storage are to be taken into account. Several authors have addressed this question (see Low, 1974, Tompa, 1976, and references in footnotes 4–6).

If the design technique is to be general, the operation set, O, cannot be tied to one application. This leads one to attempt to identify a set of "basic" or "universal" operators with which any specified operation can be easily expressed. The characteristics of a particular application are determined by the relative importance, or weights, attached to the various operators. The generic operations discussed in Section 2.5 are obvious candidates for the basic operators. These include such functions as

---

[4]C. C. Gotlieb and F. W. Tompa, "Choosing a Storage Schema," *Acta Informatica*, **3** (1974), 297–319.

[5]J. T. Schwartz, "Optimization of Very High Level Languages": "I. Value Transmission and Its Corollaries," *Computer Languages*, **1** (1975), 161–194; "II. Deducing Relationships of Inclusion and Membership," *Computer Languages*, **1** (1975), 197–218.

[6]J. Low and P. Rovner, *Techniques for the Automatic Selection of Data Structures* (Rochester, N.Y.: Computer Science Department, University of Rochester, 1975).

"add," "search," and "delete," which are certainly valid in Example 7.1.[7] Given the basic operators, the cost, in time and storage, of programming an application using different data structures is determined.

Let O_i, $1 \leq i \leq n$, be a set of basic operators, and R_j, $1 \leq j \leq m$, be a set of "standard" data structures. The data structures specify detailed mappings of value sets into storage, and from an analysis of the coded algorithms which realize the O_i, determine:

(a) $e_{ij} \cdot F_{ij}$—the cost of executing the ith operator when the jth structure is used.
(b) $s_{ij} \cdot G_{ij}$—the storage costs for implementing the ith operator using the jth structure.

In these expressions, F_{ij} and G_{ij} are complexity functions in which the parameters of the structure appear, and e_{ij} and s_{ij} are multiplicative iteration constants. Costs, measured in dollars, vary from computer to computer. Storage costs can be expressed as charge per byte (or per addressable cell). For execution costs, the expressions resulting from the algorithm analysis have to be derived as equations in which the time to carry out machine operations appears as a factor. The built-in operation set is specific to a computer, but simplifying assumptions can be made, for example that only a few times need be taken into consideration:

- M—the time to access a cell in main memory.
- A—the (average) time for an arithmetic or logical operation.
- T—the time for a transfer of control.

As an example, the cost of locating a key in a lexicographic tree with N nodes is given by

$$(c_{11}M + c_{12}A + c_{13}T) \log N + (c_{21}M + c_{22}A + c_{23}T).$$

The c_{ij} are determined by an analysis of Algorithm 6.5, in which each of the "high-level" instructions which appear there is replaced by a linear form $(mM + aA + tT)$, where m, a, and t are found from the machine-code realizations of the high-level instructions. Determining the tables for e_{ij}, F_{ij}, s_{ij}, and G_{ij} is tedious, but it has to be done only once, given O and R, and with a program for algebraic manipulation, a computer can be used to help.

Given an application, and the availability of the tables, an optimization procedure for choosing data structures follows. First it is necessary to determine f_i, the relative frequency or importance of O_i in the application. If these are not known, a priori values are assigned to them, using the best available information, and it is assumed that a monitoring program can be attached to the application while it is running, from which

---

[7]Actually the operations have to be defined more precisely than is done in Section 2.5. For example, the time to carry out a search operation, which might be designated as "Get," depends on whether the search is being initiated at the root of the structure involved, or it is being requested for a key that follows one which has just been retrieved. Thus it is necessary to have at least two search operations, say "Get" and "Get next." Still others, characteristic of the structure, might be needed. For example, when using trees, it might be desirable to have a search "Get father," which would require the presence of threaded links.

more realistic values for the f_i can be determined eventually. The execution cost E_j for the jth structure is given by

$$E_j = \sum_{i=1}^{n} f_i e_{ij} F_{ij}.$$

Similarly, the storage cost, S_j, is

$$S_j = \sum_{i=1}^{n} f_i s_{ij} G_{ij}.$$

The toal cost, C_j, for the jth structure is

$$C_j = w_e E_j + w_s s_j,$$

where w_e and w_s are factors for the cost of storage and execution time. The optimal structure is given by C_{opt}, such that

$$C_{\text{opt}} = \min_j C_j.$$

An evaluation process along these lines underlies most of the proposals for systematic design of data structures.[8] While a formal minimization, as described here, is not always present, the essential features of selection and comparison are.

- It is assumed that there is a library of "standard" structures and the design is realized by choosing among the alternatives.
- A comparative evaluation, based on execution time and storage requirements, is performed.
- The application for which the design is being undertaken is in some sense limited or closed. It is difficult to express this more precisely, but it means, for example, that the operation set that has to be considered is predetermined, or that the problem is that of optimizing one specified program.

In the references cited, there are only a few illustrations of how the methodology for data structure choice is actually used to carry through a design, and no claims are advanced that the techniques have been used as a regular working tool. There *are* recognized situations where the choice of a particular data structure has been of crucial importance in deriving an efficient algorithm; the algorithm for determining whether a graph is planar is a case in point.[9] But the data structures that are arrived at in such problems are not the result of an optimized selection procedure. They are determined, rather, as part of the algorithm derivation, and the data structure design is not separated as a distinct process. This suggests one reason why no "handbook method" or standardized engineering approach to data structure design emerges. The design has to be regarded as part of algorithm design (i.e., part of the methodology for solving problems), and there is, of course, no standarized approach for solving

---

[8]See Low (1974), Tompa (1976), and the references cited in footnotes 4 and 6. Schwartz (footnote 5) addresses himself to a different set of problems involving data structures, problems relating to the minimization of storage when assignments are made and when there are inclusion relationships in sets.

[9]J. Hopcroft and R. Tarjan, "Efficient Planarity Testing," *Journal of the ACM*, **21**, no. 4 (Oct. 974, 549–568.

problems in a general situation. It might be argued that the methodology outlined above can be applied iteratively, especially if the frequencies, *f*, can be reassessed periodically, and in this way the data structure design is integrated with algorithm evolution to produce improved structures. But the effectiveness of attempting to separate the design of data structures from the design of algorithms remains problematical.

The last of the features mentioned above points to another factor that limits the usefulness of the design process as described. In a real application, the possible savings to be realized through optimal or near-optimal structures have to be great enough to offset the costs of going through a formal optimization procedure (as compared with using simple composite structures). In practice this means that the programs must be large and repetitive, which in turn means that they will be complex enough to require several interrelated substructures. But these properties are characteristic of data-processing applications where, invariably, the volume of data requires the use of secondary storage. In effect, this says that the most important aspect of data structure design is file design, involving secondary storage, and even beyond that, data base design, where large, multiple files are needed. Therefore, to pursue data structure design further, it is necessary to study secondary storage devices, with particular attention to data access, which plays such a large role in the searching, addition, and updating operations of file processing. These topics are discussed in Chapters 9 and 10. However, to show in somewhat more detail how data structures are selected in an application close to a real situation, a design problem is discussed at some length in Appendix 1. This example illustrates many of the choices regarding data structures presented in Chapters 2 through 7.

7.2 Set Processing Languages

Notwithstanding the argument just made that there is no best way of representing sets, there have been several sustained efforts at designing general-purpose languages and systems that would be efficient for set applications. Childs based a set representation on ordered lists, and provided for the inclusion of tuples, sets whose members could be sets, and set generators.[10] Another set programming language is described by Elcock.[11] However, sets are so primitive, and have so many uses, that any attempt to realize a universal implementation encounters built-in inefficiencies to the extent that the system becomes impractical for some important special class of problems. Those set manipulation systems which have gained currency have been directed at specific applications, or have included features that allow one to bring in special facilities for dealing with particular classes of problems.

The LEAP language, developed by Feldman and Rovner (1969), is basically a set processing language, designed with graphic and artificial intelligence applications in mind. Its most interesting feature is the ability to perform *associative searches* (i.e.,

[10]D. L. Childs, "Description of a Set-Theoretic Data Structure," *Proceedings of the 1968 Fall Joint Computing Conference*, Vol. 33 (Washington, D.C.: Thompson Book Co.), pp. 557–564.

[11]E. W. Elcock and others, "ABSET, a Programming Language Based on Sets: Motivation and Examples," *Artificial Intelligence*, **6**, no. 10 (1971), 467–492.

carry out a simultaneous scan on a set to determine which members satisfy selected criteria). SETL, developed by Schwartz and coworkers at the New York University (Schwartz, 1973), was designed so that its compiler could (eventually) produce different representations of a set, according to the application area in mind. As its name suggests, it is a language based strongly on set notation, and it has been tested comprehensively with a set representation based on hash tables. In the remainder of this section we consider LEAP and SETL in greater detail.

7.2.1 Attributes, Objects, and Values in LEAP

LEAP is embedded in ALGOL, and besides having ALGOL-like types and statements, there are operators for inserting a member into a set (**put**), deleting a member (**remove**), and a loop statement of the form **foreach** x **in** S **do**, which allows one to process a set. Its most interesting constructs are built around a universe of *items* (or objects), which may be regarded as members of sets, and *associations* between items, which may be regarded as ternary relations defined on a Cartesian product of sets.

In the discussion of lists in Chapter 4 we described objects (identified by keys), and their attributes, which might be represented in a part of storage distinct from the directory where the objects are listed. The problem of ascertaining whether an object possesses a certain attribute and of determining the value of the attribute is a very common one, not only in data processing but in many other applications. In list-processing languages for artificial intelligence studies, for example, it is common to attach a *property list* to objects, and such lists are frequently searched. There are many ways of representing property lists, and the usual choices between storage and execution efficiency appear. The fastest way of testing for the presence of a particular property would be to use an indexed system where, for example, color is stored in the third field in the attribute list, in which case the value can be determined without having to do a sequential search. But for objects that have no color, it is wasteful of storage to reserve a field for that attribute; a better approach might be to represent the property by a type code followed by the value. This saves storage, but attribute search and determination is more costly, so we have the familiar trade-off. When searches for some attributes are particularly important, inverted lists and multilists can be used to advantage.

In LEAP there is special provision for representing an associative triple, F0, relating attribute, object, and value. Such a relation can be written

$$\text{F0:} \quad a \cdot o \equiv v$$

and read "the value of the attribute a possessed by the object o is v." Once this relation is declared, it is possible to ask whether object o has value v for attribute a and, more generally, to pose questions whose answers are in the form of values or set members which satisfy the relation. Thus, if x is an unspecified element in a ternary relation, another form, F1, is

$$\text{F1:} \quad a \cdot o \equiv x,$$

which requests the values x for the attribute a of object o.

Going back to the inverted list example in Table 4.2, suppose that employees are "objects" and the city of residence is an attribute. Then an instance of F0 corresponds to

"The residence · employee 105–26 ≡ N.Y."

If it is decided to *make* (i.e., establish) this association in the system, an enquiry of whether the residence of a employee 105–26 is N.Y. will yield the value *true*. The system can also keep historical information, so that not only is the city of current residence recorded, but also earlier residences. Then a query of the form

F1:   residence ∘ 105–26 ≡ x

will produce the set of cities satisfying the ternary relation (i.e., the set of cities in which employee 105–26 lived).

Other forms of the association are:

F2: $a \cdot x \equiv v$ Which employees live in N.Y.? This corresponds to a request for an inverted list on the N.Y. value of the residence attribute. The result, given the data of Table 4.2, is {105–26, 329–51, 341–90}.

F3: $x \cdot 0 \equiv v$ Which attributes of employee 105–26 have N.Y. as value? If "place of birth" is an attribute and if 105–26 had been born in N.Y., the result of the query would be {residence, place of birth}.

F4: $a \cdot x \equiv z$ List all pairs, x, z, for the attribute "city of residence" (i.e., the cities of residence for all employees). This corresponds to a set of inverted lists (i.e., an inverted list for each attribute value of residence).

F5: $x \cdot z \equiv v$ List all pairs ⟨attribute, object⟩ for which N.Y. is a value (e.g., the list of employees who *live* in N.Y., and also the list of employees who were *born* in N.Y.)

F6: $x \cdot o \equiv z$ List all attributes and values for employee 105–26. In effect, print all data about him or her.

The queries above are called *associative searches*, because they specify the retrieval of data tuples based on their contents rather than on identifiers or addresses. In Section 4.5.2 we assumed that data items were stored to permit fast access on a particular *key* field, and considered techniques (inverted lists, multilists) for looking up tuples according to other field values. These methods could be used to implement associative retrieval in LEAP, but while they avoid scanning the whole file for a particular request, their search performance is slow compared to lookup on the field used as the basis for tuple allocation. Moreover, keying data according to one particular field or attribute would conflict with the LEAP goal of preserving symmetry among attributes, objects, and values, that is, not favoring any of the a, o, or v components in a triple.

The solution adopted to maintain symmetry is to keep *three copies* of triple storage, each a hash table keyed, respectively, on the combinations Attribute–Object, Object–Value, and Value–Attribute. To illustrate how this achieves fast response for the various query types, we will describe the organization of the Attribute–Object table. Suppose that there are two triples (residence, 105–26, N.Y.) and (residence, 105–26, CHI), reflecting places where employee 105–26 has lived. Then a request of the form "residence · 105–26 = X" is answered as follows.

During compilation, unique integer internal names are assigned to every item identifier. The two high-order digits of the name for "residence" specify the page in the Attribute table where chains of the form "residence–object" reside. To find the start of the chain wanted here, "residence–105–26," the remaining digits of the residence internal name are hashed together with those of the name for 105–26. The result is the address for a list header of the type shown in Fig. 7.3(a). It points to the list of values completing the triple whose first two components are residence and 105–26 [Fig. 7.3(b)], and can be part of other chains as well. The fields of the header are:

- O—the internal name for the object identifier, in this case, the one for 105–26.
- #—a code for identifying the type of storage block (here 4, for association triplet).
- Conflict list—The address of the header for "residence–105–26" is determined by hashing parts of the internal names of the two items. This means that no other residence–object pair can map to the same location, but there might be other (attribute, object) pairs that will. Each such pair needs its own value list, and so must be given a header; the conflict list links such headers together. The situation where three pairs (A_1,O_1), (A_2,O_2) and (A_3,O_3) all hash to the same address is illustrated in Fig. 7.3(c). Note that because of the additive nature of the hashing function, the attribute values associated with O_2 and O_3 are uniquely determined given the starting address of the whole chain.
- Value list—contains either a single value, or a pointer to a list of values associated with the attribute–object pair.
- A-Use—The structure illustrated makes it easy to answer an F1-type query such as "residence–105–26 = x." However, if an F4 request (residence · $x \equiv z$) is made, we must find all the value lists for pairs of the form (residence, object). The search procedure just described needs actual object, as well as attribute values to work, and is therefore inadequate. The problem is solved by chaining together all (residence–object) headers through the A-Use field.

In Fig. 7.3(c) an extra field attached to the value blocks contains internal names assigned to *bracketed* triples, here (A_1,O_1,V_1) and (A_2,O_2,V_2). Triples are bracketed when they themselves are used as items in an association triple. For example, it might be desirable to associate a date of last residence with every place employee 105–26 has lived. This is done with the triple assignments

$$\text{residence\_ended} \cdot [\text{residence} \cdot 105\text{--}26 \equiv \text{N.Y.}] \equiv \textbf{new } (1975)$$

$$\text{residence\_ended} \cdot [\text{residence} \cdot 105\text{--}26 \equiv \text{CHI}]) \equiv \textbf{new } (1970)$$

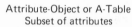

Attribute-Object or A-Table
Subset of attributes

residence-employee # table

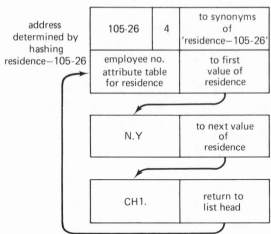

address constructed by hashing (attribute-object)	object identifier	code for identifying blocks as an association triple	pointer to synonym on attribute-object
	0	# triple	conflict list
			Value
	pointer to other associations on attribute		value for object if unique-else pointer to first entry in synonym list
	A-use		list

(a) Format for hash table entry

address determined by hashing residence—105-26	105-26	4	to synonyms of 'residence—105-26'
	employee no. attribute table for residence		to first value of residence
	N.Y		to next value of residence
	CH1.		return to list head

(b) Hash table and value entries on 'Residence-105-26'

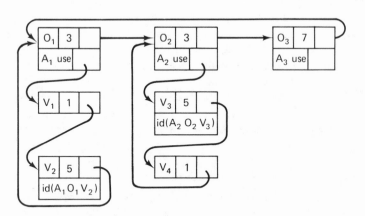

(c) Structure for multiple values and conflicts

Fig. 7.3   Storage structure for association entries in LEAP

These new triples are stored in the Attribute table as just described, and to do this, internal names are needed for the triples in brackets. The names would be assigned and stored in the value list associated with (residence, 105–26).

The Attribute table thus makes it possible to answer queries of types F1 and F4. A similarly organized Object table (hashed on object–value pairs) is used for queries F3 and F6, while a Value table ensures fast response to requests of the form F2 and F5. Queries of Type F0, which ask whether a certain tuple is in the system, can be handled using any of the tables.

Further details on LEAP can be found in Feldman and Rovner (1969), and in the references cited there.[12] The interesting contribution of the language is its handling of associative retrieval at the implementation and query levels, subjects to which we return in Chapter 10.

7.2.2 SETL

SETL is a high-level, fully developed language intended for applications ranging from constructing compilers to solving combinatorial problems. Its chief architect is J. Schwarz of New York University. Cardinal among its features are the special emphasis placed on operations for defining, generating, and manipulating sets, and a very conscious separation of the language definition from the representation for sets used by the compiler. This separation has led to a highly systematic development of the language, and among other benefits, means that the language has the potential of being highly portable (i.e., capable of being easily implemented on different computers). During the early stages, attention was focused on the choice of primitive and composite data types, and on the operations desirable for the types in the light of at least some of the applications for which the language is intended. In the intermediate stage, the language was implemented by a modular package of programs which realized the intent of the operations but which was not particularly efficient. Later, careful attention was paid to optimizing the control structures of programs and to the design of data structures. Producing a compiler that can automatically choose among alternative data structures is a long-term goal, but the advantages of allowing users to provide information that can guide the choice is recognized.

It is not possible here to provide, even in brief form, enough explanation so that one can write and fully understand SETL programs; for that it is necessary to go to the language manuals.[13] Instead, we shall attempt, as we have done for SNOBOL and APL, to present the principal features that orient the language to its special data type, sets in this case, and to illustrate how the data structures were designed in the initial implementations so that the chosen operations could be realized with acceptable efficiencies.

The types as seen by the user of SETL, along with designators for them, are shown in Table 7.4. There are no declarations but an operation *type x* returns the designator.

[12]Later developments in LEAP are to be found in J. A. Feldman and others, "Recent Developments in SAIL—An ALGOL Based Language for Artificial Intelligence," *Proceedings of the 1972 AFIPS Fall Joint Computing Conference*, Vol. 41, Part II, pp. 1193–1202. (Montvale, N.J.: AFIPS Press).

[13]For a user's manual on a preliminary version of the language, see H. Mullisk and M. Goldstein, *A SETLB Primer* (New York: Courant Institute of Mathematical Sciences, New York University, 1973).

TABLE 7.4   Types in SETL

Type	Designator
Primitive	
integer	*int*
real	*real*
bit-string	*bool*
character string	*char*
blank atom	*blank*
procedure	*subr*
label	*lab*
Composite	
set	*set*
tuple	*tupl*

Sets may be defined by enumerating the members and by using "set-former" operations expressed in standard mathematical notation. For example, $\{x \in a \mid C(x)\}$ defines the subset of a for which $C(x)$ is true; $\exists \; x \in a \mid C(x)$ sets x to the first member of a such that $C(x)$ is *true*. If no such value is found, then x is assigned Ω, the null value.

In the language there are the usual algebraic, logical, and relational operators on variables. Control structures for specifying statements, subroutines, and scope of variables, are present in variant forms, many of them very concise because of the availability of set notation. Examples of some of the basic operations on sets and tuples are shown in Table 7.5.

TABLE 7.5   Operations on sets and tuples in SETL

Notation	Meaning	Example
$\in$	Membership test	$a \in \{a, b\}$ is t
$\ni$	Selection of an element (through a built-in, deterministic selection)	$\ni \{a, b\}$ is either a or b
#	Number of elements	$\#\{a,b\}$ is 2; $\#nl$ is 0
with	Insertion	$\{a\}$ *with* $\{b\}$ is $\{a,b\}$
less	Deletion	$\{a,b\}$ *less* b is $\{a\}$
incs	Inclusion	$\{a,b\}$ *incs* $\{a\}$ is t
pow	Power set	$pow(\{a,b\})$ is $\{nl,\{a\},\{b\},\{a,b\}\}$
npow	Elements of power set with n members	$npow(2,\{a,b,c\})$ is $\{\{a,b\},\{b,c\},\{c,a\}\}$
*	Set intersection	$\{a,b\}*\{b,c\}$ is $\{b\}$
+	Tuple concatenation; set union	$\langle a,b \rangle + \langle a,c \rangle = \langle a,b,a,c \rangle$ $\{a\} + \{b\}$ is $\{a,b\}$
$t(k)$	Selection	$t(2) = b$, where $t = \langle a,b,a,c \rangle$
$t(i:j)$	Selection—j components starting with ith	$t(2:2) = \langle b,a \rangle$
hd	First component of tuple (cf. *car*)	$hd \langle a,b \rangle$ is a
tl	Remaining tuple after removal of first component (cf. *cdr*)	$tl \langle a,b \rangle$ is $\langle b \rangle$

A compound operator (similar to / in APL) is provided by the notation
$[op: x \in S]e(x)$, which means $e(x_1)op\ e(x_2)op \ldots op\ e(x_n)$ where $S = \{x_1, \ldots, x_n\}$.
For example,

$$[max: x \in \{1,3,2\}](x+1) \quad \text{is } 4$$

and

$$[+: x(n) \in a]x \quad \text{is } \sum_{i=1}^{n} a_i.$$

Three functional operators operate on sets of ordered pairs. Since any tuple can be regarded as a first member followed by the rest of the tuple, the operators are really defined on sets of tuples. Of the three, the first operator is most important since the results of the other two can be expressed as terms of it. They will be illustrated on the set

$$f = \{\langle A,P,U\rangle, \langle A,Q,V\rangle, \langle A,R,W\rangle, \langle B,P,X\rangle, \langle B,Q,Y\rangle, \langle B,R,Z\rangle\}.$$

- $f\{a\}$ is the set of all x such that $\langle a,x\rangle \in f$. Thus $f\{A\} = \{\langle P,U\rangle, \langle Q,V\rangle, \langle R,W\rangle\}$. Multiple arguments are permitted, so $f\{A,P\} = (f\{A\})\{P\} = \{U\}$.
- $f(a)$ is the unique element of $f\{a\}$ if $f\{a\}$ is a singleton, or else it is undefined. Thus $f\{A\}$ (P), which can also be written as $f(A,P)$, is U.
- $f[a]$ is the union over $x \in a$ of the sets $f\{x\}$. Thus, if $S = \{A,B\}$, $f[S] = \{\langle P,U\rangle, \langle Q,V\rangle, \langle R,W\rangle, \langle P,X\rangle, \langle Q,Y\rangle, \langle R,Z\rangle\}$.

These functions seem to be abstract and artificial, but if we remember that functions and maps on finite domains can be regarded as sets of ordered pairs $\langle\text{argument}, \text{value}\rangle$ or, $\langle x,y\rangle$, where y is the image of x, it can be seen that these operators are methods of obtaining the value corresponding to the argument, or the image of a point in a mapping. Thus suppose that f is the set (see Example 1.4) given by

$$\{\langle\text{red, cylinder}\rangle, \langle\text{red, sphere}\rangle, \langle\text{green, cube}\rangle,$$

$$\langle\text{green, cylinder}\rangle, \langle\text{blue, sphere}\rangle, \langle\text{blue, cube}\rangle\}.$$

Then $f\{\text{red}\}$ yields the set {cyclinder, sphere}, the members related to red in the binary relation COLOR $\times$ SHAPE, where

$$\text{COLOR} = \{\text{red, green, blue}\} \quad \text{and} \quad \text{SHAPE} = \{\text{cylinder, sphere, cube}\}.$$

$f(\text{red})$ yields the undefined atom, since the relation is not a function, $f[\text{COLOR}]$ yields {cylinder, sphere, cube} (i.e., $f\{\text{red}\} \cup f\{\text{blue}\} \cup f\{\text{green}\}$).

Another way of stating these evaluations is that $f\{\text{red}\}$ yields the inverted list on red, or is the result of an associative search on the attribute COLOR with value red, so we have another formulation of associative searches.

Because of the ordering present in a tuple (or a binary relation), there is a lack of symmetry between the first and second components. Thus while $f\{\text{red}\}$ resulted in {cylinder, sphere}, we cannot do a similar evaluation for $f\{\text{sphere}\}$ because SHAPE is the *second* set of the relation. To achieve symmetry the ability to reverse ordered pairs is provided. This is done by the statement

$$g = \{\langle x(2), x(1)\rangle, x \in f\},$$

which has the effect of defining the set

$$g = \{\langle \text{cyclinder, red}\rangle, \langle \text{sphere, red}\rangle, \ldots, \langle \text{cube, blue}\rangle\}.$$

Now $g\{\text{sphere}\}$ results in $\{\text{red, blue}\}$.

By using multiple arguments it is possible to describe functions on several variables or higher-order relations. Suppose that f is defined as the set of triples $\{\langle \text{B1,red,cylinder}\rangle, \langle \text{B2,red,sphere}\rangle, \ldots, \langle \text{B6,blue,cube}\rangle\}$ and $\text{BLOCK}=\{\text{B1}, \ldots, \text{B6}\}$, thereby introducing objects as well as attributes. Then f is a function of block number, and $f(\text{B3})$ yields the unique value $\langle \text{green, cube}\rangle$, corresponding to the argument B3. $f[\text{BLOCK}]$ yields the set $\{\langle \text{red,cylinder}\rangle, \ldots \langle \text{blue,cube}\rangle\}$ and $f[\text{BLOCK}]\{\text{red}\}$ results in $\{\text{cylinder,sphere}\}$. The effect is that of an associative search giving the SHAPE value for all red objects, or, in LEAP terms,

$$shape \cdot x \equiv red.$$

As will be seen, the representation of these sets and associations requires considerable storage in SETL (as was the case for LEAP), but the scope declarations which are a feature of the language allow the garbage collecter to recover storage for sets that are no longer needed.

In the initial implementation of SETL, the storage representation for sets is based on hash tables, since as was seen in the previous section, this allows efficient determinations for set membership, union, and intersection. Additional features are introduced to make working with tuples and functional evaluation of sets of tuples efficient. As in SNOBOL, there is a common descriptor, called a *root word*, for all types in SETL. Root words have a field for the type designator, and if the datum for the variable is short enough, it is carried in the root word. Otherwise, there is a pointer to a storage block for the value. The format for primitive types is straightforward, and we shall simply illustrate the data representations for tuples and sets [Fig. 7.4(a) and (b)]. The following comments, in addition to the notation in the figures, will help explain the structures.

- Tuples are represented as ordered lists with a growth space for additional members.
- The R field in both tuples and sets (and in other types as well) is a reference count indicating how many times the variable is referred to. Such information can be useful for garbage collection (see Section 8.3), but in SETL it is used to determine whether a variable should be copied when it is modified in certain ways (e.g., when an assignment is made to part of it).
- The hash table size S, and the number of members ($\# \ mem$) are both stored, $\# \ mem$ being updated on each insertion and deletion. If $\# \ mem/S >$ specified constant, the hash table's size is doubled. This is a time-consuming operation, since new addresses are needed for each member (an extra bit being required). A similar test is performed on deletion, but halving the table is less expensive.
- A binary hash signature is computed for each atomic member of a set, and then hashed to determine an address for that atom. A hash code for a set is calculated by forming the exclusive or (bit-by-bit addition, modulo 2) of the signatures of

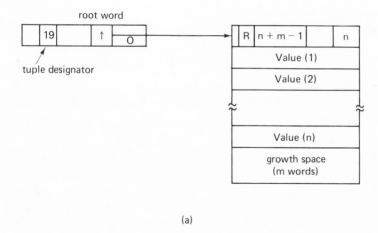

(a)

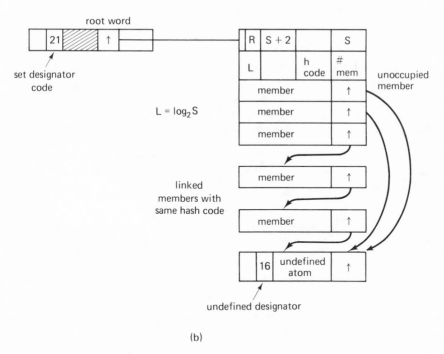

(b)

Fig. 7.4 Representations in SETL

the set members. Since the operation is associative, this code is independent of the order of formation. Each time a member is inserted or deleted in a set, the hash code is recalculated and stored. For example,

Old hash code	0 1 1 0
Code of member inserted	*1 0 1 0*
New hash code	*1 1 0 0*

Old hash code	1 1 0 0
Code of member deleted	*1 0 1 0*
New hash code	*0 1 1 0.*

The hash code for a tuple is the code of its first member. Although the code for a set is stored, for other data types it is computed as needed.

- The presence of the hash code is particularly useful when sets are being tested for equality, a test that can be recursive (since sets may have set members) and therefore expensive. Sets with distinct hash codes are unequal; if the codes are the same, a term-by-term comparison of the members must be performed. The effect is to shorten the *average* time for testing equality of sets in the situation when sets can contain set members.
- There are special representations for the null tuple and null set (not shown), and a special mapping for a set of tuples (also not shown) which allows rapid evaluation of the functional operators.

Example 7.2

We conclude the discussion of SETL by giving two short algorithms. The first is for performing an exchange sort, and the second determines the transitive closure of a binary relation. The brevity and lucidity of the algorithms are direct consequences of the language's set notation.[14] To obtain efficient algorithms, different computational processes must be used both for sorting and transitive closure.

(a) The sorting algorithm illustrates how looping is carried out by means of the quantifier $\forall$. Note how the bracketed statement specifies the domain of the variables, and how **end** specifies the range of the iteration. The entries of the tuple *seq* are sorted in place.

$$(1 < \forall j \le \# seq)$$
$$(j > \forall k \ge 1)$$
if $seq(k+1)$ *lt* $seq(k)$ **then**
$$\langle seq(k), seq(k+1) \rangle = \langle seq(k+1), seq(k) \rangle;$$
else
$\quad$ quit $\forall k$;
end if;
end $\forall k$;
end $\forall j$;

(b) The algorithm, *close(f,as)*, yields all members obtained by repeated application of the relation, *f*, to the set *as* $\subseteq S$.

---

[14]These examples are from Schwartz, *On Programming*, Installment 2, Sec. 3.

```
define f close(f,as);
im = f[as]; n = 0;
(while n lt # im) n = # im; im = im+f[im];;
return im;
end close;
```

The meaning of the key words, and of the whole program, should be obvious in each case. More sophisticated examples, which illustrate the full power of SETL, are to be found in Schwarz (1973).

7.3 Vertex-Edge-List Representation of a Graph

Graphs are second only to sets as a mathematical structure useful for applications in which there are discrete entities. The three representations of a graph described in Chapter 1 (as sets of vertices and edges, as an adjacency matrix, and as an incidence matrix) lead to a variety of data structures. As with sets, which is most suitable depends on the problem application and context. If there are n vertices and m edges in the graph, the adjacency matrix require n^2 entries, and the incidence matrix $m \cdot n$. For an undirected graph, $0 \le m \le n(n-1)/2$, and for a directed graph, $0 \le m \le n^2$. Writing $m = \rho n^2$, the *edge density*, ρ, plays much the same role for a graph as does the sparseness for a matrix. If it is small, the incidence matrix will require less storage than the adjacency matrix.

When graphs were considered in Chapter 4, the nodes carried labels which, if unique, could serve as distinct identifiers, or which might also be data carried by the nodes or pointers to such data. Because the data can be highly variable in length, it is usually convenient to maintain a node directory in which the nodes are referenced by integers and there are pointers to the labels and to the structural information. The directory already serves as a representation of the set of nodes, so that to represent a graph in terms of its constituent sets it is only necessary to add the data that specify the edges. This is done by providing for each vertex a list of its adjacent vertices. Such a representation of a graph will be called the *vertex-edge list*. It applies equally to directed and undirected graphs.

Figure 7.5(a) shows a rooted, labeled digraph (an *r.l.d.*) and Fig. 7.5(b) its logical structure in the form of a vertex-edge list. A natural storage structure for this list is an array where each entry consists of two pointers, one to the data for a vertex and one to a linked list of its outpointing edges [Fig. 7.5(c)]. This representation is economical of storage, requiring, as it does, $(n + m)$ cells. Another possibility is to use linked lists for both the node and edge lists. Figure 7.15 shows a representation for the graph of Fig. 7.5(a) when the structure is built up using LISP-type cells, consisting of atoms, and cells with pointer pairs.

In Fig. 7.5(c) the directory of nodes is an array, $out[i, j]$ where $1 \le i \le n$, and $1 \le j \le 2$, $out[i, 1]$ is a pointer to the data for the ith node, and $out[i,2]$ a pointer to the list of nodes for edges starting at node i. There is, of course, a symmetry between initial and terminal nodes, and in some problems (an example is given in the next section) it may be desirable to maintain for each node i a list of the initial nodes of

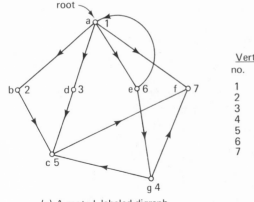

Vertex list

no.	label.	Edge list (terminal vertices of out-pointing edges)
1	a	2, 3, 6, 7
2	b	5
3	d	5
4	g	5, 7
5	c	7
6	e	4, 1
7	f	

(a) A rooted, labeled digraph

(b) Vertex-edge-list logical structure

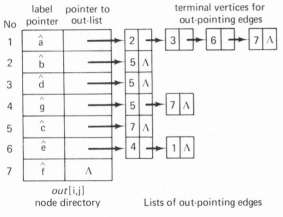

(c) Storage structure for vertex-edge list based on lists of out-pointing edges

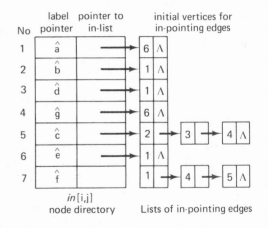

(d) Storage structure for vertex-edge-list based on lists of in-pointing edges

Fig. 7.5   Vertex-edge-list representation of a graph

edges terminating in *i*. This means keeping a node directory, $in[i,j]$, with edge lists corresponding to in-pointing edges. Figure 7.5(d) shows the storage structure using directory nodes and pointers to lists of in-pointing edges. The representation corresponds to storing the adjacency matrix of the graph, regarded as a sparse array, by the row–column method described in Section 5.4.1. When both vertex-edge lists correspond to in-pointing and out-pointing edges are maintained together, the data structure corresponds to the linked-list representation shown in Fig. 5.8. If the number of edges is less than n^2, this representation saves considerable storage over, say, the adjacency matrix representation, and in addition, provides easy access to the list of edges that either start or end at a given vertex.

Although in the logical structure of a graph the vertex lists and the edge lists are (unordered) sets, in the storage representation an ordering is imparted to the set members. In particular, there is an ordering to the edge list of each vertex. This ordering can be on the node number, or it can correspond to the lexicographic ordering on the node labels adjacent to the given vertex. But the fact that there *is* an ordering in itself means that there are several algorithms for systematic enumeration of the nodes of an r.l.d., and, as for lists, enumeration is an important process.

Two procedures for enumeration correspond to the depth-first and breadth-first searches already described in Section 6.2.2. In the depth-first enumeration of the nodes of an r.l.d., when a node is encountered, the node at the terminus of its first outgoing edge is listed (if it has not already been encountered). The same rule is then applied for the node so reached. When a node is reached for which every outgoing edge leads to an already listed node, there is a backtrack to its immediate predecessor, and the enumeration is continued from there. For the graph of Fig. 7.5(a), the depth-first listing results in

$$a, b, c, f, d, e, g.$$

In the breadth-first enumeration, all nodes (not already listed) adjacent to a vertex are listed, and the enumeration continues at the first of the adjacent nodes. For the graph of Fig. 7.4(a) the breadth-first listing is

$$a, b, d, e, f, c, g.$$

Both enumerations above yield a method for finding a spanning tree for a graph in a time that is $O(n+m)$. The spanning trees are shown in Fig. 7.6. Algorithm 7.2 gives the program for finding the spanning tree of a digraph based on depth-first search. The digraph is represented by the data structure shown in Fig. 7.7. Entries in both the node directory, and the list of outpointing edges, have a single bit field called *mark*. Initially *mark* is assumed to be set to **false** for all entries, and on termination of the algorithm *mark* is **true** for all nodes and edges in the spanning tree rooted at f (shown

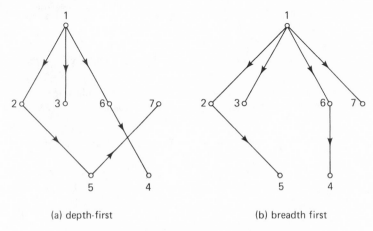

(a) depth-first   (b) breadth first

Fig. 7.6   Spanning trees for the graph of Fig. 7.5

shaded in Fig. 7.7). The declarations needed are

$$\textbf{comp node} = \langle \textbf{boolean } mark, \textbf{data-ptr } info, \textbf{entry-ptr } outlist \rangle$$

for the composite data type **node**, which describes components in the node directory, and **node-array** *nodelist*[$f:l$] to describe the node array, where $l-f+1 = n$, the number of nodes. The declaration

$$\textbf{comp entry} = \langle \textbf{boolean } mark, \textbf{integer } adjacent, \textbf{entry-ptr } link \rangle$$

describes makeup of entries in the outpointing edge list, where *adjacent* identifies a terminal node of an outpointing edge in the edge list of a node list component. The algorithm makes use of a working vector, *next*[i], which for each node indicates the next edge to be examined in the search; initially *next*[i] is set to the node at the head of the ith edge list. A stack *lifo* is used for storing the list of nodes encountered while descending. *Temp* and *edge* are temporary storage locations for an **entry-ptr** and an index to *nodelist*, respectively. The search procedure is complete when *lifo* is empty and the most recently processed node has a null link field (i.e., no additional edges). Table 7.6 shows the program trace for the graph of Fig. 7.5(a).

Algorithm 7.2   Spanning tree

```
integer l, f, i, edge; node-array nodelist[f : l]; entry-ptr temp;
integer-stack lifo; entry-ptr-array next[f : l];
do
    i ⇐ f;
    do while i ≤ l;
        next[i] ⇐ outlist (nodelist[i]);
        i ⇐ i+1;
    end /* initialize next to head of each entry-list */
    lifo ⇐ 0; temp ⇐ Λ; edge ⇐ 0; /*initialize working variables*/
    i ⇐ f; mark (nodelist[i]) ⇐ true; /*processing starts at root*/
    do while top(lifo) ≠ 0 ∨ next[i] ≠ Λ;
        if next[i] = Λ then
        pop(lifo,i); /* ascend */
        else do edge ⇐ adjacent (@ next[i]); /*take current edge*/
                temp ⇐ next[i];
                next[i] ⇐ link(@ next[i]); /*take next outgoing edge*/
                if mark(@ nodelist(edge)) = false then
                    do push(lifo,i); /*descend*/
                        mark(@ temp) ⇐ true; /*mark visited edge*/
                        i ⇐ edge;
                        mark(nodelist[i]) ⇐ true; /*mark visited node*/
                    end
            end
    end
end
end spanning_tree
```

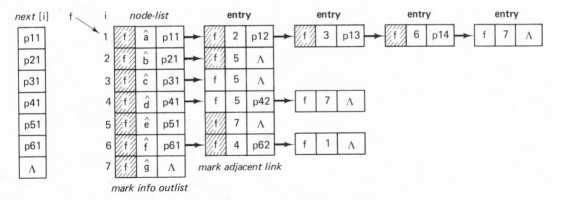

Fig. 7.7 Data structures for Algorithm 7.1

TABLE 7.6 Program trace for Algorithm 7.1

lifo	i	next[i]	edge	mark ⟸ true
·0	1	p11	0	nodelist[1]
0,1		p12	2	@ p11
	2	p21	5	nodelist[2]
0,1,2		Λ		@ p21
	5	p51	7	nodelist[5]
0,1,2,5		Λ		@ p51
	7	Λ		nodelist[7]
0,1,2	5	Λ		
0,1	2	Λ		
0	1	p12	3	
		p13		@ p12
0,1	3	p31	5	nodelist[3]
		Λ		
0	1	p13	6	
		p14		
0,1				@ p13
	6	p61	4	nodelist[6]
0,1,6				@ p61
	4	p41	5	nodelist[4]
		p42	7	
		Λ		
0,1	6	p62	1	
0	1	p14	7	
		Λ		

If the given digraph is not connected, application of Algorithm 7.2 will yield a spanning tree for the connected component rooted at f. To find another component, the node list is scanned until an unmarked node, say w, is encountered. Algorithm 7.1 is called with $w = f$, resulting in another connected component rooted at w. The process is repeated until all nodes in the node list are marked. In this way a spanning forest for a nonconnected graph is determined.

It is not difficult to show that the procedure for finding components just described takes a time which is $O(n+m)$. Each edge is visited only once, thereby introducing a term of $O(m)$, and scanning the list of nodes adds a term of $O(n)$.

The procedure outlined will also determine the connected components of an undirected graph. For an undirected graph a connected component is the transitive closure for a set of nodes related by adjacency. Thus the algorithm for finding a spanning forest or the connected components is essentially equivalent to an algorithm for finding the transitive closure of a relation, as was pointed out in Example 1.6. In that example the relation was represented by its matrix in the form of a two-dimensional array, and this results in an $O(n^3)$ algorithm for transitive closure. Transitive closure was also formulated in set terms in Example 7.2. The vertex-edge-list representation of a graph corresponds to using a combination of two different data structures for sets—an array for the node set, and linked lists for the edge set. Since $m+n < n^3$, we have an example where choosing the right data structure for the undirected graph results in a more efficient algorithm.[15] The vertex-edge-list data structure turns out to be efficient for a large number of (but not all!) procedures involving graphs, or involving lists that are equivalent to graphs. Additional examples of procedures on graphs follow in the next two sections.

7.4 Applications Using Representations for Acyclic Graphs

In this section we further illustrate the interdependence of processing efficiency and data structure by considering applications where the data takes the form of a rooted, directed *acyclic* graph. The most desirable representation for the graph depends on the calculations that come up in the application. It is clear that the incidence relation for a directed acyclic graph corresponds to a partial ordering on the nodes, since the acyclic graph is essentially the Hasse diagram for the poset (Section 1.2). The incidence relation on the nodes will be called the *precedence relation*, and the existence of an edge $\langle a,b \rangle$ in the acyclic graph corresponds to the predicate "*a* is an immediate predecessor of *b*" being *true*.

7.4.1 Parts Explosion

The first application is the *parts explosion* problem, which arises regularly in production planning. One is given a number of large products (e.g., aircraft or cars) which

---

[15] For directed graph the situation is somewhat more complicated since finding the (strongly) connected components is not equivalent to transitive closure on the adjacency relation. There may be a unilateral path between two different strongly connected components.

Besides the data structure, the working storage is another factor that greatly influences the algorithm. For example, Nijenhuis and Wilf (Chap. 14) give an algorithm for finding the spanning forest of an undirected graph without using stacks, whose complexity is $O(n \log n) + O(m)$. The literature on graph processing algorithms is extensive. (See Corneil, 1975, in the Bibliography of Chapter 1.)

are manufactured from basic components and replicated assemblies. The assemblies themselves are made up of components and subassemblies, and this continues down through many levels. At a given time there is an inventory of components and sub-assemblies on hand. Given the initial inventories and the product requirements for a time interval, the problem is to compute how many components and subassemblies of each type should be manufactured. Because there are inclusion relations between the products and their subassemblies and components, the production process is repre-sented by an acyclic graph where there is a source for each major product, and a directed edge ⟨A,B⟩ means that B is a component of A. An integer attached to the edge indicates how many copies of B appear in A.

Example 7.3

Figure 7.8 illustrates a simple parts explosion, although in a real situation the graph would consist of thousands of nodes (perhaps tens of thousands) and hun-dreds of levels.[16,17] The adjacency matrix, with integer entries corresponding to the

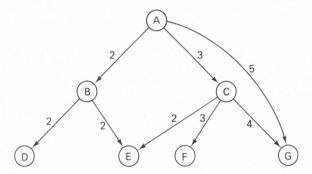

Fig. 7.8   Graph for a parts explosion

multiplicities of the edges, has zero-valued rows for basic components and columns of zeros for assemblies that are not components of anything else. It is called a *bill-of-materials* listing for the assemblies and subassemblies. The bill-of-materials listing for the production process of Fig. 7.8 is shown in Table 7.7 (next page).

The basic operation in a parts explosion is premultiplying the bill-of-materials listing by a row vector whose components are the requirements for subassemblies. This operation is repeated in stages, the successive stages corresponding to calcula-tions for subassemblies which are farther and farther distant from the source of the graph that corresponds to the largest subassembly. If five units of A are required, and the bill-of-materials matrix is designated as M, this gives rise to a requirement, on

[16]W. J. Brian, "A Parts Breakdown Technique Using List Structures," *Communications of the ACM*, **7**, no. 6 (June 1964), 362–365.

[17]F. L. Church, "Requirements Generation, Explosion and Bills of Material," *IBM Systems Journal*, **2** (Sept.–Dec. 1963), 268–287.

the first stage, of

$$\text{ABCDE FG} \qquad \text{A B CDEF G}$$
$$(5,0,0,0,0,0,0)M = (0,10,15,0,0,0,25),$$

that is, 10 units of B, 15 of C, and 25 of G. For the next stage the matrix multiplication is repeated for the new subassembly requirements. The requirements of 10 B's and 15 C's gives rise to

$$\text{A B CDEFG} \qquad \text{ABCD E F G}$$
$$(0,10,15,0,0,0,0)M = (0,0,0,20,50,45,60),$$

that is, 20 units of D, 50 of E, 45 of F, and 60 of G. There are only two stages here, corresponding to a length of two for the longest path in the graph starting at the source A. The total requirements for basic components are obtained by summing the product vectors. Thus

$$\text{DEF G} \qquad \text{D E F G} \qquad \text{D E F G}$$
$$(0,0,0,25) + (20,50,45,60) = (20,50,45,85)$$

gives the requirements.

TABLE 7.7   Bill-of-materials listing as an adjacency matrix

Bill of Material	Component						
	A	B	C	D	E	F	G
A	0	2	3	0	0	0	5
B	0	0	0	2	2	0	0
C	0	0	0	0	2	3	4
D	0	0	0	0	0	0	0
E	0	0	0	0	0	0	0
F	0	0	0	0	0	0	0
G	0	0	0	0	0	0	0

Quite aside from the size of the matrices, the actual calculations in a parts explosion are complicated by a number of factors.

- It is necessary to apply consistency checks to the matrices to ensure that there are no parts without origins (except for known sources), no diagonal elements, and no elements of out-degree 1 (the last would be redundant).
- Parts are needed for periodic intervals (e.g., weekly or monthly). Therefore, the multiplication is matrix × matrix rather than vector × matrix, where each row of the left matrix corresponds to the requirements for a period.
- There is an inventory of parts on hand which has to be subtracted from the results of the multiplication, to yield the net quantities required.
- Conditional calculations corresponding to possible requirements are often included.

Because *matrix multiplication* is the basic operation in the application, it is natural to represent the production graph by its adjacency matrix (recognizing that entries greater than 1 correspond to multiple adjacencies). Since most of the bill-of-materials entries are zero, sparse matrix techniques are used to represent the graphs. If a linked-list representation is adopted for the sparse adjacency matrix, we have, in effect, the vertex-edge list for the acyclic graph corresponding to the production explosion.

7.4.2 Topological Ordering

It is important to note that a special ordering has been chosen for the part numbers in the bill-of-material matrix. This ordering, which reflects the precedence (inclusion) relation between assemblies and subassemblies, results in the matrix M being *upper triangular*, a fact that makes the matrix multiplication efficient. In a plant in which many assemblies and subassemblies are retained over a long period of time, it is easy to see how the initial listing of the bill-of-materials might not yield a matrix that was upper triangular. The problem then arises of reordering the rows and columns so that the matrix *is* upper triangular, a problem similar to that of reducing a matrix to block triangular form, encountered in Algorithm 5.1. There, however, the reordering was required for the adjacency matrix of a general graph. In this case the reordering is to be done for the adjacency matrix of an *acyclic* graph, a difference that allows a much simpler procedure to be used. In precise terms the problem may be stated: Given a poset with numbered elements, renumber the elements so that j numerically less than i implies that j precedes i. It may be described as having to embed the partial order into a linear order, and it is a problem that arises in many situations (lattice theory, point set theory, etc.). In the context of critical-path scheduling, which is the second of the two applications discussed in this section, the process is known as *topological ordering*.

There is a very simple way of carrying out a topological ordering on the precedence matrix. The algorithm can be described informally as follows.

Step	Comment
1. Take 1 as the first sequence number.	Initialize.
2. Look for a matrix column with all zeros.	Look for a node with no predecessors.
3. If 'None', exit.	The process is complete. If the matrix is null, the relations are consistent (i.e., there are no node pairs, i, j, such that i less than j and j precedes i). Otherwise, the relations are inconsistent.
4. If 'Found', assign the sequence number to the column.	Renumber the node.
5. Delete the 'Found' row and column.	
6. Increase the sequence number.	
7. Return to step 2.	

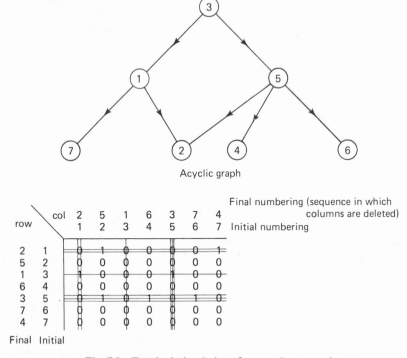

Fig. 7.9 Topological ordering of a precedence matrix

The process is illustrated in Fig. 7.9, where the graph of Fig. 7.8 is initially labeled with node numbers that do not correspond to a linear order. Although this algorithm is conceptually simple and easy to program, it is not efficient. Finding a column that is everywhere zero is easy to do by eye on a matrix, but a program for it requires a time $O(n^2)$ in the worst case, and this makes the whole procedure $O(n^3)$.

By keeping a vertex-edge list with incoming edges for each vertex, a vertex with no predecessors can be recognized in a time $O(n)$. This leads to an algorithm that is $O(n^2 + m)$, but it is possible to do better. The incoming-edge list is *only* needed to identify vertices with no predecessors, and it can be replaced by a vector, *count*[i], which gives the number of incoming edges for each vertex i (*count*[i] can be determined when the data are read in, and will be 0 for every source, of which there is at least one). When a vertex q is located such that *count*[q] = 0, all edges leading from it can be deleted. The vertex list for outpointing edges is maintained so that these edges can be located, and at the same time the count fields of the terminal nodes of the edges are decremented. The process is continued until all count fields are zero. If all edges have been deleted, the original precedence matrix was consistent (i.e., the graph was acyclic); otherwise, the matrix was inconsistent. Moreover, after an edge list is deleted, it is not necessary to search the count vector to find the next one that is zero. When a field is decremented to zero, the node number can be added to *fifo*, a queue of nodes for which *count* [i] = 0, and the members of *fifo* processed in turn (*fifo* is initialized, along with *count* during input).[18] Eliminating the need to search for nodes with no predecessors makes the process $O(m + n)$.

Algorithm 7.3 describes the topological ordering procedure, and Fig. 7.10 shows the data structures, with initial values corresponding to the graph of Fig. 7.9. *Next*[i] is a vector that stores, for *node* [i], a pointer to the terminal nodes of the next edge to be processed; it is initialized to the head of the outpointing edge list. It is assumed that *count* and *fifo* have been initialized as just described; *next* is initialized as in Algorithm 7.2. The queue *fifo* is augmented by the instruction add(*fifo*, *temp*), which adds *temp* to the rear, and decrementated by remove(*fifo*,*current*), which removes the item at the front and assigns its value to *current*. The output is a set of integer pairs, the first of which is the old node number, and the second the node number after reordering.

Algorithm 7.3 Topological ordering

```
integer f,l,p, temp, current; integer-queue fifo; boolean consistent;
integer-array count[f:l]; entry-ptr-array node[f:l], next[f:l];
comp entry = ⟨integer info, entry-ptr link⟩
/* initialization of count, next, fifo assumed complete */
do
    p ⇐ 1; /* first sequence no. */
    do while fifo ≠ 'empty';
        remove (fifo, current); /* take from queue */
        print (current, p);
        p ⇐ p+1; /* increase sequence no. */
        do while next[current] ≠ Λ;
            temp ⇐ info @ (next[current]);
            next[current] ⇐ link(@ next[current]); /*take next edge*/
            count[temp] ⇐ count[temp] − 1;
            if count[temp] = 0 then
            add(fifo, temp); /* add to queue */
        end
    end
    i ⇐ f; /* go on to test if all edges deleted */
    consistent ⇐ true;
    do while i ≤ l;
        consistent ⇐ consistent ∧ next[i] = Λ;
        i ⇐ i + 1;
    end
    print 'consistent';
end topological_ordering
```

[18]This last suggestion is due to D. E. Knuth. See *The Art of Computer Programming*, 2nd ed., Vol. 1 (Reading, Mass.: Addison-Wesley Publishing Company, Inc., 1973), pp. 258–268. The count fields themselves can be used to store the queue data, since once they go to zero they are no longer needed.

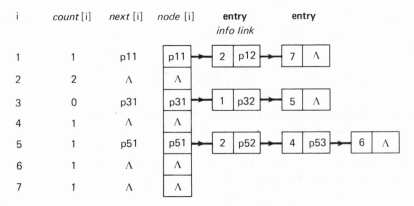

Fig. 7.10   Data structures for Algorithm 7.2

The root of the graph is referenced by f, and p is the sequence number assigned to the nodes which results in their being arranged in topological order.

7.4.3 PERT and Critical-Path Networks

As another example of an application in which the data take the form of an acyclic graph, we consider schedules constructed by the critical path method (CPM) or program evaluation review technique (PERT). This application, typical of an important class of network flow problems in which it is desired to find a path that satisfies some extremum condition, arises in project construction and planning.[19,20]

Two formulations are common, both of them based on acyclic graphs. In the first we are given an *activity matrix*, that is, a list of activities each of which has an *initial event*, *final event*, and *duration*. The diagram is a graph, called the *event-node* network, E, with labeled edges corresponding to the activities and numbered nodes corresponding to the events. In the second formulation we are given the list of activities and durations and a *precedence matrix* which indicates sequencing relations the activities must satisfy. The *activity-node network*, A, is the graph, with activities as nodes, for which the given precedence matrix holds true.

Example 7.4

A simple network is shown in Fig. 7.11 (the event-node formulation) and Fig. 7.12 (the activity-node network A). The activity and precedence matrices are given in Tables 7.8 and 7.9, respectively.

The activity matrix is the incidence matrix of the event-node graph. The precedence

[19]D. R. Fulkerson, "Scheduling in Project Networks," *Proceedings of the IBM Scientific Symposium on Combinatorial Problems*, (White Plains, N.Y.: IBM, 1964).

[20]R. L. Levin and C. Kirkpatrick, *Planning and Control with PERT/CPM* (New York: McGraw-Hill Book Company, 1966).

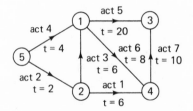

Fig. 7.11   Event-node network, *E*

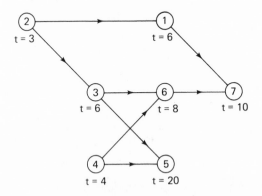

Fig. 7.12   Activity-node network, *A*

TABLE 7.8   Activity matrix

Activity	Initial Event	Final Event	Duration
1	2	4	6
2	5	2	3
3	2	1	6
4	5	1	4
5	1	3	20
6	1	4	8
7	4	3	10

TABLE 7.9   Precedence matrix

							Duration
0	0	0	0	0	0	1	6
1	0	1	0	0	0	0	3
0	0	0	0	1	1	0	6
0	0	0	0	1	1	0	4
0	0	0	0	0	0	0	20
0	0	0	0	0	0	1	8
0	0	0	0	0	0	0	10

matrix is the adjacency matrix of the activity-node graphs.[21] Given E, A is easy to construct; the number of nodes in A is equal to the number of edges in E, and if there is a path in which activity u is immediately followed by activity v in E, then there is a (directed) edge (u, v) in A. A is known as the line digraph of E.[22] Given an A network, it is possible to construct an E network for it, but the result is seldom unique, and it is usually necessary to introduce additional, *dummy* edges or nodes. Figure 7.13 illustrates a simple situation where it is necessary to introduce a dummy event, e. Any event-

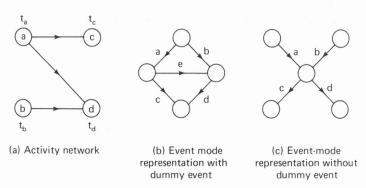

| (a) Activity network | (b) Event mode representation with dummy event | (c) Event-mode representation without dummy event |

Fig. 7.13   Introducing dummy events

node representation without a dummy event [e.g., Fig. 7.13(c)] is not acceptable since it introduces a predecessor relation not originally present, (b, c) in this case. There is no obvious way to construct the best (i.e., minimum) E network for a given A network.[23] Both the A and E representations have been used extensively in PERT and CPM.

The basic problem in CPM calculations is to find the path from source to sink of longest duration. This path is *critical* in the sense that if any activity along it takes longer than scheduled, the completion time of the whole project will be correspondingly delayed. In Fig. 7.11 the critical path is given by the activity chain $\langle 2,3,5 \rangle$. There are several different methods for finding the critical path along with other related quantities for a network. The technique generally used has four steps.

Step 1:   The A network is ordered topologically.[24] Figure 7.14(a) shows the topologically ordered network for Fig. 7.12, using Algorithm 7.3.

[21]The adjacency matrix gives the minimum list of precedences. There may also be some precedence relations which follow from transitivity. Thus in Table 7.9, activity 2 precedes activity 7. This could be given as a separate relation, but it follows from the fact that activity 2 precedes activity 1, and 1 precedes 7.

[22]F. Harary, *Graph Theory* (Reading, Mass.: Addison-Wesley Publishing Company, Inc., 1969), Chaps. 8 and 16.

[23]D. G. Corneil, C. C. Gotlieb, and Y. M. Lee, "Minimal Event-Node Network of Project Precedence Relations," *Communications of the ACM*, **16**, no. 5 (May 1973), 296–298.

[24]It is possible to do a CPM analysis without topological ordering. See M. Montalbano, "High-Speed Calculation of the Critical Paths of Large Networks," *IBM Systems Journal*. **6**, no. 5 (1967), 163–192.

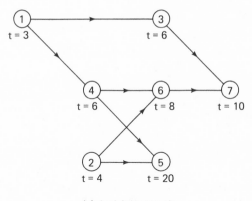

(a) Activity network

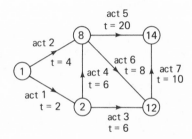

(b) Event network

Fig. 7.14 Networks renumbered after topological ordering

Step 2:   An E network is created by assigning initial and terminal event numbers $I(i)$ and $T(i)$ to each activity i. As a preliminary assignment, $I(i)$ can be taken $= 2i - 1$ and $T(i) = 2i$, but two activities, i and j, may have the same initial event $[I(i) = I(j)]$, the same terminal event $[T(i) = T(j)]$, or the terminal event $T(i)$ may be the same as the initial event, $I(j)$. There are rules for determining when these identifications can be made.

Let $A(i)$ be the set of activities that immediately succeed activity i, that is, $A(i) = \{j \,|\, r_{ij} = 1\}$, where r_{ij} is the adjacency matrix for the *immediate* successor relation. Also, $A'(i) = \{j \,|\, r'_{ij} = 1\}$, where r'_{ij} is closure of the successor matrix of the activities, that is, $A'(i)$ is the set of *all* successors of activity i. Similarly, $B(i)$ is the set of immediate predecessors of activity $i = \{j \,|\, r_{ji} = 1\}$ and $B'(i) = \{j \,|\, r'_{ji} = 1\}$. The A, A', B, and B' sets for the network of Fig. 7.14(a) is shown in Table 7.10(a). It then follows that:

(a) $I(i) = I(j)$ iff $B(i) = B(j)$.

(b) $T(i) = T(j)$ iff $A(i) = A(j)$.

TABLE 7.10   Producing the E network from the A network

$A(1) = \{3, 4\}$	$A'(1) = \{3, 4, 5, 6, 7\}$	$B(1) = \varnothing$	$B'(1) = \varnothing$
$A(2) = \{5, 6\}$	$A'(2) = \{5, 6, 7\}$	$B(2) = \varnothing$	$B'(2) = \varnothing$
$A(3) = \{7\}$	$A'(3) = \{7\}$	$B(3) = \{1\}$	$B'(3) = \{1\}$
$A(4) = \{5, 6\}$	$A'(4) = \{5, 6, 7\}$	$B(4) = \{1\}$	$B'(4) = \{1\}$
$A(5) = \varnothing$	$A'(5) = \varnothing$	$B(5) = \{2, 4\}$	$B'(5) = \{1, 2, 4\}$
$A(6) = \{7\}$	$A'(6) = \{7\}$	$B(6) = \{2, 4\}$	$B'(6) = \{1, 2, 4\}$
$A(7) = \varnothing$	$A'(7) = \varnothing$	$B(7) = \{3, 6\}$	$B'(7) = \{1, 2, 3, 4, 6\}$

(a)   Predecessor and successor sets

$I(1) = 1, \quad I(2) = 1, \quad I(3) = 5, \quad I(4) = 5, \quad I(5) = 7, \quad I(6) = 7, \quad I(7) = 13$

$T(1) = 2, \quad T(2) = 8, \quad T(3) = 12, \quad T(4) = 8, \quad T(5) = 14, \quad T(6) = 12, \quad T(7) = 14$

(b)   Initial and terminal event numbers after applying two conditions

$I(1) = 1, \quad I(2) = 1, \quad I(3) = 2, \quad I(4) = 2, \quad I(5) = 8, \quad I(6) = 8, \quad I(7) = 12$

$T(1) = 2, \quad T(2) = 8, \quad T(3) = 12, \quad T(4) = 8, \quad T(5) = 14, \quad T(6) = 12, \quad T(7) = 14$

(c)   Initial and terminal event numbers after applying all three conditions

The first condition states that the initial events for two activities can be made the same if all their immediate predecessors are the same. The second condition states that the final events for two activities can be made the same if all the immediate successors are the same. The results of applying these conditions to the initial and final events of the example network are shown in Table 7.10(b).

A third condition indicates when the initial event for one activity may be identified with the terminal event of another. It is

(c) $T(i) = I(j)$ iff $\{A'(x) \mid x \in B(j)\} \equiv A'(i)$, where $i \in B(j)$.

According to this condition, the set formed by taking the intersection of all successor sets for a member of $B(j)$ is examined. If this intersection set is equal to the successor set, $A'(i)$, of some activity i which is a member of $B(j)$, then $T(i)$ and $T(j)$ may be identified. The result of applying condition (c) to the event numbers of Table 7.10(b) are shown in Table 7.10(c), and this produces the network of Fig. 7.14(b). It can be shown that applying the above three conditions results in an event-node network having the *minimum* number of events.

Step 3:   It is then necessary to introduce dummy events so as to remove successor relationships that were not present originally. Although this is not difficult to do, it *is* difficult if one wants to introduce the *minimum* possible number of dummy events.[25] For the network of Fig. 7.14(b), no dummy events are needed.

---

[25]It turns out that there is no efficient algorithm [i.e., one in which the execution time is $O(n^c)$ when c is independent of n] to achieve the minimization. There are $O(n^c)$ algorithms if one is content to introduce close to the minimum number of dummy events (Corneil, Gotlieb, and Lee, "Minimal Event-Node Network," footnote 23).

Step 4: To find the critical path, certain auxiliary quantities are calculated for each event and activity.

The *earliest* time for a source event in the E network is taken as zero. For any other event, j, the earliest time $t_j^e = \max_i (t_i^e + d_{ij})$, where i is an event immediately preceding j and d_{ij} is the duration of the activity whose initial event is i and terminal event is j. The earliest times are calculated systematically for all events, starting with sources. In a similar way, *latest times* are calculated for every event, starting with sinks. The latest time for a sink can be taken as any time, $t_i^l \geq t_i^e$; the shortest time for the project is given by t_m^e where m is the index of the last event. For an event i, other than a sink, $t_i^l = \min_j (t_j^l - d_{ij})$, where i is an event immediately preceding event j.

Having calculated these times for *events*, then for each *activity* $\langle i, j \rangle$, there is defined the *latest completion time* $= t_j^l$, and the *earliest start time* $= t_i^e$. The *maximum available time* for an activity is $t_j^l - t_i^e$. The *float time* $= t_j^l - t_i^e - d_{ij}$ is the difference between the maximum time available for the activity and the time required to carry it out. For a *critical activity* the float time is zero, and the critical path is the chain of critical activities.

These various quantities for the network of Fig. 7.14 are shown in Table 7.11(a) and (b).

TABLE 7.11(a) Event times

Event Number	Earliest Time t_i^e	Latest Time t_i^l
1	0	0
2	3	3
8	9	9
12	17	19
14	29	29

TABLE 7.11(b) Activity times

Activity	Initial Event i	Final Event j	Duration d_{ij}	Latest Completion Time t_j^l	Earliest Start Time t_i^e	Max Time Available $t_j^l - t_i^e$	Float Time $t_j^l - t_i^e - d_{ij}$	Critical Activities
1	1	2	3	3	0	3	0	*
2	1	8	4	9	0	9	5	
3	2	12	6	19	3	16	10	
4	2	8	6	9	3	6	0	*
5	8	14	20	29	9	20	0	*
6	8	12	8	19	9	10	2	
7	12	14	10	29	17	12	2	

In summary, we can regard the CPM calculation as a problem in the conversion of one data structure to another. The data arise naturally in the form of an adjacency matrix reflecting the precedence of activities. The results of interest are obtained most readily from the event network, which is the incidence matrix of a derived graph.

7.5 Generalized Graphs

The data types that have been studied earlier, stacks and queues, simple lists, arrays, trees, and cyclic lists, are the ones commonly found in computer applications, partly because the algorithms for handling these types are efficient, but mainly because these simple (but nonprimitive) types are adequate for describing many applications. Rooted digraphs with labled nodes have served as a model for most of these types (see Section 4.1). However, general as rooted digraphs are, it is desirable to extend them so that they can serve as abstract models in other applications. One way of achieving this to produce a type that finds many applications is to attach values to the *edges* of the graph as well as to the nodes. The result is called a *network*. A network is a ternary relation, $\langle N, E, L \rangle$, on a set of nodes N, a set of edges, E, defined on $N \times N$, and a set of labels, L. We have already seen in this chapter networks for describing flows, productions systems, and event scheduling, where the labels are numbers. Matrix representations are the natural ones to deal with the quantitative problems that arise in these cases.

Networks in which the labels are names (or string values) are also very common. Figure 7.15, showing a few of the stations in the London subway system, illustrates a transportation network in which the edge labels identify the rail lines connecting the system. Here problems of routings and interchanges arise, generalizations of the path-tracing problems encountered in graphs. Representations for transportation or communication networks are obvious; a graph can be maintained for each component of the system.

Many examples of the applications of networks to social science problems are to be found in the book by Harary, Norman, and Cartwright (1965). Two situations in psychology and artificial intelligence where it is necessary to employ networks are natural-language processing and visual scene analysis. In both cases the data, sentences in one case and pictures in the other, must be structured so that meaning can be attached to the representation. For sentences this requires that concepts be identified, that the concepts in a particular sentence be related to more comprehensive concepts, that it be possible to paraphrase sentences and leave the meaning intact, and that it be possible to draw logical inferences from the data. The structure for dealing with concepts and sentences which has gained acceptance is known as a *semantic net*. A semantic net is a directed graph whose vertices are labeled with words corresponding to concepts and whose edges carry labels identifying relations between the concepts. Connecting two concepts there may be any of a very large number of relations, some of which are the ordinary relations of mathematics. Inclusion is one such example; the assertion "A dog is an instance of an animal" (colloquially, "A dog is an animal") means that a dog is a member of a set called "animals." Within the larger context of this statement can be the fact that a particular dog, for example one named *Fido*, is a member of the set of dogs. But these two set memberships are not the only types of inclusion. We can also say "A dog has a tail"; this, too, is a kind of inclusion, although it can equally be regarded as an attribute or property of dogs in general. Particular dogs also have attributes, as in "Fido has spots."

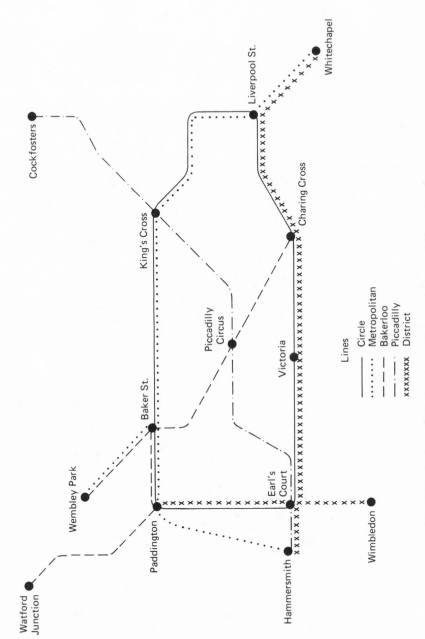

Fig. 7.15 Stations on the London underground transportation network

Example 7.5

A semantic net for the statements:

>   A dog is an animal.
>   Fido is a dog.
>   A dog has a tail.
>   A dog has four legs.
>   Fido has spots.

is shown in Fig. 7.16(a). Note that the concept for a particular dog is represented explicitly (identified by an asterisk), as well as the concept for dogs in general. By

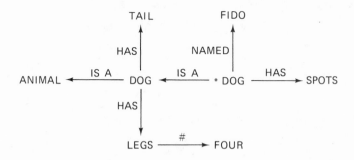

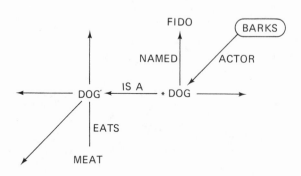

Fig. 7.16 Semantic net

applying processes that involve tracing paths and recognizing components in the graph, it is possible to make logical inferences about the data items, for example,

>   Fido has four legs.
>   Some animals have a tail.

To model concepts in natural language, the semantic net requires additional capabilities. First, one needs to represent verbs and action statements such as "Fido barks" and "Dogs eat meat." This can be done by including verbs either as concepts (suitably distinguished from nouns) or as edge labels. Both techniques are illustrated in Fig. 7.16(b). In addition it is necessary to represent time and place, causation, subject and predicate relations, and so on. Rumelhart and Norman use the term *active structural network* to describe a structure which represents both data and processes, and with such networks they attempt to construct a model of human memory.[26] In this model, memorizing a list corresponds to making assignments to the data structure, recognizing the presence of a set of concepts corresponds to locating a subgraph within a larger graph, and making inferences corresponds to tracing paths in the structure.

Networks are not the only way of generalizing graphs. Berge considers *hypergraphs*, in which an edge relation is defined on more than two nodes.[27] It is also possible to embed graphs in formal grammars for generating and manipulating them. The resulting generalizations of the context-free and context-sensitive grammars applicable to strings are called *web grammars* by Rosenfeld, and they turn out to be useful ways of describing transformations on pictures.[28]

In this chapter we have seen how the four basic storage mappings, contiguous, indexed, hashed, and linked, often used in combination, make it possible to construct representations efficient for manipulating sets and graphs. These same four mappings provide the techniques for handling the generalized data types needed to model more complex phenomena possessing richer structure.

Exercises

1. Find a set of discrete representations for the following family of subsets:

    $\{2, 3, 6, 10\}$, $\{1, 5, 10\}$, $\{2, 3, 6, 7\}$, $\{2, 4, 5, 8\}$, $\{3, 6, 7, 10\}$, $\{1, 6, 8, 9\}$, $\{3, 4, 9\}$, $\{2, 6, 7, 10\}$, $\{4, 7, 9\}$, $\{2, 3, 7, 10\}$.

2. Suppose that a set of clubs, S_i, is given and it is desired to appoint a council that has a member from every club on it, and which is of minimal size (i.e., $C \cap S_i \neq \varnothing$, $|C|$ is a minimum). Given an algorithm for determining C, what is the minimum council for the following sets?

    $S_1 = \{g, t, a, f, v\}$, $S_2 = \{a, t\}$, $S_3 = \{t, g, f\}$, $S_4 = \{v, t\}$, $S_5 = \{a, g\}$.

3. You are given a family of sets, S_i, $i = 1, \ldots, n$, and a set of elements, a_j, $j = 1, \ldots, m$, which are possible constituents. Let C_{ij} be the matrix such that row i is the characteristic vector for a_j (i.e., $c_{ij} = 1$ iff a_i is a member of S_j). Write a program that systematically generates all possible rows of C and finds all elements that correspond to a given row. Try your program using the sets for NATO (North Atlantic Treaty Organization), O.E.C.D. (the Organization for Economic Cooperation and Development), and E.E.C.

[26]D. E. Rumelhart and D. A. Norman, *Explanations in Cognition* (San Francisco: W. H. Freeman and Company, 1975). See especially Chaps. 1, 2, and 7.

[27]C. Berge, *Graphs and Hypergraphs* (Amsterdam: North-Holland Publishing Company, Inc., 1973).

[28]A. Rosenfeld and D. L. Milgram, "Web Automata and Web Grammars," in *Machine Intelligence*, Vol. 7, B. Meltzer and D. Michie, eds. (Edinburgh: Edinburgh University Press, 1972), pp. 307–324.

(the European Economic Community). In this case the row with elements 110, for example, corresponds to countries that are in NATO and O.E.C.D. but not in E.E.C.

4. (a) Each teacher $t_i \in \{T\}$ is required to meet with class $c_j \in \{C\}$ r_{ij} times. For t_i and c_j there is a set of available times $\{a_{ijk}\} \in A$, when they can meet. State necessary and sufficient conditions that:

(1) A given teacher be able to meet all his classes.

(2) A given class be able to meet all its teachers.

Why are these conditions not sufficient to ensure that all teachers can meet all classes.? State a necessary condition for this.

(b) What changes must be made in a_{ijk} when teacher $\bar{i}$ is scheduled to meet class $\bar{j}$ at time $\bar{k}$? Suggest an algorithm for constructing a timetable to satisfy the requirements matrix, r_{ij}, based on systematically carrying out such changes. [See J. Csima and C. C. Gotlieb, "Tests on a Computer Method for Constructing School Timetables," *Communications of the ACM*, **7**, no. 3 (Mar. 1964), 160–163.]

5. Suppose that a list of keys is needed for which the following operations are important.

(1) CREATE, given a set of keys $K_1, \ldots, K_n$.

(2) FIND the address of a given key K.

(3) INSERT/DELETE a given key K.

(4) COUNT the number of keys between two given keys, K_1 and K_2.

Suggest *two* possible data structures. Justify your choices (include considerations of storage requirements, and of the dependence of the times for these operations on N, the number of keys).

6. Using a particular computer, determine the coefficients of M, A, T (the times to access a cell, the average time for an arithmetic operation, and the time for a transfer of control), in Algorithm 6.2 for locating a key in a lexicographic tree. (Either write the program in assembly language or examine the compiler code produced for a transliteration of Algorithm 6.2.) Is the simplification that only three instruction times need be considered a good one?

7. Write the programs to initialize *count*, *next*, and *fifo* in Algorithm 7.3.

8. Trace the program of Algorithm 7.3 using the graph of Fig. 7.9.

9. Describe representations for networks and hypergraphs that are generalizations of the adjacency matrix, the incidence matrix, and the vertex-edge list for a graph. Give an example where each of the representations would be a good one for the needed computations.

10. Given the computer replacement schedule described by Table 7.12, determine:

(a) The critical path and minimum completion time.

(b) For each activity, the latest completion time, earliest start time, maximum time available, and float time.

11. Regarding the transportation network of Fig. 7.15 as the ternary relation LINE × STATION × STATION, express the following using the notation of (1) LEAP triplets; (2) SETL functional operators.

(a) Stations on the District Line.

(b) Lines serving the Baker Street Station.

(c) Stations accessible from Charing Cross not requiring a transfer.

12. In a semantic net, a *statement* is a relation (possibly *n*-ary) between given concepts, and an *inference* is a proposition whose truth can be established using the inference rules of the propositional calculus. What data (directories, etc.) should be included with the net in order to have an efficient way of testing and establishing inferences? Describe an

TABLE 7.12   Computer replacement schedule

Activity Number	Activity Description	Duration (days)	Predecessor Activities
1	Remove old computer	$\frac{1}{2}$	—
2	Remove old floor, partitions, etc.	$1\frac{1}{2}$	1
3	Install wiring	2	—
4	Install plumbing	2	2
5	Install steam supply	$1\frac{1}{2}$	2
6	Install computer floor	$1\frac{1}{2}$	3,4
7	Construct partitions	2	6
8	Install lighting	2	7,3
9	Install acoustic ceiling	$1\frac{1}{2}$	7,8
10	Paint	2	9
11	Install air conditioning	2	5,7
12	Install smoke-detection system	1	9
13	Move furniture	$\frac{1}{2}$	10
14	Move in computers	1	10
15	Install security system	$\frac{1}{2}$	7
16	Install cabling	2	14
17	Balance air conditioning	$\frac{1}{2}$	11,16
18	Check out system	2	17

algorithm for determining the truth of a given inference. Enlarge the net of Example 7.5 with the statements:

A parrot named Polly eats seeds.
Parrots are (instances of) birds.
An animal with a tail, two legs, and feathers is (defined to be) a bird.
A monkey is an animal with a tail and two legs.
Monkeys eat bananas.

Test your algorithm by attempting to establish the inferences:

Meat and seeds are eaten by animals.
Monkeys are birds.

13. Suppose that it were decided to use Social Security numbers instead of student numbers as a means of identifying students in the example of Appendix 1. How would this affect the design of the directory? Are there any other issues other than efficient directory design that would be involved in such a decision?

14. Recalculate Table A.3 of Appendix 1, assuming that in numeric fields 1 byte can store two decimal digits.

15. What additional data have to be carried in the subject/course substructure to allow an operation that prints the timetable of a given student?

16. Give the **comp** specification for the data type **course-data**.

17. Write algorithms for all the operations in the two groups of Table A.2 in Appendix 1.

18. It is desired to reduce the average access time in the subject directory of the tree in Fig. A.1 of Appendix 1 by assuming that the search frequencies for a given subject are proportional to the number of students registered in the subject. Using the given enrollment

statistics, design (a) nearby-optimal; (b) optimal tree directories. Compare the average search times for these trees with that for the tree in Fig. A.1 of Appendix 1.

Subject	AFS	ANT	APS	ART	AST	BIO	CHM	CLA	CSC	ECO	EDU	ENG
Enrollment	318	330	340	454	190	1262	830	251	300	718	638	1914

Subject	ERS	FRE	GER	HIP	HIS	JR	LAS	LAW	LIN	MAN	MAT	MES	MUS
Enrollment	690	329	205	408	783	902	590	843	756	919	502	264	316

Subject	ORS	PHS	PHL	PHY	POL	PSY	RLS	SLV	SOC	URB
Enrollment	385	1508	526	675	1245	741	417	241	482	568

19. The seat inventory of an airline reservation system is organized according to day and flight number. The data for every flight leg (part of a flight between a takeoff and landing) include the following:

Flight (number, flight leg, service frequency code, number of available seats)
Origin (terminal code, scheduled departure time)
Destination (terminal, scheduled arrival time)
Connecting flights (flight number, time)
Passenger list (name, address, telephone number, status, special information)
The following are some possible operations involving flights and passengers

- Reserve space for a given passenger.
- Cancel a given reservation.
- List the flights available between two cities.
- List the flight plan of a given passenger (given his or her flight number, origin, and data of departure).
- Print the passenger list for a given flight.
- List the open legs of a given flight plan (legs for which there are available seats).
- Print the waiting list for a given flight.
- List the alternatives open to a passenger whose flight has been canceled.
- List the daily flights between a given pair of terminals.

  Assuming that the two constraints present in the student/course problem (Appendix 1) are applicable here, design a (single) data structure based on flights for the application above. Which operations cannot be done efficiently? What additional substructures are needed to be able to do all the operations? What are the reasons for *not* using a substructure based on passenger's name? Write **comp** specifications for the composite types, and programs for the operations. Estimate parameter values (consult an airline schedule) and storage requirements.

Bibliography

Nijenhuis and Wilf (1975) give algorithms for a number of the combinatorial operations on sets and graphs described in this chapter. Aho, Hopcroft, and Ullman (1974) contains many illustrations of how the choice of data structure influences algorithms for manipulating sets, graphs, and other mathematical types. General problems of data structures as related to programming languages are discussed in Tou and Wegner (1971). Low (1974) and Tompa (1976) discuss algorithmic approaches to the design of data structures.

Set-processing languages have appeared periodically in the computer literature. For a discussion of some of the theoretical considerations, see Warren (1975). The documentation on the design of SETL is unusually complete. Besides extensive interim reports, a newsletter series has been published, with a catalog compiled by R. Abes (1973). For a "Precis of the SETL Language," see Schwartz (1973). The basic reference on LEAP is Feldman and Rovner (1969).

The classic work on flow networks is that of Ford and Fulkerson (1962). There are many books on PERT networks, of which two are those by Archibald and Villorin (1967), and Lombaers (1969). Graph models, especially as applied to the social sciences, are treated in Harary, Norman, and Cartwright (1965).

ABES, R., ed., *The SETL Project Master Catalogue*. New York: Courant Institute of Mathematical Science, New York University, 1973.

AHO, A., J. E. HOPCROFT, AND J. D. ULLMAN, *The Design and Analysis of Computer Algorithms*. Reading, Mass.: Addison-Wesley Publishing Company, Inc., 1974.

ARCHIBALD, R. D., AND R. L. VILLORIN, *Network-Based Management Systems (PERT/CPM)*, New York: John Wiley & Sons, Inc., 1967.

FELDMAN, J. A., AND P. D. ROVNER, "An Algol-Based Associative Language." *Communications of the ACM*, **12**, no. 8 (Aug. 1969), 439–449.

FORD, L. R., AND D. R. FULKERSON, *Flows in Networks*. Princeton, N.J.: Princeton University Press, 1962.

HARARY, F., R. NORMAN, AND D. CARTWRIGHT, *Structured Models*. New York: John Wiley & Sons, Inc., 1965.

LOMBAERS, H. J. M., ed., *Project Planning by Network Analysis*. Amsterdam: North-Holland Publishing Company, 1969.

LOW, J. R., *Automatic Coding: Choice of Data Structures* (STAN-CS-74-452). Palo Alto, Calif.: Computer Science Department, Stanford University, 1974.

NIJENHUIS, A., AND H. S. WILF, *Combinatorial Algorithms*. New York: Academic Press, Inc., 1975.

SCHWARTZ, J. T., *On Programming: An Interim Project on the SETL Project*. Installment 1. Generalities; Installment 2. The SETL Language and Examples of Its Use. New York: New York University, 1973.

TOMPA, F. W., "Data Structure Design," in *Data Structures, Computer Graphics and Pattern Recognition*, A. Klinger, K. S. Fu, and T. L. Kunii (eds.), New York: Academic Press, Inc., 1977.

TOU, J., AND P. WEGNER, eds., "Proceedings of a Symposium on Data Structures in Programming Languages." *SIGPLAN Notices*, **6**, no. 2 (Feb. 1971).

WARREN, H. S., JR., *Data Types and Structures for a Set Theoretic Language* (RC 5567). Yorktown Heights, N.Y.: IBM Research Center, 1975.

chapter 8

Storage Management

Throughout this book there has been frequent reference to the need for storage allocation; see, for example, the discussions on storage mapping in Section 2.7, and on the "create" operation for producing elements of linked lists and of sets, in Sections 4.3 and 7.1, respectively. There has also been frequent mention of the need to reclaim storage for variables that will not reoccur. In this chapter we consider techniques for storage allocation and reclamation. The responsibility for managing storage is shared between the operating system and language processor. The operating system provides storage as new programs are initiated and when it links together the various sub-routines that make up a program. The language processor may do some of its own allocation (typically, when blocks are entered on left), or it may call upon the operating system when it needs storage for a composite variable. Reclaiming storage no longer needed (i.e., deallocation) is usually incorporated with, or initiated by, the language processor.

8.1 General Strategy

Several critical questions arise as soon as the problem of storage allocation is considered:

1. When should storage be allocated? As already noted, deferring binding to execution is desirable because it ensures that only as much storage as is needed will be requested. But assigning storage dynamically means being ready to interrupt execution of the program at any time to search for and assemble

storage blocks. The time for search and assembly is likely to be less if these processes can be limited to specified points in the program (e.g., at read-in time or at compilation).

2. How important is deallocation? The answer seems to be that it is indispensible. In spite of the fact that high-speed storage has continued to decrease in cost and increase in availability as computers have evolved, this growth has been matched by the increase in storage demands made by larger and more complex programs. Unless the language processor includes some mechanism for returning memory which is no longer needed to the pool from which storage is allocated, assignment usually comes to a halt as programs execute.

3. How does a program recognize when storage can be freed? Must the user initiate the necessary processes, or can it be done automatically? This is the most challenging question.

One of the significant innovations of ALGOL 60 was the concept of block structure to delineate the scope of variables. The declaration of an identifier at the beginning of a block greatly simplifies the tasks of storage allocation (recall, for example, the role of the dope vector of an **array**, as described in Section 5.1). Moreover, the rules for the nesting of blocks in ALGOL make it possible to assign storage by means of a run time stack, consisting of uniformly sized cells linked together, with storage always taken from, and returned to, the top of this stack. Block structure and declarations allow dynamic storage management in ALGOL and provide an elegant solution to the problems of specifiying the lifetime of variables.

Useful as these ALGOL techniques are, additional ones are needed to deal with the problems of storage management in languages with a greater variety of data types. Variables of composite type need storage blocks of different sizes, so a single stack of available cells, all the same size, is not adequate as an allocation device. An obvious solution is to provide a stack, implemented as a linked list, whose constituents are multiples of a unit cell. But unless the size gradation is very fine, the allocated blocks will be somewhat larger than the storage requested; thus there is storage reserved that is not used, a phenomenon known as *internal fragmentation*. In addition, if we imagine that the available storage starts as a collection of large blocks that are partitioned to meet requests, the released storage will be in the form of smaller blocks formed as a result of the partitioning. As execution proceeds, the blocks available for allocation become smaller and smaller, until eventually many of them are too small to be useful; loss of memory in this way is called *external fragmentation*. Unless the release of memory is accompanied by some mechanism for recreating larger free blocks, memory fragmentation becomes so severe as to inhibit allocation.

There are two ways of creating larger free blocks. One is to examine the neighbors of a released block and combine them if they are free, too, a process of *consolidation*. The other is to copy allocated blocks into new, more tightly packed storage, a process called *compaction*. Even with relatively efficient methods of copying and moving lists, compaction has to be used with care. It can still be expensive, and decisions on how often it should be initiated must be made.

Weinstock (1976) identifies six subprocesses within a dynamic storage management system that uses variable-sized blocks.

1. Ordering the blocks in the available list.
2. Rounding (matching the size of the request to that of an available block).
3. Searching the available list.
4. Splitting (handling the unused part of an allocated block).
5. Consolidation.
6. Compaction.

Allocation involves rounding, searching, and splitting and, optionally, consolidation and compaction. Deallocation involves ordering and, optionally, consolidation and compaction. The literature on storage management can be viewed as a study of how varying these processes affect system performance, measured principally by the time to allocate a block, and the probability of failures to meet a request.

8.2 Allocation and Deallocation

We start by considering allocation and deallocation without consolidation or compaction, but before doing so, an important difference between the two must be noted. There is no question about the fact that storage has to be allocated; certainly it has to be done by the time a value is assigned to a variable, although, as we have noted, there is some question in determining when binding should be effected. On the other hand, if the storage is large enough, in principle deallocation does not have to be done at all. In practice it is desirable to do so, but it is a nontrivial problem to recognize when storage *can* be released. Some programming languages, for example PL/I, have "free" commands which release previously allocated storage. But one of the principal advantages of a high-level language is that the programmer can work with the logical variables of the application and leave storage management for these variables to the language processor. *Imposing* a need to include "free" commands compromises this advantage. An even more serious difficulty with such a command is that it makes it very easy to create dangling references. Consider, for example, the sequence

$$\textbf{comp node} = \langle \textbf{int } size; \textbf{ boolean } flag \rangle$$

$$\textbf{node-ptr}, \; P,Q$$

$$\text{create } \textbf{node } (@Q)$$

$$P \Leftarrow Q;$$

$$\text{free } (@Q);$$

$$size \, (@P) \Leftarrow S;$$

The statement "free $(@Q)$" leaves P pointing to a location no longer available to the program, so the subsequent size assignment is meaningless. For this reason, most high-level languages do *not* include a "free" command but leave the decisions on identification and gathering up of free storage to the implementation.[1]

A simple example will illustrate how fragmentation arises and the alternatives that can be adopted for the allocation subprocesses. In the *first-fit* allocation strategy, shown in Table 8.1(a), the available list of free blocks is not ordered with respect to block size. A search for a block request starts at the head of the list. The first block large enough to accommodate the request is accepted, and if there is a residual after the request is satisfied, it is left on the list. Eventually, there are no blocks large enough to satisfy an incoming request. (This will happen even when blocks are released and consolidated, processes not illustrated here.) The *best-fit* strategy attempts to retain large blocks by allocating the smallest block that will satisfy the request. This can be achieved by scanning the free list, or ordering the list according to increasing block size, as shown in Table 8.1(b). The block search times for the two methods are comparable, since in the former case, if N is the number of blocks on the free list, the expected number of comparisons to locate a block is $N/2$; in the latter case the same number is needed to place a released block on the list.

Another way of attempting to reduce fragmentation is to split a block only if the residual is zero or larger than a predetermined minimum [Table 8.1(c)]. In the *next-fit* technique [Table 8.1(d)], the scan for a requested block continues at the point where the previous scan left off. The idea is to distribute the small blocks throughout the free list. This affects the search time for a block but does not reduce the probability of failing to meet a request. For next-fit, the free list can be maintained as a circularly linked list, but it is necessary to recognize when the whole available list has been searched. In the *worst-fit* method [Table 8.1(e)], the largest block is used to fill the request. It is implemented by maintaining the list according to decreasing block size. This has the merit that, if a request can be filled at all, it will be met immediately, but since it always partitions the largest block, it is a strategy likely to increase fragmentation. Also, released blocks must be inserted into their correct position on the list.

In an allocation algorithm the format of blocks depends on the deallocation and consolidation processes as well, and an algorithm (based on next-fit) is given in the following section.

8.3 Consolidation

As noted, recovery of released blocks is necessary for the storage management scheme to work. Two methods are common. In the first, the available list is maintained

---

[1] The ordinary rules of block structuring partially inhibit dangling references, because assignments such as $P \Leftarrow Q$ are only valid if the scope of P is nested within the scope of Q. However, even if "free" commands are not allowed, it is still possible to create dangling references indirectly. For a discussion and method of preventation, see C. H. Correll, "A Solution to the Dangling Reference Problem in Block Structured Languages," in *First Meeting of the Working Group on Machine Oriented Higher Level Languages* J. D. Ichbiah and P. M. Cousot, eds. (Le Chesnay, France: L'Institut de Recherche d'Informatique et d'Automatique).

TABLE 8.1 Allocation Strategies

Available Block Sizes

	After Filling Request Number					
Initially	1	2	3	4	5	Features
5	3	3	1	1	1	• Blocks unordered
3	3	3	3	2	2	• Accept first large enough
2	2	2	2	2	2	• Leave unused part on list
6	6	2	2	4	1	
4	4	4	4			

Sequence of requested blocks   2   4   2   3   3   3 not available

(a) First-fit

Available Block Sizes

	After Filling Request Number (and Reordering)						
Initially	1	2	3	4	5	6	Features
2	3	3	1	1	1	1	• Blocks ordered according
3	4	5	5	2	2	2	to increasing size
4	5	6	6	6	3		• Leave unused part on list
5	6						
6							

Requested block   2   4   2   3   3   3

(b) Best-fit

Available Block Sizes

	After Filling Request Number					
Initially	1	2	3	4	5	Features
5	3	3	3	3	2	• Blocks unordered
3	3	3	3	2	4	• Accept first that leaves
2	2	2	2	4		residual 0 or ≥ 2
6	6	2	4			
4	4	4				

Requested block   2   4   2   3   3   3 not available

(c) First-fit with residual minimum

TABLE 8.1 (Cont.)

Available Block Sizes

	After Filling Request Number						
Initially	1	2	3	4	5	6	Features
·5	·3	3	3	3	·3	2	· Blocks unordered
3	3	3	3	3	2	1	· Search commences where
2	2	2	2	2	1		previous search left off
6	6	·2	·4	·1			· Accept first block large enough
4	4	4					· Leave unused part on list
Requested block 2	4	2	3	3	3		

(d) Next-fit

Available Block Sizes

	After Filling Request Number (and Reordering)					
Initially	1	2	3	4	5	Features
6	5	4	4	3	2	· Blocks ordered according
5	4	4	3	2	2	to decreasing size
4	4	3	2	2	1	· Leave unused part on list
3	3	2	2	1	1	
2	2	1	1	1		
Requested block 2	4	2	3	3	3 not available	

(e) Worst-fit

in sequence of increasing block addresses. When a block is released, its predecessor and successor in the addressing scheme are examined to see if they are on the free list, and consolidation is effected if they are. In the second method, the allocation scheme includes the ability to divide large blocks in two when needed, so that the list of free blocks can be maintained as a binary tree whose nodes are labeled with the block sizes. The two partitions into which a block is split are known as *buddies*, and the block addressing scheme makes it possible to immediately locate the buddy of a released block. If the buddy is free, consolidation takes place.

Figure 8.1 shows two ways in which the information needed to consolidate blocks can be maintained when the free list is sequenced according to address. In the method of Fig. 8.1(a), called the *boundary tag* scheme, every block carries a "head" and "tail" word which contains both the block size and an availability flag. The head also contains a link to the next available block. When a block is released, since its address and size are known, the header of the next block in memory can be located and interrogated to see if it is a candidate for consolidation. Similarly, the tail preceding the released block

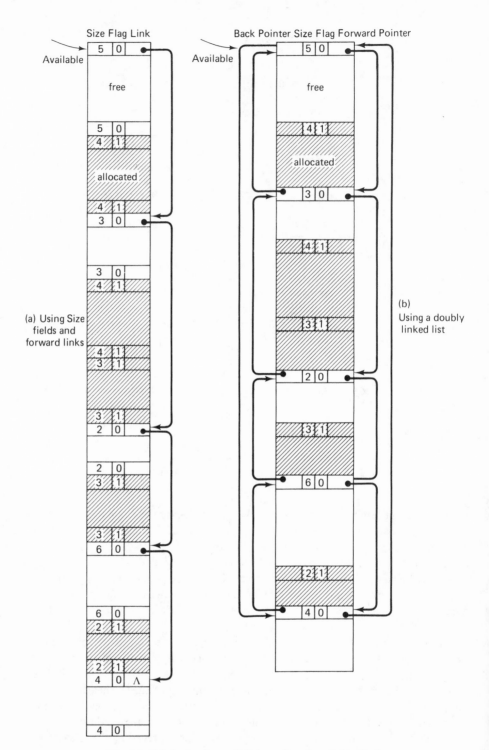

Fig. 8.1 Methods of consolidating a list of available blocks

can be interrogated and consolidation carried out, if possible. An alternative to storing both head and tail words is to keep, for each free block, forward and backward pointers to its successor and predecessor on the available list [Fig. 8.1(b)].

Programs that use the format of Fig. 8.1(b) for next-fit allocation and for block release with consolidation are given in Algorithms 8.1 and 8.2. *Available* is a pointer to

Algorithm 8.1   Allocation by next-fit

```
next_fit (available, need, found)
boolean done ; int need;
header-ptr available, start, found, temp;
do start ⇐ available;
   done ⇐ false;
   found ⇐ Λ;
   do while ¬ done;
      if size(@ available) = need then /*exact fit*/
      do temp ⇐ blink (@ available); /*remove block from chain*/
         flink (@ temp) ⇐ flink (@ available); /*reset previous
                                                       flink*/
         blink (@ flink (@ available)) ⇐ temp; /*and next blink*/
         used (@ available) ⇐ true; /*block no longer available*/
         found ⇐ available;
         available ⇐ flink (@ available);
         done ⇐ true;
      end
      else if size (@ available) ≥ need+1 then /*block larger*/
      do size (@ available) ⇐ size (@ available) − need−1;
                                     /*adjust block size*/
         found ⇐ available + size (@ available) − need; /*start of
                                                            new block*/
         size (@ found) ⇐ need;
         used (@ found) ⇐ true;
         done ⇐ true;
      end /*block larger than needed*/
      else do available ⇐ flink (@ available) /*look for room
                                             in next block*/
            if available = start then
               done ⇐ true; /*full cycle without finding a block*/
            end
   end /*while ¬ done*/
   if found = Λ then
      call help (available, need); /*block not found or available
                                        list exhausted*/
end /*first-fit*/ |
```

Algorithm 8.2 Deallocation and consolidation

```
release (available, free)
boolean next, previous; header-ptr available, free;
if free > available then
do
    do while free > flink(@ available) ∧ (available < flink(@ available));
        available ⟸ flink (@ available);
    end /* ensure no blocks on available list between available and free*/
    if (free + size (@ free)+1) = flink (@ available) then
        next ⟸ true; /*consolidate with next block*/
    if available + size (@ available)+1 = free then
        previous ⟸ true; /*consolidate with previous*/
    if next ∧ ¬ previous then /*consolidate with next only*/
        do size (@ free) ⟸ size (@ free) + size (@ flink (@ available))+1;
            used (@ free) ⟸ false;
            flink (@ free) ⟸ flink (@ flink (@ available));
            blink (@ flink (@ flink (@ available))) ⟸ free;
            flink (@ available) ⟸ free;
            blink (@ free) ⟸ available;
        end /*consolidate next only*/
    else if previous ∧ ¬ next then /* consolidate with previous only */
        size (@ available) ⟸ size (@ available) + size (@ free)+1;
    else if previous ∧ next then /*consolidate with next and previous*/
        do
            size (@ available) ⟸ size (@ available) + size (@ free)
                                  + size (@ flink (@ available))+2;
            flink (@ available) ⟸ flink (@ flink (@ available));
            blink (@ flink (@ available)) ⟸ available;
        end
    else
        do
            used (@ free) ⟸ false; /*no consolidation; insert free block*/
            flink (@ free) ⟸ flink (@ available);
            blink (@ free) ⟸ available;
            flink (@ available) ⟸ free;
            blink (@ flink (@ free)) ⟸ free;
        end /*no consolidation*/
    end /*if free > available*/
    else do /*free < available*/
        do while free < blink (@ available) ∧ (available > blink(@ available));
            (Similar sequence to that for free > available)
        end /*if free < available*/
end /*release*/
```

the first cell (of type **header**) in the circular list of blocks to be searched. A value for it is passed to the program, and on exit it will point to where the search is to commence when the program is called next. The parameter *need* specifies the size of the block requested. If a block of sufficient size is present, the pointer *found* indicates its header, and the flag in the header is set to *used*; any residual of the block is left on the available list. Note that in forming the residual, a header will be needed for the allocated block, so that *need*+1 cells must be found to partition a block. If a sufficiently large block is not available, or if the available list is exhausted after the request is filled, the program 'help' is called; in the former case *found* is set to Λ.

The deallocation program is straightforward. It divides into two distinct segments according as *free* is greater than, or less than, *available*. Only the first of these is given here (see Exercise 1 for the second). In the program segment shown, *available* is advanced until no block on the available list lies between *available* and *free*. It is then only necessary to determine whether the blocks contiguous to the one released are also free, and act accordingly. In the segment not shown (when *free<available*), *available* is stepped backward until no block on the available list lies between *free* and *available*, and similar consolidation actions are then taken. The specification and declaration global to the program are:

> **comp header** = ⟨**header-ptr** *blink*, **integer** *size*, **boolean** *used*,
> **header-ptr**, *flink*⟩
>
> **header-ptr** *available*.

With regard to consolidation methods based on the buddy system, the earlier versions of these programs partitioned each block into two equal parts, so that the block sizes were of the form 2^k, $k = 0, 1, 2, \ldots$. This makes the larger blocks very different in size from each other, a disadvantage that can be overcome by using a Fibonocci-like sequence, in which the partitions are determined by the equation

$$f_n = f_{n-1} + f_{n-k},$$

where $n \geq k$ and $f_0, f_1, \ldots, f_{k-1}$ are given initial sizes.

If $k = 1$ and $f_0 = 1$, the conventional powers of two, 1, 2, 4, 8, $\ldots$, are obtained for the block sizes. If $k = 2$ and $f_0 = f_1 = 1$, the Fibonocci sequence 1, 1, 2, 3, 5, 8, $\ldots$ gives the sizes. For $k = 3$, $f_0 = 1$, $f_1 = 3$, and $f_2 = 5$, we get the series 1, 3, 5, 6, 9, 14, 20, 29, 43. A binary tree whose nodes are labeled with the terms of this series is shown in Fig. 8.2. There are several ways in which a block can be tagged so that its buddy's tag is immediately known, and a simple one is illustrated in Fig. 8.2. The root block is given the tag 0, and if any block has tag x, its partitions have the tags $x0$ and $x1$. Thus if the 5-block with tag 01001 is released, its one-block buddy with tag 01000 is examined. If that is free, the two are consolidated into six-block 0100, and the buddy of this, the three-block 0101, is interrogated. If this is free also, there can be a further consolidation into the nine-block whose tag is 010, and so on. In the buddy system there is only one candidate block for consolidation with a released block (rather than two as is the case for the consolidation technique looked at above), but experience has shown that it is an acceptable method.

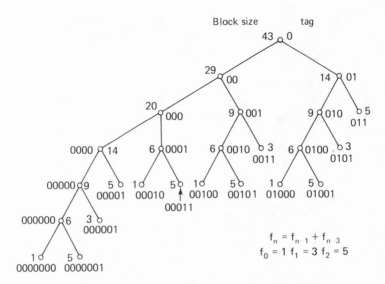

Fig. 8.2   Fibonocci tree for allocating storage block "buddies"

It is not easy to determine the conditions under which different allocation strategies should be adopted. There are so many data-related factors—distribution of block-size requests, lifetimes of blocks, interarrival rate of requests, and so on—that observations must be regarded as specific to the system studied, and simulations based on standard distributions have restricted validity. In one time-sharing system, for example, where job sizes varied widely, the block sizes were quite large, but in an application where ALGOL programs were run, post requests were for 50 words or less, and if system programs were excluded, half the requests were for less than 20 words.[2] In this latter environment the lifetime for a block was usually short, on the order of 2 per cent of the lifetime of the program. There are conflicting reports on the relative merits of first-fit, next-fit, and best-fit strategies, but on the whole, first-fit seems to be at least as good as any.[3,4] In summary, there is no best method for storage management, but given knowledge about the requests, it is possible to implement good techniques.[5] Doing so can significantly reduce the average time to satisfy a request—as much as an order of magnitude over a simple method such as that which utilizes first-fit and a lifo stack, often chosen because there are no data that would justify a more complicated approach.

[2]A. P. Batson, S. M. Ju, and D. C. Wood, "Measurement of Segment Size," *Communications of the ACM*, **13**, no. 3 (Mar. 1970), 155–159.

[3]J. E. Shore, "On the External Storage Fragmentation Produced by First-Fit and Best-Fit Allocation Strategies," *Communications of the ACM*, **18**, no. 8 (Aug. 1975), 433–440.

[4]C. Bays, "A Comparison of Next-Fit, First-Fit, and Best-Fit," *Communications of the ACM*, **20**, no. 3 (Mar. 1977), 191–192.

[5]C. B. Weinstock, *Dynamic Storage Allocation Techniques* (1976).

8.4 Garbage Collection

Having considered the techniques for allocating and deallocating storage, we return to the question, raised earlier, of deciding *when* storage is to be released and the free list augmented or reconstituted. Historically, the problem of recapturing storage was first given serious attention in list processing. Lists are dynamic data types whose lengths can vary enormously within a single program, so it is especially important to be able to reclaim unused storage when working with them. Garbage collection, the colloquial term commonly used to describe storage reclamation, can itself be thought of as having two subprocesses. These are:

1. Identifying the storage available for release.
2. Adding the storage to the free list, or alternatively, compacting it so as to reconstitute the free list.

In the context of list processing, two approaches were developed for identifying the storage available for release. In the first method, called *marking*, the program is interrupted from time to time (e.g., when the free list shrinks below a predetermined level), and the process of identifying all needed storage is initiated. First those blocks referenced within a set of basic program modules are marked; then those blocks referenced by blocks within the basic set are marked, and so on, until there are no new contributions. After the marking phase of garbage collection, free storage is collected, possibly with compaction. Algorithms for marking and compaction are given in the next subsection. The second approach to identifying storage available for release, an alternative to marking, is to carry with each block a *reference counter* which indicates how many times the block is referenced, or pointed at, throughout the program. When a block's reference count goes to zero, it is a candidate for addition to the free list; the addition may take place immediately, or be deferred and combined with compaction.

The basic technique in using reference counts is to increment the count associated with a node whenever a link is set up pointing to the node, and decrement the count whenever a link is broken. Reference counting has been used in only a few list-processing languages, principally because the cost of maintaining the counts can be high.[6] Another complication is that precautions have to be taken to avoid dangling references. The reference counts of the nodes on a circular list, for example, will never go to zero, even if the block in which the list is declared is left, and the list never referenced again. One way of handling this particular situation is to keep the reference count in the list header rather than in the individual nodes. This device has the further advantage that it may be possible to break the cycle and append it to the free list once the count goes to zero, a faster technique than processing individual nodes. The basic drawback of reference counts (whether they are maintained in nodes or list headers) is that the count must be adjusted on all insertion and deletion operations, and more-

[6]See G. E. Collins, "A Method for Overlapping and Erasure of Lists," *Communications of the ACM*, **3**, no. 12 (Dec. 1960), 655–667, and J. Weizenbaum, "Symmetric List Processor," *Communications of the ACM*, **6** (1963), 524–544.

over, the adjustment must be carried out at run time (since the number of new references cannot be determined in advance). In effect, this makes the list processor behave like an interpreter, with attendant high costs. It is true that the cost is distributed over the whole program rather than being especially high at certain times, as happens with marking, but general practice seems to favor marking for garbage collection.

8.4.1 Marking a List

A simple argument reveals why there can also be problems with garbage collection by marking. Suppose that M, A, and F are, respectively, the number of blocks in memory, the number allocated, and the number free, so that $M = A + F$. Also, let $f = A/M$. Marking programs takes a time that can be represented as aA, where a is a constant of the program. Marking is followed by an examination of all nodes, and assigning them to one of two partitions, depending on whether they are to be kept or not. This will have an execution time of the form bM, where b is another constant. The total time for a garbage collection pass is thus $aA + bM = M(b + af)$. For a given M, this increases as $f \rightarrow 1$. In other words, as the memory becomes fuller, the efficiency of garbage collection, as measured by the effort expended to recover a node, decreases. Ordinarily, of course, the garbage collection will be called just when memory is nearly full, and this argument shows that under these circumstances the process is likely to be unrewarding. The best protection is to reserve more memory than one is prepared to allocate, a precaution that also speeds up storage allocation.[7] If necessary, a program that has too large a fraction of the memory allotted to it should be swapped out and run in a larger partition, and this should be done before garbage collection and allocation become too expensive.

Even if care is taken not to wait until memory is too full before garbage collection is initiated, other factors about memory have to be considered. Examining a list by marking is essentially a form of traversing the structure. We have seen several examples where it was desirable to traverse the items of a given data structure systematically. Algorithm 4.3 for the UNION of two lists is essentially a simultaneous traversal of two simple lists; Algorithm 6.1 for enumerating the nodes of a binary tree in symmetric order and Algorithm 7.1 for finding a spanning tree are also kinds of traversals. Traversing a simple list, where every entry has only one successor, presents no problem, but for trees and graphs, where an entry can have more than one successor, it is necessary to follow one path and defer other branches for later processing. In Algorithms 6.1 and 7.1, the obvious technique for deferred processing was employed; that is, entries were placed on a stack or queue for later consideration. But garbage collection will be invoked only when storage is becoming scarce, and under such conditions it is not possible to count on unlimited blocks for use by a stack. What is wanted, therefore, is some form of marking or traversal algorithm for general lists in

---

[7]Reference count techniques for garbage collection are usually assumed to have an efficiency represented by a constant that is independent of f (Collins and Weizenbaum, footnote 6). The time to *maintain* the counts, however, might conceivably depend on f, in which case one would have to define an effective efficiency, and it is not clear what the behavior would be.

which stacks are not used. Earlier garbage collection techniques often made some use of stacks, but several algorithms that dispense with them have been developed, and we shall consider two here.

The need for a choice of algorithms arises because there are features of the data structure and of the marking process, which, if present, simplify the general procedure. By taking advantage of these features, it is possible to construct algorithms which use little or no auxiliary storage and which run very fast. The best that one can hope is that the execution time will be linearly dependent on the number of cells examined. But the iteration constant can vary, corre ponding to the fact that in some algorithms it is necessary to visit each cell several times, while in others the marking can be carried out with a single visit. Briefly, the following factors influence the running time and storage requirements.

- Is the data structure a tree (in which case the sublists of a given entry are not shared, and there are no cycles), an acyclic graph (where there are shared sublists but no cycles), or a general graph (with possible cycles)? Not surprisingly, simpler routines can be written for trees and acyclic graphs.

- Is the data structure simply to be traversed (or marked) in place, or does it have to be moved from one part of storage to another in order to perform a compaction? Also, in this latter case can the original structure be destroyed? The term *copying* is used when the original structure may *not* be altered, and the term *moving* otherwise.

- Is the use of marking bits allowed? If such bits are available, the procedure is more direct, but it is possible to dispense with them.

- Is there available a contiguous storage area into which the data structure may be copied or moved? If there is, the procedure can be simplified, because the address of a cell will indicate whether that cell is part of the old or new structure.

Most marking algorithms use an elegant technique discovered ndependently by H. Schorr and W. M. Waite, and by Peter Deutsch.[8] The technique is easily visualized for a binary tree, although it is applicable to general lists. Starting at the root, a descent of the tree is carried out, following one type of branch, say the left. On each descent the link is reversed, so as to point back to the node just visited. When an atom or null link is encountered on the left, a switch is made to the right link, and a marker in the node is set in order to indicate that after a leaf has been found, and an ascent *up* the tree started, the right link contains the information needed to retrace the path. During ascent, altered links are restored to their original values.

We shall illustrate list marking and list moving by two algorithms, neither of which uses extra storage. (The second algorithm uses a working stack, but it stores information about visited nodes in locations which have been released earlier, and therefore no *extra* storage is needed for the stack.) The simplicity of the first (based on the pointer reversal technique just described) comes from the fact that marking bits may be used.

[8]H. Schorr and W. M. Waite, "An Efficient Machine-Independent Procedure for Garbage Collection in Various List Structures," *Communications of the ACM*, **10**, no. 8 (Aug. 1967), 501–506.

The brevity of the second is due in part to the fact that a contiguous region of storage is available for the copy. Although the basic ideas of marking, moving, and copying algorithms are simple, most of the algorithms reported in the literature are highly *nonstructured*, in the sense that they have frequent *goto*'s, and apply arithmetic operations to pointers. The algorithms we give are structured implementations, based on the possible directions that can be taken on encountering a node.

In marking and copying algorithms it is common to assume the node format of LISP, in which entries consist either of atoms or of pointer pairs. It is not difficult to generalize the programs to handle nodes that contain more than two pointers, or to the case where the data may be either stored in an atomic node or referenced by a pointer which is stored in that node. The algorithm will be illustrated using the graph of Fig. 8.3. Figure 8.3 shows the data structure for that graph, using LISP-like cells. Although the data comprise a graph rather than a tree, it is still meaningful to speak of down and up during the traversal; these directions correspond to away from, and toward, the root.

The marking algorithm is given by Algorithm 8.3. It proceeds by a descent from the root, the left branch being taken first as long as that path is not blocked (which happens if the pointer is null, or reference is made to an atom or an already marked node). During descent, pointers are reversed. When the left branch is blocked, the right link is taken (if *that* path is unblocked), and the marker at the switched node is set to **true**, to indicate that the right pointer has been reversed. After a node is passed on ascent, the marker is set to **true**. Thus the markers (which are initially assumed to be set to **false**) serve multiple purposes; on descent they are set to identify the retrace path and also used to identify blocked paths; at the end they identify nodes reachable from the root. Figure 8.3 shows the nodes and pointers during traversal when the node farthest from the root (number 7) has been reached. (Reversed pointers are shown with double arrows.) In Algorithm 8.3, a general node with two pointers, each of which references a general node (e.g., *p11* in Fig. 8.3), is encountered three times (once when it is reached from a predecessor, once from its left link, and once from its right link); other nodes are visited less often (e.g., once for atoms). Since each node is visited at most three times, the running time will be bounded by an expression of $O(n)$, where n is the number of cells visited.

The **comp** declarations which specify the required node types are:

> **comp p-node** $=$ $\langle$**boolean** *marked*, **node-ptr** *llink*, **node-ptr** *rlink*$\rangle$
> **comp atom** $=$ $\langle$**boolean** *marked*, **string** *data*$\rangle$
> **comp node** $=$ **p-node** $\cup$ **atom**

The predicate **atom** $(@q)$ returns **true** if q points to an **atom**, and **false** if q points to a **p-node**.

8.4.2 Compaction

Marking, accompanied by compaction, involves moving the marked cells into some new region of store, so as to make it possible to assemble large storage blocks for

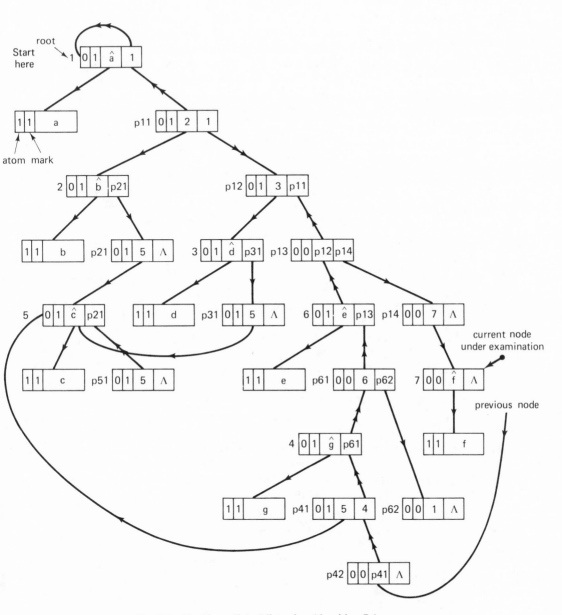

Fig. 8.3 Marking a linked list using Algorithm 7.4

subsequent use. There has been a steady appearance of algorithms for copying and moving lists without stacks since Cheney produced the first such routine.[9] G. Lind-

[9]C. J. Cheney, "A Non-Recursive List Compacting Algorithm," *Communications of the ACM*, **13**, no. 11 (Nov. 1972), 677–678.

Algorithm 8.3   Marking a list

```
mark (root)
boolean finished; node-ptr root, prev, current, leftlink, rightlink, temp;
prev ⇐ root; current ⇐ root; finished ⇐ false; /* initialization*/
if atom(@current) then marked(@ current), finished ⇐ true;
                        /* exit if root is atomic */
do while ¬ finished;
    leftlink ⇐ left(@current); /*avoid redundant selection*/
    rightlink ⇐ right(@current);
    if leftlink ≠ Λ ∧ atom(@leftlink) then marked(@leftlink) ⇐ true;
    if ¬ ((leftlink=Λ) ∨ atom(@leftlink) ∨ marked(@leftlink)) then
    do; /* follow left link*/
        temp ⇐ leftlink;
        left(@current) ⇐ prev; /* reverse link */
        prev ⇐ current;
        current ⇐ temp;
    end
    else if ¬ ((rightlink=Λ) ∧ atom(@rightlink) ∧ marked(@rightlink)) then
    do; /* follow right link */
        marked(@current) ⇐ true;
        temp ⇐ rightlink;
        right(@current) ⇐ prev; /* reverse link */
        prev ⇐ current;
        current ⇐ temp;
    end
    else
    do; /* both paths blocked so must go up */
        if rightlink ≠ Λ then marked(@rightlink) ⇐ true;
        marked(@current) ⇐ true;
        if current = root then finished ⇐ true;
        else if marked(@prev) then
        do; /* right path was taken */
            temp ⇐ right(@prev);
            right(@prev) ⇐ current; /* restore link */
        end
        else
        do; /* left path taken */
            temp ⇐ left(@prev);
            left(@prev) ⇐ current; /* restore link */
        end
        current ⇐ prev;
        prev ⇐ temp;
    end /* back up */
end /* while not finished */
```

strom[10] describes procedures for copying an arbitrary n-item list into an arbitrary set of storage cells, in $O(n \log n)$ time if a mark bit is available, and $O(n^2)$ time if there are no mark bits. D. A. Fisher described an algorithm not requiring a stack or marking bits, which copies a list into a contiguous region in a time that is $O(n)$,[11] and a similar $O(n)$ algorithm for moving a list is described by D. W. Clark.[12] Algorithm 8.4 given here is Clark's, slightly modified to improve the structuring. The **comp** declarations are as above, but there is no *marked* field.

In Algorithm 8.4, *original* points to the head of the list and *copy* to the first cell of a new, contiguous storage region to which the list is to be moved. At the end, a pointer *count* indicates the first cell in the new region available for subsequent use. It is assumed that there are two special subroutines, new (p), which yields *true* if p points to a cell in the new region, and inc (p), which yields a pointer to the cell address that follows p. As in Algorithm 8.3, the basic technique is to follow a chain of pointers making up a *segment* (right pointers are followed this time) until an atom, or a pointer to a previously met cell, is encountered. During traversal of this segment path, left links which later have to be followed are placed on a stack called *lifo*. *Lifo* links together items *of the original list* for which further action is needed; no *additional* working storage is required for it, an important feature that distinguishes the algorithm from simple list traversal methods which use a stack. When a segment is ended, *lifo* is popped, and the procedure continues with this popped entry as the start of a new segment. The algorithm is finished when *lifo*'s initialized entry of Λ is encountered.

Figure 8.4(a) illustrates a list that is to be moved, and Fig. 8.4(b) shows the situation after the first three cells have been copied and moved, and segment becomes **false**. At this time the following conditions hold:

- The left link of each original item points to the item's copy in the new storage area. (Later, discovery of a new location where an ordinary *llink* value is expected prevents the creation of duplicate copies of shared cells.)
- In the copy, links pointing to atoms have their final values.
- In the copy, *llink* values which reference lists point to the original lists in the old area.
- In the copy, *rlink* values which reference lists have their final values, all pointing to the next consecutive cell in memory.
- In the segment just completed, *llink* values which reference lists have been placed on *lifo* which was initialized to Λ.

When *segment* becomes **false**, *lifo* is popped and *llink* (@ *llink* (@ *lifo*)) is the possible head of a new segment. If this points to an already copied cell, *lifo* is popped again; otherwise, a new segment chain is entered. The process continues until *lifo* is exhausted. Figure 8.4(c) illustrates the situation after the moving has been completed.

[10]G. Lindstrom, "Copying List Structures Using Bounded Workspace," *Communications of the ACM*, **17**, no. 4 (Apr. 1974), 198–201.

[11]D. A. Fisher, "Copying Cyclic List Structures in Linear Time Using Bounded Workspace," *Communications of the ACM*, **18**, no. 5 (May 1975), 251–252.

[12]D. W. Clark, "An Efficient List Moving Algorithm Using Constant Workspace," *Communications of the ACM*, **19**, no. 6 (June 1976), 352–354.

Algorithm 8.4 Moving a list

```
move (original, copy);
node-ptr current, count, left, right;
bool segment, copying;
current ⟸ original; count ⟸ copy;
copying, segment ⟸ true; /*looping variables*/
lifo ⟸ Λ; /*looping variables*/
do while copying;
    do while segment;
        left ⟸ llink (@ current); /*save left, right links*/
        right ⟸ rlink (@ current);
        llink (@ current) ⟸ count; /*left link of original
                                              points to copy*/
        if ¬ atom (@ left) ∧ left ≠ Λ then /*if left link points
                                                    to list*/
            do rlink (@ current) ⟸ lifo; /*place current node
                                                  for stack*/
                lifo ⟸ current;
            end /*add new sublist to lifo*/
        llink (@ count) ⟸ left; /* left link of copy points
                                          to original*/
        if atom (@ right) ∨ new (llink(@ right)) then
            do; /*end of segment*/
                if atom (@ right) then rlink (@ count) ⟸ right;
                        /*because of atom*/
                else rlink (@ count) ⟸ llink (@ right);
                        /*because of previously copied list*/
                segment ⟸ false;
            end
            else
            do; /*continue copying the segment*/
                rlink (@ count) ⟸ inc(count);
                        /*set rlink in copy to next consecutive cell
                          in copy*/
                current ⟸ right;
            end
        count ⟸ inc(count);
        end /*while segment*/
    if lifo = Λ then copying ⟸ false;
    else do; /*get new sublist to copy*/
            current ⟸ llink (@ llink (@ lifo)); /*from stack*/
            temp ⟸ lifo;
            lifo ⟸ rlink (@ lifo); /*pop lifo*/
            if new (llink (@ current)) then /*try again if sublist
                                                    already copied*/
```

llink (@ *llink* (@ *temp*)) ⇐ *llink* (@ *current*);
else do *llink* (@ *llink* (@ *temp*) ⇐ *count*;
segment ⇐ **true**;
end /*llink of popped lifo entry now correct*/
end /*find new segment*/
end /* while copying */

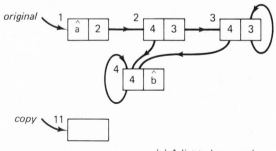

(a) A list to be moved

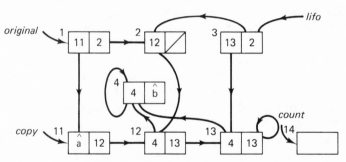

(b) The lists after the first three cells have been moved

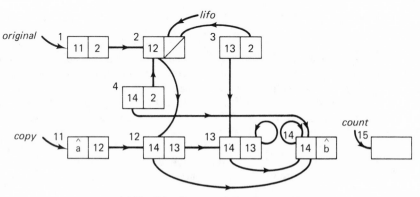

(c) The lists after completing the move

Fig. 8.4 Moving a list

311

Only cells that have llinks and rlinks both pointing to sublists have to be visited twice, so that Algorithm 8.4 is already very fast. Clark points out techniques and certain features which, if present, speed up the algorithm even further.[13]

In concluding this section on compaction, some additional remarks are in order. If the free list is compacted into one large available block, allocation and deallocation become very simple. Instead of keeping a list of different-sized blocks, it is only necessary to maintain a pointer that separates the free region from allocated storage. Given enough storage to honor a request, the required block will be immediately available. Periodically, garbage collection is initiated, marking and compaction are carried out, and the position of the pointer is adjusted accordingly. Attractive as this scheme is, it has not generally been adopted for programming languages because compaction algorithms, or at least earlier versions of them, have been regarded as too expensive. Nevertheless, it is the garbage collection method used in many implementations of LISP and SNOBOL, and it becomes even more attractive with the emergence of the fast compaction methods just presented. One final caveat is necessary. There are list-processing algorithms which also use the pointer reversal technique of Schorr and Waite to temporarily alter the pointers in a list, restoring the connections at the end. If marking is initiated in the middle of one of these algorithms, the correct list structure may never be recovered. It is therefore necessary to be able to recognize those programs which manipulate links in such ways that recovery cannot be effected, and suspend the initiation of garbage collection once such a program has been entered.

The success of programming languages such as LISP, SNOBOL, and ALGOL 68 is very much dependent on the fact that efficient garbage collections have been incorporated into them. Contrariwise, there is little doubt that PL/I is at a disadvantage because there is no garbage collection built into it; programmers are expected to provide their own, or to use the FREE and ALLOCATE commands to manage storage. If older programming languages such as COBOL and FORTRAN are to be replaced, successors will undoubtedly have to include good methods of storage management and garbage collection among the advantages.

Exercises

1. In Algorithm 8.2, program the sequence for *free* < *available*.
2. Show how first-fit and best-fit allocation would work with the buddy system for determining block sizes. What arguments are there for preferring one over the other? Rewrite Algorithms 8.1 and 8.2 using a buddy system.
3. What would happen in Algorithms 8.1 and 8.2 if the list of available blocks contained a block that was incorrectly placed in the ascending sequence of addresses? Should the programs be altered to guard against such a possibility? (Give reasons for your answer.)
4. Generalize the technique for handling reference counts of cyclic lists (Section 8.4) to handle composite, rooted substructures. How does the resulting technique for garbage collection compare with one based on marking?

[13]Clark, "Efficient List Moving Algorithm."

5. List a number of possibilities for conditions under which marking should be initiated. What are the arguments for each?
6. Complete the trace of Algorithm 8.3 from the point shown in Fig. 8.3.
7. Write an algorithm for copying a list, without using auxiliary storage or mark bits, and without changing the original list. (See the reference in footnotes 11 and 12.)
8. Trace Algorithm 8.4 for the example of Fig. 8.4.
9. Obtain expressions for the bounds on the execution times of Algorithms 8.3 and 8.4. (Consider list types for which the times will be least and greatest in each case.)

Bibliography

Although storage allocation and deallocation is a classic problem in list management, it is of such importance that it continues to receive serious attention. A good summary, to the time of writing, is given in Knuth (1973). Other surveys are to be found in Lindstrom (1973), Weinstock (1976), and Clark (1976).

CLARK, D. W., *List Structures: Measurements, Algorithms and Encoding*. Pittsburgh, Pa.: Department of Computer Science, Carnegie-Mellon University, 1976.

KNUTH, D., *The Art of Computer Programming*, Vol. 1, *Fundamental Algorithms*, 2nd ed. Reading, Mass.: Addison-Wesley Publishing Company, Inc., 1973, Sec. 2.5.

LINDSTROM, G., "Scanning List Structures Without Stacks or Tag Bits." *Information Processing Letters*, **2** (June 1973), 47–51.

WEINSTOCK, C. B., *Dynamic Storage Allocation Techniques* (Ph.D. thesis). Pittsburgh, Pa.: Department of Computer Science, Carnegie-Mellon University, 1976.

chapter 9

Files

In data processing, it is normal to handle large amounts of information, much of which is permanent in nature. Since a computer's main memory is rather limited in capacity and not suited to long-term data storage, secondary, or external memories (tapes, disks) are used. A data structure that resides in secondary storage is called a *file*. Files are commonly structured as arrays or simple lists, but they can take more complicated forms. The constituent items of a file are called *records*; hese may be composite, with fields (also called *attributes*), as described in Chapter 2.

Access times for external memories are high compared to internal processing times; the time to find and read in a character from a specific location is typically measured in milliseconds, while the speed with which a computer instruction is executed is on the order of microseconds. Therefore, files must be designed to minimize the number of external data accesses required for various operations. Up to now, however, we have ignored memory references and simply counted representative machine operations when evaluating data structure operations. This measure is reasonable if the information is assumed to reside in the main memory of a computer, but it is inadequate when the storage medium is external (i.e., when data access costs are high). Thus it is not clear which of the data structures presented in preceding chapters are suitable for use as files.

The purpose of this chapter is to show how some of the data structures and techniques discussed previously are adapted for secondary storage. The presentation is not intended to be complete; indeed, there is an extensive and growing body of literature on file organization. Rather it is a reconsideration of earlier topics in the light of the two basic realities of the file environment:

1. Files are too large to fit into the main memory of a computer.
2. It is too expensive to access individual records when carrying out operations that can range over the whole file.

Point (2) is somewhat vague. It is meant to suggest that techniques such as exchange sort and binary search will not be practical for files, but it remains to be seen how files should be designed so that sorting and retrievals can be carried out efficiently. Additional information about file sizes and device access times is needed, so we begin with a discussion of secondary storage characteristics.

9.1 Secondary Storage Characteristics

Up to now, discussion of the storage component $\langle G, M, S \rangle$ of a data structure has been confined to the mapping $S: G \Rightarrow M$. The focus of this section is the memory, M. Logically, it can be viewed as a set of cells, each capable of holding a byte, or character. Of interest here are the mechanics of retrieving a cell's contents once the address has been determined.

Present memory technology provides four kinds of access. These are:

1. *Serial*—Records are positioned one after another, in linear order. To get record i, it is necessary to read records 1 through $i - 1$, so access times can vary greatly. Moreover, they can be quite high in real terms; the time to scan a magnetic tape, a good example of serial memory, is on the order of minutes. On the other hand, magnetic tape is very inexpensive, the cost per bit being about $\$10^{-7}$.
2. *Random*—In this type of memory, access time is constant. The magnetic core and semiconductor main memories of today's computers are truly random access, and they are also very fast compared to other memory technologies; cell read times range from 50 to 1000 nanoseconds (ns). Memory access costs are included in instruction times (when applicable) and therefore do not appear explicitly when operations on data that reside in main memory are evaluated. The cost of random access memory is around $\$10^{-1}$ per bit, and the largest memories hold about 10^7 characters.
3. *Direct*—Often inaccurately labeled as random access, this type of memory is a compromise, in speed and cost per bit, between serial and truly random access stores. A good example is a drum, essentially a collection of magnetic strips, or *tracks*, located on a rotating cylinder. Each track has its own read/write head, so record access is random (and essentially instantaneous) to a track, and sequential within one. Moreover, the sequential search is fast because the drum rotates at high speed. Disks and drums are discussed in more detail below.
4. *Content Addressable*—The memories just described take an address or relative record position and return the data at the specified location. But data processing typically involves requests to locate records with given attribute values (e.g., "Find the owners of blue Chevrolets registered in 1976"). This content-based

retrieval of data is the inverse of the process by which conventional memories work. It can be simulated with software, for example by using hash tables, multilists, or inverted lists. Alternatively, content-addressable memories have been built. Given a search argument, they indicate locations whose contents match the argument. Because they are expensive, such memories are small and have not been put into wide production. Although not suitable as auxiliary storage, they are potentially useful for file operations. This aspect is discussed in Section 9.4.

The devices most commonly used for file storage are magnetic tapes, disks, and drums. We now describe these in order to appreciate how their characteristics can affect file design.

9.1.1 Magnetic Tape

The most common serial-access memory is magnetic tape. The tape itself is a magnetic recording strip, $\frac{1}{2}$ inch wide and roughly 2400 feet long. It is formatted lengthwise into tracks on which bits are recorded in sequence. A character is encoded by the cross section of bits at a track position. An extra track is included for parity, so machines with the EBCDIC character set, for example, use nine-track tapes.

The tape is stored in reel form and mounted on a tape unit for reading and writing. Depending on the unit (and tape quality), data is recorded at densities ranging from 200 to 6250 characters (bytes) per inch (cpi, bpi).[1] Reading speeds range from 10 to 200 inches per second (ips). A typical medium performance tape unit, the IBM 2420–5, reads (and writes) 1600-bpi tape at 100 ips, giving it a capacity of 23 million bytes and a maximum data rate of 160,000 bytes/second.

In practice, not all of a tape contains data; time, and therefore space on tape, is needed for the drive to reach speed before, and stop after, read and write commands. Sections of tape reserved for this purpose are called *interrecord gaps* (IRG's), and the information between two gaps constitutes a *physical record*. The basic tape unit operations involving data are read-, write-, and skip physical record.

Record gap size depends on the tape drive; on the 2420–5 it is 0.6 inch, which accounts for 960 characters at 1600 bpi. This means that physical records must be well over 1000 bytes, or a significant portion of tape will be taken up by gaps, and much of the input/output (I/O) time will be spent starting and stopping the tape. However, the "logical" records making up a file are often much smaller than gap size; typical is the card file that has been transferred to tape, in which case the logical records may be 80-byte card images. The solution in such cases is to *block* logical records, that is, group several of them together to make a physical record; for example, with a 960-character gap, blocks of 100 80-byte card images would result in a gap wastage of only 12 percent.

---

[1] Sometimes density is stated in terms of bits per inch. In such cases, track density is being described, so the measure is the same.

Blocking is an important technique for tape because record gaps tend to be large; more generally, it is used when the cost of reading logical records is too high to allow them to be accessed individually. If the records in a block can be related so that any processing required can be performed on them while the block remains in memory, the average read cost per record will be reduced. This happens naturally with tape because records are normally processed sequentially; to achieve the same effect with direct-access devices, it may be necessary to ensure that blocked records are functionally related.

Blocking has some disadvantages in the way of overhead. First, software is needed to perform blocking and *unblocking* (i.e., extracting a desired logical record from the containing physical one). Just as important, buffer space must be available to hold the blocks. Unless all the records in a block are being processed, the storage occupied may represent a significant amount of wasted space, especially on small machines (8–32K). For efficiency, I/O routines dealing with blocked files should consult the buffer(s) before issuing any actual commands; a request for a given record should be preceded by a search of the input buffer to see if a copy of the record is present there, and updates to records in a buffer should affect only the buffer until such time as the whole block is written out. Naturally this increases the complexity of the I/O programming, and also means that a buffer must be retained throughout file processing, instead of just long enough to block or unblock.

9.1.2 Disks and Drums

Even fast tape drives take over 2 minutes to read a tape, so that medium is unsuitable for applications that require rapid (in terms of seconds) nonsequential access to individual records. Disks and drums provide this capability, while often improving on the high data rates achievable with tape.

A disk unit (meaning a disk pack mounted on a drive) is a revolving stack of disks, the surfaces of which contain a fixed number of concentric tracks upon which characters can be recorded. For each surface there is a read/write head; these are arranged in a comblike access arm that can be positioned over individual tracks. The heads move together, so each position defines a set of tracks—one from each surface—called a *cylinder*. The number of cylinders is the number of tracks on a surface.

As an example, consider a unit of the IBM 3330 storage facility (a bank of up to 8 disk drives). It consists of 10 disks, 19 surfaces of which are used. A surface has 404 tracks, so there are 404 cylinders of 19 tracks each. A track can hold 13,030 characters, making the total capacity of a pack of about 100 million bytes.

As with tapes, some space on a track is taken up by information needed to delineate physical records. On IBM disks there are two basic record formats: count area followed by data, and count area, key, data. An address marker precedes each record, and all fields—marker, count, key, and data—are separated by gaps. (The gaps are of varying size and have functions different from those on tape.) To get an idea of how much space can be used up by "administrative" information (nondata fields and gaps), note that on a 3330 pack, a track containing a single physical record can hold 13,030 data bytes, while one with 30 records has capacity for only 9090.[2] Much of this loss can be avoided by blocking logical records together as the data area, and only maintaining count (and possibly key) information for the block.

The count area for each record contains, among other things, an identifier giving the cylinder and track numbers, and record number within the track. Records can be selected according to identifier (i.e., relative track position) or key values. For all operations, starting cylinder and track numbers must ultimately be determined. The access arm is moved to the specified cylinder, the read/write head for the track is activated, and track positions become available for reading or writing as the disk revolves. The access time for a record therefore has two device-dependent components—access motion (*seek*) time, and rotational delay. (Head selection is electronic and effectively instantaneous.) Seek time is roughly a linear function of the number of tracks traversed. Rotational delay, or *latency*, varies from zero to the time required for a full rotation, depending on how far away the desired track location is from the read/write head once the seek is finished. The rotational speed is also the speed with which data are read and written.

On the IBM 3330, seek time ranges between 10 and 55 milliseconds (ms) and averages 30 ms. The disk rotates once every 16.7 ms; at 13,030 bytes/track, this means a data rate of 806,000 bytes/s, or 1.2 microseconds/byte. Assuming average seek time, and taking half a rotation as the average latency, the time to read n consecutive characters from a selected track is $38.4 + 0.0012 \cdot n$ ms.

The overhead for disk access is clearly high. It cannot be avoided when a specific record is required, but may be reduced if it can be arranged for data to be requested in sufficiently large amounts. For example, latency will be eliminated if whole tracks are always read or written. Suppose instead that only a fraction f, $0 < f \le 1$, of a track is wanted. Following the seek, it may be possible to start reading as long as any portion of f is under the read head, and pick up the initial segment when the disk comes around again; the proper order can be reconstructed once the data are in memory. With probability f, reading will start in the desired portion, and therefore a whole rotation will be needed for completion, $1 - f$ of which represents rotational delay (i.e., wasted time). With probability $1 - f$, the undesired portion of track will be first encountered; assume that we have to wait through $(1 - f)/2$ of it on the average. Then the average latency incurred by this strategy will be $f(1 - f) + (1 - f)(1 - f)/2 = 1/2(1 - f^2)$, and the total of read and delay is never more than a revolution. Naturally this method requires more sophisticated buffer management than if the I/O program simply waits for the start of the data area.[3]

[2]*Introduction to IBM Direct-Access Storage Devices and Organization Methods*, Form C20-1649, Fig. 3.4 (pp. 3–9) (Dec. 1975).

[3]Actually, these two strategies cannot always be successfully used. On IBM units, the savings they achieve are reduced, paradoxically, as the degree of blocking on a track increases. This is because reads and searches cannot start until an address marker (or index point, indicating the start of a track) has been detected. Thus if the whole track is one physical record, reading will not occur until the beginning, making the total time actually greater than one revolution by the amount of latency. To

Usually, through a combination of hardware and operating system features, it is possible to read (or write) more than one track of a cylinder in one command. Another useful instruction is a search that automatically proceeds through successive tracks of a cylinder. Thus a large amount of data is available at the cost of only one seek.

Drums are essentially like disks, but the access arm does not move; rather it is confined to one cylindrical surface. Therefore, what has been said about disks, with the exception of remarks on access arm motion, applies to drums. Because the read/write heads are stationary, access to data on a drum is an order of magnitude faster. In addition, some drums (e.g., the IBM 2305 series) rotate more quickly than most disks, so even rotational delay may be less. The data rate for the 2305-I is 3000 kilobytes/s, five times that of the 3330; on the other hand, the capacity is only 5 million bytes, compared to 100 million for the disk.

The characteristics of drums are such that they are rarely used for long-term storage. Their capacity is too small, and the performance they provide is higher than needed for most file processing. In discussing direct-access file organization, we shall usually assume that storage consists of disks.

9.1.3 Other Hardware Influences on File Design

Given the kind of secondary storage just described, the time for a file operation can be estimated by

$$T_p + T_a + T_t,$$

where

$T_p =$ internal processing time
$T_a =$ cost of record accesses (seek + average rotational delay)
$T_t =$ time taken for data transfer.

All three components are device-dependent and are normally functions of file size. Although we shall use this model for evaluations, it is not entirely adequate, because there are factors that affect performance but in a way that is difficult to quantify. Two of particular interest—overlap and virtual memory—are the subjects of this section.

Overlap: If the central processing unit (CPU) were responsible for I/O as well as internal processing, it would spend much of its time waiting for seeks to be completed and tapes to stop and start. This is avoided by using specialized processors called *channels* to control transmission between the I/O devices and main memory. Typically, the CPU starts the channel executing a program and resumes its own processing until notified (by the channel) that the operation is complete (or that an error has occurred).

---

ensure that reading can start without too much delay (this is what the above methods depend on), several physical records must be allocated to a track. On a 3330 track, 15 equally sized records (with keys) would permit data transfer to start roughly 0.5 ms after seek completion (on the average); at the same time, the data capacity of the track would be reduced 20 percent over the one-record case.

Thus computing and I/O can be performed concurrently, subject to the following limitations:

1. The CPU must assemble the channel program and do any blocking or unblocking necessary.
2. The channel must be given access to main memory (over the CPU) when it is ready to transmit data. Because the memory can only be accessed from one source, this "stealing" of memory access cycles by the channel slows down the processor, depending on what kind of instructions the latter is executing, and depending on the data rate of the device.

With one channel providng full overlap (the limitations above notwithstanding), the time for a file operation can be reduced to max $(T_p, T_a + T_t)$. If two channels are available, input can be overlapped with output, so an even lower bound is (theoretically) achievable. Moreover, files can be split into parts that reside on devices attached to different channels, so different portions can be read simultaneously. Thus by exploiting the characteristics of an installation, a designer can achieve significantly better performance for file operations than the upper bound of $T_p + T_a + T_t$; without detailed knowledge about system features, however, the improvement is hard to estimate.

Given the ability to overlap processing and I/O, there is the problem of keeping the processor busy while requested data is being read (or written), and, conversely, ensuring that the processor is ready to process new data when the channel makes them available. On multiprogrammed systems, these requirements present no serious difficulty: requests for the channels are queued, so the latter are busy as long as there is work, while programs waiting for I/O operations to finish can be suspended in favor of others. Suppose, however, that only one job is running at once and that records are being read in, processed, and written out. In such a case, overlapping is accomplished by *buffering*, that is, providing an area to which (or from which) the channel can transmit while processing is going on in another section of storage.

Assume that the cost of reading (or writing) a block of K records is $t_a + K \cdot t_t$ (where t_a is the access overhead/block and t_t is the transfer time/record). Also, the *processing* time for a block is $t_o + K \cdot t_r$, where t_o represents overhead and t_r is the time spent on a record. The question of how much buffer space to provide naturally arises. Ideally, K should be large enough that the processing time for a block is exactly block read/write time. [Pictorially, this means that the line $t_a + K \cdot t_t$ intersects $t_o + K \cdot t_r$ for $K > 0$—Fig. 9.1(a).] Then the processor and channels will be always busy and never waiting for each other. Note, however, that the value of K gets larger as the two equations get closer in slope, that is, as the transfer time/record approaches processing time per record [compare Fig. 9.1(a) with Fig. 9.1(b)]; thus the buffer requirement for 100 percent overlap may be too high to be practical.

Consider now the case where the equations do not intersect for positive K. If $t_a + K \cdot t_t$ stays greater than $t_o + K \cdot t_r$ [Fig. 9.1(c)], it means that the channel can never supply blocks fast enough to keep up with the processor. If an extra channel is available, it, too, can be used for input; two blocks are read in (simultaneously) in

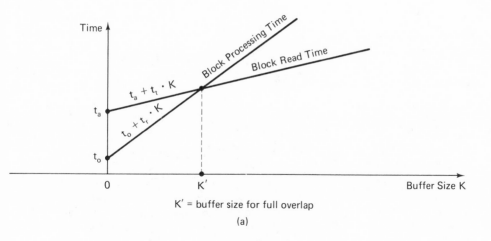

K' = buffer size for full overlap

(a)

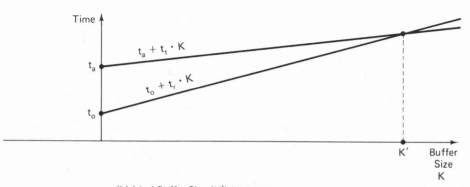

(b) Ideal Buffer Size (K') increases as
process time/record (t_r) nears transfer time/record (t_t)

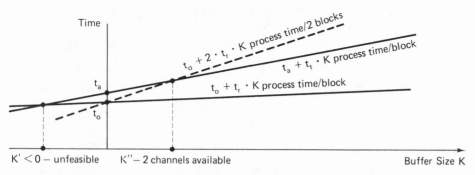

K' < 0 – unfeasible   K'' – 2 channels available   Buffer Size K

(c) Processor Too Fast for Channel—Using two channels
to achieve full read/process overlap

Fig. 9.1 Determination of buffer size

321

time $t_a + K \cdot t_t$ and processed in time $t_o + 2K \cdot t_r$, so we can look for the $K > 0$ for which these two lines intersect. If $t_a + K \cdot t_t$ is always less than $t_o + K \cdot t_r$, then blocks become available faster than the processor can dispose of them, in which case less than 100 percent over lap is unavoidable in a single processor system.

Virtual Memory: Although we have classified conventional memories into three kinds (random, direct, and serial-access), the distinction can get blurred somewhat by a feature called *virtual memory*. Basically, a virtual memory is a set of abstract or logical addresses that appear to a program as the computer's main memory. (For the rest of the section, we shall use the unqualified term "memory" to denote "main memory.") Instructions and data are assembled in the virtual address space, in the sense that all storage references are to virtual, rather than real locations. The contents of the virtual memory are kept in auxiliary storage, and the portions of it relevant to an executing process are mapped into actual memory locations.

With a suitable method of address translation, it is possible to maintain a virtual address space that is larger than the actual one. Besides mapping virtual locations to real ones, it must be possible to determine at any time which virtual locations have been brought into memory, and which to displace from main storage when ones not present are called for. If these functions can be carried out efficiently enough so that a program runs almost as fast in its virtual address space as it would in a real memory of equivalent size, then main storage effectively extended; more important, in a multi-programming environment it is possible to give *several* concurrently executing programs the illusion that they each have more real memory than is actually available, a result that could not be achieved simply by adding on random-access storage.

For the kind of performance which would make virtual memory practical, two problems have to be overcome:

1. There must be a way to ensure that, in an executing program, only a small percentage of storage references are to virtual locations which are not present in memory; otherwise, since the virtual store resides externally, the system would spend all its time bringing in the contents of virtual addresses.
2. References to virtual addresses not present in memory must be resolved as quickly as possible.

One technique that has been used successfully to meet these problems is *paging*. The virtual and actual address spaces are divided up into fixed-size blocks called *pages*. When an executing program references a virtual location not present in memory (an event called a *page fault*), the whole page containing that location is brought in. If necessary, a page not needed is written back out to make room for the incoming one. The advantage of bringing in a block of virtual memory (rather than simply the location requested) is that it tends to forestall future page faults, since often a reference to one location is followed by a reference to one nearby (e.g., when a program is looping). The frequency of page faults can be further reduced by reserving, for each running program, room in memory for some fixed number of pages from its virtual address space. If the number is large enough, the program will run for a "usefully" long time before needing a new page and paging overhead will be acceptable. Finally, the system may attempt to reduce the likelihood of faults by bringing in a page before it is called for, and by not writing a page back out if it seems likely to be referenced in the near future.

Regarding point 2 above, a small associative memory can be used to rapidly determine when a virtual reference represents a page fault, while the use of a direct-access device with a high data transfer rate as the virtual store enables pages to be read and written quickly.

Paging can be used to provide virtual secondary storage as well as virtual memory; for example, a drum can be made to look larger than it really is by backing it up with a disk. The IBM 3330, already a large-capacity high-performance bank of disks, can be backed up by the IBM 3850 (a random-access tape cartridge system) to give the appearance of several 3330's. In this case, the purpose is to extend secondary storage for data, rather than main memory for programs, and the term *staging*, rather than "paging," has been used to denote the technique.

For a detailed discussion of virtual memory, the reader is referred to Denning[4]; our purpose in raising the subject is simply to point out that virtual storage (main and auxiliary memories) can affect the performance of file operations. Basically, this can happen in two ways:

1. In a virtual memory, buffers and work areas are subject to paging; thus a block which has been read in from secondary storage by a user program will incur additional I/O costs if the system decides to remove any portion of it to make room for some other section of the virtual store.
2. A reference to a virtual device (e.g., a drum) may be more expensive than a reference to the equivalent real device, because of the need to bring in data from the slower, backup store.

The amount of overhead from these sources depends, among other things, on the number of users simultaneously contending for the storage devices being backed up, the page sizes and system policies for minimizing page faults, and the reference patterns for programs and data. Not surprisingly, these factors are hard to quantify, and we shall make no attempt to do so here; however, their contributions must be considered when file operations in a system with virtual storage are analyzed.

In this section we have outlined various hardware features that affect file organization and manipulation. Their influence will be felt in succeeding sections, although, for reasons of complexity, they cannot be taken into detailed consideration. The point to remember is that with files, the realities of the system hardware are critical. We shall discuss various file *structures*, but their actual performance depends on factors such as device speeds, number of channels, availability of buffer space, and degree of multiprogramming. This should be kept in mind throughout this chapter and the next.

[4]Peter J. Denning, "Virtual Memory," *Computing Surveys*, **2**, no. 3 (Sept. 1970), 153–189.

9.2 File Layout

Any of the data structures described so far can be used for files, and there are systems in which files appear, variously, as simple lists, trees, and general lists (graphs). There is somewhat less variety in physical organization because of constraints imposed by performance requirements, device characteristics, data reference patterns, and the like. For example, structures which use pointers extensively are undesirable because it is expensive to follow pointer chains in secondary storage.

This distinction between logical and physical organization is not new: it arose in the data structure model (Chapter 2); in Section 5.2, where the appearance of LISP-type lists in APL was maintained through the only available data type, arrays; and in the discussion of virtual memory at the end of the last section. In this section and the next we examine various physical aspects of file organization; the relevant data structures and concepts have been introduced, and it remains to interpret them in the light of secondary storage characteristics. Discussion of the logical nature of files is deferred to Chapter 10.

The simplest file consists of fixed-length records of the same type (e.g., defined by the same **comp** declaration), placed one after another in secondary storage. (This organization is sometimes called "physical sequential.") It can be thought of as an externally stored array, especially if direct access by record number is possible. Usually, however, more elaborate formats are needed. In particular, it may be desirable to have variable-length records.

On some systems, variable-sized records present no problem because the block-size (from above, the amount of data transferred during a read or write operation) is allowed to vary [Fig. 9.2(a)]. If the number of characters per block must be fixed in advance, the objective can still be realized by allowing records to cross block boundaries [Fig. 9.2(b)]. This technique requires considerable flexibility in buffer allocation, because the system will not know until it has reached the end of one block whether an additional one must be read in. A more modest approach is to fit as many records as possible into a fixed block and pad out to the required size [Fig. 9.2(c)]. This allows records to vary up to a maximum length. The larger the block compared to the average record, the less space will be wasted due to padding.

An operating system can process fixed-length records more efficiently than variable ones; in particular, unblocking is faster and does not require count information to be stored with the data. Therefore, if the variance in record length is not too high, it may be worth specifying fixed records of some average length, and allocating extra units to a record that is larger than average [Fig. 9.2(d)]. This makes the programmer (or program) responsible for retrieving the overflow or *trailer* records, and also requires an overflow bit in each record. However, the scheme is simple and can be used to implement variable-length records when that feature is not supported by the operating system.

Whether records are fixed or variable in size, provision must normally be made for their insertion and deletion. We first consider the case when the storage is serial access (in which case the only practical organization is physical sequential). Deletion

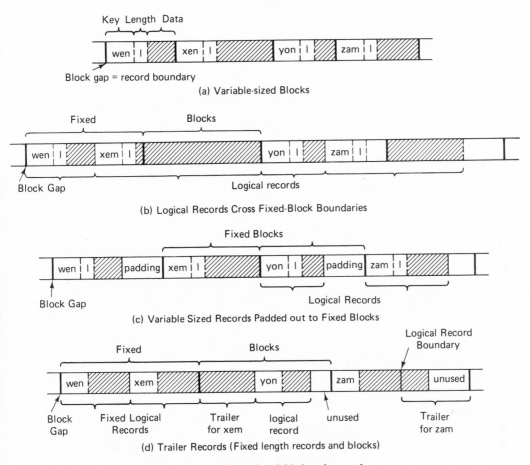

Fig. 9.2   Implementation of variable-length records

(or record shrinkage) is not difficult, because the portion to be removed can be marked as unused. There may even be a good chance of recovering the space (e.g., if record order is unimportant and records are fixed in length). In any case, the file can be compacted when space loss due to deleted records becomes too high.

Insertion into a serial-access file is more of a problem than is deletion. If order does not matter, additions can simply be appended, but more often the file is ordered on a key. Since insertions then require a complete rewrite, it is normal to accumulate additions and updates in a separate file and merge it periodically with the original. Another possibility is to initially distribute free space about the file so that inserts require only a few records to be shifted. As the file grows, additions will cause more and more work, and at some point it will be worth reorganizing. The rate of deletions will naturally affect the point at which this occurs.

With direct-access devices, it becomes practical to use pointers, and as seen in Section 4.3.1, insertion and deletion for linked lists are both quite simple. There are three kinds of pointers used in file applications—machine addresses, relative addresses, and record identifiers. A machine address gives the location of a physical record; on a disk it would consist of a cylinder and track number, and relative position on the track. [Before such a pointer is used, the address of the unit containing the file must be supplied to the I/O hardware; this is the responsibility of the program using the file, which might, for example, inform the operating system of the name of the disk pack(s) on which the file resides.]

A relative address is a number indicating the position of a record (logical or physical) relative to the start of a file. To be used, it must be converted to a machine address in much the way array indices were mapped to storage addresses in Section 5.1.

Strictly, a record identifier is *any* combination of field contents that uniquely identify a record within a file. However, files are usually organized so that records can be quickly located given their keys (e.g., by hashing or search trees). Thus in practice, record identifier pointers are keys that can be converted to machine addresses by the addressing mechanism for the file.

The three pointer types each have their merits and disadvantages. Machine addresses provide the fastest record access (they can be used directly in an I/O command) but are device-dependent, and become invalid, for example, when a file is moved from a disk of one size to a disk another size. Moreover, they are impractical in linked structures which are stored on disk but used in main memory, because it would be necessary to individually translate disk addresses to main storage references; in such a case, relative address pointers would be used.

Relative address pointers provide a degree of machine independence without sacrificing too much in access speed. As an example, consider a file of 500 fixed-length records numbered 0–499, and stored sequentially, 5 to a block, 10 blocks per track, on tracks 3–12 of a cylinder. To determine the actual location of the logical record number 267, first divide by 50 (logical records/track) and add the quotient to 3 for the track number ($3 + \lfloor 267/50 \rfloor = 8$). Then divide the remainder by the blocking factor and add to get the block number on the track ($\lfloor 17/5 \rfloor + 1 = 4$). The remainder of this division plus 1 is the relative position in the block. If the file were relocated on tracks 1–5 of a drum holding 10 blocks of 10 records each per track, the computation would simply be repeated using the new base track number (1), records/track figure (100), and blocking factor (10).

The example above indicates the versatility of relative pointers and shows that they can be converted to machine addresses fairly quickly. Naturally, as file layout becomes less "uniform" (e.g., spread over nonconsecutive tracks), the translation algorithm increases in complexity and requires more information to be maintained (as happened with the storage mappings for sparse matrices, Section 5.4). However, the computation is still fast compared to even one I/O operation, so the access times using relative and machine addresses are comparable.

Pointers to a record location become invalid when that record is moved or deleted. Record identifiers (i.e., keys) provide machine independence, which is desirable when records are moved frequently and when a file with a large number of pointers has a high rate of insertions and deletions. The cost is usually extra disk accesses in order to look up the record address, although such is not always the case (cf. hashing, Section 9.3.3). As a general rule, though, identifier pointers are unsuited for use in chained structures; they should be employed only when device independence is essential.

Consider now the situation where records are to be placed in direct-access storage in order of ascending key value. They could be chained together but the only gain—simplified insertions and deletions—would be more than offset by the possibility that each pointer reference could cause a disk seek. A better approach is to use pointers only when an insertion would otherwise require'extensive data movement. Suppose, then, that records have been initially allocated on tracks in physical sequence. As was true of a file stored on a serial-access device, deletions are straightforward; for insertions, there are several techniques, which we now describe:

1. *Deferred Insertion*—insertions can be accumulated and merged into the file when an update is considered necessary.

2. *Distributed Free Space* [Fig. 9.3(a)]—as a general rule, space should be distributed so that the unit of data read in has a good chance of accommodating an insertion; otherwise, an extra disk access will be needed and the overflow technique (below) might as well be used. Thus if data are transferred in blocks, blocks should have extra room. Of course this also depends on the growth rate of the file; if insertions are rare, it may be worth simply reserving space on each track and rewriting the whole track when there is no room in a block.

3. *Overflow* [Fig. 9.3(b)]—records that will not fit into the main file can be placed in a separate overflow area. These areas are typically located to lessen the likelihood of an extra disk access (e.g., on the same track, on the same cylinder), but the possibility of an extra seek must be accepted. Strictly, the method does not require pointers; all that is needed is a way of determining where to search when a record cannot be found in the main file. However, to list the file in sequence, each overflow area would have to be merged into the main file at the appropriate place, a rather awkward process. Thus it is usual to *chain* overflow records in key order, to preserve the key sequence. Figure 9.3(b) illustrates a setup in which each block can have an overflow chain. Insertion for this scheme will be illustrated when ISAM is discussed, below.

    The chained overflow method works well as long as following chains does not cause too many extra disk accesses. The possibility of this can be reduced by careful distribution of overflow space, for example, by having an overflow area on each track and assigning an overflow track to groups of primary tracks. This keeps the areas small enough to be read in, so that chains can be (quickly) followed in main memory. When it appears that too much time is spent following chains, the file can be reorganized.

4. *Cellular Splitting* [Fig. 9.3(c)]—suppose that a record is to be added to a full track. An elegant solution that does not require record chaining is to get a new track, link the full one to it, place half the records from the full track on the new one, and link the new track to the successor of the old one. The insertion can be made into the appropriate track and space has been provided for future

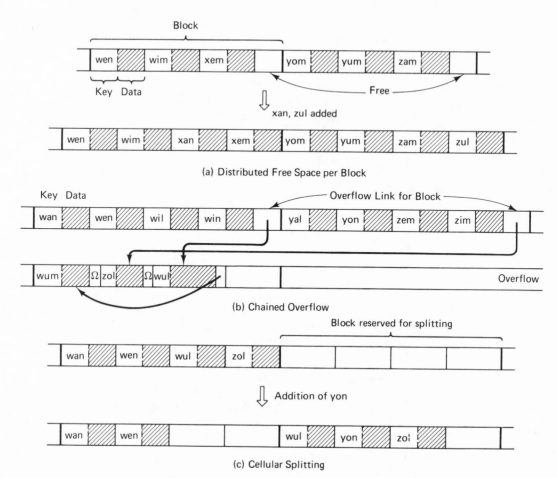

Fig. 9.3   Methods for insertion into ordered, sequential files

additions. Moreover the technique can be used at different levels: if no tracks on a cylinder are available to accommodate a split, a new cylinder can be found and half the tracks from the full one moved to it. Also, free blocks can be reserved on each track, and tracks split only when block splitting is no longer possible. Finally, the choice of cell sizes can be device-independent.

As with the methods above, cellular splitting requires that space be reserved (and, in fact, distributed throughout the file) for expansion. However, it keeps records at the smallest cell level in physical sequence, and cells are linked only where splits occur. Moreover, it lets the pattern of insertion determine how the file grows; in particular, clustered additions (groups of keys that arrive together and are close lexicographically) will not cause imbalances in search times, as can happen when the overflow method is used. We have actually seen cellular splitting earlier (the 2–3 tree, in Example 6.9) and will encounter it in the next section, when B trees and VSAM (IBM's virtual storage access method) are discussed.

The discussion above covers the basics of record allocation, but there are situations in which it is desirable to have a file organization more complicated than sequentially allocated records. For example, one or more fields of a record may be required to assume an arbitrary number of repeated values. (These are usually called *repeating groups.*) Consider a SALES file of records with two fields, PART# and TRANSAC-TION. There is an instance of TRANSACTION for each sale of the part, and more-over, that field is itself a record type, with subfields BUYER and ORDER. Finally, ORDER is a record type with three fields, DATE, QUANTITY, and PRICE, and there is an instance of ORDER for each request from the BUYER. The situation is illustrated in Fig. 9.4; the file is logically a tree structure, or *hierarchy*.

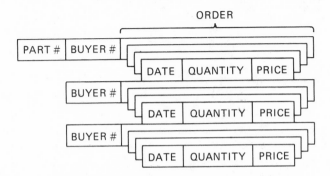

Fig. 9.4   Record with two levels of repeating groups

Now SALES could be implemented, say, as a sequential file of variable-length records whose growth is accommodated by cellular splitting. However, this would not be taking advantage of the fact that certain relationships in the file are, by their nature, more permanent than others. For example, the list of customers for a given part might be fairly static (i.e., there may always be at least one order outstanding from each regular buyer), whereas ORDER records are added and deleted as requests arrive and are filled. If it is considered undesirable to shift about information associat-ing customers with part numbers each time an order changes, the orders could be kept in a separate file. Going a step further, we could have a file of part numbers, with each part linked to a customer list (on a separate file) and each customer linked to a group of records in the ORDER file. In other words, here is a case where it might be worth making the physical organization correspond more closely to the logical structure.

9.3 File Indices and Directories

We have considered the details of record placement but not the strategy behind it. In fact, files are placed on direct-access storage (the assumed medium, in this section and the next) so that individual records can be quickly located, as well as easily moved about. Thus there is the problem of locating a record in acceptable time, given its key. Now admittedly, what is considered acceptable depends on the application. The best performance one could ask for in looking up an arbitrary record is one disk access. With hashing, an average of slightly more than one is achievable, while with trees, files of 1,000,000 records can be searched at a cost of about four disk reads. Therefore, any scheme that averages more than five seeks to find a record can be considered noncompetitive; 10 would be unacceptable. [Note that even on a "slow" disk (100-ms average seek), four seeks takes well under a second.]

In view of the standards just cited, it should be clear that a sequential search of a file is impractical. To appreciate how much so, consider 100,000 100-character records residing on an IBM 3330 disk. It would take roughly 10 s to *transfer* the data into main memory, and unless the buffer is large (100,000 bytes), seeks would account for even more than that. Another technique that turns out to be too expensive is the binary search; if the (ordered) records of this example could be read in blocks of 1000, it would require $\lceil \log(10^5/10^3) \rceil = 7$ probes (disk accesses) before the search space was reduced enough to fit into main storage.

9.3.1 Indexed-Sequential Files

If a file is ordered, it is possible to achieve fast searching by indexing. Suppose that there are N ordered records, and K can fit into a given reserved space in main memory. Then the file can be partitioned into N/K blocks, and it is only necessary to search a table of N/K endpoint values to determine the block of size K in which a particular record lies. That block can then be brought in and searched. The N/K endpoint keys along with pointers to their respective blocks can be maintained as a separate index. This type of file organization is called *one-level indexed-sequential* (Fig. 9.5). It enables a record to be located with two accesses if main memory can hold max $(K, N/K)$ records, and one if the index is kept in main storage during file processing.

A simple computation determines the optimum number of keys to be kept in the index. Suppose that the cost of performing a binary search of a table with K entries is $a + b \cdot \log K$. If file records are w_1 characters wide, and an index record (key + pointer) takes w_2 bytes, then the cost of reading a block of the file and the directory are, respectively, $t_a + t_c \cdot w_1 \cdot K$ and $t_a + t_c \cdot w_2 \cdot N/K$ (t_c is the transfer time/character). The total cost of the search is, therefore,

$$= \text{directory search time} + \text{block search time}$$

$$= t_a + t_c \cdot w_2 \cdot N/K + (a + b \cdot \log N/K)$$

$$+ (t_a + t_c \cdot w_1 \cdot K) + (a + b \cdot \log K).\text{[5]}$$

---

[5] Actually, the step constant b for the binary search could be different for a block of the file from what it is for the index, since the size of the items is different for the two. However, in both cases, it is only the key field being examined, so we assume that the search cost depends only on the number of entries.

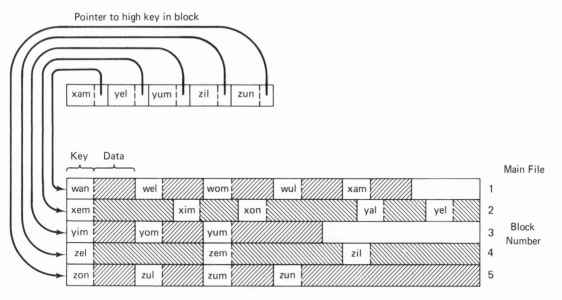

Fig. 9.5 One-level indexed-sequential file

Minimizing this with respect to K (thereby determining the directory size, N/K) gives

$$w_1 = w_2 \, N/K^2$$

or

$$K = \sqrt{(w_2/w_1) \cdot N}.$$

If the calculation above gives either a directory or block size that is too large to be practical, a two-level index can be considered. Suppose that the second (highest) level has K_2 entries, each pointing to a level one index block of size K_1, the keys of which identify a block of $N/(K_1 K_2)$ records in the file. Then the cost of a search is

$$t_a + w_2 \cdot t_c \cdot K_2 + a + b \log K_2 \text{ (level 2 search)}$$
$$+ t_a + w_2 \cdot t_c \cdot K_1 + a + b \log K_1 \text{ (level 1 search)}$$
$$+ t_a + w_1 \cdot t_c \cdot \frac{N}{K_1 \cdot K_2} + a + b \log \left(\frac{N}{K_1 \cdot K_2}\right).$$

Minimizing with respect to K_1 and K_2 gives two equations,

$$K_1 K_2^2 = \left(\frac{w_1}{w_2}\right) N$$

$$K_1^2 K_2 = \left(\frac{w_1}{w_2}\right) N.$$

Equating left sides gives $K_1 = K_2$, from which

$$K_1 = K_2 = \sqrt[3]{(w_1/w_2)N}.$$

The indexed sequential organization, although conceptually simple, is complicated by the need to accommodate changes to the file. Deletions can be restricted to the file itself; since they do not degrade search performance, the index can be left alone. For insertions, any of the techniques described in the above section can be used. However, if the file is permitted to expand (by overflow chaining, or splitting) without corresponding growth in the index, progressively more searching will take place at the file level, and the index will become less and less useful. In particular, clustered insertions could leave portions of the file effectively unindexed. Therefore, an insertion discipline is needed for the file and index together. We shall describe two approaches to maintaining indexed-sequential files—ISAM (IBM's indexed sequential access method) and B trees.

Indexed-sequential files are easily tailored to device characteristics, and this is what is done in ISAM. Records of the file are loaded sequentially (in key order) on tracks of a disk. The first track of each cylinder is an index (*track index*) to the records on that cylinder. For each track there are two entries in the index—a pointer to the track together with the highest key value on it, and a pointer to the start of the overflow chain for the track, along with the final (high) key value in the chain. The second-level index, that is, the index to all the track indexes, is the *cylinder* index; it contains the high key for each cylinder of the file. If this index is too large (suggested size is four tracks), it can be indexed by a *master index*, which contains the largest key value on each track. The master index can itself be indexed by track, and there can be up to three levels of master index.

The tracks on which the file is initially allocated (or rewritten, on reorganization) constitute the *prime data area*. Prime tracks may have free space, either by design or as a result of deletions. Records to be inserted are placed in the prime area if there is room. If the addition results in a new high key for the track, the track index for the cylinder is changed appropriately. Similarly, changes to the track index are propagated up through the cylinder and master indexes if necessary.

When a prime track is full, ISAM uses the chained overflow technique to accommodate insertions. Overflow tracks may be reserved on each cylinder to eliminate the need for an extra seek when an overflow record is retrieved. In addition, whole cylinders can be set aside as an independent overflow area. It is common to use both types of overflow, letting the independent area handle spills from the cylinder overflow tracks.

Overflow handling will be described with the aid of Fig. 9.6. Key *wul* arrives, but there is no room for it on track 1 [Fig. 9.6(a)]. Rather than place *wul* itself in overflow, thereby requiring that *win*, *wul*, and *xal* be chained together, track 1 is shifted right, stating at *xal*, to make room for *wul*, and the record that "falls" off the end, *xim*, is placed in overflow. Now *xal* is the new high key for the track, so it replaces *xim* in the index. At the same time, the overflow entry for track 1, previously null, is set to the address of *xim*, the first element in the overflow chain for the track, and its key field is set to *xim*, the largest key in the chain [Fig. 9.6(b), changes bordered].

Suppose now that *xol* is to be added. It lies between *xim* and *zum* on the track index [Fig. 9.6(b)] and so should be placed on track 2. All of that track is shifted to

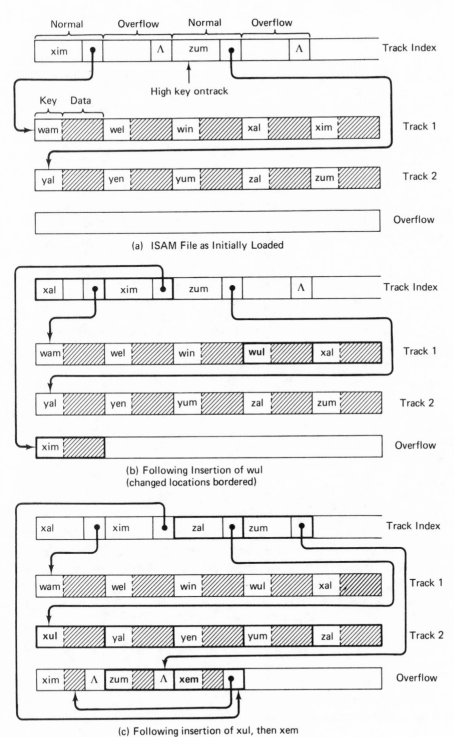

(a) ISAM File as Initially Loaded

(b) Following Insertion of wul
(changed locations bordered)

(c) Following insertion of xul, then xem

Fig. 9.6 ISAM overflow techniques

333

make room, forcing *zum* into overflow and making *zal* the new high key for the track. These changes are reflected in the index [Fig. 9.6(c)]. Finally, *xem* arrives. Since it falls between *xal* and *xim*, it has to go on the overflow chain for track 1. It is placed on the overflow track and linked to the previous head of the chain, while the overflow index entry is reset to point to it [Fig. 9.6(c)]. Note that the high key value for the chain remains unchanged.

When the cylinder overflow fills, records are inserted in the independent overflow area. After this happens for a track, all overflow searches for that track will require an extra seek, because the chain starts on another cylinder. Moreover, as records can be inserted anywhere in the chain, searches may involve jumping back and forth between cylinder and independent overflow areas. Eventually (as the chains get longer), search performance will deteriorate enough so that reorganization is necessary. The interval between reorganizations can be prolonged by reserving enough tracks per cylinder to accommodate the expected overflow (remember that the deletion rate is a factor to be considered), and by careful placement of records in the independent area (e.g., overflows from a cylinder on the same track, where possible).

An interesting feature of ISAM is the similarity between a prime track and its overflow chain. By having an entry for both in the track index, the overflow looks like a prime track, the differences being in allocation and the fact that the high key in overflow never changes. The logical equivalence is particularly evident in a search, when either one area or the other is examined; compare with hashing, where the overflow is not searched unless a record cannot be found in the prime area. Note also that when additions are made to a prime track, overflow management is extremely simple: the previous high record for the track is inserted at the front of the overflow chain, so for many insertions, the chain really behaves like a stack or queue.

9.3.2 B Trees

ISAM has the disadvantage that as overflow chains grow, search performance deteriorates to the point where reorganization is necessary. By allowing the file and index to grow by cellular splitting instead, it is possible to keep search performance within a constant factor of optimal, thereby avoiding the need for periodic maintenance. This is what happens with *B trees*, a class of multiway search trees designed especially for use in secondary storage[6]. We now describe B trees and their relation to indexed-sequential files.

A *B tree of order m* is a multiway lexicographic search tree where:

1. Every node has $\lceil m/2 \rceil - 1 \le K \le m - 1$ keys, appearing in increasing order from left to right; an exception is the root, which may have as few as one key.
2. A node with K keys either has $K + 1$ pointers to sons, which correspond to the partition induced on the key space by those K keys, or it has all pointers null, in which case it is terminal.
3. All terminal nodes are on the same level.

[6]R. Bayer and E. McCreight, "Organization and Maintenance of Large Ordered Indices," *Acta Informatica*, **1**, no. 3 (1972), 173–189.

A B tree of order 5 is illustrated in Fig. 9.7. Note that so far, only keys in the nodes are mentioned; record storage will be considered below.

To see how good search performance is guaranteed by the properties above, consider the number of keys in a B tree of order m. There is at least one at the root (property 1) which by property 2 has at least two sons, unless it is terminal. Suppose that it has two sons; by (1), each has at least $\lceil m/2 \rceil - 1$ keys. Now either both of these sons (the only nodes at level 2) are terminal (3), or they each have at least $\lceil m/2 \rceil$ sons (2). Similarly, the $2\lceil m/2 \rceil$ nodes at level 3 have at least $\lceil m/2 \rceil - 1$ keys each, and unless they are all terminal, they each have at least $\lceil m/2 \rceil$ successors as well. If there are l levels in the tree, the number of keys, N, is at least

$$1 + 2(\lceil m/2 \rceil - 1) + 2\lceil m/2 \rceil (\lceil m/2 \rceil - 1) + \ldots + 2\lceil m/2 \rceil^{l-2}(\lceil m/2 \rceil - 1)$$
$$= 1 + 2(\lceil m/2 \rceil - 1) [1 + \lceil m/2 \rceil + \ldots + \lceil m/2 \rceil^{l-2}]$$
$$= 1 + 2(\lceil m/2 \rceil^{l-2+1} - 1).$$

Therefore,

$$\frac{N + 1}{2} \geq \lceil m/2 \rceil^{l-1}$$

or

$$l \leq 1 + \log_{\lceil m/2 \rceil} \frac{N + 1}{2}.$$

This is the same order of magnitude as the best possible performance for fixed m, since with maximum (m-way) branching in each node, the number of levels would be $\log_m N + 1$. In absolute terms, if nodes are stored as blocks of 200 keys ($m = 200$), a file of up to 1,999,999 keys can be searched with at most 4 block accesses.

Insertion into a B tree is straightforward. The terminal node where the key should be placed is found and the addition (in appropriate order) made. If overflow occurs (more than $m - 1$ keys), the node splits into two, and the middle key (along with pointers to its newly created sons) is passed up to the next level for insertion, which is handled as just described. At worst, splitting will propagate along a path to the root, resulting in the creation of a new root node. Thus insertion time is the same order as search time—$O(l)$, the number of levels. Growth of a 2–3 tree—a B tree of order 3—was illustrated in Fig. 6.23. Note that insertion does not violate any of the properties above; splitting results in two nodes of at least $\lceil m/2 \rceil - 1$ keys, and the only change in number of levels occurs when the root splits, in which case property 3 is preserved.

Deletion is slightly more complicated and will be illustrated with the removal of *zem* from the tree of Fig. 9.7. First, *zem* is removed and replaced by its lexical successor *zil*, which by construction will always be in a terminal node [Fig. 9.8(a)]. This leaves the node containing *zon* with fewer than $\lceil 5/2 \rceil - 1$ keys, so it is merged with a brother say, *zam zel* and their common father *zil*, which is removed from its node, giving the situation of Fig. 9.8(b). Now the operation could stop if the father of the newly merged node *zul* had enough keys, or if the merge node had more than four keys, in which it could split and pass the middle key back up to its parent. Neither happens here, so the merge just described is repeated with *zul*, its brother *xum yel yol*,

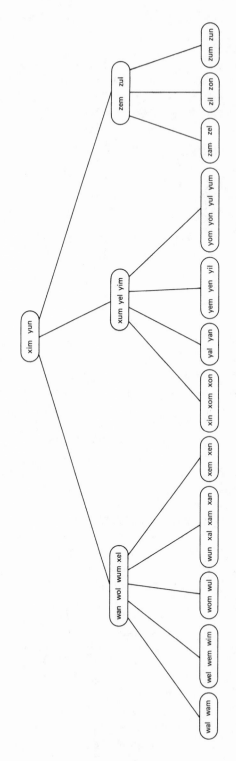

Fig. 9.7 B tree of order 5

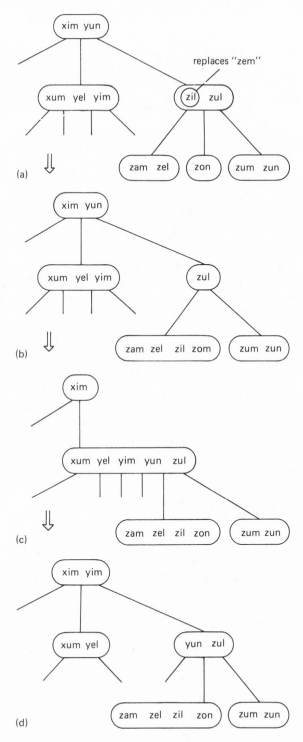

Fig. 9.8 Deletion in a B tree

and their father *yun*, giving Fig. 9.8(c). The resulting node is too full, so it splits and the middle key is moved up to replace *yun*, which just left the root [Fig. 9.8(d)]. Note that if this split did not occur and the root did not have *xim*, it would have been left empty and would have been deleted. Just as a B tree grows upward (its height increases only when the root splits), it can only contract from the top.

B trees are well suited for use in secondary storage: they provide fast searching, are self-maintaining, and their nodes are naturally implemented as tracks of a disk or pages of a virtual memory. However, their applicability to files is of interest here, so we must consider the question of record placement.

An obvious approach is to keep record data in the nodes (along with the keys). Storage management is simple and the file can be processed sequentially with reasonable efficiency, but there are two disadvantages. First, there will be unnecessary data movement whenever the tree is restructured because of insertions and deletions; with a directory, only the keys (and pointers) need to be moved about. Second, there are often practical limits on node size (e.g., track capacity), so the branching factor may not be too high. For example, it may only be possible to store 10 records in a node, in which case, with maximum branching, a search of 1,000,000 records can be expected to require $\log 10^6 = 6$ node (i.e., secondary storage) accesses. On the other hand, 100 keys and pointers to their associated data might fit into these same nodes, so that a key could be located with $\log 10^6 = 3$ node searches, and then an extra access would be needed to retrieve the record.

For fast access, then, it is probably better to use a B tree as a directory rather than a file. A directory has the additional advantage of simplifying insertion and deletion; records can be placed anywhere in the data area and can be effectively removed by setting their directory pointer to null. A disadvantage is that sequential processing can be very expensive because each record must be accessed individually. If record order as well as fast access is important, a compromise between the B-tree directory and B-tree file can be devised.

Suppose that a B tree is grown as follows:

1. Only records (and their keys) are inserted.
2. A record can never leave the level (lowest) at which it was entered; when a (terminal) node of records splits, only the middle *key* value is passed up to the next level; the associated record (plus key) stays in one of the halves (say the left).
3. Each terminal node is linked to its lexical successor (i.e., the terminal node that would follow it in a symmetric traversal of the tree).

The result is an indexed-sequential file which grows by cellular splitting. Point 3 enables the file to be processed sequentially, independent of the index (except to find the starting record). This is essentially the organization used by IBM's VSAM (Virtual Storage Access Method) to store records in key order ("key sequenced data sets"). VSAM's terminology reflects its functional correspondence to ISAM. Records are stored in *control intervals* which are the logical equivalent of tracks in ISAM and terminal nodes in a B tree. Control intervals are grouped into *control areas*, which are indexed by *sequence set* indexes (= track indexes), that is, nodes at the second lowest level of the tree. Sequence set members are linked together to facilitate sequential processing. The index levels above the sequence set are collectively termed the *index set* (ISAM master index).

When a B tree is implemented, questions of node size, placement, and creation (due to splitting) must be faced. VSAM, although hardware independent, represents specific design choices made in these regards. Each control interval is a contiguous portion of auxiliary storage; it might be a track, portion of a track, or several consecutive tracks, but it would not, for example, consist of tracks from different cylinders. Its exact size depends on record size device characteristics and the buffer space available. VSAM determines some optimal number of control intervals to be grouped into a control area. This is a basic unit in the sense that when the file grows, it does so by adding on control areas.

Perhaps the most important aspect of B-tree implementation is the way new nodes are allocated when a split occurs. VSAM requires the person setting up the file to specify the amount of free space in a control interval and the number of empty control intervals per control area. In this way, growth is achieved without major dislocation. When a control interval splits, half its records are moved to an empty interval in the same area (and the middle key is passed up a level for addition to the sequence set index). If there is no free interval, the control area splits and a new area is added at the end of the file.

Earlier, the optimal index size was computed for an indexed sequential file in which the number of levels was fixed. In a B tree with N keys, the number of levels is a function of the order, m, and we can seek the m that will minimize this number. Suppose that the nodes are stored as blocks on disk, and that maximum branching has been achieved, so that there are $m - 1$ keys/block, N in all. Assume that each key and its associated information (pointer to the next level down + either data or pointer to a record) accounts for w characters, so the costs of reading a node and performing a binary search on it are, respectively, $t_a + w \cdot t_c \cdot m$ and $a + b \cdot \log m$.[7] Since most keys are at the lowest level, the cost of a search is roughly

$$\log_m N(t_a + w \cdot t_c \cdot m + a + b \log m) = \frac{\ln N}{\ln m} \left(t_a + w \cdot t_c \cdot m + a + b \cdot \frac{\ln m}{\ln 2} \right)$$

$$= \frac{\ln N}{\ln m} (t_a + w \cdot t_c \cdot m + a) + b \cdot \frac{\ln N}{\ln 2}.$$

This is minimized with respect to m if

$$\frac{\ln N}{\ln m} \cdot w \cdot t_c = \frac{\ln N}{m \cdot \ln^2 m} (t_a + w \cdot t_c \cdot m + a)$$

or

$$m(\ln m - 1) = \frac{t_a + a}{w \cdot t_c}. \tag{9.1}$$

---

[7]Although the maximum number of keys per node is $m - 1$, we will use m in the formulas, because it simplifies minimization.

An interesting consequence of this result is that the node size for optimum m, although not constant, does not vary greatly. If $t_a = 38$ ms and $t_c = 1$ μs (respectively, average seek + average latency, and character transfer time for the 3330 disk) and a is assumed small enough compared to t_a to be ignored, then Eq. (9.1) can be partially evaluated to give

$$mw \cdot (\ln m - 1) = 40{,}000 \text{ bytes.} \tag{9.2}$$

As m goes from 100 to 1000, the node size mw ranges between 6800 and 11,000, not a very wide variance for secondary storage, and moreover conveniently close to the 3330-track capacity (13,000 bytes). The latter feature may be more than a happy coincidence: for an IBM 2314 disk ($t_a \approx 75$ ms, $t_c \approx 3$ μs), mw would range between 4200 and 7000 bytes, again close to the track capacity of that unit (7000 bytes).

The relative invariance of node size (for a given device) reflects the fact that at some point, the increase in data transfer costs starts to outweigh the advantage of higher branching factors. It also confirms a point made earlier, that storing data in the nodes adds to access costs; given a fixed node size, a larger w gives a small m, thereby increasing the number of levels. If the B tree is used as a directory, a typical value for w might be 18 (10-character key + 4-byte record pointer + 4-byte descendant pointer), which, from Eq. (9.2), would make $m = 400$. This provides good performance, but it may be more desirable to use an indexed-sequential organization, storing data in the terminal nodes. In that case $m = 400$ could be used for the index but would probably be too large a value for the data nodes. Two possible solutions are:

1. Use a reduced value of m. The minimum represented by $m = 400$ is quite flat, and a value as low as $m = 200$ will not result in significant loss of performance.
2. Use a reduced value of m for the terminal nodes only (e.g., $m = 400$ for the index and $m = 50$ for the data). This does not affect the insertion or deletion procedures, since data nodes always stay at the lowest level. It might add an extra level over that for a directory ($m = 400$ at all levels), but a directory requires an extra access to get a record anyway, so the retrieval performance of the two schemes is comparable.

A potential disadvantage of B trees is their storage utilization: by definition it is guaranteed to be only 50 per cent. In fact, studies have shown that given random insertion of records, the nodes will average about 70 per cent full,[8] but 30 per cent is a considerable amount of unused space, especially if records are being stored. A modification that increases the minimum utilization, and probably, therefore, the ratio achieved in practice, is the following.

If a node becomes too full as a result of an insertion, make room by shifting a key to the left or right brother, whichever has space. Figure 9.9(a) illustrates this for the insertion of *yin* into the tree of Fig. 9.7. If both brothers are full, or there is only one brother and it is full, then the node and a full brother can be split into three nodes of about $\lceil 2m/3 \rceil$ keys each. The result of applying this rule for the insertion of *yol*

[8]Andrew Chi-Chih Yao, *On Random 3–2 Trees* (TR679) (Department of Computer Science, University of Illinois at Urbana/Champaign, Oct. 1974).

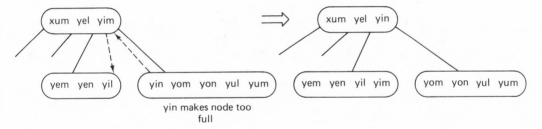

yin makes node too
full

(a) Modified insertion of yin into B-tree of Fig 9.7

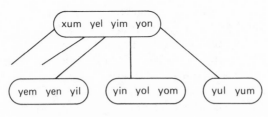

(b) modified insertion of yol into subtree
of Fig 9.9(a)

Fig. 9.9 Modified B-tree insertion

into the subtree of Fig. 9.9(a) is shown in Fig. 9.9(b). If the full node has no brothers, it is the root, and can split in the normal way. The root, and the sons that result when the root splits, will be the only nodes that are less than 66 per cent full.

9.3.3 Hash-Based File Organization

Indexed-sequential files (and their variants) provide for reasonably fast searches and updates, but it is possible to do better, at the expense of efficient sequential processing. If a file is organized as a hash table, most records can be retrieved with just one access, and insertion and deletion are similarly efficient. When hashing was discussed in Section 4.6.3, it was (implicitly) assumed that the storage was internal (i.e., random access); in this section, we are interested in hashing to secondary storage, and will therefore indicate how the characteristics of that medium affect the techniques described earlier. The choice of key-to-address transform is not influenced by storage access times and so will not be considered here; it is enough to note that "suitable" hash functions—ones that distribute records uniformly over the address space—can be devised.

For files, each hash address is typically a *bucket* capable of holding several records rather than a slot containing one. This happens because of the nature of external storage devices; as an example, consider the IBM 3330 disk. Since the interrecord gap on a track is 135 bytes, records under 200 characters should be blocked, or the space loss due to overhead will be unacceptably high. A record is therefore hashed to a relative track address giving the start of a block (i.e., a bucket containing several records). On the other hand, suppose that records are large enough to ignore the gap overhead. Then the only information needed to locate such records is track and cylinder number, since the hardware can search a track according to physical record key value.[9] Thus the number of useful addresses is effectively limited to the number of tracks available, so unless records are track-sized, each hash address will actually be a bucket location.

The collection of buckets hashed to is called the *prime area* (rather than hash table), and we speak of *overflow* (rather than collisions) to describe the situation when a bucket is full, forcing records mapped to it to be placed elsewhere. In Section 4.6.3, several strategies for locating overflow records were outlined. Briefly, they were:

1. *Open Addressing*—when a primary bucket is full, new records destined for it are placed in the first successive primary bucket with room.
2. *Combined Chaining*—overflow from a primary bucket is stored in buckets (either in the primary area or in overflow), which are then chained to the initial bucket to form a search path. If overflow from a bucket fills other primary buckets, new records destined for those buckets will be forced onto the overflow chain, hence combined chains. If a separate overflow area is used, it is not necessary to have the prime area larger than the file, so load factors of 1 and greater can be realized.
3. *Separate Chaining*—combined chaining modified to prevent records from different primary buckets from ending up on the same overflow chain. This can be done by keeping an overflow chain for each bucket in a separate overflow area, or by moving an overflow record from a full primary bucket to make room for a record which hashes to that address.

For analytical purposes, another technique, rehashing, was also mentioned. In theory, a record is hashed repeatedly using a different function each time, until a bucket with room is found. In practice, the method can be effectively implemented by double hashing, that is, rehashing just once, with a second function.

The alternatives above represent the basic ones needed for handling overflows, whether the storage is secondary or internal. However, the performance and relative merits of these methods in the file environment are influenced by factors not considered earlier—in particular, bucket size, storage accesses, and storage utilization.

Bucket Size: Grouping records into buckets turns out to be fortunate, because for a fixed prime area size and load factor under 1, the number of overflow records,

---

[9]It may be worth hashing such records to an actual track position as well as a particular track. Each surface of a 3330 disk is divided into sectors (which are transparent to the programmer). If a track contains fixed-size records, the unit can determine the starting sector from the relative address of a record, and then wait until that sector comes around before engaging the channel in a search and read operation. With this "sector addressing" feature, a channel may be able to satisfy several I/O requests in one revolution, thereby reducing the average wait for the device.

and hence the number of accesses needed to find a record, is reduced as the bucket size increases. To see this, suppose that there are N records and $b \cdot s$ record slots in the primary area. Each of b buckets can hold s records, and $N/bs = \alpha$, the load factor. If the hash function distributed records uniformly among buckets, the probability that a given record goes to any particular bucket is $1/b$. Therefore, the probability that a bucket has exactly i out N records assigned to it is

$$p_{N,b}(i) = \binom{N}{b}\left(\frac{1}{b}\right)^i\left(\frac{b-1}{b}\right)^{N-i}.$$

For large enough N and b, this is well approximated by the Poisson density function,[10]

$$p(N/b, i) = \frac{e^{-N/b}(N/b)^i}{i!}.$$

If we let s vary under the constraint that the prime area size remains fixed, $b \cdot s = N/\alpha$ always holds, so N/b can be expressed as a function of s, namely αs; then $p(N/b, i)$ can be rewritten as

$$p(s, i) = \frac{e^{-\alpha s}(\alpha s)^i}{i!}.$$

Now the probability that a bucket is assigned exactly i records *over* its capacity s is $p(s, s + i)$, and so the expected overflow per bucket of capacity s is

$$o(s) = \sum_{i=1}^{\infty} i \cdot p(s, s + i).\text{[11]}$$

The *total* expected number of records in overflow is therefore $b \cdot o(s)$

$$= \frac{N}{\alpha s} \sum_{i=1}^{\infty} i \cdot e^{-\alpha s} \frac{(\alpha s)^{s+i}}{(s + i)!}$$

$$= Ne^{-\alpha s} \frac{(\alpha s)^s}{s!}\left[\frac{1}{s + 1} + \frac{2(\alpha s)}{(s + 1)(s + 2)} + \frac{3(\alpha s)^2}{(s + 1)(s + 2)(s + 3)} + \cdots\right]$$

Each term in the sum is a decreasing function of s, and using Stirlings' approximation $s! \approx \sqrt{2\pi s} \cdot s^s/e^s$, the term outside the brackets becomes

$$Ne^{s(1-\alpha+\ln \alpha)}/\sqrt{2\pi s}.$$

For $\alpha \le 1$, $1 - \alpha + \ln \alpha \le 0$, so this is also decreasing with respect to s. Thus, for $b \cdot s \ge N$ and fixed, increasing the bucket size decreases the expected total number of records in overflow, and it follows that the average number of accesses needed to locate a record is also reduced.[12] The effect of increasing bucket size on open addressing is illustrated in Fig. 9.10. (The fact that the inequality was proved only for $\alpha \le 1$ is significant; the probability of the prime area filling up increases quickly as

---

[10]W. Feller, *An Introduction to Probability Theory and Its Applications*, 3rd ed., Vol. I (New York: John Wiley & Sons, Inc., 1968), Chap. VI.5.

[11]Note that the sum is infinite, even though the number of records is not. This is due to the nature of the approximating (Poisson) density function.

[12]J. A. Van der Pool, "Optimal Storage Allocation for Initial Loading of a File," *IBM Journal of Research and Development*, Nov. 1972, pp. 579–586.

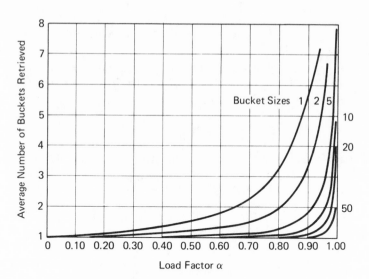

Fig. 9.10   Effect of bucket size on open addressing

α increases from 1, and once it happens, changing s subject to $b \cdot s = $ constant will not affect the number of records in overflow. Moreover, when the prime area is full, larger s means fewer but longer overflow chains, and hence a *greater* average search time per overflow record.)

Although the result above holds for hashing in general, it is particularly significant for files. In main memory, a probe is basically a compare, so there is little difference between probing two buckets of size 1 and one of size 2. In secondary storage, a probe may represent a seek, compared to which the cost of examining, say, several records on a track, is small, so it is worth having larger buckets and fewer accesses. However, s should not be increased freely at the expense of b; carried to an extreme, this would result in a single bucket containing the whole file. The advantage of increased bucket size is eventually offset by the cost of searching larger buckets. To find the optimal s for a given load, an equation incorporating device characteristics, record sizes, and the relationship of probes/record to bucket size can be formulated and minimized with respect to s. (A similar computation in the last section determined the ideal node size for a B tree.) Calculations by Severance and Duhne indicate that the optimum varies widely, from a fraction of a track to several tracks in size.[13]

Storage Accesses and Utilization: In Section 4.6.3, overflow strategies were evaluated according to the average number of probes needed to locate a record; for example, it was clear from Fig. 4.11 that separate chaining was better than open addressing for load factors greater than 0.7. Where files are concerned, this criterion is inadequate for a number of reasons:

---

[13]D. Severance and R. Duhne, "A Practitioner's Guide to Addressing Algorithms," *Communications of the ACM*, **19**, no. 6 (June 1976), 314–326.   (Fig. 9.10: Copyright 1976, Association for Computing Machinery, Inc., reprinted by permission.)

1. The reduction in accesses/record as bucket size increases can be substantial (Figure 9.10), making it hard to compare methods. When $s = 20$, open addressing averages 1.4 probes for α as high as 0.95 for records that are present, compared to 1.3 for separate chaining.[14] Since these are analytical estimates of performance, and not results based on experience, the difference in values cannot be considered enough to recommend chaining.

2. The cost of successive probes in a search is not necessarily comparable. For example, each probe generated by rehashing is random in nature, and therefore for a disk is likely to be a seek; with open addressing, successive accesses should refer to the same cylinder. Thus if rehashing averages 1.5 probes/record for given α and s, and open addressing takes 2, the latter would probably be faster on an IBM 3330, where average seek time is 30 ms and it takes 17 ms to search a track. On the other hand, with a drum, rehashing would be favored because there is no read/write head positioning associated with an access.

3. Since large amounts of data are being stored on an extended or permanent basis, storage utilization may be more important than retrieval speed. However, the load factor is only a measure of storage efficiency when all records are located in the prime area; if there is separate overflow, the expected number of overflows per bucket is needed to determine memory utilization. Also, any useful model of storage must take account of the charge for keeping the space, as well as the amount used.

As the points above suggest, the evaluation of overflow techniques for files is more detailed than it was for data in internal memory. Severance and Duhne present various tables, generated from a performance model, which can be used to select load factor, bucket size, and overflow strategy, when record length, device characteristics, and file costs are known.[15] A similar study has been carried out by Van der Pool.[16] With these guides it is fairly easy to achieve fast retrieval at reasonable storage overhead cost. The following points should be kept in mind.

1. For simplicity of overflow handling, open addressing is the best choice. It is especially attractive when the storage device has an "extended search" option, which continues the search for a record or free space from an initial track to consecutive ones on the same cylinder. In that case, open addressing is effectively a hardware function, and as long as only one or two tracks need to be searched, is very fast because only one seek is issued.

2. Rehashing, although easy to implement, is poor for disks, because the random nature of probes generated almost guarantees that records in overflow will require extra seeks to locate.

3. If fast retrieval is important, overflow should be located in the prime area, and the load factor kept around 85 per cent.

[14]D. E. Knuth, *The Art of Computer Programming*, Vol. 3 (Reading, Mass.: Addison-Wesley Publishing Company, Inc., 1973), Tables 3 and 4 of Sec. 6.4.

[15]See Severance and Duhne, "Practitioner's Guide."

[16]Van der Pool, "Optimal Storage Allocation."

4. If storage utilization is of primary concern, chained overflow should be used. Chaining in the prime area enables load factors close to 1 to be realized. Storage overhead can be reduced further by having a distinct overflow area and making the load factor greater than 1. Also, with a separate area, file growth is easy to handle and causes only a slow increase in retrieval time. On the other hand, as the number of records in overflow grows relative to that in the prime one, the chances of needing more than one seek to locate a record increase.

5. Records should be loaded in order of decreasing access probability, when that information is known.

An interesting aspect of hashing that we have not discussed is the effect on insertions and deletions on performance. The reader is referred to Olson[17] and Van der Pool[18] for analyses of this situation.

9.4 Multiple-Attribute Retrieval

Only one field (or field combination) can be used to algorithmically determine the position of records in storage. Typically, a designated attribute (usually a uniquely identifying one, selected as the key) is used either to generate addresses, or as a basis for record order. As seen in the last section, access by key is fast, especially with hashing. In practice, however, files are queried on other attributes besides the key, often on a combination of attributes. For example, given a file PERSONNEL with record format

(EMP#, NAME, DEPT, JOB, SAL),

requests of the following types might be encountered:

1. *Simple*—list all employees in the SALES department (i.e., DEPT = 'SALES').
2. *Range*—list all employees making between $15,000 and $20,000 per year $(15{,}000 \leq SAL \leq 20{,}000)$.
3. *Boolean*—list all SALES personnel except clerks and those making less than $10,000 per year [DEPT = 'SALES' **and not** (JOB = 'CLERK' **or** SAL $< 10{,}000$].

One way of satisfying such requests is an exhaustive search. This is the only choice if the storage is serial access, and may also be acceptable if immediate reply is not required, in which case queries can be batched and collectively answered with a single pass over the file. However, when fast response is needed, reading the whole file is impractical, and other techniques must be used. The best method would retrieve the records satisfying a query with only one access. This is possible with associative memory, but as far as use with files is concerned, such devices are still experimental; the potential of associative hardware will be discussed below.

[17]C. A. Olson, "Random Access File Organization for Indirectly Addressed Records," in *Proceedings of the 24th ACM National Conference* (New York: Association for Computing Machinery, 1969), pp. 539–549.

[18]J. A. van der Pool, "Optimal Storage for a File in Steady State," *IBM Journal of Research and Development* Jan. 1973, pp. 27–38.

In conventional memories, it is impossible to achieve the tight bounds on storage references for multiple-attribute searching that one finds with single-key retrieval; if a large number of records meet the search criteria, and if they are distributed throughout the file, it will take a large number of storage accesses to obtain them. The strategy behind multiple-attribute retrieval is therefore to restrict the search space as much as possible. One way of doing this is to use auxiliary structures. Inverted lists (described in Section 4.5) make it possible to retrieve exactly those records with specified attribute values, without any search of the data; multilists have a similar function. The applicability of both to files will be discussed in this section.

Another way of facilitating multiple-attribute retrieval is to make a combination of fields, rather than a single one, the basis for record allocation. The idea is to restrict the range of locations that need be searched in response to a query. Two examples of the approach—multiple key hashing and k-d trees—are described below.

9.4.1 Inverted Files

Recall from Section 4.5 that an inverted list consists of a value, together with pointers to the records having that value in a particular field. The collection of all inverted lists for an attribute A (i.e., one for each distinct value present in the A field of records in the file) will be called an *inverted file*. If the inverted attribute is the key (in which case each list has exactly one member), then the inverted file is a directory as defined in Section 4.1.3.

If enough attributes of a file are inverted, the records satisfying a query can be determined without reference to the file itself. For example, suppose, for the PERSONNEL file mentioned earlier, that there are inverted files on NAME, DEPT, JOB, and SAL. Then the above three queries can be answered as follows:

1. From the inverted file for DEPT, take the list for the value 'SALES.'
2. From the inverted file for SAL, take the union of lists for all salary values between $15,000 and $20,000.
3. Take the 'SALES' list from the inverted file for DEPT; exclude from it:
   (a) The list for 'CLERK' (from the inverted file on JOB).
   (b) The union of lists for values under $10,000 (from the inverted file on SAL).

Thus inverted files make it possible to identify the records satisfying a multiple-attribute query using basic set operations, and without referring to the data itself. As a result, they are a popular means of supporting query systems, and we now consider details of their organization. When the inverted files needed to answer a request are small enough to fit into main memory, operations on them will be fast (compared to I/O speeds), and the choice of data structure will not be critical. It is assumed here, however, that the main file has enough items, so that any inverted file for it will have to be kept in secondary storage. Therefore, the techniques described in the last two sections are needed.

An inverted file can be implemented using variable-length records. Each record has two components—a value from the field being inverted, and a repeating group (of pointers) comprising the associated inverted list. Since the value is uniquely identifying (i.e., there is exactly one inverted list per distinct value), either of the basic single-key organizations (trees or hashing) can be used to achieve rapid access by attribute value.

Hashing has the disadvantage of not being suited to range and Boolean queries; for such inquiries the records (of the inverted file) must be in physical key order so that subrange extraction, merging, and intersection can be performed efficiently. Hashing does provide fast resolution of simple queries, since the address of the inverted list for a value is quickly determined by the hash function. However, bucket organization must be treated somewhat more carefully than the case where data records (as opposed to inverted lists) are being stored. In particular, if buckets are allowed to contain more than one inverted list (which would happen because more than one value of the inverted field could hash to the same address), some way of quickly determining the list to which a pointer belongs is needed; it is too expensive to sort them out by reading in the associated data records.

The indexed-sequential organization is a natural one for inverted files, as it provides both fast access by key and the efficient sequential processing needed to handle Boolean and range queries. The physical setup was illustrated in Fig. 9.5; here the keys would be values from the inverted field, and the records' contents would be inverted lists. Records will vary in size as changes to the main file cause inverted lists to shrink and expand, but this is not hard to handle as long as provision is made for file growth. Note that in Fig. 9.5, variable-length records are pictured.

We now consider some practical aspects of inverted files. One question concerns the pointers making up the inverted lists—should they be machine addresses, relative addresses, or keys? One disadvantage of inverted files is that changes to the main file must be reflected in the inverted ones, thereby incurring maintenance costs. With key pointers, an inverted file only needs to be modified when a data record is added or deleted, or when there is a value change in the inverted field. With machine (and relative) addresses, *any* movement of records in the main file must be reflected in *all* associated inverted files. On the other hand, the reason for inverting on several attributes is usually to provide fast response to queries. If the list of pointers determined to satisfy a request consists of keys rather than actual addresses, it could take three or four storage accesses to pick up each data record instead of just one. Since this can mean the difference between unacceptable and satisfactory performance, it is common to use machine address pointers in inverted files.

A pointer type that represents a compromise between keys and machine addresses is the block address. By giving the location of a storage unit (e.g., track, page) containing the desired record rather than the exact address, the sensitivity to data movement is reduced for only a slight reduction in access speed. For example, with an ISAM file, the cylinder and track address of a record would be specified but not the position on that track. To retrieve the record, the whole track would have to be read and searched. The cost over using the full address could be as much as a rotation per access, plus buffer space, but the pointer remains valid even if records are shifted about within the track. (Note that when logical records are grouped into physical blocks, any type of pointer will only resolve to a block address, following which unblocking will take place in main memory.)

So far, nothing has been said about the nature of the field being inverted on. In fact, the size of the value space for an attribute should be taken into account when the inverted file for that field is organized. Consider a payroll file with a field, NET-PAY, giving an employee's salary after deduction of withholding taxes, pension-plan contributions, and the like. Because of the individual nature of many deductions, it is quite possible that the net earnings for each employee will be unique. However, queries on the field are unlikely to involve exact values—requests might take the form "Which employees have net pay between \$15,000 and \$16,000?" but not "Who takes home \$15,621.32?"

This is a situation where the number of distinct values present for a field is comparable to the number of records in the file. As a result, each inverted list will likely contain only one pointer—the effect is as if a key were being inverted. When this degree of detail is not needed, it is wasteful to keep so many separate inverted lists; space (and therefore I/O time) can be saved by combining them. In the example, range values could be inverted on so that there would be a list of (pointers to) employees in the \$10,000–\$11,000 bracket, the \$11,000–\$12,000 bracket, and so on. The ranges can be chosen to make the resulting lists of "manageable" size (e.g., a track, or page); if the most common net-pay bracket is \$16,000–\$17,000, that range can be broken up, whereas the "over \$25,000" bracket might be accommodated by a single list.

Complementing the situation where the inverted domain resembles a key is that in which the value space is small compared to file size. For example, the possible values for a field COLOR might be confined to {white, black, red, orange, yellow, green, blue, brown}. In this case, organizing an inverted file on COLOR so that the list for a particular value can be quickly located is not a problem, since there are only eight lists. However, barring extensive clustering of color values, using any of the lists would be tantamount to scanning the file, so it is not worth inverting just for simple or range queries. Moreover, if the file contained on the order of 1 million records, using an inverted list (likely having thousands of entries) in a Boolean query would be expensive.

Perhaps the best approach in situations such as the one just described is not to invert if it appears that the resulting inverted lists will be too large (e.g., more than a track or two). During query processing, conditions involving noninverted attributes can be checked by reading in and testing the actual data records; naturally this is delayed until the search space has been reduced as much as possible using the inverted files available.

If it is desirable to invert on fields with small value spaces, bit maps can be used. Consider the attribute COLOR. There are only eight values, but the field requires six characters, or 48 bits at 8 bits/byte, to store them in literal form. By encoding them as bit positions in an 8-bit field, the COLOR field is compressed, and records of a given color are identified through a bit string. (In fact, only 3 bits are needed, but selection is simpler when 6 are used.) Moreover, suppose that other fields are recorded in the same way—for example, in Fig. 9.11, where there is only a small number of values for MANUFACTURER, BODY-STYLE, and YEAR-OF-MAKE. Then a complex request such as "Find all blue American Motors sedans made between 1971 and 1973" can be resolved by the following bit-string operations:

1. OR the 71, 72, and 73 columns from the YEAR-OF-MAKE field (giving a string that indicates cars made in the desired period).
2. AND the result of operation 1 with the "B" column from the COLOR field, the "AMC" column from MAKE, and the "Sedan" column from BODY-STYLE (removing from operation 1 all cars that are not blue AMC sedans).

In theory, the map of Fig. 9.11 compresses fields and makes it easy to process queries on those fields as well. In practice, the functions of compression and query processing must be assigned to separate maps because of the nature of storage. Since virtually every computer is equipped to operate on bit strings in byte- and often word-sized units, we can AND, OR, and complement columns efficiently only if they are each stored as contiguous bit strings. On the other hand, for quick retrieval of the data associated with a record, each *row* of the map must be stored as a contiguous unit. Here, bit maps are being examined as an alternative to conventional inverted files (i.e., ones with pointers), so while we continue to speak of rows and columns as they appear in Fig. 9.11, it will be assumed that the map is actually stored in *transposed* form—column by column. The result is sometimes called a *transposed file*.

A question of interest is the nature of the savings offered by bit maps over conventional inverted files. Consider a file of N records, with a field that assumes one of v values. A bit map for the field would be of size Nv bits, while an inverted file would require $N \cdot \lceil \log N \rceil$ bits ($\lceil \log N \rceil$ bits are needed to address N records) plus space for the v inverted list headers. Disregarding the latter component, the bit map saves space if $v < \lceil \log N \rceil$. Performance is more difficult to compare. As a general rule, the bit map can be expected to save I/O and processing time if it represents a space compression over the equivalent inverted file. When the two alternatives are close in terms of storage, a point that favors bit maps is the fact that operations on them tend to be simpler, and therefore faster, than equivalent operations on inverted lists. For example, to intersect two columns of a map, corresponding segments from each are loaded into a register and AND'ed to form the result. The process is then reapplied to succeeding portions of the strings. To intersect two inverted lists (with pointers stored in order of increasing value), pointers from each are retrieved and compared. If equal, a copy is placed in the result list; otherwise, the smaller pointer is replaced by the next one in the list where it came from and the comparison repeated. More decision making is required, and therefore the code is basically slower.

One type of query to which bit maps are particularly well suited is the negated simple condition. With inverted files, a request such as "Find all cars that are not blue" requires a merge of all inverted lists on the color field except the one for blue; with bit maps, the string for blue is simply complemented. Now a query as general as this would not likely be posed, but it does suggest a complication introduced when negations are handled using inverted files—unless the solution space is first reduced as much as possible by applying nonnegated conditions, complementation can require

Fig. 9.11 Bit map for four attributes

Record Number	Year-of-Make								Color								Make						Body-Style			
	70	71	72	73	74	75	76	77	W	Bl	R	O	Y	G	B	Br	AMC	Chrys	Ford	GMC	Datsun	VW	Sedan	H.T.	Convertible	Wagon
1	0	0	0	1	0	0	0	0	1	0	0	0	0	0	0	0	0	1	0	0	0	0	0	1	0	0
2	0	1	0	0	0	0	0	0	0	0	0	0	0	1	0	0	0	0	1	0	0	0	0	0	0	1
3	0	0	0	0	1	0	0	0	0	1	0	0	0	0	0	0	0	0	0	0	0	1	0	1	0	0
4	0	0	0	1	0	0	0	0	0	1	0	0	0	0	0	0	0	0	1	0	0	0	1	0	0	0
5	1	0	0	0	0	0	0	0	1	0	0	0	0	0	0	0	0	0	0	1	0	0	0	0	1	0
6	0	1	0	0	0	0	0	0	0	0	0	0	0	0	1	0	1	0	0	0	0	0	0	0	0	1
7	0	0	1	0	0	0	1	0	0	0	0	1	0	0	0	0	0	0	0	0	0	1	0	0	1	0
8	0	0	0	0	0	0	0	0	0	0	0	0	1	0	0	0	0	0	0	0	1	0	1	0	0	0
9	0	0	0	0	0	0	1	0	0	0	0	0	0	1	0	0	0	0	0	1	0	0	1	0	0	0
10	0	1	0	0	0	1	0	0	0	0	0	0	0	0	1	0	0	1	0	0	0	0	0	1	0	0
11	0	0	0	0	1	0	0	0	1	0	0	0	0	0	0	0	0	0	0	0	1	0	0	0	1	0
12	1	0	1	0	0	0	0	0	0	0	1	0	0	0	0	0	0	1	0	0	0	0	0	0	0	1
13	0	0	0	0	0	0	0	0	1	0	0	0	0	0	0	0	1	0	0	0	0	0	1	0	0	0
14	0	0	0	0	1	0	0	0	0	0	1	0	1	0	0	0	0	0	0	0	0	0	0	1	0	0
15	0	0	0	0	0	0	0	0	0	0	0	0	0	0	0	0	1	0	1	0	0	0	0	0	0	1
16	0	0	0	0	0	0	0	0	0	0	1	0	0	0	0	0	0	0	0	0	0	0	0	0	1	0
17	0	0	0	0	0	1	0	1	0	0	0	0	0	0	0	0	0	0	0	1	0	1	1	0	0	0
18	0	0	0	0	0	0	0	0	0	1	0	0	0	0	0	1	0	0	0	0	1	0	0	0	1	0
19	0	0	1	0	0	1	0	1	0	0	0	0	0	0	1	0	0	1	0	0	0	0	0	1	0	0
20	0	0	0	0	0	0	0	0	0	1	0	0	0	0	0	0	0	0	0	0	0	1	1	0	0	0

351

the merging of large numbers of inverted lists. With bit maps, exclusions require no special treatment and can be resolved as they appear during evaluation.

A bit map saves space over a conventional inverted file only when v, the number of possible attribute values, is less than $\lceil \log N \rceil$, the number of bits needed to address the file, but this threshold can be raised by further compression. Since only one bit in v is turned on, the map is already quite sparse for $v \geq 5$, and moreover, compression will be increasingly effective as v grows. Naturally, the technique used must preserve the ability to process the information represented by the columns of the full map efficiently. The methods of Section 5.4 are not really applicable here, since they are designed to compress arrays with word-sized entries while preserving the indexing capability.

One possibility is to do run-length encoding (Section 3.5.2). Since there are no special characters, it is necessary to indicate the presence of uncompressed data as well as encoded runs of zeros; otherwise, it would be impossible to tell whether a sequence of bits were to be regarded as compressed or not. One bit is sufficient to describe the nature of subsequent text (encoded, or not). Suppose that v attribute values are uniformly distributed throughout the file, so that each column of the map has roughly N/v bits, dividing it into runs of zeros averaging $v - 1$ in length. We shall assume that runs of longer than average are uncommon, and will therefore use a field of $\lceil \log(v - 1) \rceil$ bits to specify the length of such runs. Two bits suffice for uncompressed groups, if we assume that more than two successive ones in a column occurs only rarely.

For a pessimistic estimate of overhead, assume that each compressed sequence is always followed by an uncoded one (i.e., that runs of zeros longer than average never occur). Then the compression overhead for each run of $v - 1$ zeros will be 1 (flag) $+ \lceil \log(v - 1) \rceil$ (length of run) $+ 1$ (flag, to indicate that the following two bits represent uncompressed data) $= \lceil \log(v - 1) \rceil + 2$ bits. For a net saving this must be less than the $v - 1$ zeros eliminated, which will be true if $v > 6$; for significant compression, v would have to be greater still.

Even if the run-length encoding reduces the map size, and therefore the read time, the net effect might not be a saving once the cost of decoding is considered. The code that operates on encoded bit-string portions is so simple that the addition of instructions to test flags and interpret length fields will increase the internal processing time several fold. Thus the practicality of compressing a particular map by run-length encoding depends on the data (which determine the space savings achievable) and hardware features (I/O and certain instruction times).

A way to retain the efficiency of bit map operations while saving space is to compress with loss of information. OR'ing columns, rows, or both together in groups gives a contracted but less precise map.[19] Suppose, for example, that the map of Fig. 9.11 is condensed by OR'ing pairs of columns, that is, 70 and 71, 72 and 73, Black and White, and so on, so that the map of Fig. 9.12 results. The immediate savings are

[19]Oscar Vallarino, "On the Use of Bit Maps for Multiple Key Retrieval," *SIGPLAN Notices,* **8,** no. 2 (1976), 108–114.

	Year-of-Make				Color				Make			Body-Style	
	70-71	72-73	74-75	76-77	W-Bl	R-O	Y-G	B-V	AMC-Chrys	Ford-CMC	Datsun-VW	Sedan H.T.	Convertible-Wagon
1	0	1	0	0	1	0	0	0	1	0	0	1	0
2	1	0	0	0	0	0	1	0	0	1	0	0	1
3	0	0	1	0	1	0	0	0	0	0	1	1	0
4	0	1	0	0	1	0	0	0	0	1	0	1	0
5	1	0	0	0	1	0	0	0	0	1	0	0	1
6	1	0	0	0	0	0	0	1	1	0	0	0	1
7	0	0	0	1	0	1	0	0	0	0	1	0	1
8	0	1	0	0	0	0	1	0	0	0	1	1	0
9	0	0	0	1	0	1	0	0	0	1	0	1	0
10	1	0	0	0	0	0	0	1	1	0	0	1	0
11	0	0	1	0	1	0	0	0	0	0	1	0	1
12	0	0	1	0	0	1	0	0	1	0	0	0	1
13	1	0	0	0	1	0	0	0	1	0	0	1	0
14	0	1	0	0	0	1	0	0	0	1	0	1	0
15	0	0	1	0	0	0	1	0	1	0	0	0	1
16	0	0	0	1	0	1	0	0	0	1	0	0	1
17	0	0	1	0	1	0	0	0	0	0	1	1	0
18	0	0	0	1	0	0	0	1	0	0	1	0	1
19	0	0	1	0	0	0	0	1	1	0	0	1	0
20	0	1	0	0	1	0	0	0	0	0	1	1	0

Fig. 9.12 Bit map condensed by OR'ing column pairs

in storage and data-transfer costs, since the compressed map is half the size of the full one. If, in addition, the compressed version can fit into the main memory available while the original cannot, then access costs are also saved when the map is read in for query processing.

The price of these economies is a relatively high number of *false drops* per query. A false drop is a record that does not meet the search criteria but is, nevertheless, indicated as doing so by the map. For example, the answer to "Which cars were made in 1973?", as determined from the second column of Fig. 9.12, is a list of five records—numbers 1, 4, 8, 14, and 20; however, numbers 8, 14, and 20 are false drops because they are present as a result of being in the column for 1972, in the full map. In fact, for any single-value query on a given attribute, we can expect Fig. 9.12 to yield roughly 50 per cent false drops. The percentage would be greater if more than two columns had been compressed into one, or if the query were an "AND" of several attributes. The savings offered by this technique must therefore be weighed against the expected cost of eliminating false drops introduced by the compression.

If the map is compressed by rows rather than columns, a natural grouping is the rows corresponding to the records of a block. The resulting columns then indicate the blocks in which particular values are found. For the result to be useful, however, the number of records in a block must be less than the number of values; otherwise, the compressed map will be mostly 1's signifying only that each block has most of the possible values present. In cases where the map is particularly sparse, row *and* column compression can be performed. The effect is to replace a rectangle of positions in the original map by a 1 if there were any 1's present, and 0 otherwise.

9.4.2 Multilists

With multilists (illustrated in Table 4.4), records are chained to other records having the same value in a particular field. If there are v values present for an attribute, each record in the file will belong to exactly one of v lists. Records in a chain could be in any sequence, but the cost of traversal is lowest if they are linked in order of their physical position in the file.

Multilists are effective for simple queries, since the only records retrieved (i.e., the ones on a chain) are those which satisfy the search condition. Range queries require that the contents of several chains be retrieved. This can be done efficiently by traversing the lists in parallel—at each step, the list followed is the one that points to the next address in sequence; if that address is in the block last read in, no additional storage access is needed. The process is equivalent to merging inverted lists and reading in each record indicated in the result.

For queries that specify the *union* of lists (range and OR conditions), multilists are as efficient as inverted files; once AND clauses are introduced, however, they are less useful. Consider the request for cars for which COLOR = 'blue' AND YEAR-OF-MAKE = '1971'. This requires that the chain for blue be intersected with that for 1971. There is no point in traversing both lists, since the records that satisfy the query will all be on one of them; the most efficient method is to traverse the shorter list and test each record encountered to see if it satisfies the remaining conditions. This means that records that do not meet all the search conditions can be examined, and that the number of records retrieved in response to a query will not go down as the number of restricting (AND) conditions increases. Inverted files do not exhibit these properties since pointers, not records, are manipulated, and are therefore superior to multilists for evaluating general Boolean conditions.

A problem with multilists is that they are expensive to update. If the field in a record is changed, that record must be transferred from one list to another. To do this, two chains must be followed from their beginnings, a procedure that may reference a substantial portion of the file. Insertion and deletion, which require a record to be added to, or removed from, the list for each chained field may cause even more storage accesses.

A modification to multilists that has improved update and retrieval properties is the *cellular multilist*.[20] The idea is to restrict chains so that they do not cross specified hardware boundaries, for example, a track, or cylinder. This breaks a single chain into several segments, the starting addresses of which can be kept in a table. Figure 9.13 illustrates cellular multilists on two fields of the data of Fig. 9.11. To find the

[20]See D. Lefkowitz, *File Structures for Online Systems* (New York: Spartan Books, 1969), Chap. 7.

Year	Starting Record Adresses of Chains
1970	$\hat{5}, \hat{13}$
1971	$\hat{2}, \hat{6}$
1972	$\hat{8}, \hat{14}, \hat{20}$
1973	$\hat{1}$
1974	$\hat{3}, \hat{12}$
1975	$\hat{11}, \hat{17}$
1976	$\hat{7}$
1977	$\hat{16}$

Color	Starting Record Addresses of Chains
White	$\hat{1}, \hat{11}$
Black	$\hat{3}, \hat{17}$
Red	$\hat{12}, \hat{16}$
Orange	$\hat{7}$
Yellow	$\hat{8}, \hat{15}$
Green	$\hat{2}, \hat{9}$
Blue	$\hat{6}, \hat{19}$
Brown	$\hat{18}$

List Headers

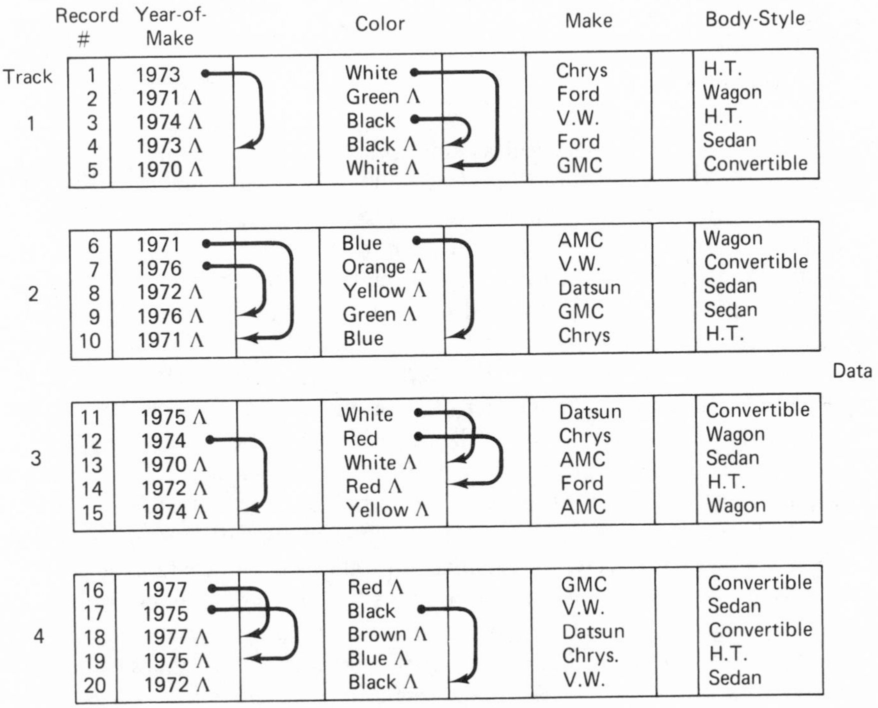

Fig. 9.13 Cellular multilists

cars made in 1974, look in the YEAR table to get the starting chain addresses for that attribute (record addresses 3 and 12 in this case), read in the appropriate blocks (one and three), and follow the chains. To find 1974 cars that are red, search those blocks common to the "1974" list from the year table, and the "red" list from the color table; in this case, only one block (three) has chains for 1974 and red, so only one chain in that block needs to be traversed. Adding, deleting, and changing records are likewise simplified; each chain affected will be in only one block of storage, and by consulting the appropriate tables, its starting address can be located without searching in the file itself.

By breaking up chains and keeping directories to the resulting segments, multilists can achieve the efficiency of inverted lists for general queries and updates. However, this begs a question: Since these directories are simply inverted lists with block addresses rather than full ones, why chain records within blocks at all? The 2 μs it might take to test a 10-character field of a 100-character record is only a fraction (2 per cent) of the time needed to transfer in that record from a fast disk. Since whole blocks, rather than individual records, are always read in, the savings from following a chain of records with a common field value over testing each record for the presence of that value are questionable, particularly when the extra I/O cost of the pointers is considered. Therefore, the variant of multilists most suited to secondary storage would appear to be the inverted file with block pointers, sometimes called the *cellular inverted file*.

9.4.3 Multifield Allocation

Trees and hashing were conceived as single-key allocation techniques, but they can be extended to use several fields. Consider 50,000 records with fields $F_1, F_2, \ldots, F_8$. If H stands for a function which maps a value into a 2-bit result, the concatenation $H(F_1) \| H(F_2) | \ldots | H(F_8)$ produces a 16-bit string that will serve as a hash address. Collisions are handled as described earlier, and the total number of locations ($2^{16} = 65,536$) gives a reasonable load factor, just under 70 per cent.

Now let values for fields F_2, F_3, and F_6 be specified. Then the candidate records are at addresses of the form xxH(F_2)H(F_3)xxxxH(F_6)xxxx, where x represents a zero or one. Since there are 10 x's, the number of locations to be checked is $2^{10} = 1024$; the search space has been reduced by 2^6, 6 being the number of bits determined by the query. In general, suppose that there are $N \approx 2^h$ records with k fields. If k divides h, each field can be hashed to an h/k-bit value which makes up part of an h-bit address. Then if t fields are specified in a query, the search space is reduced by a factor of $(2^{h/k})^t = 2^{ht/k} = N^{t/k}$; conversely, the number of locations left to examine is $N^{(k-t)/k}$.

In the example just given, all fields were hashed to the same number of bits. In practice, only those fields expected to be queried on would be used as the basis for allocation. Moreover, the contribution of a particular attribute to the hash address will depend on the size of its value set. As a general rule, a field with v values should not be mapped to a bit string longer than $\lceil \log v \rceil$; otherwise, the potential of that address segment to partition the search space into more than v parts will be lost (due to unused locations).

For equality conditions, then, multiple-field hashing is better than the straight scan. The improvement is achieved without auxiliary structures and becomes increasingly effective as more fields are specified. However, there are some features of the method that should be noted. The first concerns range queries. Consider the request for records with values between $12,000 and $13,000 in a field, SALARY. Since we do not know exactly what salaries are present in the file, each value in the desired range—1000 if amounts are only specified to the dollar, 100,000 otherwise—must be hashed. Suppose that the result of a hash is an 8-bit field, a reasonable size considering that 20 bits is enough to address 1,000,000 records, and assuming that several fields are being hashed. Then mapping a range of 1000 values with any satisfactorily random function will almost certainly result in each of the $2^8 = 256$ possible bit configurations; in other words, the range condition does nothing to restrict the search space. A possible solution is to hash only the high-order digits of SALARY values, thereby converting the salaries in a range (defined by the number of digits truncated) to the same bit string. However, if values are clustered in certain ranges, this will lead to a high number of collisions at some locations.

Multiple-field hashing is not well suited to negated conditions; as with inverted lists, such queries tend to be ineffective in reducing the search space. If a field is hashed to b bits, a simple equality condition confines the search space to addresses with one particular value (out of a possible 2^b) in a certain segment, and therefore cuts searching by $1/2^b$. On the other hand, a negated simple condition only rules out the string fixed by the hash and leaves the segment free to assume any of the $2^b - 1$ remaining values, so the savings factor is only $(2^b - 1)/2^b$.

Because different fields map to different-sized address portions, the performance achievable using multiple-field hashing for a particular query type (e.g., simple equality on one attribute) will vary according to the field involved. However, for records on secondary storage, there is another source of asymmetry which is more important. Suppose that four-field records are mapped to 16-bit addresses by concatenating the 4-bit hash of each field. Records are grouped 256 to a block, so that the 8 high-order bits of an address give the block number. Then a query in which values for the two leftmost fields are given specifies a single block whose contents (256 records) are to be examined. Fixing the two rightmost fields also leaves 256 records to be checked, but each in a different block. Assuming that block access time is the dominating factor in search cost (over internal processing), the second query effectively causes the whole file to be searched. Thus the theoretical efficiency of multiple-field hashing is not always achievable in practice; the effectiveness of the method depends very much on the fields involved in a query, particularly on the portion of the address they represent.

9.4.4 Multidimensional Search Trees

The k-d (k-dimensional) search tree, developed by J. L. Bentley,[21] extends the binary search tree to multiple-attribute retrieval. Its performance is comparable to that of multifield hashing, and it has some additional advantages. Consider a record R, with k fields. When R is being inserted in a binary search tree, the value of one, predetermined field (the key) is used to decide, at each level, whether R is to be added to the left or right subtree. Suppose, instead, that a *different* field is used as the basis for decision at each step; for example, let field 1 be used at the root, field 2 at level 2,

---

[21] J. L. Bentley, "Multidimensional Trees Used for Associative Searching," *Communications of the ACM*, **18**, no. 9 (Sept. 1975), 509–516.

and so on down to level $k + 1$, at which point, since there are no new fields, the deciding field recycles to field 1.

A tree built in this way is illustrated in Fig. 9.14; it is called a k-d tree, where k is the number of fields in a node. The nodes are the four-field records from Fig. 9.11. (In practice, the record number would be a field, but it is not being used as an attribute here, so it is simply shown alongside the nodes.) At level 1, the first field (YEAR-OF-MAKE) is the *discriminator*, that is, the field used for branching. Thus all cars in the left subtree were made in or prior to 1973, while those in the right were manufactured later. (Equality can be resolved either way, as long as it is done consistently.) At level 2, field 2 (COLOR) becomes the discriminator. This splits the left subtree into two parts —records whose COLOR value is alphabetically $\leq$ 'Green' (record 2 and its left subtree), and those whose values are greater (the subtree rooted at record 5). Similarly, the right subtree of the root is partitioned according to whether COLOR is $\leq$ or $>$ 'Black'. At level 5, the discriminator recycles to YEAR-OF-MAKE; thus record 11 and its right subtree contain cars made in 1975, and cars in the left subtree (rooted at record 16) were made later.

Physically, k-d trees are the same as binary search trees, and therefore they share many of the characteristics of those structures. For example, the optimal (unweighted) k-d tree is one that is balanced in the sense of Section 6.4.1, in which case the maximum search length for N nodes is roughly $\log (N + 1)$. Also, the expected maximum path length for a randomly constructed k-d tree of N nodes is the same as for the binary tree, namely $1.386 \log N$. Now consider a request for 1977 brown Datsun convertibles. These must be in the right subtree of the root (since YEAR-OF-MAKE is later than 1975), the right subtree of the one rooted at record 3, since Brown $>$ Black (alphabetically), the left subtree of the one rooted at 7, since 'Datsun' $\leq$ 'V.W.', and so on. This continues until record 18 is found to be the (only) one satisfying the query. Thus requests where all field values are specified define a single path from the root to a leaf, and so can be answered in average time $O(\log N)$ for a random tree.

Suppose, however, that a query fixes fewer than k fields, for example MAKE = 'Chrys.' *and* BODY-STYLE = 'H.T.'. Since MAKE does not become the discriminator until level 3, all records in the tree must be searched down to that point. At level 3, MAKE = 'Chrys." can be used to restrict further searching to the subtrees rooted at records 6, 8, and 9. There, BODY-STYLE = 'H.T.' further narrows the search space to the subtrees rooted at records 10, 13, and 11. All records in these trees must be examined since the discriminator does not recycle to MAKE again until the lowest level (7), below which no branching occurs.

From the last paragraph it should be clear that if a request specifies $t < k$ field values, the maximum amount of searching will occur if these values are for the last t fields; this minimizes the number of levels at which the discriminator can be used to make branching decisions. For a simple analysis, suppose that the tree contains $N = 2^{hk} - 1$ nodes, $h \geq 1$, with all leaves at level hk. Then, as in the example above, the search begins by checking all nodes down to and including level $k - t$; the number of these is

$$1 + 2 + \ldots + 2^{k-t-1} = 2^{k-t} - 1.$$

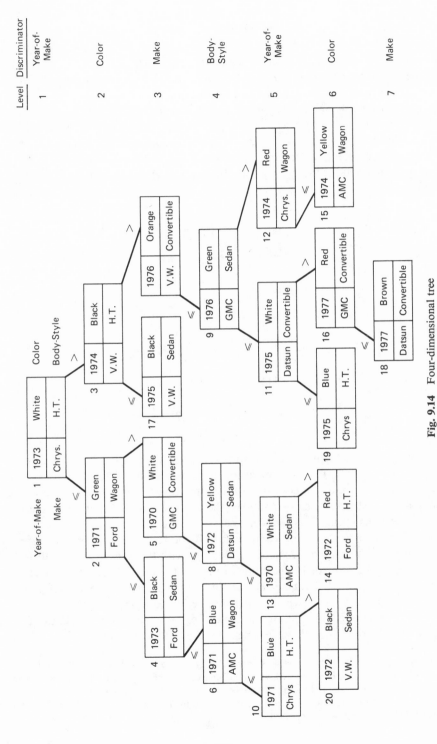

Fig. 9.14 Four-dimensional tree

Level	Discriminator
1	Year-of-Make
2	Color
3	Make
4	Body-Style
5	Year-of-Make
6	Color
7	Make

At level $k - t + 1$, there are 2^{k-t} branches to follow, corresponding to the successors of nodes at level $k - t$. Now, the values specified in the query can be used for the next t levels down, so each branch is, in fact, a unique path of t nodes; the number of nodes examined in the process is thus $t(2^{k-t})$. After the 2^{k-t} paths have been followed down t levels, level $k + 1$ is reached and the discriminator recycles to field 1. No value was supplied for this or the following $k - t - 1$ fields, so the search down the next $k - t$ levels covers 2^{k-t} subtrees of $2^{k-t} - 1$ nodes. Then the t values can be used again, confining the search to $2^{k-t}(2^{k-t}) = 2^{2(k-t)}$ paths of the nodes each. The cycle of alternately searching whole subtrees for $k - t$ levels and then single paths of length t repeats h times, since there are hk levels. The total number of nodes examined is, therefore,

$$2^{k-t} - 1 + t \cdot 2^{k-t} \qquad\qquad\qquad \text{cycle 1}$$

$$+ \ 2^{k-t}(2^{k-t} - 1) + t \cdot 2^{2(k-t)} \qquad\qquad \text{cycle 2}$$

$$\vdots$$

$$+ \ 2^{(h-1)(k-t)}(2^{k-t} - 1) + t \cdot 2^{h(k-t)} \qquad\qquad \text{cycle } h$$

$$= \sum_{i=0}^{h-1} (2^{k-t} - 1 + t \cdot 2^{k-t}) 2^{i(k-t)}$$

$$= (2^{k-t} - 1 + t \cdot 2^{k-t}) \sum_{i=0}^{h-1} 2^{i(k-t)}$$

$$= [(t + 1)2^{k-t} - 1](2^{(k-t)h} - 1)/(2^{k-t} - 1).$$

Now

$$2^{(k-t)h} = 2^{((k-t)/k) \cdot hk} = (2^{hk})^{(k-t)/h}$$

$$= (N + 1)^{(k-t)/k},$$

so the worst-case performance of k-d trees for queries which specify values for t of k fields is $O(t \cdot N^{(k-t)/k})$, that is, comparable to that of multiple-field hashing.

Insertion into a k-d tree consists of following a path from the root to a leaf. For a randomly constructed tree of N nodes, the average cost is $O(\log N)$; if the tree is balanced, this also represents the worst case.

Deletion is somewhat more complicated. If the root is to be removed from the tree of Fig. 9.14, it must be replaced by the node with the largest YEAR-OF-MAKE value in its left subtree (or smallest one in the right), since YEAR-OF-MAKE is the discriminator at level 1. Because the discriminator changes at every level, however, the replacement may be anywhere in the subtree,[22] and moreover could be a root, in which case a successor for it has to be found. For example, in the left subtree (rooted at record 2), the only possible replacement for the root is record 4. Now with a binary

---

[22]Actually, not necessarily the *whole* subtree; it may be deep enough that the discriminator will recycle to that of the node being deleted, which will enable the search space to be restricted somewhat. If, in the example here, the right subtree were being searched for the closest year to 1973, the right subtree of record 11 could be eliminated from consideration. To get an upper bound, we will assume that the whole subtree must be searched.

search tree, 4 could be promoted to the root and its whole right subtree moved up a level, but here that subtree is rooted at level 4, where BODY-STYLE, not MAKE, is the discriminator. Thus the tree must be searched for a predecessor to record 4 with respect to the MAKE field, to take 4's old position at level 3. In this case, 10 would replace 4, and 20, not having any descendents, could move up to level 5. More generally, suppose that the root of a balanced tree with $N = 2^h - 1$ nodes is to be removed, and that the $2^{h-1} - 1$ nodes of its right subtree are examined to find a successor. The worst case occurs when the root of that subtree turns out to be the successor, because its removal will cause all the nodes in *its* right subtree ($2^{h-2} - 1$ in number) to be checked. Assuming, then, that the worst case always occurs, that is, the successor is always the root of the subtree examined, the total number of nodes examined will be

$$\sum_{i=1}^{h-1} 2^i - 1 = 2^h - (h + 1) = N - h, \quad \text{which is } O(N).$$

(In fact, because of what was said in footnote 22, the cost may be slightly less; see the reference of footnote 21 for details.)

Although deletion of the root is $O(N)$, the situation is not as bad for a randomly selected node; for the balanced tree of height h, a node at level i, $1 \leq i \leq h$, is the root of a balanced tree of height $h - i + 1$, and thus costs $2^{(h-i+1)} - (h - i + 2)$ to delete. The average deletion cost is, therefore,

$$\frac{1}{N}\left[\sum_{i=1}^{h} (\text{cost of deletion at level } i) \cdot (\text{number of nodes at level } i)\right]$$

$$= \frac{1}{N}\sum_{i=1}^{h} [2^{h-i+1} - (h - i + 2)] \cdot 2^{i-1}$$

$$= \frac{1}{N}\left[h \cdot 2^h - (h + 2)(2^h - 1) + \sum_{i=1}^{h} i \cdot 2^{i-1}\right]$$

$$= \frac{1}{N}[h(2^h + 1) - 3(2^h - 1)]$$

$$\approx h - 3,$$

which, since $N = 2^h - 1 \approx \log N$. A similar result would hold for randomly constructed trees, so, on the average, deletion is as efficient as insertion.

A type of query to which k-d trees seem well suited is the nearest-neighbor search. If k-field records are regarded as points in k-dimensional space, it is natural to speak of the distance between records. A common class of distance measures are the p-norms, which define the distance $d(u, v)$ between points $u = (u_1, \ldots, u_k)$ and $v = (v_1, \ldots, v_k)$ to be $\left[\sum_{i=1}^{k} |u_i - v_i|^p\right]^{1/p}$, where $p > 0$; if $p = 2$, this is the familiar Euclidean norm.

Given a distance measure d and a record R, we can ask for the nearest neighbor(s) of R, that is, the record(s) S for which $d(R, S)$ is a minimum. With multifield hashing, the nearest neighbors of R are likely to be spread throughout the file, because the hash function for each field is designed to assign different bit segments to values that are close together. It is possible to find the nearest neighbor along a given coordinate without examining too many records but, as remarked above, the efficiency will vary widely, according to which field is being left to vary.

On the other hand, there is evidence that k-d trees can be constructed that allow closest match queries to be resolved in $O(\log N)$ time, where N is the number of records. To optimize a tree for this purpose, the discriminator for the root of each subtree is chosen to be the field with the largest spread of values in the subspace represented by that subtree. Then the record whose discriminator value is the median for the value set of the chosen discriminator is selected as the root. The process continues until a level below which all subtrees would have less than some number b records; the record groups are then stored as buckets. For a description, see Friedman.[23]

K-d trees are a promising class of structures, but they have some potential drawbacks. One concerns range conditions. With hashing, these can be handled by mapping values in the same range to the same address portion, although this is not entirely satisfactory because of possible value clustering. In theory, k-d trees are well suited to range queries, because, as one descends in the tree, the bounds satisfied by the field values of a record shrink. However, since the discriminator changes at each level, this happens slowly with respect to a single field. Suppose that the tree is balanced and has 20 levels of six-field records. A range condition on the first field *may* enable half the tree to be eliminated, providing that the discriminator value at the root is outside the range. In any case, for one of the subtrees of the root, all records must be searched down to level 7, where the discriminator recycles; then the search space can be cut by at most half again. Field 1 is the discriminator at levels 13 and 19, so, in total, at least 1/16 of the file must be examined.

Two points are worth noting here. First, although 1/16 of 2^{20} records is still a large number, the portion would be even greater if the records had more fields; for example, with 10 attributes, the discriminator would only recycle once, so a query fixing one field would leave 1/4 of the file to be searched. Thus the appropriateness of a k-d tree will depend on how the number of records (which determines the minimum number of levels) compare to the number of fields.

Second, the number of records examined does not accurately reflect the search cost, because k-d trees exhibit the same asymmetry with respect to multiple-attribute queries that hashing does. If the tree is allocated in secondary storage so that the records in a block form a single subtree (a good strategy, since this ensures that a block partitions its portion of the search space to the maximum extent), then the number of blocks examined increases with the number of paths searched in the upper levels of the tree; a query that fixes the first t of k fields, $t < k$, will be answered more cheaply than one that specifies the last t.

The limits to the effectiveness of multifield hashing and k-d trees reflect the one-dimensional nature of storage; since the records can be physically positioned accord-

---

[23]J. H. Friedman, J. L. Bentley, and R. A. Finkel, "An Algorithm for Finding Best Matches in Logarithmic Time," *ACM Transactions on Mathematical Software*, **3** no. 3 (Sept. 1977), 209–226.

ing to only one logical grouping, selection according to any other criterion means retrieval of items which are not close together, an operation that is inherently expensive. The techniques for attribute-based organization described in this section are representative of those found in general use (the exception being k-d trees, which are relatively new and untested), but there are more elaborate methods that can do better. For example, by hashing on some fields and inverting on others, it is possible to gain the advantage of multiple field hashing (efficient retrieval on high-order fields) without the main drawback (poor performance on low-order ones), and without the need for a full complement of inverted files. The problem is deciding which fields to hash and which to invert on, a choice that must be made carefully for a clear improvement to be realized.[24] Another possibility is to keep multiple copies of a file, each ordered a different field or field combination. The redundancy is expensive (usually prohibitively so), due to added space and update costs, but if enough attribute combinations are present, query evaluation can be efficient.[25]

9.4.5 Associative Processing

File operations are often set-oriented ("Increase the salary of each employee by 8 percent"), and information requests are usually associative in nature (general Boolean queries). *Associative processors*, which can operate on several data items at once, and access storage by content rather than address, would appear to be particularly well suited to these types of processing.

The associative processor organization shown in Fig. 9.15 is typical. Searching is carried out on the 10 words in parallel. (Here, the words are shown divided into fields, reflecting the data used as an example, but in fact they would simply be cells of a fixed bit size.) Words that match the search argument (in the Data Register) in those positions indicated by the Mask are indicated by a "1" bit in the Search Results Register. The Match Count gives the number of ones in the Results Register, and the Multiple Match Resolver points to the first "1." In the figure, all 1971 wagons have been requested, so all the bits in the Select Register are on; fields 1 and 4 of the Data Register are loaded, respectively, with "1971" and "Wagon," while fields 2 and 3 are masked out.

Following a search, the words flagged in the Results Register can be read out; another possibility is to use that register as the basis of a subsequent search. For example, referring to Fig. 9.15, it might be decided that what is really wanted is a 1971 *Datsun* wagon; to find out if one is present, the Word Select Register is loaded from the old Results Register, and the Data and Mask Registers are set to look for "Datsun" in the third field.

---

[24]J. B. Rothnie and T. Lozano, "Attribute-Based File Organization in a Paged Environment," *Communications of the ACM*, **17**, no. 2 (Feb. 1974), 53–67.

[25]Recall the discussion of LEAP in Section 7.2.1; see also V. Y. Lum, "Multiple-Attribute Retrieval with Combined Indices," *Communications of the ACM*, **13**, no. 11 (Nov. 1970), 660–665, and B. Schneiderman, "Reduced Combined Indexes for Efficient Multiple Attribute Retrieval," *Information Systems*, **2**, no. 4 (1977), 149–154.

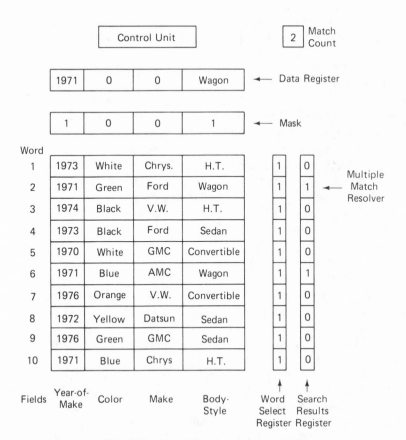

Fig. 9.15   Associative processor searches

Other features of the processor illustrated in Fig. 9.15 might include the ability to write (in parallel) into specified bit positions of selected words, and the ability to perform operations between fields of a word (simultaneously), for selected words.

The Goodyear STARAN processor is a commercially available associative processor which functions much as just described. The basic configuration consists of a 256-word × 256-bit associative array and control memory, connected to a PDP 11.[26] Other options are available, including up to 31 additional arrays. A STARAN system for file processing, implemented by Moulder,[27] is illustrated in Fig. 9.16. Four associative arrays (and their processing logic) receive instructions from (and send results to) an XDS Sigma 5 computer. Only the first 64 words of the first array are actually used; each of these is connected by its own I/O channel to the read/write head of a head-per-

[26]For details, see K. E. Batcher, "Staran Parallel Processor System Hardware," in *AFIPS Proceedings NCC* **43** (Montvale, N.J.: AFIPS Press, 1974), pp. 405–410.

[27]R. Moulder, "An Implementation of a Data Management System on an Associative Processor," in *AFIPS Proceedings NCC* **42** (Montvale, N.J.: AFIPS Press, 1973), pp. 171–176.

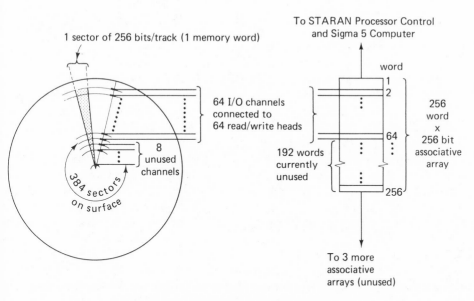

Fig. 9.16 STARAN associative processor

track disk. The surface of the disk has 72 tracks, 64 of which are used, and is divided into 384 sectors of 256 bits (one array word) per track. It takes 100 μs to read a sector and the same amount of time to search memory, so by processing alternate sectors, the surface in use (6.3 million bits) can be examined in two revolutions.

A small data management system implemented on the hardware just described includes facilities for:

1. *File definition and creation*—naming files, defining record formats, specifying how records are to be mapped onto the fixed size (256-bit) associative memory words.
2. *Interrogation*—"Print ⟨names⟩ where ⟨conditional⟩," where ⟨names⟩ is a list of one or more attribute names, and ⟨conditional⟩ is a general Boolean query, lists the named fields (and their values) for all records satisfying the condition.
3. *Update*—there are four functions: Change, Add, Delete, and Move. "Change ⟨name⟩ to ⟨value⟩, where ⟨conditional⟩" changes the named field in all records satisfying the condition. "Move" enables the user to restructure the data base by changing links between records.

It is estimated that most queries can be processed at a rate of 100 μs/sector, thereby enabling a request to be processed in two revolutions, about 80 ms; however, this is only for one disk surface, with a capacity of under 1 million characters. An actual file could account for several million bytes, and a collection of files making up a data base might contain on the order of 100 million. If the above system were coupled to 10 head per track disk surfaces, all sharing the 64 available channels, the process time for a query goes up by a factor of 10, resulting in performance that might not be competitive with software associative retrieval methods. On the other hand, increasing the amount of associative memory and number of channels to serve it is costly; the associative arrays are expensive because they require search and I/O logic for every cell, and 64 channels is already a high number compared to the three or four that might be found on a large conventional computer. Thus the practicality of a STARAN-based associative system for data-base processing remains to be determined.

In the system just described, the associative arrays do not replace conventional memory, but rather supplement it with a parallel search capability. A good deal of time is spent loading these arrays, and considerable expense (in the form of multiple I/O channels) is incurred to do this efficiently. Yet most of the data loaded are not passed on to the main computer. By moving the search logic to where the data are read from, in this case the read/write heads of a disk, unnecessary transfer of data is avoided, and the number of channels can be reduced to whatever is needed to accommodate the information actually wanted by the main processor. The intermediate associative memory is eliminated, and updates can be performed in place (i.e., without having to read an item in, change it, and write it out again).

The idea of equipping a disk with search and arithmetic logic on each track was first proposed by Slotnick,[28] who suggested that such a device would provide an effective form of associative memory for file processing. RAP (relational associative processor) is a unit based on this principle.[29] It is a logic-per-track device designed to enhance the data-management facilities of a general-purpose computer. Specifically, the goals are the elimination of access paths (e.g., inverted files) and a hardware implementation of the data base which is fairly close to the logical view presented to the user, and therefore naturally efficient. The "Relational" in the name refers to the fact that the processor represents and operates on data in close conformity with the relational data-base model (Chapter 10); for present purposes, this simply means that the basic data item is a fixed-size record with fields, and that records of the same type are stored together to make up a file.

Figure 9.17 illustrates the RAP architecture. The components of a cell include:

1. A microprocessor designed for data-base operations (the information storage management unit, ISMU, and arithmetic logic unit, ALU).
2. A circulating, sequential, bit-string memory (disk or drum track, charge-coupled device, bubble memory, etc.).
3. Read and Write heads, and a shift-register buffer capable of holding on the order of 1000 bits.

The memory for each cell (which we shall henceforth call a "track") passes by the read head, is transmitted to the buffer, processed (possibly modified), and written back

[28]D. L. Slotnick, "Logic per Track Devices," in *Advances in Computers* (New York: Academic Press, Inc., 1970), pp. 291–296.

[29]E. A. Ozkarahan, S. A. Schuster, and K. C. Smith, "RAP—An Associative Processor for Data Base Management," in *AFIPS Proceedings NCC* **44** (Montvale, N.J.: AFIPS Press, 1975), pp. 379–387.

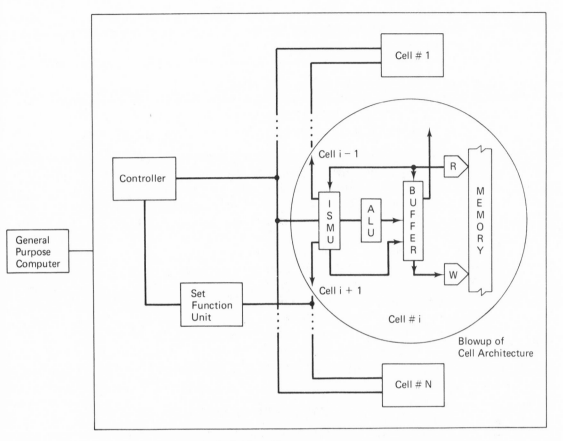

Fig. 9.17　RAP architecture

out. A number of cells connected together and driven in parallel thus provide an associative processing capability. The set function unit carries out statistical functions (e.g., SUM, MAXIMUM) over all the cells.

The basic unit of data stored by RAP is a record, which is simply an item of composite type with fixed-size fields. Records are stored sequentially on tracks, and a file consists of one or more tracks of records of the same type. Associated with each record occurrence is a deletion bit and 4 *mark-bits*. The latter have the functions of the Word-Select and Search-Results Registers shown in Fig. 9.15; certain instructions set mark bits, and others can restrict operation to records with specified bits "on," so the effect is to let one instruction use the results of others.

There are seven categories of instructions:

1. *Selection*—locating and marking subsets of records.
2. *Retrieval*—transferring selected information to the main computer.
3. *Update*—changing field values of records.

4. *Statistics*—such as AVERAGE, COUNT, and MINIMUM.
5. *Schema*—definition of record types.
6. *Insertion and deletion.*
7. *Branching*—for transfer of control, since RAP is a computer capable of processing instruction sequences.

The instructions themselves are fairly close to the level of a data-base query language that might be supplied to a user; the format is

⟨OPCODE⟩ (⟨MARK-BITS⟩) [⟨OBJECT⟩: ⟨QUALIFICATION⟩].

⟨OPCODE⟩ is an operation (one of the above seven types) to be applied to those items in the domain ⟨OBJECT⟩ (either a file or a subset of the fields of a file) that satisfy ⟨QUALIFICATION⟩, which is a Boolean predicate of conditions on mark bits and field values. Certain retrieval and update operations may change mark bits associated with a record; the particular combination to be affected is given by ⟨MARK-BITS⟩.

To illustrate how the RAP commands are tailored to the kind of queries anticipated, we present a program for a sample request. Suppose that CARS(PLATE#, YEAR-OF-MAKE, COLOR, MAKE) is a file with a record describing each vehicle for which a license plate was assigned, and OWNERS(PLATE#, NAME, ADDRESS) gives particulars of each person issued a plate. Then the query "List the name and address of each person who owns a blue AMC car made between 1972 and 1974" can be answered by the following commands:

1. MARK(A)[CARS: (CARS.COLOR = 'BLUE') ∧

   (CARS.MAKE = 'AMC') ∧

   (CARS.YEAR-OF-MAKE ≤ 1974) ∧

   (CARS:YEAR-OF-MAKE ≥ 1972)].

2. CROSS_MARK(B)[OWNERS: OWNERS.PLATE# =

   CARS.PLATE#: CARS.MKED(A)].

3. READ[OWNERS.(NAME, ADDRESS): OWNERS.MKED(B)]

   [WORK AREA].

In command 1, the first mark bit (A) of each record in the CARS file that satisfies the Boolean condition is turned on. Next, the second mark bit (B) is set for records in the OWNERS file whose PLATE# matches a record in the CARS file marked in step 1. Finally, the desired fields of records in the OWNERS file marked during 2 are transferred to a storage area of the main computer.

Most RAP instructions can be executed in one rotation of the cell memories. Notable exceptions are READ, which may need extra revolutions, depending on the number of channels available to transmit data from selected records, and operations such as CROSS_MARK, which use records from one file as a basis for selection from a second. Analytical studies suggest that RAP will perform significantly better than inverted files (implemented on conventional hardware) for associative update and retrieval problems.[30]

The associative processors described here are typical of the machines that might render obsolete many of the data-structuring techniques discussed earlier. Of the two approaches, the logic per track device appears more promising than the associative memory loaded from external storage, since, among other things, it requires less data to be transferred, avoids the problem of fitting various-length records into fixed-size memory words, and is well suited to updating data in place. RAP's instruction set is more powerful than the query language implemented on the STARAN-based system, but it should be remembered that RAP was designed for data-base operations, while the latter is an attempt to test the adaptability of an existing small-capacity associative processor to larger-scale applications. In any case, the factor determining the practicality of associative processors for the problems of interest here is not so much quality of design as economics; component prices are still high for the quantities that would be needed, so software techniques continue to remain important.

9.5 External Sorting

In this section we study the sorting of files that are too large to be accommodated in the internal memory. Auxiliary storage is used not only to store the file, but also as working storage during the sort, and the process is called *external sorting*, as opposed to the internal sorting studied in Section 4.7. Historically, magnetic tapes became available as inexpensive auxiliary storage before drums and disks, and therefore external sorting methods using tapes were developed first. We start by examining these and then look at the modifications that make them applicable for direct-access devices.

An external sort is preceded by an internal sort and consists of several stages. To see how these originate, consider a file to be sorted, consisting of three reels of magnetic tape, with N records in random order. Techniques such as Exchange sort and Quicksort described in Section 4.7 cannot be used directly, because the time to access records on tape is prohibitively long. Assuming at this stage that two tape drives are available, one for input and one for output, and that a block of high-speed storage sufficient to hold B records is available, it is not difficult to see how to get the sort started. Blocks of B records are read from an input tape, sorted by one of the internal methods, and written onto the output. The result will be $\lceil N/B \rceil$ runs, each of length B. By reserving some additional high-speed storage for input and output buffers, input, processing and output can be overlapped. Assuming the usual situation that the speed of the computer is fast enough to process B records in less time than the tape takes to read them, and that more than two tape drives are available so that mounting and dismounting reels are overlapped, then the time to produce the $\lceil N/B \rceil$ runs will just be the time needed to read the three-reel file.

---

[30]E. A. Ozkarahan, S. A. Schuster, and K. C. Sevcik, "Performance Evaluation of a Relational Associative Processor," *ACM Transactions on Database Systems*, **2**, no. 2, (June 1977), 175–195.

To complete the sort, a single run has to be produced from the $\lceil N/B \rceil$ runs, and all the methods for doing this are variations of tape merging. The more tapes available, the higher the order of the merge; at least four drives are generally devoted to this, and eight or ten are not uncommon. The merging proceeds in two stages. In what might be called the *intermediate merge*, each reel is processed individually, using all available tape drives, with the result that there is a single, sequenced run on each of the tapes. In the final stage, called *multireel merging*, the sequenced reels are merged to bring the whole file into order. In the present example, the multireel merge would be a three-way merge, resulting in one, sorted, three-reel file. Multireel merging has already been illustrated in Example 1.9. The optimal tree that specifies the merge strategy can be constructed using Algorithm 3.4 for Huffman encoding, and it is not necessary to say anything more about this last stage of the sort except to note that if a partial reel is produced in the intermediate stage, it contributes a leaf of fractional weight to the multiway merge tree.

There are many variant techniques that can be used to produce the sorted single reels of the intermediate merge. Among the basic methods that will be considered here are:

- The balanced merge (where the available tape drives are divided equally between the input and output).
- Polyphase and cascade merges (where there are $k - 1$ input and one output tapes).
- The oscillating sort (where there is an alternation between external and internal sorting).

Before turning to these, a method of internal sorting called *replacement selection* will be explained. The fewer runs (and the longer the length of the runs) produced by the internal sort, the shorter will be the time needed for later merging. Given a working store sufficient for B records, replacement selection produces runs whose length is larger than B; hence it is a good choice as an internal sorting method.

Replacement Selection: To start, B records are read from the external medium into main memory. In practice B can be quite large, but the method will be illustrated (Table 9.1) for $B = 3$, using the data of the example in Section 4.7. From the B records the one with the smallest key is selected for output. (The selection, for large B, is carried out by constructing a binary selection tree, but this is a detail that can be ignored here.) The selected record is then replaced by the next record from the external store. If the key of this replacing record is greater than that which has first been output, this new record will form part of the run currently being generated. If the replacement is less (as is the case in the first replacement that occurs in Table 9.1, since 146 is less than 711), *stepdown* is said to have occurred, and the new record is held for the next run. Next, the smallest key greater than the one written out is output and replaced. This is repeated until all keys in memory are less than the one that has just been selected. Since none of them can continue the run, a new run is started. The process continues until the whole tape is exhausted. Without replacement, the runs would be of length B; with replacement the average length is $2B$.[31] In the example of Table 9.1, four runs of lengths 3, 10, 1 and 2, respectively, are produced. A feature of replacement selection is that runs already present in the initial file are lengthened, so that advantage is taken of the commonly occurring situation that there is some ordering in the file to start with.

TABLE 9.1 Sorting by replacement selection

Start

Memory

Start															
711	711	802	855	146	802	855	146	302	855	146	302	053	146	302	150
802	146			302		711	053		711	150		711	516		711
855	302			053			150		802	516		802	537		802
146	053			150			516			537		855	569		855
302	150			516			537			569			860		053
053	516			537			569			591			215		146
150	537			569			591			860			988		
516	569			591			860			215			187		
537	591			860			215			988			201		
569	860			215			988			187					
591	215			988			187			201					
860	988			187			201								
215	187			201											
988	201														
187															
201															

Memory | | | | | | | | | | | | | | | End

															End
516	302	150	516	302	537	516	569	537	591	569	537	591	569	860	711
537		711	569		711	591		711	860		711	215		711	802
569		802	591		802	860		802	215		802	988		802	**855**
591		**855**	860		**855**	215		**855**	988		**855**	187		**855**	053
860		053	215		053	988		053	187		053	201		053	146
215		146	988		146	187		146	201		146			146	150
988		150	187		150	201		150			150			150	302
187			201		302			302			302			302	516
201					516			516			516			516	537
											537			537	569
															591
															860
															988
															215
															187
															201

[31]Knuth, *Searching and Sorting*, Sec. 5.4.1.

Balanced Merge: Sorting a single tape reel by a balanced merge is a straightforward application of techniques discussed in Chapter 4. If $2k$ tapes are available, k of the tapes are designated as inputs and k as outputs. The internal sort is designed so that as runs are produced, they are distributed onto each of the k input tapes in turn, so that if there are N runs initially, all the inputs have either $\lfloor N/k \rfloor$ or $\lceil N/k \rceil$ runs. (Their runs can be of varying length.) A k-way merge is performed onto k output tapes, the effect of which is to increase the average run length by a factor k. Assuming that tapes can only be read and written on in the forward direction, all tapes are rewound, the output tapes become the inputs, the old inputs become outputs, and another pass over the file is initiated. (A pass is completed when all the data have been moved.) The merging is repeated until there is a single run on one tape. Only the first and last passes require tape mounts or dismounts.

For N initial runs, the number of passes is $\lceil \log_k N \rceil$. The time for each pass is the time required to write the file on the outputs (equal to the time to write one complete tape if the initial file was a full tape's worth), plus tape rewinding times that will vary slightly from pass to pass.[32] The process is illustrated in Fig. 9.18 for a three-way merge on a file consisting of 23 runs, initially distributed onto tapes T_1, T_2, T_3.

Polyphase and Cascade Merges: In a balanced k-way merge, although k tapes are used during input,[33] at any time only one output is being used. In the polyphase sort, k-way merging is done with $k + 1$ tapes. In the first pass k input tapes, with varying numbers of runs computed in a manner to be described shortly, are merged onto an output, until one of the input tapes is exhausted, completing a *phase*. The output tape is rewound to become an input, the empty input tape becomes the new output, and the merge is continued until a second tape is exhausted and a second phase completed. As before, the pass is complete when all the input tapes have been scanned. When the last input has been exhausted, all tapes are rewound and a new pass is initiated.

If k-way merging is to be done at every pass and phase, the number of runs on each input tape has to satisfy an exact condition. The requirement is illustrated in Table 9.2, for a polyphase merge of order 3, using four tapes. The first row of this table indicates that initially T_1, T_2, and T_3 have 24, 20, and 13 runs, respectively, and that the average lengths of these runs are all the same, say 1 unit. T_4 is initially empty. After the first merge, phases T_1 and T_2 have 11 and 7 runs, T_3 is empty, and T_4 has 13 runs of (average) length 3. T_4 and also T_3 are rewound, and the merge continues with the second phase. At the end of the first pass, T_2 has 4 strings of length 9, T_3 has 3 strings of length 5, T_4 has 2 strings of length 3, T_1 is empty and all tapes have been rewound. The sort is complete at the end of the second pass.

During the first phase of the first pass, the fraction of the file that was processed is

---

[32]Rewinding speed is faster than reading or writing speed. In addition, some tape units have a high-speed rewind which is used if there is enough length of tape to make it worthwhile, and this makes rewinding time somewhat variable.

[33]More precisely, any of the k input buffers may become exhausted first, and thus *any* of the k input tapes may be called upon for the next input block.

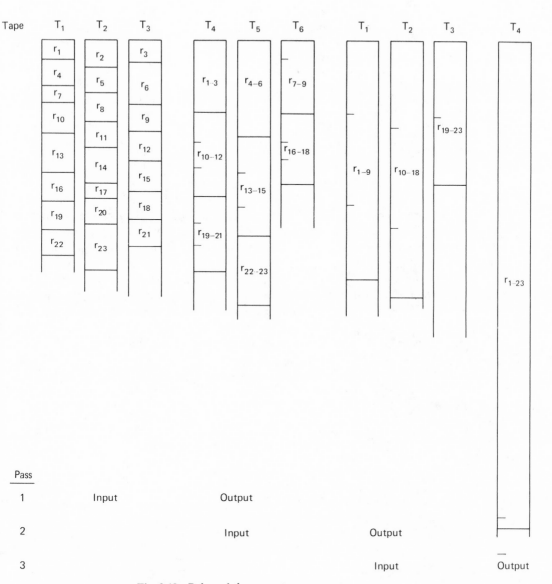

Fig. 9.18 Balanced three-way tape merge

approximately equal to $13 \times 3/(24 + 20 + 13) = 39/57$; on succeeding phases the fractions merged are $35/57$, $36/57$, $34/57$, $31/57$, and $57/57$. Neglecting rewinds, then, the six phases can be regarded as being equivalent to $(39 + 35 + 36 + 34 + 31)/57 \approx$ 4.07 passes over the file. Had the four tapes been used to perform a balanced two-way merge, the number of passes needed for 57 runs would be $\lceil \log 57 \rceil = 6$. Thus the polyphase sort is appreciably more effective.

TABLE 9.2 Polyphase sort on four tapes

Number of Runs

T_1	T_2	T_3	T_4	Pass	Phase	Comments
24^{1*}	20^1	13^1	—			Initial distribution
11^1	7^1	—	13^3	1	1	Rewind T_4, T_3
4^1	—	7^5	6^3		2	Rewind T_3, T_2
—	4^9	3^5	2^3		3	Rewind all tapes
2^{17}	2^9	1^5	—	2	1	Rewind T_1, T_4
1^{17}	1^9	—	1^{31}		3	Rewind T_4, T_5
—	—	1^{57}	—		3	Rewind all tapes

*Note that 24^1 indicates 24 runs of (average) length 1.

To derive the initial run distribution needed for the polyphase merge, we construct a table. The rows, corresponding to the phase, are numbered consecutively from zero, and the column's a, b, c ($a > b > c$) give the number of runs at the beginning of each phase for the tapes being merged. In each row the largest number, a_n, is equal to the smallest number, c_{n+1} of the row that follows (since the first phase of a pass is complete when the tape with the smallest number of rows is exhausted). Table 9.3 shows the values of a_n, b_n, and c_n for the polyphase merge on four tapes just considered.

TABLE 9.3 Run distribution on four-tape polyphase sort

Number of Runs

n	a	b	c	
0	0	0	1	Total Number
1	0	1	0	of Runs
2	1	0	0	Starting Matrix
3	1	1	1	3
4	2	2	1	5
5	4	3	2	9
6	7	6	4	17
7	13	11	7	31
8	24	20	13	57

It is apparent that

$$a_n = c_{n+1}$$
$$b_n = a_{n+1} - a_n \qquad n \geq 3 \tag{9.3}$$
$$c_n = b_{n+1} - a_n.$$

Eliminating the b's and c's from Eq. (9.3) gives

$$a_n = a_{n-1} + a_{n-2} + a_{n-3} \quad \text{where } n \geq 6, a_5 = 4, a_4 = 2, \text{ and } a_3 = 1. \tag{9.4}$$

If we write $a_2 = 1$, $a_1 = 0$, and $a_0 = 0$, Eq. (9.4) holds for $n \geq 3$; that is, we start the a column by writing 0, 0, 1 and then each entry is the sum of the preceding three entries. For the b's and c's also, each entry is the sum of the previous three, with starting values as shown. The starting matrix is the unit matrix, reflected.

This sum property for the number of runs generalizes with the number of tapes, and in a k-way polyphase merge, at each phase the number of runs on each tape is given by

$$f_n^k = f_{n-1}^k \cdots f_{n-2}^k + \cdots + f_{n-k}^k \qquad \text{for } n \geq k. \tag{9.5}$$

For the first tape, having the greatest number of runs,

$$f_{k-1}^k = 1 \quad \text{and} \quad f_n^k = 0 \qquad \text{when } 0 \leq n \leq k-2.$$

The numbers are derived by writing a string of $k-1$ zeros and a single 1, and then each term is the sum of the previous k entries. The runs on the other tapes are calculated similarly, using the reflection of the unit matrix to obtain the starting values.

Equation (9.5) defines the *Fibonocci series of order k*, a more general case of the Fibonocci series of order 2 previously encountered [Eq. (6.17)]. Equation (9.5) governs the number of runs there must be on each tape if the polyphase merge is to perform a k-way merge at all times, and this in turn determines the total number of runs at each phase. For a three-way merge, as seen in Table 9.3, the total number of runs should be a member of the series $(3, 5, \ldots, 57, \ldots)$; for a five-way merge, the total number of runs must be one of $(5, 9, 17, 33, 65, 129, \ldots)$. Given a number of available tapes it is not likely that when merging has to be done, the number of runs will be precisely equal to one of the perfect Fibonocci numbers for the merge order. However, the merge can be effected by adding "dummy" runs as needed, and the question then arises as to how these dummy runs should be allocated to the different tapes. An optimal allocation for the dummies can be calculated (with some difficulty), but it turns out that a good working rule is to distribute the dummies as evenly as possible among the tapes, in which case the increase in sorting time over the optimum is only about 3 per cent.

Although the polyphase merge maximizes the order of the merge at each phase, a significant time is spent in waiting for tapes to rewind (and in mounting and dismounting reels). By adopting different strategies for the merging it is possible to overlap some rewinding time with merging, and in certain cases achieve an overall faster sort. In a *cascade merge*, k-way merging is performed first. When one of the tapes is exhausted, $k-1$ merging is carried out while the tape that has just been written on is rewound; following that, $k-2$ merging is performed, and the process continues in this way, with the merge order being reduced by one on each phase of the pass. Table 9.4 illustrates a cascade merge using four tapes. The initial run distribution is determined by a calculation similar to that for the polyphase sort. Successively, there takes place a three-way merge, a two-way merge, and a one-way merge or copy. (Actually the copies need not be performed.) Most of the time is spent on three-way merging, and during the two-way merges, a tape is rewinding. When sorting is done with six or fewer drives the polyphase merge is faster, but for more drives the cascade sort can be better.[34] More complex strategies that can be utilized to overlap rewind time with other tape operations are described in Knuth.[35]

[34]D. L. Shell, "Optimizing the Polyphase Sort," *Communications of the ACM*, **14**, no. 11 (Nov. 1971), 713–719.

[35]Knuth, *Searching and Sorting*, Sec. 5.4.6.

TABLE 9.4   Cascade sort of four tapes

Number of Runs

T_1	T_2	T_3	T_4	Merge Order	Comments
31^1	25^1	14^1	—		Initial distribution
17^1	11^1	—	14^3	3	
6^1	—	11^2	14^3	2	T_4 rewinding
—	6^1	11^2	14^3	1	Copy; T_3 rewinding
6^6	—	5^2	8^3	3	
6^6	5^5	—	3^3	2	T_1 rewinding
6^6	5^5	3^3	—	1	Copy; T_2 rewinding
3^6	2^5	—	3^{14}	3	
1^6	—	2^{11}	3^{14}	2	T_4 rewinding
—	1^6	2^{11}	3^{14}	1	Copy; T_3 rewinding
1^{31}	—	1^{11}	2^{14}	3	
1^{31}	1^{25}	—	1^{14}	2	T_1 rewinding
1^{31}	1^{25}	1^{14}	—	1	Copy; T_2 rewinding
—	—	—	1^{70}	3	

Oscillating Sort: The only other variation of tape sorting that will be illustrated here is the oscillating sort. It is of interest because it combines internal and external sorting, and because it is applicable when tapes can be read in both the forward and reverse directions, a feature that is often present. When ascending runs are merged onto an output tape, the output can read without rewinding, but the run on it will have its keys in descending sequence. Thus programs using tapes which can be read and written in both directions must be able to handle both ascending and descending sequences of runs.

Table 9.5 illustrates an oscillating sort on four tapes. In the first phase a single run in ascending sequence (represented as 1^1A) is produced from the unsorted input by the internal sort and distributed on each of the first three tapes. The second phase is a merge, done by reading these tapes backward to produce a descending run of length 3 on tape 4. This is followed by another internal sort which produces three runs of (average) length 1, and these runs, in ascending order, are distributed onto T_2, T_3, and

TABLE 9.5   Oscillating sort on four tapes

Number of Runs

Phase	T_1	T_2	T_3	T_4	Comments
1	1^1A	1^1A	1^1A	—	Distribution
2	—	—	—	1^3D	Merge
3	—	1^1A	1^1A	1^3D 1^1A	Distribution
4	1^3D	—	—	1^3D	Merge
5	1^3D 1^1A	—	1^1A	1^3D 1^1A	Distribution
6	1^3D	1^3D	—	1^3D	Merge
7	—	—	1^9A	—	Merge

T_4. Next there is a backward read merge onto T_1, followed by an internal sort, and so on, until the sort is completed. In this example, for nine initial runs the number of merge passes is $\lceil \log_3 9 \rceil + 1 = 4$. If T tape units are available, the number of merge passes with an oscillating sort is, essentially, $\lceil \log_{T-1} N \rceil$; this compares favorably with the balanced merge, which requires $2(T - 1)$ tapes to achieve essentially the same effect.

9.5.1 Sorting with Disks and Drums

Merging is still the general strategy when sorting with disks and drums, and the methods are similar to those just discussed for sorting with tapes, but now the time taken to access a record must be taken into account. There *are* cases when the access time is negligible, for example when a drum is used or when the file resides on one cylinder of a disk that can be reserved for exclusive use by the sort routine. In these situations there is no seek time, and if latency can be eliminated by reading whole tracks, tape methods apply, essentially without change.

As an illustration, suppose that a file containing 640 200-character records is stored, 40 records to a track, on a cylinder of an IBM 3330 disk pack. If two internal work areas, each capable of storing 160 records, are provided, the following is a straightforward way of carrying out the sort.

1. By internal sorting produce 16 runs with 40 records per run.
2. Perform a four-way balanced merge. This will require $\lceil \log_4 16 \rceil = 2$ passes. In the first pass the 16 runs, of length 40, are merged to produce four runs of length 160 written onto the output cylinder. In the second pass, the four runs are merged to produce one run containing 640 records.

Figure 9.19(a) illustrates the arrangement and Fig. 9.19(b) the merging tree. In this scheme reading and writing are not overlapped (this is not possible on the same disk), but processing can be partially overlapped with both. For example, where the first partial run occupying one track is produced during the merge, it can be written onto the disk while the remainder of the run is being generated. Neglecting the nonoverlapped processing, the time for a pass is determined, as it is in a tape sort, by the time taken to transfer the file from disk to memory. Since no seeks are required, this is the length of the file divided by the data transfer rate. For disks, the transfer rate is generally greater than for tapes (although there are high-performance tape units for which the data rates are comparable), in which case the disk sorting speed is correspondingly faster. Assuming, for example, the disk access time for the IBM 3330 quoted earlier, $38.4 + 0.0012n$ ms for n characters, the transfer time for the file (ignoring seeks) is 0.1536 s.

If the order of the merge is increased to eight, two passes are still needed (the second is a two-way merge). Provided that twice the working storage is available, so that eight full-track runs can be accommodated in both the input and output regions, the total sorting time is the same. If the working storage cannot be increased, the eight inputs of the first merge will consist of half a run each, read from half a track. Reading the

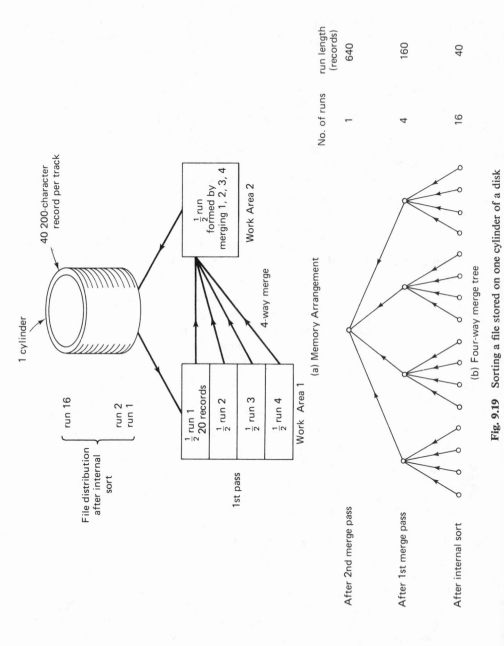

Fig. 9.19 Sorting a file stored on one cylinder of a disk

378

whole run will require two such reads, latency will come into play, and the data transfer time will be increased. The increase will not happen on the second pass (since full tracks are read), but the sorting time for the eight-way merge will be greater than that for the four-way merge. If the merge order is increased to 16, only one pass over the file is required, but the advantage would be offset by still more loss due to latency. For a merge order of two, four passes over the file are needed, but full tracks are always read so that the time would be approximately double that for a merge order of four. In general, if enough working storage is available, increasing the merge order decreases the sorting time, but if the working storage is held constant, latency effects become important when partial tracks are read.

The dependence on the block size of a data transfer becomes even more important when the file becomes too large to be stored on a single cylinder, for in this case seek times enter into the picture. Suppose that the file in the example just considered has 64,000 records. If the block size is 40 records, then 1600 blocks will be accessed each time the file is read or written. Allowing for the fact that the file can be allocated on the disk so that it is read sequentially, in which case only a slight arm movement would be needed to access a new block, the average access time will be less than the random access of 38 ms. Suppose that it is estimated as 15 ms. The file is 100 times larger, but the transfer time of $0.1536 \times 100 = 15.36$ s is less than the seek time of $1600 \times 0.015 = 24$ s. A way to reduce the effect of seeks is to provide more working memory and larger buffers. If the work areas and buffer are doubled in size, half as many seeks are required, but the seek time may still be greater than the data transfer time.

Because of seek time, the dependence on the merge order, m, is complex. If m is increased, so that more runs are being merged, while the memory and buffer sizes are kept constant, a smaller fraction of a run is read in with each block and the effective block size is decreased. This means that more blocks have to be read on each pass, so that the seek time increases. On the other hand, increasing the merge order (generally) decreases the number of passes, and this makes the data transfer time less. The total time for an input of the file will be the sum of seek times plus data transfer times. Since the first of these terms is increasing with merge order, and the second decreasing, the sum will go through a minimum; that is, for a given situation, there will be an optimum order. These balancing considerations are very similar to those we encountered in the optimum page size of a directory, or the optimum order of a B tree. Table 9.6 shows how the seek and transfer times vary as the merge order goes from two to eight for the example. For this table it is assumed that the number of runs produced by the internal sort is 1600. Further, when the merge order is four, the block size is 40 records, so that there are $64,000/4 = 1600$ blocks. For $m = 4$, the number of passes required to complete the sort is $\lceil \log 1000 \rceil = 6$. This means that altogether $32,000 \times 6 = 19,200$ blocks are read in, and at 15 ms average per seek, the block seek time is 144 s. The time to read the file of $64,000 \times 200$ characters once at a speed of 0.0012 ms per character, is 15.36 s, so the total transfer time (due to six passes) is 92.2 s, and the total time for seek plus transfer is 238 s. The numbers in the other rows of Table 9.6 are calculated in a similar way.

TABLE 9.6   Disk file transfer times for different merge orders

Merge Order m	Number of Passes[1]	Block Size[2] (Records)	Number of Blocks Read[3]	Seek Time[4] (s)	Data Transfer Time[5] (s)	Total Transfer Time[6] (s)
2	11	80	8,800	132	169	301
4	6	40	9,600	144	92	236
8	4	20	12,800	192	61	253
16	3	10	19,200	288	46	334

The file contains 64,000 200-character records.
The internal sort produces 1600 runs.
The memory is 320 records.
The (average) disk access time is $(15 + 0.0012n)$ ms for a transfer of n characters.

[1] Number of passes $= \lceil \log_m 1600 \rceil$.
[2] Block size $=$ memory size$/2m = 160/m$ records.
[3] Number of blocks read $=$ number of blocks/pass $\times$ number of passes
$\qquad\qquad\qquad\qquad\quad = 400m \times$ number of passes.
[4] Seek time $= 0.015$ s $\times$ number of blocks moved.
[5] Data transfer time $= 15.36$ s $\times$ number of passes.
[6] Total transfer time $=$ seek time $+$ data transfer time.

The total sort time will depend on the extent to which processing can be overlapped with reading and writing. To a reasonable approximation, process time can be taken to depend only on the file length, in which case it will be the same for all merge orders. With these assumptions, Table 9.6 shows how the sort time fails to decrease monotonically as the merge order is increased. Here four is the best value shown, but a merge order of five is actually best.

Based on the argument just given, it is not difficult to obtain an expression for the sort time of a disk merge in terms of the file parameters (N, the number of records; L, the length per record in characters), the configuration parameters (M, the size of high-speed memory; a and b, the constants in the equation for disk access), and the sort tree chosen. Given these parameters, the optimum merge tree for different values of merge order m can be constructed systematically using the principle that every subtree of an optimal tree must itself be optimal.[36] The validity of these calculations depends very much on the validity of the assumptions (e.g., the extent to which an average seek time is a useful measure), the extent to which average is acceptable for the length of initial runs, and so on. More detailed treatments of the calculations for disk sorting are to be found in Lorin (1975) and Black.[37] However, the examples given here illustrate how the features of secondary storage considered at the beginning of this chapter—data transfer rates, seek times, and blocking factors—affect the sort, and how these, together with estimates about the file makeup, can be used to estimate sort times and design efficient methods for external sorting.

[36] Knuth, *Searching and Sorting*, Sec. 5.4.9.
[37] N. A. Black, "Optimum Merging from Mass Storage," *Communications of the ACM*, **13**, no. 12 (Dec. 1970), 745–749.

9.5.2 Sort Generators

Sorting is both amenable to mathematical analysis and finds important everyday application. A consequence is that sorting programs have been highly developed, and it is seldom that a programmer is required to write a sort or merge program for himself. The almost invariable situation is that he is expected to draw upon a library program and provide information that will enable the program to work well. This is true for internal sorting, where programs such as Quicksort are commonly available, and even more so for external sorting. For both, the best program is very much dependent on such factors as file makeup, hardware configuration, and available high-speed storage.

Packaged sorting programs are of the type known as *generators*. Given configuration and file parameters supplied by the user, the program generates a particular sort/merge routine for the application out of prefabricated program modules. Sort generators have been available since the early 1960s, and they have evolved to the point where they are capable of being adapted to most needs. One such generator, the IBM OS Sort/Merge,[38] will be described briefly to give an indication of how sorting is actually done currently.

As illustrated in Fig. 9.20, the sort/merge program, SM1, consists of four phases: a definition/optimization phase during which the program is generated, a sort phase for the internal sort, the intermediate merge for carrying out all but the last merge of the external sort, and the final merge, distinguished because it is often combined with user-specified actions. To ensure that SM1 will be applicable in a wide variety of situations, a large number of options are incorporated in it; for example:

- Keys, represented in EBCDIC or ASCII character sets, can extend over several fields. When keys are complex, they are extracted and grouped into a single field to simplify comparisons.
- Different hardware configurations can be accommodated. These include different partition sizes of the internal store for use as buffers and working space, either tapes or disks for intermediate storage, multiple channels, the presence or absence of channel switches which allow the intermediate storage to be attached to different channels, and so on.
- Besides required data (e.g., the device location for the input and output files, the description of the key) there is provision for accepting optional data which

[38]The program product is described in a number of manuals which are revised periodically as improvements are incorporated. For the user, the following four provide the essential information:

		Program Version		
Manual Type	Name	Number	Manual Number	Date
General information	OS Sort/Merge	5734-SM1	GC33-4022-1	3rd ed., Apr. 1973
Programmer's guide	OS Sort/Merge	5734-SM1	SC33-4007-5	6th ed., Dec. 1975
System information	OS Sort/Merge	5734-SM1	SC33-4004	
Program logic	OS/US/Sort-Merge	5740-SM1	LY33-8042-4	5th ed., Mar. 1976

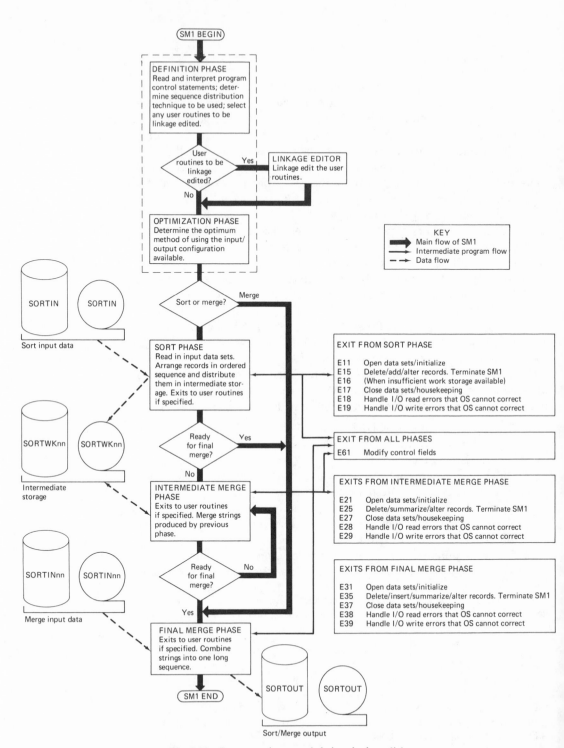

Fig. 9.20 Program phases and their exits in a disk sort program (Courtesy of International Business Machines Corporation)

382

the program can use to optimize the sort when possible. Examples of the latter type of data are the file record description (number of records, record size, whether fixed or varying, and in the latter case the maximum, minimum and modal sizes), and blocking factors.

- A variety of sorting techniques are built in, and the program performs calculations and consults tables to choose which is best. The internal sort is by replacement selection (combined, possibly in later versions of SM-1, with a technique for combining strings called a "peerage" sort). When intermediate storage is on tape, a choice is made among a balanced merge, polyphase merging, and an oscillating merge for the external phase; when disk is available, a choice is made among a balanced merge, a peerage merge, and "crisscross," a variation of the oscillating merge.[39] The programmer may force a particular method to be used, although it is not advisable to do so unless there is good reason. Advice is given on how to estimate and assign buffers, but the program will do so automatically if no instructions are given to it.
- There are some 20 program exits which permit the user to insert own-coding routines at numerous points (see Fig. 9.20). Such tasks as handling I/O errors not correctable by the operating system, selection and editing of records during input or output, and modification of the key fields can be specified.

Comprehensive tables allow the user to estimate the sorting times for varying configurations records and file size, and memory space. Some representative times which illustrate the dependencies are shown in Table 9.7. Interpolation can be used to estimate times for parameter values not in the tables.

In conclusion, it can be said that for both internal sorting, when the number of records being sorted is small, and for external sorting of files, the best sorting method is highly dependent on the file structure and available hardware. With an understanding of the various techniques it is possible to aid standardized sort generators in selecting good methods.

Exercises

1. Suppose that in an application the (average) time to process a 100-character record is 250 μs and that the calling sequence and initialization for the record processing program 6 ms. Determine the optimum blocking factor, so that processing is overlapped with I/O when the file is stored on:
   (a) The IBM 3330 disk store.
   (b) The IBM 2305 drum.
2. What does the indexed sequential "file" of Fig. 9.6 look like after each step in the following sequence of insertions and deletions?
   (a) Insert "*wem*".
   (b) Insert "*zil*".
   (c) Delete "*xim*".
   (d) Delete "*wul*".
   (e) Insert "*yon*".

[39]For details on the crisscross merge and peerage sort, see Lorin, *Sorting and Sort Systems.*

TABLE 9.7 Estimated sort/merge times on the IBM 370 Model 155*

Main Storage (bytes)	Record Length (bytes)	Auxiliary Storage				Estimated Sort/Merge Time (minutes) File Size (megabytes)			
		Devices	Model	Number of Channels	Switching	0.6	2.4	9.6	38.4
47,000	20–39	4 tapes	3420–7	1	No	0.8	2.4	8.9	
47,000	20–39	4 tapes	3420–7	2	Yes	0.8	2.4	8.5	
47,000	20–39	10 tapes	3420–7	2	Yes	1.0	1.7	5.5	
47,000	20–39	6 disks	3330	1	No	1.0	2.3	11	
200,000	20–39	4 tapes	3420–7	1	No	0.8	2.4	79	
200,000	20–39	10 tapes	3420–7	2	Yes	0.7	1.5	4.6	
20,0000	20–39	6 disks	3330	1	No	0.6	1.0	3.3	
200,000	160–319	6 disks	3330	1	No		1.0	3.4	12
404,000	160–319	10 tapes	3420–7	2	Yes		1.0	4.0	17
404,000	160–319	6 disks	3330	1	No		1.0	2.5	9.9

*Input/output block size, 4800 bytes; input medium, magnetic tape, Model 3420–7.
Source: IBM General Information Manual GC33-4022-1. See footnote 38.

3. What does the B tree of Fig. 9.7 look like after each step in the following sequence of insertions and deletions?
   (a) Insert "*yin*".
   (b) Insert "*xol*".
   (c) Insert "*xul*".
   (d) Delete "*xim*".
4. (a) Will insertion of a key that has just been deleted from a B tree always restore the original tree? Justify your answer. (b) Why might the restoration property be useful?
5. In Section 9.3.2, the optimal size in characters, $m \cdot w$, for a B-tree node, was close to the track capacity for an IBM 3330 disk, and also for an IBM 2314 pack. Look up the relevant times for the following devices, and see if the same is true.
   (a) IBM 2311 disk.
   (b) IBM 2305-II drum.
   (c) Digital RS03 fixed-head disk.
   (d) CDC 853 disk.
6. Compare bit maps to inverted files with respect to the following operations:
   (a) Change of field value in a record.
   (b) Addition of a record.
   (c) Deletion of a record.
7. Apply the run-length compression scheme described on page 352 to year-of-make and color fields of the bit map in Fig. 9.11. (Remember that the columns are scanned.) What savings, if any, are effected?
8. Suppose that the bit map in Fig. 9.11 is compressed by OR'ing columns together as follows:

Year-of-Make	4 columns into one
Color	2 columns into one
Make	3 columns into one
Body-Style	2 columns into one.

   (a) What does the resulting map look like?
   (b) What percentage of false drops can we *expect* (assuming uniform distribution of each attribute value throughout the file) when the compressed map is used to answer the following requests:
   (1) Find all cars made in 1972.
   (2) Find 1975 cars which are white or yellow.
   (3) Find all blue 1974 AMC cars.
   (4) Find all white Ford hard-tops made in 1971, 1972 or 1973.
   (c) How many false drops *actually* result from the requests above?
9. What does the 4-d tree of Fig. 9.14 look like after each step in the following sequence of insertions and deletions?
   (1) Insert ⟨1970, green, Ford, h.t.⟩.
   (2) Delete record 1 (the root).
   (3) Insert ⟨1970, white, GMC, sedan⟩.
   (4) Delete record 9 (⟨1976, green, GMC, sedan⟩).
10. Look up the rewinding times for a typical tape drive (e.g., the IBM 2420-5). Assuming that there are initially 500 runs on a full reel of 2400 feet, calculate:
   (a) The number of passes for a four-way balanced merge.

(b) The read/write time for each pass.

(c) The rewinding time for each pass.

11. Develop the equations that govern the initial run distributions for k-way cascade merging.

12. Construct a table that shows, for orders up to 10 of a polyphase merge, the number of runs necessary to have a maximum order merge at every phase (see the last column of Table 9.3).

13. Construct an optimal merge tree, using three-way merging, for a tape file consisting of 11 complete reels and 3 reels each 3/15 full.

14. (a) Estimate the influence of the latency effects on the merge order when sorting the 640-record file of Section 9.5.2, assuming that the working storage is kept constant.

    (b) Does the sort time go through a minimum as the order of the merge is increased?

15. Suppose that P, the number of passes required to carry out a disk merge using an optimal tree, is available from a table. Give an expression for the merge time in terms of the parameters N, M, L, a, b, P (see page 380). Show how to calculate the table for determining P (see footnote 36).

Bibliography

General references for files are Martin (1975) and Wiederhold (1977). Knuth (1973) contains material on B trees, external hashing, and in particular, external sorting and multiple-attribute retrieval. For a somewhat device-oriented coverage of Sections 9.1 through 9.3, see IBM Form GC20-1649-8 *Introduction to IBM Direct Access Storage Devices and Organization Methods* (1975).

Information on channels, buffers, paging, and other operating system and hardware features can be found in Madnick and Donovan (1974). Olson (1969) gives an introduction to hashing as it applies to files, while Severance and Duhne (1976) provide a useful reference for the practitioner. Behymer et al. (1974) compare the indexed-sequential organization to hashing.

A survey of associative and parallel processing hardware is given by Thurber and Wald (1975). Associative processors designed for data-base management are the subject of Moulder (1973), Ozkarahan et al. (1975), and Lin et al. (1976).

Cardenas (1973) discussed evaluation and selection of file organizations, while Cardenas (1975) looks at the performance of inverted files, two aspects of file design not discussed here.

Lorin (1975) is a good reference on sorting.

The references cited here and in the footnotes, together with their bibliographies, should provide an entry to the extensive (and growing) literature on files.

BEHYMER, J. A., R. A. OGILVIE, and A. G. MERTEN, "Analysis of Indexed-Sequential and Direct Access File Organizations," in *Proceedings of ACM SIGMOD Workshop on Data Description, Access and Control*, Randall Rustin, ed. New York: Association for Computing Machinery, 1974, pp. 389–418.

CARDENAS, A. F., "Evaluation and Selection of File Organization—A Model and System." *Communications of the ACM*, **16**, no. 9 (Sept. 1973), 540–548.

CARDENAS, A. F., "Analysis and Performance of Inverted Data Base Structures." *Communications of the ACM*, **18**, no. 5 (May 1975), 253–263.

Introduction to IBM Direct Access Storage Devices and Organization Methods, Form GC20-1649-8, Dec. 1975.

KNUTH, D. E., *The Art of Computer Programming*, Vol. 3, *Searching and Sorting*. Reading, Mass.: Addison-Wesley Publishing Company, Inc., 1973.

LIN, C. S., D. C. P. SMITH, and J. M. SMITH, "The Design of a Rotating Associative Memory for Relational Database Applications." *ACM Transactions on Database Systems*, **1**, no. 1 (Mar. 1976), 53–65.

LORIN, H., *Sorting and Sort Systems*. Reading, Mass.: Addison-Wesley Publishing Company, Inc., 1975.

MADNICK, S. E., and J. J. DONOVAN, *Operating Systems*, New York: McGraw-Hill Book Company, 1974.

MARTIN, J. A., *Computer Data-Base Organization*, 2nd ed., Englewood Cliffs, N.J.: Prentice-Hall, Inc., 1977.

MOULDER, R., "An Implementation of a Data Management System on an Associative Processor." *AFIPS Proceedings NCC* **42**. Montvale, N.J.: AFIPS Press, 1973, pp. 171–176.

OLSON, C. A., "Random Access File Organization for Indirectly Address Records." *Proceedings of the ACM National Conference*, 1969, pp. 539–549.

OZKARAHAN, E. A., S. A. SCHUSTER, and K. C. SMITH, "RAP—An Associative Processor for Data Base Management." *AFIPS Proceedings NCC* **44**. Montvale, N.J.: AFIPS Press, 1975, pp. 379–387.

SEVERANCE, D., and R. DUHNE, A Practitioner's Guide to Addressing Algorithms." "*Communications of the ACM* **19**, no. 6 (June 1976), 314–326.

THURBER, K. J., and L. D. WALD, "Associative and Parallel Processors." *ACM Computing Surveys*, **7**, no. 4 (Dec. 1975), 215–255.

WIEDERHOLD, G., *Database Design*, New York: McGraw-Hill Book Company, 1977.

chapter 10

Data-Base Models

In applications where computers are used most widely—those in business data processing—data organization and management are of paramount importance. In these situations the mathematical procedures are usually simple compared to those found in engineering or science (although the decision paths for determining which procedures to apply can be complicated), but the data is typically large in volume and complex in the sense that it exhibits numerous and varied relationships. All of the techniques we have studied for structuring and organizing stored data find use in business data processing; many of them were developed in the context of these applications. Some aspects are particularly important. For example, it is a major task to assemble the files and get the data correct, for premium accounting in life insurance or for maintaining driver license records in a government motor vehicle office. The lifetime of such files is considerably larger than the life of the usual computer or its software. It therefore becomes critically important to develop methods of referring to files and their contents, and of expressing operations on file data in ways that are not tied to whatever computer system is available. The separation between logical structure as embedded in the data type, and storage structure as implemented by the mapping into multilevel storage, must be as great as possible. There is still another reason why the distinction is important. Most file users are not programmers and they are not knowledgeable about software or file organization. The more it is possible to separate the logical concepts relating to the application from the physical concepts relating to the computer operation, the greater are the possibilities for wide-scale use of computers.

In this chapter we consider methodologies, all of them in a state of current development, for managing data bases—large files collections designed to be accessible to many users for multiple purposes. There are essential features of these systems we shall *not* discuss. For example, techniques to control who can access and change records have to be established, and safety measures for reconstructing files in case of loss or damage are important. We focus our attention on how the data is described and structured, and how retrieval, searching, and updating procedures can be specified in ways which are as independent of the computer system as possible and yet which can be interpreted by the system so that implementation is effected. Most of the concepts we shall encounter have already been presented in earlier chapters, although sometimes the terminology is new. In fact, the principal point in this chapter is to illustrate how data-base management systems are the logical extension of the techniques for defining and handling data types and structures presented in earlier chapters.

One of the earliest attempts to enable a relatively unsophisticated user to produce reports from a file and update fileds, without writing I/O programs and doing complicated formatting, was the Report Program Generator (RPG).[1] The desired results were described on a set of tabular, preprinted forms, which were subsequently key-punched and run. (Languages such as RPG, in which the programmer specifies the results of a computation, rather than the sequence of steps required to carry it out, are called *nonprocedural*). RPG (in modern versions) is still widely used, but it has the disadvantage that it provides virtually no *physical data independence*—that is, insulation of user programs from the way in which data are stored. In fact, it requires a complete physical description of each file used in a run—including such details as the name of the device on which the file resides, and the relationship between logical and physical records. This information is irrelevant to the subject of a query, and its presence ensures that requests must be modified to suit the slightest changes in the implementation.

The Mark IV File Management System[2] retains the (nonprocedural) form of RPG, while providing a considerable degree of physical data independence as well. This is accomplished by maintaining a description of each file (a *data dictionary*), including the information necessary to map it onto storage. To extract data from a file, the user need only know the field names, which can be found by consulting an abbreviated, readable printout of the dictionary. At execution time, the system uses the dictionary to resolve these names to storage addresses. Therefore, as long as the directory is kept up to date, changes in storage details will not affect user programs.

Mark IV is primarily designed for sequential processing of files; it can be used to determine relationships between records in separate files, but the procedure is awkward and requires a fairly skilled user. Yet there are many situations where connections between records of different types are as important as the contents of the records themselves. This is natural when records represent real-world objects such as people, houses, and cities, among which relationships are significant. A collection of stored

[1] *IBM System/360 Operating System RPG Language Specifications*, IBM Form GC24-3337, March 1970.

[2] *Mark IV File Management System General Information Manual*, (Canoga Park, Calif.: Informatics, Inc.).

data modeling some aspect of the real world is called a *data base;* software facilities that enable users to manipulate relationships among data items (as well as the item contents) are called *data-base management systems* (DBMS).

10.1 DBMS Concepts

To understand data-base management systems, it is helpful to review some of the terms we have used earlier to describe stored information. A data base contains two kinds of information: descriptions of entities and representations of relationships.

An *entity* is an object that has independent existence, in the context of the application for which the data base is intended. Figure 10.1 illustrates the entities (or more accurately, entity *types*), which might appear in a university data base, together with relationships among them. An entity is described by a set of characteristics, or *attributes.* An attribute may be a property that is meaningless by itself (e.g., *age* of student, *capacity* of room), or it may be an object that could be an entity, but whose sole purpose in the present context is descriptive (e.g., *parent* of student).

A *relationship* is a named association among sets of entities. In Fig. 10.1, a directed arc between two entity types denotes a binary relationship between a single entity of the source, or *parent* type, and a set of entities of the target, or *child* type. For example, the arrow (labeled "advises") from staff to students reflects the fact that a staff member may advise several students. Relationships of this kind are said to be 1:*n*, or *hierarchical*. The pair of arrows going from students to courses and back indicates that a student can take several courses while, conversely, a course can have several students

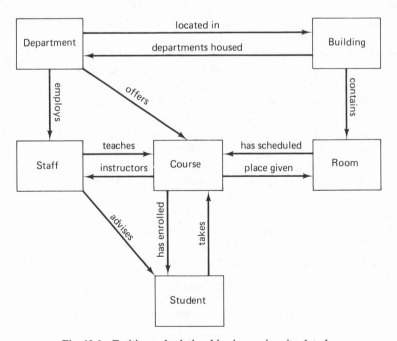

Fig. 10.1 Entities and relationships in a university data base

enrolled in it. This type of relationship is called *m:n*, or *many to many*. Finally, there are 1:1 binary relationships, in which both entity sets can have only one member. These are rarer in data bases than the 1:*n* and *m:n* kinds, because when such relationships exist, there is a tendency to make one entity an attribute of the other. If we allow a staff member to advise at most one student, and a student to have only one advisor, then "advises" becomes a 1:1 relationship between staff and students. Note that there can be more than one relationship between two entity types; for example, students could tutor courses as well as take them.

The relationships illustrated in Fig. 10.1 are binary, but there are many instances where information can only be expressed with more general ones. For example, the fact that a student takes a particular course in a particular room is a ternary relationship among the entities student, course, and room, which is not derivable from Fig. 10.1; following the "takes" and "place given" arcs from student to room in that figure simply produces the set of rooms where a student could take a course. A meaningful ternary relationship cannot always be derived from the composition of two binary ones.

A data-base management system maintains a data structure representation of entities and relationships. The storage structure is hidden from the user as much as possible, and if insulation is complete, the DBMS is said to provide physical data independence. The logical structure, or *data model*, together with its operation set, constitutes the interface through which the data base is accessed. If the interface permits the user to operate entirely in terms of the way he views the information, and imposes on him no artificial structure on the data that is not present in the real world, then the DBMS is said to provide *logical data independence*. Logical data independence is best illustrated with reference to specific data models, so we defer further discussion of it to the sections that follow.

Data-base management systems employ the basic techniques for mapping information into storage, and for providing access to it, that we discussed in Chapters 2 and 9. Entities are represented by physically grouping attribute values together to form records. Relationships are expressed through *proximity* (e.g., records in the same block are related), *position* (e.g., the *i*th record in file A is related to the *i*th one in file B), and *pointer mechanisms* (e.g., pointer values and hash tables). What characterizes DBMS, and what we shall concentrate on the rest of this chapter, is the data model they support. Currently, there are two main approaches to data modeling, *network* and *relational*. In the network model (to be described), entities and relationships appear explicitly. Entities are represented by records, and relationships by named *links* which, in the most general form, are *m:n* mappings connecting sets of records together. Figure 10.1 can be regarded as the schematic of a network data base. A special case of networks occurs when all the links are 1:*n* and directed away from a *root* record type; this restricted model is called *hierarchical* and is the one supported by the one of the most widely used DBMS's, IBM's Information Management System (IMS).[3]

---

[3]*Information Management System/360 Version 2, General Information Manual*, IBM Form GH20-0765.

In the relational model, there is no logical distinction between entities and relationships. The basic element is a relation in the mathematical sense—a set of *n*-tuples—and it is a matter of interpretation whether a relation represents a set of entities or a relationship. On the one hand, a tuple can be regarded as a record, with each component assuming the role of a field; then the relation appears as a table in which the rows represent entities, and the columns, attributes. Alternately, each tuple component can identify a row of some other relation, so that a relation with pointers as column values functions as an *n*-ary association among entity sets.

Figure 10.2(a) shows relations for the entities "student" and "course." The columns are assigned *role names* to indicate the attributes they represent, and the relation is named as well. Figure 10.2(b) is an *m:n* binary relation depicting enrollment of students in courses; it relies on the fact that each STUDENT# value identifies a unique tuple in the STUDENT relation, as does the pair of values DEPT, COURSE# in the COURSE relation.

76001	Macdonald	John	1
76086	Smith	Michael	1
77016	Tremblay	Jean	2
77918	Wilson	David	2
78195	Richard	Marc	3
79322	Jones	Alan	4

ENG	100	English Composition
FRE	100	French Composition
GER	200	Modern Authors
HIS	430	20th Century Russia
STA	300	Sampling Techniques

STUDENT (Student, Last-Name, First-Name, Year)   COURSE (Dept, Course #, Title)

(a) Relations describing entities

76001	ENG	100
76001	FRE	100
76066	ENG	100
76086	FRE	100
77016	ENG	100
77016	GER	200
77918	STA	300
78195	HIS	430
79322	GER	200
79322	HIS	430

ENROLLED (Student #, Dept, Course #)

(b) Relation for enrollment of students in courses

Fig. 10.2 Relations describing entities and associations

The operation set of the data model is presented to the user as a *data manipulation language* (DML). The DML may be embedded in a more general *host language* (e.g., PL/I, COBOL), or it may be a self-contained, English-like *query language*. The nature of the DML generally reflects the underlying model type. The basic relational operations (to be described below) are set-oriented, and any information desired can be specified by algebraic expressions involving relations and operators. Relational DML's are built on these operations and hence tend to be descriptive or nonprocedural in format. Networks, on the other hand, are generalized graphs with information represented by the links as well as the nodes. Accordingly, network DML's provide instructions for traversing paths through the network to locate desired records and to determine relationships that connect records together. The process of extracting data by following chains through a network data base has been termed *navigation*.[4]

When the DML is embedded in a compiled language, the user must supply definitions of the data model elements referenced (e.g., the relations), for the same reason that he must declare host language variables. The source of these definitions is the *schema*, a description of the data base as structured by the data model. If the model is relational, the schema contains definitions for all the relations, if network, declarations for all record and link types. The schema may also contain information on storage mapping (e.g., whether records of a given type are to be ordered on a field), access paths (e.g., whether a record is accessed sequentially, or directly, by key), and security (e.g., which users have access to certain information, which are allowed to modify the data base).

The schema is defined using a *data definition language* (DDL), which may be self-contained or may be implemented through an existing programming language. The DML user also employs a data definition language to describe the portion of the data base relevant to his application; if the DML is embedded in a host language, this user-DDL is likely to be an extension of the declaration facilities of the host. The description written in a user-DDL is called a *subschema*, and with current DBMS, the model described by the subschema must be of the same type as the one defined by the schema; moreover, it cannot introduce information not derivable from the schema. It is expected that future DBMS will relax the first restriction somewhat and allow some choice in the type of model that a user can specify. The model defined by the subschema is sometimes called the *data sub model* (if it is the same type), and also the *user view*.

The remainder of this chapter is a discussion of the network and relational models of data. We point out the main features of these models, and indicate how data manipulation and definition are carried out in systems which support them. The description is not comprehensive; rather it is intended to illustrate the data-base concepts mentioned in this section and to emphasize the logical nature of data, as opposed to its physical organization. For detailed coverage of data models and data-base management systems, the reader is referred to the Bibliography at the end of the chapter.

[4]C. W. Bachman, "The Programmer as Navigator," *Communications of the ACM*, **16**, no. 11 (Nov. 1973), 653–658.

10.2 Network Data-Base Management Systems

In 1971, the Data Base Task Group (DBTG) of the Conference on Data Systems and Languages (CODASYL) published specifications for a network data model. Although the report did not represent a standard, it has become the basis for a number of implementations, and the term "DBTG system" has become synonymous with "network DBMS." Accordingly, we shall base our discussion of networks on the DBTG proposals.

The DBTG report contains specifications for three data languages: one for defining the schema, one for defining subschemas, and one for data manipulation. The schema DDL is self-contained and is used to define record and link types and to supply information about storage mapping and data security. The subschema DDL and DML are intended for use with a host language; in the case of the Report, that language is COBOL. The subschema is a proper subset of the schema, in that it cannot contain information not explicitly defined in the latter; in particular, links cannot be introduced if they are not declared in the schema.

The basic elements in the DBTG model, corresponding to entities and relationships, are, respectively, *record types* and *sets*. A record type is a named collection of fields. Each field may be primitive or composite (in the sense of Chapter 2), and may be allowed to repeat an arbitrary number of times. The term "record" will be used to denote either "record type" or "instance of record type." when the meaning is clear from context.

A *DBTG set* is a named $1:n$ link among record types. It is declared to have an *owner* record type, and one or more *member* record types, with the restriction that the owner must be of different type from the members.[5] A particular instance of a set is called a *set occurrence* and consists of exactly one owner record, together with zero or more records of the member types.

The linking function of a set is realized by three basic operations. For each set occurrence, it is possible to

1. Retrieve the members, knowing the location of the owner.
2. Retrieve the owner, given a member.
3. Retrieve a fellow member, given a member.

These provide the basic capabilities needed to traverse paths through the network. If a record were a member of more than one occurrence of the same set, however, the determination of owner in (2) would be ambiguous: similarly, if a record were permitted to own more than one occurrence of a given set, (1) would not be well defined. Accordingly, *records are not allowed to participate in more than one occurrence of a given set.*

10.2.1 DBTG Data Definition

To show how record types and sets are formally defined in a DBTG system, we present a schema for a portion of a university data base, containing information

---

[5]The term "set" is a poor choice, since a DBTG set is not a set in the mathematical sense but a *composite data type*, constructed from record types.

about students and courses (Tables 10.1 and 10.2). Each course is represented by a COURSE record, which might contain such information as course code, title, pre- and co-requisites; similarly, each student is represented by a STUDENT record containing personal information. Courses are offered in sections, and it is these which students are enrolled in (and which instructors teach); accordingly, there is a SECTION record for each section, giving timetable information. For brevity, only two or three fields are actually defined for each record type in Table 10.1; in a real schema the declarations would be longer.

The relationship between COURSE and SECTION records is $1:n$, since each course has zero or more sections (zero if not offered), and a section is only meaningful in that it represents an offering of a single course. To model this, a set is defined with COURSE as its owner and SECTION records as its members. The relationship between students and sections is $m:n$, because students can take several courses (and so will be enrolled in one of the sections associated with each course); conversely, a

TABLE 10.1　Record type definitions for UNIVERSITY schema

```
1.  SCHEMA NAME IS UNIVERSITY.
2.  AREA NAME IS COURSE-AREA.
3.  AREA NAME IS STUDENT-AREA.

4.  RECORD NAME IS STUDENT;
5.        LOCATION MODE IS CALC USING STUDENT-NO
                DUPLICATES ARE NOT ALLOWED;
6.        WITHIN STUDENT-AREA.
7.        02 STUDENT-NO; TYPE IS FIXED DECIMAL 5.
8.        02 STUDENT-NAME;
9.              03 LAST-NAME; TYPE IS CHARACTER 20.
10.             03 FIRST-NAME; TYPE IS CHARACTER 10.
11.       02 YEAR; TYPE IS FIXED DECIMAL 1.

12. RECORD NAME IS COURSE;
13.       LOCATION MODE IS CALC USING DEPT, COURSE-NO
                DUPLICATES ARE NOT ALLOWED;
14.       WITHIN COURSE-AREA.
15.       02 COURSE-ID;
16.             03 DEPT; TYPE IS CHARACTER 3.
17.             03 COURSE-NO; TYPE IS FIXED DECIMAL 3.
18.       02 TITLE; TYPE IS CHARACTER 20;

19. RECORD NAME IS SECTION;
20.       LOCATION MODE IS VIA COURSE-SECTION SET
21.       WITHIN AREA OF OWNER.
22.       02 SECTION-NO; TYPE IS CHARACTER 2.
23.       02 SECTION-SCHEDULE; OCCURS 3 TIMES.
24.             03 BLDG; TYPE IS CHARACTER 2.
25.             03 ROOM; TYPE IS FIXED DECIMAL 3.
26.             03 DAY; TYPE IS CHARACTER 3.
27.             03 TIME; TYPE IS FIXED DECIMAL 2.

28. RECORD NAME IS ENROLLED;
29.       LOCATION MODE IS VIA STUDENT-ENROLLED SET;
30.       WITHIN AREA OF OWNER.
31.       02 GRADE; TYPE IS CHARACTER 1.
```

TABLE 10.2 Set definitions for UNIVERSITY schema

1. SET-NAME IS COURSE-SECTION;
2. OWNER IS COURSE.
3. ORDER IS PERMANENT SORTED BY DEFINED KEYS;
4. MEMBER IS SECTION MANDATORY AUTOMATIC
5.   KEY IS ASCENDING SECTION-NO
6.   DUPLICATES ARE NOT ALLOWED;
7.   SET SELECTION IS THRU COURSE-SECTION
8.   OWNER IDENTIFIED BY CALC-KEY.

9. SET NAME IS STUDENT-ENROLLED;
10. OWNER IS STUDENT
11. ORDER IS LAST;
12. MEMBER IS ENROLLED MANDATORY AUTOMATIC;
13.   SET SELECTION IS THRU STUDENT-ENROLLED
14.   OWNER IDENTIFIED BY CALC-KEY.

15. SET NAME IS SECTION-ENROLLED;
16. OWNER IS SECTION.
17. ORDER IS NEXT;
18. MEMBER IS ENROLLED MANDATORY AUTOMATIC;
19.   SET SELECTION FOR SECTION-ENROLLED
20.   IS THRU COURSE-SECTION OWNER IDENTIFIED
21.   BY CALC-KEY
22.   THEN THRU SECTION-ENROLLED WHERE OWNER
23.   IDENTIFIED BY SECTION-NO.

section will have several students enrolled in it. The obvious representation of this link would employ two sets, one with owner STUDENT and member SECTION and the other with SECTION records as the owner type, and STUDENT records the members. The problem with this is that as there is exactly one STUDENT record per student, and one SECTION record per section offered, all students taking a section would have to be owners of that SECTION record, and all sections in which a student is enrolled would have to own the record for that student. Since both situations violate the abovementioned restriction that a record participate in at most one occurrence of a given set, some other way of implementing many-to-many relationships is needed.

One solution is to introduce an intermediate record type, ENROLLED, and two sets, STUDENT-ENROLLED and SECTION-ENROLLED. Each STUDENT record is the owner of a STUDENT-ENROLLED set occurrence, containing an ENROLLED record for each section taken. At the same time, each of those ENROLLED records is a member in a SECTION-ENROLLED set occurrence, owned by the SECTION in which the student owner is enrolled. Since member records can be found given owners, and vice versa, the courses taken by a student can be determined from the (owners of the) SECTIONS that own his ENROLLED records, and the enrollment in a section is given by the student owners of that section's ENROLLED records.

The situation is illustrated for some particular records in Fig. 10.3. The records for entities are shown as rectangles, and the intermediate ENROLLED records as ovals. There are two instances of COURSE records, and each is the owner of a COURSE-SECTION set occurrence containing two SECTION records as members. Each

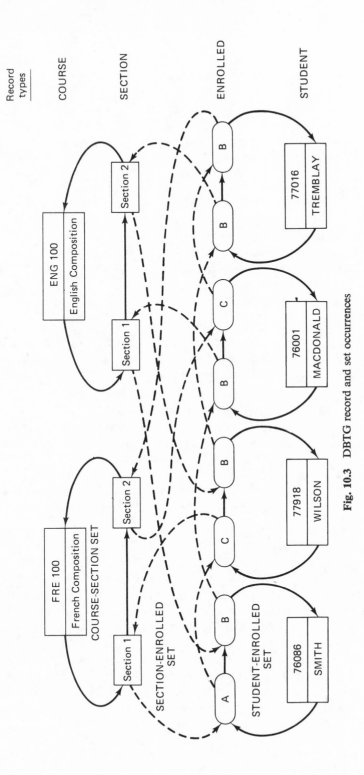

Fig. 10.3 DBTG record and set occurrences

ENROLLED record is a member in two set occurrences, one of type STUDENT-ENROLLED and the other of type SECTION-ENROLLED. (This is perfectly legal; what is *not* permissible is for an ENROLLED record to be a member of two set occurrences of the *same* type, for example the SECTION-ENROLLED occurrences belonging to Smith and Wilson.) The directed lines connect the participants of each set together and represent the fact that for the set, it is possible to go from owner to members, member to member, and member to owner. Thus to find the courses taken by "Smith." follow the line from the STUDENT record with "Smith" in it to the ENROLLED records, and from each of those, trace the dashed line up to the owning SECTION record, then the solid line up to the owning COURSE record. Although the ENROLLED records are only intermediaries and not entities, they are a natural place to store information that is associated with the links but not the owners; in Fig. 10.3, the letter in every such record represents the grade obtained by the student in the section.

Record definitions in the schema DDL are shown in Table 10.1. A record declaration contains field definitions and instructions for the system to follow when storing newly created instances of that record type. The field definition part is similar to a PL/I structure declaration, except that a subfield may repeat a fixed (or in some cases, variable) number of times by writing an OCCURS clause after its name. In line 23, the SCHEDULE subfield of the SECTION record is declared as "OCCURS 3 TIMES." so that data on three weekly meetings can be recorded.

Information on record placement is supplied by the LOCATION MODE and WITHIN clauses. When a record is created and subsequently stored for the first time, it is assigned a unique data-base key that effectively serves as its address. Since it may be desirable for processing efficiency to keep members in certain sets close together, or to quickly find a record on the basis of one or a combination of its fields, the schema designer can tell the system to follow certain strategies in placing (i.e., computing the data-bases key for) each type of record. There are four alternatives:

1. The address of a record is computed from one or more of its fields. The phrase "LOCATION MODE IS CALC USING STUDENT-NO" (line 5) causes STUDENT records to be placed according to their STUDENT-NO values; similarly, COURSE records are stored on the basis of two fields (line 13). When CALC USING *field1*, . . . , *fieldn* is given for a record type, the system must know what to do with records that have the same *field1*, . . . , *fieldn* contents as ones already stored. The CALC procedure would produce the same data-base key as the original, and since more than one record cannot be stored at the same address, the duplicate must either be rejected or be given a different key. The DUPLICATES ARE/ARE NOT ALLOWED tells the system which of these choices to make. In lines 5 and 13, DUPLICATES ARE NOT ALLOWED is used to ensure that there will never be more than one STUDENT (COURSE) record in the data base per student (course) in the university.

2. The record is placed as close as possible to other members in one of the sets in which it may become a member. The phrase "LOCATION MODE IS VIA

COURSE-SECTION SET" (line 20) causes SECTION records to be stored near other members of some COURSE-SECTION set occurrence. The means for determining which occurrence, and the exact placement in the set, are detailed in the COURSE-SECTION set definition (below).

3. The programmer may supply data-base keys, which the system will try to use for storage purposes (LOCATION MODE IS DIRECT).

4. Record placement strategy is left to the system (LOCATION MODE IS SYSTEM).

The WITHIN clause (together with the AREA NAME statement) enables the schema designer to divide the database into named portions, called *areas*, and restrict the placement of records to specified areas. As defined, the area is a logical subdivision that can be assigned privacy locks to enhance security; however, it is also intended as a physical partitioning, in order to provide locality of reference, efficient record allocation, and other conveniences. In Table 10.1, separate areas are defined for STUDENT and COURSE records. SECTION records are placed in the same area as the owner of the COURSE-SECTION set to which they belong (line 21), which turns out to be the COURSE-AREA, since COURSE is the owner type for that set; similarly, ENROLLED records will be stored in the STUDENT-AREA.

The set definitions in Table 10.2 have three basic parts:

1. OWNER—A previously declared record type.

2. ORDER—A set can be regarded logically as a simple circular list, with the owner at the head. There is a FIRST member record, a LAST record, and from any point in the set, the NEXT and PRIOR records are uniquely defined; in particular, the NEXT record following the owner is the FIRST member, and the NEXT following the LAST member is the owner.

   The "ORDER IS PERMANENT SORTED BY DEFINED KEYS" clause in the COURSE-SECTION definition (line 3) tells the system to keep the sequence of member records defined by FIRST, NEXT following FIRST, and so on to LAST, ordered numerically or lexicographically on the fields to be named in the MEMBER clause as new members are inserted. ORDER is LAST means that a new member is to be inserted following the LAST member in the set, and ORDER IS NEXT specifies that a new member is to be inserted following a set member that will be designated by the inserting program.

3. MEMBER—The MEMBER clause names a member record type and puts conditions on its membership in the set. MANDATORY means that once a record has been placed in a set as a member, it cannot be removed, except for deletion or transfer to another occurrence of the same set. Thus a SECTION record, once inserted into a COURSE-SECTION set, must always be in one COURSE-SECTION set or another. The alternative to MANDATORY is OPTIONAL, which permits a record to be removed from sets for which it has been named an OPTIONAL member. In Table 10.2, all members are MANDATORY because, for the application, they have no meaning outside their partici-

pation in sets; for example, an ENROLLED record contains only a single letter value and so has no use by itself; its function is to link STUDENT and SECTION records, and therefore must always be in one STUDENT-ENROLLED set occurrence and one SECTION-ENROLLED occurrence.

AUTOMATIC means that when a record is stored, it will automatically be placed by the DBMS in an occurrence of each set for which it has been declared an AUTOMATIC member. The alternative, MANUAL, leaves membership in a set to be established by the programmer, using an INSERT command.

The MEMBER clause in the COURSE-SECTION definition (lines 4–6) also says that the insertion of a SECTION record into the set will preserve the existing order of the members, which is by increasing SECTION-NO value ("KEY IS ASCENDING SECTION-NO"), and should the new member have the same SECTION-NO as one already present, the system will reject the duplicate ("DUPLICATES ARE NOT ALLOWED").

Since inclusion of members in COURSE-SECTION sets is AUTOMATIC, the system must have a way of determining the COURSE-SECTION occurrence to which a newly stored SECTION record is to be added. The SET SELECTION clause (lines 7 and 8; there is one per AUTOMATIC member) informs the system how this set is to be found; for SECTION records it will be identified by its owner ("THRU COURSE-SECTION OWNER"), a COURSE record that is uniquely determined from values in the CALC fields (DEPT, COURSE-NO) named in the LOCATION MODE clause of the record definition ("IDENTIFIED BY CALC-KEY").

Set selection for insertion of ENROLLED records into SECTION-ENROLLED sets (lines 19–23) is slightly more complicated. We cannot directly indicate the SECTION-ENROLLED occurrence into which an ENROLLED records is to be inserted, because the LOCATION MODE for SECTION records is neither CALC nor DIRECT; the SECTION-NO field only serves as a key *within* a particular COURSE-SECTION set. Therefore, to enable the system to select a SECTION-ENROLLED occurrence, we provide CALC field values for a COURSE record, to identify a COURSE-SECTION set ("COURSE-SECTION OWNER IDENTIFIED BY CALC-KEY") and a SECTION-NO field value which identifies a particular SECTION record (and, therefore, SECTION-ENROLLED occurrence) within that set ("THEN THRU SECTION-ENROLLED WHERE OWNER IDENTIFIED BY SECTION-NO").

10.2.2 DBTG Data Manipulation

As might be inferred from the discussion above, data manipulation in a DBTG system consists of creating and deleting records, inserting them in and removing them from sets, and locating them in the data base, either by contents or through their participation in one or more set occurrences. To illustrate how some of these operations are expressed in the DML, we present a sample program, involving the schema types declared above, with the "data-base" portion shown in Table 10.3. The program is COBOL-like because the Data Base Task Group designed the subschema DDL as a COBOL extension. However, no knowledge of COBOL is required here, and it should also be pointed out that other languages can be developed to serve as a DBTG host language, as well.

TABLE 10.3   DBTG DML code to "Move Student #76086 to Section 2 of French 100"

```
 1.      MOVE '76086' TO STUDENT-NO IN STUDENT.
 2.      FIND STUDENT RECORD.
 3. LOOP. FIND NEXT ENROLLED RECORD OF
                STUDENT-ENROLLED SET.
 4.      IF ERROR-STATUS = "end-of-set" GOTO NOT-ENROLLED.
 5.      FIND OWNER IN SECTION-ENROLLED OF
                CURRENT OF STUDENT-ENROLLED SET.
 6.      FIND OWNER RECORD OF COURSE-SECTION SET.
 7.      GET COURSE; DEPT, COURSE-NO.
 8.      IF DEPT = 'FRE' AND COURSE-NO = '100' GOTO SWITCH.
 9.      GOTO LOOP
10. SWITCH. MOVE '2' TO SECTION-NO IN SECTION.
11.          FIND CURRENT OF STUDENT-ENROLLED SET.
12.          MODIFY ENROLLED; USING DEPT IN COURSE,
                COURSE-NO IN COURSE,
                SECTION-NO IN SECTION.
```

Before any DML operations can be performed, the schema elements to be referenced must be identified to the host language program. For this purpose, the COBOL declaration facilities have been extended to form a subschema data definition language. With the subschema DDL, the user selectively indicates those areas, record types, and sets in the schema that will be needed by the application program. The subschema may differ from the schema in several respects: among other things, records, fields, sets, and areas can be renamed; fields may be reordered, omitted, or given new types; and set members may be dropped or assigned different means for SET SELECTION. However, what is defined must be self-consistent; for example, if a record type is named as a set member, it must be declared.

When the program is run, the DBMS sets up a User Working Area (UWA) to serve as a communication buffer between the user and the data base. Each record in the subschema is assigned a location in the UWA and can be referenced there by name. When a particular record occurrence in the data base has been identified for retrieval, the GET command brings a copy of it into the UWA location reserved for that type; to create a record and place it in the data base, the values for its fields, and information needed to insert it in the sets for which it is an AUTOMATIC member, are assembled in the UWA and a STORE is issued. Other instructions that transfer information from the UWA to the data base are INSERT (place a record in one or more sets), its inverse REMOVE, and MODIFY (change a record's fields and/or move it to a different set).

The capability for searching through the data base is provided by the FIND command. There are two basic versions of FIND, corresponding to the two basic ways of locating a record. The first looks up a record directly, using either its data-base key or, if the LOCATION MODE for the record type is CALC, the field values that enable the key to be computed. The second starts from a previously determined record, and moves to one of the following:

1. The owner of a set for which the record is a member.
2. Another member of a set for which that record is a member.
3. A member in a set owned by that record.

The "previously determined" record used in the second type of FIND is one of a number of location references, called *currency indicators*, which are continuously updated by the system to keep track of a user's position in the data base. For each area, record type, and set in the subschema, a "current" record occurrence is defined. It is usually the record of that area, record type, or set most recently located by a FIND, but there are other ways in which currency can be established; for example, when a record is STORED, it becomes the "current of" every set into which it has been automatically inserted, as well as current of its area and record type. It also becomes the "current of run unit," which is the currency indicator for the record most recently accessed by the program. Except for the "current of run unit," updating of currency indicators may be selectively suppressed, so an indicator does not necessarily represent a "most recently accessed" record.

Table 10.3 shows a sample DML instruction sequence to "Move the student with student number '76086' to section '2' of course 'French 100' " (refer to Fig. 10.3). The code illustrates the use of currency indicators and various forms of the FIND command but is not a complete program. In particular:

1. We have not declared a subschema, but instead use the names from the schema (Tables 10.1 and 10.2).
2. After every DML operation, there should be an ERROR-STATUS check and provision for exceptional conditions. This is done only once (line 4), and even then the action that would be taken at statement NOT-ENROLLED is unspecified.
3. Details such as COBOL DIVISION definitions, and area OPEN and CLOSE commands have been omitted.

The steps performed to satisfy the request are the following. First, the desired STUDENT record is located by initializing the CALC field in the User Work Area location for that record type (STUDENT-NO) with the identifying value (line 1), and then issuing the FIND used for record types whose LOCATION MODE is CALC (2). The FIND establishes the STUDENT record with student number 76086 as the current STUDENT-ENROLLED set (the "current" of a set identifies a set occurrence, but actually refers to a record, either the owner or one of the members), and line 3 selects the NEXT member ENROLLED record of that set. The first time the line is executed, the current of the set is the owner, so the first member (i.e., the NEXT following the owner) is selected. If the FIND fails because the end of the set has been reached, it means that the student in question is not enrolled in French 100, and an appropriate transfer is taken (4).

If line 3 succeeds, the ENROLLED record found becomes the current of all sets in which it participates—in particular, SECTION-ENROLLED. Line 5 locates the owner of this SECTION-ENROLLED set—a SECTION record which then becomes the current COURSE-SECTION set. The owner of this current COURSE-SECTION set is a COURSE record that is located (line 6), retrieved (line 7, only the DEPT and COURSE-NO fields are needed), and examined to see if it is the record for French 100. If so, the current ENROLLED record must be moved to the SECTION-ENROLLED set (of COURSE French 100) owned by SECTION '2'; otherwise, the next ENROLLED record owned by student 76086 is checked (GOTO LOOP).

The move is carried out by the MODIFY command, which transfers the record that is the current of run unit from one set occurrence to another. Line 11 establishes the ENROLLED record to be moved as the current of run unit. To identify the set occurrences that are the target of the move, the system matches the identifiers in the USING phrase (line 12) with those named in SET SELECTION clauses of sets for which the current of run-unit record type is declared a member. In Table 10.2, SET SELECTION for new ENROLLED records in SECTION-ENROLLED sets was defined to be through course identifier (DEPT and COURSE-NO) and section number (SECTION-NO), so those fields are named in the USING clause and loaded with the appropriate values (lines 7 and 10). The target sets determine the sets from which to remove the current of run-unit record (in this case, the current SECTION-ENROLLED set), and the transfer from present to new set occurrences can be made.

10.2.3 Summary

The appeal of the network approach lies in the conceptual simplicity with which it treats data representation and manipulation. Schema definition is relatively easy because entities and relationships can be translated directly to record types and owner-member sets, while the basic idea of navigation—moving along chains connecting records—can be grasped by anyone with an elementary understanding of data structures. Naturally, any implementation of the model must compromise this simplicity to some extent, and the DBTG proposal is no exception. However, there are many who feel it goes too far in imposing system-related details on the user. Three issues on which criticism has been focused are of interest here:

1. Lack of physical data independence. The programmer must know how and where records are stored. If, for purposes of optimization or other reasons, the LOCATION mode of a record type or the AREAS in which it is located are changed, all DML programs which refer to that record type (either explicitly or through SET SELECTION that depends on the LOCATION MODE) must be correspondingly modified.

2. Lack of logical data independence. We can make the definition given earlier more precise by calling logical data independence the degree to which the subschema (the user view of the schema) and the DML (the user facility for operating on the subschema) are isolated from the schema (the system's view of the data base). The dependencies described in issue 1 are logical as well as physical, because they are schema properties that must be reflected in the subschema and DML commands. Examples of other schema changes that affect the user's program but are not really relevant to it are:

(a) Information added to the schema can affect programs, even if they do not use the new data. If an existing record type is declared an AUTOMATIC member of a new set, programs which store records of that type must provide information for SET SELECTION of the new set, regardless of whether they reference it or not.

(b) There are actually two ways of representing $1:n$ relationships—with sets, or by repeating groups. Recall that we depicted buildings and rooms as separate entities in the university schematic of Fig. 10.1, but in Table 10.1 used a field declared as "occurs 3 times" to represent the association of sections with buildings and rooms. The programmer must know which of these two ways is used to represent a relationship, and must change his program if the method of representing the hierarchy is changed in the schema.

3. Although the idea behind navigation is simple, the DML itself is complex—currency indicators are hard to keep track of because they can be changed in subtle ways and cannot be directly examined for validity because they are data-base keys, not records. Complications arise because in some operations, currency indicator updates must be selectively suppressed.

These complaints are legitimate, but they should be considered in perspective. First, although the DBTG DML does tend to shift the focus of data operations somewhat from the information represented to the intricacies of the schema, it is still a great improvement over the highly parameterized subroutine calls that characterize data manipulation in other data-base systems (e.g., IMS, TOTAL[6]). Second, the Report was produced with the expectation that implementations would soon follow; for example, repeating groups are included in the schema DDL to maintain compatibility with the data definition facilities of likely host languages—COBOL, PL/I, and even FORTRAN. The decision to sacrifice some data independence in order to ease the task of the implementor is at least partially vindicated by the appearance of commercial DBTG-type systems only a few years after the appearance of the Report. Finally, many of the problems above could be avoided if the DML were designed to be more descriptive and less procedural; for example, it might be modified so that the request of Table 10.3 reads:

> MOVE *ENROLLED*
> IN *STUDENT-ENROLLED*
>   WHERE *STUDENT-NO* = '76086'
> AND IN *SECTION-ENROLLED*
>   IN *COURSE-SECTION*
>   WHERE (*DEPT, COURSE-NO*) = ('FRE', '100')
> TO *SECTION-ENROLLED*
>   WHERE *SECTION-NO* = '2'
>   IN CURRENT *COURSE-SECTION*.

[6]CINCOM SYSTEMS, "TOTAL/7 Reference Manual—Application Programming", *Publication P02-1321-2*, June 1974.

The information necessary to execute this code is in the schema; considerations of SET SELECTION and LOCATION MODE are eliminated, and the user need know only that STUDENT records are uniquely identified by STUDENT-NO, COURSE records by DEPT and COURSE-NO, and SECTIONS by SECTION-NO within a COURSE-SECTION set. This more abstract form of data manipulation can be found in the relational data model, which we now describe.

10.3 Relational Data Model

The relational approach to data management derives largely from the work of E. F. Codd,[7] who adapted the mathematical notion of a relation to data-base use and formally developed it as a basis for data representation and retrieval. The philosophy of the approach can be expressed by three main points:

1. The entities and relationships making up a database can be represented by *n*-ary relations that are:
   (a) *Time-varying*, in the sense that tuples may be changed, inserted, or deleted.
   (b) *Normalized*, or *flat*, in the sense that each component of a tuple is either of primitive type or a character string (but not a set, relation, or otherwise composite).
2. By a process of successive decomposition (further normalization), a relation can be split into several relations which behave in a consistent manner when modified, and from which the information in the original can be reconstructed without loss.
3. It is possible to develop relational data languages that are highly data independent and which can, for practical purposes, express any query whose answer is contained in the data base.

Before discussing these points in more detail, we present some definitions and relational terminology. Let $D_1, D_2, \ldots, D_n$ be a collection of sets, not necessarily distinct. Each D_i represents a space of values, or data type, and is called a *domain*. A relation R on the domains $D_1, D_2, \ldots, D_n$ is a subset of the Cartesian product $D_1 \times D_2 \times \ldots \times D_n$, that is, a set of *tuples* $(x_1, x_2, \ldots, x_n)$ where x_i, the *i*th *component*, is an element of D_i. The number of components in a tuple is called the *degree* of R, and the number of tuples in R is called its *cardinality*.

Frequently, a relation will be pictured as a table in which rows correspond to tuples, and columns to domains (e.g., Fig. 10.2). Since the relation is actually a set, identical rows are not permitted, and the ordering of rows is considered immaterial. The order of columns is significant, reflecting the fact that, in general, the *i*th and *j*th components of a tuple cannot be changed without affecting the meaning. To enable the user to reference components by function, rather than position (and thereby avoid unwanted dependence on the order of domains in the cross product $D_1 \times \ldots \times D_n$), columns are assigned unique *role names*. The role names may be the domain names,

[7]E. F. Codd, "A Relational Model for Large Shared Data Banks," *Communications of the ACM*, 13, no. 6 (June 1970), 377–397.

but in practice are not, for two reasons:

1. A domain can appear several times in the cross product, in which case the column names would not be unique.
2. The name of a domain will be, more often than not, a type designation that would be of no descriptive value [e.g., **char** (30), **int**, **fixed decimal** (6)].

The role names correspond to the field names of a record in other models, and columns are often called *attributes*, even when the relation does not represent an entity.

A *key* (or *candidate key*) *K* of a relation *R* is any attribute or attribute combination of *R*, with the following time-independent properties:

1. *Unique identification*: Each tuple in *R* is uniquely identified by its K value.
2. *Nonredundancy*: No attribute in *K* can be dropped without destroying property 1.

Time independence means that a key is determined from the semantics of the relation, and not simply by the fact that at some point, a column or column combination exhibits properties 1 and 2. Thus, for the STUDENT relation of Fig. 10.2(a), STU-DENT# would be a key because each student would be assigned a unique student number; (LAST-NAME, FIRST-NAME) would not, even though that combination uniquely identifies the tuples in the relation as shown, unless it could be determined in advance that two students with the same first and last names could not simultaneously be enrolled in the university.

A relation always has at least one key, because all the columns in combination satisfy property 1, and if no smaller group does, then 2 as well. There may be more than one key, in which case one is usually designated as the *primary key*. For logical and physical reasons, a tuple may not be added to a relation unless its primary key is completely supplied; other attributes may be left unspecified. An attribute or attribute combination in one relation that is a key for another is called a *foreign key*. A foreign key is not necessarily a key in its own relation, and need not have the same attribute names as the keys it corresponds to in other relations.

Two aspects of the relational model should be noted here. First, the term "relation" is used in a dual way. As defined above, it represents an actual set of tuples; however, it also refers to the *definition* (or data type) of the tuples in the set—the column names and domains. Thus the STUDENT relation of Fig. 10.2 denotes the *entity type* "student" and also a set of (student) entities. Similarly, the relation ENROLLED in the same figure represents a relationship between the student and course entity types, and also a set of connections, or links between specific students and courses. The interpretation—set or definition—is usually clear from context, but it is important to understand that we frequently talk about a relation without having particular tuples in mind.

The second point is that the relation is a logical structure and does not necessarily have physical connotations. It should not be assumed that flat relations (e.g., those in Fig. 10.2) are stored as pictured, and as a corollary, the redundancy that is introduced at the logical level, when a relation is normalized, might not be reflected in the physical structure. There are advantages in implementing relations in flat form (e.g., avoidance of variable-length records), but the model does not require it.

10.3.1 Data Representation

The idea of using relations as a logical structure is not particularly new; for example, LEAP, discussed in Section 7.1, is a "prerelational" system which employs relations (binary in appearance, but in fact more general, since components themselves may be ordered pairs) to store facts about objects and associations among them. The point of the relational approach in that a data model based on flat relations is powerful enough to represent the information in a data base and that the tabular format of such relations is a natural one for data retrieval and manipulation.

The relations in Fig. 10.2, depicting students, courses, and enrollment were flat because we were careful to avoid attributes that took on sets or relations as values. A more common structure for representing entities and relationships is the hierarchical record type, with fields at different levels, and repeating groups. To demonstrate that information in hierarchical form can be expressed as flat relations, we show how to normalize COBOL record definitions. The statement of the procedure will be simplified by imposing two conditions on the source record:

1. A primary key must be defined for the record (i.e., at level "02") and also for every repeating group; each key is defined from one or more simple fields (fields without subfields) which are at the same level and belong to the same group.
2. Only composite fields may be repeating (declared OCCURS).

(A COBOL record can always be trivially modified to satisfy these conditions. The first can be met by adding a numeric group identifier field if a suitable key does not already exist. As for the second, any simple field that is declared OCCURS can be made into a hierarchy by introducing a lower-level field to hold the value; for example,

02 HRS-WORKED FIXED DECIMAL(2) OCCURS 5 TIMES

⇒ 02 HRS-WORKED OCCURS 5 TIMES;

03 HRS-WORKED-VAL FIXED DECIMAL(2).)

A record to be converted is shown in Table 10.4. The primary keys are italicized. A course has two prerequisites (P-REQ), and two sections. The instructor of a section will be referred to by name here [hence the CHAR(10) type], although in a real application, a unique identifier, such as employee number, would probably be used. INSTR-STATUS is a code based on the academic position and teaching experience of the instructor. A section meets twice weekly, and there is at most one meeting a day, so DAY is a key for the SCHEDULE subgroup.

The conversion proceeds as follows[8]:

1. *Construct a definition tree for the record type.* This is simply a matter of translating one representation of a hierarchy (level numbers, also shown by indentation), to another (a multiway, rooted, directed tree with labeled nodes). The root is labeled with the record name (COURSE in this instance), and for each level

---

[8]The procedure used is basically that suggested by Codd, "Relational Model."

TABLE 10.4   Record type to be converted to normalized relations

```
COURSE
    02 DEPT; CHAR(3);
    02 COURSE #; FIXED DECIMAL(3);
    02 TITLE; CHAR(50);
    02 P-REQ OCCURS 2 TIMES;
        03 P-DEPT; CHAR(3);
        03 P-COURSE #; FIXED DECIMAL(3);
    02 SECTION OCCURS 2 TIMES;
        03 SECTION #; FIXED DECIMAL(1);
        03 INSTRUCTOR; CHAR(10);
        03 INSTR-STATUS; FIXED DECIMAL(2)
        03 SCHEDULE OCCURS 2 TIMES;
            04 DAY; CHAR(3);
            04 TIME; FIXED DECIMAL(2);
            04 BLDG; CHAR(2);
            04 RM; FIXED DECIMAL(4);
```

"02" field in the record definition is given a son labeled with the corresponding field name. Sons which are themselves composite (P-REQ, and SECTION, here) are treated similarly, and the process stops when all the leaves correspond to simple fields. Figure 10.4(a) shows the result; the key combinations from Table 10.4 are underlined.

2. *Determine the relations and their primary keys.* Each internal node in the tree defines a relation. The primary keys for these are established by the following rules:

   (a) The primary key at the root is the primary key at level 2.

   (b) The key at any internal node is the key of its father, concatenated with the key, if any, defined by its noncomposite sons.

   In the example, there will be four relations, corresponding to the nodes COURSE, P-REQ, SECTION, and SCHEDULE. The keys determined by rule (b) are shown in parentheses, next to the internal node names in Fig. 10.4. By rule (a), (*DEPT, COURSE #*) becomes the primary key for the COURSE relation; from rule (b), the key for SCHEDULE is that of its father (*DEPT, COURSE #, SECTION #*), together with its own key at level four, *DAY*.

3. *Generate the relations.* For each internal node, add to the key list the noncomposite sons not already in the list.

Step 3 produces the relations shown in Fig. 10.4(b). Figure 10.5 illustrates data in the (unnormalized relational) form of COURSE records, and Fig. 10.6 shows the equivalent flat relations that result from the conversion illustrated in Fig. 10.4.

10.3.2 Further Normalization

The procedure just described is the first in a sequence of refinements by which an unnormalized relation (one with domains that are relations) can be broken down into

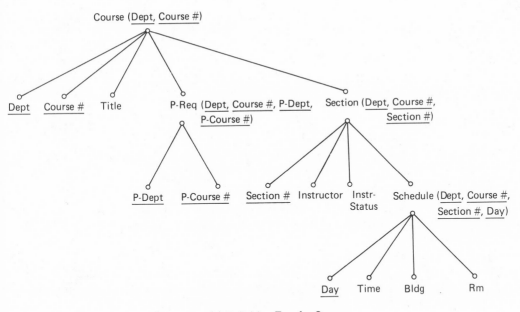

(a) Definition Tree for Course

COURSE (Dept, Course #, Title)
P-REQ (Dept, Course #, P-Dept, P-Course #)
SECTION (Dept, Course #, Section #, Instructor, Instr-Status)
Schedule (Dept, Course #, Section #, Day, Time, BLDG, RM)

(b) Relation Definitions from Tree

Fig. 10.4   Conversion of COURSE record type to flat relations

relations that exhibit certain "desirable" update properties.[9] The flat relations that result from the first step are said to be in *first normal form* (1NF). Successive decompositions aimed at eliminating relationships among nonkey attributes in a relation produce second, and then third normal form. Although the relational approach does not insist on normalization beyond first normal form, there may be good reasons for doing so. To see why, consider the following anomalies the SECTION relation (Fig. 10.6) can exhibit when tuples are modified, added, or deleted:

1. *Update anomaly.* Because the INSTR-STATUS was defined as a property of INSTRUCTOR alone, any change in that value in one tuple of the SECTION relation must be reflected in all other tuples with the same instructor; otherwise,

[9]E. F. Codd, "Further Normalization of the Data Base Relational Model," *Courant Computer Science Symposium 6 on Data Base Systems, New York, May 1971*, R. Rustin, ed. (Englewood Cliffs, N.J.: Prentice-Hall Inc., 1972), pp. 33–64.

COURSE

DEPT	COURSE #	TITLE	P-REQ		SECTION						
			P-DEPT	P-COURSE #	SECTION #	INSTRUCTOR	INSTR-STATUS	DAY	TIME	BLDG	RM
ENG	160	Critical Writing	ENG	20	1	Andrews	18	Mon	10	UC	201
			ENG	51				Thu	11	UC	202
					2	Thomas	67	Mon	10	NC	14
								Wed	9	NC	20
ENG	220	Shakespeare	ENG	120	1	Andrews	18	Wed	1	TR	20
			ENG	121				Fri	12	TR	21
					2	Brown	56	Tue	10	NC	517
								Thu	11	NC	517
FRE	340	19th Cent. Fiction	FRE	100	1	Dubois	40	Tue	2	UC	202
			FRE	240				Thu	1	UC	201
					2	Armand	22	Mon	3	VC	118
								Thu	3	VC	120

Fig. 10.5   Unnormalized relation from COURSE record definition

the relation will be inconsistent, in the sense that information in one row contradicts that in another.

2. *Insertion anomaly.* We cannot record INSTR-STATUS information about an instructor unless that person teaches some section; a tuple with only INSTRUCTOR and INSTR-STATUS cannot be inserted because it would lack a value for its primary key (DEPT, COURSE #, SECTION #).

3. *Deletion anomaly.* If the instructor in a tuple being deleted teaches other sections, nothing happens, but if the tuple deleted represents the only section taught by that instructor, we lose the INSTR-STATUS information for that person, probably an unintended side effect, especially if the data is not stored elsewhere.

The basic reason for these anomalies is that INSTR-STATUS is a property of the instructor and not the tuple as a whole. Since a SECTION tuple represents an instructor–section association, any components in it other than the instructor and section identifiers must be attributes of the link itself, or inconsistencies of the above kind will occur. To make this explanation more precise and state conditions under which anomalies can be avoided, we employ the notion of *functional dependency*.

If A and B are attributes, or attribute collections, of a relation, and there is a time-independent, functional relationship with domain A and range B, we write $A \longrightarrow B$ and say that B is *functionally dependent* on A (alternately, B *depends* on A, or A *determines* B). "Functional" is used in the mathematical sense, that is, for each value of A there is only one B value. Time independence, introduced for keys, means that the functionality holds by definition; thus in SECTION, INSTRUCTOR $\longrightarrow$ INSTR-STATUS because INSTR-STATUS is a code which describes the instructor, a property that might be guessed by looking at the relation, but which in fact must be determined in advance. It follows from the definition above that all attributes in a relation are dependent (individually, or in combination) on each key.

Now suppose that B is a collection of one or more attributes in a relation R, A is an attribute collection from $R - B$ (i.e., in R but outside of B), and $A \longrightarrow B$.

If A is *not* a key, there can be several tuples in R with the same A value, say a. It follows that the B value associated with a will only be lost if all such tuples are removed, a deletion anomaly of the type just described. An update anomaly occurs because any change in the B value associated with a must be reflected in each tuple with a as its A value, in order to preserve the $A \longrightarrow B$ dependence. Finally, since A is not a key, an (A, B) value association can be established only if a new tuple is added—an insertion anomaly (unless B happens to be the primary key).

These problems are eliminated if we require that A be a key for every functional dependency of the form $A \longrightarrow B$, where B is an attribute (collection) in R and A is in $R - B$. Then if a dependent attribute in a tuple is changed, each attribute (combination) on which it depends is a key which uniquely identifies that tuple, and so anomalies do not occur. An attribute that is nondependent must be a key, and therefore any change in it is confined to the tuple, by definition. A relation which has the property that every determining side of a functional dependency is a key is said to be in *Boyce–Codd normal form* (BCNF).[10]

The section relation in Fig. 10.6 can be converted to BCNF by dropping the INSTR-STATUS column and storing it in a separate relation, say INSTR-INFO (*INSTRUCTOR*, INSTR-STATUS). (Keys are shown in italics). It is easy to see that the new relations are in BCNF and, as a result, cannot exhibit any of the anomalies described above.

Boyce–Codd normal form is, in fact, a "fourth" normal form, since between it and 1NF there are two steps (second and third normal forms) which successively eliminate

[10]E. F. Codd, "Recent Investigations in Relational Data Base Systems," *Information Processing*, **74**, *Proc. IFIP Congress*, Aug. 1974, Vol. 5 (Amsterdam: North-Holland Publishing Company, 1974), pp. 1017–1021.

P-REQ

DEPT	COURSE #	P-DEPT	P-COURSE #
ENG	160	ENG	20
ENG	160	ENG	51
ENG	220	ENG	120
ENG	220	ENG	121
FRE	340	FRE	100
FRE	340	FRE	240

P-REQ

COURSE

DEPT	COURSE #	TITLE
ENG	160	Creative Writing
ENG	220	Shakespeare
FRE	340	19th Cent Fiction

COURSE

SCHEDULE

DEPT	COURSE #	SECTION #	DAY	TIME	BLDG.	RM
ENG	160	1	Mon	10	UC	201
ENG	160	1	Thu	11	UC	202
ENG	160	2	Mon	10	NC	14
ENG	160	2	Wed	9	NC	20
ENG	220	1	Wed	1	TR	20
ENG	220	1	Fri	12	TR	21
ENG	220	2	Tue	10	NC	517
ENG	220	2	Thu	11	NC	517
FRE	340	1	Tue	2	UC	202
FRE	340	1	Thu	1	UC	201
FRE	340	2	Mon	3	VC	118
FRE	340	2	Thu	3	VC	120

SCHEDULE

SECTION

DEPT	COURSE #	SECTION #	INSTRUCTOR	INSTR-STATUS
ENG	160	1	Andrews	18
ENG	160	2	Thomas	67
ENG	220	1	Andrews	18
ENG	220	2	Brown	56
FRE	340	1	Dubois	40
FRE	340	2	Armand	22

SECTION

certain types of functional dependencies. We went directly to BCNF from first, since it is the most restrictive, and also the easiest to formulate; however, there are times when BCNF does not exist, while the slightly weaker third normal form (3NF) does, and ensures, for practical purposes, that there will be no anomalies.

To see this, observe that BCNF divides the attributes of a relation into two groups: *prime*, which are, or are part of keys, and *nonprime*, which are neither. Furthermore, the *only* functional dependencies in which a nonprime attribute participates are ones where it depends on a key. Now if, in Fig. 10.6, INSTR-STATUS is dropped from SECTION, then INSTRUCTOR is left as the only nonprime attribute. The relation as defined is in BCNF, but if the condition that each instructor teaches courses in only one department is added, a functional dependency INSTRUCTOR → DEPT is introduced. Since INSTRUCTOR is not a key, SECTION would no longer be in BCNF, and yet it cannot be broken down into anything smaller. Moreover, the new dependency does not really cause anomalies, because a change in the department affiliation of an instructor cannot be indicated by changing the DEPT component of tuples representing sections taught by that person; that would simply make some of the course identifiers in SECTION incorrect.

Because this kind of situation is not unusual, it often suffices to make *third normal form*, which relaxes the BCNF conditions by allowing prime attributes to depend on nonprime ones, the target of normalization (when normalization is carried out). BCNF is sometimes presented as a restatement of 3NF, but as this example shows, it is somewhat stronger and not always achievable.

10.3.3 Relational Data Languages

In the relational model, a query is answered by deriving a relation from existing ones. For example, referring to Fig. 10.6, the answer to "Which instructors teach the 'Shakespeare' course?" is obtained from COURSE and SECTION, and is given by the one-column relation

SHAKESPEARE (*INSTRUCTOR*)[11]

Andrews

Brown

A relational data language provides the user with the ability to specify relational derivations. The specification can take the form of an algebraic expression composed of relations and relational operators, or it may be a sequence of qualifications that characterize tuples in the result. Languages that employ the latter type of specification are more descriptive than those based on the algebraic approach, because the system is given more freedom to carry out the derivation; in the former case, the system is forced to work with the expression supplied.

---

[11]The relation name "SHAKESPEARE" is chosen for descriptive purposes and is not part of the answer to the query. Note also that the model allows relations of degree 1, which are not strictly relations in the mathematical sense, because they do not contain tuples.

Relational data languages are sometimes classified according to whether they are self-contained. Those that are called *query languages*, while those designed to be embedded in a host language are known as *data sublanguages* (DSL's). The distinction between the two types is not always obvious, however, because the query facilities of both are self-contained and because some query languages can serve as data sublanguages. The difference is usually that a DSL relies on its host for data-manipulation facilities, whereas a query language, if it has any, will have its own.

We shall illustrate the query facilities of three relational languages—the *relational algebra*, the *relational calculus*, and SEQUEL (Structured English Query Language).

Relational Algebra[12]:   Relational algebra is comprised of a set of operators that produce new relations from old ones. It includes set operations such as union and intersection and operators that apply specifically to relations. The most important of these latter are:

1. *Projection*—takes a relation and returns only the columns specified, with duplicates removed. For example, to "List the courses and buildings they are taught in," we project the DEPT, COURSE#, and BLDG columns out of SCHEDULE (Fig. 10.6), by writing SCHEDULE[DEPT, COURSE#, BLDG]. The result is

(*DEPT*,	*COURSE#*,	*BLDG*)
ENG	160	UC
ENG	160	NC
ENG	220	TR
ENG	220	NC
FRE	340	UC
FRE	340	VC

2. *Restriction*—selects from a relation those tuples that meet a given condition. For example, the answer to "Which classes are taught Monday at 10?" is given by the restriction SCHEDULE[DAY = 'Mon'][TIME = '10']. The result is

(*DEPT*,	*COURSE#*,	*SECTION#*,	*DAY*,	TIME,	BLDG,	RM)
ENG	160	1	Mon	10	UC	201
ENG	160	2	Mon	10	NC	517
ENG	220	2	Mon	10	NC	510

   Since the request is really for class names alone, we can project the desired columns out of the result, by writing

   (SCHEDULE[DAY = 'Mon'][TIME = '10'])

   [DEPT, COURSE#, SECTION#],

---

[12]Codd, "Relational Completeness."

to get

$$(DEPT, \ COURSE\#, \ SECTION\#)$$

ENG	160	1
ENG	160	2
ENG	220	2

Note the bracketing in the expression, to specify that projection is to follow restriction.

3. *Join*—From relations R and S, the join forms a new relation by concatenating a tuple of R with a tuple of S, whenever a given condition holds between the two. Formally, let A be a collection of attributes in R and let $r[A]$ denote the A value of a tuple $r \in R$; similarly, for B and $s[B]$ in S. The *equi-join* of relations R and S on their respective domains A and B is written $R[A=B]S$, and defined as the relation $\{(r, s) \mid r \in R, s \in S, \text{ and } r[A]=s[B]\}$, where (r, s) denotes the concatenation of tuples r and s. There are more general definitions for the join (e.g., any mathematical relation can be substituted in place of equality), but this is the one most commonly referred to; as can be seen, it is very similar to function composition.

The join is the key operation in the relational algebra, since by correlating tuples in two relations, it provides the ability to establish relationships between entities of different types. The following expression employs the join to answer the query posed at the start of this section: "Which instructors teach the 'Shakespeare' course?":

$$((COURSE[TITLE = \text{'Shakespeare'}]) \ [(DEPT, \ COURSE\#) =$$
$$(DEPT, \ COURSE\#)] \ SECTION)[INSTRUCTOR]$$

The restriction (COURSE [TITLE $=$ 'Shakespeare']) creates a relation of COURSE tuples which have the desired title (there is only one such tuple in this example). This is joined with SECTION, on the condition that concatenated tuples have the same DEPT and COURSE$\#$ values. The result is the relation

(DEPT,	COURSE#,	TITLE,	DEPT,	COURSE#,	SEC TION#,	INST RUCTOR,	INSTR_STATUS)
ENG	220	Shakespeare	ENG	220	1	Andrews	18
ENG	220	Shakespeare	ENG	220	2	Brown	56

(In some versions of the join, the join columns are eliminated from the result; here we include them, since they can always be removed by projection. Also, it is not necessary that the join columns have the same names, as they do here; the only requirement is that the corresponding domains be comparable.) Finally, the desired field, INSTRUCTOR, is projected out, to get the result shown earlier:

$$(INSTRUCTOR)$$

Andrews

Brown

Relational Calculus: Relational calculus is a notation with which the relations to be derived are described by first-order predicates. The description takes the form of a condition constructed from logical connectives ($\wedge$, $\vee$, $\rceil$), quantifiers ($\exists$, $\forall$), and variables which range over the tuples of relations. We will show how the queries posed above are expressed in ALPHA, a calculus-based DSL developed by Codd.[13]

Q1. List the courses and buildings they are taught in.

GET W: (SCHEDULE.DEPT,

SCHEDULE.COURSE#,SCHEDULE.BLDG)

W is a workspace into which the selected information is placed. Following the workspace name is the *target list*, giving the attributes of the relation which are to be returned.

Q2. Which classes are taught Monday at 10?

RANGE SCHEDULE *sc*

GET W: (*sc*.DEPT, *sc*.COURSE#, *sc*.SECTION#)

: (*sc*.DAY = 'Mon' $\wedge$ *sc*.TIME = '10')

The RANGE statement declares *sc* to be a variable that refers to tuples in SCHEDULE. The *qualification* that follows the target list sets the conditions which tuples from the target relation must satisfy.

Q3. "Which instructors teach 'Shakespeare'?"

RANGE COURSE *c*

RANGE SECTION *sn*

GET W *sn*.INSTRUCTOR:

($\exists c$: (*c*.TITLE = 'Shakespeare' $\wedge$

c.DEPT = *sn*.DEPT $\wedge$

c.COURSE# = *sn*.COURSE #))

This reads "Get the INSTRUCTOR component of SECTION tuples for which there is a COURSE tuple with the same DEPT and COURSE# values, and the title 'Shakespeare'." The existential quantifier ($\exists$) performs a function similar to that of the join, in the relational algebra. Variables bound by quantifiers must be declared in RANGE statements (*c* in this case). Others (*sn* here) may be declared RANGE for shorthand purposes.

The relational calculus sets a standard for other relational languages, in the following sense: A language is said to be *relationally complete* if it permits the specification of any derivation that can be described by a first-order predicate. This is a precise way of saying that a user can derive any desired relation from ones present in the data

---

[13]E. F. Codd, "A Data Base Language Founded on the Relational Calculus," *Proceedings of the ACM—SIGFIDET Workshop on Data Description, Access and Control*, Nov. 1971 (New York: Association for Computing Machinery, 1971), pp. 35–68.

base. ALPHA is defined so as to be complete, and other languages can be proved complete by demonstrating their ability to express any query definable in ALPHA. In particular, the relational algebra is complete,[14] as is the query language, SEQUEL, to be illustrated next.

SEQUEL[15]: SEQUEL is a query language that uses English keywords and nested structure to achieve the power of ALPHA, without quantifiers. Queries Q1, Q2, and Q3 are expressed as follows:

Q1: SELECT DEPT, COURSE#, BLDG

     FROM   SCHEDULE

Q2: SELECT DEPT, COURSE#, SECTION#

     FROM   SCHEDULE

     WHERE DAY = 'Mon'

     AND   TIME = '10'

Q3: SELECT INSTRUCTOR

     FROM   SECTION

     WHERE ⟨DEPT, COURSE#⟩ =

          SELECT DEPT, COURSE#

          FROM   COURSE

          WHERE TITLE = 'Shakespeare'

These are fairly self-explanatory. Note, in Q3, how the inner SELECT achieves the effect of ALPHA's existential quantifier.

The foregoing illustrates the basic retrieval capabilities of relational data languages. These languages have additional features which cannot be covered here but which are worth mentioning as part of the relational approach. Some of them are as follows.

More Complex Queries: There are useful queries which cannot be expressed by first-order predicates or relational algebra, because they require not the assembly of a relation from existing ones, but rather information computed from a relation's contents. For example, referring to Fig. 10.6, we might ask for the number of lectures given in each room. This requires the ability to count, for each BLDG and RM value combination in SCHEDULE, the number of tuples with that value. SEQUEL provides for this; the statement

       SELECT BLDG, RM, COUNT(*)

       FROM SCHEDULE GROUP BY BLDG, RM

---

[14]See Codd, "Relational Completeness."

[15]D. D. Chamberlin and R. F. Boyce, "SEQUEL: A Structured English Query Language," *Proceedings of the ACM—SIGMOD Workshop on Data Description, Access and Control*, May 1974 (New York: Association for Computing Machinery, 1974), pp. 249–264.

will produce the desired result. The GROUP BY specifies that COUNT is to be performed on groups of tuples with identical BLDG and RM components. Other statistical functions available in SEQUEL are AVG, MAX, MIN, and SUM. ALPHA was also defined with these extended query facilities, but the relational algebra does not appear to be well suited for them.

Updates: A tuple is added to a relation by assembling components and calling an insert function; the particular form of the function and the way the new tuple is created will depend on the relational (and host) language, but the basic procedure does not vary much. Similarly, deletion is a matter of using the query facility to select the subset of a relation to be removed.

The procedure for update varies from one language to another. In SEQUEL, the tuples to be modified can be identified and changed with one command. For example, to reassign classes using 'UC 201' to 'UC 204', one writes

> UPDATE SCHEDULE
>
> SET RM = '204'
>
> WHERE BLDG = 'UC'
>
> AND RM = '201'

In ALPHA, the same tuples would be brought into a workspace by a HOLD command (which is like GET but tells the system that the target information is to be updated), changed there using host language statements, and then written back out. This is similar to the update procedure in a DBTG system.

In relational algebra, the set operators UNION and DIFFERENCE can be used to change a tuple if all the component values for that tuple are known. It is also possible to modify a set of tuples by describing it and supplying the new component values, but the procedure is complicated and inefficient (Exercise 6); in any algebra-based implementation, some kind of "update-in-place" facility would have to be provided.

Views: In the network model proposed by the DBTG, a user does not have much flexibility in defining the subschema; new relationships cannot be introduced, and although the Report does allow new record types to be created from existing ones, most implementations do not support this feature. A relationally complete data language, on the other hand, gives the user considerable freedom in defining new entities and associations, but with one qualification: a relation produced by a query represents a portion of the data base at the time the query was executed only, and remains unaffected by subsequent changes to the relations from which it was defined. In some systems a relation can be added to the data model by defining it as a *view*; such a relation is constructed using the query facility and is dynamic in the sense that it continually reflects updates to the relations on which it is based.

As an example of view definition, suppose that we want, from the data of Fig. 10.6, a relation of timetable information for instructors of English courses. With SEQUEL statements, it could be specified as follows[16]:

DEFINE VIEW ENG-SCHEDULE AS

SELECT INSTRUCTOR, DAY, TIME

FROM SECTION, SCHEDULE

WHERE SECTION.DEPT = 'ENG'

AND   SCHEDULE.DEPT = 'ENG'

AND   SECTION.COURSE# = SCHEDULE.COURSE#

AND   SECTION.SECTION# = SCHEDULE.SECTION#

Except for the first line, this is a normal query. ENG-SCHEDULE is constructed by joining SECTION and SCHEDULE on (DEPT, COURSE#, SECTION#) with the condition that the DEPT code be that for English, and then projecting the appropriate columns. Where ENG-SCHEDULE differs from the result of a normal query is in the following:

1. It is stored in the table of relational definitions and is available to other users.
2. When referenced, it appears as if the derivation specified in the SELECT clause had just been performed.
3. It can be used in queries and as the basis for other views.

Under certain conditions, views can be updated. The basic requirement is that a change to a tuple in a view not affect other tuples in that view, as a result of the change in the underlying relation. In practice, this means that only views derived from a single relation may be modified.

10.3.4 Summary

The relational approach has a number of features that make it well suited to the "casual" user—a person who requires direct and immediate access to computer-stored information but has little knowledge of programming and data structure concepts. Some of these features are:

1. Physical data independence—no assumptions are made about the storage of relations, and therefore queries are not affected by details of physical organization.
2. Logical data independence
   The user must know the relation names, column names, and sometimes the column data types of the relations he or she plans to reference—in other words, which information is in what relation. This means, for example, that if a relation is broken down as a result of normalization, queries based on that relation

---

[16]This is how views are defined in System R, a relational implementation. See M. M. Astrahan et al., "System R: A Relational Approach to Database Management," *ACM Transactions on Database Systems*, **1**, no. 2 (June 1976), 97–137.

must be modified (unless a view that will serve as an acceptable substitute can be defined). Other than this, the model exhibits a high degree of logical data independence. In particular:

(a) There are no access path considerations, as was true in the DBTG model. A user may be expected to *specify* access paths (e.g., inverted lists on various columns) so that queries can be answered efficiently, but these are for the system's use and are never referred to in data language statements.

(b) User programs are not affected by the addition of new relations to the model, in contrast with point 2 of Section 10.2.3.

(c) Symmetric exploitation of relationships—Suppose that enrollment information is represented by hierarchical records of the following type:

COURSE

    02 DEPT; CHAR(3)

    02 COURSE-NO; FIXED DECIMAL(3);

    02 ENROLLED OCCURS 100 TIMES;

       03 STUDENT-NO; FIXED DECIMAL (6);

       03 GRADE; CHAR(1);

Then it is easy to see that in a highly procedural query language, the request for students with a given grade in a given course must be handled differently from one for the courses in which a given student got a particular grade. The queries are symmetric (one fixes course and grade, the other student and grade), but the code to answer them is not. On the other hand, if the representation took the form of a relation ENROLLED (*DEPT, COURSE-NO STUDENT-NO*, GRADE), both requests would be handled in the same way. There are systems which use hierarchical record types and provide a high-level query language which eliminates the asymmetry inherent in the record structure,[17] but in the relational model, the symmetry is present independent of the query facility.

3. Flexibility in data definition—the user can augment his or her own data submodel by deriving new relations, and also introduce new relations (views) into the data model. These capabilities are not supported in a DBTG system.

The relational approach has some potential drawbacks, the most important of which concerns performance. Because the model permits a relation to be queried on any attribute or attribute combination, a fast associative retrieval capability is essential if an implementation is to compete with existing, nonrelational facilities. Some of the techniques mentioned in Section 9.4 have been used in experimental systems, but it remains to be seen whether these will prove satisfactory on a larger scale. Commercial

[17]For example, SYSTEM 2000; see MRI Systems Corp., *SYSTEM 2000 General Information Manual* (Austin, Tex., 1972).

relational systems may not become practical until large-capacity associative memories along the lines of those described in Section 9.4.5 become available.

Another problem with the relational model is its semantics: it is just as easy to derive a relation that has no interpretation in the context of the application as it is to produce a meaningful one. A derivable relationship exists between *any* two relations with comparable attributes, because such relations can be joined; however, the result will not necessarily correspond to a true association in the portion of the real world being modeled. In a DBTG system, relationships, in the form of owner–member sets, are decided in advance, as part of the schema definition process. This limits flexibility but offers some protection against producing meaningless information. Extensions of the relational model that make relationships more explicit have been proposed by Chen,[18] and by Schmid and Swenson.[19]

In this chapter we have presented the two principal data-base models. The network approach, as proposed by the DBTG, offers direct representation of entities and relationships. Data manipulation is complicated by physical and logical data dependences and currency indicators, but the effect of these can be lessened by a higher-level DML than the one proposed. The relational model represents a systematic and rigorous attempt to understand the design of data-base management systems. Potentially, it offers a high degree of data independence, and in consequence, simplified data retrieval and manipulation; currently, however, the only existing full relational implementations are developmental.

The ideal DBMS would combine the best features of these and other data models, and it may be that a synthesis will evolve; alternatively, future systems may let the user choose from a variety of models through which to view the data base. In any case, the area of data-base management systems continues to provide a rich source of examples and problems for the subject of data types and structures.

Exercises

1. The schema of Tables 10.1 and 10.2 is to be expanded by adding a new entity, INSTRUCTOR. Supply appropriate record and set definitions, assuming that
   (a) Instructors teach several sections, and conversely, a section may be shared by more than one instructor.
   (b) An instructor may advise several students, but a student may have only one advisor.
2. For the schema defined by Tables 10.1 and 10.2, write DBTG DML code to:
   (a) List the students enrolled in section 1 of 'ENG 100'.
   (b) List the students who got an 'A' in 'FRE 100'.
   (It may help to refer to Fig. 10.3 and the DML code of Table 10.3.)

[18]Peter P. Chen, "The Entity-Relationship Model—Toward a Unified View of Data," *ACM Transactions on Database Systems*, **1**, no. 1 (Mar. 1976), 7–36.

[19]H. A. Schmid and J. R. Swenson, "On the Semantics of the Relational Data Model," *Proceedings of the ACM SIGMOD International Conference on Management of Data*, W. F. King, ed., May 1975.

3. Use the procedure described in Section 10.3.1 to convert the following record definition to flat relations (keys are italicized):

> EMPLOYEE
>> 02 *EMPLOYEE-NO*; FIXED DECIMAL (9);
>>
>> 02 NAME; CHAR (50);
>>
>> 02 BIRTHDATE; FIXED DECIMAL (6);
>>
>> 02 JOB-HISTORY; OCCURS 3 TIMES;
>>> 03 *JOB-DATE*; FIXED DECIMAL (6);
>>>
>>> 03 TITLE; CHAR (30);
>>>
>>> 03 SALARY-HISTORY; OCCURS 3 TIMES;
>>>> 04 *SALARY-DATE*; FIXED DECIMAL (6);
>>>>
>>>> 04 SALARY; FIXED DECIMAL (6);
>>
>> 02 CHILDREN; OCCURS 6 TIMES;
>>> 03 *CHILD-NAME*; CHAR (20);
>>>
>>> 03 BIRTHYEAR; FIXED DECIMAL (6);

4. Give relational algebra expressions to answer the following queries, based on the relations in Fig. 10.2.
    (a) What courses is 'Macdonald' enrolled in?
    (b) List the students enrolled in 'HIS 430'.
    (c) List the students enrolled in 'French Composition'.
5. Give SEQUEL expressions to answer the following queries, based on the relations in Fig. 10.6.
    (a) What are the prerequisites for 'Creative Writing'?
    (b) What is Andrews' timetable (day, time, location)?
    (c) What instructors teach on Mondays?
6. Show how the relational algebra can be used to modify a set of tuples in a relation by describing that set and supplying the new component values (as was done with SEQUEL in Section 10.3.3). (*Hint:* The solution requires a sequence of steps, involving the construction of intermediate relations, and the relational operations selection, projection, join, set union, set difference, and *permutation*, which switches around the columns of a relation.)

Bibliography

Three textbooks on data-base management systems are Martin (1976), Date (1977), and Tsichritzis and Lochovsky (1977); the latter two describe in detail the network, relational, and hierarchical approaches to data management. The March 1976 issue of *Computing Surveys* is devoted entirely to data-base management systems, and each article contains an extensive bibliography, including references to experimental and commercial systems.

The defining document for the DBTG network model is the April 1971 DBTG report. A revised schema DDL is presented in the *Data Description Language Journal of Development* (1973).

The relational model was developed by E. F. Codd in a series of papers. Most of the material in these can be found in Date (1977), and Tsichritzis and Lochovsky (1977), but for the more detailed aspects of relational completeness, see Codd (1971). A large-scale relational implementation (System R) is described by Astrahan et al. (1976).

ASTRAHAN, M. M. et al., "System R: A Relational Approach to Database Management." *ACM Transactions on Database Systems* **1**, no. 2 (June 1976), 97–137.

CODASYL DATA BASE TASK GROUP, *April 1791 Report*. New York: Association for Computing Machinery.

CODASYL DATA DESCRIPTION LANGUAGE COMMITTEE, *Data Description Language Journal of Development* (Document C136/2:113). Washington, D.C.: Government Printing Office. 1973.

CODD, E. F., "A Relational Model for Large Shared Data Banks." *Communications of the ACM*, **13**, no. 6 (June 1970), 377–397.

CODD, E. F., "Relational Completeness of Database Sublanguages." *Courant Computer Science Symposium 6 on Data Base Systems, New York, May 1971*, R. Rustin, ed. Englewood Cliffs, N.J.: Prentice-Hall, Inc. 1972, pp. 65–98.

DATE, C. J., *An Introduction to Database Systems*. Second Edition, Reading, Mass.: Addison-Wesley Publishing Company, Inc., 1977.

MARTIN, J., *Principles of Data-Base Management*. Englewood Cliffs, N.J.: Prentice-Hall, Inc., 1976.

TSICHRITZIS, D. C., and LOCHOVSKY, F. H., *Data Base Management Systems*. New York: Academic Press, Inc., 1977.

appendix 1

Example of Data Structure Design

The example, although hypothetical, contains many of the elements of a real application. The data is the student file of a small college, assumed to have about 4000 students, containing information that identifies the students and describes their current subjects of study. In a real situation the total amount of data recorded about a student might include many items not present in this example (e.g., data on entrance standings, subjects taken in previous sessions, fees payment, medical history). In such cases the data would be recorded in secondary storage, even for a small student body, and most certainly for a larger number of students. Data structures involving secondary storage were considered in Chapter 9. Here we have kept the volume of data small enough so that it is not unreasonable to think of them as being stored in fast access (or virtual) memory, and problems connected with access to secondary storage can be ignored. Nevertheless, many of the aspects of choosing a data structure manifest themselves in the problem as outlined here, aspects encountered in Chapters 2 through 7, and ones that reappear in modified forms when secondary storage is considered. Because the application is one which, if expanded, would naturally require auxiliary storage, we use the terms "file" and "record," which are normally associated with secondary storage. The former refers to the whole collection of data, and the latter to the data about an individual student or course.

Table A.1 shows the data recorded about each student and the description of the courses he or she takes. In Table A.1 the term *subject* is used to refer to a discipline, and also to the department which teaches that discipline. The term *course* refers to a particular offering of the department, identified by the subject code and a three-digit number, the first of which is the *level* of the course (0 for make-up, 1 for first year, etc.). Each course is described by its course identifier group. A course is taught in a number

TABLE A.1 Student and course data

Student Data	Field Size (bytes)
Surname, given name, middle initial	26
Sex	1
Age	2
University address	21
Student number	
Year of first registration	2
Serial number	4
Number of courses in current session	1
Course description (one for each course taken)	
Course identifier	
Subject code	3
Level number	1
Serial number	2
Session description (one for each session)	
Code (L lecture, T tutorial, Y lab)	1
Section number (where applicable)	1
Time	
Day	1
Hour	2
Place	
Building	3
Room	3
Instructor	15
Grade	
Status (N normal, A aegrotat,	
R raised, I incomplete)	1
Term mark	3
Examination mark	3
Final mark	3

of weekly *sessions* (each described by a session group), scheduled at a given time and place. Following the practice of this book, the student and course records are regarded as instances of types, called **student-data** and **course-data**, and it is necessary to specify the operations which are to be applied to these types. Table A.2 illustrates operations that take as their arguments student records, course records, or fields from such records. The operations are placed in two groups, and they may regarded as those which occur most frequently, but it may be expected that there are additional ones, not shown.

Any realistic design must be carried out in the presence of constraints which are essentially economic in nature. We assume two:

1. It is too expensive to search or traverse the whole file to carry out an operation.
2. Data are not to be replicated.

The first of these might not be necessary for a small file such as is being dealt with here, but it would be applicable in the extended situation where there were more data and a larger number of students. In practice, the second constraint is often relaxed so that

TABLE A.2   Operations on **student-data** and **course-data**

Group 1.	Operations requiring selection of a single record and, possibly, changes to selected fields of the record.
(a)	Print the course list of a given student.
(b)	Drop or add a course for a given student.
(c)	Update the mark in a given course for a given student.
(d)	Locate the classroom (or list of possible classrooms) of a given student at a given hour.
(e)	Change a value in a field of the personal data for a given student.
Group 2.	Operations to be applied over a defined subset of records.
(a)	Find the grade average for all students enrolled in a given subject at a given level.
(b)	List alphabetically all students taking a given subject.
(c)	Update the grades of all students enrolled in a given course.
(d)	List alphabetically all students with a given year of registration.
(e)	List the courses offered by a given department at a given level.

portions of a record can be kept in several places, in order to speed up important operations.

A.1 Access Paths and Substructures

A look at the operations of Table A.2 reveals that two distinct access paths to the data are needed. The first is access by student *identity*—many of the operations and queries specify an individual student. The second is access by *subject* or *course*, required by most of the operations in the second category. Each of these access paths determines what might be called a *substructure*. The data must be organized so that there are routes to them defined by student identity and by subject or course. We can regard the substructures as independent, even though they share some of the same data. Other types of queries or operations would have produced the need for additional substructures. For example, if an operation to list all the courses taught by a given instructor had been specified, the prohibition against searching the whole file would have dictated a third substructure or access path, based on instructor identity. Similarly, had there been an operation to list all the hours a given classroom is occupied, a substructure based on classrooms (or perhaps time) would be needed. In the study of searching in earlier chapters we saw that access is provided through directories implemented by arrays, hash tables, inverted lists, linked lists, multilists, various types of trees, and so on, so that each substructure must be realized by one of these forms. The question is: Which? We must examine the various alternatives.

A.1.1 Student Substructure

It will be observed that there are two ways to identify a student: by name and by student number. In the absence of any information as to which is to be expected in a query, we must be prepared to use either. Names are usually distinct, but occasionally they are duplicated, even to given names (consult the telephone book!). The student numbers are constructed to be unique and they are true keys.

Consider first access by student number, and suppose that $Y_1Y_2X_1X_2X_3X_4$ is a key. All keys can be grouped according to the first two digits Y_1Y_2, which specify the first year of registration; within each registration year the serial numbers $X_1X_2X_3X_4$, starting from 0001, form a consecutive run (except perhaps for some missing numbers due to withdrawals). Using the notation of Table A.3, which shows various parameters associated with the data, the numbers Y_1Y_2 form a consecutive sequence, and the numbers $X_1X_2X_3X_4$ densely fill the range 0 to TYR. This is precisely the situation in which a multidimensional index is efficient for both access and storage. The student numbers can be regarded as occupying a two-dimensional array in which Y_1Y_2 is the index for one dimension, and $X_1X_2X_3X_4$ the index for the other. Access through student number in thus obtained by dissecting the number and taking Y_1Y_2 and $X_1X_2X_3X_4$ as the indexes of a directory array [Fig. A.1(a)]. Needless to say, the efficiency achieved in this way is not coincidental. Student number is the one data item about the student that can be assigned arbitrarily, and this mode of numbering was chosen so as to permit construction of a compact, fast-access directory. The address in the student number directory array will point to the variable-length student record containing the data of Table A.1.

TABLE A.3 Parameters for student record file

Quantity	Symbol	Minimum	Value Expected	Maximum
Number of students	T	—	4000	4500
Number of students registered in year YR	TYR	600	1000	1200
Number of courses taken by a student in a semester	CTS	1	5.2	7
Number of departments (also number of subjects)	D	—	35	—
Number of courses offered	C	—	400	—
Number of students in course COR	TCOR	10	50	200
Number of session/week for course COR	SCOR	1	3.5	5
Number of students registered in subject SUB at level n	TSUB_n			
Total number of students registered in subject $\text{TSUB} = \sum_{n=1}^{5} \text{TSUB}_n$	TSUB			

Let us now consider access by student name. If any of the binary tree variants are used to construct a name directory, it will require approximately log 4000, or about 12 comparisons, to locate a key when the tree is completely filled, and more if it is not. A trie is ruled out because of storage requirements.[1] A hybrid tree would require fewer comparisons, but it was seen in Chapter 4 that for a chained hash table with $\alpha = 0.8$,

[1]Because of the alphabet size and number of characters in a name; also the expected number of comparisons, determined by the average number of letters in a name, is too large.

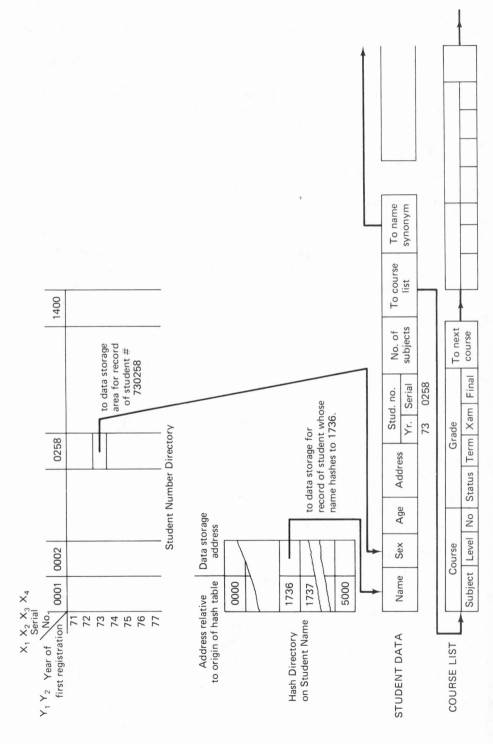

$X_1 X_2 X_3 X_4$ Serial No.

$Y_1 Y_2$ Year of first registration

	0001	0002		0258		1400
71						
72						
73						
74						
75						
76						
77						

to data storage area for record of student # 730258

Student Number Directory

Address relative to origin of hash table

Data storage address

0000	
1736	
1737	
5000	

to data storage for record of student whose name hashes to 1736.

Hash Directory on Student Name

STUDENT DATA

Name	Sex	Age	Address	Stud. no. Yr. Serial	No. of subjects	To course list	To name synonym
				73 0258			

COURSE LIST

Course Subject Level No	Grade Status Term Xam Final	To next course

(requiring therefore some 5000 entries), the average number of comparisons will be less than 1.5. Unless some factor makes a hash table unsuitable,[2] a name directory based on a hash table is to be preferred, and this form of directory is therefore adopted. There is still some choice in the method of resolving synonyms, but the differences in performance are not great, and a chained table will be assumed. There is also a choice about where the chaining address is stored. In Table 4.6 the chaining address was stored in the hash table, but here it is also possible to keep it with the student record. Synonyms are resolved by examining the student number, and since this number is already present in the record, keeping the synonym chaining address in the student record saves storage by making it unnecessary to store it also in the hash table. We thus arrive at the dual directory shown in Fig. A.1 for accessing a student, given iden-tification, either in the form of a student number, or a name.

The main part of the student substructure is the storage area containing a student's identification data, along with his or her list of subjects. As explained above, this is organized as a set of linked lists, each list consisting of the synonyms for a given hash value on the name. Since CTS, the number of courses in which a student is enrolled for a given session is variable, and for part of the year at least, courses can be dropped and added, the repeating group of courses will be recorded as a linked sublist to the main student entry. Figure A.1 illustrates the student substructure, with its directories and student data. Based on this substructure, most of the operations of group 1 can be carried out efficiently. Some operations, however (e.g., printing a student's timetable), require access to information not available in the student data, and access to the course substructure is needed to carry these out.

A.1.2 Subject/Course Substructure

Given that the main body of student data is organized according to student identi-fication, operations that require access to all students taking a given subject or course will require either inverted lists on the subject and course or a multilist structure. As pointed out in Section 4.5, the relative merits of these two are difficult to assess without a detailed comparison of how the different operations would be programmed for each. We shall choose the inverted lists, on the grounds that keeping the subject structure as a distinct entity in the inverted list is, overall, likely to make for simpler operations than embedding this structure into the student data as a multilist. Deleting a course from the course list of a student, for example, involves performing the following steps:

1. Find the designated course.
2. Search through the list of registrants, until the designated student is located.
3. Delete the entry.

Step 1 will require a search in a directory of courses which can be of the same form for either inverted lists or multilists. Step 2 requires a search in a localized inverted list (the student list for the course being deleted) and throughout the student file for the

---

[2]For example, names are often given incorrectly, and it may be necessary to have reasonably effi-cient searches, even for misspelled names.

multilist. Step 3 requires changes in both the course directory and student data for the inverted list, and only in the student data for the multilist. But the changes are somewhat more complicated in the latter case, and as the number of students increases, it becomes more desirable to reduce operations on student records in favor of operations on the more compact directories.

The directory for accessing a given subject and course can take any of the forms we have studied. But this is another case where the encoding system (for courses this time) is at the disposal of the designer. With the chosen encoding, a composite directory based on a lexicographic tree for finding subjects, a pointer array for locating the link number, and a linked list for finding the specific course is particularly effective. Figure A.2 illustrates the directory. The string nodes of the lexicographic tree contains the subject. It would be possible to guard against skewed tree formation by constructing a height-balanced or weight-balanced tree, but by the simple expedient of entering the subjects in the correct order, the tree can be made complete, in which case the number of comparisons to locate any subject is at most $\lceil \log_2 34 \rceil$, or 6. The next step in locating a course is taken by following a pointer in a pointer vector for which course level is the index. This pointer leads to a linked list, which is followed to the particular course sought. Thus to find the students enrolled in ENG 201, a search through the six-level lexicographic tree locates the ENG subject, an indexing operation points to the 200 level courses, and a search through the linked list locates ENG 201. The result is a pointer to the course data and to the inverted list containing students enrolled in that course. The advantage of this organization is that operations such as

- List all students enrolled in any history course.
- Delete CHM 205 from the list of offerings of the chemistry department.

are easily effected on the directory without extended searches. If the subject directory were a hash table, the first of these would be expensive, and if it were a contiguous ordered list, the second would be expensive. If the list of departmental course offerings were fairly static, a binary search of an ordered list to determine pointers to the different course levels would be quite satisfactory. Since the number of courses within a subject level is variable and changes are allowed, a linked list connecting these courses is favored. There are D departments, offering C courses at five levels, so the average length of one of the lists is $C/5D$, which, from Table A.3, is expected to be less than 3, so the time for searching a linked list to find a particular course is acceptably short.

Another decision regarding the inverted lists is whether the entries should contain student identifiers or pointers to the storage area containing the data about a student. The fact that many of the operations based on the inverted list require access to the record (e.g., to determine the student name, or update a grade) is an argument for storing pointer addresses, thereby avoiding the need to go through the student number directory. On the other hand, the student number is permanent, so storing it makes it unnecessary to calculate the addresses every time the program is read in or to replace the address by a meaningful value whenever a printout is made. We shall assume that student numbers are stored. Figure A.2 illustrates the subject substructure with its directory and inverted list.

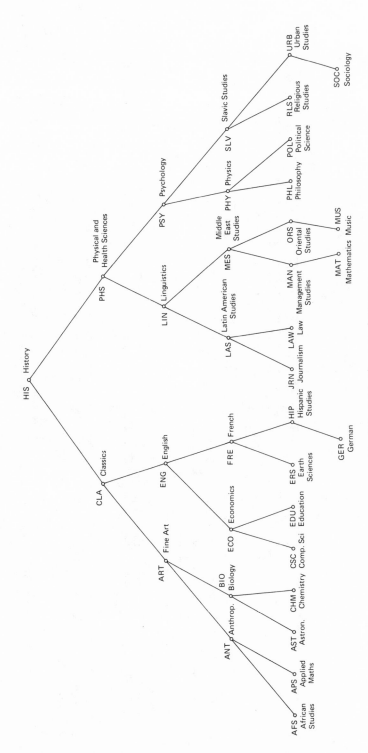

Fig. A.2 Subject/course substructure

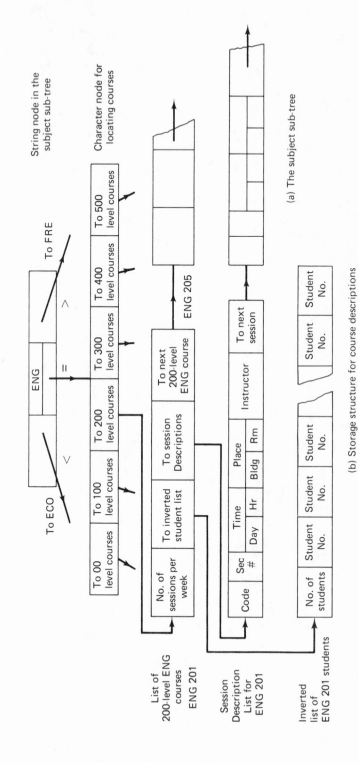

String node in the subject sub-tree

Character node for locating courses

To ECO

ENG

To FRE

| To 00 level courses | To 100 level courses | To 200 level courses | To 300 level courses | To 400 level courses | To 500 level courses |

ENG 205

(a) The subject sub-tree

| No. of sessions per week | To inverted student list | To session Descriptions |

| To next 200-level ENG course |

List of 200-level ENG courses ENG 201

| Code | Sec # | Time | | Place | | Instructor | To next session |
| | | Day | Hr | Bldg | Rm | | |

Session Description List for ENG 201

| No. of students | Student No. | Student No. | Student No. | Student No. | Student No. |

Inverted list of ENG 201 students

(b) Storage structure for course descriptions and student lists

Fig. A.2 (Cont.)

432

A.2 Storage Requirements

Estimating the storage requirements is an essential part of the data structure design. Table A.4 shows the requirements for the various constituents of the two substructures in terms of the parameters defined in Table A.2. Estimates on number of bytes are based on the expected values for these parameters (pointers are assumed to require 4 bytes). The total storage requirement is about 1000 kilobytes, confirming that the data (for this contracted file) could be contained within high-speed memory.

TABLE A.4   Data storage requirements for example

Constituent	In Terms of Parameters*	In Kilobytes, Using Estimated Values
Student substructure		
Student data	$(65+20 \cdot \text{CTS}) \cdot \text{T}$	676
Student number directory	6T	24
Hash directory	5T	20
Subject substructure		
Inverted lists	$(1 + 6\overline{\text{TCOR}})\text{C}$	120
Session description	$30 \cdot \overline{\text{SCOR}} \cdot \text{C}$	42
Subject and course directory	$39\text{D} + 13\text{C}$	7
	Total	889

*$\overline{\text{TCOR}}$, average number of students per course; $\overline{\text{SCOR}}$, average number of sessions per week per course; other parameters from Table A.2.

A.3 Operation Set

Having arrived at the detailed storage mapping for all the variables that arise in the application, it becomes a straightforward exercise to write programs which carry out the operations in the two groups. The first step is to write the specifications for the composite data types. Those needed for the student data can be written down from Fig. A.1. We have:

comp student-data = ⟨**string** *name*, **boolean** *sex*, **int** *age*,
       string *address*, **int** *student-no*,
       int *subject-no*, **course-entry-ptr** *head*,
       student-data-ptr *synonym*⟩

comp course-entry = ⟨**course-id** *course*, **grade** *result*,
       subject-entry-ptr *next*⟩

comp course-id   = ⟨**string** *subject*, **int** *level*, **int** *serial-no*⟩

comp grade   = ⟨**char** *status*, **int** *term*, **int** *exam*, **int** *final*⟩

In a similar way, specifications can be written for the type **course-data.** Two variables, with names *student-record* and *course-record*, of types **student-data** and **course-data**, respectively, are declared in the programs for the operations. All the operations are based on searching, adding or deleting records, and changing the values of selected

433

fields, so the programs will be very similar to those encountered in Chapters 3 to 6. Some of the operations [e.g., 2(b)] will call upon sorting routines.

Although the general dependence of the times for the operations is known for the data structures chosen, detailed expressions for timing have to be derived. The iteration constants in the timing expressions will depend on the parameters of the data. Some of the parameters have already appeared in the estimate of storage requirements, but there are others which have to be determined if times are to be calculated. For example, operation 2(a), "Find the grade average for all students enrolled in a given subject at a given level," is easily computed, since the subject directory contains the header to the linked list of all courses at each level, and each course contains a pointer to the inverted list of students enrolled in it. The time to carry out this operation will be simply proportional to the number of students registered in the subject at that level. This parameter is called $TSUB_n$, where SUB is the subject and n the level number. The number of students in a given subject at all levels, $\sum_{n=1}^{5} TSUB_n$ is TSUB (see Exercise 18, Chapter 7), and this appears in the timing expression of operation 2(b).

If still more statistics are available, it becomes possible to examine more closely the choices that were made at particular points of the design and so determine if these were made wisely. For example, in Fig. A.2 the inverted list of students enrolled in a given course is shown as a contiguous list. The number of entries in the list is given by TCOR, and since courses gain and lose students, the declaration for the list size must include the maximum number of entries. This maximum is dependent on the specific course, and a question arises whether to use a single value for it or whether to estimate individual maxima for each course. Another alternative would be to represent the inverted lists by linked lists, on the argument that the extra storage for the links simplifies the storage management. If the unused storage in contiguous inverted lists exceeds the used storage, it is advantageous to go to linked lists. Another decision, applicable to both contiguous and linked lists, is whether the lists should be ordered in any way. It will be recalled that for unordered lists, additions are inexpensive (they can be made at an end) but deletions are costly. For ordered lists, deletions are less costly but additions more so. Given the relative frequencies of additions and deletions, detailed coding of the two alternatives will determine which is better.

The important point is that as more precise knowledge is gained about the files and their usage, the data structures can be refined to reduce the operation times and execution cost of the application.

Index